READING ASSESSMENT AND INSTRUCTION FOR ALL LEARNERS

SOLVING PROBLEMS IN THE TEACHING OF LITERACY

Cathy Collins Block, *Series Editor*

Recent Volumes

Vocabulary Instruction: Research to Practice
Edited by James F. Baumann and Edward J. Kame'enui

The Reading Specialist: Leadership for the Classroom, School, and Community
Rita M. Bean

Multicultural and Multilingual Literacy and Language: Contexts and Practices
Edited by Fenice B. Boyd and Cynthia H. Brock, with Mary S. Rozendal

Teaching All the Children:
Strategies for Developing Literacy in an Urban Setting
Edited by Diane Lapp, Cathy Collins Block, Eric J. Cooper, James Flood, Nancy Roser, and Josefina Villamil Tinajero

Conceptual Foundations of Teaching Reading
Mark Sadoski

The Literacy Coach's Handbook: A Guide to Research-Based Practice
Sharon Walpole and Michael C. McKenna

Comprehension Process Instruction: Creating Reading Success in Grades K–3
Cathy Collins Block, Lori L. Rodgers, and Rebecca B. Johnson

Adolescent Literacy Research and Practice
Edited by Tamara L. Jetton and Janice A. Dole

Tutoring Adolescent Literacy Learners: A Guide for Volunteers
Kelly Chandler-Olcott and Kathleen A. Hinchman

Success with Struggling Readers: The Benchmark School Approach
Irene West Gaskins

Making Sense of Phonics: The Hows and Whys
Isabel L. Beck

Reading Instruction That Works, Third Edition: The Case for Balanced Teaching
Michael Pressley

Narrowing the Literacy Gap: What Works in High-Poverty Schools
Diane M. Barone

Reading Assessment and Instruction for All Learners
Jeanne Shay Schumm

READING
ASSESSMENT AND INSTRUCTION FOR ALL LEARNERS

Edited by JEANNE SHAY SCHUMM

THE GUILFORD PRESS
New York London

A Division of Guilford Publications, Inc.
72 Spring Street, New York, NY 10012
www.guilford.com

Printed in the United States of America

This book is printed on acid-free paper.

Last digit is print number: 9 8 7 6 5 4 3 2 1

Library of Congress Cataloging-in-Publication Data

Reading assessment and instruction for all learners / edited by Jeanne Shay Schumm.
p. cm. (Solving problems in the teaching of literacy)
Includes bibliographical references and index.
ISBN-10: 1-59385-290-8 ISBN-13: 978-1-59385-290-0 (paper)
ISBN-10: 1-59385-291-6 ISBN-13: 978-1-59385-291-7 (cloth)
1. Reading (Elementary)—United States. 2. Reading teachers—Training of—United States. I. Schumm, Jeanne Shay, 1947– II. Series.
LB1573.R2783 2006
372.58—dc22

2005028087

First, this book is dedicated to my godmother, Janis Shay Minford, who taught me at an early age about loving and teaching the children of the world.

Second, this book is dedicated to Sam J. Yager, former Dean of the School of Education at the University of Miami. Sam died suddenly in the fall of 2005. Sam was very aware of this book and very proud of each and every faculty member and graduate student who participated in its development.

—J. S. S.

About the Editor

Jeanne Shay Schumm, PhD, is Professor and Chair of the Department of Teaching and Learning in the School of Education at the University of Miami. She has experience teaching reading and writing to students in grades K–12 in both classroom and resource settings. Dr. Schumm has coauthored or authored over 75 chapters and articles, and has recently coedited *Promising Practices for Urban Reading Instruction* (International Reading Association, 2005) and coauthored the fourth edition of *Teaching Exceptional, Diverse, and At-Risk Students in the General Education Classroom* (Allyn & Bacon, 2003).

Contributors

Maria Elena Arguelles, PhD, Department of Teaching and Learning, School of Education, University of Miami, Coral Gables, Florida

Mary A. Avalos, PhD, Department of Teaching and Learning, School of Education, University of Miami, Coral Gables, Florida

Jeanne Bergeron, PhD, Department of Teaching and Learning, School of Education, University of Miami, Coral Gables, Florida

William E. Blanton, EdD, Department of Teaching and Learning, School of Education, University of Miami, Coral Gables, Florida

Yvonne C. Campbell, MEd, School of Education, University of Miami, Coral Gables, Florida

Michele Mits Cash, PhD, Academic Services, Farquhar College of Arts and Sciences, Nova Southeastern University, Fort Lauderdale, Florida

Lina Lopez Chiappone, PhD, Department of Teacher Education, College of Education, Florida Atlantic University, Davie, Florida

Elizabeth D. Cramer, PhD, Department of Special Education, College of Education, Florida International University, Miami, Florida

Peggy D. Cuevas, PhD, Department of Teaching and Learning, School of Education, University of Miami, Coral Gables, Florida

Jodi Crum Marshall, MEd, School of Education, University of Miami, Coral Gables, Florida

Adriana L. Medina, MEd, Department of Teaching and Learning, School of Education, University of Miami, Coral Gables, Florida

Rita M. Menendez, MEd, School of Education, University of Miami, Coral Gables, Florida

Paola Pilonieta, MEd, School of Education, University of Miami, Coral Gables, Florida

Ana Maria Pazos Rego, PhD, Department of Teaching and Learning, School of Education, University of Miami, Coral Gables, Florida

Jeanne Shay Schumm, PhD, Department of Teaching and Learning, School of Education, University of Miami, Coral Gables, Florida

Preface

We live, teach, and conduct our research in Miami–Dade County, Florida. Our public school system is the fourth largest in the United States. We have a wide range of cultural, linguistic, and academic diversity among our student population. Our diversity is a source of pride for us. It also presents a challenge for teachers in classroom and resource settings who are responsible for guiding students on the road to literacy. Because the needs of our students in learning to read and write are varied, it is imperative that their teachers have the best professional development possible to identify their needs and respond with appropriate instruction.

In the state of Florida, both general and special education teachers graduating from approved teacher education programs are required to have a minimum of four courses in the teaching of reading, as well as a strong foundation in teaching English to speakers of other languages (TESOL). This is true at graduate and undergraduate levels. Moreover, both general education and special education teachers are required to develop an understanding of their roles and responsibilities in working in inclusion settings, as well as in coordinating efforts when traditional classroom and pull-out or self-contained resource models are used to provide special education, Title I, or bilingual education services. In other words, the state of Florida is requiring teachers to be prepared for what they are actually going to do—to teach diverse students in diverse settings.

Research in best practices for the teaching of reading has emerged from multiple disciplines: psychology, reading, special education, gifted education, and TESOL. In addition, many times reading, writing, special education, gifted education, and TESOL courses are taught as separate classes—sometimes by professors from different departments. Therefore, putting all this together rests on the shoulders of the individual teacher. We believe that teachers who are best prepared to teach in diverse settings are familiar with instructional practices from different fields and are prepared to make critical and informed evaluations about what is best suited for their students.

Reading Assessment and Instruction for All Learners takes an interdisciplinary approach to the teaching of reading and writing. Some of us are reading specialists; others are special educators; others are TESOL experts; and one has training in gifted education. Still others are cross-trained in two or more areas. All of us have taught in K–12 settings that include students who are English-language learners (ELLs) and students who have exceptional needs in learning to read and write. Many of us have learned to read and write in English as a second language.

Contents

I

FOCUS ON THE LEARNER

ONE

Understanding Our Role as Teachers

Facing the Challenges of Helping All Students Learn to Read and Write

JEANNE SHAY SCHUMM
MARIA ELENA ARGUELLES

VIGNETTE

Vivian Varga teaches third grade at an urban elementary school that houses over 1,500 students. This year her class size is 30 students. About one-third of her students are recent immigrants who are English-language learners (ELLs). Vivian also teaches two students with learning disabilities who receive special education services. As a result, student reading levels in her class range from preprimer to fifth grade. Recently her state mandated passing a state achievement test as a requirement for promotion to fourth grade. This mandate includes immigrant students who have lived in the United States for two or more years.

Vivian has been teaching for 15 years and recently completed the requirements for National Board certification. She is a seasoned professional who thrives in the classroom and puts her students first. Nonetheless, like many of her colleagues, she is concerned about what she can do to help all of her students make steady progress in learning to read and write.

Vivian describes her concerns as follows: "The high-stakes tests keep getting higher and higher for my students and for me. Even though the state and school district have become more prescriptive in terms of what is expected with standards-based instruction, I still find myself faced with making critical decisions on a daily basis. I make decisions about my students' needs, how to group students for instruction, what instructional methods I use, and how to report progress to parents. My biggest decision is how to best use every second of instructional time to help all students learn. I know the decisions I make will have a large impact on the lives of the children I teach."

ANTICIPATION QUESTIONS

- What are the major challenges classroom teachers face in helping all students learn to read and write?
- What resources do classroom teachers have to meet these challenges?

- What is the classroom teacher's role as a decision maker in planning assessment and instruction for all learners?
- What assessment tools can teachers use as a starting point for getting to know their students?

INTRODUCTION

Vivian Varga realizes that "teaching to the middle" will leave some of her students lagging behind—or ignored. Some student needs are more specific and extreme than others. This chapter begins with a discussion of the challenges classroom teachers face in helping all students learn to read and write. It continues with resources for meeting these challenges, and suggestions for building reading profiles for students that will serve as the groundwork for planning assessment and instruction in reading and writing.

CHALLENGES IN HELPING ALL STUDENTS LEARN TO READ AND WRITE

It's no secret: Some children simply have a tough time learning to read and write. As early as the 1930s, Marion Monroe's research pointed out that there is no one reason for this (Monroe, 1932). This is still true today. There is no one cause of difficulty in learning to read and write. Some learners have physical problems; others exhibit cognitive or language disorders; others have language or cultural differences; and still others experience home situations that are not conducive to learning. One sad reality is that some children do not learn to read and write because they are not well taught. For most students with problems in learning to read and write, there are usually multiple causes for their difficulties.

According to the 1992 National Adult Literacy Survey (*http://nces.ed.gov/naal/*), low literacy skills can have dire consequences, including increased changes for incarceration, likelihood of unemployment, and lower potential for higher wages. Trying to resolve this national dilemma is a daunting mission. The task has become even more difficult due to three challenges: accountability, changing classrooms, and controversy about how reading should be taught (see Figure 1.1).

Accountability

The first challenge is an increased emphasis on accountability. States and school districts have administered standardized tests in reading, mathematics, and other content subjects for decades. These tests were given to provide policymakers and taxpayers with information about how students were performing overall. In recent years, however, standardized

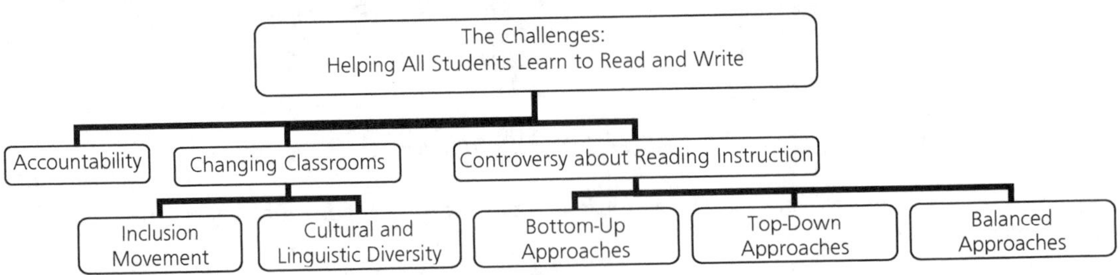

FIGURE 1.1. The challenges: Helping all students learn to read and write.

tests have become "high-stakes," in that student outcomes have an impact on whether or not students will be retained in designated grades or will graduate from high school. Test scores are made public and in many cases are used as a primary component of formulas to identify high- and low-performing schools. Low-performing schools are required to make substantive changes in personnel, curriculum, and/or allocation of resources in attempts to turn schools around.

The national movement toward greater accountability was accelerated through the passage of the 2001 reauthorization of the 1965 Elementary and Secondary Education Act. According to the Executive Summary (*www.ed.gov/nclb/overview/intro/execsumm.html*), this new authorization, entitled the No Child Left Behind Act (NCLB) of 2001, is based on four themes:

- Accountability
- Choices for parents and students
- Flexibility for states, school districts, and schools
- Putting reading first

NCLB requires that states conduct statewide assessments in reading and mathematics. Science testing is also required as of 2006. Actual test instruments vary from state to state, but all must be aligned to state academic standards in the given area of assessment. NCLB also requires states to define criteria for students' *adequate yearly progress* (AYP) in reading. Based on individual state standards, each state is required to document how subgroups of students are making progress in achieving target levels in reading by the year 2014. These criteria vary considerably from state to state (Allington, 2006), so it is important for teachers to be aware of their own states' standards as well as requirements for AYP.

States, school districts, schools, and individual teachers are being held more accountable for the quality of teaching and its impact on student learning. This includes the learning of *all* students—even students who have been historically "waived" from standardized testing: students with disabilities and students who are ELLs.

The increased emphasis on high-stakes testing and accountability has not gone without criticism, both in the mass media and in the professional literature. In a policy brief written for the National Reading Conference, Afflerbach (2004) points out some of the dangers of high-stakes testing, such as restriction of the reading curriculum, student and teacher disengagement and demoralization, and potential misplacement or labeling of students. This policy brief (Afflerbach, 2004, pp. 12–15) concludes with a series of recommendation for improved assessment:

- Reading assessment should reflect performances over multiple time points with various tests and purposes.
- Assessment should measure a wide range of skills with a variety of formats and responses.
- Assessments should follow ethical guidelines of the American Educational Research Association, standard practices of the American Psychological Association, and recommended practices of the International Reading Association.
- Assessments should provide clear distinctions between the acquisition of reading skills and the effective use of these skills for various purposes.
- Assessments should provide students with useful information about their developmental accomplishments, as well as with clear suggestions for improvement.
- Assessments should provide teachers with useful diagnostic information that can be linked to classroom instruction.

- Assessments should provide parents with comprehensible explanations of their children's progress and achievement, as well as with suggestions for enhancing their involvement in their children's literacy development.
- Assessments should provide administrators with data related to specific criteria and standards of performance in order to assess annual progress.
- Assessments should be aligned with curricula and instruction.
- Assessments and testing procedures should be reviewed and revised by school boards, teachers, and parents on a regular basis.

While some of these recommendations are beyond the realm of individual teacher's responsibilities, most are not. There is a great deal that individual teachers can do to improve not only the quality of assessment, but implementation and reporting practices.

Changing Classrooms

A second challenge is the changing nature of classrooms in the United States. Classrooms have changed for three major reasons. First, there has been an increase in the numbers of students with disabilities included in the general education classroom for all or part of the school day. According to the National Education Association, "Three out of every four students with disabilities spend part or all of their school day in a general education classroom. In turn, nearly every general education classroom across the country includes students with disabilities" (*www.nea.org/specialed/*, p. 1). Why has this occurred? The 1997 reauthorization of the Individuals with Disabilities Education Act (IDEA) mandated greater access to the general education classroom for students with special needs. As a result, rather than receiving instruction in pull-out (resource) classrooms or self-contained classrooms, students with disabilities are increasingly included in the general education classroom for all or part of the school day.

Until recently, pull-out (resource) classrooms were also more common for students receiving Title I funding. Schools with high numbers of students from low-income families are eligible for additional funding from the federal government under Title I of the Elementary and Secondary Education Act. Students in such schools who were reading below grade level (whether from low-income families or not) were frequently placed in resource settings for additional instruction in basic reading skills. While some schools receiving Title I funds maintain resource settings, others are moving to schoolwide models for improving the quality of reading instruction for all students.

This shift of service delivery for students with disabilities and students in Title I schools has necessitated that general education teachers learn ways to accommodate individual differences, and that special education teachers and reading specialists learn more about the content of instruction (Vaughn, Bos, & Schumm, 2003). As you will read in Chapter 2, the range of students' instructional needs can be vast, and teachers must be prepared to respond accordingly.

A third reason why classrooms have changed is the influx in diverse populations migrating to the United States. The number of students with cultural and linguistic differences in our classrooms is increasing daily. While immigrant populations were typically limited to certain areas in the United States, the population is beginning to shift and disperse. As you will learn in Chapter 3, more classroom teachers are being faced with how best to teach reading and writing to children with cultural and linguistic backgrounds other than their own. Responding to these differences can be rewarding and enlightening for teachers, but can be demanding as well. Taken together, the increased range of students' needs in the general education classroom has required that teachers learn to diversify instruction. A one-size-fits-all mentality for teaching reading simply does not work (Schumm, Vaughn, & Moody, 2000).

All children have the right to read. The International Reading Association has taken a very strong stance in proclaiming this right in the form of a position statement, *Making a Difference Means Making It Different: Honoring Children's Rights to Excellent Reading Instruction* (see Figure 1.2). As Mason and Schumm (2003) have stated,

> How to make those rights a reality for children who attend overcrowded urban schools, for children who do not have access to technology, for children of poverty with limited family resources, and for children of cultural and linguistic backgrounds that are different from the mainstream are the challenges for education students in the new millennium. The United States, its educational system and its professional organizations have a moral obligation to make those rights a reality for all children in this country and beyond. (p. iv)

Controversy about How Reading Should Be Taught

A final challenge is the ongoing debate about how best to teach reading. The field of reading has been riddled with controversy for decades, and the controversy continues. This controversy can be baffling to teachers concerned about providing the best for their students. For professionals who have been in the field for some time, frustration can arise when instructional practices come, go, and come back again. For new teachers, conflicting information can provide confusion in terms of how to get started on the right foot.

**MAKING A DIFFERENCE MEANS MAKING IT DIFFERENT:
HONORING CHILDREN'S RIGHTS TO EXCELLENT READING INSTRUCTION**

IRA asserts that, to meet the challenges of teaching literacy in the 21st century, it is time to build reading programs on a set of comprehensive principles that honor children's rights to excellent instruction. We believe that all children have a right to

1. Early reading instruction that meets individual needs
2. Reading instruction that builds skill and the desire to read increasingly complex materials
3. Well-prepared teachers who keep their skills up to date
4. A variety of books and other reading material in classroom, and in school and community libraries
5. Assessment that identifies strengths as well as needs and involves students in making decisions about their own learning
6. Supplemental instruction from professionals specifically prepared to teach reading
7. Instruction that involves parents and communities in students' academic lives
8. Instruction that makes meaningful use of first-language skills
9. Equal access to instructional technology
10. Classrooms that optimize learning opportunities

Meeting our obligation to provide excellent reading instruction to every child means that classrooms need to be rethought, sufficient financial investments must be made, and communities must wholeheartedly support school and instructional reform efforts.

FIGURE 1.2. Children's rights to excellent reading instruction. From International Reading Association. (2000). *Making a Difference Means Making it Different: Honoring Children's Rights to Excellent Reading Instruction* (*www.reading.org/resources/issues/positions_rights.html*). A Position Statement of the International Reading Association. Newark, DE: International Reading Association. Reprinted with permission of the International Reading Association.

Frequently known as the "reading wars," the controversy centers on phonics (a bottom-up perspective) versus more language-based approaches (a top-down perspective). In other words, advocates at one end of the spectrum promote a phonics-first approach, while those at the opposite end of the spectrum encourage language-based approaches based on authentic reading and writing tasks. As with most educational issues, there are policymakers, researchers, teacher educators, teachers, and parents who represent the two ends of the spectrum, and others who are somewhere in the middle. In thinking about these different perspectives, think about a mountain. The top of the mountain is meaning—being able to comprehend and respond to text. The bottom of the mountain is the sounds of letters. Opinions about the pathway to the top of the mountain vary considerably from one perspective to another.

The bottom-up perspective is built on the premise that learning to read is a process of breaking the code in a systemic way, starting with the sounds of letters. Reading instruction is viewed as a linear, systematic process with letter sounds taught first (phonemic awareness), followed by letter–sound correspondence (phonics), and then syllables, words, sentences, and so on. Spelling and language arts are taught as separate subjects. Bottom-up advocates see rapid, context-free word recognition as the hallmark of a proficient reader. The historical roots of this approach go back to the Greeks, when the teaching of reading was delegated to slaves (Mathews, 1966). In more modern times, Rudolph Flesch's (1955) book *Why Johnny Can't Read* drew public attention to the importance of phonics first. Two research summaries—Jeanne Chall's (1967) *Learning to Read: The Great Debate*, and Marilyn Adams's (1990) *Beginning to Read: Thinking and Learning about Print*—both brought public and professional attention to the importance of systematic, intensive phonics instruction. Advocates of a bottom-up perspective believe that learning to read starts at the bottom of the mountain, and that there are systematic steps to get to the top. The teacher must have a clear road map for leading students from the bottom to the top.

The top-down perspective is just the opposite. Advocates of this point of view start at the top of the mountain with meaning. The notion is that early readers are empowered with their growing knowledge of language. Students are exposed to a wide variety of literature and authentic reading materials. Word recognition is taught—but more incidentally, as individual students need and are ready for it. Students who are learning to read are considered emergent readers and writers; there are legitimate stages of learning to read, and all stages of reading development are important. Top-down advocates see facile use of context (meaning) as the hallmark of a proficient reader. Historically, the top-down perspective is associated with the progressive movement led by John Dewey (Edelsky, Altwerger, & Flores, 1991; Goodman, 1986). Later, Kenneth Goodman's (1967) "Reading as a Psycholinguistic Guessing Game" suggested that good readers use only minimal cues from print and use the context and structure of language to decode and make meaning. Goodman's own research and his understanding of linguistics (Chomsky, 1965), psychology (Piaget & Inhelder, 1969), and psycholinguistics (Vygotsky, 1978) led him to develop the theoretical framework for the whole-language movement. Many definitions of *whole language* exist. Therefore, Betty Bergeron (1990) synthesized over 64 definitions and crafted the following set of common characteristics:

> Construction of meaning, wherein an emphasis is placed on comprehending what is read; functional language, or language that has a purpose and relevance to the learner; the use of literature in a variety of forms; the writing process, through which learners write, revise, and edit written works; cooperative student work; and an emphasis on affective aspects of the students' learning experience, such as motivation, enthusiasm, and interest. (p. 319)

Within the top-down perspective, each student takes an individualized route to developing proficiency in reading. Teachers can serve as facilitators and provide assistance (*mini-lessons*) when individual students need guidance. Authentic literature and writing tasks are emphasized in whole-language approaches, as opposed to commercial basal readers and supplementary materials.

There is a middle ground between the phonics and whole-language approaches. The theoretical model that undergirds this middle ground evolved out of the work of David Rumelhart (1976) and later Keith Stanovich (1980). Stanovich's *interactive–compensatory model* recognizes that the hallmark of a good reader is rapid, context- free word recognition. Unlike Goodman's point of view, the research of Stanovich and his colleagues indicates that proficient readers process print quickly, efficiently, and completely (Stanovich, 2000). Good readers also use context better than poorer readers. The difference is that good readers use context for two purposes—for deriving word meanings, and as a backup system when word recognition doesn't seem to work. Good readers use cue systems interactively and know how to compensate when one cue system fails. Poor readers have weaker word recognition skills, so they overrely on context; it is the primary cue system they have for reading. Of particular importance is the role of *phonological awareness*. Phonological awareness is "the ability to deal explicitly and segmentally with sound units smaller than the syllable" (Stanovich, 1993–1994, p. 283). Students who develop or are explicitly taught phonological awareness have the best chance for success in learning to read in the early grades.

So what does the interactive–compensatory model suggest for reading instruction? First, it suggests that students should receive early intensive instruction in phonological awareness and phonics, but with an emphasis as well on real reading and writing. The two are not mutually exclusive. Second, it is important for teachers to have data about students' strengths and areas for improvement in reading and writing. Assessment is critical. Third, it suggests that teachers have to be prepared to differentiate instruction based on individual students' needs. Critical to this model is ongoing assessment with differentiated instruction as needed. Fourth, it suggests that teachers should look to science—research—when they consider what to teach and how to teach it.

Some researchers refer to this moderate perspective as the *radical middle* (Morrow, 1997; Pearson, 2001a); others call it *balanced instruction* or *balanced literacy*. Balanced instruction pulls the best from both bottom-up and top-down perspectives (Pressley, 2006). "Balanced-literacy teachers combine the strengths of whole-language and skills instruction, and in doing so create instruction that is more than the sum of its parts" (Pressley, 2006, p. 2).

Of course, there is a danger in trying to "balance." Balance suggests equal portions of whole-language and skill instruction, which are not always appropriate for individual students, or always even possible. Moreover, as Fletcher (2004) has pointed out, balance is more than simply having students in a literature-based program fill out phonics workbooks. Staresina (2003) puts it this way: "Today, the reading debate no longer centers on which approach is better, but the proper mix of each in a comprehensive reading program" (p. 5). Perhaps what makes sense is thinking about what Cromwell (1997) calls a "careful combination" (p. 4).

After many years of debate, we now know more about effective reading instruction than ever before. We have well over 30 years of converging scientific research, making this a very exciting time in the field of reading. Several consensus documents, like those developed by the National Reading Panel and the National Research Council, provide us with clear information on how children learn to read, what factors impede reading development, and which instructional approaches provide most benefit (Fletcher & Lyon, 1998). You will learn more about these important documents throughout this book.

This book's chapters include specific ideas for planning and implementing this careful combination, with particular emphasis on assessment, monitoring student progress, grouping for student success, and evidence-based instructional practices. What is most critical to making this combination a success is a well-prepared, reflective teacher. As Duffy (1997, p. 363) has stated, "I fear that teachers are often set up to follow a particular instructional model rather than being taught to thoughtfully combine models according to the demands of the instructional situation. This, I believe, is part of the reason why we see fewer creative classroom teachers of literacy than we would like."

RESOURCES FOR MEETING THE CHALLENGES

Meeting the challenges described above cannot happen without well-prepared teachers. As Louisa C. Moats (1999) wrote in her monograph *Teaching Reading IS Rocket Science*, "Teaching reading is a job for an expert. Contrary to the popular theory that learning to read is natural and easy, learning to read is a complex linguistic achievement. For many children, it requires effort and incremental skill development. Moreover, teaching reading requires considerable knowledge and skill, acquired over several years through focused study and supervised practice" (p. 11).

In 2000, the International Reading Association issued a position statement *Making a Difference Means Making It Different: Honoring Children's Rights to Excellent Reading Instruction* (*www.reading.org/resources/issues/positions_rights.html*). This statement underscores the importance of the teacher in meeting the instructional needs of individual learners. It includes a list of qualities of excellent teachers of reading, as well as recommendations for professional preparation and practice. Key ideas from the position statement are included in this section. Five resources for meeting the challenges are assessment, evidence-based instruction, professional networking, parents and students, and self-reflection (see Figure 1.3).

Assessment

The first resource for meeting the challenges is *assessment*. According to *The Literacy Dictionary*, assessment is "the act or process of gathering data in order to better understand the strengths and weaknesses of student learning, as by observation, testing, interviews, etc." (Harris & Hodges, 1999, p. 12). Assessment can be both formal (e.g., standardized tests) and informal (e.g., teacher-made tests, checklists). Data from both formal and informal assessments are critical for teachers to make important instructional decisions. Serafini (2000–2001) defines assessment as inquiry—a process of collecting data to make decisions about instruction: "When assessment becomes a process of inquiry, an interpretive activity rather than simply the 'objective' measure of predetermined behaviors, teachers will be able

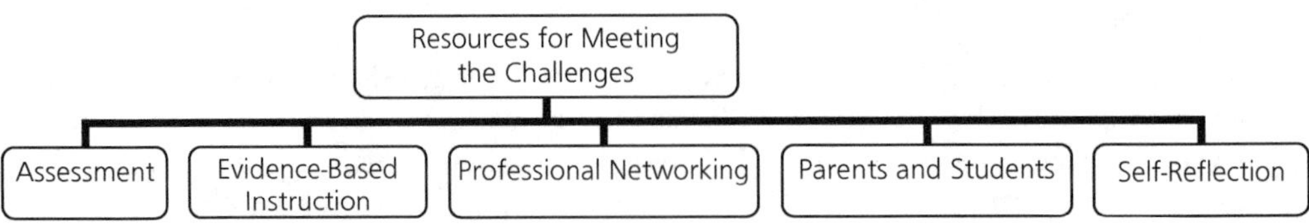

FIGURE 1.3. Resources for meeting the challenges.

to use assessment to make informed decisions concerning curriculum and instruction in their classes" (p. 392). Assessment and instruction need to work hand in hand.

When asked, "How will literacy be assessed in the next millennium?", Sheila Valencia, an expert in literacy assessment, made two predictions that underscore the importance of formal and informal assessment. "One future trend that seems most certain is that high-stakes, large-scale assessment will continue to dominate the assessment scene" (Valencia, 2000, p. 247). "A second future trend I predict is the strengthening of classroom-based assessment, much of it in the form of [student] performance assessment" (Valencia, 2000, p. 248). Therefore, it is critical for classroom and clinical teachers to know how to administer and interpret data from a variety of assessment tools. In Chapter 2 and throughout this book, you will learn more about the purposes for assessment and how you can use appropriate assessment tools to plan appropriate instruction for all students.

Evidence-Based Instruction

The second resource teachers have is *evidence-based instruction* (Stanovich & Stanovich, 2003). Evidence-based (also referred to as *research-based* or *scientifically based*) instruction puts an "emphasis on implementing education programs and practices that have been clearly demonstrated to be effective through rigorous scientific research" (*www.ed.gov/nclb*). In an article entitled "Romance and Reality," Stanovich (1993–94) wrote, "Nothing has retarded the cumulative growth of knowledge in the psychology of reading more than the failure to deal with problems in a scientific matter" (p. 287). While much still needs to be learned about how best to teach all students to read and write, a strong foundation of reading research does exist. This research provides evidence about "what works" in terms of understanding the psychology and physiology of reading and producing positive student achievement outcomes in reading.

With increased public interest in best practice in reading instruction, in 2002 the International Reading Association issued a position statement about evidence-based reading instruction (*www.reading.org/resources/issues/positions_evidence_based.html*). The position statement describes five criteria for good evidence. These criteria can be used to evaluate any particular practice.

- *Objective*—data would be identified and interpreted similarly by any evaluator.
- *Valid*—data adequately represent the tasks children need to accomplish to be successful readers.
- *Reliable*—data will remain essentially unchanged if collected on a different day or by a different person.
- *Systematic*—data were collected according to a rigorous design of either experimentation or observation.
- *Refereed*—data have been approved for publication by a panel of independent reviewers.

In addition, the position statement emphasizes that administrators and teachers need to keep the needs of their particular students and schools in mind when selecting instructional practices for implementation. Chapter 2 provides more discussion of evidence-based practice and how to differentiate instruction based on assessment of students' strengths and areas for improvement. Other chapters (Chapters 4–12) in this book are organized topically by key components of a reading curriculum (e.g., phonological awareness, phonics, reading comprehension). These chapters provide specific suggestions for assessing students in multiple ways and for increasing the intensity of instruction as needed.

RESEARCH BRIEF Best Practice in Reading Instruction

What do we know about best practice in reading instruction? What does research indicate about best practice? To answer these questions, in 1997 the National Institute of Child Health and Development, in collaboration with the U.S. Department of Education, selected a panel of 14 prominent researchers to synthesize existing research in reading instruction. The National Reading Panel's (2000a) final report (also available at *www.nationalreadingpanel.org*) provides a summary of what we know about effective reading instruction and what we still need to learn. Findings emphasize the importance of systematic and intensive instruction in the following areas: phonemic awareness, phonics, fluency, and reading comprehension. The National Reading Panel report has not been without critics (Allington, 2002; Krashen, 2001). Concerns have been registered about the criteria used to select studies and the applicability of findings to ELLs and struggling readers. In an attempt to dispel some of the "myths" about the National Reading Panel, one of the panel members, Timothy Shanahan (2003a), wrote, "It would be best if educators and policymakers read the NRP report themselves and drew their own conclusions" (p. 654).

Professional Networking

After five years of teaching, Willa Hart was beginning to feel isolated in her teaching and in need of a boost—she wanted some fresh ideas. When one of the teachers in her school invited her to attend the local reading council meeting, she jumped at the chance. What Willa discovered was that attending meetings several times a year helped bring new resources to her class, and that she could share some of her own good ideas with other professionals. At the school level, Willa organized a professional reading group. Each group member subscribed to a different professional journal. Once a week at lunchtime, a group member provided highlights and teaching tips from the newest edition of her journal to other members of the group.

What Willa learned is that even a little time spent in *professional networking* is time well spent. Professional organizations provide a lifeline for teachers. Through publications, conferences, and the promotion of ongoing research, professional organizations provide opportunities for teachers to stay current and to keep abreast of trends, issues, and best practices. Some national organizations, such as the International Reading Association and the Council for Exceptional Children, have state and local chapters. Table 1.1 provides information about several professional organizations, including a brief description of each, contact information, journals, and additional services.

TECH TIP Online Reading Resources

It's becoming easier than ever to tap into the resources available through professional organizations. In addition to books, newsletters, and journals, many organizations have expanded their online resources. For example, the International Reading Association's website includes an archive of past publications, as well as current issues of *Reading Research Quarterly.* In addition, this organization publishes a peer-reviewed online journal, *Reading Online* (*www.readingonline.org*). *Reading Online* is particularly useful for professionals interested in integrating technology into the teaching of reading.

Parents and Students

In meeting today's challenges in helping students learn to read and write, it is critical that *parents and students* feel involved and have ownership in the educational process (Turner & Kim, 2003). In terms of parent involvement, Edwards (2003) put it this way: "Parent involvement in education is no passing fad; it is here to stay. It is center stage within policy circles, professional organizations, and the media" (p. 308). Beginning with the efforts of former First Lady Barbara Bush, the importance of parental involvement in reading has come into the national spotlight in recent years.

Certainly there is a strong positive relationship between parent involvement in children's education and academic achievement (Hannon, 1987; Henderson, 1987; Southwest Educational Development Laboratory, 2002), and children who are successful readers have supportive and interested parents, guardians, and/or siblings who value reading (Spiegel, Fitzgerald, & Cunningham, 1993). However, parents of children with disabilities often do not know how to participate in children's education effectively (Harry, 1992). Similarly, parents of children who are ELLs have a great deal of confusion about what schools expect academically, and they often feel frustrated about how to help their children (Delgado-Gaitan, 1990). Research indicates that reading achievement of children with special needs improves when parents become actively involved in assisting their children in reading (Hourcade & Richardson, 1987). Also, when parents of ELLs are guided on how to conduct home reading activities, their children increase their reading achievement (Goldenberg, 1987). Parents often want to help, but need the guidance of professionals to provide leadership and to suggest specific ways of helping their children at home (Hughes, 1995; Hughes, Valle-Riestra, & Arguelles, 2002). Fortunately, research-based practices in parent engagement are beginning to emerge. Throughout this book, we provide Parent Pointers that describe specific ways to communicate and collaborate with parents.

When you are working with children who appear to be having challenges in learning to read and write, bringing in parents or guardians as partners is vital. The Student Background Information forms, Figure 1.4 (English version) and Figure 1.5 (Spanish version), provide templates for gathering information from parents or guardians, either in writing or through a personal interview. Such detailed information is not likely to be necessary for all students. However, for students who are struggling, you'll want to have insights about their strengths and challenges from a home perspective. The information you gather can provide valuable insights into how your students read, write, and learn. Because some of the information can be quite sensitive, you may want to clear the use of forms such as these with an administrator at your school. Parents need to be told who will see this information and how it will be used. Consider the Student Background Information forms as sources of items that you can develop further for your own use.

In addition to getting parent input, students need to be involved in the assessment process. In a web page called "A Guide to the Developmentally Appropriate Assessment of Young Children" (*www.beyond-the.book.com/strategies/strategies_090705.html*), the importance of student involvement is described. Form 1.1, the Getting to Know You Survey, provides a starting point for getting to know your students. You can have students fill out the form during the first few days of class. The Getting to Know You Survey can serve as a springboard for getting to know your students' feelings about reading and writing, as well as their interests. If possible, you may want to follow up with an individual or small-group discussion about interests. In addition, you may want to customize this survey to meet your own needs.

TABLE 1.1. Professional Organizations

Professional organization	Description	Contact information	Professional journals	Additional services
International Reading Association (IRA)	IRA is a professional membership organization dedicated to promoting high levels of literacy for all by improving the quality of reading instruction, disseminating research and information about reading, and encouraging the lifetime reading habit.	International Reading Association Headquarters Office 800 Barksdale Road, P.O. Box 8139 Newark, DE 19714-8139 Phone: 302-731-1600 Fax: 302-731-1057 *www.reading.org*	*The Reading Teacher, Journal of Adolescent and Adult Literacy, Reading Research Quarterly, Reading Research Quarterly Online, Lectura y Vida, Reading Online*	Journal subscriptions; discounts on books and on registration for meetings; access to grants and awards; a wealth of online resources; opportunities to connect with colleagues around the world.
College Reading Association (CRA)	CRA promotes professional standards, self-development, and growth; and encourages the improvement of college and university curricula, programs, and administrative, clinical, diagnostic, and instructional practices related to the learning process.	College Reading Association *www.collegereadingassociation.org*	*Reading Research and Instruction, The Reading News*	Acts as a resource for the consideration and dissemination of information related to the field of literacy; prepares and distributes professional publications; sponsors conferences and meetings to meet the professional needs of members.
National Reading Conference (NRC)	NRC is a community that engages in literacy research and dialogue around literacy and related topics. Its purpose is to support the professional development of	National Reading Conference Headquarters 7044 S. 13th Street Oak Creek, WI 53154-1429 Phone: 414-768-8000	*Journal of Literacy Research, National Reading Conference Yearbook*	Holds an annual conference; serves as a forum for the dissemination or reading research; confers awards for outstanding reading research and service to the reading community.

	emerging and established scholars and advocate research-informed improvements in education.	Fax: 414-768-8001 *www.nrconline.org*		
Council for Exceptional Children (CEC)	CEC supports special education professionals and others working on behalf of individuals with exceptionalities by advocating for appropriate governmental policies, setting professional standards, providing professional development, and helping professionals achieve the conditions necessary for effective professional practice.	Council for Exceptional Children 1110 North Glebe Road, Suite 300 Arlington, VA 22201 Voice phone: 703-620-3660 TTY: 703-264-9446 Fax: 703-264-9494 email: *service @cec.sped.org* *www.cec.sped.org*	*Exceptional Children, Teaching Exceptional Children*	Professional development opportunities; 17 divisions for specialized information; journals; conventions; special education publications; information services, including ERIC Clearinghouse, National Clearinghouse on Careers Serving Children with Disabilities, and IDEA Partnerships.
Teachers of English to Speakers of Other Languages (TESOL)	TESOL's mission is to ensure excellence in English-language teaching to speakers of other languages.	Teachers of English to Speakers of Other Languages 700 South Washington Street, Suite 200 Alexandria, VA 22314 Phone: 888-547-3369 Fax: 703-836-7864 or -6447 *www.tesol.org*	*TESOL Quarterly, Essential Teacher*	Serial publications; member communities; electronic-only newsletters and announcements lists; discounts on publications; convention and professional development event registrations; free career services; awards, grants, and other funding.

STUDENT BACKGROUND INFORMATION

Child's name: ______________________________

Birth date: ______________ Birthplace: ______________

Languages spoken in home: ______________________________

Address: ______________________________

Phone number: ______________________________

Parent/guardian email: ______________________________

1. Does your child generally listen attentively when you talk to him/her? __________
2. Does s/he follow directions well? __________
3. Does your child generally see tasks through to completion? __________
4. Has your child had many ear infections? __________
5. Has s/he had his/her hearing examined by a doctor? __________
6. Do you think your child hears well? __________
7. Do you feel your child has any speech or language problems? If so, describe. __________
   ____
8. What is your child's attitude toward school? __________
9. What is your child's attitude toward reading? __________
10. What is your child's attitude toward writing? __________
11. What is his/her usual disposition? __________
12. How does s/he usually react to authority? __________
13. Are there situations in which your child becomes easily frustrated? If so, explain. __________
    ____
14. How does your child get along with siblings? Others his/her age? __________
15. List any childhood disease, serious injury, or surgery and the age that each occurred: ____
    ____
16. Does your child have any health problems? Explain. __________
    ____
17. When was your child last examined by a physician? __________

(cont.)

FIGURE 1.4. Student Background Information (English Version). From Bader, Lois A. (2005). *Bader Reading and Language Inventory* (5th ed.). Copyright N/A. Reprinted by permission of Pearson Education, Inc., Upper Saddle River, NJ. Note: In Chapter 2 you will read more about factors that influence reading and writing difficulties. The data you collect from parents can give you insight about possible factors that may have an impact on a child's learning to read and write. Although there is potential for overlap, items on this background form relate to the following factors:
Items 1–3—Cognitive factors
Items 4–7—Language factors
Items 8–14—Social/emotional factors
Items 15–21—Physical factors
Items 22–24—Educational factors
Items 25–30—Family factors

18. List any types of medication s/he is now receiving. ______________________________

____
19. Does your child wear, or has s/he ever worn, glasses? __________________________
20. When was your child's last vision check? __________ Results? ___________________
21. Do you think your child gets enough rest? __________ Does s/he become easily fatigued? ____
22. What are his/her best subjects? _____________ Worst subjects? _________________
23. Has your child experienced any difficulty in learning to read? Please describe. _________

____
24. Has your child experienced any difficulty in learning to write? Please describe. ________

____
25. Does your child read voluntarily? __________ What? ___________________________
26. Are there reading materials in your home that are appropriate for your child? ________
27. Does your child spend time on his/her schoolwork at home? ___________________
28. Does s/he have a quiet place to study? _______________________________________
29. Is there anyone at home who can help him/her read and write? _________________
30. Is there any family history of reading or writing problems? _____________________

Other

Please add any information that you feel will aid in understanding and helping your child. _______

Name of person completing form: ____

Relationship to child: ____

FIGURE 1.4. *(cont.)*

Self-Reflection

The final way to meet the challenges is through *self-reflection*. We teachers must constantly strive to become even better—we owe it to our students and ourselves. Teaching in general, and teaching reading and writing in particular, are not easy. We can and must do our best, and then try to do even better the next class session and the next year.

The National Board for Professional Teaching Standards (*www.nbpts.org*) is a nonprofit organization that has developed teaching standards to guide professional development for educators. One of the core propositions of National Board certification is reflective teaching: "Teachers think systematically about their practice and learn from experience" (*www.nbpts.org/standards/know_do/intro.html*). "Accomplished teachers draw on their knowledge of human development, subject matter and instruction, and their understanding of their students to make principled judgments about sound practice. Their decisions are not only grounded in the literature, but also in their experience. They engage in lifelong learning which they seek to encourage in their students" (p. 3).

This book provides opportunities for you to reflect about your own teaching and how to make it better. Take time to do this. Self-reflection about your professional practice and ongoing professional development are pathways to growth—growth that can benefit you and benefit your students, both present and future. Features in each chapter to assist you include Reflection and Action (activities to promote self-reflection), Read On! (recommended professional reading), and Sharpening Your Skills: Suggestions for Professional Development (tips for professional growth).

INFORMACIÓN DE LA CASA DEL NIÑO/A

Nombre del niño/a: ______

Fecha de nacimiento: ______ Lugar de nacimiento: ______

Idioma(s) hablado en casa: ______

Dirección: ______

Teléfono: ______

Correo electrónico de padres/guardianes: ______

1. En general, ¿su niño/a escucha atentamente cuado usted le habla? ______
2. ¿Su niño/a sigue instrucciones bien? ______
3. Generalmente, ¿su niño/a hace sus trabajos hasta completarlos? ______
4. ¿Ha tenido su niño/a muchas infecciones de oído? ______
5. ¿Ha sido su niño/a examinado del oído por un médico? ______
6. ¿Usted piensa que su niño/a oye bien? ______
7. ¿Usted cree que su niño/a tiene algún problema al hablar o de lenguaje? Si es así, descríbalo. ______
8. ¿Cuál es la actitud de su niño/a hacia la escuela? ______
9. ¿Cuál es la actitud de su niño/a hacia la lectura? ______
10. ¿Cuál es la actitud de su niño/a hacia la escritura? ______
11. ¿Cuál es su temperamento usual? ______
12. Usualmente, ¿cómo reacciona él/ella a la autoridad? ______
13. ¿Hay situaciones en las cuales su niño/a se siente frustrado/a fácilmente? Si es así, explíquelo. ______
14. ¿Cómo se lleva su niño/a con sus hermanos? ¿Con otros de su edad? ______
15. Apunte cualquier enfermedad infantil, herida grave, o cirugía, y a qué edad ocurrió cada una: ______
16. ¿Tiene su niño/a algún problema de salud? Explique. ______
    ______
17. ¿Cuándo fue la última vez que su niño/a fue examinado por un médico? ______
18. Apunte cualquier tipo de medicina que su niño/a toma actualmente. ______
    ______
19. ¿Su niño/a usa o ha usado anteojos? ______ Si es sí, ¿porqué? ______
20. ¿Cuándo tuvo su niño/a el último examen de la vista? ______ ¿Cuál fue el resultado? ______
21. ¿Usted piensa que su niño/a descansa lo suficiente? ______
    ¿Se fatiga su niño/a fácilmente? ______
22. ¿Cuáles son las mejores asignaturas de su niño/a? ______ ¿Las peores asignaturas? ______

(cont.)

FIGURE 1.5. Student Background Information (Spanish version). From Bader, Lois A. (2005). *Bader Reading and Language Inventory* (5th ed.). Copyright N/A. Reprinted by permission of Pearson Education, Inc., Upper Saddle River, NJ. See the *Note* in the caption to Figure 1.4.

23. ¿Ha presentado su niño/a alguna dificultad aprendiendo a leer? Por favor describala. ______

24. ¿Ha presentado su niño/a alguna dificultad aprendiendo a escribir? Por favor descríbala. ______

25. ¿Lee su niño/a voluntariamente? ________ ¿Qué lee? ________
26. ¿Hay en su casa materiales de lectura apropiados para su niño/a? ________
27. ¿Pasa su niño/a tiempo en casa haciendo su tarea? ________
28. ¿Tiene su niño/a un lugar tranquilo para estudiar? ________
29. ¿Hay alguien en casa que pueda ayudarlo/a a leer y escribir? ________
30. ¿Hay alguien en la familia que haya tenido algún problema aprendiendo a leer o a escribir? ________

Other

Por favor, agregue cualquier información que usted considere nos ayudará a entender y atender mejor a su niño/a. ________

Nombre de la persona llenando el formulario: ________

Relación al niño/a: ________

FIGURE 1.5. *(cont.)*

RESEARCH BRIEF Best Practice: A View from the Past

The quest to find the "best way" to provide reading instruction is not new. In an attempt to identify the optimal way to teach reading, in the 1960s the United States funded a series of 27 individual research projects under the umbrella title of the Cooperative Research Program in First-Grade Reading. Guy Bond and Robert Dykstra from the University of Minnesota served as principal investigators for the studies. Findings from the studies were published in 1967 in the *Reading Research Quarterly*. Thirty years later, the editors of this journal devoted an entire issue to reflections of this landmark research. Today researchers are using new tools to continue the quest for finding best practices and, in some cases, are making great strides. Nonetheless, one finding from the First-Grade Reading studies still holds true—the importance of the individual classroom teacher. As Bond and Dykstra (1967) concluded, "The tremendous range among classrooms within any method points out the importance of elements in the learning situation over and above the methods employed. To improve reading instruction, it is necessary to train better teachers of reading rather than to expect a panacea in the form of materials" (p. 416).

DEVELOPING STUDENT READING AND WRITING PROFILES

As Vivian Varga's vignette at the beginning of this chapter illustrates, even in times of high accountability, standards-based instruction, and high-stakes tests, teachers still are decision makers. As a matter of fact, the current emphasis on data-based decision making makes the role of the teacher even more central and demands a high level of professionalism. In this book, we encourage teachers to develop student reading and writing profiles to help them organize data for decision making. Our discussion of these profiles begins in the next section and grows from chapter to chapter. A comprehensive profile form is included in Appendix A at the end of the book. We encourage you to think and reflect about the components of the profile included in each chapter, to use them as a guide, and then to adapt the components to meet your local assessment, curricular, and individual student needs. You may also want to make adaptations based on whether you teach in a classroom or a resource setting. We begin with gathering input from students and parents. Let's get started.

Getting to Know Your Students

As teachers, our primary responsibility is to provide the best instruction possible to our students and to monitor how our students are learning. For this to happen, we need to know students' learning needs from multiple sources. Formal and informal assessment tools can provide a great deal of detail about what students know and what they need to learn. This book will provide detailed information about how to conduct such assessment.

However, the first and best way to get started is to get to know your students on an informal level. The Getting to Know You Survey (Form 1.1) is a good starting point. You may also want to gather information from parents/guardians. We have included parent/guardian information sheets in both English and Spanish versions (see Figures 1.4 and 1.5). Additional instruments for gathering information from students and parents are included throughout this book.

Use the data you gather from students and parents/guardians to start a Student Reading and Writing Profile for each of your students. The cover sheet for the Student Reading and Writing Profile is included in Form 1.2 in this chapter; subsequent chapters will include additional summary pages for this profile. Some teachers keep such profiles in file drawers, in notebooks, or in databases on the computer. Whatever you decide, make certain that the data are kept in a secure place.

CHAPTER SUMMARY

Literacy is power. Those who are literate—who "know the code"—are in a better position to obtain advanced education, desirable jobs, and leadership positions in our society. Those who know the code are also in a better position to teach their own children the power of the written word. Those who do not know the code are likely not only to have opposite experiences in terms of quality of life, but to be in danger of perpetuating their lack of knowledge to future generations. In our society and in this day and age, all students should have the opportunity to learn how to read and write. Without that opportunity, their lives and the lives of their children are restricted in many ways. We need to provide high-quality literacy instruction for all students—to help all students learn how to read and write. Increased accountability, diversity of students in the classroom, and controversy about how best to teach all students to read and write are formidable challenges. Fortunately, there are resources to help teachers meet these challenges. Assessment, evidence-based instruction, professional networking, parents and students, and self-reflection can provide teachers with support in making vital instructional decisions. To guide teachers in decision making, it is important to have a reading and writing profile to serve as a guide for planning and instruction for each student. A reading and writing profile begins with getting to know students through input from parents and students. The profile begins in this chapter (see Form 1.2) and grows and develops throughout this book.

KEY TERMS AND CONCEPTS

Adequate yearly progress (AYP)
Assessment
Balanced instruction
Bottom-up perspective
Children's rights to read
Evidence-based instruction
Interactive–compensatory model
National Board for Professional Teaching Standards
No Child Left Behind Act (NCLB)
Self-reflection
Top-down perspective

REFLECTION AND ACTION

1. Each of us has a story about how we learned to read and write. Think about your own journey as a reader and writer. Write a two-page reflective paper about your own literacy biography.
2. What are your beliefs about the teaching of reading? Complete the questionnaire about beliefs about the teaching of reading in Figure 1.6 on the next page. Then write a one-page belief statement expressing your own views about how reading should be taught.
3. This chapter introduces challenges teachers face in helping all students learn to read and write. The chapter also suggests resources teachers can tap for meeting those challenges. List additional challenges that teachers face and productive ways that teachers are meeting those challenges. Also list barriers that keep teachers from doing the good job they would like to do.
4. Form 1.1 presents a Getting to Know You Survey that is appropriate for students in upper elementary and secondary grades. Think about how you might assess interests and background information for students in primary grades. Develop a Getting to Know You format for younger readers and writers, and add this format to your assessment file.
5. Identify the standards for reading, guidelines for determining AYP, and high-stakes assessment methods in your state.

READ ON!

Edwards, P. A. (2004). *Children's literacy development: Making it happen through school, family, and community involvement.* Boston: Allyn & Bacon.

This book was written by one of the nation's leading experts in parent involvement in reading. It provides practical, research-based ideas for encouraging family involvement in a wide range of literacy activities.

National Reading Panel. (2000). *Teaching children to read: An evidence-based assessment of the scientific research literature on reading and its implications for reading instruction.* Rockville, MD: National Institute of Child Health and Human Development.

The National Reading Panel report provides findings of a federally mandated committee. Congress charged the committee with the responsibility to summarize research in reading in the following areas: alphabetics, fluency, comprehension, teacher education, and computer technology. (The executive summary is available at *www.nationalreadingpanel.org*)

Pressley, M. (2003). A few things educators should know about instructional experiments. *The Reading Teacher, 57*, 64–71.

This article presents 12 important points that teachers should know in considering what constitutes evidence-based instructional practices. The author emphasizes the importance of using instructional practices in reading that have a research base. However, he also describes cautions that teachers should attend to in considering the merit of potential practices.

QUESTIONNAIRE AIMED AT BELIEFS REGARDING HOW READING ABILITY DEVELOPS

Name: ______________________________ Date: ____________

Purpose: The purpose of this exercise is to help you reflect on your beliefs about how reading ability develops. Your beliefs can impact your decision making about assessment and instruction.

Directions: Circle the five statements below that most reflect your beliefs about how reading ability develops. Then write a one-page belief statement expressing your own views about how reading ability develops and how reading should be taught.

1. It is important for teachers to provide very clear presentations during reading instruction.
2. Children should receive many opportunities to read materials unrelated to specific school learning tasks.
3. When deciding how to teach reading, one should carefully consider the nature and abilities of the children.
4. Reading, writing, speaking, and listening are closely related learning tasks.
5. Children learn reading best when the task is broken down into specific skills to be taught.
6. Children should be tested frequently to determine if they have learned what was taught. These tests should match very closely the nature of the instruction.
7. Some children read by reading widely and often; others learn best through direct instruction
8. Children should frequently read while they are young so they acquire a "feel" for what reading is like.
9. Opportunities should be created in the classroom to provide children with a reason to read.
10. Less proficient readers often benefit from more direct and structured learning experiences.
11. Teachers should have a list of separate reading skills appropriate for their grade level and make certain that each student masters these skills, and only these skills.
12. Much of what children learn about reading can be attributed directly to what a teacher taught in the classroom.
13. It is important to individuals' reading instruction as much as possible by taking into consideration the children's reading abilities.
14. Children learn a great deal about reading by watching their parents at home.
15. A teacher should generally spend greater time in the classroom with less proficient readers than with more proficient readers.

Interpreting your results:

Items: 1, 5, 6, 11, 12—are related to a bottom-up perspective
Items: 2, 4, 8, 9, 14—are related to a top-down perspective
Items: 3, 7, 10, 13, 15—are related to an interactive compensatory perspective

FIGURE 1.6. Questionnaire aimed at beliefs regarding how reading ability develops. From Leu, Donald J., and Kinzer, Charles K. (2003). *Effective Literacty Instruction, K–8: Implementing Best Practice* (5th ed.). Copyright 2003. Reprinted by permission of Pearson Education, Inc., Upper Saddle River, NJ.

Pressley, M. (2006). *Reading instruction that works: The case for balanced teaching* (3rd ed.). New York: Guilford Press.

Provides more information about different perspectives on the teaching of reading, with related research. Builds a rationale for a balanced-literacy approach that builds on the strengths of bottom-up and top-down approaches.

Stahl, S. A., & Hayes, D. A. (Eds.). (1997). *Instructional models in reading*. Mahwah, NJ: Erlbaum.

This volume is a collection of chapters describing and reflecting about various models of reading instruction.

Stanovich, K. E. (2000). *Progress in understanding reading: Scientific foundations and new Frontiers.* New York: Guilford Press.

This book includes many of Stanovich's landmark publications, as well as his insights about current issues in reading research and policy. Of particular interest is his perspective on the "reading wars."

Stanovich, P. J., & Stanovich, K. E. (2003). *Using research and reason in education: How teachers can use scientifically based research to make curricular and instructional decisions.* Jessup, MD: National Institute for Literacy.

This monograph provides a clear description of the importance of evidence-based practice and guidelines for teachers to use in evaluating the merit of instructional practices.

SHARPENING YOUR SKILLS: SUGGESTIONS FOR PROFESSIONAL DEVELOPMENT

1. There is a popular statement floating around: "Goals set, goals met." Look at the International Reading Association's position statement on *Excellent Reading Teachers* (*www.reading.org/resources/issues/positions_excellent.html*). Use this statement to set five goals toward becoming a better teacher of reading. What is your action plan to meet those goals?
2. Mark your calendar to make regular visits to the websites of two or three professional organizations. Making a habit of checking the websites regularly will help you get in touch with new resources and updates.

RESOURCES FOR ASSESSMENT AND INSTRUCTION

Cunningham, P. M., & Allington, R. L. (2002). *Classrooms that work: They can all read and write* (3rd ed.). New York: Longman.

Provides practical suggestions for putting a balanced literacy program into action in elementary classrooms. The authors emphasize multilevel strategies to help all students learn.

Harp, B. (2000). *The handbook of literacy assessment and evaluation* (2nd ed.). Norwood, MA: Christopher-Gordon.

Gives descriptions of many commonly used reading and writing assessments—both formal and informal. Advantages and disadvantages of each assessment are provided, as well as implications of data for literacy instruction.

Kame'enui, E., Simmons, D., & Cornachione, C. (2000). *A practical guide to reading assessments.* Newark, DE: International Reading Association.

Describes tools for assessing reading for English- and Spanish-speaking students for the areas of reading outlined in the National Reading Panel report. Includes information about linking assessment to instruction, administration requirements, and ordering information.

International Reading Association. (2002). *Evidence-based reading instruction: Putting the National Reading Panel report into practice.* Newark, DE: International Reading Association.

A collection of articles from *The Reading Teacher*, organized by the National Reading Panel's five major areas of focus: phonemic awareness, phonics, fluency, vocabulary, and reading comprehension.

Mason, P. A., & Schumm, J. S. (Eds.). (2003). *Promising practices for urban reading instruction.* Newark, DE: International Reading Association.

A collection of articles from International Reading Association publications, focusing on promising practices for teaching of reading. Articles are organized according to the 10 Children's Rights to Excellent Reading Instruction identified by the Association. Also includes an extensive annotated bibliography and list of related websites.

Vaughn, S., & Linan-Thompson, S. (2004). *Research-based methods of reading instruction: Grades K–3*. Alexandria, VA: Association for Supervision and Curriculum Development.

A collection of research-based practices for addressing the major areas of reading instruction outlined in the National Reading Panel report.

RECOMMENDED WEBSITES

Barbara Bush Foundation for Family Literacy
www.barbarabushfoundation.com

This website houses information about the former First Lady's foundation activities. The Barbara Bush Foundation funds projects related to the promotion of home literacy, including the reading and writing of parents and their children. The site includes lessons learned from previous projects, publications, and guidelines for submitting grants to the foundation.

Big Ideas in Beginning Reading
http://reading.uoregon.edu

This site provides information on the ongoing work of researchers in reading and special education at the University of Oregon as part of its Institute for the Development of Educational Achievement. Specific evidence-based suggestions for assessment and instruction in phonemic awareness, alphabetic understanding, fluency, vocabulary, and comprehension are provided. Particular emphasis is placed on grades K–3.

Florida Literacy and Reading Excellence (FLaRE)
flare.ucf.edu

The FLaRE website is housed at the University of Central Florida. This site serves as a clearinghouse for information about reading assessment and instruction. It provides links to multiple websites and provides excellent recommendations for teacher resources, both online and in print.

ReadWriteThink
www.readwritethink.org

This website is a joint effort of the International Reading Association, the National Council of Teachers of English, and the MarcoPolo Foundation. The site includes lesson plans, Web resources, and student materials to help educators design and implement standards-based instruction in reading and writing.

Wisconsin Literacy Education and Reading Network Source (WiLEARNS)
http://wilearns.state.wi.us

WiLEARNS provides practical resources for parents and teachers for assessment and teaching of all aspects of reading. The site includes special sections on struggling readers, ELLs, and family involvement.

FORM 1.1. Getting to Know You Survey

Getting to Know You Survey

Name ______________________ Age ____________ Date ____________

1. My favorite TV show is ______________________
2. My favorite kind of music is ______________________
3. If I could get one person's autograph, I'd get one from ______________________
4. On the weekend I like to ______________________
5. My favorite sport is ______________________
6. I like to read about ______________________
7. My favorite magazine is ______________________
8. The best story I ever heard is ______________________
9. The best storyteller I know is ______________________
10. The person who does the best job reading me stories is ______________________
11. The best book I ever read was ______________________
12. In the evening I ______________________
13. I like to collect ______________________
14. I first got a library card when I was ____________ years old.
15. I go to the library about ____________ times a month.
16. I like to write stories about ______________________
17. I like to write letters to ______________________
18. My favorite subject in school is ______________________
19. My hardest subject in school is ______________________
20. My favorite person to talk with is ______________________
21. The most fun I ever had was ______________________
22. My favorite color is ______________________
23. My favorite food is ______________________
24. I wish I could go to ______________________
25. If I had three wishes, I'd wish for
    1. ______________________
    2. ______________________
    3. ______________________

FORM 1.2. Student Reading and Writing Profile (Part I)

Student Reading and Writing Profile

Part I: Getting to Know Your Student

Student's name ____

School ____________________ Grade __________ Age __________

Teacher's name ____

Summary Data from Parents/Guardians

Student strengths in reading and writing ______________________________

____

Student areas for improvement in reading and writing ______________________

____

Possible reasons for difficulties ____________________________________

____

Parent/guardian goals for student improvement in reading and writing ______________

Summary Data from Student

Student strengths in reading and writing ______________________________

____

Student areas for improvement in reading and writing ______________________

____

Possible reasons for difficulties ____________________________________

____

Student goals for improvement in reading and writing ______________________

____

TWO

No Two Learners Learn Alike

The Importance of Assessment and Differentiated Instruction

JEANNE SHAY SCHUMM
MARIA ELENA ARGUELLES

VIGNETTE

Maabel Morales has been a third-grade teacher for 13 years. She enjoys her work and takes pride in the achievements of her students. She instills in them a love of reading as they share different kinds of books for various purposes. Maabel usually considers her class to be a well-oiled machine.

However, this year things are not running as smoothly as they usually do. Harold, a student identified as having an emotional disorder, was placed in her class for most of the day. The first day of school, Harold ran into the classroom and pushed others aside as he yelled, "Hello! Hello!" Most of his classmates backed away. Harold can be aggressive and has a hard time controlling his outbursts. He desperately wants to make friends, but because he throws tantrums and is impulsive, most students keep their distance. Maabel's greatest concern is that Harold's misbehavior prevents him from spending any significant amount of time on classroom tasks. *Informal reading inventory* (IRI) assessments indicate that Harold is reading at the kindergarten level. Maabel is determined to help Harold improve his reading, but she isn't sure where to begin.

Across the hall, Diane Peterson, a second-grade teacher, is also struggling with concerns about the fact that a few of her students are not making progress. Diane has three students, Tammy, Emily, and Julian, who have each been identified as having a learning disability. All three are reading significantly below grade level. Tammy looks at the first letter of a word and guesses the rest of the word. Emily insists on decoding every single word, even those that have been taught as sight words and should be recognized automatically. She draws no clues from pictures or from syntactic or semantic cues. Julian still confuses some letters and doesn't know all the letter–sound correspondences. The individual needs of these students are varied, and Diane worries about how she will meet their needs and of her 25 other students, while covering all of the state grade-level standards.

ANTICIPATION QUESTIONS

- What are some of the reasons students experience difficulties in learning to read and write?
- What are some of the major purposes for assessment?
- What is the role of the classroom teacher in the assessment process?
- What is "different" about differentiated instruction?
- What is a framework for differentiating instruction for students with a wide variety of needs?

INTRODUCTION

In 1908, Edmund Burke Huey wrote in his classic book *The Psychology and Pedagogy of Reading*, "And reading itself, as a psycho-physiological process, is almost as good as a miracle" (1908/1968, p. 5). Like many teachers across the United States, Maabel and Diane perform miracles every day in helping students to become competent readers and writers. Their students have a wide range of backgrounds and needs. As both Maabel and Diane have realized, no two learners learn alike, and "teaching to the middle" will not ensure that all students' needs are met or that all students will learn. This chapter begins with a discussion of why the phenomenon of reading and writing is difficult for some students to achieve. The next two sections provide insights into how assessment and differentiated instruction can help. The chapter concludes with an overview of how data from a student's cumulative folder can serve as a base for further development of a reading and writing profile.

WHY STUDENTS HAVE DIFFICULTY LEARNING TO READ AND WRITE

For some children, learning to read and write occurs in a flash, with little or no adult supervision. For others, with the help of teachers and parents, the process evolves over a period of years. For still others, the miracle just never happens. The answer for why this does not occur is not simple. For most individuals with problems in learning to read and write, it is difficult to isolate one single cause for problems in learning to read and write (Kibby, 1995). As Figure 2.1 indicates, many factors have an impact on success or difficulty in acquiring basic literacy skills.

The types of assessment needed to determine the underlying causes of difficulty in acquiring these skills (see Table 2.1) are typically beyond the expertise of classroom teachers and reading coaches. To determine if a child is dyslexic or in need of special education services, assessment procedures as outlined in federal, state, and local mandates should be followed. Some argue that rather than focusing on underlying causes, a teacher's time is better spent in reading-related academic assessment, systematic instructional interventions, ongoing monitoring of student progress, and referrals to specialists when more in-depth assessment is warranted (Kibby, 1995). Throughout this book, we discuss specific factors that may explain why students may have difficulty learning a particular aspect of reading or writing.

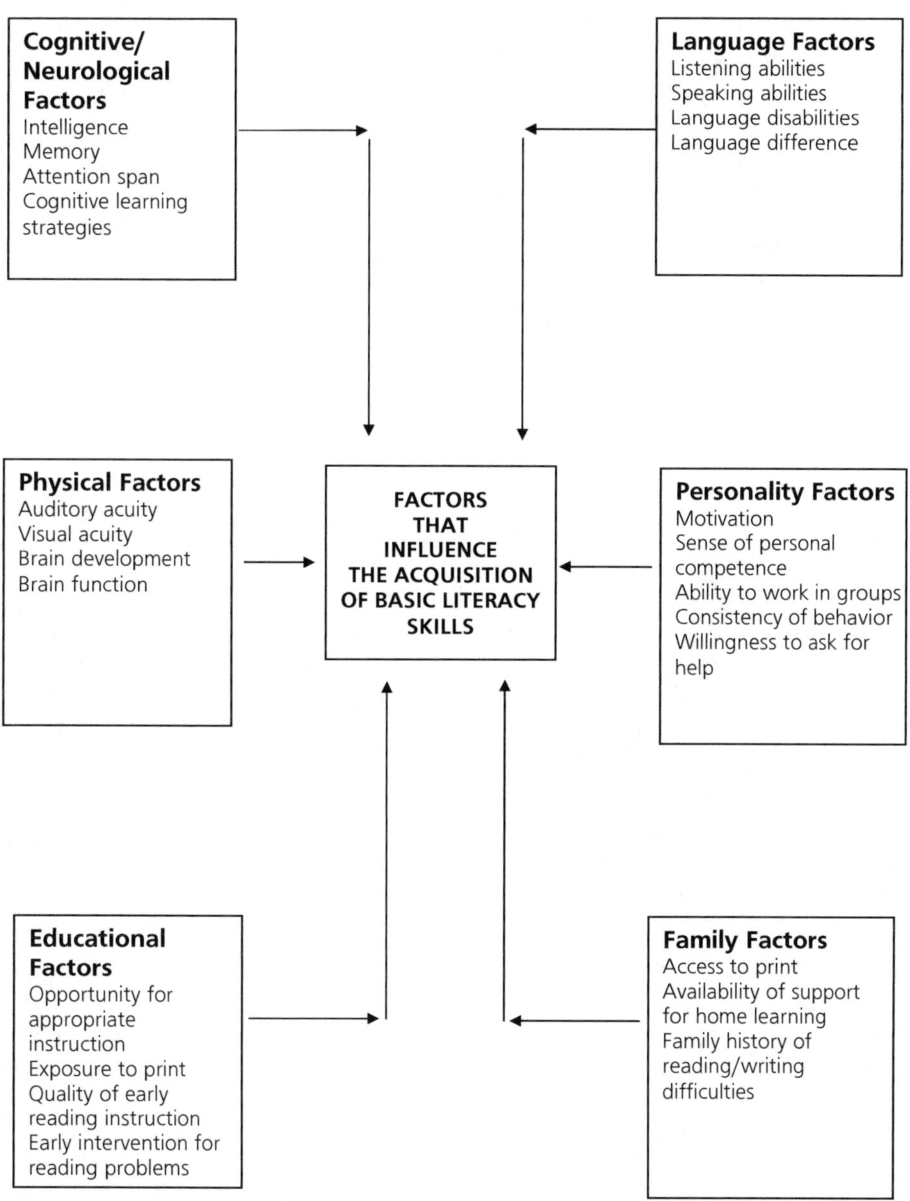

FIGURE 2.1. Factors that influence success or difficulty in acquiring basic literacy skills. Data from Hiebert and Taylor (1994); Johnson and Allington (1991); McCormick (1994); Stanovich (1986); and Vaughn, Bos, and Schumm (1997).

TABLE 2.1. Factors That Influence Success or Difficulty in Acquiring Basic Literacy Skills

Factors that influence the acquisition of basic literacy skills	Indicators	Assessment methods	*Appropriate assessor (referral)*/Instructional strategy
Cognitive/neurological factors	Trouble with memory (encoding, storage, retrieval); need for repetition; need for slower than average pace; difficulty maintaining attention; difficulty understanding	Stanford–Binet Intelligence Scale S–5 (SB5) Woodcock–Johnson III (WJ III) Wechsler Intelligence Scale for Children–IV (WISC-IV) Wechsler Preschool and Primary Scale of Intelligence Cognitive Abilities Test (CogAT) Otis–Lemon School Ability Test Iowa Test of Basic Skills Iowa Tests of Educational Development Detroit Tests of Learning Aptitude–4 (DTLA-4) Informal student observation Portfolio assessment Recall letter/item tasks Time on/off task	*Classroom teacher, school psychologist, testing specialist* Small groups that target specific problematic skills; memory exercise/games; breaking tasks down to small segments; highlighting to emphasize important details; summarizing while reading; semantic mapping; mnemonics and other memory strategies; test-taking, planning, and organizing strategies
Language factors	Delay in learning language; limited vocabulary; trouble with phonological awareness; trouble with articulation; slowness to recognize; overrelying on phonics; trouble retrieving letters/sounds; long pauses in speech; trouble thinking of words; trouble spelling and/or identifying words that are spelled similarly; prolonged sounding out with irregular words; confusing similar words; phonetic spelling; trouble retrieving irregular words; mixing up letter order in words	Comprehensive Receptive and Expressive Vocabulary Test–2 (CREVT-2) Oral and Written Language Scales (OWLS) Peabody Picture Vocabulary Test–III (PPVT-III) Tests of Language Development–3 (TOLD-3) Comprehensive Test of Phonological Processing (CTOPP) Rapid automatized naming (RAN) Tap number of syllables in words Physical medical exam Reading assessments: Informal reading inventory (IRI) Stanford Diagnostic Reading Test–4 (SDRT4) Woodcock Reading Mastery Tests—Revised (WRMT-R) Woodcock Diagnostic Reading Battery (WDRB) Durrell Analysis of Reading Difficulty (DARD) Error analysis (informal)	*Classroom teacher, school psychologist, testing specialist, speech pathologist, medical doctor* Expanding vocabulary; establishing relationships between words; teaching and using cues; sounding out words; preview of vocabulary before reading; word walls and labels; additional wait time; increasing experiences with print; teaching letter patterns; exposure to a variety of print materials

Physical factors	Increased illness; increased absences; medicine side effects; anxiety; fragility; child abuse; allergic conditions; neurological conditions; malnutrition *Hearing*: talking loudly; repeating; ear infections *Vision*: myopia; hyperopia; astigmatism; strabismus; amblyopia; daltonism; headaches while reading; squinting; rubbing; copying; prolonged reversals; rotation errors; mirror imaging; transposition; trouble with directionality	Attention instruments: Attention Deficit Disorders Evaluation Scale–2 (ADDES-2) ADD-H Comprehensive Teacher's Rating Scale (ACTeRS) Attention-Deficit/Hyperactivity Disorder Test (ADHDT) Children's Attention and Adjustment Survey (CAAS) Bender Visual–Motor Gestalt Test (BVMGT) Test of Visual–Motor Integration (TVMI) Written tasks Oral reads Medical examination Eye examination Hearing examination	*Classroom teacher, school psychologist, testing specialist, medical doctor, psychologist/psychiatrist/therapist* Activities in which students are able to work slowly with the shape of letters (using keyboard, etc.); vision therapy; tracing letters; always following left–right, up–down pattern; referral for testing; visual therapy; large print; practice in forming sounds with mouth; speaking slowly and clearly; assistive technologies; adequate lighting; nutritious meal plans in the school
Personality factors	Distractibility; need for significant amount of attention; disruptive behavior; refusal to read; asking peers for help rather than reading; bad self-image; learned helplessness, withdrawal; rejection by classmates; poor physical appearance (i.e., clothing, personal hygiene)	Thematic Apperception Test (TAT) Children's Apperception Test (CAT) Education Apperception Test (EAT) Tasks of Emotional Development (TED) Piers–Harris Children's Self-Concept Scale Student Self-Concept Scale (SSCS) Personality Inventory for Children–2 (PIC-2) Minnesota Multiphasic Personality Inventory–2 (MMPI-2) Functional behavior assessment Behavior Rating Profile–2 (BRP-2) Achenbach System of Empirically Based Assessment (ASEBA) Devereux Behavior Rating Scale—School Form (DBRS-SF) Behavioral and Emotional Rating Scale Drawing	*Classroom teacher, school psychologist, testing specialist, psychologist/psychiatrist/therapist* Creating a comfortable and nonthreatening classroom environment; referral to the guidance counselor/school psychologist; building self-efficacy; specific feedback; reprimanding in private; allowing silent reading before oral reading; providing choices; acknowledging differences; promoting independence; helping students apply strategies independently; appropriate materials; more answer time; prompts

(cont.)

TABLE 2.1. *(cont.)*

Factors that influence the acquisition of basic literacy skills	Indicators	Assessment methods	*Appropriate assessor (referral)*/Instructional strategy
Educational factors	Inadequate teacher, unvaried instruction, inappropriate materials (too difficult/easy), poor educational planning, lack of access to resources, substandard schools,	Grade-level achievement tests Standardized tests Observation Informal assessments *Interview*	*Classroom teacher, school psychologist, testing specialist, school administrator, educational agencies* Workshops; professional organizations; high standards in university programs; direct instruction; professional development; rigorous certification exams; early intervention programs
Family factors (social/cultural factors)	Cultural or social traditions incongruent with those of the instructor (e.g., beliefs about eye contact, education); few or no school supplies; no access to medical needs (e.g., glasses); poor parental reading skills; working family (no time or help at home); parents who do not speak school language; no support (emotional) for schoolwork; low parental expectation of achievement	Reading discussions Question–answer sessions Interview Observation Home language survey *Parent conference*	*Classroom teacher, school psychologist, social service agencies, social worker* A variety of methods; materials that reflect the cultural heritage/diversity of students in the class; creation of a learning community; not requiring materials for home learning that cannot be made in class; cooperative groups; multicultural activities; encouraging use of public library and other public or free facilities and institutions; community organizations; family literacy programs; involving family members whenever possible; encouraging reading at home; encouraging parents to hold high expectations (not pressure); providing reading and writing materials for home use

The Matthew Effect and Reading Difficulties

What is clear is that when young children get off to the wrong start in learning to read and write, for whatever reason or combination of reasons, problems escalate and compound. Walberg and Tsai (1983) and Stanovich (1986) refer to this impact of early reading difficulties on subsequent success in reading as the *Matthew effect*. Their thinking is based on the following passage from the Gospel of Matthew: "For unto every one that hath shall be given, and he shall have abundance: but from him that hath not shall be taken away even that which he hath" (XXV:29). Children who learn the alphabet early, develop a sensitivity to the sounds of the language, are exposed to a wide variety of print, and have a solid early childhood education (at home and at school) have better chances for learning to read and write and for succeeding academically. These children learn to read and write, thus widening their vocabulary and conceptual development. Children who do not have such opportunities and experiences may not catch on to reading and writing; they can get stuck behind and, unfortunately, are likely to stay behind. The Matthew effect is the Biblical version of "the rich get richer while the poor get poorer."

Children come to school with a wide variety of experiences in oral language. Hart and Risley (1995) found that by the time children entered school, the number of vocabulary words the children had been exposed to varied greatly: Some had been exposed to 13 million words, but those on the other end of the spectrum had heard 45 million words. Children from homes with less exposure to oral language heard many more directives, while children who came from homes with high exposure to oral language were engaged in interactive conversations that centered on the children's interests. These gaps in vocabulary and exposure to oral language are difficult to close and seem to be one of the contributing causes for the Matthew effect. Children who come from homes where they have engaged in lots of conversations, they have been read to, have heard lots of rhymes and songs, and have been exposed to lots of words have a solid background knowledge base and are better prepared for learning to read and write.

Phonological awareness is of particular importance in thinking about the Matthew effect. As noted in Chapter 1, *phonological awareness* is the ability to detect and manipulate the speech sounds in language. Eventually, young readers link speech sounds to how the sounds are represented in print. In the past 20 years, research has underscored the importance of phonological awareness in early reading (Torgesen, Wagner, & Rashotte, 1997). As Stanovich (2000) concluded, "I have hypothesized that if there is a specific cause of reading disability at all, it resides in the area of phonological awareness. Slow development in this area delays early code-breaking progress and initiates the cascade of interacting achievement failures and motivational problems" (p. 200). In short, research indicates that lack of phonological awareness is the primary catalyst of the Matthew effect for many students.

SERVICES FOR STUDENTS WITH READING AND WRITING DIFFICULTIES

Students with reading and writing difficulties can be categorized in terms of the types of services they are likely to receive. Five general categories are students with disabilities, students with other exceptionalities, students with cultural and linguistic differences, students with economic challenges, and garden-variety poor readers. As you can see, the range of services is vast and often school-specific. It is important to learn what services are available at the school and district level, and how providers of those services coordinate and collaborate among each other.

Students with Disabilities

In 1975, the U.S. Congress passed Public Law 94-142, the Education for All Handicapped Children Act. This landmark act provided funding for free and appropriate education of students with special needs. This included students with high-incidence disabilities (i.e., communication disorders, learning disabilities, and behavioral disabilities) and low-incidence disabilities (i.e., multiple disabilities, sensory impairments, physical or health disabilities, traumatic brain injury, or autism). One of the key components of this law was the requirement of an *individualized education program* (IEP) for any student receiving federal funds for special education. The reauthorization of this legislation in 1990 and 1997, entitled the Individuals with Disabilities Education Act (IDEA), included emphasis for education of students with disabilities in the *least restrictive environment*, thus increasing the numbers of students with disabilities included in the general education classroom for all or part of the school day. Students with disabilities may receive services in inclusion classrooms, part-time resource settings, self-contained classrooms, or special schools.

While any student with disabilities may experience difficulties with learning to read and write for any of the reasons mentioned earlier in this chapter, students with the most severe literacy problems may be diagnosed as having *dyslexia*. In 2002, the International Dyslexia Association's Board of Directors and the National Institute of Child Health and Human Development defined dyslexia as follows:

> Dyslexia is a specific learning disability that is neurological in origin. It is characterized by difficulties with accurate and/or fluent word recognition and by poor spelling and decoding abilities. These difficulties typically result from a deficit in the phonological component of language that is often unexpected in relation to other cognitive abilities and the provision of effective classroom instruction. Secondary consequences may include problems in reading comprehension and reduced reading experience that can impede growth of vocabulary and background knowledge. (*www.interdys.org*, p. 1)

Students with Other Exceptionalities

Students with exceptionalities that are not included under the umbrella of IDEA may qualify for special services, depending on local and state funding and initiatives. One such group is students identified as gifted and talented. Identification procedures for students who are gifted and talented vary considerably from state to state (Davis & Rimm, 2004). Service provision varies as well. Students who are gifted and talented or who are high-achieving have particular needs in terms of reading and language arts (VanTassel-Baska, 1994), whether they are placed in general education settings or in gifted education settings for all or part of the school day.

Section 504 of the Vocational Rehabilitation Act of 1973 provides support for students who have certain conditions that inhibit academic activities (e.g., chronic health problems, attention disorders). Some students who cannot receive assistance through IDEA can get support through Section 504. The largest group of students who qualify for Section 504 are students with attention-deficit/hyperactivity disorder (ADHD). Although

Section 504 gives qualifying students the right to receive appropriate accommodations, it does not provide additional funds to do so. Thus the majority accommodations are made in the general education setting.

Students with Linguistic Differences

Students who are English-language learners (ELLs) may have access to additional support in language and literacy learning. As you will read in Chapter 3, the nature of that support varies widely from state to state, from district to district, and even from school to school. Types of services may include reading and writing instruction in self-contained classrooms, pull-out instruction, instruction from a language specialist in the regular classroom, or no special services at all. The support may be more intensive in early years of language learning and then diminish as the student becomes more proficient in English.

Students with Economic Challenges

In 1965, the U.S. Congress approved sweeping compensatory education legislation, the Elementary and Secondary Education Act; as noted in Chapter 1, this was reauthorized in 2001 as the No Child Left Behind Act (NCLB). Title I of the act provides funding for the education of students in high-poverty schools. Keep in mind that the funding is allocated by school, not by student. The funding is intended to help compensate for the possible challenges that students from homes with limited economic resources might face in education—particularly in the learning of basic reading, writing, and computational skills. The act has been reauthorized periodically since 1965, and the more recent reauthorizations have given local school districts more flexibility in how the funds are to be spent. Some schools use the funding for resource rooms and reading coaches; others hire reading coaches to work with general education teachers in classroom settings; still others use Title I funds to hire more teachers, thus reducing class size.

Garden-Variety Poor Readers

Some children have a tough time learning to read, but do not qualify for special programs. For the most part, general education teachers are responsible for meeting the needs of these students. This book is organized in a way to provide you with resources for working with garden-variety poor readers. However, some schools have planned for programs for all students with reading challenges, regardless of whether they qualify for funded programs or not. Chapter 14 describes tutoring programs, resource rooms, and other ways to provide support for all struggling readers and writers.

HOW ASSESSMENT CAN HELP

Chapter 1 has included a discussion of the increased accountability for education in the United States. The companion to accountability is high-stakes testing. The emphasis on standardized tests has often overshadowed teacher-generated, classroom-based assessment. This does not need to be the case. In fact, classroom-based assessment is more important now than ever. Such assessment helps to build student profiles and helps teachers better meet individual needs. As Klingner (2003) has written,

> It is important to remember that there are different purposes for assessment, for different audiences, and that high-stakes testing does not and cannot take the place of other forms of testing, such as assessment as inquiry. So then the question becomes how to fit it all in, how to administer the mandatory high-stakes tests and still have time for meaningful assessment and instruction. And that is where teachers do have some choices. (p. 227)

The remainder of this section on assessment is organized by teachers' most frequently asked questions:

- What are the purposes for assessment?
- What expertise is necessary to conduct literacy assessment and to analyze assessment results?
- What tools can be used for assessment?

What Are the Purposes for Assessment?

There are six general purposes for assessment:

1. To screen students for initial grouping, instruction, and needs for further assessment.
2. To identify individual students' strengths and areas in need of improvement in reading and writing.
3. To monitor ongoing progress in reading and writing development.
4. To determine student outcomes in reading.
5. To evaluate the strengths and weaknesses of instructional programs at the classroom, school, district, state, and national levels.
6. To account to parents, administration, community, and policymakers.

The first four purposes for assessment focus on individual students and can assist in making instructional decisions. Screening provides a first step. Screening measures are typically brief in terms of administration time, but provide teachers with initial information for making decisions about grouping, instruction, and needs for additional assessment.

The second purpose for assessment is to determine individual students' strengths and areas of difficulty in reading and writing. Assessments to address this purpose are called *diagnostic instruments*. Classroom teachers and reading coaches can implement and interpret the diagnostic instruments described in this book. However, when students fail to make satisfactory progress as gauged with regular in-class assessment, a recommendation for bringing the case to a school-level prereferral intervention team may be made with parental consent (Friend & Bursuck, 2002). The team will suggest in-class instructional practices or accommodations that the teacher may try to provide for appropriate instruction. If the suggested intervention is not successful, then the student may be recommended to a school psychologist or other specialist for additional individual assessment. Diagnostic assessment may address specific academic areas, as well as factors that affect learning to read and write (cognitive/neurological, physical, educational, language, social/emotional, and family). Based on assessment outcomes, a multidisciplinary team that includes general educators, special educators, school administrators, and parents will determine if special education services are warranted. In addition, the team will craft an IEP to outline specific instructional goals, strategies, and accommodations that are suited for the student.

The third purpose for assessment is to provide ongoing monitoring of student progress. Progress monitoring can serve as a powerful tool for informing instruction. For those students who are receiving intervention or supplemental instruction, ongoing progress monitoring should be more frequent than for those students who have met established benchmarks. The use of ongoing progress monitoring with struggling readers lets you know whether the instruction you provide is effective and whether changes need to be made. The Dynamic Indicators of Basic Early Literacy Skills (DIBELS; Good, Kaminski, Smith, Laimon, & Dill, 2001), is a short, easy-to-administer, and accurate progress-monitoring tool that is very helpful when you are working with young, struggling readers. This one-minute assessment tool can be used on a weekly or biweekly basis to inform you whether students' progress is on track or whether changes to instruction need to be made. The DIBELS is discussed more fully in Chapters 4, 5, and 7.

The fourth purpose for assessment is to determine individual students' progress in reading for the purpose of determining grades, promotion, and placement in remedial classes or special education services. Measures for determining grades can be identified by individual teachers. However, increasing demands of state standards in reading have sometimes limited teacher choices for outcome measures. With the passage of NCLB, standardized tests are increasingly being used to determine grade-level promotion and eventually graduation from high school (Jimerson, 2001). While classroom teachers may be asked to provide evidence of formal and informal assessments as part of a data package to place a student in a special program, school psychologists typically administer the formal assessments need to make such decisions. Clearly, it is important for teachers to know what measures they are both qualified and responsible for administering, and what measures are the responsibility of individuals with specialized training.

The fifth and sixth purposes for assessment are both related to evaluation and accountability issues. For the most part, student outcome data can be used to evaluate the strengths and weakness of instructional programs at multiple levels (classroom, school, district, state, and national; purpose 5) and to provide information to policymakers and to the public (purpose 6). The community at large is interested in whether tax dollars are being well spent and whether children are learning to read and write. At the federal level, the National Assessment of Educational Progress (NAEP) provides a global picture of reading achievement of students in grades 4, 8, and 12 (*http://nces.ed.gov/nationsreportcard*). Since 1969, NAEP (also known as The Nation's Report Card) has provided data about long-term trends in reading performance. These data represent assessment of a sample of students who mirror the national student population.

At the state and local levels, formal assessments are conducted to provide information about student performance in reading. Individual student data are reported to parents, teachers, and administrators. School, district, and overall state data are reported to the general public via websites, public documents, and the mass media. For example, in the state of Florida, the Florida Comprehensive Assessment Test (FCAT) is administered annually to gauge student progress in meeting state-identified reading and writing standards, the Sunshine State Standards (*www.firn.edu/doe/curric/prek12/index.html*). At the student level, test scores on the FCAT are used to determine eligibility for promotion and ultimately graduation from high school. At the school, district, and state levels, data are used to hold teachers and administrators accountable to the public.

RESEARCH BRIEF Why Do Children Fail State Reading Tests?

Riddle Buly and Valencia (2002) attempted to find out more about the reading profiles of 108 fourth-grade students who failed a state high-stakes examination. The research team administered a battery of tests of phonemic awareness, word identification, comprehension, rate, and fluency. Findings indicated that the range of student difficulties was vast, but that these difficulties fell into six general clusters of reading problems. Riddle Buly and Valencia categorized the students as "word callers," "struggling word callers," "word stumblers," "slow comprehenders," "slow word callers," and "disabled readers." A disproportionate number of students who failed the test were ELLs. The findings from this study underscore the importance of classroom assessment to go beyond what standardized test results reveal. Findings also indicate that differentiated instruction is mandatory to meet the varied needs of individual readers, including students who are learning to speak English as a second language.

What Expertise Is Necessary to Conduct Assessments and to Analyze Assessment Results?

The International Reading Association has a Code of Ethics for its members and a set of guidelines for professional practice entitled *Standards for Reading Professionals*. The Code of Ethics states:

> Professionals in reading must possess suitable qualifications for engaging in consulting, diagnostic, or remedial work. Unqualified persons should not engage in such activities except under the direct supervision of one who is properly qualified. Professional intent and the welfare of the person seeking services should govern all consulting or clinical activities such as counseling, administering diagnostic tests, or providing remediation. (*www.reading.org/association/about/code.html*, p. 1)

The newly revised *Standards for Reading Professionals* (International Reading Association, 2003; also available at *www.reading.org/resources/issues/reports/professional_standards.html*) recommend that classroom teachers know how to administer and interpret a variety of formal and informal assessment tools. This includes technology-based assessment tools and assessments appropriate for students from diverse cultural and linguistic backgrounds. In general, the classroom teacher should be familiar with basic assessment terms and be capable of interpreting assessment results in comprehensible language to parents. Figure 2.2 provides a brief quiz to determine your knowledge of common assessment terms. In addition, Figure 2.3 is an assessment primer from *The Reading Teacher's Book of Lists* (Fry, Kress, & Fountoukidis, 2000). This primer defines basic terms that you need to know and that you may need to explain to parents. Additional assessment terms and guidelines for interpreting assessment results are provided throughout this book.

Many informal assessment tools are fairly straightforward and easy to use with little training. Others, such as an IRI (see Appendix B of this book), take more supervised training and practice. The amount of expertise needed for formal assessment, however, varies considerably. Some assessment tools (such as intelligence tests) are appropriate only for professionals who have had special training, and in some cases a professional or state license may be required. Others are intended for teacher use, with the understanding that standardized administration and scoring procedures will be followed. When you are

HOW MUCH DO YOU KNOW ABOUT TESTING?

Below is a matching test designed to determine how much you do and do not know about testing terminology. The column on the left is a list of measurement terms. In the space before each term on the left, enter the number of the appropriate definition from the column on the right.

____ Raw score

____ Norms

____ Stanines

____ Norm-referenced test

____ Standardized tests

____ Mean

____ Standard error of measurement

____ Validity

____ Diagnostic test

____ Reliability

____ Standardized score

____ Achievement test

____ Criterion-referenced test

____ Percentile rank

____ Grade equivalent

1. The degree to which a test gives consistent results when administered repeatedly, usually expressed by some form of coefficient.
2. Administered and scored according to a uniform procedure and measured against a norm.
3. Expected variation in test scores if the test were to be given repeatedly to the same person. It is both added to and subtracted from an individual's score to obtain the range with which the individual's true score really lies.
4. A test typically containing many subsections and designed to analyze an individual's specific strengths and weaknesses.
5. The year and month of school (grade level) for which the raw score is the median score on a standardized test.
6. The statistics that describe the test performance of the groups on whom the test was standardized, groups considered representative of those for whom the test is intended.
7. A general term for referring to a variety of transformed raw scores that can be compared across other individuals and tests.
8. A test whose results are meant to be compared with previously established norms.
9. The degree of accuracy with which a test measures what it is intended to measure.
10. The number of items answered correctly.
11. Compares one score with other scores of individuals on that level.
12. A measurement of the mastery of certain academic skills.
13. Normalized standardized scores with a mean of 5 and a range of 1–9.
14. A test of specific content, measuring individual performances without comparison to the entire group.
15. The arithmetic average of a group of scores.

Answer key: 10, 11, 13, 8, 2, 15, 3, 9, 4, 1, 7, 12, 14, 6, 5

FIGURE 2.2. How much do you know about testing? From Lyndon W. Searfoss & John E. Readence, *Helping Children Learn to Read* (3rd ed.). Published by Allyn and Bacon, Boston, MA. Copyright 1994 by Pearson Education. Reprinted by permission of the publisher.

TESTING TERMS

Most school districts give tests. Most teachers get the results of those tests. What do those test scores mean? How do you interpret them? One place to start is with an understanding of the terminology that test makers use. Familiarity with these terms will help you to explain test results to interested and sometimes anxious students and parents.

Achievement tests. Tests that measure how much students have learned in a particular subject area.

Aptitude tests. Tests that attempt to predict how well students will do in learning new subject matter in the future.

CEEB test scores. College Entrance Examination Board test scores. This type of score is used by exams such as the Scholastic Aptitude Test. It has a mean of 500 and a standard deviation of 100.

Correlation coefficient. A measure of the strength and direction (positive or negative) of the relationship between two things.

Criterion-referenced tests. Tests for which the performance of the test taker is compared with a fixed standard or criterion. The primary purpose is to determine if the test taker has mastered a particular unit sufficiently to proceed to the next unit.

Diagnostic tests. Tests that are used to identify individual student's strengths and weaknesses in a particular subject area.

Grade equivalent scores. The grade level for which a score is the real or estimated average. For example, a grade equivalent score of 3.5 is the average score of students halfway through the third grade.

Mean. The arithmetical average of a group of scores.

Median. The middle score in a group of ranked scores.

Mode. The score that was obtained by the largest number of test takers.

Normal distribution. A bell-shaped distribution of test scores in which scores are distributed symmetrically around the mean and where the mean, median, and mode are the same.

Norming population. The group of people to whom the test was administered in order to establish performance standards for various age or grade levels. When the norming population is composed of students from various sections of the country, the resulting standards are called *national norms*. When the norming population is drawn from a local school or school district, the standards are referred to as *local norms*.

Norm-referenced tests. Tests for which the results of the test taker are compared with the performance of others (the norming population) who have taken the test.

Percentile rank. A comparison of an individual's raw score with the raw score of others who took the test (usually this is a comparison with the norming population). This comparison tells the test taker the percentage of other test takers whose scores fell below his or her own score.

Raw score. The initial score assigned to test performance. This score usually is the number correct; however, sometimes it may include a correction for guessing.

Reliability. A measure of the extent to which a test is consistent in measuring whatever it purports to measure. Reliability coefficients range from 0 to 1. In order to be considered highly reliable, a test should have a reliability coefficient of .90 or above. There are several types of reliability coefficients: *parallel-form* reliability (the correlation of performance on two different forms of a test), *test–retest* reliability (the correlation of test scores from two different administrations of the same test to the same population), *split-half* reliability (the correlation between two halves of the same test), and *internal-consistency* reliability (a reliability coefficient computed using a Kuder–Richardson formula).

(cont.)

FIGURE 2.3. Testing terms. From Fry, E. B., Kress, J. E., & Fountoukidis, D. L. (2000). *The Reading Teacher's Book of Lists* (4th ed.). Paramus, NJ: Prentice Hall. Copyright 2000 by John Wiley & Sons. Reprinted by permission.

Standard deviation. A measure of the variability of test scores. If most scores are close to the mean, the standard deviation will be small. If the scores have a wide range, then the standard deviation will be large.

Standard error of measurement (SEM). An estimate of the amount of measurement error in a test. This provides an estimate of how much a person's actual test score may vary from his or her hypothetical true score. The larger the SEM, the less confidence can be placed in the score as a reflection of an individual's true ability.

Standardized tests. Tests that have been given to groups of students under standardized conditions and for which norms have been established.

Stanine scores. Whole number scores between 1 and 9 that have a mean of 5 and a standard deviation of 2.

True score. The score that would be obtained on a given test if that test were perfectly reliable. This is a hypothetical score.

Validity. The extent to which a test measures what it is supposed to measure. Two common types of validity are *content validity* (the extent to which the content of the test covers situations and subject matter about which conclusions will be drawn) and *predictive validity* (the extent to which predictions made from the test are confirmed by evidence gathered at some later time).

FIGURE 2.3. *(cont.)*

in doubt about the expertise needed to administer a particular assessment tool, ask a reading specialist, administrator, or school psychologist.

PARENT POINTER ☞ Interpreting High-Stakes Test Scores to Parents

Eissenberg and Rudner (1988) suggest that teachers be prepared to explain the following during conferences when test scores are reported:

- The purpose for the test and how results are to be used
- The types of scores reported
- How the child's scores compared with a norming population
- How the child's scores compared with his or her scores from previous years
- How the child's scores compared with other classroom assessments and classroom performance

What Tools Can Be Used for Assessment?

When J. P. Williams was in undergraduate school, he started a file as an assignment for a reading methods course. The file is a collection of reading assessments—some individually administered, some group-administered. Over the years, J. P. has added to the file as he gathers more instruments from the school system, professional journals, and other teachers. He says, "It's my professional toolbox. I couldn't do without it."

Throughout this book, you will be reading about a variety of assessment tools and adding them to your professional toolkit. Each chapter highlights particular measures and includes an annotated bibliography of Resources for Assessment and Instruction. Appendix C of this book provides references for the assessment tools cited in the text of these chapters. A variety of tools is vital for a comprehensive, multidimensional assessment program that includes screening, diagnosis, progress monitoring, and outcomes

(Carnine, Silbert, Kame'enui, & Tarver, 2004). Assessment tools fall into three general categories: norm-referenced, criterion-referenced, and informal assessments.

Norm-Referenced Tests

Norm-referenced tests compare an individual student's performance with that of his or her peers. When norm-referenced tests are developed, the test is given to a sample or norming population of students. The emphasis of norm-referenced tests is on the relative standing of an individual among students of a norm group of the same age or grade level. Norm-referenced tests can be administered on a group or individual basis. They are typically recommended as program evaluation tools and as screening tools (to be followed with measures more appropriate for individual assessment). The Stanford Achievement Test and the Iowa Tests of Basic Skills are examples of norm-referenced tests. Although norm-referenced tests vary, most offer standard, percentile, stanine, and sometimes grade equivalent scores.

Some norm-referenced tests are writing production measures in which students respond in writing to a prompt. Norms for these tests are often local ones created on the spot when a team scans through a set of papers to establish "anchor" or typical papers at each scoring level—say, from 1 (unacceptable) to 6 (exemplary). Once this norming takes place, other papers are scored to determine where they fall in relation to the anchors.

Criterion-Referenced Tests

Criterion-referenced tests assess student mastery of specific goals. They are less global than norm-referenced tests and are typically more closely linked to a particular curriculum or set of competencies. A student's score on a criterion-referenced test is not compared to those of a norming population; instead, it is compared to a predetermined criterion. Criteria need not be traditional ones, such as correctly completing 7 out of 10 items on a test. For example, a criterion could be using correct punctuation "most of the time" or including at least three types of writing in one's portfolio.

Criterion-referenced tests typically serve as tools to aid in individualizing instruction, grouping for instruction, and assessing individual progress. Criterion-referenced tests accompany many basal reading programs. More generic criterion-referenced tests are also available commercially.

Informal Assessments

Informal assessment devices are the heart of a comprehensive assessment program. They are informal in that administration and interpretation of results are flexible. Both teacher and student reports of evaluation of student reading and writing are incorporated. Chapters in this book provide multiple examples of informal assessments including interviews and checklists.

With all the informal assessments available, how does a teacher choose? In some cases, the choice will be made by the state or school district. On many occasions, however, teachers have the flexibility to choose. Indeed, the choices are vast, but, "We must pick, choose, adapt, and adopt the measures that provide us with the information that fits our vision of reading and writing" (Winograd, Paris, & Bridge, 1991, p. 110). Figure 2.4 provides a set of questions to guide your decision making about which assessment tool to use.

QUESTIONS FOR SELECTING ASSESSMENT TOOLS: A BAKER'S DOZEN

1. What is my purpose in using this measure (screening, diagnosis, progress monitoring, outcomes)?
2. Do I have the professional training to administer and interpret the data from this measure?
3. Are the format and content of the measure consistent with my purposes and goals and state or school district standards?
4. Is the type of measure (formal or informal) consistent with my purposes and goals?
5. Is a commercially prepared assessment or local/teacher-prepared assessment tool most appropriate for my goals and purpose?
6. Is the administration and scoring time reasonable in terms of what I hope to learn?
7. Is the measure biased against any linguistic or cultural group?
8. Does the measure assume prior knowledge that the target student(s) may not possess?
9. In the case of a standardized test, are adequate reliability and validity data available?
10. Are directions for administration, scoring, and interpretation of the measure clear and easy to follow?
11. Is an individual measure necessary, or will a group assessment tool suffice?
12. Are multiple forms and levels of the measure available?
13. Can the results of this measure be communicated easily to parents, administrators, and the community at large (depending on the assessment purpose)?

FIGURE 2.4. Questions for selecting assessment tools: A baker's dozen. From M. C. Radencich, P. G. Beers, and J. S. Schumm, *A Handbook for the K–12 Reading Resource Specialist*. Published by Allyn and Bacon, Boston, MA. Copyright 1991 by Pearson Education. Reprinted by permission of the publisher.

HOW DIFFERENTIATED INSTRUCTION CAN HELP

Researchers at the University of Miami conducted observational studies of reading lessons in general education classrooms that included students with disabilities (Schumm, Vaughn, & Moody, 2000) and in special education resource settings (Vaughn, Moody, & Schumm, 1998). Observations revealed that in both settings, teachers conducted mainly whole class lessons and that the individual needs of students with reading problems were not being met. In fact, individual administrations of pre- and posttests indicated that students made very little progress during the academic year in their reading. A later observational study with students with emotional or behavioral disorders indicated similar results with an additional note (Levy & Vaughn, 2002). Teachers in these classrooms spent more time on behavioral issues with less time on reading instruction. Clearly, the one-size-fits-all instructional pattern simply was not working in these classrooms.

Differentiated instruction has become emphasized more and more in recent years. Hall (2003) defines differentiated instruction as follows:

> To differentiate instruction is to recognize students' varying background knowledge, readiness, language, preferences in learning, interests, and to react responsively. Differentiated instruction is a process to approach teaching and learning for students with differing academic needs in the same class. The intent of differentiating instruction is to maximize each student's growth and individual success by meeting each student where he or she is, and assisting in the learning process. (p. 1)

The remainder of this section is organized by frequently asked questions regarding differentiated instruction:

- What is "different" about differentiated instruction?
- How can teachers organize and implement differentiated instruction?

What Is "Different" about Differentiated Instruction?

Differentiation of instruction varies in terms of the level of intensity of instruction provided for each student. Differentiated instruction can occur in classroom or resource settings. Five major dimensions have an impact on the intensity of instruction and thus on differentiation (Table 2.2). These dimensions can be escalated either independently or in a variety of combinations depending on student needs and what instructional goals have been identified. These five dimensions are incorporated in the instructional suggestions included throughout this book.

Instructional Grouping

Instructional groups vary in terms of size (whole class, small groups, pairs, individuals) and composition (homogeneous or same ability vs. heterogeneous or mixed ability). Although there are exceptions, in general, the larger and more diverse the group, the lower the intensity of instruction. As discussed earlier in this chapter, the third purpose for assessment is to provide teachers with data for grouping students for instruction. Using a variety of grouping patterns (known as *flexible grouping*) is essential to address student difficulties in learning to read and write (Vaughn, Bos, & Schumm, 2003). Assessment data can provide information about students' instructional needs. Based on this information teachers can make grouping decisions about the most appropriate group size, composition, materials, purposes, and leadership to meet students instructional needs. Throughout this text we provide specific suggestions for grouping students based on assessment data, as well as practical tips for organizing the classroom for flexible grouping.

TABLE 2.2. Intensity Index: The Five Major Dimensions of Instruction

Dimension	Low	Medium	High
Grouping			
Size	Whole class	Small groups, pairs	Individuals
Composition	Mixed ability	Mixed or same ability	Same ability
Strategies and materials	No evidence	Moderate scientific evidence or proven track record with classroom implementation	Strong scientific evidence with a similar population of students
Instructor	Untrained volunteer	Classroom teacher	Reading specialist
Time	Low length, frequency, duration	Moderate length, frequency, duration	High length, frequency, duration
Practice			
Support	None	Peer-supported	Teacher-guided
Feedback	None	Delayed and/or nonspecific	Immediate and specific

Instructional Strategies and Materials

INSTRUCTIONAL STRATEGIES

High-intensity strategies are those with a strong research base, consisting of data drawn from populations similar to the target group of students. Medium-intensity strategies and materials are research-based—but perhaps with a different population of students—or are based on solid classroom practices with positive student outcomes in the past. Low-intensity strategies are simply untested. They may prove to be powerful, but need to be monitored for effectiveness. Figure 2.5 provides a series of questions you can ask to determine which instructional strategies might be best for your instructional purposes.

INSTRUCTIONAL MATERIALS

Role of Basal Readers. Basal readers are the staple materials of most reading programs around the country. The historical scarcity of children's literature forced early educators to rely on basal readers, thus giving them a prominent role in reading instruction that continues to endure today (Martinez & McGee, 2000). Woodward and Elliott (1992) note that the majority of instruction, approximately 85–95%, still revolves around textbooks such as these.

Whereas basal reading series of the early 1900s were composed of student anthologies and a few instructional suggestions, today's basal series are more complex and have a plethora of ancillary material. Modern-day basal series include student anthologies of literature, practice workbooks, teacher's manuals filled with instructional suggestions and cross-curricular activities, leveled reading and decodable books, assessment kits, and supplemental materials to meet the needs of all learners.

QUESTIONS FOR SELECTING INSTRUCTIONAL PRACTICES: A BAKER'S DOZEN

1. What is my purpose in using this instructional practice?
2. Does the practice have a research base?
3. Do I have the professional training to implement the instructional practice?
4. Is the instructional practice consistent with standards and objectives outlined by the state or school district?
5. Is the practice most appropriate for whole-class instruction or for an alternative grouping configuration?
6. Do I have the instructional materials necessary to implement the practice? If not, is the cost reasonable in terms of what I hope to accomplish?
7. Is the instructional time reasonable?
8. Does the practice assume skills that the target student(s) may not possess?
9. Will I need additional human resources (e.g., paraprofessionals, volunteers) to implement this practice?
10. Will adaptations need to be made for students with disabilities or students who are ELLs?
11. How will I monitor student progress using this instructional practice?
12. Does the practice offer a home learning component?
13. Overall, is this instructional practice desirable in terms of promoting student learning and feasible to implement, given the realities of my classroom?

FIGURE 2.5. Questions for selecting instructional practices: A baker's dozen.

The content of basal readers has also changed dramatically over the past decades. Whereas moralistic and patriotic passages made up the content of early basal readers, basal readers of the early 20th century consisted of stereotypical narratives (better known as "Dick and Jane" stories), which were later replaced by excerpts and adaptations from children's literature (Pearson, 2001b). Using authentic pieces of children's literature came into vogue as a result of the whole-language movement of the 1990s. However, publishers of basal readers continued to struggle with finding a balance between the amount of decodable text and the amount of authentic children's literature that should be included in the anthologies. This struggle was not limited to the content of the student textbooks, but also spread to the type of instruction that should accompany the textbooks: Should it be whole-language or phonics-based? Today's basal readers have a more balanced content (Martinez & McGee, 2000). Basal readers still include authentic texts, but there is also a heavy emphasis on writing, literature, and comprehension, along with specific instruction in phonics, spelling, comprehension strategies and writing. In addition, more basal readers are including suggestions for ELLs and students with disabilities.

Alternative Texts. Basal readers should not be the only reading material to which students have access. Trade books, or authentic literature, should also be part of all students' literary diets. Smith, Tracey, and Weber (1998) found that elementary students watch television for 2.3 hours a day, but read for only 8 minutes per day! This is appalling, considering that the amount of time spent reading is a good predictor of reading achievement (Caldwell & Gaine, 2000). One way to help increase the amount of time children spend reading is to provide children with engaging and high-quality reading material. The easiest way to do this is through the classroom library. Classroom libraries should include at least 10 books per student. The books need to be in good condition and have bright, attractive covers and illustrations (Hack, Hepler, & Hickman, 2001). The literature selection should include books from all genres and should cover a wide range of topics. Children should be encouraged to read a variety of genres, because early exposure to a wide assortment of reading materials enhances students' ability to comprehend texts in later grades (Cunningham & Stanovich, 1997).

While providing diverse books for your students, it's also important to think of diversity in terms of reading difficulty. You should have some books that challenge your brightest students and others that are simple enough for your students with reading difficulties. Finding suitable books for older readers reading below grade level can be quite a challenge. These students need high-interest easy books that will build fluency, offer rich content and vocabulary, and present sophisticated concepts and stories (Ivey, 2002). Ivey (2002) recommends the *Bullseye Chiller* series or some of Roald Dahl's books (*The Magic Finger* [1996] or *Fantastic Mr. Fox* [2004]), because they're easy to read but still maintain an engaging story line that will give students a chance to practice their comprehension strategies.

Instructor

Increased intensity of instruction is aligned with the level of training and experience of the person providing the instruction. The more professional development that an individual has in terms of instruction, assessment, and intervention, the more intensive. The previously mentioned International Reading Association (2003) *Standards for Reading Professionals* document includes professional preparation guidelines for paraprofessionals, classroom teachers, reading specialists/literacy coaches, teacher educators, and administrators. It is important to be aware of these guidelines, as they constitute an excellent blueprint for professional goals and preparation.

Instructional Time

Instructional time can vary in terms of length, frequency, and duration. *Length* refers to the number of minutes in a particular lesson. *Frequency* refers to the number of lessons per week. *Duration* refers to the overall period of time that an instructional series occurs. Obviously, the more time spent on instructional tasks, the more likely it is that learning will take place.

Type of Practice

Intensity of practice after instruction can vary in terms of type of support and feedback provided. High-intensity practice is teacher-directed, with opportunities for immediate and very specific feedback about student performance. Intensity decreases when less knowledgeable support is available and when feedback about performance is delayed or nonspecific.

How Can Teachers Organize and Implement Differentiated Instruction?

The majority of students will learn to read and write if they are given well-planned classroom instruction. Others may need only supplemental instruction. Yet some students may require more. How can teachers organize instruction to accommodate individual students' needs?

In developing a program for primary grade students to prevent reading failure, Dickson and Bursuck (1999) proposed a five-tier reading system that included multiple levels of intensity of instruction. The five-tier reading system was designed for the restoring of a beginning reading program, but has implications for instructional planning throughout elementary grade levels. The system provides a structure for defining a continuum of instruction from general education (tier 1) to special education (tier 5). Students are not "locked" into tiers, but rather are placed in appropriate levels of instruction based on individual needs as determined by ongoing assessment and monitoring of response to instruction.

Clearly, the Dickson and Bursuck model goes beyond individual teacher planning and looks at instruction from a systemic perspective. However, their model can guide teachers' decision making. The system can be adapted to represent a spectrum from typical grade-level instruction, supplementary instruction, and additional instruction based on support services available within a particular school setting (e.g., special education, bilingual education, paraprofessional support, volunteer tutors, Title I reading initiatives).

Another possible model is the three-tier reading model, developed as an early reading model in grades K–3 (Vaughn, Linan-Thompson, & Elbaum, 2004). Tier 1 is essentially a core reading program, based on principles of effective teaching and focused on the key areas of reading instruction outlined in the National Reading Panel (2000a) report. Based on results of ongoing assessment, students who are not making sufficient progress move to a second (supplemental) or third (intensive intervention) tier. The content is presented in different ways during these two tiers, and to reach students who need extra support.

In Chapters 4–12 of this book, we provide research-based instructional practices for use in three levels of instruction: high-quality core reading and writing instruction, supplemental instruction, and intensive support. The book is organized topically by key components of a reading curriculum (e.g., phonological awareness, phonics, reading comprehension). The chapter on each topic provides specific suggestions for assessing students in multiple ways and for increasing the intensity of instruction as needed. Chapter 14 provides specific suggestions for organizing for multiple levels of instruction in classroom settings (with and without inclusion models) and in resource settings.

Level 1: High-Quality Core Instruction

The first level consists of high-quality instruction in reading and writing for the whole class. High-quality instruction includes the use of a comprehensive reading program that addresses the five big areas of reading instruction outlined by the National Reading Panel (2000a): phonemic awareness, phonics, vocabulary, fluency, and comprehension. How much of each of these components is addressed will depend on the grade you are teaching and the needs of your students. Schools vary in their process for selecting programs. In your school, you may be part of a team of teachers asked to review various programs and then to select one. In addition to addressing the five components of reading, evaluate your program to make sure that it incorporates evidence-based instructional practices and that it presents information in a systematic, explicit manner. As you consider various programs, look for things such as how much practice is provided, whether concepts are presented from simplest to most difficult, what type and amount of feedback students receive, how much modeling is provided, and so forth. A high-quality core instructional program includes explicitness, systematic instruction, scaffolding, feedback, maximum student engagement, opportunities for students to read and write, time on task, flexible grouping, and ongoing progress monitoring.

EXPLICITNESS

Reading proficiency is difficult for many students to acquire. To facilitate their learning, make sure to make your instruction as explicit as possible. Explicit instruction fully and clearly explains what is being taught. It involves the overt teaching of steps needed to complete a task, followed by guided practice.

According to Arguelles, Morris, and Ross (2003), explicit instruction promotes efficient learning for all students and includes the following:

- Thinking processes that are visible through modeling.
- Lessons that introduce a few ideas or skills and provide practice activities for each idea or skill until mastery is achieved.
- Instruction that varies the pace.
- Background information provided before new knowledge is introduced.
- Preteaching of key vocabulary and concepts, using tools such as pictures or word maps.
- Visual support for auditory information—for example, the use of graphic organizers to connect the ideas being presented.
- Immediate, corrective feedback and reteaching, if needed.
- Systematic coverage of reading components.

Let's look at two classroom examples.

EXAMPLE A

The teacher says, "Today we are going to read a new book. The name of our new book is Mmmarvelous Mmmary." The teacher reads the entire book, and each time she encounters a word with the letter M, she prolongs the sound. At the end of the reading, she says to the students, "Boys and girls, what do you think today's sound will be?"

EXAMPLE B

The teacher says, "Today we are going to learn a new letter and its sound." The teacher shows the students a capital M and lowercase m, and says, "This is the capital letter M [as she points to the capital M]. What letter?"

The children say, "M."

The teacher continues, "The letter M makes the mmm [exaggerates the sound] sound. What sound does the letter M make?"

The children respond, "Mmm."

The teacher calls on several students and asks each, "What sound does the M make?" She provides corrective feedback as needed. Then she takes out the book and says, "Today's story has many words with our new letter and sound: Mmmmarvelous Mmmmary. As I read the book, I want you to give me a thumbs up every time you hear a word that begins with the mmm sound. Juan, when are you going to give a thumbs up?"

Juan says, "Every time we hear the mmm sound."

"Excellent," says the teacher, "and Mary, what is today's letter?"

Mary answers, "M."

"Great. Everybody get ready to hear those mmm sounds!"

The teacher begins by reading the first sentence and modeling a thumbs up each time she reads a word that begins with the /m/ sound. She then continues reading the story.

Clearly, Example A does not typify explicit instruction. In the first example, the students have to figure out what the new sound for the day will be. This task may be easy for those students who come from backgrounds where they have been read to a lot, but may be more difficult for those who have limited experiences with books or with oral language. The second example includes explicit instruction, so that the students have a clear understanding of what they needed to do; that is, the students did not have to infer or guess what was required of them.

SYSTEMATIC INSTRUCTION

Systematic instruction refers to well-thought-out, planned instruction. Systematic instruction does not skip from concept to concept, but is delivered in a sequenced manner, beginning with easier concepts and moving to more difficult ones. The use of systematic instruction ensures that there are no gaps in your teaching and that no important concepts are missed. As an example, let's examine the frequency of various phonics patterns. Research informs us that some phoneme–grapheme patterns are more common than others (Bear & Templeton, 1998). The use of systematic instruction in the primary grades will take into consideration this knowledge and arrange the introduction of these patterns in order of frequency (high-frequency patterns first).

SCAFFOLDING

When we are learning a new skill or concept, it is important for most of us to have some support along the way. The writings of Vygotsky (1978) have helped educators to understand the important role that educators play in providing assistance to guide learners toward independence and proficiency. Brown and Palincsar (1989) describe this assistance as *scaffolding*: "The metaphor of a scaffold captures the idea of an adjustable and temporary support that can be removed when no longer necessary" (p. 122). Indeed, scaffolding is an instructional technique that enables teachers to provide guidance and assistance in a graduated manner. That is, this guidance and assistance are slowly removed as students become more and more proficient in the task (see Figure 2.6). The key to scaffolding is that teacher support is responsive to students' performance. Some students will need more scaffolding, while others will be able to perform a task independently soon after being introduced to it.

RESEARCH BRIEF Reciprocal Teaching and Scaffolded Instruction

One line of research that has made a substantive contribution to educators' understanding of scaffolded instruction is the work of Palincsar and Brown on *reciprocal teaching*. Palincsar and Brown (Brown & Palincsar, 1989; Palincsar, 1984) conducted a series of intervention studies designed to improve students' use of a set of reading comprehension strategies. A key component of the reciprocal teaching intervention was the use of scaffolded instruction. At first the teacher modeled use of the comprehension strategies while students observed. Eventually, students participated more in the use of the strategies, but still with teacher support and guidance. Finally, students were able to implement strategy use on their own. The use of reading comprehension strategies combined with scaffolded instruction enabled students to perform better on researcher-made tests that resembled typical classroom assessment, as well as on standardized tests. You'll read more about reciprocal teaching and its variations in Chapter 8.

Arguelles and colleagues (2003) suggest providing good models and using think-alouds. These techniques will make thinking visible and facilitate students' understand-

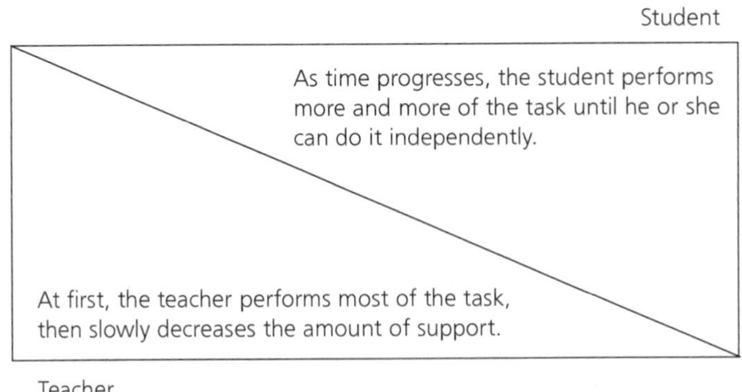

FIGURE 2.6. Scaffolded instruction.

ing of the concepts being presented. As you scaffold students' learning, provide them with multiple opportunities to respond. Give students frequent and specific feedback as they perform tasks or complete assignments. When students are learning a new concept or skill, it is preferable to provide guidance as they complete related assignments, rather than waiting until a student makes repeated mistakes and has to "unlearn" material. Scaffolding also includes systematic review that leads to more difficult applications.

The research of Pressley (2006) and his colleagues underscored the importance of using scaffolding techniques: "By providing more intensive scaffolding for students who were struggling, the excellent teachers were able to run classrooms in which all students experienced pretty much the same curriculum while receiving instruction appropriate to their needs and progress" (p. 204). Teacher guidance is only one form of scaffolding. Dickson, Simmons, and Kame'enui (1995) suggest using four types of scaffolding:

- *Teacher/peer scaffolding* occurs across a continuum, with more support occurring when new concepts, tasks, or strategies are introduced. Support is slowly removed as students gain proficiency and assume more responsibility. One example of peer scaffolding is to pair a lower-performing reader with one who is reading at a slightly higher level.
- *Content scaffolding* occurs as the teacher introduces simpler concepts and skills first, and slowly guides students through more challenging concepts and skills.
- *Task scaffolding* occurs as students move from easier to more difficult tasks and activities .
- *Material scaffolding* occurs when a variety of materials are used to guide student thinking (e.g., story maps, graphic organizers, study guides). Brown (2000) explains how different types of text can be used to scaffold young students' reading. For younger students, you may want to use predictable books with lots of illustrations and few words per page. As students become more proficient, they will begin to read *transitional* texts (texts that rely less on illustrations or patterns and are decodable). Once students have become proficient reading transitional texts, they can begin reading *easy reader* texts (texts that highlight certain patterns and high-frequency words).

FEEDBACK

Providing feedback includes much more than just letting students know that they've done a good job. Although positive feedback is certainly an important aspect of teaching, feedback is also a way to let students know if they are on the right track and, if not, how to correct their errors. As you provide feedback, be sure to make it specific, clear, and immediate. Instead of "Well done," consider "I really like how you have included a punctuation mark at the end of each sentence." Similarly, instead of "You need to try harder," say, "Take a look at each sentence and make sure to include a punctuation mark at the end of each." Often students spend years making the same error because they never received clear feedback. When a student provides an incorrect answer, teachers often call on another student to provide the correct answer, assuming that the first student will learn from the second one. For many struggling readers, this is not the case. If a student provides an incorrect answer, have the student repeat the correct answer; later on during the same day or week, ask the same question to make sure the student has internalized the information.

MAXIMUM STUDENT ENGAGEMENT

Student engagement refers to the number of opportunities that each student has to respond. In large classes, many students only have one or no opportunity to respond to teacher questions or prompts. Instead of calling individual students, consider asking every student to turn to a neighbor and share the answer. If you are asking questions that require yes or no responses, instead of calling on one or two students, ask students to use thumbs up for yes and thumbs down for no. This allows more students to participate and become actively involved in their learning. Think of other ways that your lessons can be full of opportunities for students to respond and demonstrate what they are learning. One activity that students enjoy is the use of eraser boards. You can have all students write their responses on the eraser boards and then, when prompted, raise their boards for you to see. Not only does this increase the number of students participating; it also ensures that all students have the same wait time, giving students who need more time and students who are ELLs the opportunity to process information.

OPPORTUNITIES FOR STUDENTS TO READ, AND TIME ON TASK

Sadly, the time students spend reading in many classrooms is disturbingly small. In Durkin's (1984) classic study, students spent between 7 and 15 minutes reading per day. Likewise, the 1996 NAEP report indicated that about 25% of youngsters reported reading five or fewer pages per day in school and for homework, and only 25% of 17-year-olds reported reading for pleasure on a daily basis. To ensure growth in reading, students must spend a large portion of each class period reading connected text (McCormick, 2003). The amount of time students spend engaged in academic tasks is directly related to student progress. Consider strategies that increase the time students spend reading each day. For example, *classwide peer tutoring* (Mathes, 1995; see Chapter 7) is a strategy in which students read in pairs for 20 minutes daily, using text that is at their instructional or independent level.

FLEXIBLE GROUPING

Use flexible grouping so that all students are engaged in learning and your own time is used most effectively. Flexible grouping will afford you the opportunity to meet individual needs and tailor your teaching to particular students. The key of successful grouping is that the members in each group change frequently in response to information about student performance gathered from progress-monitoring tools. Students can belong to different groups at the same time, depending on the goal or activity. Make sure to stay away from tracking, in which students are always kept in the same group. For lower-performing students, being locked into a low-level track can lead to watering down of curriculum and lower-level tasks.

ONGOING PROGRESS MONITORING

Frequent progress monitoring can provide you with valuable information on students' levels of mastery of the various concepts being studied. You can use the results from progress monitoring to plan new lessons, to reteach unclear concepts, and to group students for instruction

Level 2: Supplemental Instruction

Despite the use of a high-quality program and careful planning, some students will need "booster sessions" to become more proficient in reading and writing. These students receive what we refer to as *supplemental instruction*. Students who need supplemental instruction may require more opportunities for practice, reteaching of certain concepts, or instruction that is broken down into further manageable steps. It is possible that these students are missing some of the appropriate preskills or prior knowledge necessary to master new concepts or skills. Ongoing progress monitoring will provide you with the information needed to place students into small groups, where you can provide the instruction that will meet their needs. During your reading block, you can begin by providing instruction to the whole class; later, you can divide the class into small groups. Some students will work independently, while others meet with a teacher or paraprofessional and receive additional instruction. You can also utilize centers that focus on building certain skills. For example, for students who are having difficulty with fluency, a listening center will allow students to reread books at a comfortable reading level several times. Various computer software programs that target particular areas can be used to provide additional practice.

Level 3: Intensive Support

A small number of students will need intensive support. These are students who are below grade level in one or more areas of reading or writing. Using the five dimensions of intensity, you will be able to plan lessons that will meet these students' needs. This may include the use of intervention programs that are more intensive. Many current reading programs include suggestions for additional support that are aligned with core instruction and that help students develop proficiency in specific areas of instruction. You may also want to work with other professionals in your school, such as the special education teacher or reading specialist, to develop plans for these students.

PARENT POINTER ☞ Talking with Parents about Differentiated Instruction

The idea of differentiated instruction may be new to some of your students' parents and frightening to others. Some parents who were taught in classes that implemented undifferentiated whole-class instruction, or in systems where students were "tracked" according to achievement levels, may not be aware of the potential benefits of differentiated instruction. Parents of high-achieving students may fear the *Robin Hood effect*—that instructional time is being taken from the "rich" (higher-achieving students) to give to the "poor" (lower-achieving students). Parents of low-achieving students may fear that a "spotlight" is being put on their students when they receive intensive support in the classroom. Parents of students in the middle may feel that their children are being overlooked.

When parents ask about differentiated instruction, provide them with information about their own child and your instructional plan for meeting their child's needs. Many questions and fears will subside when you provide data that indicate you are monitoring their child's performance regularly and that you have a solid plan for a high-quality program to meet their child's needs.

CONTINUING TO DEVELOP STUDENT READING AND WRITING PROFILES

Chapter 1 has provided a starting point for developing reading and writing profiles for students: data from students and their parents/guardians. The next source of data is students' cumulative folders to learn about previous assessments. Cumulative records can provide information about previous testing, grades, retention, attendance, placement in special classes, as well as previous schools attended. If you are a school employee, check procedures for access to data both in paper files and in electronic databases. If you are not a school employee, you should keep in mind that the Family Education Rights and Privacy Act (Buckley Amendment, Public Law 93-380, 1974) requires parental consent (in writing) for examination of school records. Moreover, as with all student data, confidentiality should be maintained. Part II of the Student Reading and Writing Profile (see Form 2.1) provides a generic format for cumulative records. Actual data will vary considerably from school district to school district.

CHAPTER SUMMARY

No two learners learn alike. This is what makes the job of a teacher interesting. Building on individual students' strengths and providing appropriate instruction to overcome problem areas is what makes the job of a teacher rewarding. It's trite, but true. Teachers frequently talk about "the light bulb going on." When a student "gets it," the joy of teaching is boundless. An understanding of the factors that influence individual challenges in learning to read and write, of appropriate classroom assessment, and of differentiated instruction are the keys to turning on the light bulb. Starting with information from parents/guardians and students (Chapter 1) and continuing with the cumulative folder, you can begin to develop profiles of your students as readers and writers. Subsequent chapters will provide you with tools for getting to know more about your students and how best to help them become proficient in reading and writing.

KEY TERMS AND CONCEPTS

Criterion-referenced tests
Diagnostic instruments
Differentiated instruction
Dyslexia
High-stakes tests
Informal assessment tools
Individualized educational program (IEP)
Least restrictive environment
Levels of intensity
Matthew effect
National Assessment of Educational Progress (NAEP)
Norm-referenced tests
Outcome measures
Phonological awareness
Progress-monitoring measures
Scaffolding
Screening measures
Standards for Reading Professionals

REFLECTION AND ACTION

1. You have read about some of the reasons why students struggle in learning to read and write. Explain what areas of student difficulty would provide you with the greatest challenges as a teacher.

2. Make a list of the pros and cons of high-stakes testing. Then write a one-page position statement about how you think high-stakes testing might affect how you teach reading.
3. Work with a team of two colleagues to role-play a parent conference with the purpose of interpreting high-stakes test results. One person plays the role of teacher, one of parent, and one of observer. After the role play, critique the conference and offer suggestions for improvement.
4. Make a list of barriers that you think might inhibit teachers from differentiating instruction. Then think of some resources teachers can use to overcome those barriers.

READ ON!

Barrentine, S. J., & Stokes, S. M. (Eds.). (2005). *Reading assessment: Principles and practices for elementary teachers* (2nd ed.). Newark, DE: International Reading Association.

A collection of articles from *The Reading Teacher* with practical suggestions and instruments for classroom use. Includes an appendix written by a panel of experts in reading assessment, discussing the pros and cons of high-stakes tests.

Gunning, T. G. (2005). *Assessing and correcting reading and writing difficulties* (3rd ed.). Boston: Allyn & Bacon.

Chapter 2 is entitled "Factors Involved in Reading and Writing Difficulties." This chapter provides a description of a number of factors that influence success or failure in learning to read and write.

Klingner, J. K., Harry, B., & Felton, R. K. (2003). Understanding factors that contribute to disproportionality. *Journal of Special Education Leadership*, *16*, 23–33.

Educators and parents have expressed concern about the overrepresentation of minority students in special education. This article is part of a line of investigation conducted by Klingner and Harry to address this important issue.

McMillan, J. H. (2003). *Classroom assessment: Principles and practice for effective instruction* (3rd ed.). Boston: Allyn & Bacon.

This book provides an excellent overview of classroom assessment and how to use data to inform instructional decision making. It includes chapters on assessing students before, during, and after instruction. It also includes a chapter on the assessment of students with disabilities included in the general education classroom.

International Reading Association, Professional Standards and Ethics Committee. (2003). *Standards for reading professionals—revised 2003.* Newark, DE: Author.

Outlines criteria for professional preparation requirements for the teaching of reading for paraprofessional, classroom teachers, reading specialists, and teacher educators. Recommendations for professional preparation of administrators who supervise reading programs are included as well.

Shaywitz, S. (2003). *Overcoming dyslexia: A new and complete science-based program for reading problems at any level.* New York: Knopf.

Written for a lay audience, this book provides an overview of the nature of dyslexia and other severe reading problems. It also includes research-based instructional practices to teach reading to children who have the most difficulty in learning to read and write.

Vaughn, S., Bos, C. S., & Schumm, J. S. (2005). *Teaching exceptional, diverse, and at-risk students in the general education classroom* (3rd ed.). Boston: Allyn & Bacon.

Here is a textbook that provides an overview of differentiated instruction across a wide range of subject areas. Provides detailed information for what the classroom teacher needs to know about diverse learning needs and practical suggestions to help all students learn.

SHARPENING YOUR SKILLS: SUGGESTIONS FOR PROFESSIONAL DEVELOPMENT

1. Start developing a professional toolkit for assessment. Keep hard copies of assessment instruments in a file drawer or portable file box, so that they are handy and ready to use.
2. Examine the International Reading Association's (2003) *Standards for Reading Professionals.* Make a list of professional goals you can set for yourself to meet those standards.
3. Interview a school psychologist. Ask what his or her roles and responsibilities are, and how classroom teachers and reading coaches can work with school psychologists to best meet the assessment needs of students.

RESOURCES FOR ASSESSMENT AND INSTRUCTION

Council for Exceptional Children. (1999). *ERIC/OSEP mini-library: Adapting curricular materials* (3 vols.). Reston, VA: Author.

This three-volume set includes suggestions for making instructional and curricular adaptations for students with disabilities in the general education classroom. The first volume (Kame'enui & Simmons) provides general guidelines for "The Architecture for Instruction." Volumes 2 (Schumm) and 3 (Lenz & Schumacher) include more specific strategies for making adaptations.

Ganske, K., Monroe, J. K., & Strickland, D. S. (2003). Questions teachers ask about struggling readers and writers. *The Reading Teacher, 57,* 118–128.

Ganske and her colleagues surveyed 191 teachers to gain insights about their most pressing concerns in teaching struggling readers and writers. This article provides excellent suggestions for addressing those concerns and provides teachers with suggestions for helping all students become successful learners.

Idol, L., Nevin, A., & Paolucci-Whitcomb, P. (1999). *Models of curriculum-based assessment: A blueprint for learning* (3rd ed.). Austin, TX: PRO-ED.

This book provides examples of curriculum-based assessment with specific tips for how to develop assessment that reflects curricular goals. Includes suggestions for how to implement curriculum-based assessment in inclusion classrooms.

Kibby, M. W. (1995). *Practical steps for informing literacy instruction: A diagnostic decision-making model.* Newark, DE: International Reading Association.

This monograph provides a step-by-step guide to using assessment to guide instructional decision making. The diagnostic decision-making model (based on an interactive view of the reading process) was developed at the University of Buffalo Reading Clinic and provides an assessment "road map" for teachers in classroom and resource settings.

Tomlinson, C. A. (2003). *Fulfilling the promise of the differentiated classroom: Strategies and tools for responsive teaching.* Alexandria, VA: Association for Supervision and Curriculum Development.

Planning and implementing instruction that is responsive to diverse student needs can be a daunting task for classroom teachers. This book provides specific suggestions that are realistic and "doable."

Tyner, B. (2004). *Small-group reading instruction: A differentiated teaching model for beginning and struggling readers.* Newark, DE: International Reading Association.

Provides a comprehensive word study program for students who are early readers and students in the elementary grades who need more support in learning to read. Based on a stages model of reading development, this book includes instructional suggestions in a clear, well-sequenced manner.

RECOMMENDED WEBSITES

Children with Special Needs
www.children-special-needs.org

Need information about vision and how it affects learning? Check this page sponsored by the Optometrists Network. It includes vision checklists for parents and teachers, as well as descriptions of various vision disorders that may impact performance in school.

Hello Friend/Ennis William Cosby Foundation
www.hellofriend.org

The Ennis William Cosby Foundation is dedicated to people for whom learning is different or difficult. The website provides resources for parents and teachers, including links to professional organizations for students with reading and learning differences. The site also includes a newsroom that includes descriptions of foundation activities.

International Dyslexia Association (IDA)
www.interdys.org

This is the website for the International Dyslexia Association (IDA), formerly known as the Orton Dyslexia Society (which was named in honor of one of the initial researchers in the area of dyslexia, Dr. Samuel T. Orton). The site provides a wealth of information about dyslexia, including definitions and resources for parents, teens, adults, and teachers.

Southwest Educational Development Laboratory
www.sedl.org/reading/rad

The Southwest Educational Development Laboratory has a searchable database that includes information about 125 assessment tools. The database includes both norm- and criterion-referenced measures for use with children in grades K–2 (some measures for grade 3 are also included).

FORM 2.1. Student Reading and Writing Profile (Part II)

Student Reading and Writing Profile

Part II: Gathering Existing Data

Summary Data from Cumulative Records

Retentions (grades) ______

Special education placements or referrals ______

Remedial placements ______

Academic grades in reading and language arts

Grade	K	1	2	3	4	5	6	7	8	9	10	11	12
Reading													
Language arts													

Scores on high-stakes tests

Grade	K	1	2	3	4	5	6	7	8	9	10	11	12
Reading													
Language arts													

Other previous testing

Name of test	Date	Score
______	______	______
______	______	______
______	______	______
______	______	______
______	______	______
______	______	______
______	______	______

Recommendations from previous teachers in cumulative folders

Student strengths in reading and writing ______

______

Student areas for improvement in reading and writing ______

______

Possible reasons for difficulties (cognitive/neurological, physical, educational, language, personality, family)

______

______

THREE

No Two Learners Are Alike

Learners with Linguistic and Cultural Differences

MARY A. AVALOS

VIGNETTE

"What is it with Josie, Felix, and Claude Jean? They usually get the main idea of the text, but stare blankly at me when I ask questions about supporting details," muses Robert Franco. A first-year fifth-grade teacher, Robert has recently completed his reading education courses. The instructors of these courses typically spent one or two class periods speaking about strategies for second-language readers; many of these strategies were applicable to other special-needs students. At the start of the school year, Robert thought he was prepared to work with second-language readers. He has tried several comprehension strategies with these three *English-language learners* (ELLs), but none of them seems to be working. Robert has many other ELLs in his classroom; sometimes they also stare blankly at him, but they don't appear to have the challenges that these three students face in comprehending various texts. Is it a language issue? Do they need to be referred for exceptional student education? "What else can I do to reach my ELLs, especially Josie, Felix, and Claude Jean?" Robert ponders. He puts his head in his hands and sighs deeply.

ANTICIPATION QUESTIONS

- What are some of the issues specific to second-language learners learning to read in English?
- Is there one best way to approach reading instruction with ELLs in K–12 classrooms?
- How can teachers reach out to parents of ELLs?
- What about formal testing and ELLs? How can teachers best prepare ELLs for norm-referenced or standardized testing?

INTRODUCTION

A growing number of ELLs in our schools have fulfilled predictions of a changing U.S. population. The growth of diverse populations (i.e., those of other than European American descent) is expected to continue throughout the 21st century. The National Center for Education Statistics (2000) states that over 37% of K–12 students are culturally, linguistically, and ethnically different from the mainstream U.S. population, whereas 90% of the teaching population is European American, female, and from a middle-class background. While certain regions are affected more than others, the growing number of diverse students throughout the United States warrants an understanding of students who are different from the majority teaching population. Moreover, differences between the teaching and learning populations are not simply based on cultural, linguistic, and ethnic background; more and more teachers are finding themselves in schools with students who have differing socioeconomic backgrounds as well. Such educators must be prepared to teach all their students. Although all teaching assignments are challenging and teachers everywhere deserve respect, teachers in urban, high-poverty schools who are faced with many types of diversity face the additional challenge of leaving their comfort zones in order to better meet their students' needs.

This chapter begins with an overview of the growing diversity in the United States. Next, issues related to second-language literacy are discussed, followed by a description of the second-language acquisition process. The next section provides information about the impact of culture on literacy learning. This is followed with a discussion of assessment and particular issues regarding assessment as it relates to ELLs. General instructional guidelines and best practices for ELLs follow, although more specific suggestions are provided throughout this book.

OVERVIEW OF GROWING DIVERSITY IN THE UNITED STATES

Immigrants come to the United States for various reasons: They may simply be hoping for better opportunities for their children, or they may also be fleeing war-torn lands, oppressive governments, or economic hardships (Ovando, Collier, & Combs, 2006). Children who have experienced trauma (war, life-threatening journeys, etc.) will need extra patience and counseling upon their arrival. Our calling as teachers should be to educate the whole child, not just the mind. When new students enroll, every attempt should be made to find out as much as possible about their background.

Excerpts from three parent interviews are transcribed in Figures 3.1–3.3 to provide a taste of the many different backgrounds encountered in work with ELLs. (All three interviews are used with the permission of the interviewers, and family members' names have been concealed or changed.) The first family interviewed comes from Venezuela; both parents are highly educated and were affluent in their native country. This excerpt demonstrates some of the adjustments that need to be made even when family members have prior knowledge of the United States (in this case, they used to vacation here) and plenty of family and financial resources to assist them with the transition to their new life. The second family interviewed is from rural Nicaragua; both parents attended school through the sixth grade. They currently own a home in a working-class neighborhood. This excerpt is included because there are many issues facing immigrants that mainstream Americans cannot relate to, such as the desire to return to the native country, and the reality that it will probably never happen. The third interview excerpt is included to dem-

Family background: The teacher interviewing this parent teaches kindergarten in a large urban school district. The family is from Caracas, Venezuela, where many political changes are occurring at the time this interview takes place. Both parents were attorneys in Venezuela; however, the mother has not worked outside the home since her eldest child was born nine years ago.

Question (Q): Do you plan on returning to Venezuela?

Answer (A): I honestly cannot answer that right now. We have invested everything we have into businesses here in the U.S. Right now we are trying to legalize our status here and establish our business in order to secure our economic future. I love my country, but I cannot live in a system that is not free.

Q: Tell me about your children's education in Venezuela.

A: My children went to a very expensive private school in Caracas. This school is supposed to be one of the best in my country. The class size is about eight students to one teacher. Every teacher had an assistant in the class. The curriculum was very student-centered; it was based on the Montessori method of teaching.

Q: Is the U.S. what you imagined it to be?

A: No! I came to the United States for vacations every year. I went to Texas to visit my sister and here to visit my brother, but living here is very different from being on vacation. Life here is very rigid and structured—you are always on a schedule. For someone who comes from a Latin American country where things are very "laid back," it is a very big shock. On a positive note, it is an amazing country. . . .

Q: What are your aspirations and dreams for your children?

A: I want my children to be productive members of this society. I want them both to be educated professionals.

FIGURE 3.1. Transcript from an interview with a Venezuelan parent.

Family background: The teacher interviewing this parent from rural Nicaragua teaches 4th grade in an urban school district. Both parents attended school up to the sixth grade; there were no secondary schools in their town. The mother being interviewed left her parents, brothers, sisters, and extended family to come to the United States; her mother passed away two years ago, but she could not return for the funeral because she and her husband could not afford the airfare. The student's mother does not work outside the home. The father works in construction and brings home a "steady paycheck." They own a car and a modest home that they are very proud of. Their oldest son will graduate from high school this year and attend the local community college the following fall.

Q: Why did you decide to leave your country and come to the United States?

A: We decided to leave and come live in this great country full of possibilities, of liberty, especially for our son and later for our daughter born here in the United States. This has been a great move. Life is not easy here, but we have a much better life here.

Q: Do you have any hope of returning to live in your country?

A: As for me, no. My husband still has hope, but I know my children have become Americanized and will never go back. I cannot leave my children. Everything changes; you cannot go back.

FIGURE 3.2. Transcript from an interview with a Nicaraguan parent.

Family background: This family was originally from Taiwan, but came more recently from Japan, as they moved there to open businesses. The family immigrated to the United States for the same purpose—to open and begin a business. Family members speak Mandarin and Japanese, and are now learning English. Mei is in the 12th grade at the time of this interview. Both parents attended and graduated from high schools in Taiwan. The person conducting the interview is from China; note the different tone and style of questioning she uses when posing her questions at the beginning of the interview, as compared to the questioning style from the previous two interviews.

Teacher (T): Hi, Mr. Chin, I am sorry to take your time, but can I ask you some questions?

Parent (P): No problem.

T: Thank you very much. . . . Can I know how long have you been in the U.S.?

P: It's been almost five years.

T: By the way, is it proper to ask about your occupation here in the U.S.?

P: Oh, no problem. Now I own a shoe company.

T: So why did you decide to leave . . . Japan and come to the U.S.?

P: I think it was business that drove me to come to the U.S., because, in my opinion, in the U.S., as long as you have great ability, you can earn everything you want.

T: Since you brought Mei here, what is your expectation for her?

P: I hope she can learn what she wants and learn happily here.

T: Will you help Mei with her schoolwork?

P: If I can help, I will do as much as possible to help her. However, if I can't, I hope she can gain as much help as possible from her school. For example, when we were just arriving here, I had hired a tutor for Mei.

T: OK, the final question. Do you hope to return to live in your home country, Taiwan, or Japan?

P: Yes, I will. I will spend my retired life in Taiwan after my children can support themselves, because Taiwan is my real home country.

FIGURE 3.3. Transcript from an interview with a Taiwanese parent.

onstrate the difference in questioning styles between the first two interviewers (mainstream Americans) and the third (a graduate student from China). Understanding how language is used by different students' cultures will assist teachers in knowing how to speak with families. Note that these excerpts provide only a small glimpse of diversity; there are many other situations and possible student backgrounds. It is important that we keep abreast of world events and their impact on global population shifts in order to best serve our students.

SECOND-LANGUAGE LITERACY: ISSUES SPECIFIC TO ENGLISH-LANGUAGE LEARNERS

ELLs are unique in their needs not only because they come from different language groups (variation *across* languages), but because they have varying needs *within* their language groups. Teachers like Robert Franco are not alone in wondering what they can do to best serve their ELLs. Faced with the challenges of teaching the English language and curriculum content comprehensibly, they must also teach students to read in a non-native language they are in the process of acquiring. The following issues are important to remember in considering ELLs' academic progress and planning for their instruction.

Importance of Primary-Language Literacy and Structure

Students who are ELLs have a first, native, or primary language (also known as language 1 or L1) and are acquiring a second language (also known as language 2 or L2—English, for this chapter). Research demonstrates that children need to learn the process of reading and writing only once (Au, 1993; Cummins, 2003; Hudelson, 1984; Snow, 1990). In other words, when children learn to read, regardless of their L1, they typically do not need to learn to read again if they are learning to read in their L2; rather, they need to acquire the L2 vocabulary and knowledge about the structure of the language. It is not the concept of reading that is new to L2 readers who are proficient readers in their L1; rather, the language and structure are unfamiliar. Furthermore, it is acknowledged that building upon what students know with regard to literacy, language, and experiences is important in successful L2 instruction (Au, 1993, 2002; Ovando et al., 2006). For this reason, it is of utmost importance to assess the reading proficiency of children in their L1 in order to best serve them in their L2.

L1 Literacy

Not all state policies or districts recognize the importance of L1 literacy and its impact upon L2 literacy learning. If a district does not have a policy to assess ELLs in their L1 upon enrollment, teachers are denied access to valuable information that would assist them with setting appropriate instructional goals. An alternative to assessing L1 literacy (although not as accurate) for a teacher in a district that lacks this type of policy would be to find out how many years of formal schooling a child has had in his or her country of origin. Cummins's (1981) *interdependence hypothesis* explains that the degree of knowledge and processes evident in the L1 will determine the ease of transfer to the L2. Many studies have since substantiated Cummins's claim in the area of L2 reading proficiency (e.g., Avalos, 2003; Cummins, 1991; Freeman & Freeman, 1992; Hudelson, 1984; Wong Fillmore & Valadez, 1986).

If the interdependence hypothesis could be visualized within the context of reading, it would look something like Figure 3.4. Oral language proficiency in L1 and L2 are on each side, and L1/L2 literacy proficiencies, or levels, run along the top. The X's represent a bilingual student who is just learning to read in L1 *and* L2, while the Y's represent a bilingual student who is a more proficient reader in L1 and L2. One side of the chart mirrors the other to indicate the transferability effects of L1/L2 reading. The point at which the student begins his or her journey toward fluent English reading (the target) will influence how long it takes the student to reach that goal. For example, a student who is an L2 emergent reader at the L2 speech emergent stage (X^1), but an L1 emergent reader at the L1 intermediate fluency stage of language proficiency (X^2), will have a longer path to fluent English reading than an L2 early fluent reader (Y^1) or an L1 early fluent reader (Y^2) at the same language proficiency levels. In other words, if Linda is a native Spanish speaker with age-appropriate L1 oral language development but limited Spanish reading skills, she will take longer to become a proficient L2 reader than Xiomara, who has the same L1 oral language proficiency, but stronger L1 reading skills.

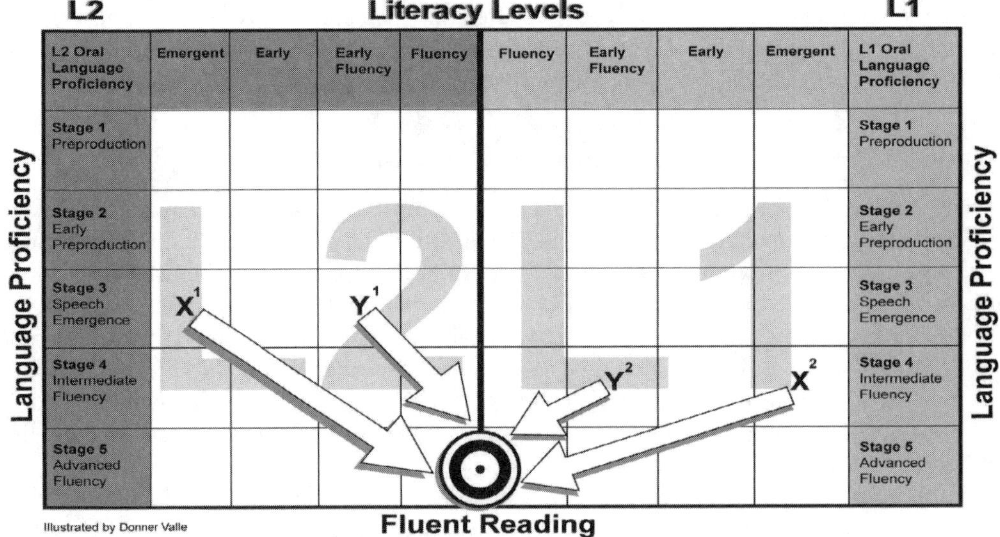

FIGURE 3.4. Literacy levels and oral language proficiency. Adapted and revised Rigby ELL Chart, used with permission by the author, Adel Nadeau.

L1 Structure

We need to factor not only in the amount of L1 reading proficiency and/or formal education, but also the differences in structure between the L1 and L2 (Birch, 2002; Moats, 2003). When instructing ELLs, we should ask questions such as these: Is the L1 writing system logographic (e.g., Arabic), syllabic (e.g., Cherokee), or alphabetic (e.g., English or Greek)? How does the L1 syntax (language structure or word order) compare with the L2's? Are the spelling patterns phonetic with consistent grapheme–phoneme (letter–sound) relationships (e.g., Spanish or French), or are there multiple vowel sounds (e.g., English)? Do students read from left to right and from top to bottom in their L1? Are there *cognates* (friendly or false) that would assist or inhibit the student in understanding texts (e.g., *internacional* in Spanish is a friendly cognate of *international* in English)? What are the discourse patterns and writing styles of the L1 as compared to the L2? Are questions asked with known answers at home (the type most teachers ask), or, as Heath (1983) found among working-class families, are rhetorical questions used? Is the L1 writing style circular, with long sentences and many details (e.g., Spanish), or linear, with the minimum number of facts or supporting details needed to establish support for the main idea (e.g., English)? Table 3.1 includes examples of different writing systems.

Knowing about our ELLs' L1 structure and style enables us to validate and show that we value what students already know and bring with them to class. At the same time, this knowledge broadens our own understanding of why certain L2 errors might be made, and it guides us in our language teaching to include instructional objectives dealing with comparison/contrast between languages. Interestingly, students who read in a different writing system have been found to transfer general reading skills (e.g., strategies, habits, and attitudes) to the L2 (Ovando et al., 2003). Table 3.2 provides a list of problematic English sounds for speakers of other languages (see Birch, 2002, for a comprehensive explanation of linguistics' impact on reading).

TABLE 3.1. Examples of Different Writing Systems

<table>
<tr><th>Writing system</th><th colspan="2">Example</th></tr>
<tr><td>Logographic: Each symbol or character represents one idea.</td><td colspan="2">Arabic: As logographic texts are transliterated (written using an alphabetic system), different marks are used to retain the logographic theory of one symbol per idea. (Example from Sagally, 1997.)<table><tr><th>7-bit input</th><th>transcription</th><th>Arabic script</th></tr><tr><td>i^star_A ^gu.hA ‘a^saraTa .hamIriN</td><td>ištarā ǧuḥā ʿašarata ḥamīrin</td><td>إشترى جحا عشرة حمير</td></tr></table></td></tr>
<tr><td>Syllabic: Each symbol or character represents a syllable.</td><td colspan="2">Cherokee: Selected symbols representing syllables with a, e, and i sounds (Example from Ager, 1998.)<table><tr><th>a</th><th>e</th><th>i</th></tr><tr><td>Ꭰ a</td><td>Ꭱ e</td><td>Ꭲ i</td></tr><tr><td>Ꭶ ga Ꭷ ka</td><td>Ꭸ ge</td><td>Ꭹ gi</td></tr><tr><td>Ꭽ ha</td><td>Ꭾ he</td><td>Ꭿ hi</td></tr><tr><td>Ꮃ la</td><td>Ꮄ le</td><td>Ꮅ li</td></tr><tr><td>Ꮉ ma</td><td>Ꮊ me</td><td>Ꮋ mi</td></tr></table></td></tr>
<tr><td>Alphabetic: Each symbol represents a sound or sounds.</td><td>Spanish: Transparent (generally a 1:1 grapheme-to-phoneme representation). (Example from Wald, 2000.)
A = /ah/ as in Caracas (kah-rah-kas)
E = /eh/ as in pelo (peh-lo) [hair]
I = /ee/ as in piña (pee-nyah) [pineapple]
O = /oh/ as in coco (coh-coh) [coconut]
U = /oo/ as in fruta (froo-tah) [fruit]</td><td>English: More opaque (multiple grapheme-to-phoneme representations).
The vowels in the following words make different sounds:
beach vs. bet
sale vs. Sam
hop vs. toad</td></tr>
</table>

TABLE 3.2. Problematic English Sounds for Speakers of Other Languages

Native language	Problematic English Sounds
Chinese	b, ch, d, dg, f, g, j, l, m, n, ng, ō, sh, s, th, TH, v, z, l clusters, r clusters
French	ā, ch, ē, h, j, ng, oo, oy, s, th, TH, s, schwa
Greek	aw, b, d, ē, g, i, j, m, n, ng, oo, r, s, w, y, z, schwa, end clusters
Italian	a, ar, dg, h, i, ng, th, TH, v, schwa, l clusters, end clusters
Japanese	dg, f, h, I, l, th, TH, oo, r, sh, s, v, w, schwa, l clusters, r clusters
Korean	b, l, ō, ow, p, r, sh, t, TH, l clusters, r clusters
Spanish	b, d, dg, h, j, m, n, ng, r, sh, t, th, v, w, y, z, s clusters, end clusters
Urdu	ā, a, d, ē, e, f, n, ng, s, sh, t, th, TH
Vietnamese	ā, ē, k, l, ng, p, r, sh, s, y, l clusters, r clusters

From Kress, J. (1993). *The ESL Teacher's Book of Lists*.

RESEARCH BRIEF ✎ The National Reading Panel's Findings and ELLs

The National Reading Panel's (2000a) report has been deemed controversial (see also Chapter 1). Reasons for the criticism include the methods utilized to select studies for the meta-analyses of the phonics and fluency research, the narrow population of those studies, and consequently the reliability and validity of such findings (Garan, 2001; Krashen, 2003). More recently, federal funding provided the resources for a National Reading Panel on Language Minority Children and Youth to investigate literacy acquisition among language minority populations (August 2003). The panel was made up of six subgroups of L2 reading experts, who were commissioned to investigate the literature regarding (1) the relationship between oral language proficiency and literacy; (2) transfer of L1 to L2 literacy; (3) L2 literacy development (e.g., sequence of development, processes as compared to native speakers, etc.); (4) social and cultural influences on L2 literacy; (5) strategies and professional development for promoting L2 literacy; and (6) L2 literacy assessment. A final report from this panel was anticipated during late summer 2004, although a dearth of studies with L2 populations that met the established selection criteria for inclusion in the meta-analyses had restricted the panel's findings. Unfortunately, at the time this book went to print, the report still hadn't been released, and according to the website, the report is in the "latter stages of the drafting process." More research is needed in all of the L2 areas targeted by the National Reading Panel (Shanahan, 2003a).

Oral Language versus Literacy Proficiency

Undeniably, research shows that students who have the opportunity to learn to read in their L1 are more successful L2 readers (Collier & Thomas, 1989; Ovando et al., 2003; Snow, Burns, & Griffin, 1998). There has been some question, however, about the role that L2 oral language proficiency plays in learning to read in the L2. Must a student be "orally proficient" in the L2 before beginning to read that language? Bilingual education models support the acquisition of the L2 to at least a speech emergent level of L2 proficiency before L2 reading instruction is begun. On the other hand, some believe that due to the increasing diversity among the U.S. school-age population, it is no longer conceivable (or equitable) to wait for oral language proficiency to develop before beginning to read in the L2 (English); therefore, L2 reading should be "promoted" for certain L2 learners and "not avoided" for others (Anderson & Roit, 1998, p. 51). When instruction is well planned and takes individual students' needs into account, all students can benefit from learning to read in the L2, regardless of their oral proficiency levels.

Teachers certainly play an important role in social and academic language acquisition. With proper instructional methods, students can learn strategies that will enhance their reading ability in the new language while increasing oral proficiency. Establishing solid reading strategies seems to be a more important variable than L2 oral proficiency in comprehending L2 texts (Langer, Bartolomé, Vásquez, & Lucas, 1990). These strategies include predicting, making connections, monitoring and correcting, word solving, inferring, and summarizing (Pinnell & Scharer, 2001). Also, the process of learning to read and reading itself have been shown to provide a reciprocal relationship between oral language proficiency and L2 reading ability (Barrera, 1983). In other words, learning to read in the L2 assists and develops oral language proficiency, while increasing oral proficiency assists and improves L2 reading ability (Figure 3.5). Learning to read in the L2 with limited L2 oral proficiency is possible, although it is not the route shown to be most effective; however, again, L1 literacy proficiency will play a major role in determining successful L2 reading progress for students who are acquiring an L2. From Figure 3.5, it is evident that the more orally proficient a student is in the L2, the faster the path to the goal of fluent L2 reading.

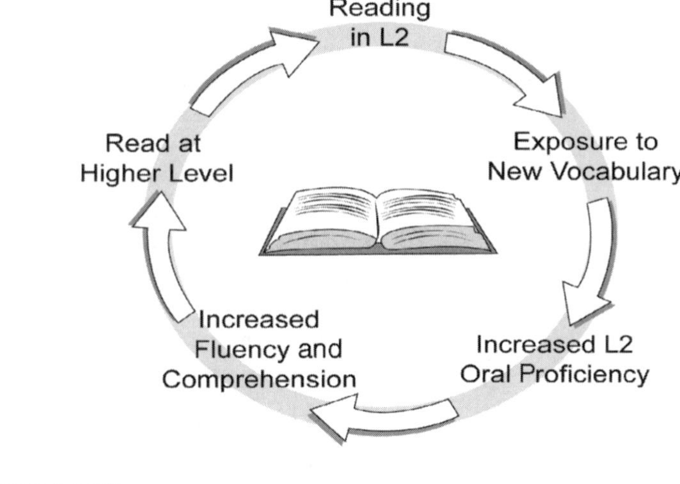

FIGURE 3.5. The reciprocity of L2 reading and oral language proficiency.

RESEARCH BRIEF Emerging Research Base

It is important to note that the scientific research base is "emerging rather than firmly established" with regard to ELLs (Baker, Linan-Thompson, & Arguelles, 2003, p. 2). A major challenge in designing a research study with ELLs as participants is to acknowledge the diversity that they bring to our institutions or schools, while applying a Western-based framework for data analysis. Because much reading research has monolingual students as participants, it is problematic to generalize its findings to diverse populations (Bernhardt, 1991; Taylor, Anderson, Au, & Raphael, 2000). L2 learners are similar to one another in that they are acquiring a second language, but as previously mentioned there are typically many differences within and among these students, making it difficult to generalize findings even among same-language L2 populations (Segalowitz & Hébert, 1994).

THE SECOND-LANGUAGE ACQUISITION PROCESS

There are many misconceptions regarding language acquisition (McLaughlin, 1990). Most people believe that young children have an advantage over older learners when acquiring an L2, or that once *orally* proficient in the L2, ELLs should be able to work on the same academic level as native English speakers with limited support. Both of these beliefs are false. As McLaughlin points out, older learners of an L2 have several advantages over younger learners:

- Typically, the more proficient a learner is in L1, the more the learner understands about language structures and is able to use that knowledge to help make language choices when communicating in the L2.
- The level of cognitive conversational demands becomes much higher as the learner matures; therefore, children appear to "soak up" the language when acquiring an L2. In reality, age wouldn't affect acquisition if we all spoke using the lower cognitive conversational level of younger children.

- Older learners can use their world experiences to assist them in L2 comprehension and communication, whereas younger children cannot use this resource. Carey (1985) has shown that although children have thought processes similar to those of adults, their lack of experiences prohibits them from being able to think as adults do.

It is a fallacy to assume that once students are able to communicate in the L2, they are ready for mainstreamed, general education classrooms. In demonstrating why this common misconception is a myth, Cummins (2003) has defined three levels of language proficiency. The first level is oral proficiency in the form of *basic interpersonal conversation skills* (BICS), defined as "the ability to carry on a conversation in familiar face-to-face situations" (Cummins, 2003, p. 4). Generally BICS takes between one and three years to acquire, depending on the individual. There is a great deal of implicit support for those acquiring BICS. Conversational partners' facial expressions, gestures, rate of speech, high-frequency words, and/or common phrases are a few examples of why this level of language proficiency is the first acquired.

Following BICS, the next level of proficiency is termed *discrete language skills* by Cummins. This includes those skills learned as a result of formal instruction (e.g., phonological awareness, grammar rules, conventions of writing) and practice. Reading is an example of how discrete language skills can affect a student's academic progress, since formal reading instruction is usually not sufficient to create a reader. Independent reading, or practice, must also be present in order for a student to become a good reader. This level of language proficiency begins at an early age (i.e., the alphabetic principle) and continues throughout the learner's schooling (conventional spelling, grammatical rules, appropriate writing style, etc.). In addition, discrete language skills in the L2 can be acquired simultaneously with BICS and content vocabulary learning. Some discrete language skills readily transfer from the L1 to the L2 (e.g., the concepts of phonemic awareness and decoding similar symbol systems), strengthening the argument for L1 literacy instruction whenever possible.

The third level of language proficiency is known as *academic language proficiency* (ALP) or *cognitive academic language proficiency* (CALP). Low-frequency words of Greek or Latin origin (found primarily in texts), abstract expressions, and complex syntax are examples of what is included at this level of proficiency. Without consistent exposure to texts where the majority of ALP or CALP components can be found, ELLs are not likely to acquire this level of proficiency. The absence of this third level of language proficiency is seen as the reason why students who appear to be orally proficient still need support with academics—specifically, ELLs who have not been exposed to texts or this level of proficiency in their L1 (Cummins, 2003).

Cummins goes on to explain that all three levels of language proficiency are important: BICS to enable communication, discrete language skills to enable reading or other complex academic tasks, and ALP or CALP to enable academic success parallel to that of native English speakers. He cautions, however, that a focus on discrete language skills in isolation could lead to ELLs' developing proficient decoding skills with little to no understanding of the text. For this reason, application of discrete language skills within meaningful contexts should be emphasized daily in classrooms. In other words, for those students who need instruction in phonemic awareness, phonics, vocabulary, fluency, and comprehension, explicit instruction should always be bridged by scaffolding and guided practice with texts (Dole, 2003); these skills should not be taught in isolation without meaningful applications.

CULTURAL/EXPERIENTIAL DIFFERENCES

Acknowledging and valuing the differing experiences of our ELLs are seen as facilitative variables for L2 acquisition (Ovando et al., 2003). For those of us who are native-born, mainstream Americans, immigration experiences are something we cannot relate to personally, since we have never had to flee our country or leave it permanently; however, by making an effort to know our ELLs and their families, we can understand these experiences much more than by merely acknowledging that Maria is from Cuba, Pierre is from Haiti, and Ghada is from Saudi Arabia. As Table 3.3 indicates, there are multiple stages of the acculturation process. Here are some suggestions on how we can come to a better understanding of ELLs and their experiences:

1. *Giving our students a voice in the classroom.* Krashen (1982) emphasizes the *affective filter* as the factor that will encourage or inhibit L2 acquisition. That is, the amount of input (exposure) turned into intake (learning) is determined by the learner's motivation, self-confidence, or anxiety. Students with high motivation and self-confidence, but low anxiety, have low filters and therefore the greatest intake or learning possibilities. On the other hand, low motivation, little self-confidence, and high anxiety limit the intake or learning opportunities. Teachers have the power to acknowledge and value children's diverse experiences or languages by encouraging them and allowing interaction (creating a low filter). They also have the power to squelch motivation and increase anxiety by interrupting students or not allowing mistakes (creating a high filter). Furthermore, if ELLs are not communicating, teachers are not aware of their linguistic needs (Wong Fillmore, 1991) or their cultural/experiential knowledge base. All students' experiences should be expanded upon, if necessary, so that they are successful in the classroom. Often, expanding experiences involves direct teaching; however, when the majority of activities are teacher-centered, restricting student interaction, teachers are limited in their interaction with students as well. Asking students what they think the main idea is, or for their predictions, allows teachers to probe their understandings of text at a deeper level if their initial responses do not appear to make sense. This interac-

TABLE 3.3. Stages of Acculturation

Stage	Description
Honeymoon stage	Everything looks bright and positive. The family or individuals have just arrived and are ready to begin a new chapter in their lives. All are eager to please, ready to interact, and happy to be in their new home.
Hostility stage	Frustration begins to set in as reality hits. The language, unknown daily survival tasks (e.g., navigating the transportation system), foods, and new ways of doing are unfamiliar and seen as problems inherent within the new society. Depression, anger, anxiety, and a longing to go "home" are generally felt during this stage.
Humor stage	Accomplishments bring on a triumphant feeling that the new society might not be so bad. As families or individuals begin to experience success and adjust to life's new demands, they are able to laugh at themselves or their previous frustrations.
Home stage	Allegiance to the "old homeland" is retained while accepting the "new home." A successful transition from the old to the new norms has occurred, and the new location is seen as "home."

Note. Data from *Help! They Don't Speak English Starter Kit for Primary Teachers: A Resource Guide for Educators of Limited English Proficient Migrant Students, Grades Pre-K–6.* (2003). Oneonta, NY: ESCORT.

tion provides valuable information and a rich data source for teachers to build on ELLs' knowledge base in a sensitive way, as well as the opportunity to further develop a positive relationship and affective environment.

TECH TIP Computer Access

Children of immigrants are typically living close to or below the poverty level (Reardon-Anderson, Capps, & Fix, 2002); thus their families face many socioeconomic challenges, in addition to cultural, economic, and linguistic transitions. Only 11% of students in low-income households (earning less than $20,000 annually) own a personal computer (Otterbourg, 1998). In addition, schools serving low-income populations generally have fewer computers, with a national average of nine students for every available computer. Parents of ELLs need additional support and encouragement with technology; however, many do not have access to the most current technologies and are unaware of how technology can support their children's learning. See the Recommended Websites at the end of this chapter for two sites designed to empower ELLs with technological literacy with a focus on reading (Wiggle Works and Hangman for ELLs).

2. *Interviewing family members.* Another way to understand ELLs is to speak with their parents or guardians within the first month of enrollment. Interviewing allows ELLs to be seen as individuals, parents as people interested in and concerned about their children's academic progress, and teachers as professionals wanting to reach out and understand how to best serve ELLs. If you do not speak a family's L1, the school district should have someone to translate for you, or perhaps a friend or relative of the family could do so. New immigrants often work more than one job and are likely still adjusting to a new life; be sensitive and work around their schedule when you invite them to come to the school. Also, keep in mind that if recently arrived, they are probably experiencing culture shock and might share some disillusionment about life in the United States. Typically, when one arrives in a new country (or even a new city or state, for that matter), various stages of adjustment are experienced (see Table 3.3). The amount of time each stage lasts will depend on the individual.

PARENT POINTER Family Interview

An interview with family members can be a rich source of knowledge regarding ELLs and their experiences. It is important for immigrant parents to understand the expectations that U.S. teachers hold for the parents of their students, although the way the expectations are described will determine how they are understood. If these are relayed in a cold, artificial way, parents may feel inhibited or defensive about their largely culturally and experientially based views of education. On the other hand, if the expectations or resources are explained in a sensitive, caring way, parents are more likely to appreciate the suggestions and do what they can to meet them. One way of showing sensitivity is to provide a suggestion in the form of a question. For example, instead of "Here in the United States, parents are expected to come to school events, check homework, and be involved in their child[ren]'s education," a better response would be "Did you know that teachers in the United States feel the education of your child[ren] is a partnership effort between parents and schools?" This latter question leads to opportunities to provide suggestions that parents will be open to hearing. It represents a true partnering effort from the onset, rather than an authoritative view that excludes parents as partners. As noted in the text, a family interview guide is provided in Forms 3.1 and 3.2. You will need to establish a rapport with the family before asking these questions; some of them are personal and will require a sense of trust before the family members will open up and discuss them. The questions will provide you not only with a chance to better understand and know the families of your ELLs, but also with opportunities to suggest resources or support for those areas of our educational system that are not clear.

A Parent Interview Checklist is provided in Form 3.1, with a Spanish version of the checklist in Form 3.2. While somewhat difficult to do logistically, interviews at the beginning of the year or at the time a student is enrolled in the school can provide rich information from parents that will help you get to know your students better. Forms 3.1 and 3.2 are geared for immigrant parents, so you may want to make adaptations to meet your local needs. Note that the items invite parents to respond through the use of prompting questions that are open and stated positively, allowing parents to provide answers beyond "Yes" or "No." At times, however, yes–no questions are a good option if you are just getting to know the family and need to break the ice.

ASSESSMENT AND ENGLISH-LANGUAGE LEARNERS

There are several important issues to address with regard to ELLs and assessment (Goh, 2004; Valdez-Pierce, 2003). Goh (2004) points out that while there are federal statutes requiring ELLs to be provided with nondiscriminatory assessment opportunities, there are problems associated with how this is carried out from state to state, due to the loose definition of ELLs and the lack of guidelines provided by the legislation. According to the statutes, ELLs must be provided opportunities to participate in reliable and valid assessments, be supplied with reasonable testing accommodations, and be administered tests that accurately reflect their aptitude and achievement.

Reliability and Validity

The constructs of *reliability* and *validity* are especially important in assessing ELLs. The reliability of an assessment is the degree of consistency obtained in producing the same result with the same student in different settings, with different assessors, or at different points in time. Reliability can be established by using multiple assessment measures, objective tests, multiple raters, and clearly specified scoring criteria (Valdez-Pierce, 2003). In order for a test to be valid, it must first be reliable (Goh, 2004). With the recent emphasis on high-stakes testing (tests that are used to make important decisions about schools, teachers, and students), it is crucial to determine whether the assessment is not only reliable, but also valid. Content validity ensures that the assessment reflects the curriculum and objectives it states it is evaluating. Because ELLs are still developing their English proficiency (both oral and academic), it is often difficult to get a true measure of the content being assessed. In other words, tests almost always become language or literacy measures, rather than measures of science, mathematics, and so on (Goh, 2004). In addition, bias can be a threat to the validity of an instrument (Goh, 2004; Valdez Pierce, 2003). Three different types of bias are defined below:

1. *Cultural bias* is acquired knowledge from participating in and sharing particular values or experiences of a culture. An example of cultural bias on an assessment would be including a question pertaining to birthday or holiday celebrations that

expects an answer relevant to mainstream, middle-class families. Often immigrant children do not celebrate birthdays or holidays in the same manner as mainstream American populations, either because they live in poverty or because they celebrate differently (with piñatas or extended family members rather than friends from school, etc.).

2. *Attitudinal bias* is a negative attitude displayed by the assessor toward a language or dialect. Just as low expectations from teachers predict low achievement, negative attitudes conveyed by the assessor, teacher, or school culture can have damaging effects on test results.
3. *Test bias* or *norming bias* refers to excluding ELLs or diverse populations from the population used to norm results. When this occurs, the test results of ELLs are compared with those of children from the cultural and linguistic mainstream. In effect, this is like comparing apples and oranges, as the ELLs' results will not be accurately interpreted against the normed population.

A fourth type of bias includes literally translating tests from the L2 to the L1 via interpreters or paper/pencil translations. Translations will not be equivalent to the original assessments, since it is difficult to translate cultural concepts, and using interpreters for testing requires more research (Valdés & Figueroa, 1994). Valdez Pierce (2003) suggests conducting dual-language tests (designed for the L1 and the L2) to limit bias; however, when students are not receiving instruction in both languages or have never received instruction in their L1, this could also be problematic, because the L1 might not be the dominant language.

L2 Acquisition Issues or Learning Disabilities?

As Robert Franco's situation demonstrates, many teachers wonder whether their ELLs are experiencing academic delays due to L2 acquisition issues or learning disabilities. ELLs have such diversity within and among groups that it is nearly impossible to outline what teachers can expect in identifying special needs. Schools typically have waited to refer ELLs for special education services until they are in the middle grades, due to criticisms of special education programs for an overrepresentation of ELLs "dumped" or misplaced into special education environments (Ovando et al., 2003; Yates & Ortiz, 1998). The problem with waiting until a student has some English proficiency is that it restricts much-needed assistance for those who really need special services at an earlier age (Yates & Ortiz, 1998); yet the overrepresentation of ELLs in special education classes demonstrates that teachers have difficulty distinguishing true learning disabilities from the process of language acquisition (Ortiz, 2001). Add to the mix the lack of appropriate instruments and personnel (knowledgeable about language acquisition and cultural nuances) trained to administer these assessments, and the identification of ELLs for special services becomes even more tenuous. Early intervention, however, is the key to appropriate identification and placement for ELLs (Ortiz, 2001).

Using response to instruction rather than IQ–achievement discrepancy as the criterion for placing students in special education might be the answer to this problem (Speece, 2003). This approach involves teachers and others on the child study team agreeing to implement systematic, scientific-research-based interventions in the classroom with the referred children. Implementing the interventions, conducting and interpreting assessments, and charting the data (results) will provide the criteria for determining whether the children are responding to instruction. If progress has been made, the students will not need to be unnecessarily labeled and placed in special education classes. If the children do not respond to instruction, they can then be placed in a special education environment that will focus on their needs. This procedure has been field-tested and examined as an alternative to IQ testing for students referred to special education (Speece, 2003).

Gifted and Talented Program Identification and ELLs

While there is an overrepresentation of ELLs identified with learning disabilities, there is an underrepresentation of ELLs in programs for gifted and talented students. Again, this can be attributed to testing bias and the common practice of using one measure or assessment for identification purposes (Bermúdez & Márquez, 1998). Also problematic are the many definitions of *giftedness* used by districts (Office of Educational Research and Improvement, 1998). Some districts strictly use test scores; others include teacher judgment; and still others include "high achievers" in their gifted programs. In addition, although many teachers know that children acquiring a language may be too inhibited to speak much, their expectations of silent, unquestioning children are generally low, clouding their perceptions of ELLs' academic performance (Office of Educational Research and Improvement, 1998). For example, until Carla, a fourth-grade ELL with two years of English instruction and low grades, was asked to write an acrostic poem about her native country, her teacher did not understand that she should have had high expectations for her all along, even though Carla was quiet and a low performer in the class. The teacher had coursework that explained theories of language acquisition as part of her teacher training, but the connection between L2 acquisition and student expectation theory was not made. Here is Carla's poem about her life in Honduras:

> How wonderful it was
> On the boat
> Near the mouth of the river at
> Dawn. The sun was pointing at me
> Under the roof of the boat. The
> River was wonderful when the sun was pointing at me
> And the boat was soft in the water,
> Soft, very soft in the water.
> (Robisheaux, 1997, as cited in Office of Educational Research and Improvement, 1998)

As a result of this assignment that allowed for creativity and self-expression, Carla's teacher gained a whole new understanding of students with different cultural and linguistic backgrounds. The teacher became an advocate for ELLs and expanded the established identification procedures for the gifted and talented programs in her district.

Bermúdez and Márquez (1998) suggest the use of multiple measures rather than one test score to place students in gifted programs. The following are suggested as alternatives to the sole use of IQ/testing for identification:

- Collect background data and work samples for each student. Asking for parental input regarding their child's background and previous work prior to enrolling in U.S. schools is valuable information.
- Observe the child's language and social behaviors, using a behavioral profile that takes cultural background into consideration. Many gifted and talented programs use a profile to record and evaluate students under evaluation to be placed in

gifted programs, with the understanding that a child's background will have an impact on language and social behaviors.

- Examine the cultural and linguistic behaviors of the child, and determine if they can be masking the child's potential identification into a gifted program. For example, particular cultural canons such as "don't speak unless spoken to" might inhibit the child from participating in class or providing his or her opinions.
- Examine standardized test scores in light of the demographic data: Are test scores consistent with the rest of the information collected? (If not, test bias may be to blame.)

Testing Accommodations

There are six possible accommodations when tests are administered to ELLs, although, as previously mentioned, states are not uniform in providing the same accommodations (Goh, 2004). The first possibility, *modification of setting*, refers to the changing of location, environment, or condition of testing for ELLs while taking the exam. For example, in Florida, ELLs (or their parents, if the ELLs are underage) are given a choice of taking state or district exams in their regular classroom or with their heritage-language or English as a second language (ESL) teacher. *Modification of presentation format* is the second type of accommodation and involves changing the medium of test administration, test items, or both. Examples of this include oral reading of directions, explaining directions, or reducing the number of items per page. In Florida, the heritage-language teacher may answer questions pertaining to general test directions or explain a word or phrase that might be difficult for ELLs to understand in the heritage language; however, the teacher is not permitted to provide information that would assist the students in correctly answering the question or solving the problem. Third, *modification of response format* enables ELLs to answer in their preferred modality of communication. This includes the use of the L1 orally or in writing by a student, or the use of an interpreter to translate the student's responses into English. It also involves providing heritage-language/English dictionaries for use during exams, as is the case in Florida. *Modification of timing and scheduling* is the fourth type of accommodation. Allowing additional time to complete the test, offering breaks, or administering the test in multiple sessions are examples of modifying the timing or schedule of an exam. ELLs in Florida are given extra time to complete the exams; however, all exam sections scheduled to be administered that day must be completed by the students on that same day. Students are not permitted to continue testing within a section or session from one day to another.

Another possible modification is the *elimination of portions of tests or subtests* that are not valid due to a language barrier, interfering with the accuracy of student achievement results. This option is typically used for students with disabilities rather than ELLs by states or districts. Finally, the *testing of limits* is the last type of accommodation permitted for diverse learners when completing exams. This involves having ELLs first complete the exam using the standard administration criteria, then taking the exam a second time with a series of accommodations (e.g., eliminating time restrictions, use of bilingual dictionaries) to determine if performance can be improved using different criteria for administration. Again, this type of accommodation is not typically used with ELLs and is problematic, in that "learning" from the first testing administration can influence the results of the second.

Accommodations can be useful tools for ELLs who are taking high-stakes tests; however, teachers' and parents' lack of knowledge about them can inhibit their use. If students are not exposed to these types of accommodations during regular classroom assessments or instruction, they will probably not be useful during an exam. For example, if students are not provided with bilingual dictionaries for daily assignments, the dictionaries may not be used adequately during an exam. Another possible problem with accommodations is that teachers, parents, and students may not even be aware of them. With the move toward inclusive classrooms, regular classroom teachers are generally unaware of possible testing accommodations for diverse learners (Goh, 2004). Immigrant parents coming from different countries' school systems are not knowledgeable about these accommodations, and therefore cannot advocate for their children. There also needs to be more research investigating the effects of accommodations with diverse learners. Not many studies have been conducted with ELLs to document the effects of accommodations on testing results, reliability, or validity. Finally, the lack of consistency across states and districts in using accommodations calls for legislation to standardize procedures, so that comparisons of ELLs' performance can be made across districts within the same states, as well as nationwide.

Aptitude and Achievement

As noted earlier, many standardized or high-stakes tests ultimately become language tests (Goh, 2004). Classroom-based assessment is generally a better measure of ELLs' aptitude and achievement when teachers use student-centered teaching and principles of authentic assessment. According to Ovando and colleagues (2003), teachers who are more student-centered in their approach to learning focus more on students' needs and interests, as well as on their learning processes (strategies used to decode words in text), than on products (test scores). Collaboration among students is important in order for the student-centered teacher to foster a learning environment where students learn from each other. Teachers can prepare ELLs for standardized or norm-referenced tests by defining learning outcomes for each student according to the standards or outcomes from which the tests are based. Once individual needs have been identified, instructional plans addressing those needs can be prepared and used to guide lesson planning. Classroom-based assessments should be used to indicate when new learning objectives can be incorporated into the instructional plan. Ovando and colleagues (2003, pp. 341–345) include five fundamental assumptions to guide classroom-based assessment for ELLs:

1. *It must be based on what we know about how language learners learn—in particular, about how they acquire reading and writing processes.* Important to remember are the three levels of language proficiency, actively engaging prior knowledge, student knowledge of text structure, collaborative learning, and related concepts.
2. *It is integral to instruction, informs teaching, and improves learning.* Classroom assessment must be conducted on a regular and systematic basis; must be integrated within instruction (not just conducted at the end of a unit); and must be used to inform instructional decision making, as well as to provide an evaluation tool for teachers to assess their teaching. Teachers should assess often (daily, weekly or biweekly) to determine student progress in achieving the planned objectives.
3. *It uses multiple sources of information on a regular and systematic basis.* Different measures that vary in format should be used before decisions regarding student progress are made. Examples of classroom-based assessments include oral reports, essays, multiple-choice tests, reading logs, portfolios, and miscue analyses. Multiple measures

provide a bigger picture of student progress, ultimately leading to more sound instructional decisions.

4. *It is culturally and developmentally appropriate.* Culturally relevant instruction involves understanding students and how they learn best. For example, students from cultures that do not value competition might be best assessed in collaborative learning contexts. While this suggestion is not always possible or appropriate, students who prefer cooperation to competition should be allowed to use this context for assessment if it is the most accurate way to assess their aptitude and achievement. Developmentally appropriate assessment involves using materials and activities that are in line with the age, interests, and language proficiency of the students.

5. *It provides valid, reliable, and fair measures of learning.* Students should be assessed on the instructional objectives and classroom activities in order to provide information for teachers to improve their instruction. It is unfair for teachers to assess students on material covered in class using high-level thinking skills, when lower-level skills were used during instruction. It is also unfair for teachers to show bias in their grading, awarding better grades to students who have done well in the past. So-called "blind" scoring (assigning students numbers) rather than putting their names on tests can be used to avoid grade biases. Also, a criterion-referenced assessment that uses a rating scale or a checklist can guide teachers in scoring against specific criteria rather than knowledge of past student performances. Finally, teachers must set clear criteria, scaffold instruction, use benchmarks (or exemplars), and involve the learners in the assessment process to create reliable and valid assessment measures.

Teacher-Administered Tests for ELLs

Teachers are often required to administer district- or state-mandated assessments to ELLs. ESL teachers are generally responsible for this, but with the implementation of inclusion, classroom teachers also need to be aware of these tests, how often they are to be administered, and the reporting procedures. All districts are required to report on the English-language proficiency of each child once per year. In addition, all states receiving federal funds for ELLs must monitor their programs to ensure compliance with state and federal laws. Not all districts administer the same tests, since the law does not explicitly state that a certain assessment be given; therefore, the names of the assessments will vary from district to district.

Most districts emphasize L2 oral language proficiency as a measure to determine program placement, language-learning progress, language of reading instruction, and level of support to be provided to the students. This is unfortunate, since it is now known that there are different tiers of language proficiency, and using oral language as a program exit criterion cuts support from ELLs when they are still acquiring the academic language needed for success in classrooms. The Student Oral Language Observation Matrix (SOLOM) is used by some districts to ascertain oral language proficiency and is usually administered by teachers. Five areas are assessed: comprehension, vocabulary, fluency, grammar, and pronunciation. Teachers mark the cell on the SOLOM that best describes the student's use of language based upon the child's interaction within different contexts (playground, class discussions, conversations, etc.). The SOLOM does not take much time to complete; however, teachers need to keep in mind what is typical for L1 students at the same grade level, in order for the results to reflect accurate language growth and progress through the grade levels. See the Recommended Websites list at the end of this chapter to access more information on the SOLOM.

Other tests require specialized skills/procedures and are only administered by those who have received this training. The Woodcock–Muñoz Language Survey (Woodcock & Muñoz-Sandoval, 2005) is an example of such a test. It can be administered in English or Spanish and assigns students to one of five academic language proficiency levels. One negative point about the Woodcock–Muñoz is that the English items were translated into Spanish to create the Spanish items. As previously mentioned, this is problematic, since the underlying assumption with translation is that all items are equal in discrimination across languages (Crocker, 2000). Woodcock–Muñoz test scores can be used to determine student eligibility for bilingual services, classify students by language proficiency for instructional purposes, assess progress or readiness for English-only instruction, evaluate ESL program effectiveness, or assess the language proficiency of participants in research studies. With training, the assessment is generally easy to administer, and the scores are computerized.

GENERAL INSTRUCTIONAL GUIDELINES AND BEST PRACTICES FOR ENGLISH-LANGUAGE LEARNERS

All ELLs and dialect speakers benefit from comprehensible input (Krashen, 1985). *Sheltered instruction* is a way to provide comprehensibility of content, as well as a means to model or demonstrate while scaffolding language instruction. In sheltered instruction, the content of the lesson is made comprehensible when the teacher embeds the L2 learning principles (e.g., context clues, modified speech rate and tone, extensive modeling) within the learning environment (Echevarria, Vogt, & Short, 2000). Tools that help teachers embed L2 learning within content instruction include graphic organizers, visual aids, cooperative learning, peer tutoring, vocabulary previews, predictions, and native-language support. Echevarria and colleagues (2000) are careful to note that sheltering instruction is more than using additional tools or modifying techniques when teaching. There is a high level of engagement and interaction between teachers and students, between text and students, and among students, creating an environment conducive to instructional conversations and higher-order thinking activities. Sheltered instruction works particularly well when there is a mix of L1 languages in the class, since all instruction is in English (see Echeverria et al., 2000, for specific lesson, instructional, and assessment guidelines).

In addition to sheltered instruction, other best practices include reading aloud daily, structuring independent reading and writing, planning around interdisciplinary themes, teaching the writing process, and expecting higher-order thinking (Lopez-Reyna, 2002). For older ELLs in middle or high school, explicitly teaching phonics and phonemic differences between the L1 and the L2 provides the students with knowledge of the English letter–sound system and increases confidence when L2 oral proficiency is low; however, it is extremely important to apply phonics lessons to authentic texts for meaningful instruction. Finally, pronunciation should not be stressed over meaning and comprehension, as L2 acquisition is a lengthy process. Over time, the more ELLs speak, read, write, and listen, the more orally proficient and comfortable they will become.

Although this information is meant to help teachers with general instructional guidelines, the most important actions a teacher can take to assist ELLs in acquiring L2 structure and content are (1) to make the information meaningful and comprehensible, and (2) to know each child as an individual. Most teachers responsible for ELLs will tell you that this population is very eager to learn and wants to succeed in school. In my opinion, the high dropout rate of minority populations stems not only from the economic need for children to contribute to the families' income, but also from the way some teachers approach instruction. All students must see the relevancy of what they are learning to their lives in order for them to remain motivated and engaged in learning. As teachers, we are responsible for engaging our students and helping them make connections that might not be evident, especially for ELLs, who typically have different experiences from those of mainstream-culture students.

Teachers can make reading content or skills *meaningful* by constantly applying what is being learned to authentic texts and personal writing assignments. This goes beyond the practice pages of workbooks and isolated exercises to authentic use of the skills within the context of "real" applications. For example, when teachers select books for guided reading, they should keep in mind the students' instructional level and needs; from the text should come the objectives for phonological awareness and other teaching points. Using differentiated instruction (see Chapter 2) will best meet all students' needs. Teachers can make the content *comprehensible* by using visuals, using role playing, planning around universal and culturally congruent themes, and integrating subject matter (e.g., teaching science or social studies concepts throughout the day, not just during the time designated for content area instruction). If possible, the L1 should be used to support comprehension. Finally, teachers can begin to know their children as individuals by interviewing family members and rethinking the popular attitude about parental involvement in schools. Many, if not most, teachers view parental involvement in schools as something that parents are supposed to initiate. The popular attitude goes something like this: "If parents feel it is important, they will come to school and ask about how they can help their child, or how they can become involved." This attitude must be changed to something like this: "All parents want the best for their children. Together, parents and teachers must work hard to see that every child reaches his or her fullest potential. Teachers should invite parents into classrooms, have regularly scheduled communication or conferences, and suggest ways parents can support their children's learning at home." This new attitude is especially important for children of diverse backgrounds, who are more than likely to come from places with different attitudes about parental involvement.

FURTHER DEVELOPING STUDENT READING AND WRITING PROFILES

The Parent Interview Checklist (Forms 3.1 and 3.2) will provide you with more in-depth information about your students' backgrounds and how you might structure instruction to meet your students' needs. You can use this information to expand the parent/guardian data summary included in Part I of the Student Reading and Writing Profile. Part III of the Profile (Form 3.3) provides a place for you to record language assessment results, as well as areas of strength and improvement in language learning.

CHAPTER SUMMARY

The number of ELLs in U.S. public schools is increasing. We have much to learn about how to best serve them in our classrooms; however, from what is currently known, students acquiring an L2 need teachers who are knowledgeable about their L1 (both its structure and their L1 reading ability), the different levels of L2 proficiency, and how the L1 is the base upon which students grow and learn. In addition, ELLs need teachers who will provide a positive affective classroom environment, are willing to interact with them (and their families), and will advocate on their behalf to ensure equity. Assessment issues (accommodations, biases, portfolios) and curriculum development needs of ELLs are also important to remember in serving this population.

ELLs bring many strengths with them to U.S. schools, although these strengths may not be readily recognized and valued by the mainstream population. It is important that we get to know our ELL students and build upon what they know to expand their experiences for success in classrooms.

KEY TERMS AND CONCEPTS

Academic language proficiency (ALP) or cognitive academic language proficiency (CALP)
Basic interpersonal conversation skills (BICS)
Cognate
Comprehensible input
Culturally relevant
Discourse patterns
Discrete language skills
English-language learners (ELLs)
Primary language (L1)
Secondary language (L2)
Sheltered instruction

REFLECTION AND ACTION

1. Research the political climate concerning English-language and bilingual instruction in public schools. Compare and contrast the different positions with what is known from research about language acquisition and learning. Write an essay that outlines your philosophy regarding instruction for those learning English in the K–12 school system. Be sure to substantiate your assertions with research.
2. Select a story that could serve as an interactive read-aloud for ELLs. Analyze the text and identify possible literacy challenges for L2 readers with regard to the following:
   a. Vocabulary
   b. Figurative language
   c. Homophones
   d. Complex syntax
   e. Cultural relevance
   f. Concepts or content from the text that might be new information

READ ON!

Au, K. H. (1993). *Literacy instruction in multicultural settings.* Orlando, FL: Harcourt Brace.

Au's book is an excellent resource for understanding sociocultural aspects of learning to read in an L2, as well as ways we as teachers can advocate on behalf of ELLs.

Birch, B. M. (2002). *English L2 reading: Getting to the bottom.* Mahwah, NJ: Erlbaum.

Birch's book focuses on bottom-up or text-based issues of teaching L2 reading and writing. That is, her approach is based on differing L1 structures, including the transfer of those processes as students begin to read in the L2. Many practical suggestions are included at the end of each chapter.

Brock, C. H., & Raphael, T. E. (2005). *Windows to language, literacy, and culture: Insights from an English-language learner.* Newark, DE: International Reading Association.

Using the case of an elementary student from Laos, the authors provide insights about the needs of linguistically diverse students. The case serves as a catalyst for reflection about purposeful learning for English-language learners.

Drucker, M. J. (2003). What reading teachers should know about ESL learners. *The Reading Teacher*, *57*, 22–29.

Provides a good overview of basic understandings of teaching ELLs and an explanation of appropriate reading strategies.

Harry, B., & Klingner, J. (2005). *Why are so many minority students in special education? Understanding race and disability in schools*. New York: Teachers College Press.

This book examines the disproportionate representation of minority students in special education. Based on their research in a large, urban setting, the authors provide moving examples as well as recommendations for instructional practice, assessment, teacher education, and policy.

Ovando, C. J., Combs, M. E., & Collier, V. P. (Eds.). (2006). *Bilingual and ESL classrooms: Teaching in multicultural contexts* (4th ed.). Boston: McGraw-Hill.

This is an excellent, comprehensive resource concerning L2 learners and their education in the United States. Vignettes throughout the text give the reader a better understanding of the construct/content from the perspective of an ELL in our school system.

Peregoy, S. F., & Boyle, O. F. (2005). *Reading, writing, and learning in ESL: A resource book for K–12 teachers* (4th ed.). New York: Longman.

Peregoy and Boyle have compiled a comprehensive look at L2 literacy instruction, including background chapters on ELLs in general, and the process of acquiring an L2.

SHARPENING YOUR SKILLS: SUGGESTIONS FOR PROFESSIONAL DEVELOPMENT

1. Identify a language other than English with a high number of speakers in your area. Make an attempt to learn the language, or at least some common phrases and the alphabet or symbol system. Analyze and investigate possible ways the L1 speakers of that language could experience interference (both positive and negative) while learning English as an L2 (see Birch, 2002, for examples).
2. Examine the excerpted family interview transcripts in Figures 3.1–3.3, or transcripts from your own family interviews. What are the themes that run through each interview? What other information would you want to obtain in order to better understand your students' backgrounds or learning needs? How are the students' needs different? How are they the same?

RESOURCES FOR ASSESSMENT AND INSTRUCTION

Fradd, S. H., & Klingner, J. K. (1995). *Classroom inclusion strategies for students learning English*. Austin, TX: PRO-ED.

This book is a collection of instructional strategies for classrooms that include both ELL and native English speakers.

Kress, J. (1993). *The ESL teacher's book of lists*. Upper Saddle River, NJ: Prentice Hall.

This book provides a great way to get organized with practical applications, checklists, charts, and suggestions for teachers of ELLs.

Tiedt, P. L., & Tiedt, I. M. (2001). *Multicultural teaching: A handbook of activities, information and resources* (6th ed.). Boston: Allyn & Bacon.

This handbook includes activities appropriate for ELLs, but also includes lesson plans and thematic units.

RECOMMENDED WEBSITES

English Language Learner Knowledge Base
www.helpforschools.com/ELLKBase/index.shtml

This site includes the latest information regarding ELLs, including upcoming conferences, program evaluation, legislative initiatives, parent outreach, and a searchable knowledge base. For information on the SOLOM, go directly to *www.helpforschools.com/ELLKBase/forms/SOLOM.shtml*

Hangman
http://server1.billsgames.com/hangman

This site provides domain-free software to help ELLs learn vocabulary words in a game format.

WebQuests
http://webquest.sdsu.edu

Theme-based learning is beneficial for all learners, especially ELLs. Teaching with a theme provides students the opportunity to hear vocabulary throughout the school day and in other content areas, providing a more complete picture to support language and concept learning. WebQuests (Dodge, 1997) provide teachers with a scaffold for building inquiry-based theme units, using the Internet as a learning tool and provider of information.

Wiggle Works
www.ed.gov/pubs/TechStrength/scholastic.html

An early-literacy, bilingual series that incorporates universally designed CD-ROMs for each book within the database. (Sponsored by Scholastic, Inc., and the Center for Applied Special Technology.)

FORM 3.1. Parent Interview Checklist (English Version)

Parent Interview Checklist

Name of student ______________________________ Date ____________

School ____________________ Name of teacher ____________________

Name(s) of parent(s) Mother ______________________________

Father ______________________________

Other family members or people residing in the home:

Name Relationship

____

____

____

____

____

____

____

1. Family background information
   a. Tell me about your homeland and why you decided to come to the United States. (If necessary, prompt with: What country was [student's name] born in?)
   b. Where did you live? (If necessary, prompt with: Did you live in a rural or urban area? Was this a city or town? Did you have a lot of family members in that same area?)
   c. What other countries has your family lived in and for how long?
   d. Do you still have family in that [those] country [countries]?
   e. What were the highest grades completed [for parents and older siblings of the student]?
   f. What were your occupations in the homeland?
   g. Was the journey to the United States frightening or traumatic for [student's name]?
2. Life in the United States
   a. Tell me about your experience in the United States so far. (If necessary, prompt with: How long has it been since you left your homeland? Are you receiving assistance as a refugee or from other sponsors?)
   b. Is this country what you imagined it would be?
   c. What cities/states have you lived in since arriving in the United States?
   d. How many schools has [name of student] attended in this country?
   e. What is [are] your occupation(s) in the United States?
   f. What would you do differently with regard to immigrating to the United States if you could go back in time?

(cont.)

3. Student's educational background:
   a. Tell me about [name of student's] formal education in your homeland. (If necessary, prompt with: How many years did [name of student] attend school before coming to the United States?
   b. What language[s] were teachers using for instruction?
   c. Was their instruction provided in a second language?
   d. What was [name of student's] favorite subject or activity in school?
   e. Were the instructional methods used traditional [requiring memorization, teacher-centered activities] or constructivist [student-centered, process learning emphasis]?
4. Future hopes and dreams
   a. Tell me about your hopes and aspirations for your children, specifically [name of your student]. (If necessary, prompt with: Do you expect them to finish high school? Do you expect them to go to college?)
   b. Do you know who can help you if you have questions about your children's future? (The idea here is to see how much is known about our system of education—high school counselors, community organizations, college recruiters, etc.)
5. Perspectives on language learning and support
   a. Tell me how you feel about [name of student] learning English. (If necessary, prompt with: Do you plan on maintaining [name of student's] L1? If so, how?)
   b. How do you feel about [name of student] possibly becoming English-dominant?
   c. How will you or someone at home support [name of student] with homework or projects that are in English?
   d. Are you aware of the differences between the school system where you once lived and the school system here? (This is to assist you in determining the amount of support the family will need as they make the transition to a new culture and school system.)

FORM 3.2. Parent Interview Checklist (Spanish Version)

Lista de Verificación para la Entrevista de los Padres

Nombre del/la estudiante ______________________ Fecha ____________

Escuela ______________________ Nombre del profesor ______________________

Nombre de los padres Madre ______________________

Padre ______________________

Nombres de otros parientes u otras personas que viven con el/la estudiante:

Nombre Relación

____

____

____

____

____

____

____

1. Información familiar
   a. Cuénteme de su patria y por qué decidió venir a Estados Unidos. (Si fuera necesario, empiece con: ¿En qué país nació [nombre del/la estudiante]?)
   b. ¿Dónde vivía? (Si fuera necesario, empiece con: ¿Usted vivía en un área rural o urbana? ¿Era ésta una ciudad o un pueblo? ¿Tenía mucha familia o parientes en esa misma área?)
   c. ¿En qué otros países ha vivido su familia y por cuánto tiempo?
   d. ¿Todavía tiene familia en ese [esos] país [países]?
   e. ¿Hasta qué grado escolar llegaron los padres y hermanos mayores del estudiante?
   f. ¿Cuáles eran sus oficios en su país?
   g. ¿Cómo fue el viaje a Estados Unidos para el estudiante?
2. Vida en los Estados Unidos
   a. Cuénteme de su experiencia en Estados Unidos hasta ahora. (Si fuera necesario, empiece con: ¿Cuánto tiempo hace que salieron de su país? ¿Están recibiendo ayuda del gobierno como refugiados o de otros patrocinadores?)
   b. ¿Es Estados Unidos como usted se lo imaginó?
   c. ¿Dónde ha vivido desde que llegó a Estados Unidos?
   d. ¿A cuántas escuelas ha asistido [nombre del/la estudiante] en Estados Unidos?
   e. ¿Cuál es/son sus oficios en los Estados Unidos?
   f. ¿Qué hubiese hecho diferente en respecto a la inmigración a Estados Unidos si pudiese volver al pasado?

(cont.)

3. Historia de la instrucción del/la estudiante
   a. Cuénteme de la instrucción formal de [nombre del/la estudiante] en su país. (Si fuera necesario, empiece con: ¿Cuántos años asistió [nombre del/la estudiante] a la escuela antes de llegar a Estados Unidos?).
   b. ¿Qué lenguaje usaban sus maestras/os en la escuela?
   c. ¿Se enseñaba en un lenguaje secundario?
   d. ¿Qué asignatura o actividad era la favorita de [nombre del/la estudiante]?
   e. ¿Qué métodos de instrucción se usaban—los tradicionales [memorización, actividades enfocadas en la maestra/o] o los constructivistas [actividades enfocadas en el/la estudiante, énfasis en el proceso de aprender]?
4. Futuro y ambición
   a. Cuénteme de sus esperanzas y aspiraciones para sus hijos, en específico [nombre del/la estudiante]. (Si fuera necesario, empiece con: ¿Usted espera que sus hijos terminen la escuela secundaria? ¿Espera que sus hijos asistan a un instituto o una universidad?)
   b. ¿Sabe quién le puede ayudar si tiene preguntas sobre el futuro de sus hijos? (Queremos saber cuánto conoce acerca de nuestro sistema de educación—consejeros de secundaria, organizaciones comunitarias, reclutadores para la universidad, etc.)
5. Perspectivas sobre adquisición de idioma y apoyo
   a. Cuénteme cómo le hace sentir que [nombre del/la estudiante] aprenda inglés. (Si fuera necesario, empiece con: ¿Usted piensa mantener vigente el primer idioma de [nombre del/la estudiante]? ¿Si es así, cómo lo piensa lograr?)
   b. ¿Cómo le hace sentir que para [nombre del/la estudiante] posiblemente el inglés sea el idioma dominante?
   c. ¿Cómo apoyan en casa a [nombre del/la estudiante] con la tarea o proyectos escolares en inglés?
   d. ¿Está consiente de las diferencias entre nuestro sistema escolar y el de su lugar de origen? [Esto es para ayudar a determinar la cantidad de apoyo que la familia necesitará durante la transición a la nueva cultura y el sistema escolar.]

FORM 3.3. Student Reading and Writing Profile (Part III)

Student Reading and Writing Profile

Part III: Data Pertaining to English-Language Learners

Summary Data from Cumulative Records

Previous placements in English as a second language or bilingual programs ________________

____

____

____

____

Previous language testing

Name of Test	Date	Score
________________	__________	__________
________________	__________	__________
________________	__________	__________
________________	__________	__________
________________	__________	__________
________________	__________	__________
________________	__________	__________

Recommendations from previous teachers in cumulative folders

Student strengths in language learning ______________________________

____

Student areas for improvement in language learning ____________________

____

Possible reasons for difficulties ____________________________________

____

II

FOCUS ON THE FOUNDATIONS OF READING

FOUR

In the Beginning

Phonological Awareness

ELIZABETH D. CRAMER

VIGNETTE

Gonzalo is a kindergarten student at River Rock Elementary School. His teacher, Anita Sotomayer, has had concerns about his preparedness for learning to read from the beginning of the school year. When she reads stories to the children, Gonzalo is one of the few students in the class who is not familiar with any of the literature, even the most popular children's stories in the classroom library. Additionally, when Gonzalo engages in free reading time, he often holds the book upside down and sometimes turns the pages from right to left.

Anita often makes up silly stories with her students, where each child takes a turn coming up with a word that rhymes to complete a sentence. One day, when it was Gonzalo's turn to come up with an animal that rhymed with *big*, his reply was, "cow." His classmates giggled and anxiously raised their hands to volunteer "pig." Gonzalo didn't understand why "cow" wasn't a good choice.

By spring, Anita is debating whether Gonzalo needs to be referred for further testing, or whether perhaps he is just a slow learner, or whether he has just come to school without some of the same exposure to literature and print-rich environments as some of his peers. Gonzalo is wondering why so many of his classmates are learning to read, and he still can't make sense of the words on the page.

ANTICIPATION QUESTIONS

- What are early signs that students are learning to read?
- What challenges might students face in their early reading?
- What does the research show to be the most important predictor of reading success?
- What assessment tools can be used to determine a child's level of phonological awareness and determine suspected areas of future reading difficulty?
- How can classroom teachers help students improve their phonological awareness?

INTRODUCTION

Like many students, Gonzalo shows early signs that he is struggling with the basic prereading concepts that most students have mastered by the time they reach kindergarten. This chapter begins with a discussion of emergent literacy and indicators that students are on the way to learning to read and write. It continues with a discussion of the importance of phonological awareness as a precursor to reading instruction. Finally, resources are provided to enable teachers to effectively meet the challenge of preparing young children for assessment and instruction in phonological awareness and other areas of emergent literacy.

EMERGENT LITERACY

When should young children begin to learn to read and write? Traditional educators espoused a maturational view of early reading, known as *reading readiness*. Harris and Sipay (1980) defined reading readiness as follows: "Reading readiness may be defined as a state of general maturity, based on attitudes and learned knowledge and skills, which allow a child to learn to read under given instructional conditions" (p. 19). The notion was that reading and writing instruction should begin when a child was developmentally ready to learn—for most students, in first grade. Indeed, some contended that rushing a child into a highly structured reading and writing curriculum could be harmful if the child was not developmentally ready (Elkind, 1981). The acronym PIES was often used to describe reading readiness. That is, proponents felt that reading and writing should begin when a child was Physically, Intellectually, Emotionally, and Socially ready.

However, withholding reading and writing instruction until a child reaches school age can prevent the child from the benefits of exposure to rich literacy experiences. Most children are naturally curious and are natural learners, simply through interacting with their environment. By observing their peers, older children, and adults, and through exposure to print, children begin to develop concepts and behaviors that will later serve as the foundation for reading and writing. These concepts and behaviors may include learning how to hold a book, pointing at pictures, and scribbling. Providing structured opportunities to foster early reading and writing can build on this natural curiosity and provide success in the early stages of literacy. The work of Marie Clay (1966) triggered the idea that children learn about language, reading, and writing before beginning formal instruction in school, and that these early learnings are important and legitimate stages of emerging competency in literacy. The term *emergent literacy* is defined as "the reading and writing concepts and behaviors of young children that precede and develop into conventional literacy" (Sulzby & Teale, 1991, p. 728). Emergent literacy includes awareness of environmental print, book and print awareness, and the sounds of the language (phonological awareness).

Environmental Print

One of the easiest ways to expose young children to literacy early on is through the use of *environmental print*. Environmental print surrounds children each day on items such as cereal boxes, restaurant signs, food labels, cleaners, magazines, street signs, and stores. This type of print is often a child's first exposure to print, and often children as young as two can begin to recognize or "read" familiar environmental print (though usually only

1. Find 10 logos from stores or restaurants, food products, or other brands in magazines, newspapers, or coupons. Identify logos of national or local brands that students are likely to encounter in your community.
2. Paste the logos on index cards and laminate.
3. Present the index cards to students in individual sessions—ask students to identify each.

FIGURE 4.1. Assessing children's grasp of environmental print.

in the context of the style of writing or sign in which a child often sees it). Figure 4.1 provides a description of how you can assess children's grasp of environmental print. Parents can take the opportunity to point out such print to their children early on, and teachers of young children can label items all around preschool classrooms. Children who learn at an early age that symbols come together to form words, as in environmental print, will be able to carry that connection into the reading involved in books.

Book and Print Awareness

Book awareness is another indicator of emergent literacy. Book awareness entails knowing how to hold a book, identifying the front and back of the book, and mastering how to turn pages. Early exposure to books and read-aloud experiences at home and in preschool settings provides children with the opportunity to develop book awareness. Developing a print-rich environment in the classroom is also vital to the development of book and print awareness (see Chapter 14).

Another early sign that students are on the road to reading and writing is *print awareness*. Print awareness involves the ability to recognize and form both upper- and lower-case letters. Usually, students will learn the alphabet by singing the traditional alphabet song; later, children begin to recognize alphabet symbols as the representation of those letters. Print awareness also involves identifying letters, developing a concept of *word*, and learning that there are spaces between words. Form 4.1 is a checklist designed to assess student understanding of book and print awareness. Form 4.2 can be used to record student mastery of upper- and lower-case letters.

Once students have mastered print awareness, they will be able to master the idea of the *alphabetic principle*—that is, the awareness that there is a systematic relationship between speech sounds and words in print (Adams, 1990). An extension of the alphabetic principle is the understanding that spoken words are made up of sequences of sounds. In Chapter 5, you'll read more about letter–sound correspondence and how the understanding of this correspondence leads to reading. This chapter focuses primarily on how children learn the sounds of language: a concept called *phonological awareness*.

PHONOLOGICAL AWARENESS

The National Reading Panel (2000a) identified over 50 scientifically credible studies that documented the importance of *phonemic awareness* in learning to read and in preventing and treating reading difficulties. Phonemic awareness is the ability to notice, think about, and work with the individual sounds (*phonemes*) in spoken words—for example, the ability to realize that the word *man* comprises three distinct sounds, /m/, /a/, and /n/.

There are 44 phonemes in the English language. Phonemic awareness is one component of the larger concept of *phonological awareness.*

Phonological awareness refers to the understanding of different ways that oral language can be divided into smaller segments and manipulated. Once children are aware of these sounds, they can put this awareness into practice by actually picking out and manipulating sounds and words. This manipulation may be demonstrated through breaking sentences apart into words, words into syllables, or words into phonemes. Words can be divided by syllable; for example, the word *hammer* is composed of two syllables: *ham-mer*. The word *cat* is composed of one syllable, but can be divided into two: onset /k/ and rhyme /at/. Furthermore, *cat* can be divided into three different phonemes: /k/, /a/, and /t/. Phonological awareness is also the awareness that if the last sound is removed from the word *cart*, the result is the word *car*.

Components of Phonological Awareness

Research seems to indicate that phonological awareness is a general ability with multiple dimensions (Smith, Simmons, & Kame'enui, 1995; Yopp, 1988). A diagram demonstrating the range of difficulty of these dimensions is provided in Figure 4.2.

Onset and Rhyme

Onset is the initial phoneme in a word. For example, in the word *tip*, the onset is /t/. (The use of two or more words with the same onset in a phrase or sentence—e.g., "*tip* the *top* to *Tony*"—is known as *alliteration.*) *Rhyme* refers to the remaining portion of a word, beginning with the vowel (in *tip*, the rhyme is *ip*). In the word *cat*, the onset is the sound /k/, and the rhyme is the *at*. When the onset and rhyme are blended together, the result is *cat*.

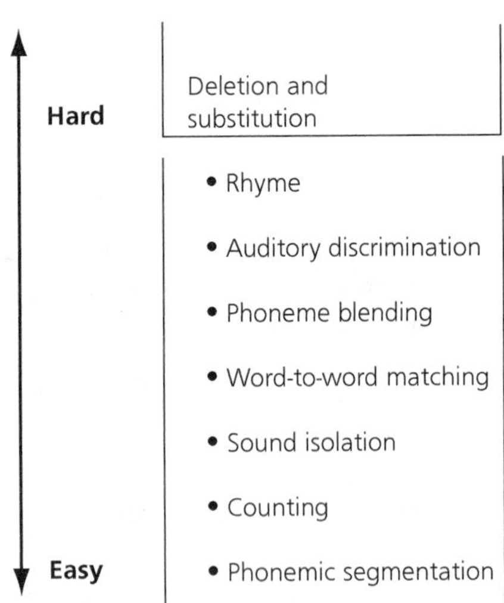

FIGURE 4.2. Range of difficulty for phonological awareness dimensions. From Yopp, Hallie Kay. (1988, Spring). The validity and reliability of phonemic awareness tests. *Reading Research Quarterly*, *23*(2), 159–177. Copyright 1988 by the International Reading Association. Reprinted with permission of Hallie Kay Yopp and the International Reading Association.

Manipulation of Phonemes

McCormick (2003) describes two levels of phonemic awareness: *simple* and *compound.* Simple phonemic awareness refers to the knowledge that words can be broken into sounds and syllables. Students demonstrate simple phonemic awareness through the ability to manipulate phonemes through *segmenting, counting, isolating*, or *blending* sounds. Segmenting sounds refers to recognizing and separating the distinct sounds in a word; for example, in the word *top*, a student can be asked to break the word into its three distinct sounds, /t/, /o/, and /p/. Counting is simple: counting the number of distinct sounds in a word. Isolating a sound refers to the ability to set apart a specific sound in a word; for example, a student asked to isolate the first sound in the word *dog* should isolate the /d/ sound. Blending sounds refers to combining separate sounds to form words—for example, blending the separate sounds /d/, /o/, and /g/ together to form the word *dog*.

Compound phonemic awareness involves tasks that are more difficult for students to master: *phoneme deletion*, *substitution*, and *word-to-word matching*. Phoneme deletion refers to isolating one sound in a word and blending the remaining sounds. For example, a student may be asked to identify what will remain if the /t/ sound is removed from the word *stock*. A student with an awareness of phoneme deletion will correctly answer "sock." Substitution is the process of replacing one phoneme with another—for example, replacing the /b/ in *back* with an /r/ to make the word *rack*. Word-to-word matching refers to the ability to isolate a sound in the same position in two distinct words and compare the sound. For example, to demonstrate awareness of word-to-word matching, a student may be asked if *pig* and *pen* begin with the same sound. Simple phonemic awareness skills are precursors to reading and writing, while compound phonemic awareness skills often develop after some experience with reading and writing.

What Does Research Say about Phonological Awareness?

Although phonological awareness most recently came into the general spotlight with the National Reading Panel's (2000a) report, the relationship between phonological awareness and the ability to read has been researched for over 50 years. In the 1960s and 1970s, research was linking sound awareness to success in learning to read. By the 1980s and 1990s, the notion that reading disabilities may be due to a lack of phonological awareness was being discussed in the literature. Now in the 21st century, phonological awareness has been widely accepted by researchers and practitioners as a crucial component of early reading. Phonological awareness is a strong predictor of the success a child will have in learning to read, especially in learning to decode words. In fact, phonological awareness has been called the strongest single determinant of a child's success in learning to read (Stanovich, 1986).

Over the past three decades, research has been consistently citing the importance of phonological awareness in early reading. Research in the 1980s found activities promoting phonological awareness, combined with instruction in the relationship between sounds and symbols, significantly increase reading and writing ability (Blachman, 1988; Bradley & Bryant, 1983; Hohn & Ehri, 1983). Other research has found that phonological awareness predicts reading success because English encodes speech into phonemes (Yopp, 1992). Researchers believe that learning to read and spell requires children to understand that spoken words are made up of phonemes, which can be manipulated, and that phonemes correspond to letters (Ball & Blachman, 1991; Yopp, 1992). The consensus in the literature is (1) phonological awareness gives children an understanding of the structure of sound, so that they can later learn from experiences with print and direct instruction on letter–sound relationships (Juel, Griffith, & Gough, 1986); and (2) that children who understand that words can be broken into sounds (i.e., they are phonologically aware) tend to be better readers than children with low phonological awareness (Bradley & Bryant, 1983, 1985; Lundberg, Olofsson, & Wall, 1980).

RESEARCH BRIEF ✎ Predictors of Reading Success

Carson, Kirby, and Hutchinson (2000) investigated the effects of phonological processing, family support, and academic self-concept on the reading achievement of first-grade students. Sixty-eight first-grade students in Ontario, Canada, were assessed for phonological processing at the beginning of the school year. Families were interviewed to determine the amount of family support in the children's reading and literacy. Students were given measures to determine their academic self-concept. The authors found that the strongest and only statistically significant predictor of reading success was phonological processing.

Torgesen and Mathes (1998) point out three ways that phonological awareness is important in learning beginning word-reading skills. First, phonological awareness helps children to understand the alphabetic principle. This serves as the basis for their later ability to "sound out" words and learn the way that individual letters sound. Without this skill, students will have difficulty learning to decode or spell new words.

Second, phonological awareness helps children to notice the regular ways letters represent sounds in words. Once children are able to notice each of the distinct phonemic sounds in a spoken word, they can understand the way the letters in the written word correspond to these sounds. This promotes individual letter–sound correspondence. Children without phonemic awareness will not understand what written letters represent in words. In addition, this allows reading to make sense for students, so that they can begin to easily recognize and remember a word when they come across it again. This recognition is the foundation of the sight word recognition that is present in proficient, fluent readers.

Third, phonological awareness makes it possible for students to generate possibilities for words in context that they are only able to partially sound out. When students encounter a word that they can't recognize and can't completely sound out, their foundation in phonological awareness will enable them to search their own mental dictionary for words that begin with a similar sound to the one they see in print and that would appropriately fit into the context of the rest of the passage.

RESEARCH BRIEF ✎ A Common Vocabulary for Speech and Reading

In 2002, Scarborough and Brady sought to establish a common vocabulary for discussing issues related to phonological awareness. A panel of 18 experts in the field served together, reviewing definitions for accuracy and objectivity. A glossary was established to make sure that researchers, educators, and other professionals will have the same understanding of important words related to oral language and written language. These terms were divided into four parts: Speaking and Listening, Metalinguistic Awareness of Phonological Elements, Phonological Memory and Naming Skills, and Terms Pertaining to Written Language. The authors of this article hope that this glossary will serve to reduce the miscommunications and misunderstandings that have arisen in the past from the lack of clear and consistent definitions of these terms among professionals.

Recognizing the importance of phonemic awareness in a comprehensive literacy program, in 1998 the International Reading Association approved a position statement regarding phonemic awareness (*www.reading.org/resources/issues/positions_phonemic.html*). The statement emphasizes the role of phonemic awareness as an early predictor of reading acquisition, and suggests that phonemic awareness can be taught successfully. It also cautions that phonemic awareness instruction should not be overemphasized to the point of sacrificing a balanced reading and writing curriculum.

Why Do Some Students have Problems with Phonological Awareness?

Most typically developing children will know some nursery rhymes, silly songs, and alliterations by the time they are three years old. By the end of kindergarten, most children can begin to manipulate words into syllables and delete initial syllables from words. By the end of first grade, most children can count, segment, and delete phonemes from words. By the end of second grade, most children can segment all sounds of a word, including sound clusters, and they can also delete beginning and ending sounds from words (see Table 4.1).

But what about the 20% of children who are not catching on to phonological awareness by the middle of first grade? In a recent synthesis of the research on phonological awareness, Smith and colleagues (1995) concluded that "phonological processing (awareness, coding, and retrieval) is the basis for many differences in learner characteristics" (p. 8). Phonological awareness is a complex process that involves perception of auditory input, the ability to code or translate the auditory input into short-term memory, and then the ability to retrieve that coded message from memory at a rapid rate. Thus perception, cognition, and memory are important for developing phonological awareness. Any breakdown in this process can inhibit early success. Difficulty with phonological awareness can occur among students with and without learning disabilities.

For these students, early identification of the difficulty and intensive programs of direct instruction in such phonological awareness skills are important. For example, in one study of first and second graders with phonological processing deficits, children received direct instruction in segmenting and spelling as part of the intervention, and these students showed significant gains in blending (Shepard & Uhry, 1997). However, Torgesen, Treason, Wagner, and Rashotte (1994) note that some students may not

TABLE 4.1. Development of Phonological Awareness through Early Childhood

Developmental stage	Typical phonological abilities
At 3 years of age	Many children know some nursery rhymes and some other ways of playing with sound, such as alliteration (e.g., *a pretty pink pig*) or some sequences of nonsense words (e.g., *helicopter–helebopter–helipopter*).
After a year of kindergarten	Most children can rhyme, identify syllables, break words into syllables, and delete the first syllable of a multisyllabic word.
By end of first grade	Most children can count phonemes and segment or delete phonemes at the beginning of words containing one, two, and three phonemes to make new words (Pratt & Brady, 1988).
By end of second grade	Most children can segment all sounds of a word (including sound clusters such as sk, ch, and sh) into individual sounds, and can delete beginning or ending sounds of words and tell the remaining word.

respond to phonological awareness training as described in typically instructional materials, and may need even more intensive support in learning to read and write.

Phonological awareness can pose particular challenges for English-language learners (ELLs). Some phonemes may be unfamiliar to them, and students may not have developed phonemic awareness in their own language. However, there is emerging evidence that phonological awareness training in English can benefit ELLs. For example, Quiroga, Lemos-Britton, Mostafapour, Abbot, and Berninger (2002) conducted two studies of Spanish-speaking first graders. These students were administered Spanish and English measures of phonological awareness, in addition to other cognitive and academic measures. The results suggested that phonological awareness in a student's first language may transfer to the second language. A second intervention study with phonological awareness training in both languages yielded positive outcomes in reading performance. An earlier intervention study with second-semester kindergarten students (Giambo, 1999) compared the reading performance of students in a phonological training program with students in a story-reading contrast group. Students in the phonological group outperformed the contrast group in phonological awareness and on oral English proficiency measures as well. While much more research is needed to improve our understanding of how best to teach phonological awareness to ELLs, this initial research is promising.

RESEARCH BRIEF Interventions with Older Students

Bhat, Griffin, and Sindelar (2003) examined the prevalence of phonological deficits in middle school students with reading disabilities. They also studied whether middle school students with learning disabilities who were deficient in phonological awareness could develop their phonological skills after direct instruction, and whether these skills would then improve the students' word recognition abilities. Sixty-four middle school students were given tests to measure their word identification and phonological awareness skills before, during, and after the instruction. The researchers found that the students did have deficits in phonological awareness, but that their phonological awareness skills did improve after instruction. However, the students did not make statistically significant improvements in word identification abilities as a result of their improved phonological awareness. The researchers believed that the age of the students and severity of their reading problems contributed to the lack of improvement in word identification. This study shows that even older learners with reading difficulty may be lacking in basic phonological awareness and can benefit from such instruction; however, the impact may not be as potent as if the instruction had been introduced in early years.

What are Formal Assessments of Phonological Awareness?

Test of Phonological Awareness—Second Edition: PLUS

The Test of Phonological Awareness—Second Edition: PLUS (TOPA-2+; Torgesen & Bryant, 2004) is a norm-referenced test of phonological awareness for children from five to eight years of age. The measure can be individually administered or group-administered. There are two versions, the Kindergarten and the Early Elementary. Each of these can be administered in 15–20 minutes. Typically, kindergarten students are not assessed until the second semester.

The Kindergarten version contains two subtests: Initial Sound—Same and Initial Sound—Different. In the first test, students are shown an initial picture and then three other pictures. They are asked to mark the picture that begins with the same sound as the first picture. The examiner says each of the words that represent each of the pictures aloud. In the second subtest, students are asked to mark the picture that begins with a different sound than the initial picture.

The Early Elementary version contains two subtests: Ending Sound—Same and Ending Sound—Different. These tests are administered exactly the same way as the Kindergarten version, only the students are asked to mark the pictures with the same and different ending sounds rather than beginning sounds. On each of these tests, students receive one point for each correct answer. These total points are tallied to form a complete score. Norms can help you decide what students will benefit from regular classroom instruction and what students may be in need of supplementary or intensive support.

Test of Early Reading Ability–3

The Test of Early Reading Ability–3 (TERA-3; Reid, Hresko, & Hammill, 2001) is a norm-referenced test for children ages three to eight. It is an assessment designed to tap early reading skills. Subtests include measures of alphabet, conventions of print, and meaning. This is an untimed, individually administered test that takes 15–30 minutes, depending on a child's age.

What Are Informal Assessments of Phonological Awareness?

Many informal assessments exist that can quickly screen components of a child's phonological awareness. Teachers often create their own systems for monitoring a student's ability through simple activities in the classroom routine. One widely used informal assessment of phonological awareness is the Yopp–Singer Phoneme Segmentation Test (Yopp, 1995; see Form 4.3). A second measure that can be used for ongoing monitoring of student progress in learning phonological awareness is the Dynamic Indicators of Basic Early Literacy Skills (DIBELS; Good & Kaminski, 2002). Three additional measures for informal assessment of rhyme identification (Form 4.4), rhyme production (Form 4.5), and phoneme counting (Form 4.6) are also included in this chapter.

Yopp–Singer Phoneme Segmentation Test

The Yopp–Singer Phoneme Segmentation Test (Form 4.3) is administered individually and takes approximately 5–10 minutes to administer. The examiner asks the student to "break apart" the word, telling each sound in the word in order. It is a measure of phoneme isolation. The examiner gives the student examples (*old* should be said /o/ /l/ /d/; other examples include *ride*, *go*, and *man*). The examiner indicates whether the student segments each word correctly without assistance.

Bruce Phoneme Deletion Test

The Bruce Phoneme Deletion Test (Bruce, 1964) is individually administered in approximately 10 minutes and is another measure of phoneme isolation. It is somewhat more difficult than the Yopp–Singer. The examiner asks the student to name what word would remain when a specific letter is removed from the word—for example, "What word would be left if the /t/ were removed from the word *stand*?" (The correct answer would be *sand*.) Other examples include *cat* (remove the /k/), *bright* (remove the /r/), *cried* (remove the /d/). It is important that the examiner indicate the letter sound to be removed and not the actual letter. The examiner records correct and incorrect responses.

Dynamic Indicators of Basic Early Literacy Skills

DIBELS is a set of standardized, individually administered measures of early literacy that was developed based on the report from the National Reading Panel (2000a). It contains measures for each of the five "big ideas" about literacy (including phonemic awareness). The two subtests associated with phonological awareness are Initial Sounds Fluency (ISF) and Phonemic Segmentation Fluency (PSF).

When administering the ISF, the examiner presents four pictures to the child, names each picture, and then asks the child to identify the picture that begins with particular sounds produced orally by the examiner. The child is also asked to orally produce the beginning sound for an orally presented word that matches one of the given pictures. The amount of time taken to identify or produce the correct sound is recorded, and the total number of correct initial sounds in one minute produces a score. The ISF measure takes about three minutes to administer and has over 20 alternate forms to monitor progress.

The PSF measure assesses a student's ability to segment three- and four-phoneme words into their individual phonemes fluently. To administer this measure, the examiner says words that contain three or four phonemes and asks the student to verbally produce each of the individual phonemes for that word. For example, the examiner says "cat," and the student says "/c/ /a/ /t/" to receive three possible points for the word. After the student responds, the examiner proceeds to the next word. The total correct number of phonemes produced in one minute becomes the student's final score. The PSF measure takes about two minutes to administer and has over 20 alternate forms for monitoring progress.

These measures are short and quick to administer, and are intended to be used regularly to monitor the status and development of early reading in children. When these measures are given frequently, individual student development can be monitored. The measures are available for free downloading (*http://dibels.uoregon.edu*).

How Do You Provide Differentiated Instruction in Phonological Awareness?

Many students will develop phonological awareness during their early childhood years simply by interacting in language-rich environments. Nursery rhymes, children's songs, and everyday conversations all automatically teach children about the sounds of language and how sounds are manipulated to form different words. Studies have shown that children who know more nursery rhymes at age three tend to have more highly developed phonological and phonemic awareness when they enter kindergarten (Bryant, MacLean, Bradley, & Crossland, 1990). When parents or caregivers read books with rhymes or alliteration, children are exposed to early phonological awareness. However, for many other students, this incidental learning through exposure to language is not enough. Blevins (1997) estimates that 20% of young children lack phonemic awareness. Whether students have not been given the opportunity to interact in a language-rich environment or whether they simply did not pick up on the language cues present without direct instruction, it is clear that many children enter kindergarten and first grade without an awareness of or the ability to manipulate the sounds of the English language. Students vary in their ability to develop phonological awareness, just as they vary in their abilities in all other areas. For some students, informal language activities will help to develop their skills. For other students, direct instruction in phonological awareness is critical to later reading success.

Level 1: High-Quality Core Instruction

Phonological awareness is taught in kindergarten through frequent, brief, playful activities. These activities are often only seconds or a few minutes in length; students may not even realize that a lesson is taking place. Children can become actively involved in this instruction, often moving their bodies or clapping their hands as they manipulate phonemes. When the manipulation of phonemes takes place, there is no connection between the sounds children hear and the actual symbol letter that is often representative of that sound; for example, when students hear the /k/ sound, the fact that there are two letters (K and C) that can represent this sound is irrelevant at this point. However, Cheyney and Cohen (1999) note the importance of tying phonological awareness activities to real literature, to allow students to develop this understanding and insight in a connected practice. Many kindergarten and first-grade basal readers now include sequenced phonological awareness activities and assessments.

Yopp (1992) offers the following recommendations for teaching phonemic awareness:

1. Keep a sense of playfulness and fun; avoid drill and rote memorization.
2. Use group settings that encourage interaction among children.
3. Encourage children's curiosity about language and their experimentation with it.
4. Allow for and be prepared for individual differences.
5. Make sure the tone of the activity is not evaluative, but informal and fun.

CONSIDERATIONS FOR TEACHING PHONOLOGICAL AWARENESS

Teachers often ask if a set sequence should be followed in the teaching of phonological awareness. Basal reading programs typically do have a set scope and sequence. However, Yopp and Yopp (2000) caution that for early readers, initial instruction should be flexible. As they put it, "It is not the case that teachers should engage exclusively in rhyme activities for weeks before they engage in syllable activities. Likewise, we do not believe that children must 'pass' one type of operation (e.g., matching) before having experiences with another (e.g., blending). Phonemic awareness development is not a lockstep process" (p. 7).

Catts (1995) describes seven considerations in teaching phonological awareness. These considerations are paraphrased below:

1. The level of difficulty of phonological awareness varies across activities. For example, saying that *bat* and *cat* rhyme is easier than finding a word that rhymes with *bat*.
2. Tasks at the syllable level are easier than those at the phoneme level. For example, it is easier to break the word reading into syllables (*read-ing*) than it is to break the word *cat* into phonemes (/k/ /a/ /t/).
3. Isolating a phoneme is easier than phoneme segmentation. For example, identifying the first sound of *man* as /m/ is easier than identifying all of the phonemes as /m/ /a/ /n/.

4. Blending and segmenting are easier with continuant phonemes, such as /s/, /sh/, /l/, than with noncontinuant or stop phonemes, such as /p/, /b/, /t/.
5. Blending and segmenting is easier with initial consonants than it is with final consonants; for example, it is easier to remove the /c/ sound from the beginning of *car* then it is to ask students to remove the /r/ sound from the end.
6. Manipulatives can be used in phoneme segmentation/manipulation activities. For example, students may move disks, tokens, counters, or chips apart to represent the segment, the onset, and the rhyme, and then move the manipulatives back together when blending these components.
7. Phonological awareness activities have a greater effect on success in reading if they are combined with letter–sound correspondence instruction. After the sounds have been mastered, then it becomes time to tie the sounds to the letters that represent them.

INFORMAL ACTIVITIES TO PROMOTE PHONOLOGICAL AWARENESS

Classroom Activities. Flett and Conderman (2002) suggest 20 ways to promote phonemic awareness through classroom activities. Here are some of their innovative ideas:

1. Playing the "I Spy" game with the initial sounds of words as the clues. Rather than saying, "I spy something that begins with the letter S," the teacher says, "I spy something that begins with /s/."
2. Creating a "sound box" in the classroom, where students bring objects from home that begin with particular sounds. These become the focus of the lesson for an abbreviated show and tell.
3. Playing "change a name" (adapted from Chard & Dickson, 1999), where students sit in a circle and select a student and "change" the student's name by deleting the initial sound (e.g., Joseph becomes Oseph). The other students try to guess who the student is. Another variation would be to substitute the initial sound with a different sound (e.g., Joseph becomes Moseph).
4. Calling students to line up or transition based upon the ending sounds of their names—for example, saying "All students whose names end with /k/ may line up."
5. Presenting phoneme substitution tasks in riddle format, such as "What rhymes with 'cat' and starts with /h/?"

PARENT POINTER ☞ Phonological Awareness: On the Go!

Jack DeFraites is three years old. Like most youngsters these days, he spends time in a car seat. Keeping a lively three-year-old boy strapped in during family errands or during trips to his grandparents' house in another state is tough. One "family favorite" that saves the day is Jack's rhyme game. Jack and his mom and dad take turns making rhyme sets. At first it was random rhymes (*fat/sat*); then the game evolved to "meaningful sets" (e.g., *fat cat, small ball*), and then to "thematic sets" (e.g., vegetables–*carrot/parrot*). Each rhyme usually ends with a giggle or two.

In working with parents, encourage them to engage in word play with their children. Such family word play builds on children's natural curiosity about language and helps them engage in the joy of learning.

Literature Connections. Phonological awareness instruction should include regular reading of books to help students to connect students to print. Murray, Stahl, and Ivey (1996) found that young readers improved their knowledge of phonological awareness with regular (daily) reading of alphabet books. Given the rich array of alphabet books on the market (see Figure 4.3 for examples), kindergarten teachers could read one a day and still not hit the bottom of the barrel with available books. Rhyming books are also important for developing phonological awareness. A list of rhyming books appears in Figure 4.4.

Base, G. (1987). *Animalia.* New York: Harry N. Abrams.

Crane, C. (2000). *S is for sunshine: A Florida alphabet* (M. G. Monroe, Illus.). Chelsea, MI: Sleeping Bear Press.

Dragonwood, C., & Aruego, J. (1992). *Alligator arrived with apples: A potluck alphabet feast* (A. Dewey, Illus.). New York: Simon & Schuster.

Ernst, L. C. (2004). *The turn-around, upside-down alphabet book.* New York: Simon & Schuster.

Inkpen, M. (2000). *Kipper's A to Z: An alphabet adventure.* San Diego, CA: Harcourt.

Martin, B., & Archambault, J. (1989). *Chicka-chicka boom boom* (L. Ehlert, Illus.). New York: Simon & Schuster.

Musgrove, M. (1980). *Ashanti to Zulu: African traditions* (L. Dillon & D. Dillion, Illus.). New York: Puffin Books.

Pallota, J. (1987). *The icky bug alphabet book.* (R. Masiello, Illus.). Watertown, MA: Charlesbridge.

Shannon, G. (1999). *Tomorrow's alphabet* (D. Crews, Illus.). New York: Morrow.

Wood, A. (2001). *Alphabet adventure* (B. R. Wood, Illus.). New York: Scholastic.

FIGURE 4.3. Alphabet books.

Battaglia, A. (1973). *Mother Goose.* New York: Random House.

Bemelmans, L. (1958). *Madeline.* New York: Viking.

Brown, M. W. (1984). *Goodnight moon.* New York: Harper & Row.

Butler, A., & Neville, P. (1987). *May I stay home today?* Crystal Lake, IL: Rigby.

Cameron, P. (1961). *"I can't," said the ant.* New York: Coward-McCann.

Cowley, J. (1990). *Dan the flying man.* Bothell, WA: Wright Group.

De Paola, T. (1985). *Tomie De Paola's Mother Goose.* East Rutherford, NJ: Putnam.

Emberley, B. (1992). *One wide river to cross.* Boston: Little, Brown.

Kuskin, K. (1990). *Roar and more.* New York: HarperTrophy.

Mayo, D. (2001). *The house that Jack built.* Cambridge, MA: Barefoot Books.

Patrick, G. (1974). *A bug in a jug.* New York: Scholastic.

Patz, N. (1983). *Moses supposes his toeses are roses.* San Diego, CA: Harcourt.

Sendak, M. (1962). *Chick soup with rice.* New York: Scholastic.

Seuss, Dr. [Geisel, T.] (1957). *The cat in the hat.* New York: Random House.

Silverstein, S. (1964). *A giraffe and a half.* New York: HarperCollins.

FIGURE 4.4. Rhyming books.

Level 2: Supplemental Instruction

For students who are not learning phonological awareness through the same classroom activities as their peers, these activities can be modified to target the specific needs of these students. Small-group instruction may be needed to provide additional instruction. Teachers should model sounds or strategies to students, beginning with easier words and gradually moving on to more difficult ones (Chard & Osborn, 1998). Kame'enui (1995) identifies five characteristics that determine the difficulty of a word:

1. The size of the phonological unit: It is easier to break larger structures into units (e.g., it is easier to break a sentence into words than syllables into phonemes).
2. The number of phonemes in the word: Words with fewer phonemes are easier than words with sound clusters.
3. Phoneme position in words: Initial consonants are easiest, final consonants are more difficult, and middle consonants are most difficult.
4. Phonological properties of words: Certain sounds are easier (e.g., continuant sounds like /s/ and /m/ are easier than brief sounds such as /t/).
5. Phonological awareness challenges: Rhyming is easier than blending, which is easier than segmenting.

In addition to modifying the activities used, combining phonological awareness instruction with explicit instruction in letter–sound correspondence can be effective for students struggling to master these sounds in isolation. Linking phonological awareness activities to writing activities can serve the same purpose. Involving other sensory modalities, such as tactile and kinesthetic, can be helpful as well. Students can clap out syllables in words, stand up or sit down each time they hear a syllable, or move tiles together or apart to segment or blend phonemes in words.

ELKONIN BOXES

Students needing supplemental instruction in phonemic awareness activities (beginning in second grade and up) may benefit from the use of *Elkonin boxes* or variations of these (Clay, 1985; Griffith & Olson, 1992). Elkonin boxes are simple, recognizable pictures, along with boxes drawn below (see Figure 4.5). For activities related to phonemic awareness, the number of boxes should correspond to the number of phonemes in the word (not the number of letters). Students are given chips to move into each box as they hear the teacher pronounce each sound when saying a word. If a student has a picture of a kite, as in Figure 4.5, there are three boxes below, and the student would place one chip for each of the three sounds heard: /k/, /ī/, /t/. Once the student is able to manipulate the chips effectively, then he or she can combine the movement of the chips with the pronouncing of the sounds.

MIAMI PHONOLOGICAL AWARENESS

Miami Phonological Awareness (MPA; McKinney, Schumm, & Hocutt, 1999) is an adaptation of Torgesen and Bryant's (1994) Phonological Awareness Training for Reading program. While the Torgesen and Bryant program was designed for clinical settings, MPA was designed for use in small, teacher-led groups of five or six children. Like the

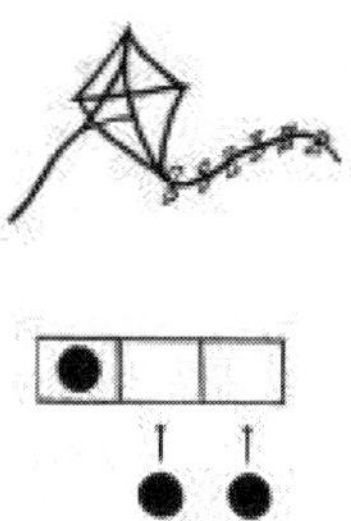

FIGURE 4.5. Elkonin box used for phonemic manipulation. (Picture obtained from *www.ldonline.org/ld_indepth/teachers/cid_howno.html.*) Reprinted with permission from Patricia Edelen-Smith.

other program, however, MPA emphasizes rhyme, initial/middle/ending sounds, and phoneme manipulation. Lessons are fast-paced and take about 20 minutes, three times a week. Puppets, puzzles, and silly stories that put words in context help to make the lessons active and fun. Lessons were designed in collaboration with kindergarten teachers who have large numbers of ELLs in their classes.

KINDERGARTEN PEER-ASSISTED LITERACY STRATEGIES AND FIRST GRADE PEER-ASSISTED LITERACY STRATEGIES

Kindergarten Peer-Assisted Literacy Strategies (K-PALS; Mathes, Clancy-Menchetti, & Torgesen, 2001) and First Grade Peer-Assisted Literacy Strategies (First Grade PALS; Mathes, Torgesen, Allen, & Allor, 2001) are supplemental programs to assist young readers in developing letter knowledge, phonological and phonemic awareness, and initial phonics. As the names of these programs indicate, the key to the lessons is peer-assisted learning. Students are placed in pairs to work through a carefully sequenced set of game-like activities. A lesson is typically about 20 minutes long, and the series is 20 weeks in length. The lessons are scripted and basically ready to go.

Level 3: Intensive Support

Some students may need even more intensive support in learning phonological awareness. Adams, Foorman, Lundberg, and Beeler (1998) note that in some cases, teachers might want to consult with a speech–language pathologist to get additional insights about how best to provide instruction. For students needing more help with phonological awareness, individual instruction or instruction in groups of two to three students is warranted. Structured programs such as Phonological Awareness Training for Reading can be used. In Chapter 5 you'll read more about students with severe difficulties in learning to read and write, and how best to support those students.

PHONOLOGICAL AWARENESS TRAINING KIT FOR READING

The Phonological Awareness Training for Reading (Torgesen & Bryant, 1994) program is designed to increase young children's level of phonological awareness. This program contains four sets of activities: warm-up, sound blending, sound segmenting, and reading and spelling. This formal training program features activities that teach students to blend, segment, and apply these skills to reading and spelling. It is designed for use in one-on-one instruction for students who need extra support.

READING RECOVERY

Reading Recovery is an intensive early intervention program that emerged from the work of Marie Clay in New Zealand (Clay, 1985, 1987). Teachers go through intensive professional development to prepare for teaching this program. Reading Recovery involves one-on-one sessions with students in primary grades showing early signs of reading difficulty. Sessions are held daily for about 30 minutes over a period of 15 weeks. Each session contains a set of activities, including rereading of predictable books, introduction of new books, writing activities, and phonemic awareness activities taught in context. Teachers are trained to keep running records of student reading as a part of a diagnostic–teaching model. Teacher observations and notes are used to plan subsequent lessons.

TECH TIP Using Technology to Promote Phonological Awareness

Technology can be used in many ways to promote phonological awareness in young children. When a simple nursery rhyme or children's song is played on a CD player, students can be taught to jump up or clap their hands each time they hear a rhyming word or a specific beginning sound to a word. For classrooms with access to computers, Don Johnston Incorporated produces a series of computer programs called *Earobics.* This program is designed to provide extensive practice and skills training for students who are struggling with phonological awareness. There are different "steps" in the program: Software is available for children ages 4–7 (Step 1) and 7–10 (Step 2), and a series has also been specifically developed for adolescents and adults. Step 1 stresses skills such as syllables, sound blending, rhyming, and sound discrimination through the use of motivating, interactive games. Step 2 focuses on insertion, deletion, and substitution of sounds through games geared at older students. This step also reviews and advances the skills taught in Step 1. The adolescent and adult version uses more sophisticated multimedia to appeal to older learners, yet still focuses on all of the basic skills associated with phonological awareness. Resource guides and data tracking are available for teachers to supplement and monitor students' progress.

SNAPSHOTS

Phonological Awareness Assessment and Instruction in a Kindergarten Classroom

Erika Garcia teaches kindergarten to approximately 25 children. Her classroom provides students with a print-rich environment. Objects around the room are labeled, and she has lots of examples of environmental print sprinkled around the room. During the first semester, Erika focuses on establishing classroom routines, especially how to work in centers. She pretests students on print awareness, book awareness, and environmental print. She reads to the students at least twice daily—including the reading of one alphabet book each day.

At midterm, Erika screens all students for phonological awareness. During center time, Erika works with groups of five students to teach phonological awareness. For students who need less direct instruction, Erika meets with the groups two days a week; for students who need more assistance, Erika meets with the groups three days a week. Erika monitors students carefully and sometimes switches students from group to group, depending on their performance. Small-group instruction occurs during center time, when a part-time paraprofessional is in the room. In addition to the small-group instruction, Erika includes phonological awareness activities and songs as part of her daily routine.

Phonological Awareness Instruction in a Resource Setting

Deltona Park is a large urban school with over 1,500 students. Allison Peters, a reading coach funded through Title I resources, is assigned to work with students in grades 1–3 who need intensive instruction in phonological awareness. The school has developed entrance and exit criteria for the "Phono Lab." Teachers identify students who appear to be having difficulty in phonological awareness, and refer them to Allison for further assessment and development of individual instructional plans. Allison typically pulls 10 students at a time for an hour each day. During each session, Allison plans group and individual lessons as well as computer-based activities. She communicates regularly with teachers to assure that the lessons she plans are coordinated with classroom activities. Allison also plans Phono Lab home learning activities to provide students with additional reinforcement.

FURTHER DEVELOPING STUDENT READING AND WRITING PROFILES

You can record assessment results for all components of phonological awareness, as well as a student's awareness of environmental print, book awareness, and print awareness, on Part IV of the Student Reading and Writing Profile (Form 4.7). Keep in mind that frequent ongoing informal assessment, using measures such as the DIBELS, is also important. If your school or school district does not have a set of benchmarks for student mastery of phonological awareness or other areas of early reading and writing, you'll need to establish "decision rules" about who needs instruction at different levels of intensity.

CHAPTER SUMMARY

Young children develop literacy through their interactions with the environment. Hearing stories, scribbling on paper, and engaging in songs and nursery rhymes are all ways that children start to become readers and writers. Critical to later reading ability is the development of phonological awareness. Children's ability to understand that words are made up of sounds, and then to be able to manipulate these sounds, is the foundation for their later ability to connect sounds to letters and letters to words. For some children, this awareness will come naturally through language-rich environments; for others, more direct instruction will be necessary. Assessment and instruction of phonological awareness can and should be done quickly and frequently to ensure that all children become successful readers. As Smith and colleagues (2004) point out, while phonological awareness instruction is necessary, it is not sufficient to ensure that students will become proficient readers. As you will read in Chapter 5, for students to become proficient in the use of the alphabetic principle, instruction in phonological awareness and letter–sound correspondence is necessary.

KEY TERMS AND CONCEPTS

Alliteration
Alphabetic principle
Blending
Book awareness
Counting
Emergent literacy
Environmental print
Grapheme–phoneme correspondence
Isolating
Onset
Phoneme deletion
Phonemic awareness
Phonological awareness
Print awareness
Reading readiness
Rhyme
Segmenting
Word-to-word matching

REFLECTION AND ACTION

1. Now that you have read about early reading and phonological awareness, think about the potential students that you will encounter in your classroom. What do you think their early literacy experiences may have been? What impact do you think these have had on the students they are today? What can you as the teacher do to try to ensure that all of your students become proficient readers? How can you implement daily activities that will foster increased phonological awareness in your students?
2. Have you ever learned to speak a foreign language? For students struggling with phonological awareness, learning to read or spell in English is comparable to learning to read or spell in a foreign language to many of us. Write a one-page reflection statement about how you felt when you were learning to navigate in a new language that was difficult for you.
3. Think about how you could ideally expose a young child to literacy early on, so that he or she would be more likely to develop a strong understanding of the alphabetic principle and phonological awareness. Develop a plan for a literacy-rich classroom environment, and draw this on paper.
4. Try to remember a favorite rhyming book of yours from your childhood. Think about what it was about that book that made you enjoy reading it. Find that book at your local library, and develop a list of all the rhymes in the book to be used with students.

READ ON!

Bryant, P., MacLean, M., Bradley, L., & Crossland, J. (1990). Rhyme and alliteration, phoneme detection and learning to read. *Developmental Psychology*, *26*, 429–438.

This article looks at longitudinal findings on phonological awareness and progress in reading and spelling of 65 young children (ages four to six). The results of this study show the importance of rhyme in learning to read.

Chard, D. J., & Dickson, S. V. (1999). Phonological awareness: Instructional and assessment guidelines. *Intervention in School and Clinic*, *34*, 261–270.

This article provides an overview of phonological awareness, as well as sample activities and assessments that can be used to assess children's understanding of this important concept.

Lane, H. B., Pullen, P. C., Eisele, M. R., & Jordan, L. (2002). Preventing reading failure: Phonological awareness assessment and instruction. *Preventing School Failure*, *46*(3), 101–110.

This article links phonological awareness research with practical classroom usage, including phonological awareness development and its relationship to beginning reading and formal and informal assessments. Strategies are described for classroom-based instruction in phonological skills with emergent readers.

Liberman, I. Y., Shankweiler, D., & Liberman, A. M. (1989). The alphabetic principle and learning to read. In D. Shankweiler & I. Y. Lieberman (Eds.), *Phonology and reading disability: Solving the reading puzzle* (pp. 1–33). Ann Arbor: University of Michigan Press.

This book chapter focuses on proper application of the alphabetic principle, particularly with students who are having difficulty in developing phonological awareness and in learning to read.

Snow, C. E., Burns, M. S., & Griffin, P. (Eds.). (1998). *Preventing reading difficulties in young children.* Washington, DC: National Academy Press.

This book reviews an extensive literature of sometimes discrepant research findings, to provide an integrated picture of the development of reading and how this should guide reading instruction. This book has a strong emphasis on the prevention of reading difficulty and failure.

Stanovich, K. E. (1986). Matthew effects on reading: Some consequences of individual differences in the acquisition of literacy. *Reading Research Quarterly*, *21*, 360–407.

This landmark article presents a unique framework for conceptualizing development of individual differences in reading ability. This popular framework is then used to explain some persisting problems in the literature on reading disabilities and to suggest remediation.

Yopp, H. K. (1992). Developing phonemic awareness in young children. *The Reading Teacher*, *45*, 696–703.

This popular article describes the concept of phonemic awareness and offers practical suggestions to teachers on how to enhance phonemic awareness development in their students through easy activities.

SHARPENING YOUR SKILLS: SUGGESTIONS FOR PROFESSIONAL DEVELOPMENT

1. Start compiling a reference list or personal library of books that will enhance phonological awareness in young children. These may include books that use alliteration, word families, or rhyme patterns. Decide which of these books you are most likely to use with your students.
2. Practice using some of the tests of phonemic awareness included in or discussed in this chapter. You can create your own tests as well. Try administering your own self-made tests to colleagues or friends, and see how "phonemically aware" your acquaintances are.

RESOURCES FOR ASSESSMENT AND INSTRUCTION

Adams, M., Foorman, B., Lundberg, I., & Beeler, C. (1998). *Phonemic awareness in young children: A classroom curriculum.* Baltimore: Brookes.

This supplemental language and reading curriculum contains fun, adaptable activities and games for preschool, kindergarten, and first-grade students. The developmental sequence begins with simple listening games, and gradually moves on to more advanced sound manipulation exercises such as rhyming, alliteration, and segmentation. The book also contains reproducible assessment activities to evaluate language and listening skills.

Blachman, B., Ball, E. W., Black, R., & Tangel, D. (1999). *Road to the code: A phonological awareness program for young children.* Baltimore: Brookes.

Road to the Code is an 11-week program for teaching phonemic awareness and letter–sound correspondence to kindergartners and first graders who are having difficulty with their early literacy skills. This program contains 44 lessons (15–20 minutes each) that feature scripted instructions and reproducible materials for three activities: Say-It-and-Move-It, Letter Name and Sound Instruction, and Phonological Awareness Practice.

Blevins, W. (1997). *Phonemic awareness activities for early reading success*. New York: Scholastic.

This book features easy, playful activities that prepare young children for phonics instruction through rhymes, oddity tasks, orally blending words and splitting syllables, segmenting words, and phonemic manipulation tasks.

Cheyey, W. J., & Cohen, E. J. (1999). *Focus on phonics: Assessment and instruction*. Bothell, WA: Wright Group.

This book features a balanced, integrated model for teaching phonics and phonemic awareness skills directly and systematically. It provides a discussion of research, combined with detailed assessments and model lesson plans that focus on the components of phonological awareness, print awareness, synthetic and analytic phonics, and structural analysis.

Erickson, G. C., Foster, K. C., Foster, D. F., Torgesen, J. K., & Packer, S. (1992). *DaisyQuest*. Austin, TX: PRO-ED.

DaisyQuest is a software package designed to improve phonological awareness skills (rhyming words; beginning, middle, and ending sounds; blending sounds; etc.). This program has an excellent research base to support student progress.

Erickson, G. C., Foster, K. C., Foster, D. F., Torgesen, J. K., & Packer, S. (1993). *Daisy's castle*. Austin, TX: PRO-ED.

Daisy's Castle is a software package designed to teach more complex forms of phonological awareness, such as two-part blending, whole-word blending, and segmenting. Again, this program has an excellent research base to support student progress.

Lane, H. B., & Pullen, P. C. (2004). *Phonological awareness assessment and instruction: A sound beginning*. Boston: Allyn & Bacon.

This handbook provides a range of informal measures for components of phonological awareness assessment including ongoing progress monitoring. It also provides an overview of commercial materials, as well as many classroom activities.

Robertson, C., & Salter, W. (1995). *The phonological awareness kit*. East Moline, IL: Linguisystems.

This kit uses a multisensory approach to help students ages five to eight learn to use phonological information to process oral and written language through activities for direct instruction of rhyming; segmenting sentences, words, and syllables; identifying sound placement in words; and blending sounds to make words.

RECOMMENDED WEBSITES

Phonological Awareness Resources and Links
http://ca.geocities.com/phonological

This website provides links to various tests of phonological awareness and to other websites, articles, and resources related to phonological awareness.

Songs That Build Phonological Awareness
www.songsforteaching.com/PA.html

This website provides a list of songs, lyrics, and sound clips that can be used to help teach phonological awareness.

Reading Recovery Council of North America
www.readingrecovery.org/sections/reading/phonics.asp

This is the website for the Reading Recovery Council of North America. Lesson plans and information about the Reading Recovery program are available.

Tampa Reads' Reading Key
www.tampareads.com/phonics/phonicsindex.htm

This website provides links to 56 phonics and phonemic awareness worksheets designed to improve memorization of important consonant and vowel sounds.

Patti's Electronic Classroom
http://teams.lacoe.edu/documentation/classrooms/patti/k-1/activities/phonemic.html

This website provides many activities to promote phonological awareness for students in kindergarten through third grade.

ProTeacher
www.proteacher.com/070171.shtml

This website provides a series of links to games, activities, and songs that can be used to promote phonemic awareness in students.

Manatee Public Schools Reading Workshop
www.manatee.k12.fl.us/sites/elementary/palmasola/rcompindex1.htm

This website, from a Florida school district, provides a host of information about different component of phonological awareness and sample activities that can be used to illustrate each of the various components.

Teachers.net
http://teachers.net/archive/phonemicarchive.html

This website is a discussion site about phonemic awareness, where you can either read through past discussion archives or click to participate in a new discussion about this topic.

Mega Phonemic Awareness Links
www.expage.com/page/woodshop13

This website provides a host of links to information about phonological awareness, activities to use, research on the topic, and examples of effective programs.

Institute for the Development of Educational Achievement
http://reading.uoregon.edu/pa

This website provides detailed information about the importance of phonological awareness and its link to early reading. Information is provided about how to assess for and teach these skills.

Nevada Reading First: Educational Reform
http://literacy.edreform.net/portal/literacy/phonemicawareness

This website is a series of links to other websites about phonemic awareness that provide information and activities.

FORM 4.1. Checklist for Assessing Concepts of Book and Print Awareness

Checklist for Assessing Concepts of Book and Print Awareness

Student's name ______________________________

Date ______________________________

	Always	Sometimes	Never
Knows how to hold a book	_____	_____	_____
Knows print is read from left to right	_____	_____	_____
Knows what a letter is (point out on page)	_____	_____	_____
Knows what a word is (point out on page)	_____	_____	_____
Knows there are spaces between words	_____	_____	_____
Reads environmental print	_____	_____	_____
Can identify upper-case letters	_____	_____	_____
Can identify lower-case letters	_____	_____	_____
Attempts reading by using pictures	_____	_____	_____
Attempts reading by sounding out letters	_____	_____	_____
Attempts reading by sight words	_____	_____	_____

FORM 4.2. Letter Recognition Checklist

Letter Recognition Checklist

Student's name ______________________________

Date ______________________________

Directions: Present letters in random order on index cards.

	Upper-case	Lower-case	Sound
A	______	______	______
B	______	______	______
C	______	______	______
D	______	______	______
E	______	______	______
F	______	______	______
G	______	______	______
H	______	______	______
I	______	______	______
J	______	______	______
K	______	______	______
L	______	______	______
M	______	______	______
N	______	______	______
O	______	______	______
P	______	______	______
Q	______	______	______
R	______	______	______
S	______	______	______
T	______	______	______
U	______	______	______
V	______	______	______
W	______	______	______
X	______	______	______
Y	______	______	______
Z	______	______	______

FORM 4.3. Yopp–Singer Test of Phoneme Segmentation

Yopp–Singer Test of Phoneme Segmentation

Student's name ______________________________ Date ____________________

Score (number correct) ________________________

Directions: Today we're going to play a word game. I'm going to say a word and I want you to break the word apart. You are going to tell me each sound in the word in order. For example, if I say "old," you should say "/o/ /l/ /d/." *(Administrator: Be sure to say the sounds, not the letters, in the word.)* Let's try a few together.

Practice items: (*Assist the child in segmenting these items as necessary.*) ride, go, man

Test items: (*Circle those items that the student correctly segments; incorrect responses may be recorded on the blank line following the item.)*

1. dog	_______	12. hay	_______
2. keep	_______	13. race	_______
3. fine	_______	14. zoo	_______
4. no	_______	15. three	_______
5. she	_______	16. job	_______
6. wave	_______	17. in	_______
7. grew	_______	18. ice	_______
8. that	_______	19. at	_______
9. red	_______	20. top	_______
10. me	_______	21. by	_______
11. sat	_______	22. do	_______

FORM 4.4. Rhyme Identification

Rhyme Identification

Student's name ____________________

Date ____________________

Directions: Explain to the student that you are going to play a rhyming game. When words rhyme, the ends of the words sound the same. You are going to say two words, and you want the student to say if the words rhyme. Start with two examples: "When I say *cat* and *rat*, do those words rhyme? When I say *car* and *bike*, do those words rhyme? Now you try."

If the student has difficulty, provide more examples. Stop when the student makes five errors in a row.

1. fat/mat _______
2. bake/ball _______
3. cub/rub _______
4. wide/ride _______
5. win/fin _______
6. fax/fish _______
7. pet/met _______
8. cut/rut _______
9. hide/hit _______
10. tall/call _______
11. rice/room _______
12. hit/fit _______
13. skip/trip _______
14. cake/make _______
15. smile/small _______
16. stop/hop _______
17. rain/gain _______
18. goat/boat _______
19. pill/bill _______
20. rock/rain _______
21. fight/night _______
22. fox/fog _______
23. run/fun _______
24. rock/rake _______
25. slide/skip _______
26. moon/soon _______
27. sail/pail _______
28. life/leaf _______
29. team/scream_______
30. wiggle/giggle_______

	Rhymes	Non-rhymes	Total
# correct	__/20	__/10	__/30
% correct			

FORM 4.5. Rhyme Production

Rhyme Production

Student's name ______________________________

Date ______________________________

Directions: Explain to the student that you are going to play a rhyming game. When words rhyme, the ends of the words sound the same. You are going to say a word, and you want the student to say a word that rhymes. Start with two examples: "When I say *cat*, a rhyming word is *rat*. When I say *bike*, a rhyming word is *hike*. Now you try."

If the student has difficulty, provide more examples. Stop when the student makes five errors in a row.

1. bat ________
2. wet ________
3. pig ________
4. fog ________
5. bug ________
6. call ________
7. fell ________
8. fish ________
9. jail ________
10. team ________
11. hike ________
12. coat ________
13. slow ________
14. nice ________
15. light ________

correct ________

% correct ________

FORM 4.6. Phoneme Counting

Phoneme Counting

Student's name ____

Date ____

Directions: Explain to the student that you are going to play a listening game. You are going to say some words, and you want the student to say how many sounds he or she hears in each word. Start with two examples: "When I say *cat,* I hear three sounds, /c/ /a/ /t/. When I say *go*, I hear two sounds, /g/ /o/. Now you try."

If the student has difficulty, show the student how to clap with each new sound.

1. dog _______
2. wet _______
3. bee _______
4. chip _______
5. bed _______
6. cow _______
7. sea _______
8. rake _______
9. bag _______
10. float _______
11. skip _______
12. rat _______
13. still _______
14. zoo _______
15. truck _______

Total correct: _______

Observations:

FORM 4.7. Student Reading and Writing Profile (Part IV)

Student Reading and Writing Profile

Part IV: Emergent Literacy

Environmental Print Awareness

Name of test	Date	Score

Student strengths in environmental print ____________________

Student areas for improvement in environmental print ____________________

Instructional recommendations ____________________

Book Awareness

(Book awareness areas: book holding, page turning, front and back of book)

Name of test	Date	Score

Student strengths in book awareness ____________________

Student areas for improvement in book awareness ____________________

Instructional recommendations ____________________

(cont.)

FORM 4.7. *(page 2 of 2)*

Print Awareness

(Print awareness areas: letter names, left-to-right orientation, knowledge of "word")

Name of test	Date	Score

Student strengths in print awareness ____________________

Student areas for improvement in print awareness ____________________

Instructional recommendations ____________________

Phonological Awareness

(Phonological awareness areas: onset, rhyme, isolation, counting, segmentation, blending)

Name of test	Date	Score

Student strengths in phonological awareness ____________________

Student areas for improvement in phonological awareness ____________________

Instructional recommendations ____________________

FIVE

The Alphabetic Principle, Phonics, and Spelling

Teaching Students the Code

ANA MARIA PAZOS REGO

VIGNETTE

Joshua is a bright boy in Andrea File's third-grade class. Andrea has noticed that Joshua has difficulty decoding words. She sees little progress, despite the intensity of the reading curriculum and the amount of time she dedicates to reading instruction in her classroom. Andrea has also noticed that Joshua is the kind of student who does not read with fluency; instead, he seems to read word for word, as if reading a list very slowly. His errors are mainly mispronunciations of words. They sound like the words he is looking at in the text, but either they do not make sense given the context, or are the wrong part of speech. For example, Joshua may read "hose" for *home*, or "bad" for *bed*, or "hat" for *hate*. When he stumbles on a word, Andrea will ask him to try and figure out what the word is in the sentence. Joshua tries to give each letter a sound, blends the sounds together, and repeats them quickly. This strategy results in nonsense words, and rarely does Joshua pronounce the correct word. Andrea believes that she needs to help Joshua master decoding skills. She knows that development of phonics is an important component of literacy in beginning readers, because strong word recognition skills lead to better comprehension. In fact, children like Joshua, who initiate their reading experience with poor decoding skills, rarely become proficient readers. Andrea would like to employ strategies that will benefit not only Joshua but other students as well. "My biggest challenge is to determine which strategies to employ to help Joshua to read."

ANTICIPATION QUESTIONS

- What are the principles of exemplary phonics instruction?
- What are the phases of reading and spelling development and their implications for students?

- What formal and informal measures can be used to assess student proficiency in using the code?
- How can teachers provide differentiated instruction in learning the code?

INTRODUCTION

The main goal of reading is to comprehend. The process that leads to comprehension is decoding of words. The reader needs to "conquer the code in order to master the meaning" (Cohen, 1996, p. 76). As you have already read, phonological awareness and print awareness are important precursors to reading and writing. When children develop the connection between the spoken and written word, they master the idea of the alphabetic principle. *Phonics* instruction emphasizes the teaching of sound–symbol relationships and patterns. The teaching of phonics is also highly related to spelling instruction.

Like many others, Dechant (1993) stresses the important role that teaching phonics plays in the reading development of children, because it helps children to clearly see the relationship between letters and sounds. It clarifies that letters actually mimic the phonemic sequences of words. Dechant explains that phonics instruction is what leads to automatic semantic activation, to the complete understanding of the alphabetic principle, to proficient word identification, to better reading and spelling, and finally to the ultimate goal of reading: comprehension.

Phonics is one aspect of word recognition instruction. *Word recognition* refers to the instant recall of words that occurs during reading. It involves knowledge of phonics, sight words, structural analysis, and the use of context clues (including picture clues). During the reading process, the recognition of words needs to be automatic enough that the reader can focus on understanding the meaning of the text (Chall, 1991). When readers recognize words without pausing, they have attained *automaticity* (LaBerge & Samuels, 1974). When word recognition has become automatic, the processes underlying recognition of words are still taking place in the brain; however, these operations are not obvious to the reader. Once readers develop word recognition strategies, they can focus more on the comprehension of text. The reader who needs to concentrate on decoding words will not be able to engage in the processes involved in comprehending the text. In addition to identifying words automatically, the reader must be fluent; if the reader is stopping frequently during a reading, the meaning is more likely to be lost. Effective word recognition will allow for more fluent reading, which in turn will facilitate comprehension.

Andrea File, like so many teachers, faces the challenge of teaching children like Joshua to read. These students do not understand the letter–sound connection, or how they can use this link to facilitate reading. Therefore, they are unable to comprehend what they read. Consequently, the main focus of phonics instruction is to help beginning readers understand letter–sound correspondences and spelling patterns, and to help them learn how to apply this knowledge in their reading and writing (National Reading Panel, 2000a). Early development of the alphabetic principle and phonics proficiency is important for literacy among beginning readers. In fact, children who start off with poor decoding skills seldom become strong readers (Cunningham & Stanovich, 1998). It is therefore imperative that teachers provide systematic instruction for teaching the code to their students.

The chapter begins with an overview of principles of strong phonics instruction—phonics instruction that includes an understanding of the alphabetic principle and connections with the written word (spelling). It continues with suggestions for assessment and differentiated instruction in working with the code.

LEARNING THE CODE: THE ALPHABETIC PRINCIPLE, PHONICS, AND SPELLING

What Does Research Say about Teaching the Code?

As you will recall from Chapter 1, there is a range of perspectives about how reading should be taught. The bottom-up perspective is built on the premise that learning to read is a process of breaking the code in a systematic way. Good readers are good decoders. The primary approach for the teaching of phonics associated with a bottom-up perspective is *synthetic phonics*. Synthetic phonics emphasizes part-to whole instruction, because children are taught sounds in isolation and are then asked to blend these sounds together to form words. A teacher following a synthetic phonics program may ask children who have mastered certain letter sounds to blend or synthesize them to form words. For example, if children are familiar with the sounds /b/, /a/, and /t/, they can blend them to form the word *bat*. Most practice of synthetic phonics occurs out of context, at least at the initial stages. Eventually, practice continues in books specifically designed to provide exposure to the particular sounds and patterns being taught. There is little emphasis on "naturally occurring" text at initial stages of reading.

RESEARCH BRIEF What about Teaching Phonics Rules?

"When two vowels go walking, the first does the talking." Remember this phrase from elementary school? It's a kid-friendly version of a phonics rule: When two vowels are together, they form a long vowel sound using the sound of the first vowel letter. How useful are phonics rules, and should they be taught?

Theodore Clymer (1963) examined this question in a now-classic study. First, Clymer did make reference to phonics *generalizations* rather than phonics *rules*. Because the English language has evolved from multiple sources, there are many exceptions to the rules. Therefore, the word *generalization* is more appropriate.

Clymer identified the most common phonics generalizations taught in basal readers and then developed a word list from the readers to test the generalizations (20 words for each generalization). Of the 45 generalizations identified, only 18 were considered "high utility" in terms of applying to at least 75% of the target words. The "walking vowel" partners didn't make the high-utility list.

Should generalizations be taught? Teaching common word patterns can help students to learn the consistency among words in the English language better than teaching generalizations can.

According to the top-down perspective, reading is primarily meaning making fueled by the reader's growing knowledge of the spoken word. Good readers are good meaning makers. Top-down advocates rely on an *analytic phonics* approach. Analytic phonics emphasizes whole-to-part-to-whole instruction. This means that children are given whole words with similar patterns, and they make generalizations about the parts of the words that are similar. For example, when introducing the word *bat*, the teacher reminds the students about words they already know. They know the word *boy*, and they know the word *cat*. If they take the beginning of the word *boy*, and the ending of the word *cat*, they have a new word, *bat*. Within an analytic approach, words are introduced in context. Context cues are considered vitally important. Naturally occurring text is important as well. As children become more familiar with word parts, they are able to form other words with the same information.

The *linguistic phonics* approach is a variation of the analytic phonics approach (Bloomfield & Barnhard, 1961). In linguistic phonics, beginning instruction usually focuses on the word patterns found in words like *cat*, *rat*, *mat*, and *bat*. These selected words are presented to the students. Children need to make generalizations about the short a sound by learning these words in print. Consequently, linguistic phonics lessons are based on decodable books that present repetitions of a single pattern ("Mat saw a cat and a rat"). Thus linguistic phonics instruction includes fostering an awareness of onsets and rhymes, and showing children how to recognize words through analogy. The onset of a syllable is the initial consonant sound that comes before the vowel. For example in the one-syllable word *chat*, the onset is /ch/. The onset sound in *sun* is /s/; the onset sound in *smile* is /sm/. A *rhyme*, also called a *phonogram* or *word family*, is a group of letters composed of a vowel and the consonants that follow the vowel. For example in the word *stick*, the onset would be *st* and the rhyme would be *-ick*. Rhymes are quite regular from word to word and form a great many words. Fry (1998) states that the main problem for teachers is to determine which rhymes to teach first. One way to address this dilemma is to teach the ones that occur more commonly. Linguistic phonics is like synthetic phonics in that there is an emphasis on structured decodable texts. It is like analytic phonics in that it emphasizes word patterns rather than individual letter sounds. However, linguistic phonics is not typically espoused by top-down advocates, because it does not emphasize naturally occurring text.

Advocates of the *interactive–compensatory* perspective view reading as a complex system where readers use a variety of cue systems to construct meaning. Good readers have strong, rapid, context-free word recognition abilities, but can use context and meaning for decoding if necessary. Because good readers can read individual words so efficiently, they have more cognitive capacity to make meaning of text. The major differences among the various perspectives lie primarily in how good reading of words is viewed and how word recognition should be taught.

Strict bottom-up and top-down models of the reading process are linear in fashion, emphasizing print to meaning (bottom-up) or meaning to print (top-down). Interactive models recognize both bottom-up and top-down processing, but in a different way. Based on her extensive review of research on word recognition, Marilyn Adams (1990) developed a model of the reading process (see Figure 5.1). The model includes four components: the *orthographic processor* (letter forms and sequences), *phonological processor* (individual phonemes and phonological patterns), *meaning processor* (prior knowledge and vocabulary), and *context processor* (ongoing construction of the meaning of a text). The reader initially gets input from print (or from speech, in the case of listening comprehension). The reader then interactively uses knowledge of print conventions (spelling or orthography), knowledge of speech sounds (phonology), personal background knowledge about the topic and semantics (meaning), and knowledge of syntactics (language structure) and text structure (context) to process the input. The Adams model illustrates

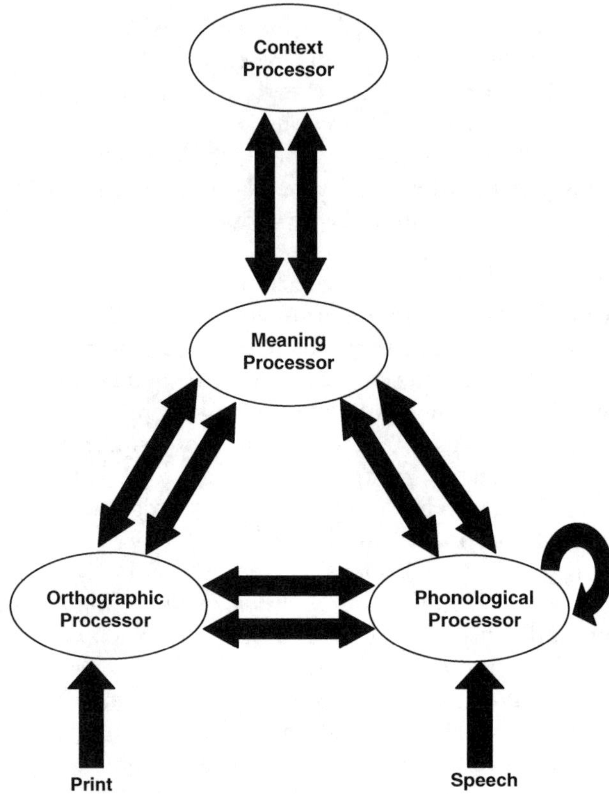

FIGURE 5.1. A model of the reading system: Four processors. From Adams, M. J. (1990). *Beginning to Read: Thinking and Learning about Print*. Cambridge, MA: MIT Press. Copyright 1990 by the MIT Press. Reprinted by permission.

how various cue systems work interactively to help the reader decode and comprehend text. A breakdown in any one component can occur, but facile readers will be able to use other cue systems to compensate and move on.

In Chapter 4 you have read about phonological processing. In Chapter 8 you'll read about contextual and meaning processing. This chapter focuses on orthographic processing, and on phonics instruction as the bridge between orthographic and phonological processing.

Orthographic Processing

Fluent identification of letters facilitates word recognition, which in turn facilitates reading comprehension. In fact, letter name knowledge is one of the best predictors of reading acquisition (Chall & Popp, 1996; Snow, Burns, & Griffin, 1998; Torgesen & Wagner, 1998). Letter-naming fluency (identifying letters in less than one minute) is also predictive of word-reading ability (Stage, Sheppard, Davidson, & Browning, 2001). The ability to identify letters is a first step toward reading, because readers must initially discriminate a letter visually and then name it before they can identify and decode a word (Treiman, Tincoff, Rodriguez, Mouzaki, & Francis, 1998). Treiman and colleagues (1998) suggest that children can use their knowledge of letter names to read words. For example, a preschooler who recognizes the letters f and t may understand that f is the first letter in the word *fan* and t is the first letter in the word *team* (Bowman & Treiman, 2002).

Letter identification may seem to be a simple task for students. However, the direction and orientation of letters are vital. The lower-case letter b when turned to the left becomes the letter d and says /d/. If turned upside down, it says /p/, and p turned to the left is q and says /k/. Upper- and lower-case letters may appear different in various printed materials, depending on the font used. Variations in letters can also occur between printed forms and in handwritten forms, causing further confusion.

Alphabet knowledge can be divided into recognition, identification, and formation. A child is able to recognize a letter when a teacher asks the student, "Show me the letter B," and he or she finds the particular grapheme among a group of other letters. Identification occurs when students are able to identify a letter without hearing the name of the letter. For example, the teacher points to a letter and the child says, "This is the letter B." Finally, as students become more comfortable in identifying letters, they form letters themselves without prompting. Teachers often question when and how to move children from recognition to identification and finally to formation. Kindergarten children are generally ready to learn letters and letter–sound correspondence. Vail (1991) suggests that teachers can make this task "painless and a joyfully solid opportunity" (p. 15) by allowing children to experience each letter in connotation and providing opportunities for them to play with what they are learning.

Phonics Instruction

Phonics instruction forms the bridge between orthographic processing and phonological processing. The National Reading Panel (2000a) identified phonics as one of the five components that are essential for successful reading. The Panel concluded that systematic phonics instruction does have a strong impact on reading and spelling performance for both younger readers and older readers experiencing reading difficulty. While the Panel did recommend explicit phonics instruction as part of the reading curriculum beginning in kindergarten, it did not endorse any one method of phonics instruction. Here are the key recommendations about phonics from the National Reading Panel:

- Programs that include systematic phonics make a bigger contribution to reading growth than programs that do not provide this type of instruction.
- There are many different specific systematic phonics programs. Despite the variations in these programs, they all have the same effects on reading achievement.
- Systematic phonics instruction is effective when delivered in various settings—tutoring, small groups, or whole classes.
- 2.Have one child give designated letters to each child. Give out only the letters needed for the lesson. If the children have their own magnetic letter sets, ask them to select letters for the activity. This process can also help review letter identification for students who need this sk
- Phonics instruction helps to remediate the reading needs of students with disabilities and helps to prevent reading difficulties in students at risk.
- Regardless of socioeconomic status, all students benefit from phonics instruction.
- Phonics instruction proves to be helpful in developing spelling ability in kindergarten and first grade.

The International Reading Association (1996–1997) has pointed out that phonics instruction has become more of a political issue than an educational strategy for teaching children to read. Indeed, the debate over how reading should be taught has been the focus of much public attention in recent years (see Chapter 1). Much of this debate has focused on the role of phonics in reading instruction. In fact, the mass media, parents, state legislatures, and school districts constantly evaluate and discuss the potential benefits of phonics instruction. The International Reading Association is concerned with and warns against the following: (1) the fact that many media reports have exaggerated the lack of phonics instruction in the early grades; (2) the growth in legislation that requires teachers to follow prescriptive phonics instruction plans; (3) the misinformation from professional literature surrounding the place of phonics instruction in a well-rounded reading program; (4) the creation of a rift between literature and phonics, as if they cannot coexist inside the same program; and (5) the exaggerated and inaccurate claims by the media that many students fail to read due to a lack of phonics instruction. In fact, the Association mentions that research shows that teachers do teach phonics.

Although performance of students on national achievement measures and on international comparison tests needs to be improved, the International Reading Association calls for the recognition of the tremendous strides being made by teachers in reading instruction, and offers three main assertions regarding phonics and reading instruction. First, it affirms that the teaching of phonics is an important component of beginning reading instruction. Second, it concludes that classroom teachers in the elementary grades do teach phonics as part of their reading programs. Third, it asserts that phonics instruction needs to be rooted in the context of a total reading/language arts program in order to obtain positive outcomes. Richard Vacca, who was President of the International Reading Association in 1996–1997, stated:

> Phonics is a tool needed by all readers and writers of alphabetically written languages such as English. While I am not a proponent of isolated drill, overreliance on worksheets, or rote memorization of phonics rules, I support the teaching of phonics that children actually need and use to identify words quickly and accurately. These strategies need to be taught systematically in well-planned lessons. (*www.reading.org/pdf/commission_summary.pdf*)

Systematic phonics instruction has shown to have a positive effect on reading. Although the benefits of phonics instruction are clear and evident in various studies, it is important to emphasize that systematic phonics instruction should not be taught in isolation. It is not the total reading program, but a part of a balanced model (Lapp & Flood, 1997; Stahl, Duffy-Hester, & Stahl, 1998).

RESEARCH BRIEF Letter Knowledge and Oral Reading Fluency

Stage and colleagues (2001) found that letter identification and letter sound knowledge significantly predicted oral reading fluency in first grade. However, this study showed that letter sound knowledge affects reading skills more than letter name knowledge does. Letter sound knowledge differs from letter name knowledge, for in the former, the reader not only identifies the letter by name, but also associates the letter with its sound when it is written in words. The grapheme–phoneme correspondence is a better predictor of reading ability, because the rapid processing of grapheme–phoneme codes demonstrates a deeper understanding of the alphabetic principle (McBride-Chang, 1999; Stage et al., 2001). Because prevention is the best antidote to reading difficulties, it is crucial for teachers to offer effective letter instruction and to make sure that all their students master letters by the end of the year before formal reading instruction begins. Moats (1999) suggests that instruction should begin by teaching the sound of a letter first and then making the connection to the abstract letter symbol that represents that sound, because children can move naturally from a familiar sound to an unknown symbol. This process respects the learning process itself. When we humans learn something new, we move from the known to the unknown. Oral language precedes written language so, it is natural to move from oral to written and not the other way around.

Stahl and colleagues (1998) conducted a review of the word recognition literature and developed a set of principles for sound phonics instruction. The authors point out that these principles are applicable to any approach to phonics instruction—traditional approaches or contemporary approaches. Understanding that the readers of this book may be using any one of the approaches described earlier (e.g., synthetic, analytic, linguistic, or a combination), we have used these principles to choose instructional activities for providing differentiated instruction in learning the code, regardless of the approach that you, your school, your school district, or your state might select. The principles are as follows:

- Build upon a child's rich understanding of how print works.
- Teach students the alphabetic principle that letters stand for sounds.
- Build upon students' phonemic awareness.
- Provide students with a firm grasp of letter recognition.
- Explicitly teach students the letter–sound relationships.
- Provide students with sufficient practice in reading words in and out of context.
- Give students daily opportunities to practice writing where phonic principles are used and reinforced.
- Encourage students to develop automatic word recognition.

The research on phonics instruction and English-language learners (ELLs) is more limited (Gersten & Baker, 2000). Systematic phonics instruction in meaningful contexts is generally recommended (Peregoy & Boyle, 2001). Teaching of word patterns and making reading–spelling connections seem to be particularly important in planning phonics instruction for ELLs.

For children who have been identified with reading-related learning disabilities, rapid context-free word recognition is of primary concern. Students with dyslexia often experience difficulties not only with phonological awareness, but also with identifying words under timed conditions (Fuchs, Fuchs, Mathes, & Lipsey, 2000). For students with more severe reading problems, intensive direct instruction and instruction in strategies are recommended (Swanson, 2000), along with opportunities to develop automatic word recognition and fluency (Fuchs et al., 2000). You will read about some approaches for students needing more direct instruction in word recognition in the "Level 3: Intensive Support" section of this chapter.

Keep in mind that the amount of phonics instruction students need will vary considerably. Some students who are fluent readers may need little or no phonics instruction. Others may need more intensive and direct teaching. Assessment and differentiated instruction are particularly important when you are planning phonics instructional activities.

Why Do Some Students Have Trouble with Learning the Code?

The factors influencing reading that you have read about in Chapter 2 certainly can have an impact on students' ability to break the code. As Adams's (1990) model suggests, difficulties in phonological, orthographic, contextual, or meaning processing can make reading difficult. In addition to these factors, it is important to discuss the phases of word learning in reading and spelling, because they need to be considered in teaching a child who is struggling to read and write. While students typically move through these developmental stages smoothly, some students get "stuck" and need additional instruction to move to the next level of development.

The Phases of Reading Development: Implications for Students

Ehri (1995, 1998) proposes five phases of word recognition development that young children go through in learning to read.

PREALPHABETIC PHASE

The first phase is called *prealphabetic*, because alphabetic knowledge is not used to read words. Most students are in this phase during their prekindergarten or early kindergarten year. Children this phase have very limited knowledge of letters, and they have not made the connection between letters and sounds. In fact, the main characteristic of children experiencing this phase is their lack of knowledge about letters and the sounds associated with the letters. They see words as pictures (Adams, 1990).

Prealphabetic readers read words from memory. They do not employ decoding skills to decipher words. For example they may identify a sign for McDonald's, but not by reading the word. In fact, studies have shown that if a letter in a familiar logo is altered, children in the prealphabetic phase will continue to read the word as if the change has not occurred (Adams, 1990). They are not employing context clues, but instead are using the context to decipher a word. This process is called *visual cue reading* (Ehri & McCormick, 1998; Masonheimer, Drum, & Ehri, 1984).

During this phase children may also learn some words out of context, because they may memorize a particular feature in the word. For example, they may look at the word *tall* and remember it by looking at the two tall letters at the end of the word.

PARTIAL ALPHABETIC PHASE

Most students enter the *partial alphabetic* phase during kindergarten. Here children begin to recognize more words. These words are usually learned by recognizing and connecting with one or more of the actual letters in the word (often a beginning sound and/or ending sound). A student in this phase may recognize *boat*, but also mistake it for *bat*, *but*, *beet*, *beat*, and perhaps even *bit*, because they all start with a b and have a t at (or near) the end.

FULL ALPHABETIC PHASE

Children typically enter the *full alphabetic* phase during first grade. As students increase in their phonological awareness, they are able to remember how to read specific words. They do so by forming connections between the written letters they see in the text and the phonemes present in the pronunciation of the word (Morris, Bloodgood, Lomax, & Perney, 2003). For example, now when a child encounters the word *tall*, he or she recognizes that there are three distinct sounds in this word—/t/, /a/, and /l/—and is able to see and hear the connection between the letters on the page and the sounds he or she hears when reading this word. This relationship between written letters and the spoken sound is known as *grapheme–phoneme correspondence* or the *alphabetic principle*. Obviously, once this connection has been established, the student is able to read, decode, and recognize many more words, and to do so more consistently and accurately.

CONSOLIDATED ALPHABETIC PHASE

The next phase of development occurs when children begin to experience more words, and find that the features that they relied on to identify words in the prealphabetic phase begin to overlap. This phase emerges in second grade and beyond. The visual distinctiveness of some words is no longer enough to help children in word recognition. During this phase students begin to make associations between letters and sounds. These associations allow for students to begin deciphering and remembering words in a systematic fashion (Bowman & Treiman, 2002). According to Ehri and McCormick (1998),

> . . . during this stage, readers typically know the sounds of consonants whose letter names contain these sounds: b, d, f, j, k, l, m, n, p, r, s, t, v, z, including the "soft" sounds of c (/s/) and g (/j/). However, they may not know the hard sounds of c (/k/) and g (/g/), or the sounds of h, w, and y, whose names are not informative about sounds and may even mislead (e.g., initial /w/ sound in the name of letter Y). Also, they may not know graphemes involving more than one letter to symbolize a phoneme: sh, wh, th, ch, ck. (p. 138)

Ehri and McCormick (1998) refer to this developmental reading phase as the *consolidated alphabetic* phase or *orthographic* phase. The focus during this phase is on decoding. Knowledge of the major grapheme–phoneme correspondences—including phonemic awareness and understanding the importance of vowels—enables readers to match up phonemes in pronunciations of words to graphemes seen in the conventional spellings of words. Initially the decoding process can be slow and laborious for readers, because they are literally reading and sounding out letters as they decode. However, with practice, this process allows readers to become familiar with frequently occurring sounds and how they are typically found in words. In turn, their reading becomes more and more fluent. The students' sight word vocabulary also increases significantly during this phase, because they encounter these words several times during reading and decode them slowly. After a few times experiencing a word, the students are able to recognize it as a sight word without decoding it, because it is stored in memory. At this phase, students also become able to read unfamiliar words by analogy to familiar words they know by sight—for example, reading *mouse* for *house*.

AUTOMATIC ALPHABETIC PHASE

The final phase of development identified by Ehri (1995) is the *automatic alphabetic* phase. Most students in this phase are considered to be mature readers, because they recognize most words in text automatically by sight. Furthermore, they routinely apply various strategies to attack unfamiliar words.

The Phases of Spelling Development: Implications for Students

Together with developing the ability to read, students develop the ability to spell words. The history of the English language helps us to understand why there are so many spelling patterns. Bear, Invernizzi, Templeton, and Johnson (2000) explain that English has been enriched by many other languages, and therefore has also imported various spelling patterns. Not only have we borrowed words from other languages, but also we have also developed various dialects within the English language and pronounce words differently. It is therefore important to provide children with ample opportunities to work on developing skills in letter–sound association. Gentry and Gillet (1993) have defined five developmental stages of spelling (for examples, see Figure 5.2).

PRECOMMUNICATION STAGE

During the *precommunication* stage, the writer is trying to portray a message, but only the child can read it, and the child can do so only immediately after writing it. Children in this stage have not mastered the alphabetic principle yet. Children mix real upper- and lower-case letters with other symbols or marks (in random order).

SEMIPHONETIC STAGE

Children begin to develop the alphabetic principle during the *semiphonetic* stage. Letters may represent whole words, particularly initial consonants (like M for *Mother* or J for *Jack*). Children begin to get a sense of letter directionality and to grasp the idea that words are spelled from left to right, and their markings more closely resemble actual letters.

PHONETIC STAGE

At the *phonetic* stage, children fully understand the alphabetic principle and know that letters represents all sounds. Words are spelled strictly on the basis of sound, with sounds consistently spelled the same way. Others can often understand these invented spellings.

Word	Precommunicative	Semiphonetic	Phonetic	Transitional	Conventional
1. monster	Random letters	MTR	MOSTR	MONSTUR	Monster
2. united	Random letters	U	UNITD	YOUNIGHTED	United
3. dress	Random letters	JRS	JRAS	DRES	Dress
4. bottom	Random letters	BT	BODM	BOTTUM	Bottom
5. hiked	Random letters	H	HIKT	HICKED	Hiked
6. human	Random letters	UM	HUMN	HUMUM	Human
7. eagle	Random letters	EL	EGL	EGUL	Eagle
8. closed	Random letters	KD	KLOSD	CLOSSED	Closed
9. bumped	Random letters	B	BOPT	BUMPPED	Bumped
10. type	Random letters	TP	TIP	TIPE	Type

FIGURE 5.2. Developmental Spelling Test, with student spelling responses indicating stage of development. From "You Can Analyze Developmental Spelling—and Here's How to Do It!" by J. Richard Gentry, *Teaching K–8* Magazine, May 1985, pp. 44–45. Reprinted with permission of the publisher, Early Years, Inc., Norwalk, CT.

Also, children utilize their phonemic awareness skills, saying words aloud to hear the sounds as they spell them.

TRANSITIONAL STAGE

During the *transitional* stage, writers begin to pay attention to whether a word is spelled correctly, although they may not always be accurate in the determination. They include vowels in spelling attempts, rather than relying only on consonant sounds. Children begin to apply rules of language and meaning, such as using prefixes and suffixes, and dropping or doubling final consonants. At this stage common sight words are spelled correctly, and these patterns are applied to spelling other words.

CONVENTIONAL STAGE

At the *conventional* stage, most words are spelled correctly, and children apply the rules they know about spelling and apply them consistently to words. Children begin to notice when words "don't look right." Writers show increased awareness of the rules of morphology, compound words, homonyms, and contractions. At this stage writers benefit from systematic spelling instruction.

What Are Formal Assessments of Phonics and Spelling?

Several formal assessments of phonics and spelling are available. Before using these measures or using results to make curricular decisions, make certain that you understand how the phonics and spelling tests are constructed. The formats and tasks of these tests vary greatly and may or may not relate to your curriculum in a classroom or resource setting.

The Woodcock–Johnson III Diagnostic Reading Battery

The Woodcock-Johnson III Diagnostic Reading Battery (Woodcock, Mather, & Schrank, 2004) is an individually administered measure used to diagnose student strengths and areas for instruction. It includes a Brief Reading screening subtest, as well as subtests in Reading Comprehension, Phonics Knowledge, and Oral Language Comprehension. The Broad Reading subtest is a combination of fluency and comprehension. The Basic Reading subtest is a combination of vocabulary and phonics. The battery is appropriate for students in grades K–12.

Stanford Diagnostic Reading Test, Fourth Edition

The fourth edition of the Stanford Diagnostic Reading Test (Karlsen & Gardner, 1995) is a group-administered standardized test that can be used to assess student proficiency in decoding, vocabulary, comprehension, and scanning (grade 1–college). Subtests at the early levels enable teachers to diagnose detailed information about phonics skills.

Fox in a Box

Fox in a Box (CTB/McGraw-Hill, 2004) is a set of assessment tools intended for students in grades K–3. The kit includes assessments for phonological awareness, phonics, fluency, comprehension, and vocabulary. The brief measures are individually administered twice a year—at the beginning of each semester. The kit offers an electronic management option.

Roswell–Chall Diagnostic Reading Test

The Roswell–Chall Diagnostic Reading Test (Roswell & Chall, 1997) is a standardized measure of letter recognition, phonics, and other word recognition skills. The test is short (four pages) and easy to administer. It has two forms, so it can be used for pre- and posttesting. The test is appropriate for children in grades 1–4 and for older readers who are experiencing difficulties with decoding.

Decoding Skills Test

The Decoding Skills Test (DST; Richardson & DiBenedetto, 1985) is designed for children and adults with reading levels between grades 1 and 5. The individual measure takes approximately 15–30 minutes to administer. It provides criterion-referenced scores that relate directly to the reading curriculum and provide valuable information, including (1) reading achievement level, (2) frustration level, (3) phonic pattern knowledge, (4) phonic decoding deficiencies, (5) the effect of context on a child's word recognition and decoding skills, (6) oral fluency at various reading levels, and (7) oral reading errors. The DST provides a diagnostic profile of the child's decoding skills and shows the particular area in which an individual needs help. Subtest 1 (Basic Vocabulary) measures the ability to recognize words taught in most basic reading programs. Subtest 2 (Phonic Patterns) assesses the ability to decode words by using letter–sound correspondence. Subtest 3 (Contextual Decoding) assesses the effect of context on decoding skills. More information and ordering instructions can be found on the DST website.

Test of Written Spelling–4

The Test of Written Spelling–4 (TWS-4; Larsen, Hammill, & Moats, 1999) is a standardized test of spelling for students in grades 1–12. Unlike some standardized tests of spelling that are actually editing tests, the TWS-4 requires the student to spell words with predictable and unpredictable spelling patterns via dictation. There is a graded word list of 50 predictable and 50 unpredictable words. Test administration typically begins at the student's present grade-level placement. Test administration stops when students miss five words consecutively. Some schools use the TWS-4 as a screening measure to determine which students need more support in learning to spell.

What Are Informal Assessments of Letter Knowledge, Phonics, and Spelling?

Informal assessments of letter knowledge, phonics, and spelling are often included in the teacher's editions of basal reading and spelling textbooks. Other informal assessments follow, including an overview of the informal reading inventory (IRI), a multifaceted tool for assessing student's strengths and challenges in reading.

Assessing Letter Knowledge

LETTER-NAMING SKILLS

Stage and colleagues (2001) administered an informal measure of letter-naming skills to help them determine how strong these skills were in 59 kindergarten students (see Form

5.1). This measure has three versions (though only one of these is presented in Form 5.1). Each version has lower-case and upper-case letters randomly arranged across 11 rows. Each row contains 10 letters except for the last row, which contains only 4 letters. Students are individually administered the measure to determine how proficient they are in letter recognition. Each version takes about one minute to administer, for a total of three minutes per student. Teachers should administer this measure early in the year to ensure that students are able to identify letters. This same measure can be repeated as instruction in letter identification continues throughout the year. To determine how proficient students are in letter identification, teachers can begin by directing students to recognize the letters that they ask for—for example, "Show me the letter s on this form." The question can be more specific—"Show me the capital s"—to determine knowledge of upper-case and lower-case graphemes. If a student is proficient in letter recognition, the teacher should test letter identification and then proceed to letter formation. The goal of letter identification assessment is to determine which letters the child can identify. It is not sufficient to say that the student knows "some letters," because instruction should take into account exactly what he or she knows.

LETTER SOUND IDENTIFICATION

Similar to the letter identification measure, Stage and colleagues (2001) developed a practical measure to assess letter sound identification (see Form 5.2). In addition, most IRIs contain similar simple letter recognition and letter sound identification assessment measures that may help instructors to identify what areas of strengths and needs students have in relation to these skills. These measures usually take about a minute to administer per child and can help guide teachers' plans.

Assessing Phonics

PHONICS SURVEYS

Phonics surveys can be used or constructed to determine students' initial knowledge and mastery of a variety of phonics patterns. Some surveys use real words, some use nonsense words, still others use a combination of both. Many basal reading programs include phonics surveys. The El Paso Phonics Survey (Ekwall & Shanker, 1999) is a commercial measure of knowledge of basic consonant and vowel sounds and patterns. Target words are actually nonesense words. Nonsense words are used so that the student is being assessed for decoding ability using phonics, not knowledge of sight words. Scholastic, Inc. (2002) has developed a phonics survey entitled the *CORE Phonics Survey*, which is also available online (*www.scholastic.com/dodea/Module_2/resources/dodea_m2_tr_core.pdf*). The Phonics Elements Profile (Form 5.3) can be used to summarize data from a variety of phonics surveys.

NAMES TEST

Cunningham (1990) developed the Names Test (Figure 5.3) as an alternative to nonsense word phonics assessments. The students read a list of names that represent common phonics and syllable patterns. When a student mispronounces a word, the teacher can analyze the phonic and syllable pattern to inform instruction.

THE NAMES TEST:
AN ASSESSMENT TOOL FOR DECODING ABILITY

Summary: This is an informal assessment tool used to measure and analyze a student's decoding ability. The student reads aloud a list of names (which are representative of most of the phonemes and spelling patterns in English). The teacher scores the answers and analyzes them in order to plan further, appropriate instruction for that student.

Preparation:
- Type a list of the 25 names (listed at the bottom of this page) on a sheet of paper or on individual index cards.
- Create a scoring sheet by typing the list of names in one column, each name followed by a blank line to record student responses.

Administration:
- Test each student individually, in a quiet area free of distractions.
- Tell the student that he/she is to pretend to be a teacher reading a list of student names to take attendance.
- Explain that you cannot help at all, and to make a guess if they come to a name they are not sure about.
- Have the student read the list orally.

Scoring and Interpreting:
- As the student reads, make a check on the scoring sheet for those names pronounced correctly, and write the phonetic spellings for the names that were mispronounced.
- Mark a name as correct if all syllables are pronounced correctly, no matter where the accent is placed (i.e., Yol/lan/da or Yo/lan/da–both are correct).
- When there is a vowel pronunciation that depends on which syllable the consonant is placed with, either pronunciation is counted as correct (i.e., Ho/mer or Hom/er).
- Count the number of names read correctly. Analyze those that were mispronounced, looking for patterns indicative of decoding strengths and weaknesses.

Jay Conway	Gus Quincy	Glen Spencer	Troy Whitlock
Tim Cornell	Cindy Sampson	Fred Sherwood	Vance Middleton
Chuck Hoke	Chester Wright	Ron Smitherman	Zane Anderson
Yolanda Clark	Ginger Yale	Dee Skidmore	Flo Thorton
Kimberly Blake	Patrick Tweed	Grace Brewster	
Roberta Slade	Stanley Shaw	Ned Westmoreland	
Homer Preston	Wendy Swain	Bernard Pendergraph	

FIGURE 5.3. Names Test. From Cunningham, Patricia M. (1990, October). The Names Test: A quick assessment of decoding ability. *The Reading Teacher*, 44(2), 124–129.

WORD PATTERN SURVEY

The Word Pattern Survey (Form 5.4) can be used to assess a student's knowledge of the most frequent word patterns. The survey can be used in two ways. You can assess student's reading of word patterns by presenting each word on a card and asking the child to pronounce the word. You can also use the list to assess student spelling of frequent word patterns. The survey is based on Wylie and Durrell's (1970) list of 37 basic rhymes that appear in over 500 primary words. The ability to recognize only these 37 rhymes empowers children to learn these primary words.

DYNAMIC INDICATORS OF BASIC EARLY LITERACY SKILLS

The Dynamic Indicators of Basic Early Literacy Skills (DIBELS) is a set of "individually administered measures of early literacy development. They are designed to be short (one minute) fluency measures used to regularly monitor the development of pre-reading and early reading skills" (*http//:dibels.uoregon.edu*). The results of these tests can be used to assess individual student development, as well as to direct and guide teachers in developing instructional objectives. The subtest that measures the alphabetic principle is Nonsense Word Fluency (NWF). It evaluates children's knowledge of letter-sound correspondences as well their ability to blend letters to form unfamiliar "nonsense" words (e.g., *fik*, *lig*). The DIBELS can be downloaded for free from its website (see the URL above). Each subtest has various versions, so they can be administered repeatedly to the same student. This allows the teacher to monitor progress and adapt instruction accordingly. In addition, the DIBELS developers offer a service called the DIBELS Data System. Teachers can enter their students' DIBELS data online and generate automated reports for $1.00 per student per year.

Assessing Spelling

DEVELOPMENTAL SPELLING TEST

Gentry (1985) developed a 10-word spelling test that can be used to estimate a student's spelling developmental level (see Figure 5.2, above). The test is appropriate for students from the second semester of kindergarten on, to get an idea of where students are on the spelling developmental spectrum.

DIAGNOSTIC SPELLING TEST

The Diagnostic Spelling Test (Kottmeyer, 1959) is a dictation test that can be used to estimate students' general spelling levels (by grade). The test consists of two lists of 32 words each (see Figure 5.4). The administrator dictates words to students, along with a sentence that illustrates the use of the word in context.

WORD CHOICE ASSESSMENTS

A word choice assessment is a quick measure of student understanding of conventional spelling. Students are presented with a page of word pairs (see Form 5.5 for a sample) and are asked to decide which word in each pair is "right." After completing the practice items, students are asked to check as many "right" words in each pair as possible. You

DIAGNOSTIC SPELLING TEST

Directions:

- Give List 1 to any pupil whose placement is second or third grade.
- Give List 2 to any pupil whose placement is above third grade.

Grade scoring, List 1:

Below 15 correct:	Below second grade
15–22 correct:	Second grade
23–29 correct:	Third grade

Any pupil who scores above 29 should be given the List 2 test.

Grade scoring, List 2:

Below 9 correct:	Below third grade
9–19 correct:	Third grade
20–25 correct:	Fourth grade
26–29 correct:	Fifth grade
Over 29 correct:	Sixth grade or better

Any pupil who scores below 9 should be given the List 1 test.

List 1

Word Illustrative Sentence

1. not–He is not here.
2. but–Mary is here, but Joe is not.
3. get–Get the wagon, John.
4. sit–Sit down, please.
5. man–Father is a tall man.
6. boat–We sailed our boat on the lake.
7. train–Tom has a new toy train.
8. time–It is time to come home.
9. like–We like ice cream.
10. found–We found our lost ball.
11. down–Do not fall down.
12. soon–Our teacher will soon be here.
13. good–He is a good boy.
14. very–We are very glad to be here.
15. happy–Jane is a happy girl.
16. kept–We kept our shoes dry.
17. come–Come to our party.
18. what–What is your name?
19. those–Those are our toys.
20. show–Show us the way.
21. much–I feel much better.
22. sing–We will sing a new song.
23. will–Who will help us?
24. doll–Make a dress for the doll.
25. after–We play after school.
26. sister–My sister is older than I.
27. toy–I have a new toy train.
28. say–Say your name clearly.
29. little–Tom is a little boy.
30. one–I have only one book.
31. would–Would you come with us?
32. pretty–She is a pretty girl.

List 2

Word Illustrative Sentence

1. flower–A rose is a flower.
2. mouth–Open your mouth.
3. shoot–Joe wants to shoot his new gun.
4. stood–We stood under the roof.
5. while–We sang while we marched.
6. third–We are in the third grade.
7. each–Each child has a pencil.
8. class–Our class is reading.
9. jump–We like to jump rope.
10. jumps–Mary jumps rope.
11. jumped–We jumped rope yesterday.
12. jumping–The girls are jumping rope now.
13. hit–Hit the ball hard.
14. hitting–John is hitting the ball.
15. bite–Our dog does not bite.
16. biting–The dog is biting on the bone.
17. study–Study your lesson.
18. studies–He studies each day.
19. dark–The sky is dark and cloudy.
20. darker–This color is darker than that one.
21. darkest–This color is the darkest of the three.
22. afternoon–We may play this afternoon.
23. grandmother–Our grandmother will visit us.
24. can't–We can't go with you.
25. doesn't–Mary doesn't like to play.
26. night–We read to Mother last night.
27. brought–Joe brought his lunch to school.
28. apple–An apple fell from the tree.
29. again–We must come back again.
30. laugh–Do not laugh at other children.
31. because–We cannot play because of the rain.
32. through–We ran through the yard.

FIGURE 5.4. Diagnostic Spelling Test. From Kottmeyer, W. (1959). *Teacher's Guide for Remedial Reading* (pp. 88–89). St. Louis, MO: Webster. Reproduced with permission of The McGraw-Hill Companies.

can construct word choice assessments to gauge students' understanding of regular and irregular phonics and spelling patterns.

INFORMAL SPELLING INVENTORY

Jones (2001) describes a "teacher-friendly" method for devising an informal spelling inventory (ISI) that is aligned with the curriculum being taught. First, gather copies of the school's spelling basals (grades 1–6). Using the table of contents or scope and sequence chart, identify the spelling patterns taught. Select one or two words from each grade-level book to tap each pattern. You can use an ISI at the beginning of the year to assess student needs, at midyear to assess progress, and at the end of the year to assess mastery.

Informal Reading Inventory

An IRI has long been recognized as an efficient way to discover a great deal of information about a student's strengths and challenges in reading in a relatively short period of time. IRIs are administered individually in sessions that last 30–60 minutes. For students who are nonreaders, measures to assess alphabet knowledge, phonological awareness, and concepts about books and print are more appropriate as a starting point.

IRIs have been basic tools for reading teachers since the 1940s, when Emmett Betts first developed one in his clinical work (Betts, 1941, 1957). As a starting point for teacher decision making about instructional needs of students, an IRI is hard to beat. Many commercial IRIs are now available. Appendix B of this book includes a feature analysis that compares currently available IRIs. Many now include supplemental informal assessments to assist in discovering what students know and what they need to learn. In addition, many basal readers include an IRI as supplemental material.

The overall purpose of an IRI is to determine a student's reading level. Betts set criteria for three levels of reading: *independent*, *instructional*, and *frustration*. At the independent level, a student can recognize words easily, and comprehension is excellent. In short, the independent level is just that—the student can function well on his or her own without the support of a teacher or other adult. Identifying this level is important and can assist the teacher in choosing materials for pleasurable reading. At the instructional level, the reading material is challenging but comfortable. Students may need some teacher assistance in word recognition and in understanding the text. At the frustration level, things are different: Word recognition is strained, comprehension is difficult, and the student does not read smoothly or with ease. Students should not be assigned reading material at their frustration level, because it will do just that—frustrate the students.

IRIs have subtests that enable teachers to determine independent, instructional, and frustration levels for word identification in isolation, word identification in context, oral reading comprehension, silent reading comprehension, and listening comprehension. All IRIs include a set of graded word lists and graded reading passages followed by comprehension questions. Most have multiple sets of passages that can be used for pre- and posttesting and/or as oral or silent reading assessments. Typically the graded word lists and passages range from preprimer to sixth-grade levels, but sometimes higher grade levels are also included. The graded word lists are used for assessing word identification in isolation. The graded passages are used for assessing oral reading (including word identification in context) and oral and silent reading comprehension. The teacher or test administrator can also read passages aloud to students and ask questions orally to assess listening comprehension.

Most commercial IRIs have explicit directions for administration, scoring, and interpretation. Nonetheless, we have included some generic instructions for the use of IRIs in Appendix B. The instructions are organized by frequently asked questions about IRIs.

How Do You Provide Differentiated Instruction in Phonics and Spelling?

Level 1: High-Quality Core Instruction

Most school systems are guided by state or local standards for the teaching of reading and spelling. In many cases, basal reading programs or basal spelling programs guide the instructional program for teaching of the code. Sometimes phonics and spelling are taught as separate subject areas. As Stahl and colleagues (1998) have recommended, phonics and spelling should be taught together. Weekly spelling tests can focus on the phonics patterns being taught that week, as well as on target sight words that do not follow predictable patterns. Because you are likely to have a range of spelling levels among your students, you may want to individualize spelling lists. You can focus on common patterns each week, but have a range of levels of difficulty among words using those patterns. For students with difficulties, supplemental instruction over and above the basal reading/spelling program will be necessary.

TEACHING LETTERS

Letter Naming. Vail (1991) contends that success results from a "letter of the week" approach. The sequence of how letters are presented can be any logical one; however, similar letters (e.g., lower-case b and d, or m, n, and u) should be well separated to avoid confusion. The introduction of vowels is often postponed by many teachers because they may feel that the vowels have varying sounds, which might confuse children. Vowels should be introduced gradually, with attention to both their long and short sounds. When vowels are introduced early, children will be able to form words and understand the connection between learning letters and reading. A teacher should have a rationale on which to base the order of teaching letters. The teacher may select the sequence by considering different options according to students' needs.

For example, a teacher may choose to begin with letters that occur in children's names or that occur frequently in children's books. Often teachers may find that starting with letters that are easier for children to say may be helpful. For example, the name of the letter M is more easily pronounced than the name of the letter W. It is also imperative to begin with continuant sounds like s and m, because sounds can be isolated and elongated without confusion (Bear et al., 2000). The sequence followed in presenting letters is also important to consider, in order to allow for obvious contrast. It is essential that letters with similar names be separated in order to avoid auditory confusion. For example, the letters D and W, A and H, or C and S should be taught at different times. In addition, teachers should separate letters that represent voiced and unvoiced sounds (e.g., b/p g/k d/t v/f z/s). For example, the letters B and P should be separated, because they cannot be isolated or elongated without the use of a vowel sound ("buh," "puh"). These two letters can be confusing because they are articulated similarly. In order to produce both letter sounds, lips must be pressed together in the same way. The only difference is that B ("buh") causes the vocal cords to vibrate and P does not (Bear et al., 2000; Cheyney & Cohen, 1999).

A suggested sequence that follows the principles discussed above would be the following:

M S T A F B N I P K L O D G H U C W R E Y J V Z X Q

Dechant (1993) analyzed the results of his studies and those of other researchers, and came up with a list of teaching suggestions to follow when teaching letters to children:

1. Teach capital letters before lower-case letters.
2. Present letters in the order of their difficulty. Begin with the easiest and move your way up.
3. Point out differences instead of similarities in letters.
4. Use color coding to highlight the presence of individual letters in words.
5. Use transparencies to show differences in letters.

You can record student outcomes on formal or informal assessments of the alphabetic principle, phonics, and spelling on Part V of the Student Reading and Writing Profile (Form 5.6). In addition, you can use the Phonics Elements Profile (see Form 5.3) to provide further information to guide assessment and

7. Highlight the salient features in letters.
8. Match individual letters to their duplicates in different words.
9. Find letters from memory.

Another valuable activity for children, especially those who may need additional support in developing letter identification skills, is presented by Morris and Nelson (1992): reinforcing the letters in children's names. This is a lesson that can be taught in small groups or individually. Materials for this activity include blank cards, and letter cards that have both upper-case and lower-case letters. Note that plastic letters, foam letters, or letter tiles can replace the letter cards. Using these materials, follow the steps below:

1. Spell out each child's name, using the upper-case letter cards.
2. Ask the student to form his or her name, using lower-case letters, under the name you have formed.
3. Mix up the top row and have the student unscramble the letters to form his or her name.
4. Repeat the third step with the bottom row of lower-case letters.
5. Place blank cards under each letter, and write each letter on the blank card. As you write, discuss aloud the direction and movement followed to form each letter. This step should be followed for both upper-case and lower-case letters.
6. Play Concentration with the letters in the student's name.

Letter–Sound Correspondence. Vail (1991) suggests five activities that will help with letter–sound correspondence. As with letter naming, all of these activities should be part of a "letter of the week" approach. As the sound for each letter is introduced, the teacher should include as many art projects for hands-on activities as possible.

1. *Sound–symbol cards.* For each letter taught, the class can create a clue card. The teacher should guide students in creating a large clue card and then allow students to make their own on index cards. The material of which the letter on each clue card is made should begin with that letter. For example, the letter C can be made up of cotton balls, and the letter D can be made up of tiny dots. All of the clue cards should be kept on

a ring or file box for later use. Some children will be able to grasp letter sounds quickly, while others will need to experience more hands-on activities before they can identify letter sounds or master letter–sound correspondence. Table 5.1 presents suggestions for clue materials, adapted from Vail (1991).

2. *Sound–symbol scrapbook.* A sound–symbol scrapbook contains at least one page for each letter. In their scrapbooks, children can paste cut-out pictures from magazines, catalogs, or newspapers, or can make their own drawings of objects that begin with each letter. The scrapbook is a unique project that each child develops throughout the year. Children should be encouraged to label each picture or figure they include in the scrapbook. Some teachers send the scrapbook home and assign one letter per week. Older children can deal with more letters at a time and may be assigned two or three letters weekly. The assignment might include letter formation and then the gluing of pictures in the notebook.

3. *Keeping a calendar.* Time is a concept that is difficult for children to grasp, but can be reinforced while they are learning letters. This activity may be even more helpful for students with learning disabilities, who may struggle with more abstract concepts as time. Vail (1991) suggests that the teacher keep a calendar, and that every day the class as a whole can come up with a word that starts with the letter of the week to describe the

TABLE 5.1. Clue Materials for Letter–Sound Correspondence Activities

Letter	Materials
A	Picture of apple superimposed on letter A for short A
	Animal for long A
B	Picture of balloon, or beans in shape of B
C	Cotton balls/candy in shape of C
D	Dots in shape of D
E	Egg shells in shape of E for short E
	Picture of eel in shape of E for long E
F	Feathers in shape of F
G	Gummy Bears in shape of G
H	Hearts in shape of H
I	Picture of igloo superimposed over I for short I
	Picture of ice cream for long I
J	Jelly beans in shape of J
K	Crinkled foil from chocolate kisses in shape of K
L	Lollipop sticks in shape of L
M	Mini-marshmallows or M&Ms in shape of M
N	Nails or name tags in shape of N
O	Tongue depressor decorated with O for short O
	Picture of a person jumping over a barrier for long O
P	Pieces of paper/pennies in shape of P
Q	Pieces of cloth cut out to form a quilt in shape of Q
R	Raisins in shape of R
S	String in shape of S
T	Colored tape in shape of T
U	Ugly face drawn on the card for short U
	Picture of unicorn superimposed on letter U for long U
V	Pieces of velvet in shape of V
W	Picture of window, or window cut open on the card
X	X-ray drawn on the card
Y	Yellow yarn in shape of Y
Z	Picture of zebra, or paper decorated with zebra stripes

Note. Based on Vail (1991).

day. In this way the teacher can also help children to understand such concepts as tomorrow and two days ago by saying, for example, "Tomorrow will be *fabulous*" and "Two days ago we said the day had been *fun*." Letters and time are both reinforced in this exercise.

4. *Word games.* Word games can help children in developing letter sound identification and letter-naming skills. As noted above, some children may master letter identification and letter–sound relationships quickly, while others will need more hands-on activities before they reach that point; word games are possible activities that children can engage in while other children continue to reinforce the hands-on activities. These games can also be played to reinforce skills that children have not yet mastered. Games that focus on alliteration are played to reinforce these skills. For example, children can sit in a circle, and one child is given a word to begin. The children go around the circle, each one taking a turn to give a word that starts with the same letter. The letter of the week can be the focus of the activity, and then other previously covered letters can also be reviewed during the game. With the letter card rings, a similar game can be played. Children can play among themselves or with an adult. One child or the adult can say the sound of a letter, while the others flip to the letter card that represents that sound. Playing with and manipulating letters give children the opportunity to develop beginning literacy skills. It is important to ensure that by the end of kindergarten, children have mastered letter identification and phoneme–grapheme relationships.

TEACHING PHONICS

Initial and Final Consonant sounds. Most phonics instructional programs start with the teaching of initial and final consonant sounds. This is a natural next step to follow phonological awareness instruction. Alphabetic puzzles containing letters shaped like objects or animals whose initial sounds are symbolized by those letters (e.g., S as a snake) are typically found in preschool classrooms. Some of these toys have pictures under the letters, so when children lift the letter S, they see the picture of a snake. The same picture will remind a child that the letter S belongs in that hole. In fact, mnemonics is an approach that can help children to form links between letters and sounds. Some programs designed with this approach in mind have proven helpful in teaching children to learn letter–sound relationships.

IRIs have subtests that enable teachers to determine independent, instructional, and frustration levels for word identification in isolation, word identification in context, oral reading comprehension, silent reading comprehension, and listening comprehension. All IRIs include a set of graded word lists and graded reading passages followed by comprehension questions. Most have multiple sets of passages that can be used for pre- and posttesting and/or as oral or silent reading assessments. Typically the graded word lists and passages range from preprimer to sixth-grade levels, but sometimes higher grade levels are also included. The graded word lists are used for assessing word identification in isolation. The graded passages are used for assessing oral reading (including word identification in context) and oral and silent reading comprehension. The teacher or test administrator can also read passages aloud to students and ask questions orally to assess listening comprehension.

Short and Long Vowel Sounds. Teaching short and long vowel sounds is an important part of letter sound recognition and a crucial component of reading. Vowel sounds are essential aspects of reading, because they determine the sounds words or syllables will have. For example, in *hop* the o is making a short sound; however, if an e is added to *hop*, the word is now hope. The o is now making a long o sound. The word *hop* is completely transformed semantically and phonologically by the position of its vowels. When you are introducing vowels, it is important to specify to beginning readers that vowels sometimes make a short sound and sometimes make a long sound. However, Cheyney and Cohen (1999) suggest referring to the different sounds as long or short, because children may confuse the sounds with big letters and small letters. It is not uncommon to see children in clinical settings writing short a as a lower-case letter and long a as capital A. A suggestion would be to refer to long vowel sounds as the letters' own names, A E I O U (say the long vowels). In contrast, vowels have special sounds when they are short (say the short vowels). The quicker children are able to master this concept, the quicker their reading skills will develop. In addition, the consonants y and w should also be included in vowel instruction, because they function as vowels when they appear after another vowel or at the end of a word or syllable. Some examples are *play*, *key*, *snow*, *toy*, *new*, *stew*, *down*, *my*, and *candy*.

Cheyney and Cohen (1999) propose that vowel sounds be emphasized using a song and by always representing vowels in a different color than consonants to emphasize their role in word formation. It is likely that most teachers are familiar with the song "Are You Sleeping, Brother John?" (the English version of "Frère Jacques"). Following this melody, children are taught to sing the vowel sound song. Each word that represents either a short or a long vowel in the song can be changed and tailored to each specific class. The sample below (based on one by Cohen, 1996) provides example of baseball words for a class whose favorite team was in the playoffs. The children were grouped and given a sound, and each group came up with a specific baseball word that started with the assigned letter.

A has two sounds, A has two sounds
Ā and Ă, Ā and Ă.
Ā is for *Ace*, Ă is for *Adversary*,
Ā and Ă, Ā and Ă.
E has two sounds, E has two sounds,
Ē and Ĕ, Ē and Ĕ.
Ē is for *Event*, Ĕ is for *Everyone*,
Ē and Ĕ, Ē and Ĕ.
I has two sounds, I has two sounds,
Ī and Ĭ, Ī and Ĭ.
Ī is for *Ice Cream*, Ĭ is for *Infield*,
Ī and Ĭ, Ī and Ĭ.
O has two sounds, O has two sounds,
Ō and Ŏ, Ō and Ŏ.
O is for *Over* [the fence], Ŏ is for *Opponent*,
Ō and Ŏ, Ō and Ŏ.
U has two sounds, U has two sounds,
Ū and Ŭ, Ū and Ŭ.
Ū is for *Uniform*, Ŭ is for *Umpire*,
Ū and Ŭ, Ū and Ŭ.

Consonant Blends and Digraphs. A blend is a spelling unit formed by two or three consonants, which appear at the beginning or end of words. These consonants retain their sounds when the blend is pronounced, yet the blend is not easily separated into phonemes, and can be difficult for children to spell and recognize. Consonant blends come from three major groups: the s blends (sn, sm, st, sk, sc, sl, sp, sw), the l blends (bl, cl, fl, gl, pl, sl), and the r blends (br, cr, dr, fr, gr, pr, tr). The easiest blends are the s blends, because s makes a continuous sound. Teaching consonant blends begins with the contrast of pictures representing words. Contrasts should include words that begin with the blend and words that begin with the first letter in the blend. For example, a sort for the sm blend should include pictures representing words that begin with sm and words that begin with the letter s (e.g., *smile* and *sand*).

A *digraph* is a combination of two letters that make a new sound. The word *digraph* itself ends with the digraph ph. The letters p and h together make the /f/ sound. Other digraphs include th, ck, sh, and wh. The same approaches explained above for teaching blends can be applied to teach digraphs. Some students will learn quickly; others may need additional reinforcement, such as presenting digraphs of sharper contrast together.

The study of digraphs and blends should begin after students have mastered initial consonant sounds. Most of the teaching of these double consonant patterns is done with the use of pictures, because children at this stage of development do not have enough sight vocabulary to work with. Most importantly, teaching digraphs and blends is done by comparing words that are represented by pictures. For example, a picture of a tree and a picture of the number 10 are used to compare the letter t and the blend tr. *Tree* begins with tr and *ten* with t.

To accurately determine what sounds to contrast, Bear and colleagues (2000) suggest looking at children's invented spelling. For example kids usually confuse ch as in *chin* with j. They may write *chin* as JN. It seems from this example that a good sort to study would include words that begin with ch, j, and even c and h. Some possible digraph contrasts include c/ch/h, s/sh/h, t/th/h, ch/sh/th, j/ch, and wh/sh/th.

Vowel Patterns. When efficient readers decode, they do not recite rules in order to decipher words. Instead, they look for patterns in words. Beginning readers need to be taught to recognize clusters of letters in words. Teachers need to provide them with strategies for finding these clusters by teaching them vowel patterns. A *vowel pattern*, also called a *spelling* or *syllable pattern* or *word family*, is a word or syllable that is decoded according to the position of its vowels and consonants. There are six different syllable types that appear in approximately 85%–88% of all English-language words (Moats, 2000). This is a significant number; therefore, it makes sense to teach children these patterns, because by learning them they will acquire the necessary skills to decode at least 85% of words they encounter.

May (1998) investigated the predictive power of four of the six vowel patterns. He concluded that "the prediction power of the patterns ranges from 77[%] to 89%, each of which is much better than predictions on the basis of chance alone, and teaching children vowel patterns can make a difference in their fluency and comprehension" (p. 189). The six vowel patterns are closed vowel patterns, open vowel patterns, silent-e vowel patterns, r-controlled vowel patterns, vowel digraphs (two vowels with a single sound), and consonant + le. Cheyney and Cohen (1999) state: "Once children realize that there are only six basic vowel patterns that can be analyzed and recognized fairly easily, the mystery of decoding disappears" (p. 31).

Vowel patterns should be introduced one at a time. Students should be offered ample opportunities to work with each pattern through a variety of multisensory lessons. As each new pattern is introduced, the preceding pattern(s) should be reviewed. This review provides teachers with an opportunity to point out similarities and differences among the patterns. This review will also emphasize the fact that vowels make different sounds according to their position in a word (Cheyney & Cohen, 1999). Cohen (1996) designed a vowel pattern chart that provides a structure on which to sort and classify patterns as they are taught. In addition, she proposes reinforcing patterns by teaching them with jingles and stories to help children remember and differentiate the characteristics of each pattern. Table 5.2 is an adapted version of the chart with suggested definitions, jingles, and stories. Patterns should be presented in the order in which they appear in the table. In other words, begin at upper left with closed patterns, and finish at lower right with consonant + le.

Other Vowel Sounds. In addition to vowel patterns, three other categories of vowels are part of the curriculum: *vowel digraphs*, *vowel diphthongs*, and *schwa*. Vowel digraphs are vowel combinations that work together to represent a single sound, such as the ea in *read*. Vowel diphthongs are vowel combinations that form new sounds, such as oi in *boil* and ou in *bout*. The schwa is a vowel sound common in unaccented syllables, such as the a in *about* and the u in *circus*.

PUTTING IT ALL TOGETHER: MAKING WORDS

Cunningham and Hall (1998) discuss Making Words, a multilevel, hands-on spelling and phonics program. Making Words provides students with the opportunity to put together all aspects of a phonics and spelling curriculum in a game-like manner. Making Words lessons can begin as early as the second semester of kindergarten and continue throughout the elementary grades.

In the Making Words lessons, children are given a group of letters individually and use these letters to make words. Each activity takes about 15 minutes. It begins with simple two-letter words and progresses to larger graphemes. The final word of the lesson employs all of the letters presented to the child. The children are usually curious and excited to discover what the last word will be. The first Making Words activities involve only one vowel, distinguished from the consonants by its color. As children progress and learn to manipulate single-vowel words, words that have two or more vowels are introduced. Because this is a multilevel activity, children can be grouped according to their needs for practice. Parent volunteers, teacher aides, or peers can lead Making Words activities. Cunningham and Hall (1994b) present steps for teachers to create their own Making Words lessons that include words connected with the content covered in their classes:

1. Decide what the final word in the lesson will be. For example, in a baseball lesson, the final word can be *baseball*. The criteria for selecting the word can include the children's interests, the nature of the curriculum, and the letter–sound patterns to be emphasized in the lesson.
2. Make a list of shorter words that can be made from the letters of the final word.
3. From all the words selected, pick about 15, including these:

TABLE 5.2. Vowel Patterns

Closed	Open	Silent-e
Definition: A word or syllable that contains only one vowel followed by one or more consonants. *Jingle*: One lonely vowel squished in the middle says its special sound [short vowel sound] just a little. *Story*: The vowel is stuck between the two consonants and cannot say its real name, so it says its special sound. *Sandwich analogy*: Use your hands as the bread and the child's hand as a sandwich filler (ham, cheese, peanut butter). Say that the consonants are the bread and that the vowel is the filler. Place your left palm up and ask the child to place his or her hand on top. Then place your right hand over the child's hand to create a "sandwich." Say: "The bread [your hands] does not allow the filler [child's hand] to come out, just like the consonant does not allow the vowel to be free to say its real name." As you say this, press down firmly on the child's hand. *Examples*: sat, fin, bed, top, gum, sand, print, shop, lunch, at, Ed, in, on, up.	*Definition*: A word or syllable that ends with one long vowel. *Jingle*: If one vowel at the end is free, it pops up and says its real name to me. *Story*: Contrast open vowels with the closed pattern already studied. Unlike the closed vowel that is stuck between two consonants, the vowel in the open pattern is free and can say its real name. *Sandwich analogy*: Use one hand as the bread and the child's hand as a sandwich filler (cheese, tuna, salad). Say that the consonant is the bread and that the vowel is the filler. Place your left palm up and ask the child to place his or her hand on top. Say: "This is an open-faced sandwich. There is only one bread before the filler. There is no bread closing the sandwich or locking in the filler. This vowel is free and can say its real name." *Examples*: me, she, hi, go, fly, flu.	*Definition*: A word or syllable that ends with e, containing the final e and one long vowel before the consonant. *Jingle*: The preceding vowel says, "I'm stuck in the middle! Please, magic e, come and free me!" *Story*: The magic e is a very generous vowel. It gives its power to the preceding vowel so that this vowel can say its real name. The e is silent because it gives away all of its power. *Analogy*: Children can work on changing words by touching them with a magic-e wand. For example, the teacher presents the word *cub*. Children are asked to touch the word with their magic-e wand and it is transformed into *cube*. *Examples*: Steve, make, ride, hope, cube.
Double vowels Double vowel talker	Bossy r	Consonant + le
Definition: A word or syllable that contains two adjacent vowels. The first vowel is long. *Jingle*: When two vowels go walking, the first one does the talking. *Story*: Two friends go walking so that the first one can tell her friend why she is so happy. The first vowel talks, and the second one listens and says nothing. *Examples*: rain, day, see, meat, pie, slow, toe, blue, green, boat, true, fruit. In the preceding patterns, children have worked with long	*Definition*: A word or syllable containing a vowel followed by r. The vowel sound is altered by r. *Jingle*: R is the boss. You must do what it says, or it will be cross. *Story*: The r is so bossy that it will not allow the vowel to say its real name or special sound, but only a different sound, as in car. *Examples*: car, her, horn, first, curl, sharp, storm.	*Definition*: The syllable ends with le and is preceded by a consonant. This pattern occurs in two-syllable words. *Jingle*: This consonant loves le. It pulls it towards itself and is filled with glee. *Story*: When a word ends with a consonant followed by le, the le grabs the consonant before it, and we break the word into two parts right before the consonant. *Examples*: bub-ble, puz-zle, ap-ple, ti-tle, ea-gle.

(cont.)

TABLE 5.2. *(cont.)*

vowel sounds. Consequently, it is easy for them to learn this pattern where vowels are long.
Double vowel whiner
Definition: A word or syllable that contains two vowels. Neither of the vowels says its long or short sound. Instead, together they say a funny whining sound: ow, aw, oy, or oo.

a. Words that you can sort for the pattern(s) you wish to emphasize.
b. Short and long words, to make the lesson multilevel.
c. Words that can be made with the same letters in different places—for example, *barn* and *bran*. This is especially important, because children will be reminded that the place of letters in words is crucial to reading and spelling.
d. One or two proper names to reinforce the use of capital letters.
e. Words that most students have in their listening vocabularies.
f. If you are working with ELLs, some cognates. As noted in Chapter 3, a *cognate* is a word that is spelled and sounds similarly in two different languages—for example, *abundant* (English) and *abundante* (Spanish).

4. Write all the words on index cards and order them from smallest to biggest. Group one letter, then two-letter words, three-letter words, and so on.
5. Once words are sorted into groups, continue sorting them by looking for similar patterns that will be emphasized in the lesson.
6. Store the cards in an envelope. Write the words in order and the patterns that will be sorted on the envelope.

Steps in teaching a Making Words lesson are as follows:

1. Place the large letter cards needed for this lesson in a pocket chart or along the chalk ledge (e.g., for the lesson on baseball, the letters a, a, e, b, b, l, l, and s).
2. Have one child give designated letters to each child. Give out only the letters needed for the lesson. If the children have their own magnetic letter sets, ask them to select letters for the activity. This process can also help review letter identification for students who need this sk
3. Write the numeral 2 (or 3, if there are no two-letter words in the lesson) on the board. Ask students to take two (or three) letters and form the first word—for example, "Take two letters and form the word *as*." Then write the numeral 3 on the board and say, "Switch the letters around and add a letter to form *sea*." Say the word and use it in a sentence if necessary: "*Sea*. I love to swim in the *sea*." Continue the process to form the other words in the lesson. (For the baseball lesson, these can include *be*, *as*, *sea*, *all*, *ball*, *bell*, *sell*, *seal*, *sale*, *bale*, *base*, *balls*, *bells*, *bales*, *label*, *labels*, and *baseball*).
4. Have the children make each word, using their letter cards or magnetic letters.
5. Call on a volunteer who has formed the word correctly to come up to the board

to form the word, using the large letter cards. At this time, encourage children who did not form the words correctly to correct their answers.

6. Continue to dictate words for students to form. Remember that for every word, you should write on the board the number of letters required to form the word. In addition, you should guide students by reminding them if they are to build a word from scratch, if they are changing a letter, or if they are just moving letters around. If a word is a name, emphasize the role of capital letters.
7. Once all the words are made, take the index cards on which the whole words are written and place them one at a time (in the same order children made them) along the chalk ledge or in the pocket chart. The children should be actively participating with you in spelling the words out orally.
8. Pick out certain patterns from some of the words and encourage the children to find other words that follow the same pattern. For example, you can point out that *base* follows a silent-e pattern. The students can point out that *bale* and *sale* also conform to the silent-e pattern.
9. To encourage spelling skills and reinforce patterns, students can be asked to come up with additional words that follow the same patterns emphasized in the lesson. This is an optional activity that you can use to provide reinforcement to children who have mastered the lesson. During this activity, you can do further work with students who still need assistance in grasping the concepts covered.

TECH TIP Computer Programs for Phonics Instruction

Computer programs can be used to provide additional practice in phonics. Many software and online programs are available to help reinforce letter identification, letter–sound association, and phonics skills. Teachers and parents can use these programs to help students reinforce skills they are in the process of mastering (Mercer & Mercer, 2005). Care should be taken to make certain that the scope and sequence of the programs are consistent with what is being taught in school. You'll read about more such programs in Chapter 13. Some of these programs include Supersonic Phonics (*www.ibsc.com/readingjoy/phonics*), Let's Go Read (*http://edresources.com*), and Reading Blaster (*http://edresources.com*).

For an annotated bibliography of comp software for teaching Early Reading and Spelling, go to *www.ed.arizona.edu/rimes2000/ComputerSoftware.htm*.

Level 2: Supplemental Instruction

TEACHING LETTERS

Letter Naming. Some children may need additional reinforcement in learning letters. Usually these children have not developed a consistent way of reproducing a letter; they may have orientation and discrimination difficulties, and/or visual-perceptual deficits. These children will benefit from direct instruction so that these skills can become automatic.

For children who have not mastered alphabet letters or letter–sound correspondence, the one-letter-a-week approach may not be enough. Bear and colleagues (2000) suggest dealing with more than one letter at a time, especially with children who reach kindergarten with neither one of these skills and need to catch up. One way in which this can be done is by sharing alphabet books, just as good literature is shared, with students and families (see Figure 4.3 in Chapter 4 for examples). Some books are simple letter-naming books; others are a bit more advanced. For example, in Base's (1987) *Animalia*, readers are asked to name all the things hidden in the illustrations that begin with a particular letter sound.

Letter Formation. Cheyney and Cohen (1999) suggest creating manipulative centers where children can trace, match, find, and form letters from all different materials. Materials may include clay; shaving cream; colored glue; glitter; gel in plastic bags; screens and wax crayons; highlighters; colored tape; and rice, salt, sand, or cornmeal trays lined with colored paper. These centers are ideal for whole-class, small-group, or individual reinforcement of letter identification skills.

TEACHING PHONICS

Consonant Sounds. Students who are having difficulty learning consonant sounds will benefit from additional instruction using alphabet books and manipulatives. While teacher-made manipulatives are more cost-effective in terms of materials, they may be less cost-effective in terms of teacher time. Commercial sets of materials using letter tiles or reading rods attached to alphabet books are available through ETA Cuisenaire (*www.etacuisenaire.com*) and can be used for teacher-directed sessions or for reading center activities.

Vowel Sounds. Learning vowel sounds is certainly an important component of learning to read and write in English; however, it is a complex process for a number of reasons. First of all, there are more sounds than there are vowels to represent them. For example, the vowel a in different words appears to have different sounds, as is the case in the words *hat*, *car*, *father*, *play*, and *claw*. In addition, different letter combinations can form the same sound. For example, the sound /a/ can be spelled in eight different ways: *cake*, *play*, *mail*, *eight*, *vein*, *steak*, *table*, and *they*. There are many vowel sounds that are spelled in a variety of patterns. These include r-influenced vowels (*cart*, *war*, *sir*), diphthongs (*brown*, *cloud*, *boil*, *toy*), vowel digraphs (*boat*, *tea*, *pie*, *play*), and vowel variants (*straw*, *paw*, *room*, *book*, *new*).

Due to the complexity of vowel sounds, some children may need additional support in mastering vowel sounds. Vail (1991) suggests that vowel rings can help these students to remember the hard-to-discriminate vowel sounds. The teacher gives each child a notebook ring and five index cards. On the bottom of each card, the teacher writes one of the five vowels. The teacher should point to the letter at the bottom of the card and say, "This is the letter a. Can you think of some words that have the letter a in the middle?" Children are allowed to give several examples. The teacher then directs students to select one of the words and to draw a picture of that example. The process is repeated for every vowel until the vowel ring is completed. Vowel rings work well in a classroom setting because all children can have them, so no one stands out, but some children will use them more than others. Most importantly, children will be using their own art to remember the vowel sounds.

Consonant Blends/Digraphs. Some children may not benefit from learning digraphs using similar blends, or initial letters in the process. Children who have difficulty distinguishing phonemes may have difficulty distinguishing between similar blends. A sharper contrast is needed to stress the significance of blends in these cases. For example children can be presented with sl and pr words to identify words that begin with sl (*sloppy*, *slow*, *slam*) and pr (*present*, *protect*).

Vowel Patterns

1. *Concentration.* This is a fun game that can be played by partners or even small groups in a class. A deck of 16–20 cards is placed face down in groups of fours or fives. The pattern being studied during the week should be featured in the deck. If other patterns are known, they can be included as well; however, students only get points for the featured pattern. Another option is to give extra points for the featured pattern and less to other matches. The first player starts the game by turning over two cards. If he or she is able to identify a common feature of the two words shown, and the other players agree, the two cards are set aside, a predetermined number of points is added to the player's scorecard, and two more cards are turned over. The same process continues until the player does not find a match. The two cards that are not matched are returned to the array of cards, and the next player proceeds in the same way. The game ends when no more matches can be made. The player with the largest number of matches wins.

2. *Word sorts.* These are excellent activities that can help teachers to reinforce knowledge of vowel patterns. For example, if the pattern studied during the week was the silent-e pattern, then a word sort containing these words can be created so that students can separate the silent-e words from other patterns. As children learn more patterns, sorts can include different vowel combinations so as to reinforce each pattern. Words that are exceptions to the rules should also be included in the sort.

3. *Word wheels.* Students needing extra support with vowel patterns can construct a word wheel. This game can be assigned for homework, as an individual classwork activity, or as a game to play for reinforcement. Parents can be encouraged to keep word wheels in the car for daily practice to and from school. A word wheel is easy to construct. Two posterboard circles (one smaller than the other) are fastened together through their centers so that they can rotate without difficulty. An initial consonant or an initial blend can be written on the inner circle with an opening next to it. The inner circle can be lined with letters to add to the blends or initial consonant letters to form words. Common basic rhymes can also be used to line the outer circle. Another variation of the word wheel is to print word endings and suffixes on the outer wheel and various root words on the inner wheel. The children can practice reading words independently, or the word wheel can be used as a game. The teacher can say a sentence and omit one of the words in the sentence. Children need to rotate the wheel to form the answer that fills in the blank and read it out loud.

4. *Flip books.* Ganske (2000) recommends that students make flip books to reinforce onsets and rhymes. The last page in the book is longer than the others and contains a rhyme. Various blends can be combined with the rhyme to form different words. Different combinations can help students to develop reinforcement materials for analytic phonics. Flip books are good for individual class activities, or homework for students who need extra help in learning these word parts as homework or class activities.

5. *Magnetic letters or similar letter sets.* Magnetic letters that differentiate between consonants and vowels by color can be purchased to teach phonics. The color selected to differentiate vowels is not relevant; however, once a color is chosen to distinguish vowels from other letters, it should be consistent. If teachers cannot purchase magnetic letter sets, or letter cubes, they can create alphabets by using index cards. Cheyney and Cohen

(1999) suggest that vowels be red, digraphs blue (referred to as Blues Brothers), and blends green. By consistently presenting these word parts in colors, teachers are helping children to better develop the ability to recognize these word parts and to differentiate between them.

As children learn to form words—for example, *cat*—they will be able to form *bat*, *rat*, *mat*, and *sat* by removing just the initial letter. The same activity will work well with ending sounds—for example, by changing the last consonant in *cat* to form *car* or *can*. The vowel sound, or medial sound, can also be modified to create other words (e.g., *cut* or *cot*). As children learn to represent the simple consonant–vowel–consonant pattern, blends and digraphs can be introduced. This substitution activity can be used in large groups, in small groups, or one-on-one with a child. The value of this activity lies in the fact that it allows children to practice and master sound–symbol connections.

MAKING WORDS PLUS

Making Words was originally designed as a whole-class activity. Our research in large, urban elementary schools with diverse student populations has led us to conclude that some adaptations need to be made for some students with disabilities or some ELLs (Vaughn, Hughes, Schumm, & Klingner, 1998). Here are some suggestions for adaptations of Making Words for students with special needs:

- Make certain that words are part of the student's listening vocabulary.
- Hold small-group mini-sessions with students before and after the large-group lesson, to provide confidence in participating in the whole-class lesson and extra reinforcement afterward.
- Make certain that each whole-class lesson includes a review of previously taught patterns.
- In classes with more than 30 students and a large range of student reading levels, you may want to hold two sessions—one for students who need more support, and one for students who need less support.

TEACHING WORD-READING STRATEGIES

Many students with decoding problems take a "shotgun" approach to reading new or difficult words. Teaching word-reading strategies can provide students with a system for reading words. Brown (2003) suggests that the strategies can be taught while listening to a student's oral reading (see the following Research Brief).

RESEARCH BRIEF Responding to Student Miscues

When primary students are engaged in oral reading, sometimes they get stuck. What's the teacher to do? The prompts that a teacher provides send messages to students about how to decode. Therefore, it seems important for the prompts to be thought of as a critical component of instruction. Kathleen Brown (2003) conducted a review of the research and a content analysis of instructional materials to see what recommendations were offered to teachers. The research literature provided very little information. The clearest recommendation was to wait to provide responses until a student has had time to self-correct, and to wait until a student finishes a meaningful phrase or sentence.

Recommendations from instructional materials for teachers were sometimes related to a particular theoretical orientation. Bottom-up-oriented authors recommended providing prompts that attend to the code. Top-down-oriented authors recommended prompts that used context cues. Other materials were just "all over the map" in terms of recommendations.

Brown has offered a template for providing prompts that reflect the reader's developmental stage in reading. All students should be given the opportunity for self-correction before a teacher intervenes.

TEACHING SPELLING

Gordon, Vaughn, and Schumm (1993) conducted a review of the literature on spelling instruction for students with disabilities. The review indicated that students with difficulties in learning to spell benefit from focusing on fewer words at a time. The typical 20-word spelling list may be just too much. Peer tutoring and using a variety of modalities (writing, tracing, letter tiles, keyboarding) also seem to help.

PARENT POINTER ☞ Cued Spelling

Topping and his colleagues at the University of Dundee in Scotland have developed a procedure for parents to assist their children with spelling. The procedure, called *cued spelling*, helps children learn to spell words through cue generation. In a cued spelling session, a student learns five words. The parent reads the word; the student reads the word. Then they analyze the word together for features that can help the student remember the word—cues. Steps for a cued spelling session, as well as materials lists and pointers, can be found online (*www.dundee.ac.uk/TRWresources/CSHTDI.htm*).

Level 3: Intensive Support

Students needing intensive support in phonics and spelling need to be identified as early as possible for intervention. The earlier such students are identified, the more likely they will be to get on the right track to reading and writing. There are a number of approaches to intensive support. Chapter 4 has discussed Reading Recovery as one method of early intervention in reading; additional approaches follow.

The approach you choose is dependent on a number of factors: (1) relevance of the approach to a student's diagnosed needs; (2) coordination of the approach with the school's reading program; (3) your own training in implementing the approach; and (4) resources in terms of time, materials, and personnel for implementing the approach.

ORTON–GILLINGHAM APPROACH

The Orton–Gillingham approach begins with the teaching of individual letters paired with their sounds through a combined visual, auditory, kinesthetic, and tactile approach (Orton, 1966). The method involves first tracing each letter while the learner says the name and sound, and then blending letters together to read words, sentences, and finally short stories constructed to contain only the sounds taught. Spelling dictation is also part of the lessons. More advanced lessons involve teaching learners to blend syllables together and read more complex selections. Teachers must be specially trained to use the Orton–Gillingham method.

If the program is followed as designed, students receive instruction five days a week for a two-year period. Sessions last one hour each, and activities are changed every 10 minutes. The latter is a plus for students with attention disorders, because it keeps them involved and the lesson moving. The advantage of this approach is that students obtain explicit instruction in sound–letter associations.

DIRECT INSTRUCTION READING

In the direct instruction (DI) approach, students are taught letter sounds (not letter names) in the beginning stages of the program through highly structured use of cueing and reinforcement procedures derived from behavioral analysis (Carnine, Silbert, & Kame'enui, 1996; Englemann & Bruner, 1969). Instruction proceeds from letter sounds to blending, to reading in context. DI is highly scripted, with the teacher using a flip book containing both the stimuli for the children to respond to and a script of what the teacher is to say. Lessons are fast-paced with high student involvement. Children practice in specially constructed books containing sounds to be taught. Students receive frequent, specific feedback.

RESEARCH BRIEF Direct Instruction Reading

DI began about 40 years ago with the work of Engelmann and his colleagues. They developed a well-known program called the Direct Instruction System for Teaching Arithmetic and Reading (DISTAR; Englemann & Bruner, 1969). Although studies demonstrated that DI was an effective approach to teaching, many educators thought of it as too scripted and inflexible, and rejected the strategy. In fact, research by some opponents claimed that children who participated in DI programs had higher rates of delinquency and emotional difficulties during their adolescence and early adult years. However, studies published in the late 1990s demonstrated that DI approach models yielded higher achievement levels in student participants (Marston, Deno, Dongil, Diment, & Rogers, 1995). However, in the late 1990s the American Institute for Research published a study that stressed the benefits of DI. Most of these investigations focused on the effects of DI reading for special education populations. The most comprehensive evidence gathered on the effects of DI on reading instruction stem from what MacIver and Kemper (2002) refer to as the "reanalysis of data from project Follow Through" (p. 108). This project was developed to analyze different teaching models. Various programs were implemented beginning in the late 1960s, and some continued for more than a decade. Evidence gleaned from these investigations showed that basic skills models, among which was DI, were the most effective in teaching reading and math. Students participating in DI models outperformed their peers in other Follow Through models. Other longitudinal studies that stemmed from this project continued to show that DI had positive effects on students' test results in the areas of math and reading. In summary, there is substantial evidence for DI's impact on decoding skills. Less evidence exists for its effects on comprehension.

LINDAMOOD PHONEME SEQUENCING

Lindamood and Lindamood (2000) have developed a sequenced program of phonological training for students with severe reading problems. It is a direct training program that focuses on vocalization of phonemes in systematic and intensive ways. Teachers need specialized training for this program.

GLASS WORD ANALYSIS

Glass (1973) developed an intensive remediation system that focuses less on phonic rules and more on student analysis of word patterns. The core of this program is a set of word lists representing high-frequency letter clusters, organized in order of difficulty. Students are presented with a target word for the day on a flash card. The teacher then leads the students through a series of word analysis questions:

- Look at the word *rain.*
- What letter has the /r/ sound?
- What letters have the /ai/ sound?
- What sound does the letter r make?
- What sounds do the letters ai make?
- What is the word?

The drill and scripts are fairly easy to follow. Teachers and paraprofessionals can learn to lead students though the drills with relatively little training.

SNAPSHOTS

Teaching the Code in a First-Grade Classroom

Meg Reynolds's school district requires benchmark testing for first graders three times a year—at the beginning, middle, and end of the year. As part of this benchmark testing, Meg administers tests in phonics individually to all 25 students. She also gives group-administered benchmark spelling tests three times a year. Meg uses the beginning and midyear assessments to make decisions about grouping students for word study instruction. Meg typically has three or four word study groups, depending on student needs. She combines phonics and spelling instruction for her students during 30-minute word study sessions each day. Meg has devised a rotation system for the groups, including teacher-led small-group instruction, computer-based practice, and word study center activities. Because parent involvement in helping students with spelling tests is so important, Meg provides parents and students with specific home learning activities to help students prepare for weekly tests. She posts these activities on her class website, so that parents can access information.

Teaching the Code in a Third-Grade Inclusion Classroom

Nichole Shea and Maria Sanchez coteach in a third-grade inclusion classroom. Maria, the special educator, rotates between two classrooms, so she is in the classroom with Nichole during reading and math periods. On Mondays, Maria works with a group of five students who are struggling readers. She introduces the word pattern for the week, using small letter tiles. Maria has developed "home versions" of *Making Words* and has trained parents in their use. This gives the five students additional practice at home. On Tuesdays through Thursdays, Nichole and Maria conduct whole-class Making Words sessions. Both Nichole and Maria circulate around the room and make note of students who need additional support. After each whole-class session, Maria pulls students for a reteaching session as needed. During the week Nicole reads books to the students that illustrate the pattern of the week. She also posts a poem that uses the pattern for choral reading during in-between moments. On Fridays she gives spelling tests, which consist of words illustrating the patterns introduced in Making Words, sight words, and a few review words illustrating patterns from previous weeks.

CONTINUING TO DEVELOP STUDENT READING AND WRITING PROFILES

You can record student outcomes on formal or informal assessments of the alphabetic principle, phonics, and spelling on Part V of the Student Reading and Writing Profile (Form 5.6). In addition, you can use the Phonics Elements Profile (see Form 5.3) to provide further information to guide assessment and

CHAPTER SUMMARY

Word recognition is the instant recall of words that occurs during reading (Chall, 1991). Although it is not the only component of the reading process, word identification has to be automatic enough to allow comprehension to take place. The National Reading Panel (2000a) defines phonics skills as the process of linking sounds to letters and then combining them to form words. This process begins with letter identification, letter–sound relationships, and letter formation. As students progress into what Ehri (1995) identifies as the consolidated alphabetic phase, systematic phonics instruction begins to take a prominent role in reading instruction. The National Reading Panel identifies phonics instruction as a crucial part of effective reading programs. However, it is imperative to realize that phonics needs to be taught as part of a comprehensive reading and language arts curriculum, and not in isolation, in order to be effective. There are different approaches to teaching phonics, including synthetic phonics, analytic phonics, linguistic phonics, and combinations of these. Teachers today face the challenge of teaching large classes of diverse learners. They need to be able to assess the needs of each student and provide adequate instruction and support to facilitate mastery of word recognition skills.

KEY TERMS AND CONCEPTS

Automaticity
Analytic phonics
Automatic alphabetic phase
Context processor
Consonant blends
Consonant digraphs
Consolidated alphabetic phase
Conventional stage
Full alphabetic phase
Informal reading inventory (IRI)
Linguistic phonics
Meaning processor
Onset
Orthographic processor
Orton–Gillingham approach
Partial alphabetic phase
Phonetic stage
Phonics
Phonological processor
Prealphabetic phase
Precommunication stage
Rhyme/phonogram
Schwa
Semantics
Semiphonetic stage
Syntactics
Synthetic phonics
Transitional stage
Vowel digraphs
Vowel diphthongs
Vowel patterns

REFLECTION AND ACTION

1. Read more about synthetic, analytic, linguistic, and combination approaches to phonics instruction. Write a position statement describing your point of view about how phonics should be taught in the elementary classroom. Is your position in agreement or disagreement with that of the International Reading Association?
2. Based on your view of phonics instruction, think how you plan to give prompts and feedback to students during oral reading. Practice giving prompts and feedback, and make note of how students respond.
3. The field of reading uses a number of different words to refer to word reading: *decoding*, *word attack*, *word pronunciation*, *word recognition*, and *word perception*. There are subtle differences among these words. Examine various definitions of these words in teacher's manuals and reading texts. What term is most aligned to your thinking about word reading?
4. Develop a personal set of goals for becoming more proficient in administering an IRI. Your goals may include observing a proficient administrator in administering an IRI, conducting practice administrations with an experienced observer, or conducting practice administrations on your own.

READ ON!

Adams, M. J. (1990). *Beginning to read: Thinking and learning about print.* Cambridge, MA: MIT Press.

This book contains Adams's comprehensive review of the literature on word recognition and provides a detailed description of the literature related to her model of the reading process.

Carnine, D. W., Silbert, J., & Kame'enui, E. J. (1996). *Direct instruction reading* (3rd ed.). Upper Saddle River, NJ: Pearson Education.

This text includes the research and instructional practices related to DI reading. It includes specifics about the method, including instruction in decoding, comprehension, and study skills.

MacIver, M. A., & Kemper, E. (2002) Research on direct instruction reading. *Journal of Education for Students Placed at Risk*, *7*(2).

The *Journal of Education for Students Placed at Risk* devoted a special issue in July 2002 to recent research on DI reading programs. It was motivated by several presentations of investigations on DI reading at the Fort Worth Reading Symposium in August 2000. MacIver and Kemper's article introduced this special issue.

Stahl, S. A., Duffy-Hester, A. M., & Stahl, K. A. D. (1998). Everything you wanted to know about phonics (but were afraid to ask). *Reading Research Quarterly, 33*

A comprehensive review of phonics research, combined with specific suggestions for the teaching of phonics.

Strickland, D. S. (1998). *Teaching phonics today: A primer for educators.* Newark, DE: International Reading Association.

Want to learn more about phonics and phonics instruction? This book provides a concise yet comprehensive overview for teachers.

SHARPENING YOUR SKILLS: SUGGESTION FOR PROFESSIONAL DEVELOPMENT

1. Need to learn more about the elements of phonological awareness and phonics instruction? Louisa Moats (2003) has written *Language Essentials for Teachers of Reading and Spelling*, a set of four books and supplementary modules that provide resources for the assessment and instruction of both areas. The package includes a videotape demonstrating pronunciation of phonemes. If you have cold feet about teaching phonics, this book will help. Written by one of the nation's leaders in reading education, the primer provides a teacher-friendly orientation to the teaching of phonics.

RESOURCES FOR ASSESSMENT AND INSTRUCTION

Bear, D. R., Invernizzi, M., Templeton, S., & Johnson, F. (2000). *Words their way: Word study for phonics, vocabulary, and spelling instruction* (2nd ed.). Upper Saddle River, NJ: Merrill.

This book provides a curriculum for a spelling approach to word recognition instruction. It includes tools for assessment and instruction.

Blevins, W. (2001). *Teaching phonics and word study in the intermediate grades: A complete sourcebook.* New York: Scholastic.

If you need ideas for making your phonics lessons for intermediate students more than just worksheets, this book can help.

Caldwell, J. S., & Leslie, L. (2005). *Intervention strategies to follow informal reading inventory assessment: So what do I do now?* Boston: Pearson Educational.

This book is written by the authors of a commercial IRI, the Qualitative Reading Inventory. It offers follow-up instructional strategies aligned with outcomes from student performance on an IRI.

Carson-Dellosa, Inc. (1994). *Introducing word families through literature.* Greensboro, NC: Author.

If you are teaching vowel patterns, this book provides lists of books and related activities to link those vowel patterns to stories.

Cunningham, P. M., & Hall, D. (1994). *Making Words: Hands-on developmentally appropriate spelling and phonics activities.* New York: Good Apple.

Cunningham and Hall's book provides all you need to get started. Includes lessons to pack a whole school year.

Fry, E. B. (1999). *Spelling book: Words most needed plus phonics by Dr. Fry.* Westminster, CA: Teacher Created Materials.

This book includes lessons in spelling and phonics for students in grades 1–6. The Teacher Created Materials company also produces materials for hands-on learning of spelling and phonics. In addition they publish other books by Edward Fry, including *Phonics Patterns by Dr. Fry* (1999) and *Informal Assessments* (2001).

Gunning, T. G. (2000). *Building words: A resource manual for teaching word analysis and spelling.* Upper Saddle River, NJ: Pearson Education.

This is a resource for teachers in grades 1–4. It's full of ideas and activities. You'll want to have it on your desk when you do your lesson planning.

Savage, J. F. (2004). *Sound it out! Phonics in a comprehensive reading program* (2nd ed.). Boston: McGraw-Hill.

This book provides a brief but compact overview of instructional practices for phonics instruction. The first chapter details historical background and political issues related to phonics. A CD-ROM phonics tutorial is included to familiarize the reader with phonics basics.

RECOMMENDED WEBSITES

International Dyslexia Association
www.interdys.org

The International Dyslexia Association is an organization that was based on the work of Dr. Samuel Orton and his work with students with language disorders. This organization also has local chapters.

Invented Spelling and Spelling Development
www.ed.gov/databases/ERIC_Digests/ed272922.html

This site provides an overview of spelling development and explains how invented spellings are an integral part of the process of learning conventional spelling.

Loops and Other Groups
www.tpc-international.com/occu/loops and other groups.htm

This website provides guidance and materials for teaching letter formation using the Loops and Other Groups writing system. Teachers have access to two levels of reproducible practice sheets. Level 1 is used to teach all students during the first year of writing instruction. Level 2 contains a review of lower-case letters and focuses on the practice of capital letters. Two other websites also focus on letter formation strategies (*www.concentric.net/~paull/bigstrokes.shtml* and *www.hwtears.com*).

Reading for the Blind and Dyslexic
www.rfbd.org

Reading for the Blind and Dyslexic is a resource for students to learn about receiving books on tape. This may be especially helpful for older students who struggle with decoding skills.

Webbing into Literacy
http://curry.edschool.virginia.edu/go/wil/#ALPHABET

Webbing into Literacy is a downloadable program designed to provide rural Head Start teachers with materials and instruction. This is a multifaceted program that addresses in-class instruction, home–school connections, and transition support for Head Start children entering kindergarten.

FORM 5.1. Letter Names

Letter Names

a j K A z u x N s l	10
d k H b b x z h G P	20
t e T c Q m Y S q S	30
R h c r n V L U q E	40
W X Q L I y P D F O	50
n F y A B a B U v v	60
j g I f l J R o M E	70
O Z p H e N Z m I V	80
w g t o C F s M k D	90
I K u w C r d T W J	100
X G p Y	104

Name:	Total letters read:	Errors:
Date:	Letters read correctly:	

FORM 5.2. Letter Sounds

Letter Sounds

D I l v X Q H o D g	10
v r G F J Q u o Z n	20
j T C M k s W t s F	30
p r p m y R f P x l	40
S O n U J d c b k A	50
u e e i w a q Z U K	60
g c E W j I f x R T	70
B E N O V y b V L q	80
z z Y L C d w m H x	90
M a i G N A t Y B P	100
h h S K	104

Name:	Total sounds read: Errors:
Date:	Sounds read correctly:

FORM 5.3. Phonics Elements Profile

Phonics Elements Profile

Student's name:____________________________________

Skill	Date	Score	Date	Score	Date	Score	Date mastered
Initial consonant sounds							
Final consonant sounds							
Consonant digraphs							
Consonant blends							
Short vowel sounds							
Long vowel sounds							
Closed vowel patterns							
Open vowel patterns							
Silent-e vowel patterns							
R-controlled vowel patterns							
Consonant plus –le patterns							
Vowel digraphs							
Vowel diphthongs							

(cont.)

FORM 5.3. *(page 2 of 2)*

Skill	Date	Score	Date	Score	Date	Score	Date mastered
Schwa							
Silent letters							
Prefixes							
Suffixes							
Compound words							
Contractions							
Other multisyllabic words							

Word Pattern Survey

Name ______________________________ Date ______________

_______	1. rack	_______	19. more
_______	2. fan	_______	20. pale
_______	3. paw	_______	21. rash
_______	4. lick	_______	22. tell
_______	5. sing	_______	23. pill
_______	6. hop	_______	24. sir
_______	7. junk	_______	25. tuck
_______	8. rain	_______	26. mall
_______	9. tank	_______	27. fat
_______	10. say	_______	28. rest
_______	11. ride	_______	29. tin
_______	12. pink	_______	30. rock
_______	13. for	_______	31. tug
_______	14. make	_______	32. same
_______	15. zap	_______	33. rate
_______	16. meat	_______	34. mice
_______	17. sight	_______	35. fine
_______	18. rip	_______	36. joke
		_______	37. hump

FORM 5.5. Word Choice Assessment

Word Choice Assessment

Name ______________________________________ Date ____________________

Directions: Look at each word pair. Decide which one is spelled correctly. Put an × on the line next to the word you think is spelled the right way.

1.	_______ car	_______ kar
2.	_______ sea	_______ cea
3.	_______ faas	_______ face
4.	_______ basket	_______ baskit
5.	_______ wagun	_______ wagon
6.	_______ play	_______ plai
7.	_______ clean	_______ cleen
8.	_______ kold	_______ cold
9.	_______ hope	_______ hoap
10.	_______ goat	_______ goot
11.	_______ photo	_______ foto
12.	_______ sity	_______ city
13.	_______ oven	_______ ofen
14.	_______ feu	_______ few
15.	_______ straw	_______ strau
16.	_______ shook	_______ shouk
17.	_______ nock	_______ knock
18.	_______ author	_______ auther
19.	_______ mission	_______ mission
20.	_______ ghost	_______ goost

FORM 5.6. Student Reading and Writing Profile (Part V)

Student Reading and Writing Profile

Part V: Word Recognition

Alphabet Knowledge

(Alphabet knowledge areas: letter recognition, identification, formation)

Name of test	Date	Score

Student strengths in alphabet knowledge __________

Student areas for improvement in alphabet knowledge __________

Instructional recommendations __________

Phonics

(Phonics areas: see Form 5.3, Phonics Elements Profile)

Name of test	Date	Score

Student strengths in phonics __________

Student areas for improvement in phonics __________

Instructional recommendations __________

Spelling

Name of test	Date	Score

Student strengths in spelling __________

Student areas for improvement in spelling __________

Instructional recommendations __________

SIX

Toward Independence

Sight Words and Structural Analysis

PEGGY D. CUEVAS

VIGNETTE

Adrianna enjoys school. Her fourth-grade teacher, Marjorie Henderson, fills the classroom with print. The class library shelves and reading tables contain books and magazines for the children to read during free time. Several computers along one wall of the room allow the children to read stories online or to complete research for school projects and reports. There are posters and pictures with captions on all of the walls.

The environmental print area is Adrianna's favorite corner of the room. It contains brochures, menus, posters, and empty food boxes from familiar attractions, locations, and restaurants around the city. She is drawn to this area because she can easily read the familiar slogans and advertisements. Frequently, Marjorie has the children go to the corner to order a meal, purchase tickets to a local attraction, or buy clothes and toys from the sale brochures. Adrianna loves to place orders. Marjorie notices that Adrianna has little difficulty reading words like *ticket*, *book bag*, and *hamburger* when she is placing an order at the environmental print center. Yet, when she encounters these same words in running text, Adrianna often stumbles, painstakingly sounds out each syllable, and sometimes simply gives up and asks for help.

When reading on her own, Adrianna sounds out even basic sight words. As a result, her reading is so slow and laborious that she frequently forgets the information in the first part of a paragraph by the time she reaches the end of the last sentence. Because she uses word-by-word reading, Adrianna does not chunk text into meaningful phrases. Consequently, she often does not understand what she reads.

Although Adrianna began the school year with enthusiasm and eagerness to read, her lack of fluency now makes her hesitant to read in front of her classmates. In social studies and science classes, she is less and less able to make sense of what she reads. Marjorie knows that without proper assessment and appropriate instruction, Adrianna will lose the enthusiasm and love for reading that characterized her in early months of the school year.

ANTICIPATION QUESTIONS

- How does a child become an independent reader?
- What instruments are available to assess a child's sight word and structural analysis knowledge?
- What are some research-based strategies for improving children's sight word and structural analysis knowledge?
- How can technology be integrated into instruction for increasing sight word and structural analysis knowledge?
- How can parents and teachers work together to increase a child's sight word and structural analysis knowledge?

INTRODUCTION

Reading text can be a slow and laborious process, almost devoid of meaning, when the student must stop and decode each and every word on the page. The less effort spent on sounding out each phoneme, the more short-term memory is left for actually understanding and remembering the meaning of the text. The ability to immediately recognize a word allows a reader to focus effort on comprehension. The work of Tan and Nicholson (1997) supports the practice of drilling students on words they will frequently encounter in reading, to the point at which those words are automatically recognized. These authors encourage teachers to focus on this challenge to develop automaticity of word recognition in the early elementary years. Teaching sight words increases fluency and makes reading an enjoyable experience rather than a frustrating one.

An awareness of word structure and the ability to define structurally complex words are also related to comprehension and reading achievement (Carlisle, 2000). By fourth grade, most children understand that a long word can be broken down into shorter words, and that these shorter parts can provide clues for the meaning of the original word. The development of this awareness of how smaller parts of words contribute to meaning continues through high school (Tyler & Nagy, 1989). Arnoff (1994) notes that teachers should spend a considerable amount of time on direct instruction in word structure. Enhancing students' spelling ability, vocabulary, and thus reading comprehension will be the result.

SIGHT WORDS

> For instructional purposes these are usually referred to as sight words or sight vocabulary because we would like our students to recognize them in less than a second. Why? Because this enhances their chance of getting to the end of a sentence in time to remember how it began. (May, 1998, p. 5)

The 100 most common words actually make up about 50% of the text we read. The 25 most common words make up about one-third of our written material (Fry, Kress, & Fountoukidis, 2000). We can enable our students to greatly increase their reading efficiency when we teach them to read half or more of the words they encounter in a quick and automatic manner.

What Does Research Say about Sight Words?

Tan and Nicholson (1997) agree that beginning and struggling readers need phonemic awareness and some basic phonics skills in order to sound out regular words like *bat* and *cop*. However, being in command of a sufficient number of sight words—particularly those that are high-frequency and/or irregular in spelling, like *which*, *where*, and *would*—enables children to increase their reading speed, which allows them to increase comprehension. Rapid, context-free word recognition is increasingly recognized as the hallmark of a skilled reader (Stanovich, 1986). Chapter 7 of this book emphasizes the importance of fluency instruction (including repeated readings to text) to help build word recognition speed and accuracy. Chapter 11 focuses on the importance of wide reading to build reading competency. However, systematic instruction in sight words is also necessary for development of reading proficiency.

Working with three matched groups of unskilled readers from 7 to 10 years of age, Tan and Nicholson (1997) presented one group with word flashcards with 20 difficult words from a 500-word story. A second group received training on flashcards with sentences from the story, and the third group (a control group) discussed the flashcard words verbally but did not read them. All of the children understood the meaning of the words. After all three groups received 20-minute training sessions, they had an opportunity to read the story independently, and then they were given a reading comprehension test. Both the word and sentence flashcard groups scored significantly better in story comprehension than the control group. Tan and Nicholson's results showed that only the children who were trained to read words quickly improved their comprehension. That is, their research showed that reading accuracy, speed, and comprehension increased when children knew some basic sight words before they read a story.

In a similar study (Rivera, Koorland, & Fueyo, 2002), a nine-year-old boy with learning disabilities was taught to illustrate his own picture prompt materials for learning basic sight words. The researcher's design measured the student's success at saying previously unknown words and reading aloud a 175-word story created to include the unknown words. The words were taken from the easier half of the original 220 on the *Dolch Basic* (to be discussed later in this chapter) list of sight words. For three sessions prior to the intervention, the student began reading at a different word on the list. After a word had been missed on three consecutive sessions, it became a target word for the study. Twenty-one target words were identified and arranged in three sets of seven. The same words were used to create a story for the student to read at the end of the three intervention sessions. The training sessions provided an opportunity for the student to practice the sight words, using a stimulus-fading procedure. (In stimulus fading, a prompt is gradually reduced by decreasing its intensity.) Each training session lasted approximately 20 minutes.

The child was shown how to make a picture for each of the 21 target words. In each of three sessions, the student dealt with seven words. After the examiner modeled making a picture of the first word, the child was allowed to create word cards for each of the remaining six words. In the modeling portion of the session, the teacher read the word aloud, discussed its meaning, again read the word, spelled the word aloud, and used the word in a sentence. Then the teacher drew and colored a picture illustrating the meaning of the target word. Next the teacher took another of the target words and, after reading the word aloud and discussing its meaning, asked the child to perform the remainder of the tasks. In the first session, large 5 × 8 index cards were used, and the child was given eight colored markers for the drawing and a black marker to write the word. In the second session, medium-size 4 × 6 cards were used, with eight crayons or colored pencils and a black marker for writing the word. In the third session, small 3 × 5 cards and the black marker were the only materials available. In this way the stimulus-fading condition was achieved. At the end of three sessions with each of the seven words, the child successfully responded to all 21 words as sight words.

Why Do Some Students Have Trouble with Sight Words?

Sight words are those words a student can identify immediately, without the use of word identification strategies. When the student must use word attack or word analysis skills to translate print into speech, attention that might be given to meaning and looking at the next words in a sentence is used to identify each troublesome word. This slows down the reading process and may negatively affect comprehension (Dowhower, 1987). Words can be identified immediately only after students are able to make associations between spelling and pronunciation—that is, to learn letter–sound relationships (Ehri, 1995). An even greater number of words can be recognized by sight when students are able to recognize sounds of multiletter, units such as onsets and rhymes. Nonetheless, some students have strong phonological awareness and phonics skills, but limited sight word vocabulary (Vellutino, 2003).

What Are Formal Assessments of Sight Words?

Wide Range Achievement Test—Revised

The Wide Range Achievement Test—Revised (Jastak & Jastak, 1993) is a formal assessment appropriate for measuring sight word ability in both elementary and secondary school students. It is a brief achievement test designed to measure reading recognition, spelling, and arithmetic computation in populations of children ages 5–12 and over. There are two levels: Level I is normed for children ages 5 years, 10 months to 11 years, 11 months; level II is normed for individuals ages 12–64 years. The authors of the WRAT-R stress that the test is designed to measure basic school discourse rather than comprehension, reasoning, and judgment processes. Test administration takes 15–30 minutes, and scoring by hand another 5–10 minutes. The reading test must be administered individually. The WRAT-R identifies performance in relation to age peers and, when used in conjunction with a comprehensive test of general ability, can be used to diagnose learning disabilities.

Peabody Individual Achievement Test—Revised

The Peabody Individual Achievement Test—Revised is designed to obtain a survey of an individual's scholastic attainment (Markwart, 1996). This untimed test is appropriate for grades K–12 and yields scores in six content areas: (1) General Information, (2) Reading Recognition, (3) Reading Comprehension, (4) Mathematics, (5) Spelling, and (6) Written Expression.

Slosson Oral Reading Test

The Slosson Oral Reading Test (SORT; Slosson & Nicholson, 1994) is designed as a rapid estimate to target word recognition levels for preschool children through adults.

The SORT is designed to assess a subject's level of oral word recognition, word calling, or reading level. This instrument is not a diagnostic measure, nor does it measure all aspects of reading (such as word knowledge and comprehension). It is a quick screening test to determine a student's reading level. A basal level is attained when a subject can pronounce all 20 words in a group. A ceiling is reached when none of the 20 words in a group can be pronounced correctly. Basic administration and scoring procedures are printed on each test protocol. Raw scores, grade and age equivalents, percentile rank, standard scores, and confidence levels can also be determined and recorded directly on the protocol. Although the primary use of the SORT is as a screening instrument, it may also be used to assess a student's progress, to determine a student's grade level in reading, and to determine if a student is in need of further diagnostic assessment.

What Are Informal Assessments of Sight Words?

San Diego Quick Assessment

The San Diego Quick Assessment (LaPray & Ross, 1969) is a quick way to gauge a student's reading ability (see Form 6.1). It is a graded word list, formed by drawing words randomly from basal reader glossaries. The graded word list can be used to detect errors in word analysis. It can also be used to determine a student's independent (no words or one word missed), instructional (two words missed), or frustration (three or more words missed) reading levels. It is limited in that it does not tap reading of words in context or reading comprehension. Even so, the results can be used to give teachers a starting point for grouping, instruction, and additional assessment. Data can also be used to determine starting points for administration of an informal reading inventory. You will need to type out each list of 10 words on an index card. Begin with a card that is at least two years below a student's grade level assignment. Ask the student to read the words aloud. If he or she misreads any on the list, drop down to easier lists until the student makes no errors; this indicates the base level. Then have the student read from increasingly difficult lists until he or she misses at least three words. The list in which a student misses not more than 1 of the 10 words is the level at which he or she can read independently. Two errors indicate his instructional level, and three or more errors identifies the level at which the reading material will be too difficult for him.

Fry Instant (Sight) Words

If you want more detailed information about what high frequency words your students know by sight, you can use the Fry Instant (Sight) Words list (see Figure 6.1) as an informal assessment tool (Fry et al., 2000). Put the words on flashcards, and then record which words your students know and need to learn.

Both formal and informal assessments can provide valuable information for the classroom teacher. Monitoring a student's progress by means of the San Diego Quick Assessment or the SORT enables teachers to frequently modify instruction based on their knowledge of a child's progress. As another informal assessment, good teachers will also watch for daily signs of improvement as students quickly read high-frequency words over which they previously stumbled. Rather than wait for the annual, schoolwide standardized testing, teachers with a repertoire of quick assessments that are easy to administer

The First 100 Words (approximately first grade)

Group 1a	Group 1b	Group 1c	Group 1d
the	he	go	who
a	I	see	an
is	they	then	their
you	one	us	she
to	good	no	new
and	me	him	said
we	about	by	did
that	had	was	boy
in	if	come	three
not	some	get	down
for	up	or	work
at	her	two	put
with	do	man	were
it	when	little	before
on	so	has	just
can	my	them	long
will	very	how	here
are	all	like	other
of	would	our	old
this	any	what	take
your	been	know	cat
as	out	make	again
but	there	which	give
be	from	much	after
have	day	his	many

The Second 100 Words (approximately second grade)

Group 2a	Group 2b	Group 2c	Group 2d
saw	big	may	ran
home	where	let	five
soon	am	use	read
stand	ball	these	over
box	morning	right	such
upon	live	present	way
first	our	tell	too
came	last	next	shall
girl	color	please	own
house	away	leave	most
find	red	hand	sure
because	friend	more	thing
made	pretty	why	only
could	eat	better	near
book	want	under	than
look	year	while	open
mother	white	should	kind
run	got	never	must
school	play	each	high
people	found	best	far
night	left	another	both
into	men	seem	end
say	bring	tree	also
think	wish	name	until
back	black	dear	call

(cont.)

FIGURE 6.1. Fry's Instant (Sight) Words list. From Fry, E. B., Kress, J. E., & Fountoukidis, D. L. (2000). *The Reading Teacher's Book of Lists* (4th ed.). Paramus, NJ: Prentice Hall. Copyright 2000 by John Wiley & Sons. Reprinted by permission.

The Third 100 Words (approximately third grade)

Group 3a	Group 3b	Group 3c	Group 3d
ask	hat	off	fire
small	car	sister	ten
yellow	write	happy	order
show	try	once	part
goes	myself	didn't	early
clean	longer	set	fat
buy	those	round	third
thank	hold	dress	same
sleep	full	fell	love
letter	carry	wash	hear
jump	eight	start	yesterday
help	sing	always	eyes
fly	warm	anything	door
don't	sit	around	clothes
fast	dog	close	through
cold	ride	walk	o'clock
today	hot	money	second
does	grow	turn	water
face	cut	might	town
green	seven	hard	took
every	woman	along	pair
brown	funny	bed	now
coat	yes	fine	keep
six	ate	sat	head
gave	stop	hope	food

The Second 300 Words (approximately fourth grade)

Group 4a	Group 4b	Group 4c	Group 4d
told	time	word	wear
Miss	yet	almost	Mr.
father	true	thought	side
children	above	send	poor
land	still	receive	lost
interest	meet	pay	outside
government	since	nothing	wind
feet	number	need	Mrs.
garden	state	mean	learn
done	matter	late	held
country	line	half	front
different	remember	fight	built
bad	large	enough	family
across	few	feel	began
yard	hit	during	air
winter	cover	gone	young
table	window	hundred	ago
story	even	week	world
sometimes	city	between	airplane
I'm	together	change	without
tried	sun	being	kill
horse	life	care	ready
something	street	answer	stay
brought	party	course	won't
shoes	suit	against	paper

(cont.)

FIGURE 6.1. *(cont.)*

Group 4e	Group 4f	Group 4g	Group 4h
hour	grade	egg	spell
glad	brother	ground	beautiful
follow	remain	afternoon	sick
company	milk	feed	became
believe	several	boat	cry
begin	war	plan	finish
mind	able	question	catch
pass	charge	fish	floor
reach	either	return	stick
month	less	sir	great
point	train	fell	guess
rest	cost	hill	bridges
sent	evening	wood	church
talk	note	add	lady
went	past	ice	tomorrow
bank	room	chair	snow
ship	flew	watch	whom
business	office	alone	women
whole	cow	how	among
short	visit	arm	road
certain	wait	dinner	farm
fair	teacher	hair	cousin
reason	spring	service	bread
summer	picture	class	wrong
fill	bird	quite	age

Group 4i	Group 4j	Group 4k	Group 4l
Become	herself	demand	aunt
body	idea	however	system
chance	drop	figure	lie
act	river	case	cause
die	smile	increase	marry
real	son	enjoy	possible
speak	bat	rather	supply
already	fact	sound	thousand
doctor	sort	eleven	pen
step	king	music	condition
itself	dark	human	perhaps
nine	themselves	court	produce
baby	whose	force	twelve
minute	study	plant	rode
ring	fear	suppose	uncle
wrote	move	law	labor
happen	stood	husband	public
appear	himself	moment	consider
heart	strong	person	thus
swim	knew	result	least
felt	often	continue	power
fourth	toward	price	mark
I'll	wonder	serve	president
kept	twenty	national	voice
well	important	wife	whether

FIGURE 6.1. *(cont.)*

and score can save valuable time and tailor strategies and activities to suit the ever-changing reading levels within their classrooms.

RESEARCH BRIEF ✎ Strategies for Reading Sight Words

How can teachers help students recognize words? What are some alternatives to simply instructing students to "sound it out"? Clark (2004) proposes that teachers become coaches, persuading students to apply developing reading skills and knowledge of strategies. Inspired by the work of Marie Clay (2001), Clark encourages teacher to observe students closely and support their use of strategic processes. Such support can come in the form of cues to prompt thought, such as "Look and think what you need to do." Cues to prompt specific action are found in statements such as "Remember, g-h can make an /f/ sound." Knowledge of the relationships between graphemes and phonemes, a conscious awareness of students' instructional histories, and an awareness of students' individual strengths and weaknesses can all contribute to a successful coaching experience. Using effective coaching, teachers can support students on a moment-to-moment basis as they increase their ability to read words at sight.

How Do You Provide Differentiated Instruction in Sight Words?

Level 1: High-Quality Core Instruction

WEEKLY SPELLING TESTS

You can introduce words from the Fry Instant (Sight) Words (see Figure 6.1) as part of your regular spelling program. Weekly spelling tests can serve as ongoing assessments of student mastery of sight words. Make certain that when you introduce the words, you introduce them in context; this is particularly important for English-language learners (ELLs). Also, provide practice during the week for rapid identification of the words in isolation.

WORD WALL

A *word wall* is an effective tool to provide additional study time for words and word patterns. It creates a classroom environment where word study is seen as important and ongoing. A word wall can be constructed by hanging a large sheet of construction paper on the wall, or simply by using an already existing bulletin board space. The words can be written on construction paper, sentence strips, or file cards.

Word walls can contain teacher-selected words that have been chosen for their frequency, or words beginning with a particular letter of the alphabet, containing a certain sound, or displaying a specific pattern. Words can also be selected by students from their reading in a unit of study or from individual texts read for pleasure. Words on the word wall should be discussed and updated on a regular basis. Discussion of words on the word wall can center not only on the meaning and correct use of the specific word, but on antonyms, synonyms, and homonyms—a wonderful way to expand vocabulary and create interest in words.

Within the classroom context, all children can benefit from the introduction of a word wall. A bulletin board display with words related to a specific unit, words children encounter in their reading, or words that share a common pattern are a few ways a word wall can be used effectively with all children.

WIDE READING

The most effective way for students to become comfortable with high-frequency words is for them to engage in lots of reading. As students read predictable books and those that are within their independent level they will encounter these words many times. Books such as *Are You My Mother?* (Eastman, 1960) and *Brown Bear, Brown Bear, What Do You See?* (Martin, 1996) will help them recognize these words in context and practice them.

PARENT POINTER ☞ Reading Predictable Books

Predictable books are fun to read together. You can encourage parents to read these texts together with their child and, as the child becomes aware of repeated phrases, let him or her be the one to chime in! Parents can help promote oral expression by reading the phrase with an exaggerated yet appropriate volume, intonation, or effect, and encouraging the child to mimic their voices. Local librarians can assist parents in locating appropriate predictable texts. Having fun while reading to children is one of the easiest ways to promote a desire to learn to read independently. Plan a parent night where you demonstrate how to read aloud to children and provide many examples of predictable books.

READING–WRITING CONNECTIONS

Engaging students in activities such as writing short sentences, paragraphs, or even stories using the basic sight word lists can provide them with creative opportunities. In a writing center filled with many types of media, these children can put their thoughts on paper; they can then share them with the class in an author's chair, or with students in other classes by means of a traveling library of student work. Giving an authentic purpose, such as reading their own story to others, provides these students with an opportunity to creatively reinforce skills and provide other students with the opportunity to see and hear the important basic sight words in a new and refreshing context. A class library of such booklets, illustrated by their author, would be a welcome addition to the class library.

Level 2: Supplemental Instruction

FLASHCARDS

For those children in grades 3 and up who need a little extra practice, flashcards may be used to turn this task into an enjoyable experience for the students as well as the teacher. In grades 1 and 2, teachers may want to consider flashcards a part of Level 1 instruction.

Preston (1997) has a unique approach. Most classroom teachers use the Dolch Basic list and teach sight words via the "look–say" whole-word approach. However, Preston recommends a precision teaching method. Since clustering of words facilitates learning, she categorized the Dolch list into 32 categories. Examples of the categories and a few members of each are as follows:

Action words	Other-people words	Question words	Feeling words
put	he	who	hurt
open	she	where	like
start	their	why	thank
buy	you	how	happy

Nicholson (1998) encourages the use of flashcards that are specific to a story or reading passage for sight word instruction. Locate a story that is suitable for the children in your class, or a reading passage required by the curriculum you are using. Select 10% of the words for training. These are words that you believe might cause some difficulty when the students attempt to read the story independently. Put the words on flashcards. Put the meaning of each word on the back of its card. Depending on the passage and the level of the children, you can use either single-word or sentence flashcards—for example, *apple*, or "I like *apple* pie." Tan and Nicholson (1997) found no difference in effectiveness between the two types of flashcards, so the choice is up to you. Present each of the 20 flashcards, one by one, to see if the children can recognize them. As you present a sentence flashcard, point to the difficult word, so the children know this is the one you are focusing on. If the children cannot pronounce the word, then you should pronounce the word or sentence and check to make sure the meaning is understood. If the children do not know what the word means, turn the card around and show the phrase. If they do appear to understand the meaning, ask them to use the word in a sentence. Once the words are well learned, ask the children to guess what the story will be about. Although they probably won't be able to guess the real plot of the story, their predictions will be fun and helpful in focusing their interest on reading.

Using flashcards with sentences or phrases rather than words can be accomplished with a basic sight word list as well. Excellent examples of phrases constructed from the Dolch list can be found online (*www.theschoolbell.com/Links/Dolch/Dolch.html*). Phrases like "*he had* to," "*but they* said," and "*you and* I" are combinations that students are likely to find in text, thus providing them with valuable experience as emergent readers. The phrase cards can be used for additional practice when a few sentences to provide context are glued onto the cards.

TECH TIP Using Downloadable Material for Sight Word Practice

Gursky (*www.theschoolbell.com/Links/Dolch/Dolch.html*) encourages teachers to provide opportunities for sight word practice during the "sponge moments" children have throughout the school day. A most helpful aspect of her website is the availability of student workbooks for sight word practice which can be downloaded. Gursky's recommendations for organization of materials and student progress records will be helpful to teachers of all levels. For example, she suggests printing materials for each list in a particular color. This makes it easy to get stray flashcards and other materials into the proper storage folder or box. You can cut construction paper to 8.5 × 11 inches and run it through the computer printer.

Level 3: Intensive Support

LIMITING THE NUMBER OF WORDS INTRODUCED

Some students truly struggle with recognizing words by sight and need even more help. In order to engage all of the senses in practicing sight words, opportunities should be provided to see the words, say them, and spell them. For students who seem to have the most difficulty, start by limiting the number of words introduced at any one time. Start by introducing three words, and provide ample opportunity for practice and mastery before introducing a second set of three words. If three words seem manageable, then increase the number incrementally.

THE FERNALD TECHNIQUE

A multisensory approach is often helpful to introduce new sight words for students with difficulty in this area. The Fernald technique (Fernald, 1943) and variations of this traditional method have been used for years to provide maximum support to students with reading and related learning disabilities (Tierney, Readence, & Dishner, 1990). Words are introduced through a combined visual, auditory, kinesthetic, and tactile approach.

First, students select a word they would like to learn. The word is written in crayon on a flashcard (visual). Next, each student traces the word by placing a finger on the card (kinesthetic and tactile). While tracing, the student pronounces each part of the word (auditory). Eventually, the card is taken away, and the student traces the word "in the air" and pronounces word parts while tracing. When the student can successfully write the word on a piece of paper without seeing the word, the flashcard is filed away in an index card box for review at later sessions.

PERSONAL WORD WALL

The classroom word wall may be a problem for children with visual tracking problems. Looking up at the word wall and transferring the information to a piece of paper can be frustrating for such students. A manila file folder can be created that a student can keep at his or her desk. When you add words to the word wall, also print those words in the folder for the student.

MAKING IT FUN

A website (*www.Literacyconnections.com/sightwordpractice.html*) provides directions for chants, cheers, songs, and pantomimes. Using an imaginary chalkboard, students say each letter as they "write" it and then say the entire word as they "erase" it. Children "pump iron" as they say the individual letters of a word, and then pretend to hang the barbell on the wall as they say the entire word. In "blast off," children squat on the floor, stand a little higher as they say each letter, and then jump into the air when they say the entire word. When students need additional practice, these activities will be of help to the classroom teacher.

STRUCTURAL ANALYSIS

Analyzing the meaningful parts of a word enhances children's ability to decode words of more than one syllable. In *structural analysis*, a child learns to identify words by breaking them down into *morphemes*, or meaning-bearing units. Free morphemes such as *judge*, *book*, and *car* can stand by themselves. Bound morphemes change the meaning of free morphemes and cannot stand by themselves. *Prefixes*, *suffixes*, *inflectional endings*, *possessives*, and *plurals* are examples of bound morphemes.

Structural analysis differs from phonics in the sizes of the parts of the word being decoded. Rather than focusing on individual letters and the sounds they represent, the student examines prefixes, suffixes, and *root* or *base words*. Knowledge of the high-frequency sight words discussed previously is certainly essential for fluency and understanding text.

Although big words are less frequent, they are usually essential for understanding the complete meaning of text. Many students tend to skip over any word of more than two syllables or more than seven letters. Here is a paragraph from *Sports Illustrated for Kids* (Cunningham & Hall, 1994a) that illustrates the importance of big words for comprehension:

> Few things feel as good as __________ the __________ of your __________ __________ __________. You __________ the thrill of __________ him face to face, and you get to take home a __________ __________.

When easily decodable two-syllable words are added, the paragraph becomes this:

> Few things feel as good as getting the __________ of your __________ baseball player. You __________ the thrill of meeting him face to face, and you get to take home a __________ __________.

Here is the whole paragraph:

> Few things feel as good as getting the autograph of your favorite baseball player. You experience the thrill of meeting him face to face, and you get to take home a valuable memento.

Children can analyze the structure of words as an aid to pronunciation or for use in meaning making. Big words carry a lot of the meaning and content of what is read. Linguists estimate that every big word a child can read, spell, and analyze enables him or her to acquire six or seven other morphemically related words. As children gain skill at structural analysis, their attitude toward big words changes. They begin to say, "I wonder what that word is?" or "Do I need it to understand this sentence?" Instead of just skipping over big words, they develop an attitude that says, "I can try it" (Cunningham & Hall, 1994a).

Brown (2003) suggests that the way readers approach unfamiliar words can illuminate where they are as readers and where they are going next. Good and poor readers differ in their awareness of morphological structure (Carlisle, 2000). Children must understand relationships such as inflected and derived word forms. However, teachers need to recognize how an awareness of word structure is related to whether or not children understand the meaning of words. For example, does a child understand that *help* and *helped* represent two different meanings in a sentence, or that *participant* is the way to describe an individual who *participates* in an action or thought?

According to Nilsen and Nilsen (2002), students are aware, by means of cartoons and video games like Mighty Morphin' Power Rangers, that *to morph* means to change. "By bringing morphology to a conscious level of understanding we can encourage students to increase their efforts to figure out how the meanings of words change" (p. 2).

What Does Research Say about Structural Analysis?

An awareness of word structure is related to the ability to define morphologically complex words, and this ability in turn contributes to reading comprehension (Carlisle, 2000). Particularly, knowledge of inflected forms such as *book*, *books*, *complete*, *completed*, or *challenge*, *challenger* is related to reading achievement. Carlisle (2000) believes that children with learning disabilities may be more dependent on structure, because they have not developed the automatic recognition of words that more skilled readers develop.

Working with 34 third graders (18 boys and 16 girls) and 26 fifth graders (10 boys and 16 girls), Carlisle administered a word-reading test, a test of morphological structure, and a test of absolute vocabulary knowledge. The results of the study demonstrated that for third and fifth graders there is a significant link between the awareness of structure and the ability to define morphologically complex words. In addition, results indicate that morphological awareness and the ability to read derived forms contribute positively to reading comprehension. Both groups were better at decomposing complex forms than at deriving them. For example, being given the word *farmer* and asked to complete the sentence "My uncle is a ___________ [farmer]" proved to be a more difficult task than being given the word *drive* and asked to complete the sentence, "Children are too young to ___________ [drive]." Carlisle concludes that while more research needs to be done on the causal factors in the relationship between morphological analysis and comprehension, his study showed that the awareness of structure and meaning and the ability to read derived words contributed significantly to comprehension at the word and text level at both third and fifth grades.

Harmon (1998) provides profiles of three middle school students that allow the reader a window into successful assessment of independent word-learning strategies and how this assessment might serve to drive instruction. She describes the independent word-learning strategies of these learners of varying ability, and the instructional actions taken to extend and refine their use of such strategies. Independent word-learning strategies such as relying on context; making connections to story events; using ideas beyond the story and language structures; employing word-level strategies (e.g., sounding out, structural analysis, and word appearance); and using the dictionary, syntax, and other relevant information were observed. Harmon concluded that whether or not students used strategies like structural analysis and reliance on context determined how successful they were in becoming independent in their reading. In order to help students become strategic readers, Harmon suggests that teachers must do three things:

1. Assess what strategies students use to figure out an unknown word.
2. Help students think more deeply about what strategies they use and how successful these strategies are.
3. Develop in the students an appreciation and awareness of words.

Harmon continues:

> Students, especially struggling readers need to know that they are capable of making good decisions about unknown words. By the time they reach middle school, these learners have developed ways to cope with unfamiliar words that are unproductive and self-defeating. . . . They must be given opportunities where they can try out new strategic maneuvers that lead to successful encounters with unfamiliar words. (p. 565)

Why Do Some Students Have Trouble with Structural Analysis?

Struggling readers may not have a strategy for decoding longer words that require structural analysis. Perhaps they have mastered the basic sight words and understand how to use word attack skills to identify many unknown words. However, when confronted with a word of more than one syllable, they may panic and simply guess based on context or visual cues. While these are workable strategies in many instances, learning to break a word into chunks that they recognize and to which basic word identification strategies can be applied will provide greater success. If students are not familiar with letter patterns that produce rhymes, they may have difficulty in pronouncing a word.

Still other readers may have difficulty with longer words because these are not part of their listening vocabulary. In addition, students who are not familiar with the pronunciation and meaning of commonly used prefixes and suffixes may have difficulty in determining the meaning of a word.

What Are Formal Assessments of Structural Analysis?

Star Early Literacy

Star Early Literacy is a computerized adaptive diagnostic assessment that can be useful for evaluating literacy development in structural analysis, as well as grapheme–phoneme knowledge, general readiness, phonemic awareness, phonics, comprehension, and vocabulary. The test, appropriate for grades K–3, classifies students as being in the *emergent*, *transitional*, or *probable reader* stage of reading development. The reliability and validity of the test were assessed on a sample of 11,000 students from 84 schools in the United States and Canada. The average completion time for the test is 10 minutes, and it has 25 multiple-choice items. An advantage of Star Early Literacy is the adaptive testing component that selects items of varying difficulty, based on the responses of the individual. Consequently, the number of items each student answers is greatly reduced, and the efficiency of the test is increased. The test is useful for teachers who want to measure early literacy, monitor student progress, and plan instruction.

What Are Informal Assessments of Structural Analysis?

Harmon (1998) provides a list of independent word-learning strategies that can be used by teachers to assess and understand what tools students use when they are confronted with an unknown word. An informal assessment of a student's structural analysis abilities can be accomplished by listening to the student read and noting the type of errors the student makes. For example, does the student easily read sight words and one-syllable words? Does the student have trouble reading words of more than one syllable?

Assessment of students' ability to read morphologically complex words can be done by preparing lists of *transparent words* and *shift words*. A transparent word is one that is fully represented (both orthographically and phonologically), such as *movement (move)* and *powerful (power)*. A shift word is a word that is different (orthographically or phonologically) from the base word, such as *natural (nature)* and *easily (ease)*. Students' ability to say and understand the two types of words may differ and thus drive instruction in a specific format.

These skills include the ability to recognize and use the following:

Inflected forms (*-s*, *-es*, *-ed*, *-ing*, *-ly*)
Contractions (*can not—can't*)
Possessives (*Jack's dog*)
Compound words (*bookshelf*)
Syllables (*computer—com-pu-ter*)
Root words (*complete*)
Prefixes (*incomplete*)
Suffixes (*completion*)

RESEARCH BRIEF Structural Analysis and Vocabulary Development

When students are able to analyze meaningful parts of words, they have the power to expand their vocabularies. Baumann and colleagues (2002) studied the effect of instruction in structural analysis on the vocabulary development of 88 fifth-grade students in a diverse public elementary school in the southeastern United States. Students were divided into four groups. The first group received instruction in structural analysis; the second group received instruction in contextual analysis; and the third group received both structural and contextual analysis instruction. The fourth group simply met to read, discuss, and respond to a young adult book. Results of the study demonstrated that participation in structural analysis lessons enabled students to infer the meaning of unknown words. These results will be of assistance to teachers as they plan and implement reading lessons.

How Do You Provide Differentiated Instruction in Structural Analysis?

Level 1: High-Quality Core Instruction

CONTEXT–STRUCTURE–SOUND–REFERENCE

All students can benefit from the *context–structure–sound–reference* system (Ruddell & Ruddell, 1995). This is a sequential approach in which students first search for meaning clues in the sentences and paragraphs surrounding the word. Next the students examine word parts and pronunciation; lastly, they consult margin notes, glossaries, or dictionaries. The purpose of this strategy is to enable students to move quickly through a passage as soon as the word makes sense within the passage, in order for the students not to forget what they read.

MAKING BIG WORDS

Chapter 5 has described Making Words as a whole-class program for word recognition. Cunningham and Hall (1994a) have developed an intermediate version of Making Words, entitled Making Big Words. Making Big Words lessons are a good way to introduce longer words to students, and to generate class discussions about syllable analysis as well as root words, prefixes, and suffixes. In some intermediate classes (grades 5 and 6) with a large range of student reading levels, Making Big Words might be more appropriate as a Level 2 activity.

GREEK AND LATIN ROOTS

Additional work with Greek and Latin roots may be appropriate for more advanced students. Teaching basic Greek and Latin roots in "teachable moments" as they appear in instruction will give students the opportunity to develop extended vocabularies. Use visual means to highlight the shared element in words that are derived from the same root. Students can illustrate booklets with similar-root words that can serve as classroom dictionaries. In addition, these students can be directed to look for root words and *affixes* (prefixes or suffixes) as they encounter them in content area studies. Hennings (2000) gives several ideas for supplemental work appropriate for more advanced students. For advanced students in the upper elementary grades, Nilsen and Nilsen (2002) encourage teachers to use the popular *Harry Potter* series to illustrate principles of structural analysis. This will allow students to understand such nonsensical words as *sneakscopes* and *omnniculars*.

CONTENT AREA CONNECTIONS

Teaching structural analysis should not be limited to the reading/language arts block. Teaching structural analysis should be a regular part of teaching technical vocabulary in science, social studies, and other content area classes. You'll read more about strategies for vocabulary instruction in Chapter 10.

Level 2: Supplemental Instruction

STRUCTURAL WORD ANALYSIS

For those students who need additional assistance in analyzing words, Harmon (1998) suggests students learn to ask the following questions when they encounter an unknown word:

1. Do I need to know this word to understand what I am reading?
2. If I think this word is important, what do I already know about it?
3. What does the word have to do with what I am reading? What is it referring to?
4. How is it used in the sentence? Does it describe or show action?
5. Do I see any word parts that make sense?

Teachers should model and explain how to separate words into meaningful parts. There is a difference between separating words into meaningful parts and separating them into syllables. For example, the word *bi-o-graph-y* has four syllables but contains three meaningful parts, *bio-graph-y*. Likewise, *chairs* has one syllable but contains two meaningful parts, *chair-s*. Often a word will contain the same number of syllables as meaningful parts, but these will be different. An example is *underplayed*, which has three syllables (*un-der-played*) and three (different) meaningful parts (*under-play-ed*). The teacher needs to model the separation of words into meaningful parts rather than syllables if students are to use these meaningful parts as clues to pronunciation and meaning. Teacher modeling by way of direct instruction often requires enormous amounts of time spent in preparing materials. Students can make a page in their notebook with morphemes that frequently appear in class and can add to the list as they notice derivatives in their reading or conversation (Harmon, 1998). Research indicates that giving students instructional choices promotes adaptive behavior, and that interventions based on student initiatives and preferences produce positive cognitive and social results (Dunlap et al., 1994). Consequently, in secondary content area classes as well as elementary language arts classrooms, allowing students to have a voice in organizing their own lists or booklets and selecting the affixes they believe will be most helpful will have positive consequences in both the academic and social realms.

SYLLABLE ANALYSIS

Syllabication is a structural analysis technique that can be taught to help beginning readers decode multisyllabic words. In syllabication, long words are broken up into smaller syllables. There are five syllabication patterns; these are presented in Table 6.1. For some students who are having difficulty with longer words, an awareness of basic syllable patterns may help.

One way to help a student with syllabication is to have the student place a hand under his or her chin and repeat the word slowly. Every time the jaw moves downwards, there is a vowel, and therefore a syllable. This simple procedure helps students to count how many syllables they need to analyze in a word. Cheyney and Cohen (1999) propose a syllabication strategy called *spot and dot*. It consists of five simple steps that facilitate the process for all children. Many activities can help to reinforce instruction in syllable patterns; the spot and dot strategy can help students to remember the patterns in order to complete the activities. These are the five steps:

1. "Spot and dot" the vowels (children find the vowels in a word and place a dot directly above each one).
2. Connect the dots with a line.
3. Look at the number of consonants between the vowels.
4. If there are two consonants, break between the consonants. If there is one, break before the consonant.
5. If the break doesn't sound right, move over one letter.

Select a few multisyllabic words from a story or poem read in class. Write the words on index cards large enough for children to cut into syllable patterns. Have children apply the spot and dot strategy to break each multisyllable word into syllable patterns. Children should then use scissors to cut the syllable parts. They can classify syllables by using a chart divided into the five syllable patterns (see Table 6.1). Children can then recreate the original words by joining the syllables together. Syllable patterns can also be

TABLE 6.1. Syllabication Patterns

Syllabication patterns	Definition	Examples
C + le	This pattern occurs in two syllable words that end in a consonant and le. The le grabs the consonant to its side before the word is broken. Since children have learned the vowel pattern c + le, this is a good starting place for teaching syllable patterns.	puz-zle bub-ble ta-ble pur-ple
VC/CV	In this pattern, two consonants appear between two vowels. The word is broken between the consonants.	doc-tor win-ter pup-py rab-bit
V/CV	In this pattern, there is only one consonant between two vowels. The word is parted after the first vowel and before the consonant.	be-gan fi-nal ti-ger mu-sic
VC/V	This pattern is similar to the V/CV; however, it is broken after the consonant. It is less frequently found, and therefore should be taught after children have mastered the V/CV pattern. Children should be told to always try separating the word before the consonant first. If this does not sound correct, then they should break the syllable after the consonant.	cab-in rob-in mel-on
V/V	This pattern occurs infrequently. It is difficult to learn and should be taught after all the other patterns. There are two vowels together in these words. The separation occurs between the two vowels.	po-et ru-in cre-ate

practiced by forming words with letter tiles or blocks. Children should be encouraged to break the words apart and recreate various words for practice.

After all words are broken, children can be encouraged to classify the various syllables into vowel patterns. For example, the word *professor* can be broken into three syllables: *pro* (open vowel pattern), *fes* (closed vowel pattern), *sor* (r-controlled vowel pattern).

Level 3: Intensive Support

VISUAL–AUDITORY LINKS

For students who continue to struggle with structural analysis, Peterson and Phelps (1991) suggest a simple technique called visual–auditory links (VALs) to expose students to common base words that will help them decode new words and decipher their meaning. The steps in this technique are as follows:

1. Use *The Reading Teacher's Book of Lists* (Fry et al., 2000) to identify words to teach. This book has an extensive list of morphemes and their meanings.
2. Locate a picture from clip art, magazines, or your own drawing to associate the meaning of the word part. Peterson and Phelps (1991) use an example of someone drawing as an appropriate link for *script* (the Latin root meaning *to write*) and a picture of twins for *duo* (Latin for *two*).
3. Create a slogan or brief saying that will help students recall the meaning. For example, "Scriptus, the Writer" can be the mnemonic slogan (auditory link) for the picture (visual link) of a rabbit writing on a chalkboard, and "Duo, the Twosome" can be a caption for the twins. A transparency for each VAL can be made, and worksheets with smaller pictures of the VALs (without the captions) can be distributed to students for note taking.
4. Create word cards that contain English words derived from the roots of the VAL pictures. The card for "Scriptus, the Writer" contains words like *prescription*, *scripture*, *inscription*, and *postscript*. The card for "Duo, the Twosome" contains *dual*, *duet*, and *duplicate*.
5. Introduce the transparencies informally by asking the students to guess what the root *script* might mean. To reinforce the slogan, the students write it on their worksheets.
6. After presenting the transparencies, have the students form groups, and distribute the word cards. Each student must pronounce a word on the card and use it within an appropriate context in a sentence.
7. Give each group several different roots and ask them to create VALs to share with the class. When they share their links, they should model the procedure used by the teacher and provide word cards for the other students.

Students' VALs can be displayed on bulletin boards or hung from mobiles. As an additional activity, students can construct collages of derivatives found and clipped from newspapers and magazines.

FOCUSING ON MEANINGFUL PARTS

A special word of caution about working with students on structural analysis is needed. Although some words look like derivatives, they are not. Words like *tricycle*, *tricolor*, *trick*, and *triangle* look as if they all have the same meaningful prefix, *tri-*. Write these words on the chalkboard and ask students to eliminate the one in which the prefix *tri-* does not mean *three*. Do this exercise once a day, perhaps asking the students to come up with similar groupings. Remind students that it is important to check each word's context, to see if what they believe is the meaning actually makes sense within the sentence. Certainly, breaking words up into meaningful parts does not always help. *Mother* is not really made up of *moth-er* or *mot-her*, nor is *father fat-her*. However, used in conjunction with other word-learning strategies, looking for meaningful parts can help students approximate meanings for new words. This is especially helpful in content area classes that have technical vocabularies.

Whether you have selected "big words" from a current reading selection or have decided to focus on your students' learning root words and affixes that appear frequently in text within your specific discipline, it is important for the students to do more than simply memorize lists. Remind students of the importance of focusing on the meaningful parts and how each part contributes to a word. You can assist students by writing words on the board and underlining the meaningful parts or by asking students to identify the parts. Cunningham, Moore, Cunningham, and Moore (2000) suggest the following steps:

1. In science, put the word *biology* on the board and underline *bio-*. Explain how the prefix *bio-* means *life* and how this contributes to the meaning of the word.
2. Place *biosphere* and *biohazard* on the board, underline *bio-*, and describe how the meaning of the prefix functions to give a similar meaning to these three words.
3. Have students construct sentences with these words.
4. Have students make a list of five words that contain *bio-* as a meaningful part and use these words appropriately in a sentence.

FURTHER DEVELOPING STUDENT READING AND WRITING PROFILES

You can record student results from formal and informal tests of sight words in Part VI of the Student Reading and Writing Profile (Form 6.2). In addition, you can use copies of the Fry Instant (Sight) Words (Figure 6.1) as a checklist to monitor sight words students have mastered.

SNAPSHOTS

Sight Word Assessment and Instruction in a Fourth-Grade Inclusion Classroom

Mary Ann Miller and Todd Jacobs coteach in a fourth-grade inclusion classroom. Mary Ann is the general education teacher, and Todd is a special educator (or, as the kids call him, a strategy teacher). Todd is in the classroom during the reading/language arts block to assist five students with learning disabilities who are included in Mary Ann's classroom on a full-time basis.

At the beginning of each day, Mary Ann starts with word wall activities for the whole class. Todd adds words to the individual word walls for students who need additional help, as determined by a pretest of the word wall words for the week. These may be students with learning disabilities or other students who need a boost. In addition, Todd supervises the students in creating flashcards to take home to practice the reading and spelling of sight words.

Structural Analysis Assessment and Instruction in a Fifth-Grade Classroom

Sharon Agassi has a class of 30 fifth-grade students. Many of her students are ELLs and are in need of strategies for learning how to decode more complex words, as well as for learning the meanings of those words. In addition to regular instruction using the basal reader, Sharon has Making Big Words lessons three times a week during the reading/language arts block. Each lesson takes about 30 minutes. These supplemental sessions help students with specific strategies for learning longer words as well as meanings of common root words, prefixes, and suffixes. Targeted Big Words are included on the weekly spelling test. During science and social studies, Sharon also makes a point of identifying words with common prefixes and suffixes, and she encourages students to apply what they have learned during Making Big Words lessons. Sharon has noticed that the structured lessons have helped her students develop "word radar," become more confident in tackling longer words, and learn to take the risk of asking questions when they encounter a challenging word.

CHAPTER SUMMARY

Children begin school with eagerness and anticipation—filled with excitement about learning to read. For most children, this eagerness and anticipation are rewarded as they learn first to recognize letters; then to read words; and finally to make sense of sentences, paragraphs, and entire stories. However, for an increasing number of children, the eagerness and enthusiasm with which they greeted the first days of school are replaced by hesitancy and discomfort in reading contexts, because they are less and less able to make sense of what they read. Fortunately, there are many strategies teachers and parents can use to help these children regain the enthusiasm and excitement about reading that characterized their early experiences. Increasing sight word vocabulary allows children to spend less time sounding out words and more time focusing on comprehension. Enhancing students' awareness of word structure and smaller, meaningful parts of words increases their spelling ability and vocabulary. The use of these strategies can thus increase fluency and makes reading an enjoyable rather than a frustrating experience.

KEY TERMS AND CONCEPTS

Affix
Base word
Derivational suffix
Dolch Basic list
Inflectional ending
Morpheme
Morphological analysis
Plural
Possessive
Prefix
Root
Shift word
Sight word
Structural analysis
Suffix
Syllabication
Transparent word
Word wall

REFLECTION AND ACTION

1. Select one of the informal assessments described in this chapter to evaluate students' ability to recognize sight words. Prepare the materials necessary to administer this assessment, and use it

to determine the sight word recognition ability of several students. Do the same with one of the informal assessments of structural analysis.

2. Select one strategy for increasing sight word recognition. Prepare the necessary materials and use this strategy with several students. Do the same with a strategy for increasing structural analysis skills.
3. Investigate several of the websites mentioned within the text and in the list at the end of this chapter. Work with a fellow teacher to locate resources that will be helpful to you in working with students who have literacy problems.
4. Prepare a handout, to be distributed at the next "Back to School" night or PTSA/PTSO meeting, providing several ideas for ways parents can work with their children at home. Use the ideas presented within this chapter, and be sure to direct parents who have personal computers to some of the interactive websites.
5. Begin a literacy website list to be shared with your fellow teachers. Ask others to contribute websites they find that might be useful to others in your school. Perhaps each faculty or grade-level meeting could include a short summary of a new website of interest to teachers.

READ ON!

Cunningham, P. M. (2005). *Phonics they use* (4th ed.). Boston: Pearson/Allyn & Bacon.

In this book you will find practical, hands-on activities and strategies for teaching reading. Rather than subscribing to a single theory, the book stresses a balanced reading program, incorporating a variety of strategic approaches tied to the individual needs of children.

Gunning, T. G. (2001). *Building words: A resource manual.* Needham Heights, MA: Allyn & Bacon.

This book provides everything you need to implement a literacy program based on word analysis skills and strategies. Each section provides songs, riddles, and puzzles to practice and reinforce word analysis skills.

SHARPENING YOUR SKILLS: SUGGESTIONS FOR PROFESSIONAL DEVELOPMENT

1. Check the International Reading Association website (*www.reading.org*) for books and articles related to sight words and structural analysis. While you're on this site, look for new study groups through which you can enhance your knowledge of best practices in reading instruction.
2. Share some of the activities mentioned in this chapter, the websites, and the books in the Read On! section with your fellow teachers. Form a group to discuss how to implement several of the activities. Have a debriefing session after working with your students to discuss things that worked, things that didn't, and ways to improve the implementation of the activity the next time you use it.
3. Work with fellow teachers to share your ideas for using sight words and structural analysis in the content areas. Present your activities to the whole faculty, to encourage others to adopt these methods in working with children in their classes.

RESOURCES FOR ASSESSMENT AND INSTRUCTION

Bear, D., Invernizzi, M., Templeton, S., & Johnston, F. (2004). *Words their way: Word study for phonics, vocabulary, and spelling instruction* (3rd ed.). Upper Saddle River, NJ: Pearson/Merrill/Prentice Hall.

This book contains practical assessment tools and techniques for word recognition and spelling skills. Based on extensive observations and experiences in real classrooms for more than 15 years, it combines discussions of theory and practical assessment tools and techniques with over 250 ready-to-use word study, spelling, vocabulary, and phonics activities. It shows how to work with picture and word sorting, how to use word banks at the beginning levels, and how to incorporate word study into reading and writing.

Callella, T., Samoiloff, S., & Tom, D. (2001). *Making your word wall more interactive.* Huntington Beach, CA: Creative Teaching Press.

This handy manual can help you bring your word wall to life. It includes excellent activities for promoting active learning.

Cunningham, P., & Hall, D. (1994). *Making Big Words: Multi-level hands-on spelling and phonics activities.* New York: Good Apple.

The text includes 150 word-building lessons, as well as reproducible pages and ideas for integrating spelling and reading instruction. The Making Big Words lessons allow teachers to introduce vocabulary, point out spelling patterns, talk about vowel variances, and talk about how words are made up, with a particular emphasis on structural analysis.

Fry, E., Kress, J., & Fountoukidis, D. (2000). *The reading teacher's book of lists.* Paramus, NJ: Prentice Hall.

This book contains over 190 of the most used and useful lists for reading teachers. The lists are organized into 15 sections, each of which contains examples, key words, teaching ideas, and activities.

Hall, R. (1984). *Sniglets: Any word that doesn't appear in the dictionary, but should.* New York: Collier Books.

Intermediate students will love *Sniglets.* This book uses common prefixes and suffixes to coin new words.

Johns, J., Lenski, S. D., & Elish-Piper, L. (1999). *Reading and learning strategies for middle and high school students.* Dubuque, IA: Kendall/Hunt.

Teaching strategies for comprehension, vocabulary, and fluency, as well as reading skills for expository text, are presented in this book.

RECOMMENDED WEBSITES

The School Bell
www.theschoolbell.com/Links/Dolch/Dolch.html

This site is compiled and maintained by a classroom teacher. It contains everything you need to teach basic sight words to your class. After reading the short discussion of the importance of teaching basic sight words go to the bottom of the page and click on "The Dolch Kit." This will open the table of contents, where you will find tips on organization and record keeping, a student practice book, and directions for activities and games. All of the materials are presented in downloadable format. Particularly helpful on this site are the printer-ready copies of game boards and student practice book pages.

Created by Teachers
www.createdbyteachers.com/sightfreemain.html

On this site, you will find free teaching materials for the Dolch Basic sight words. Also included are instructional materials for Dolch phrases and the Dolch noun list. All of the materials are presented in a format for classroom use, as well as in take-home card format. Additionally, there are word searches for each list.

Net Rover
www.netrover.com/~jjrose/dolch/intro.html

This site presents a fun interactive challenge game. Students participate in activities related to the Dolch Basic sight word list.

Quiaweb
www.quia.com/jg/66094.html

Use matching games, flashcards, Concentration, and word searches to test your knowledge of roots and prefixes. You can also create your own activities that can be emailed to friends.

VirtualSalt
www.virtualsalt.com/roots.htm

This list contains common roots and prefixes that make up the building blocks of numerous English words. Roots, prefixes, meanings, and examples of words containing each root/prefix are presented. There is also a table of math prefixes.

National Grid for Learning
www.spelling.hemscott.net

This site provides pages that encourage the development of prefix and suffix knowledge as an aid to spelling. An added resource is a page detailing suggestions for parents to work with students at home.

The Word List
www.thewordlist.com

You will find lots of word games for teachers, parents, and students.

FORM 6.1. San Diego Quick Assessment

San Diego Quick Assessment or Graded Word List (GWL)

GRADED WORD LIST (GWL) SCORING SHEET

Name ______________________ Date ______________

School ______________ Tester ______________

PP	P	1.
see ______	you ______	road ______
play ______	come ______	live ______
me ______	not ______	thank ______
at ______	with ______	when ______
run ______	jump ______	bigger ______
go ______	help ______	how ______
and ______	is ______	always ______
look ______	work ______	night ______
can ______	are ______	spring ______
here ______	this ______	today ______

2.	3.	4.
our ______	city ______	decided ______
please ______	middle ______	served ______
myself ______	moment ______	amazed ______
town ______	frightened ______	silent ______
early ______	exclaimed ______	wrecked ______
send ______	several ______	improved ______
wide ______	lonely ______	certainly ______
believe ______	drew ______	entered ______
quietly ______	since ______	realized ______
carefully ______	straight ______	interrupted ______

(cont.)

FORM 6.1. *(page 2 of 2)*

5.

scanty ____________
business ____________
develop ____________
considered ____________
discussed ____________
behaved ____________
splendid ____________
acquainted ____________
escaped ____________
grim ____________

6.

bridge ____________
commercial ____________
abolish ____________
trucker ____________
apparatus ____________
elementary ____________
comment ____________
necessity ____________
gallery ____________
relativity ____________

7.

amber ____________
dominion ____________
sundry ____________
capillary ____________
impetuous ____________
blight ____________
wrest ____________
enumerate ____________
daunted ____________
condescend ____________

8.

capacious ____________
limitation ____________
pretext ____________
intrigue ____________
delusion ____________
immaculate ____________
ascent ____________
acrid ____________
binocular ____________
embankment ____________

9.

conscientious ____________
isolation ____________
molecule ____________
ritual ____________
momentous ____________
vulnerable ____________
kinship ____________
conservatism ____________
jaunty ____________
inventive ____________

RESULTS OF GRADED WORD LIST

Independent reading level	Grade ___	Highest level at which one or no words were missed
Instructional reading level	Grade ___	Level at which two words were missed
Frustration reading level	Grade ___	Lowest level at which three words were missed

FORM 6.2. Student Reading and Writing Profile (Part VI)

Student Reading and Writing Profile

Part VI: Sight Words and Structural Analysis

Sight Words

Name of test	Date	Score

Student strengths in sight words ______________________________

____

Student areas for improvement in sight words ______________________________

____

Instructional recommendations ______________________________

____

Structural Analysis

Name of test	Date	Score

Student strengths in structural analysis ______________________________

____

Student areas for improvement in structural analysis ______________________________

____

Instructional recommendations ______________________________

____

SEVEN

Practice Makes Permanent

Working toward Fluency

JODI CRUM MARSHALL
YVONNE C. CAMPBELL

VIGNETTE

Shari Willis teaches fifth grade at an inner-city elementary school. Approximately 90% of the school population is on free or reduced-price lunch and scored below the 30th percentile on the reading comprehension portion of their state-standardized test. The school consists of primarily Hispanic and African American students, with a small population of Vietnamese and European American students. Class size is approximately 30 students. A small group of teachers at the school (including Shari) are serving on a task force that is trying to improve instruction for reading and language arts. Just recently the state implemented a retention policy so that students will no longer be socially promoted. In an effort to lead such a reform, Shari's district has mandated that all teachers give the Degrees of Reading Power, an informal reading inventory (IRI), and a fluency test each trimester to track student progress.

Shari has been teaching for eight years. She has a BA in English and an MA in English education, and she recently obtained National Board certification. However, she does not have formal training in teaching English to speakers of other languages. Shari feels pressure to get her students to succeed on state-standardized tests. Although she sees improvement in her students' reading through their class participation and in their portfolios of work, she feels it is difficult to produce the proof her district and state are looking for—improved test scores.

Shari is concerned that all the testing will cause her students to become turned off to reading. She wants to continue to motivate them to read for the sake of reading—for its intrinsic value. She also worries about each student's ability to take tests. Many of her fifth graders are reading at the second- or third-grade level and run out of time when taking timed tests. She wonders if the fluency tests her district has recently mandated really matter. Shari is concerned because she believes that comprehension must be a part of fluency, yet her district measures and reports these two aspects of reading separately. She is looking for the best way to use assessment to improve her instruction and get results from her students without turning them off to reading.

ANTICIPATION QUESTIONS

- What exactly is *fluency*?
- What does a fluent reader look and sound like?
- How do you know if a student needs fluency instruction?
- How significant a factor is fluency in determining reading comprehension problems?
- Can we measure fluency? If so, what assessment tools are available?
- How can we use assessments to guide reading instruction?
- What can classroom teachers do to help students improve fluency?

INTRODUCTION

What do you do with the nonfluent readers in your classroom? Is the rate at which a student reads important to success in reading? As in Shari's case, many teachers in classrooms today struggle with the best way to teach students the skills they need to become successful, lifelong readers. Many times, especially with older students, teachers tend to focus on *what* the students can read, and may not realize that it is also important to observe *how* the students can read. They may wonder if there is even a connection between fluency and comprehension. Students who are more fluent readers are actually able to focus less on putting sounds together to form words, and words together to form sentences; instead, they can focus on the meaning of what they are reading. If a student is reading at an extremely slow pace, chances are that he or she is not even able to remember what was read, or to make much sense of it. Some children seem to be able to read accurately yet still do not read fluently. You may have called these types of readers "word callers." This word-by-word reading limits their speed, and in many cases has a negative impact on comprehension (Allington, 2006). Many students who are unable to read fluently are also found to struggle with all aspects of reading.

FLUENCY

What exactly do we mean by reading *fluently*? Fountas and Pinnell (1999) refer to *fluency* as "the way readers put words together in phrases, the expression and intonation they use, and the speed and ease with which they read" (p. 10). In the National Reading Panel (2000a) report, fluency is defined as "reading text with speed, accuracy, and proper expression" (p. 3-1). If reading is included in the definition of fluency, then comprehension must also be included, as to comprehend is to understand what one is reading, and understanding or making meaning is a vital component of reading. Therefore, the definition of fluency for our purposes in this chapter will be the speed, accuracy, expression, and comprehension one exhibits while reading.

What does each of these components entail? *Speed* simply refers to how fast one can read, or *reading rate*. The rate at which a student reads is usually measured in *words per minute* (wpm). *Accuracy* is the percentage of words read correctly in one minute. When a student is reading words correctly, this usually means that the student is recognizing words with little effort. In regard to fluency, we want to measure how fast a student reads accurately. This is measured in *words correct per minute* (wcpm). Although fast and accurate decoding elements are usually associated with fluent reading, the manner in which a student reads and the expression used are also important. *Expression* refers to the student's *tone*, *juncture* (or phrasing), and *pitch* while reading. The goal is to have a student read in such a way that oral reading sounds like conversational speaking. Students who read fluently should sound as if they are talking. The ability to pause appropriately when reading is known as juncture (slight pauses between words, longer pauses between phrases, and even longer pauses between sentences). The pauses and changes in speed give students clues for chunking words into clauses or phrases (Clay & Imlach, 1971). The raising or lowering of the voice, which provides clues to the type of sentence being read (e.g., a question vs. a statement), is referred to as pitch. The general term most often used to describe all of these components of expression is *prosody* (Johns & Berglund, 2002). The National Reading Panel (2000a) report defines prosody as reading with appropriate rhythm, intonation, and expression. One aspect of prosody is the ability to use punctuation to group words into natural units. Reading with prosody shows an understanding of important phrasing and syntax (Rasinski, 2000).

RESEARCH BRIEF Reading Comprehension and Fluency

Comprehension, of course, is the ability to understand what one is reading. There is a close relationship between fluency and reading comprehension. LaBerge and Samuels (1974) have defined a basic theory of fluency. They believe that students who experience difficulty with fluency concentrate on decoding the text word by word and may not have enough cognitive resources available to help them obtain meaning from what they read; fluent readers decode text automatically and can apply more of their cognitive resources to the meaning of the text. Comprehension, therefore, is an essential factor in the definition of reading and should also be a part of our definition of fluency.

Helping children read quickly, accurately, and smoothly helps improve reading comprehension (National Reading Panel, 2000a). Most of the definitions and aspects of fluency discussed thus far have dealt with oral reading, but is fluency important in silent reading as well?

What Does Research Say about Fluency?

Most people associate fluency with oral reading, as that is the way teachers most often assess fluency. However, fluency is actually a factor in silent reading as well. The rate at which students can comprehend while they are reading silently is important. Think of all the different times that students must read effectively and quickly while reading silently. Students need to perform as fluent readers every time they read independently—whether they are reading a book for pleasure, reading directions on an assignment, or (of course) taking those high-stakes, state-standardized tests. As students grow older and progress through school, the amount of time they are required to read silently increases dramatically.

Why Do Some Students Have Trouble with Fluency?

As defined earlier, fluency entails several important factors, including speed or reading rate (Rasinski, 2000). Although comprehension is the ultimate aim of reading, Rasinski believes that reading rate cannot be ignored as evidence of either extremely slow processing of text or fluent reading. When given the same amount of time, slow readers read fewer words than readers who read at an age-appropriate rate. Teachers should be concerned about the amount of time and energy slow readers have to invest in reading a text, compared to the amount of time spent by their classmates who read at the appropriate level. Even when students demonstrate adequate comprehension, slow, laborious reading leads to reading frustration. Reading rate is therefore important and should not be ignored by teachers. In essence, excessively slow reading is associated with poor comprehension, poor overall reading performance, and eventual reading frustration.

Other researchers believe the most crucial element of fluency is accuracy in word recognition. Fast, accurate word recognition skills should lead to fluent reading. As described in Chapter 6, sight words are words that students correctly recognize quickly and easily. The more sight words a student knows, the more likely he or she will be to exhibit fluent reading (Johns & Berglund, 2002).

There has actually been much research on how inaccurate reading affects reading development, but much less research on the development of fluency and methods for teaching fluency. In *What Really Matters for Struggling Readers*, Richard Allington (2001) wonders if this is because accuracy in word recognition and rate of reading are the easiest elements to measure. He points to various studies on the importance of reading rate. However, he stresses an important caveat:

> We cannot get too carried away with a focus on reading rate. I do think the development of reading fluency and rate needs to be monitored and when children deviate enormously and regularly from general adequacy standards we need to explore the issue further. What I worry most about is the possibility that we literally teach some children slow reading and the slow reading becomes a habit. (p. 72)

We must remember that factors other than speed and accuracy have an impact on fluency. A study conducted with 100 beginning readers found that the early readers who made the most progress not only read accurately with greater speed, but also read with better phrasing and intonation. The students who made the least amount of progress read aloud in one- or two-word segments, while those who made the most progress read in segments of five to seven words (Clay & Imlach, 1971).

Many students have not developed reading fluency because they have not been taught. Until recently, fluency has been a neglected part of the curriculum. If fluency was taught, it was frequently incidental and not a systematic component of reading instruction. The National Reading Panel (2000a) report has ignited interest in this area. More and more tools are now available to help teachers promote fluency instruction in the classroom.

Fluent and nonfluent readers differ not only in fluency, but also in comprehension and self-monitoring. Fluent readers have the ability to group words into appropriate clause or phrase units and to express these units with the proper rhythm, intonation, expression, and pauses. These readers see clauses and phrases as chunks of text and use these chunks to read faster, allowing their oral reading to sound like conversational speaking. They read whole passages for meaning, as opposed to single words or phrases. Their ability to decode text automatically allows them to devote their attention to the meaning of the text. Finally, they are confident readers who are consciously engaged in continuous self-monitoring and are able to make the necessary substitutions and corrections, while always maintaining the meaning of what they read.

Nonfluent readers, on the other hand, read slowly and laboriously because they read each word as a single unit, thus limiting the flow of the passage. They are unable to put words together in meaningful phrases. Instead, they concentrate on putting sounds together to form words, and words together to form sentences, thus leaving little attention available for comprehending what they read. These readers also lack self-monitoring skills; their substitutions are occasionally inappropriate in maintaining the context; and they need excessive assistance when reading age-appropriate materials.

Knowing that fluency (with all of its components) is an important factor in a student's ability to read, what can a classroom teacher like Shari do? First and foremost, teachers must observe and assess students, informally and formally, to find out where they are in regard to fluency development. It is essential that both fluent and nonfluent readers be regularly assessed to ensure that they are making the necessary progress, or to provide more intensive fluency instruction if needed.

Fluency and Assessment

Fluency is considered a critical component of skilled reading and therefore an essential skill to measure. With the call for all children to be fluent readers by the end of third grade, many states and districts mandate teachers to determine students' reading levels, accuracy, and oral reading fluency as part of a comprehensive literacy assessment. In order to design effective fluency instruction, it is essential that fluency be assessed regularly and systematically. Regular and systematic assessment of oral fluency does the following:

- Allows teachers to identify strengths and weaknesses of students who experience fluency difficulties.
- Helps determine eligibility of students for special programs.
- Facilitates early intervention.
- Aids teachers in planning appropriate instructional goals and strategies.
- Determines the effectiveness of instruction.
- Guides instructional grouping.
- Helps teachers monitor student progress toward achievement of goals and objectives.

Since fluency depends on the speed of reading (reading rate), the ability to read accurately with intonation and expression, and the ability to construct meaning from written text, an assessment of reading fluency should evaluate speed, accuracy, expression, and comprehension. The ability to construct meaning from written text is strongly dependent on the development of word recognition accuracy and reading fluency; it is therefore essential that both be regularly assessed in the classroom (Snow, Burns, & Griffin, 1998).

When Should Fluency Be Assessed?

Fluency should be assessed regularly to ensure that your students are making adequate progress and to evaluate the effectiveness of your instruction. Informal fluency assessment can begin as early as the first grade by listening to students reading passages aloud. It is essential that teachers know the characteristics of fluent and nonfluent readers as described above.

What Types of Assessment Tools Can Be Used to Guide Fluency Instruction?

Fluency can be assessed both formally and informally. In its 1999 position statement *High-Stakes Assessments in Reading*, the International Reading Association recommends that teachers "create rich assessment environments in their classrooms and schools" that include both formal and informal assessment measures to advance instruction and benefit students who are learning to read. Both formal and informal assessment measures can be used to obtain various information, such as baseline data and data reflecting student progress. Formal fluency assessments measure *what* students have learned and not *how* students learn. These measures include standardized and norm-referenced tests. Informal fluency measures, on the other hand, use the same text that students read during reading instruction and can provide information on *how* students learn. Teachers can develop various informal assessment measures; when doing so, however, teachers should be sensitive to each child's language variation, culture, and life experiences. The International Reading Association (1999) recommends that teachers take responsibility to educate parents about the forms of classroom-based assessment they use, in addition to standardized tests, that can improve instruction and benefit students learning to read.

What Are Formal Assessments of Fluency?

Test of Silent Word Reading Fluency

The Test of Silent Word Reading Fluency (Mather, Hammill, Allen, & Roberts, 2004) is a norm-referenced test you can use to (1) identify children who may need further intensive assessment in fluency and (2) measure increases in reading skills. This is a timed test that can be administered individually or in a group. Students are presented with rows of words with no boundaries, and are given three minutes to put slashes in between words. This is a quick screening device that can be used to monitor student fluency throughout the academic year. The measure is appropriate for students ages 6 years, 6 months to 17 years, 11 months.

Gray Oral Reading Tests–4

The Gray Oral Reading Tests–4 (GORT-4; Wiederholt & Bryant, 2001) is a norm-referenced battery that provides an efficient and objective measure of growth in oral reading and aids in the diagnosis of oral reading difficulties. The GORT-4 measures reading rate, accuracy, and comprehension. It is individually administered to students between the ages of 6 and 18 years, and consists of two parallel forms that allow you to study an individual's oral reading progress over time. Each form contains 14 developmentally sequenced reading passages with five comprehension questions. The GORT-4 provides five scores: (1) a Rate score (time in seconds to read each passage); (2) an Accuracy score (number of deviations from print made in each passage); (3) a Fluency score (the reader's Rate and Accuracy scores combined); (4) an Oral Reading Comprehension score (number of correct responses made to the comprehension questions); and (5) an Overall Reading Ability score (a combination of the reader's Fluency and Comprehension scores). The GORT-4 has average internal-consistency reliabilities of .90 or higher. The validity research includes studies illustrating that the GORT-4 can be used with confidence to measure change in oral reading over time.

Remember our teacher, Shari, who is concerned that all the testing will cause her students to become turned off to reading and worries about her students' ability to take tests? Classroom instruction determines the success students will have on formal tests. Teachers should provide students with opportunities to learn what they will be tested on and how they will be tested. Students should know that they will be assessed on skills they have received instruction in, in a familiar way. If teachers make connections enabling students to realize that what they have been learning and doing in class is related to what is on a test, they will become more confident and motivated to take the test, and their test performance will increase.

What Are Informal Assessments of Fluency?

A variety of informal procedures can be used to assess students' accuracy levels, reading rates, and oral reading fluency. In order to meet the needs of the diverse student population in today's schools, you should be familiar with a range of formal and informal methods for assessing fluency.

Dynamic Indicators of Basic Early Literacy Skills

The Dynamic Indicators of Basic Early Literacy Skills (DIBELS; Good & Kaminski, 2002) has two subtests for assessing fluency. The Oral Reading Fluency (ORF) subtest is used to assess oral reading fluency. The ORF is a standardized test of accuracy and fluency with connected text and is individually administered to students in grades 1–3. The ORF consists of a standardized set of graded passages that are easy to administer and score.

The Retell Fluency (RTF) measure serves as a comprehension check for the ORF assessment. The RTF measure was developed to (1) prevent students from mistakenly learning that the goal of speed-reading without attending to comprehension is either desirable or the purpose of the ORF measure; (2) identify children who read fluently but do not comprehend; (3) explicitly map out the core components of early reading as identified by the National Reading Panel; and (4) increase the face validity of the ORF.

Assessing Accuracy Levels

As described earlier in this chapter, accuracy is the percentage of words read correctly in one minute. For instructional purposes, accuracy is often divided into three levels: (1) *independent*, (2) *instructional*, and (3) *frustration*. The independent level is the level at which a child can accurately pronounce or decode 99% of the words without any assistance from the teacher; the instructional level is the level at which a child can accurately decode at least 95% of the words; and the frustration level is the level at which reading simply becomes too difficult and the child can only decode 90% or fewer of the words accurately, while comprehending only 50% or less of the material. You can easily determine your students' accuracy levels. However, in order to collect reliable data, you need to ensure the following:

- Appropriate selection of passages.
- Specific directions to students, given in a consistent manner across different administrations of the test.
- Proper scoring.

The following three steps can assist you in obtaining students' accuracy levels:

1. You will need a stopwatch and two sets of two or three passages from a grade-level basal text (one set for you, and one set for your student). Ensure that your student has not read these passages previously. For each passage, give the student specific directions—for example, "I want you to read the following page. When I say 'Begin,' start at the top of the page and read across [demonstrate by pointing]. Do your best, and try to read each word. If you don't know a word, I'll tell it to you. Do you have any questions?"

2. Instruct the student to begin and start the stopwatch. If the student is unable to read the first word after three seconds, tell him or her the word and mark it as incorrect. As the student reads, mark any words read incorrectly. At the end of one minute, tell the student to stop and place a bracket after the last word read. Use the following guidelines recommended by Shanker and Ekwall (2003) to score errors:

- Circle omissions.
- Mark insertions with a caret (^).
- Draw a line through words mispronounced or substituted.
- Use parentheses ( ) for words given to the student.
- Underline repetitions.

Do not score the following as errors:

- Words that the student self-corrects—insert a check mark (✓).
- Punctuation that the student disregards—use an arched line to indicate (∩).
- Pauses the student takes before a word—indicate by drawing two vertical lines (| |).

3. To calculate the accuracy level, divide the number of words read correctly by the total number of words read. For example, if a student read 78 words correctly out of a passage that contains 120 words, the student's accuracy level is 65%. This indicates that the reading material is at the student's frustration level (see Figure 7.1).

The research of Fuchs, Fuchs, Hosp, and Jenkins (2001) indicates that having students read graded passages aloud for one minute and calculating the number of words correct per minute will provide a highly reliable and valid measure of general reading competence, as well as comprehension, for most students. By the second grade, students

---

Correct number of words read ÷ Total number of words read = Percent accuracy

Example of a student's accuracy levels:

99 ÷ 120 = (0.99) 99%	(independent level)
114 ÷ 120 = (0.95) 95%	(instructional level)
78 ÷ 120 = (0.65) 65%	(frustration level)

FIGURE 7.1. Sample calculation of accuracy level.

should be able to read grade-level material aloud with accuracy, appropriate rhythm, intonation, and expression.

Whereas accuracy is the percentage of words read correctly in one minute, reading rate is the speed and pattern of a person's oral reading. Assessing a student's oral reading fluency provides a measure of both accuracy and rate, and is an essential step in informal fluency assessment.

Curriculum-Based Measurement of Oral Reading Fluency

You can easily assess your students' oral reading fluency through curriculum-based measurement (CBM). CBM is a sequence of informal tests developed by teachers to assess basic skills in reading, writing, spelling, and mathematics. In the assessment of reading, CBM includes rate of reading. CBM can be used with all students and is particularly beneficial for use with students with special needs. Teachers can use a series of text samples drawn directly from their curriculum (e.g., samples from a basal text) to obtain oral reading fluency scores. CBM provides the following advantages over traditional norm-referenced tests:

- It is pertinent to instruction, since it is directly derived from the curriculum—in other words, from the same materials used for instruction in the classroom.
- It concentrates on repeated measurement as a means of monitoring student progress.
- It is sensitive to change and performance over time. A teacher can thus easily determine a student's progress across the school year.
- It provides reliable feedback on the effectiveness of fluency instruction.
- It does not require extensive training, needs little time to administer and score, and is inexpensive to develop.

Besides generating quantitative scores, CBM is a practical tool for the collection of qualitative, diagnostic descriptions of students' performance. In addition to obtaining the number of words read correctly in one minute, teachers can note the kinds of decoding errors students make and the types of decoding strategies students use to decode unfamiliar words. Furthermore, teachers can take note of how (1) miscues mirror students' dependence on graphic, semantic, or syntactic language characteristics; and (2) how self-corrections, pacing, and scanning reveal strategic reading processes, along with the prosodic features of a student's reading performance (Fuchs, Fuchs, Hosp, & Jenkins, 2001).

RESEARCH BRIEF ✎ CBM of Oral Reading Fluency

CBM is an effective, reliable and valid measure for assessing students' proficiency and progress in reading, as reflected by oral reading fluency. Hasbrouck and Tindal (1992) define oral reading fluency as the combination of accuracy and rate, expressed as the number of "words correct per minute" (p. 41). Most teachers know the importance of considering both accuracy and rate. When one only considers rate, a student reading 200 words per minute with no errors will show the same proficiency as a student reading 200 words per minutes with many errors. Similarly, when one only considers accuracy, a student who takes three minutes to read a passage and makes five errors will show the same skill level as a student who takes one minute to read the same passage and also makes five errors. Since oral reading fluency discriminates between the two students, it is considered more advanced than rate or accuracy in isolation. Teachers with students in grades 2–5 can use CBM to collect oral reading fluency data to inform important instructional decisions (Hasbrouck & Tindal, 1992).

HOW IS CBM USED TO OBTAIN STUDENTS' ORAL READING FLUENCY SCORES?

Oral reading fluency scores can be obtained three or more times per year—for example, at the beginning, middle, and end of each school year—depending on your school's policy and practices. Determining baseline oral reading fluency scores can assist teachers in planning instructional goals for improving fluency. The most straightforward way to obtain a student's oral reading fluency score informally is to compare one-minute samples of the student's reading to the curriculum-based oral reading fluency norms in Table 7.1. When administering the reading passage, follow the same procedures as described previously for determining students' accuracy levels as previously described. It is once again essential to pay attention to the three important considerations involved in collecting reliable fluency data:

- Ensuring appropriate selection of passages.
- Giving specific directions to the student in a consistent manner across different administrations of the test.
- Executing scoring procedures properly.

TABLE 7.1. Curriculum-Based Norms in Oral Reading Fluency for Grades 2–5 (Medians)

		Fall		Winter		Spring		SD of raw
Grade	Percentile	*n*[a]	WCPM[b]	*n*[a]	WCPM[b]	*n*[a]	WCPM[b]	scores[c]
2	75	4	82	5	106	4	124	39
	50	6	53	8	78	6	94	
	25	4	23	5	46	4	65	
	75	4	107	5	123	4	142	
3	50	6	79	8	93	6	114	39
	25	4	65	5	70	4	87	
	75	4	125	5	133	4	143	
4	50	6	99	8	112	6	118	37
	25	4	72	5	89	4	92	
	75	4	126	5	143	4	151	
5	50	6	105	8	118	6	128	35
	25	4	77	5	93	4	100	

Note. From Hasbrouck, J. E., & Tindal, G. (1992). Curriculum-based oral reading fluency norms for students in grades 2 through 5. *Teaching Exceptional Children*, *24*, 41–44. Copyright 1992 by The Council for Exceptional Children. Reprinted with permission.
[a] Number of median scores from percentile tables of districts (maximum possible = 8).
[b] Words correct per minute.
[c] Average standard deviation of scores from fall, winter, and spring for each grade level.

It is also important to ensure that the levels of the one-minute selected passages are not too difficult. Passages can be taken directly from grade-appropriate curriculum materials with the difficulty levels corresponding to end-of-year benchmarks, or you can decide on 100-word passages from the beginning, middle, and end of your basal reading series.

CALCULATING STUDENTS' ORAL READING FLUENCY SCORES

To calculate a student's oral reading fluency score, take the total number of words read in one minute and subtract the number of errors (words read incorrectly). This gives the number of words correct per minute (wcpm) or the student's oral reading fluency score. For example, a student reads a total of 95 words and makes 9 errors. The student's oral reading fluency score is 86 wcpm (see Figure 7.2).

You can obtain a more accurate oral reading fluency score when you give a student two or three different instructional-level passages to read and calculate the mean or average of the two or three readings. After you have obtained your student's oral reading fluency score, you can use the norms in Table 7.1 to guide the instructional goals for the student. You can check students' oral reading fluency at least every six to eight weeks. Students who score significantly below the 50th percentile need more intensive fluency instruction. The norms table allows you to tell parents and administrators exactly how each student's fluency compares to that of other students in the same grade across the country. Oral reading fluency scores can also be reported to meet state and local requirements.

USING THE ORAL READING FLUENCY NORMS

Hasbrouck and Tindal (1992) compiled oral reading fluency scores from eight school districts' CBM measurement norms that teachers can use to assess their students' reading fluency (see Table 7.1). These scores represent the range of oral reading fluency rates between students at the bottom (25%) and top (75%) of their grade during three periods of the school year. A *norm* represents a standardized score that is established from the scores of a large sample of students at the same grade level. A *percentile* represents the percentage of students who obtained scores equal to or lower than the given raw score. Oral reading fluency norms correlate highly with reading comprehension ability. You can use the oral reading fluency norm in various ways:

- As a screening tool, to identify students who may be at risk for achieving the desired level of skill and fluency in reading.
- To assess your students' reading fluency by comparing their oral reading fluency scores to the norms in the table.
- To identify target fluency rates.

Total number of words read – number of errors = words correct per minute (wcpm)

95 – 9 = 86

FIGURE 7.2. Sample calculation of oral reading fluency scores.

- To monitor students response to fluency instruction progress and their progress over time, particularly students whose fluency is in the at-risk range (25th percentile and below).
- To rank students' fluency performance and tailor instruction accordingly.

Assessing Prosody in Fluent Reading

As described earlier in this chapter, prosody refers to reading with appropriate rhythm, intonation, and expression, and showing an understanding of important phrasing and syntax (Johns & Berglund, 2002; Rasinski, 2000). The National Assessment of Educational Progress (NAEP) provides an integrated scale that can assist you in distinguishing fluent reading (characterized by good prosody) from less fluent reading (characterized by poor prosody). Table 7.2 describes the NAEP's scale, which consists of four levels that differentiate word-by-word reading from reading that reflects awareness of larger, meaningful phrase groups, syntax, and expressive interpretation. Students at levels 3 and 4 are generally viewed as fluent readers, while students at levels 1 and 2 are nonfluent readers. The scale also assesses accuracy and rate.

Monitoring Fluency Progress

After you have determined your students' reading levels, obtained their oral reading fluency scores, identified students who struggle with reading fluency, and tailored your instruction to improve students' fluency (as discussed later in the chapter), you should monitor your students' progress. Monitoring or assessing students' progress is part of effective instruction: It allows teachers to set instructional goals for each student, while also serving as a means to evaluate instruction. The following techniques can be used to help you monitor your students' fluency progress.

TABLE 7.2. NAEP's Integrated Reading Performance Record

Level 4

Reads primarily in large, meaningful phrase groups. Although some regressions, repetitions, and deviations from text may be present, these do not appear to detract from the overall structure of the story. Preservation of the author's syntax is consistent. Some or most of the story is read with expressive interpretation.

Level 3

Reads primarily in three- or four-word phrase groups. Some smaller groupings may be present. However, the majority of phrasing seems appropriate and preserves the syntax of the author. Little or no expressive interpretation is present.

Level 2

Reads primarily in two-word phrases with some three- or four-word groupings. Some word-by-word reading may be present. Word groupings may seem awkward and unrelated to larger context of sentence or passage.

Level 1

Reads primarily word-by-word. Occasional two-word or three-word phrases may occur—but these are infrequent and/or they do not preserve meaningful syntax.

Note. From National Center for Education Statistics. (1995). *Listening to Children Read Aloud*, *1*(1). Washington, DC: Author. (Also available at *http//nces.ed.gov/pubs95/web/95762.asp*)

KEEPING TRACK OF DISFLUENT READING

Zutell and Rasinski (1991) recommend that teachers keep track of the specific behaviors that indicate disfluent reading. To do this, a teacher simply marks a student's errors on a written copy of the selected text. This marked copy serves two purposes: (1) It compels the teacher to pay more thorough and accurate attention to the student's fluency; and (2) it serves as a permanent record of the student's reading behavior and can be used as a source in the overall rating of the student's reading performance. The specific behaviors to keep track of include the following:

- *Pauses*—inappropriate or overextended pauses that are clear breaks in the flow and pace of reading.
- *Sound-outs*—the reader's conscious efforts at figuring out a word's pronunciation
- *Multiple attempts* at a word (including repetitions of the word's correct pronunciation).
- *Run-ons*—the reader's inability to pause appropriately in order to mark a phrase or clause boundary.
- Patterns of *stress or intonation* that are inconsistent with phrase or clause structure.

You should also keep track of text sections that are read in a slow, laborious (word-by-word) manner or with numerous slight hesitations (choppiness). With some practice, you can soon become competent in using this system.

CAUTIONS ABOUT MONITORING READING RATES

Teachers should be cautious when using oral passages to monitor the reading rates of students with disabilities and English-language learners (ELLs). Additionally, when monitoring student progress with oral passages, teachers should consider students' grade level in order to establish appropriate weekly rates of improvement (Fuchs, Fuchs, Hamlett, Walz, & Germann, 1993). Research by Fuchs and Deno (1991) and Rasinski (2000) indicates that reading rate steadily increases as children progress from one grade level to the next, with the number of words increasing most in the elementary school and less in middle and high school. Fuchs and colleagues (1993) provide realistic and ambitious standards for weekly growth in number of words read (see Figure 7.3).

READING FLUENCY PROGRESS CHART

To monitor students' progress, you can use CBM (discussed earlier) and administer one-minute reading passages to determine students' wcpm scores. This can be done on a weekly basis or several times during a grading period. You can plot students' progress on a reading fluency progress chart like the one seen in Figure 7.4.

HAVING STUDENTS MONITOR THEIR OWN PROGRESS

Students can play an important role in judging their own progress. Assessing their own progress can be motivating to them, especially when they can see how their fluency

Grade level	Realistic goal	Ambitious goal
1	2.0	3.0
2	1.5	2.0
3	1.0	1.5
4	0.85	1.1
5	0.5	0.8
6	0.3	0.65

FIGURE 7.3. Standards for weekly growth in number of words per minute in grade-level text read correctly. From Fuchs, L. S., Fuchs, D., Hamlett, C. L., Walz, L., and Germann, G. (1993). Formative evaluation of academic progress: How much growth should we expect? *School Psychology Review*, 22, 27–48. Copyright 1993 by the National Association of School Psychologists, Bethesda, MD. Reprinted with permission of the publisher.

improves. You can teach students to monitor and plot their own progress on charts during fluency instruction. Provide students with a stopwatch and passages that they can read with a minimal amount of assistance. Passages can be taken from basal readers, short workbook segments, or the like. Each passage should contain 50–100 words. Students can do repeated one-minute readings of the same passage and record their wcpm scores on a chart similar to the one in Figure 7.4.

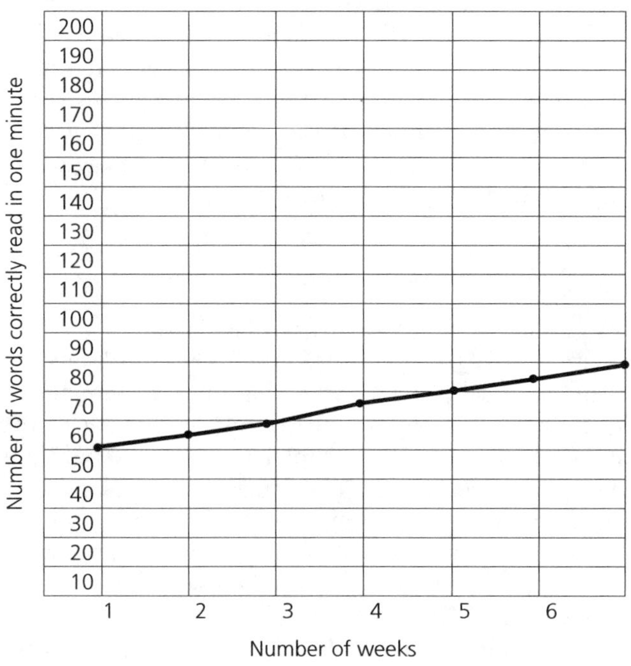

FIGURE 7.4. Reading fluency progress chart.

PAIRED READINGS

You can also teach your students to monitor their reading rate by having them work in pairs. Ensure that students are sufficiently similar in ability and that they can mutually benefit from instruction. Provide each pair of students with a stopwatch and passages that they can read with a minimal amount of assistance. Have students do multiple readings of the same passage. Partner 1 times partner 2's reading. At the end of one minute, partner 1 says "Stop" and inserts brackets around the last word read by partner 2. Partner 1 then marks the wcpm score on a chart. Partners switch and follow same procedures to obtain partner 1's wcpm score.

Research indicates that monitoring students' oral reading fluency, and having students read a text repeatedly, increase fluency and overall reading achievement (Hiebert, 2003; National Reading Panel, 2000a). Fluency should thus be monitored regularly. Teachers should remember that assessing student progress is a continual process and not a final product. Monitoring students' fluency progress through ongoing classroom assessment, and providing appropriate instruction based on the information obtained, increase the chance that students' fluency will increase satisfactorily.

How Do You Provide Differentiated Instruction in Fluency?

Once you have utilized the many different ways to assess fluency in the classroom, how do you go about using this information to implement instruction that will reach all students? If you are like Shari, the teacher described at the beginning of the chapter, you have many students who read at various levels and who are in different stages of fluency development. How do you attempt to serve all your students with strategies that will improve reading fluency? Although fluent reading is identified as an important component of proficient reading, until recently it is was often neglected in reading instruction (Allington, 1983). Fluency can and should be taught. Fluency instruction begins as early as the first grade, as soon as students can read connected text with 90% accuracy, and continues through fourth and fifth grades. However, many struggling readers need direct instruction in fluency beyond the fifth grade.

Level 1: High-Quality Core Instruction

To instruct students in fluency, it is important to be aware of your students' reading levels and to select the appropriate reading materials. This is important for helping students read texts independently, and also for ensuring that the texts you might use for shared or guided reading and for reading aloud are at the appropriate levels. (Reading aloud and shared reading are discussed later in the chapter.) Teachers should use texts that are at the students' instructional level. How to determine the instructional level has been discussed earlier in this chapter. As a general rule, at the instructional level a student will miss no more than 1 word out of 20, which translates into approximately 95% accuracy. If students are practicing on their own, with no support from a teacher, the materials should be at their independent level (98% degree of accuracy). We need to remember, however, that there are many factors involved in matching students with appropriate texts (Johns & Berglund, 2002). Motivation and interest can play just as big a part (if not bigger) in matching students to a text that is appropriate to them.

Two recent research syntheses on fluency instruction for special-needs students shed light on high-quality fluency instruction for *all* students, and provide guidelines for comprehensive instruction in fluency.

RECOMMENDATIONS FOR STUDENTS WITH LEARNING DISABILITIES

Chard, Vaughn, and Tyler (2002) conducted a synthesis of the research on effective interventions that build reading fluency in elementary school students with learning disabilities (LDs). They concluded that students with LDs who have problems with reading fluency are most likely to benefit from interventions that have several components focused on increasing reading rate and accuracy. Chard et al. suggest the following:

- Give students multiple opportunities to practice reading and rereading of familiar text independently, and with corrective feedback. Corrective feedback, combined with repeated readings, can boost students' fluency (mainly by reducing their reading errors).
- Have students practice rereading text that they can decode easily. In other words, the texts should be at the students' independent reading level.
- Provide an explicit model of fluent reading. Adult models seem to be most effective, though audiotaped or computer-generated models are effective substitutes.
- Have students listen to books on tape and on CD-ROM. This will allow children to read repeatedly in order to build automatic word recognition.
- Group proficient readers to guide less proficient readers.
- Focus students' attention on increasing both their fluency and their understanding of the text. Modeling fluent reading also seems to boost students' comprehension, since they not only hear how a proficient reader reads but are also able to comprehend the text instead of centering all their attention on decoding.
- In daily instruction, combine repeated reading with comprehension activities.
- Establish Performance criteria for increasing text difficulty.

RECOMMENDATIONS FOR ELLs

There are many factors that influence reading in another language. These may vary according to the nature of a student's primary language, oral English fluency, attitude toward reading, and specific background knowledge. Hiebert, Pearson, Taylor, Richardson, and Paris (1998) conducted a synthesis of reading research and provide the following suggestions for building fluency with ELLs, several of which also apply to young readers in general:

- ELLs should learn to read in their first language. If this is not possible, the best way of modeling fluency to ELLs is having them see and hear hundreds of books over the duration of a school year.
- Oral proficiency provides the foundation for fluent reading.
- Have ELLs engage in guided repeated oral reading. Encourage students to read passages out loud, and provide systematic and explicit guidance and feedback.
- Reading passages should be at students' independent reading level.
- Provide ample opportunity for ELLs to participate in read-alouds of big books.
- Have ELLs listen repeatedly to books read aloud.

- ELLs should read along with proficient readers.
- Teachers should not confuse fluency with accent. Sometimes the English sounds may be different from the sounds of students' home languages, and ELLs will thus read and speak English with an accent. Teachers should rectify students' mispronunciations of English sounds with care. It is not necessary to rectify mispronunciations all the time. ELLs can be taught to read fluently in English with their native language accent.
- The use of computer software with speech synthesis features allows students to listen to directions, and shows them how words are pronounced.

READING ALOUD

Richard Allington's worries about the possibility of actually teaching children *slow* reading, quoted earlier in the chapter, should remind every classroom teacher of the most basic way to model fluent reading: *reading aloud* to students! Reading aloud is simple to implement, and if the reading selections are engaging, it can be enjoyable for teachers and students alike. Furthermore, reading aloud can be implemented into any classroom and allows one teacher to easily serve the entire class of students at once.

Typically, reading aloud involves one person reading selected material aloud to others who do not have access to the material being read. To use reading aloud as a technique to foster fluency in the classroom, the teacher (or some other fluent reader) should be the person selected to read aloud. In *Wondrous Words: Writers and Writing in the Elementary Classroom*, Katie Wood Ray (1999) writes: "When we read aloud, often and well, we fill our classrooms with the sound of words, well placed and well written, and that sound wraps its arms around the work of young writers and readers who are hard at work learning their craft" (p. 47). Reading aloud allows your students to hear wonderfully well-written stories, accurately pronounced with the right expression and at the appropriate speed. It provides your students with a terrific model of fluent reading. Reading aloud to your students does not require much time (10–15 minutes is recommended) or expensive materials. It is the easiest, fastest way to build fluency!

Many students come to school lacking exposure to fluent reading, which could be a cause for poor reading ability (Allington, 2001). Reading aloud is actually often a favorite technique; it hooks students and makes them want to read on their own. To foster the development of fluency in all students, read aloud on a daily basis from a variety of texts at appropriate reading levels. Reading aloud actually has many advantages in addition to modeling fluent reading: It builds background knowledge, exposes students to a wide variety of genres, makes reading pleasurable, motivates students to read independently, guides students in choosing books, develops higher-level thinking skills, improves listening skills, connects books to students' lives, provides examples of new and different writing, teaches elements of literature, leads students in meaningful discussions, teaches students effective strategies (predicting, questioning, responding, etc.), and ideally will help lead students to a lifelong love of reading (Trelease, 2001). Modeling oral reading also stimulates oral language development, helps students move naturally into reading, stimulates students to react to what is read, encourages active listening, builds classroom rapport, and helps enlarge vocabulary (Johns & Berglund, 2002).

Modeling Fluent Reading. When you read aloud, students will hear how oral reading should sound, which will help them build fluency. It is thus important to pay close attention to the phrasing, tone, and speed you use when you are reading aloud. Accuracy is obviously vital, so make sure you have practiced all selections to be read aloud first, before you read to students. Keep in mind that most of your students read at a much slower pace than you. You will need to slow down and possibly reread sections, especially if you are reading from a copy of a text that the students do not also have available to them. On the other hand, you don't want to read too slowly—you are trying to make the selection enjoyable, as well as be a model for fluent reading.

Choosing Appropriate Read-Aloud Selections. For a successful period of reading aloud, the selections you read must be at the appropriate reading level (as discussed earlier), and should also be engaging enough to make all of your students *want* to listen. In choosing your read-aloud selections, make certain you know the interests of your students, their reading level, and their tolerance level for listening. Haven't you, at one time or another, listened to something being read aloud, only to realize you can't remember a thing about it once it's completed? Your students will get distracted too. Therefore, it is important to select short, interesting pieces to read aloud. Some characteristics of selections you might want to read include strong leads, descriptive passages, interesting or mysterious settings, humorous anecdotes, bizarre facts, or scary stories. These selections can take the format of a book excerpt, a short story, poetry, a magazine article, a newspaper article, or even an email (Marshall, 2002).

Qualities of an Effective Read-Aloud. To make your read-aloud more effective, you need to keep the following in mind:

- Choose a selection that you think your students will find interesting.
- Choose something that you also enjoy reading.
- Practice several times before reading to the class.
- Pause in appropriate places to build suspense.
- Repeat certain phrases or passages, if necessary.
- Do *not* use the read-aloud period as a time to instruct.
- Skip certain parts of the selection if they do not add to the story.
- Watch your timing—do not start reading aloud if you won't have time to finish.
- Read at an appropriate speed, and enunciate clearly.
- Provide time for discussions, so students can ask questions.

You may feel that reading aloud to your students, even on a daily basis, is not quite enough to foster fluent reading. For some students, it may be all the help they need; for other students, however, you may need to offer more support to foster fluent reading. Another type of reading used to engage students in reading is shared reading.

SHARED READING

Another simple and rather inexpensive way to improve fluency is to have children follow along in their own books, without actually reading aloud themselves, while a teacher reads aloud. Called *shared reading*, this allows students to hear fluent oral reading, while being introduced to and discussing literature they would not otherwise be able to read independently. It involves students and a teacher sharing the experience of reading by listening to and rereading text. Like reading aloud, shared reading only has to last 10–15 minutes each day to make an impact.

Don Holdaway (1979), in *The Foundations of Literacy*, calls shared reading a "shared book experience." It is crucial that students have fluent oral reading models as a support while they are following the text with their eyes. Holdaway recommends enriching the students' familiarity with the text through oral cloze, unison reading, language experience, enlarged text, whole-group readings, and repeated readings. Shared reading can be done in any classroom; it requires only a class set of books and a fluent teacher reader. The shared book experience is a way to support the literacy needs of all the learners in the classroom, especially those who are less fluent.

Materials for Shared Reading. In the elementary grades, to increase visual intimacy with print, materials used for shared book experiences are often big books (enlarged text) or text shared on an overhead projector or blackboard. Repetitive language patterns or predictable story structures are often popular and useful for building fluency with younger grades (Johns & Berglund, 2002). Shared readings usually take the form of rhymes, songs, poems, or shorter pieces in the younger grades. It is a good idea to involve the class in your reading selection by allowing the students to ask for rereadings of their favorites.

Shared reading also helps improve literacy with older students, too, although texts of course need to be age-appropriate. For example, if you are teaching older students, you might choose to use poetry, articles, or young adult novels for shared reading. Again, it helps foster a feeling of community and ownership in the classroom if you encourage your students to make suggestions for shared reading titles. We often allow our students to vote on a book (out of several that we offer) as the shared reading selection.

Goals for Shared Reading. Janet Allen (2002), in *On the Same Page: Shared Reading beyond the Primary Grades*, has summarized the goals she hopes her students will achieve through shared reading as follows: "demonstrate reading fluency, build background and content knowledge, enjoy reading, build world knowledge, increase vocabulary, and demonstrate effective use of reading strategies" (p. 7). Like texts for reading aloud, texts for shared reading should be at the students' instructional level, interesting, motivating, connected to the students' lives, and full of information on a wide variety of topics. Allen believes that shared reading texts need to have certain characteristics: They should invite personal connections, should "create intense emotional experiences for the reader, and should expand the world of the reader" (p. 20). It is also important to note that although shared reading should be considered instructional, the reading of the text should be relatively uninterrupted. Stopping occasionally to ask students questions or elicit responses is fine; stopping constantly, or actually trying to stop teach a lesson within shared reading time, is not a favorable method. Shared reading is a useful tool and, like reading aloud, should be a part of literacy instruction for students of all ages and at every level of reading and fluency development.

Round Robin Reading. Shared reading should not be confused with *round robin reading*, in which students are asked to take turns reading the same text out loud, one at a time. Typically, one student starts with the first paragraph (or page), the second student reads the following passage, the next student reads the third passage, and so on. From our personal teaching experience, we find that there is very little success with this approach to reading. Research indicates that there are in fact many drawbacks to round robin reading. Complaints are as follows: It focuses on oral reading performance and not on understanding; it engages only the student who is reading; it teaches students very little; it has little relationship to real life; and it embarrasses poor readers (Johns & Galen,

1977). We and our colleagues have found round robin reading to be extremely limiting. First, there is no guarantee that a fluent reader will be reading. Most teachers use round robin reading as a way to hear all students in the class read orally, and even if volunteers are requested, they can't be sure that these will be the most fluent readers. (How many times have your most struggling readers been the ones to volunteer?) Second, the round robin approach causes distractions, as most readers likely do not have the full attention of all students in the class; rarely are they all focused on the reading (which is the purpose)! Instead, the person reading aloud is focused on the reading; the person who is to read next is rehearsing his or her part; the person 10 seats away is trying to figure out which passage will be assigned to him or her; and so on. It is also unlikely that the text you choose will be at an appropriate level for all students in your classroom. In addition, there is no time built in for practice during round robin reading, which means that mistakes will inevitably be made, setting poor examples of reading, and possibly opening the door for students to ridicule one another. And finally, the many different voices of the various readers in your class will make for a disconnected, nonfluent reading. Students will not hear the same accuracy, phrasing, tone, and pitch from all readers, which could confuse the poorer readers in the class and do more harm than good. If your goal is to have all children read orally, understand what they read, and receive feedback from a skilled reader, then short read-alouds (see below) would be a much better approach.

CHORAL READING

Choral reading is a quick and simple approach to building fluency. Choral reading can be done in large- or small-group settings and requires a class set of the reading material. The teacher first reads the text aloud in order to model fluent reading, making sure to point out *how* it is being read (explaining pauses, inflection, etc.). For the second reading, the students join in by reading with the teacher, all together, in unison. The process of reading together can then be repeated. This procedure works particularly well with materials that are repetitive or texts that contain refrains. Repeated practice of choral reading helps develop fluency as well as fosters collaboration and confidence in students (Johns & Berglund, 2002).

READERS' THEATER

In Readers' Theater, students are assigned text, which they read aloud and act out. They are reading dramatically and with expression, as if they were actors or actresses. You need two or more readers, and it works best with narrative texts or plays (Johns & Berglund, 2002). Activities like this one, which are very demonstrative, have also been known to help ELLs.

PARENT POINTER ☞ Ideas for Home Learning that Promote Fluency

INDEPENDENT READING

It is a good idea to have students read independently at home, especially if there is no time devoted to this during the school day. Teachers might consider creating Home Reading Logs, where students track what they are reading and the amount of time they are spending reading. A good way to get parents involved is to ask for a parent signature, signifying that the parents verify the student has read or that they have listened to or read to their child.

BOOKS ON TAPE

If you have material you would like students to read that they cannot yet read independently, you should consider sending a book on tape home to be used as homework (see Figure 7.5). Students can listen to the tape, but must have a text with which to follow along. Some form of reading log is suggested so students can track what they are listening to, for how long, and where they start and stop each day.

TAPE, CHECK, CHART

The tape, check, chart procedure is an adaptation of structured repeated readings. Students listen to audiotapes of their own reading, and then record their miscues to determine the words per minute. This obviously works best with older students, since it involves complex materials (tapes, recorders, text) as well as training (to show students how to determine miscues).

MORE TIME FOR PRACTICE: INDEPENDENT READING

Fluency is not just a word recognition problem, which is why reading connected text is an important part of fluency instruction. Rehearsing word lists may help students master site words, but it will not necessarily improve fluency. This is because the training may fail to

Recorded Books, Inc. (*www.recordedbooks.com*) is a great source for books on tape. Its mailing address is 270 Skipjack Road, Prince Frederick, MD 20678. Product numbers are included below.

Bauer, Marion	*On My Honor*	95425
Byars, Betsy	*The Pinballs*	94626
Christopher, Matt	*Baseball Pals*	46789
Cleary, Beverly	*Dear Mr. Henshaw*	46792
Curtis, C. Paul	*The Watsons Go to Birmingham*	21670
Hesse, Karen	*Out of the Dust*	21731
Hunt, Irene	*The Lottery Rose*	3A320
Lowry, Lois	*The Giver*	21642
	Number the Stars	12055
Park, Barbara	*Mick Harte Was Here*	95339
Paterson, Katherine	*The Great Gilly Hopkins*	46797
Paulsen, Gary	*Hatchet*	21524
Rowling, J. K.	*Harry Potter and the Sorcerer's Stone*	21723
	Harry Potter and the Chamber of Secrets	21739
	Harry Potter and the Prisoner of Azkaban	21747
	Harry Potter and the Goblet of Fire	21762
	Harry Potter and the Order of the Phoenix	3A370
	Harry Potter and the Half-Blood Prince	22363
Sachar, Louis	*Holes*	21732
Shreve, Susan	*The Flunking of Joshua T. Bates*	3A171
Spinelli, Jerry	*Crash*	94893
	Who Put That Hair in My Toothbrush?	3A056
White, E. B.	*Charlotte's Web*	21611

FIGURE 7.5. Popular books on tape.

transfer when the words are encountered in meaningful context (National Reading Panel, 2000a). It makes sense, then, to say that more time spent practicing reading strategies in connected text will lead to improved fluency. For fluency to develop, students should be reading somewhat longer text—an entire passage or book. Therefore, we would assume that more time spent simply reading independently can lead to greater fluency. The National Reading Panel did not find evidence to suggest that engaging in *sustained silent reading* (SSR) alone would lead to improved reading. However, many researchers determined that there were too few studies to isolate a causal relationship, and that many correlational studies do link better readers to more time spent reading. It has also been found that when SSR is provided with teacher conferences and peer discussions, there is improvement in reading (Manning & Manning, 1984). Students should be given more time to read, in addition to the approaches described above, in order to practice the strategies taught during those other approaches. Students will hear great models of fluent reading in these approaches and when they hear material read aloud (during read-aloud time or small-group activities), and they need to be able to mimic these models on their own.

Giving time for independent reading also allows teachers to work with students one on one or in small groups. Of course, your students will have to be shown how to engage in this type of reading first. It is important to set expectations, help with book selections, have a large classroom library, and possibly even establish a comfortable reading corner. It takes a lot of time and effort on your part to get students accustomed to the freedom of having time to read during class—but once you do, the rewards will be worth it. Depending on the age, maturity, and reading level of the students, you might also consider encouraging students to listen to books on tape during independent reading time.

TECH TIP Using Accelerated Reader

One way to improve reading fluency with technology is through the Accelerated Reader (AR) program (*www.rosenpublishing.com/acreader.cfm*). AR has quizzes that correspond to books, and students take these quizzes after reading each book. Some schools set up incentive programs to encourage students to read more and read faster. The AR program helps determine where (at which level) a student should start reading, and it assigns points for each quiz taken. Some schools offer incentives by allowing students to use these points for various things (purchasing items from the student store, attending activities, etc.)

Although widely used, AR has not been without its critics (for a discussion, see the Jim Trelease website, *www.trelease-on-reading.com/whatsnu_ar.html*). As you will read further in Chapter 13, programs such as AR can be helpful when used as part of a comprehensive reading program with a well-trained teacher. When used in isolation, or without teacher understanding of the place of AR within an overall balanced plan for reading, the potential for misuse is present.

Level 2: Supplemental Instruction

CLASSWIDE PEER TUTORING

Classwide peer tutoring (CWPT) is a well-known instructional method for heterogeneous groups of students who function at highly varied skill levels. CWPT is a more formal, structured way of providing instruction to students. All students in the classroom are paired and work simultaneously (Greenwood & Delquadri, 1995; Mathes, Fuchs, Fuchs, Henley, & Sanders, 1994). With CWPT, the teacher's role changes from instructor to facilitator and monitor. CWPT sessions last approximately 15–30 minutes. Implementation of CWPT requires intensive initial instruction, but once students are familiar with the procedure, the prescribed activities become automatic. For the purpose of reading fluency, a CWPT program will require the teacher do to the following:

- Train students in CWPT.
- Develop a script for students that contains detailed description of the activities involved.
- Implement a daily point-earning schedule and public posting of students' performance.
- Select the content and instructional materials for tutoring sessions.
- Pair the students.

Intensive Initial Instruction. Start by explaining the purpose and rationale for the technique. It is essential to emphasize the importance of on-task behavior. It is also important to stress that CWPT requires collaboration and cooperation rather than competition between paired students. Train students in the roles of tutor and tutee by modeling appropriate behavior for both roles. Ensure that students know how to provide feedback for correct responses. Train students (1) how to provide feedback to their partners in a sensitive and useful way, (2) how to correct errors, and (3) how to keep score. Divide students into pairs. Pair less proficient readers with more proficient readers, and also check that students are socially compatible. Then provide students with the detailed script. The script helps students follow the sequence of activities and assists them in providing feedback to their partners in a sensitive and useful way. Have students practice the role of tutor. While students practice their roles, circulate around the classroom, provide feedback and reinforcement, and answer questions as they arise. Have students switch roles and then practice the role of tutee by following the same procedure.

Implementation of CWPT. The more proficient reader (tutee) begins oral reading for 5 minutes. The less proficient reader assumes the role of tutor. After five minutes, the students switch roles. Since the less proficient reader has already heard the text read by the tutee, it should now be easier. While the tutee reads, the tutor indicates errors by pointing to each misread word and stating, "You missed this word. Can you figure it out?" If the tutee identifies the word successfully, the tutor asks him or her to reread the sentence. If the reader fails to identify the word, the tutor provides it. The following are marked as errors: (1) omissions, (2) additions (i.e., words inserted by the reader), and (3) waiting longer than four seconds to supply the word. Self-corrections are not counted as errors.

CWPT also allows students to evaluate their understanding of the reading text. Students use retelling activities to improve reading comprehension. Upon completion of the reading text, students retell what they have read for two minutes. The tutor prompts the reader by asking, "What did you learn first? Second?" If necessary, the tutor may provide assistance. Students switch roles after two minutes.

As students work through the script, they can earn points as a pair. Students may be awarded points for reading correctly, self-corrections, prosody, effort, appropriate feedback, and so forth. Ten points are awarded if the partners believe they put forth a good effort (Fulk & King, 2001).

STRUCTURED REPEATED READING

Repeated reading is a general term that means just that—the reading of a text more than once. Several of the strategies discussed so far fall into the category of repeated reading. Structured repeated reading is a one-on-one strategy used with students to motivate them toward progress while engaging them in a rereading of a text. It is considered "structured" because students keep a chart that shows the progress they make (noting miscues and words per minute) each time they read (Samuels, 1979). Allington (2001) found that this was particularly effective in fostering fluent reading in struggling readers. In order to use structured repeated reading, you need time to work one-on-one with a student. The following steps have been summarized from *Fluency: Questions, Answers, Evidence-Based Strategies* (Johns & Berglund, 2002, pp. 56–57):

1. Select a brief passage (50–200 words) at the student's instructional level and have the student read it orally.
2. Note the student's miscues and time (in seconds) it took to read the passage.
3. Ask the student to retell the story (to monitor comprehension).
4. To determine the words per minute (wpm), multiply the number of words in the passage by 60 and then divide by the time (in seconds).
5. Encourage the student to practice rereading the passage independently for the next few days and then repeat this process, checking for improvement.

Students can practice by rereading on their own, silently or orally, at home or at school. Students may choose to practice repeated-reading passages during independent reading time.

RESEARCH BRIEF ✎ Repeated Reading

Repeated reading of a text is a rather popular method that lends itself to daily classroom routines. Repeated reading is "intended as a supplement in a developmental reading program, not as a method for teaching all beginning reading skills" (Samuels, 1979, p. 403). The method is simple: Students reread short, meaningful passages several times until a satisfactory level of fluency is reached. The process is then repeated with a new passage. The students should be reading interesting material in context. Comprehension may be poor initially, but should improve with each reading as decoding barriers are decreased. The theory behind repeated reading comes from the automaticity theory—that is, the idea "fluent readers decode text automatically and without attention, thus leaving attention free for comprehension" (Samuels, 1979). The teacher's role should be to help students obtain automaticity by giving instruction on how to recognize words, and then providing them with the time to practice. Repeated reading thus allows students to read fluently and understand the text in short segments before moving on.

Repeated reading can be practiced either in a read-along format or independently. A study was conducted in which these two techniques were investigated (Dowhower, 1987). Seventeen readers were selected on the basis of average or above-average decoding ability but below-average reading rate. The students were assigned to a repeated-reading group—one that used a read-along technique and the other in which students read independently. Results showed that the readers' rate, accuracy, comprehension, and prosodic reading were significantly improved with repeated reading, regardless of which technique was used. Gains in repeated reading of practiced passages did transfer to similar passages, but practice on a single passage was not as effective as practice on a series of passages. Prosody was most facilitated with the read-along technique.

Research indicates that repeated reading is also an effective way to improve the reading fluency of students with LDs. Rashotte and Torgesen (1985) compared the reading fluency of students with LDs under two different reading conditions. Students in a repeated-reading condition read stories four times with about (1) 20 words overlapping across the stories and (2) 60 words overlapping across the stories. Students in a sustained-reading condition read four different stories each day. Rashotte and Torgesen found that students in both of the repeated-reading conditions performed significantly better on a measure of reading rate than students who participated in the sustained-reading condition. Greater overlap of words resulted in more fluent reading of the text, while minimal overlap of words demonstrated no greater effects from four readings of the same passage than from readings of four different passages.

REPEATED LISTENING

Repeated listening, also known as "reading while listening," is students' listening to recorded passages (on a tape or CD) while they silently read the printed version (Kuhn & Stahl, 2000). Students need to engage in this activity with materials that are at their instructional level, with verbal cues that are specific, and at a speed they will be able to follow (Johns & Berglund, 2002). Because the model of fluent reading is being provided by a passage recorded on a tape, this approach needs less assistance from the teacher than other activities. Since students are able to engage in this activity independently, teachers must hold students accountable for reading the material assigned fluently. Studies have shown that repeated listening with this type of accountability has lead to increased gains in reading speed, accuracy, and word recognition, and that students with LDs have benefited as well (Johns & Berglund, 2002). Repeated listening can be used with *audiobooks*, or books on tape.

TECH TIP Using Audiobooks

Practicing fluency through shared reading can also be done by using books on tape (or audiobooks). Students listen to a book on tape while following along with the text. Again, the students have fluent reading modeled for them while their eyes are reading the text. While this is more expensive than shared reading (you have to purchase classroom sets of texts, personal tape recorders, headphones, batteries, and books on tape), you are enabling the students to choose their own reading material and to read this way at their own speed. They may also rewind a tape and hear parts over again. With shared reading, students must all read the same text, which inhibits their choice of reading material. Recorded Books, Inc. (*www.recordedbooks.com*) is a good company to use when purchasing books on tape as they have a variety of current popular titles and their books are unabridged and match the tapes verbatim (see Figure 7.5, above). You can also check tapes out from the library, or create tapes on your own. If you have parent volunteers, older grades at your school, or drama clubs or classes, you may also consider using these organizations to record books for your classrooms.

In addition to using audiobooks, you can also help students practice fluency by using computer-based reading programs. Read 180 (Scholastic, Inc., 1999; also available at *http://teacher.scholastic.com/read180*) is a computer-based program designed to help students improve literacy skills. Part of the program consists of books on tape set up in guided reading format. This means that the tape stops reading the story periodically and asks the reader guiding questions. The tape acts as a teacher in this scenario.

Level 3: Intensive Support

If you still have students who need extra instruction in fluency, there are many more activities you can try. Keep in mind that these are more time-intensive and may require extra involvement or attention from you. The following activities should give you a good idea of what to do, and you may eventually create your own activities, tailored specifically to your students' interests.

ECHO READING

In *echo reading*, a fluent reader reads, and students immediately echo the reading by rereading the text. This can be done in whole-class settings, small groups, or individually. Fairly easy material with patterns or repeated phrases should be used for this activity (Johns & Berglund, 2002).

ANTIPHONAL READING

Antiphonal reading is an adaptation of choral reading. Students are divided into groups, and each group reads an assigned part of a text, sometimes alternately and sometimes in unison. This activity works best with poems, rhymes, limericks, or other materials set up for more than one voice. Again, this can be done with a large class or in small groups. If you use a small group, then each person will read a separate piece of the text (Johns & Berglund, 2002).

NEUROLOGICAL IMPRESS METHOD

Neurological impress method (NIM) activities help impress words into a child's memory, assisting the child to imitate correct pronunciation, intonation, and phrasing (Heckelman, 1969; Ringenberg, 1991). To begin using NIM, pick a text with words that the child can already read. Sit side by side with the child, so that you are able to speak into the child's ear. It is important to determine which hand the child writes with and sit on that side of the child. Jointly hold the book between you. Begin by reading aloud together. Read a little faster and louder than the child. Track the words smoothly with your finger as you read. This allows the learner to hear the word just before saying it, and to imitate the intonation and flow of the language. Occasionally lower the volume of your voice to allow the learner to lead the reading. Help the learner gradually take over tracking by guiding the student's hand smoothly under the words.

PARENT POINTER ☞ Preview–Pause–Prompt–Praise

Preview-pause-prompt-praise (Allington, 2006) is an activity where children can apply independent reading strategies to smooth out choppy reading while gaining guidance in monitoring their own reading. To begin, choose a reading that is about 50–200 words long and relatively easy for the learner at first. Choose progressively more difficult materials as a child advances and gains confidence.

In *preview*, the parent and child look at the cover, title, and illustrations while discussing the question "What do you think this story is about?" Next, the child and parent begin to read aloud together. If the child is stuck or mispronounces a word, the parent literally *pauses*, counts to three silently, or waits until the child reaches the end of the sentence. This allows the child to implement learned reading strategies such as self-correction, rereading, and/or decoding. If the reading is still not correct or the child still cannot read the word, the parent *prompts* the child to "Try that again" or "Read that again." If the child still does not say the word, the parent should tell the child the word. The child should repeat the word and continue reading. If the child correctly decodes the word during the pause, the parent *praises* the child for the reading strategy used. It is important that after reading the passage, the parent and the child share their favorite parts of the passage.

SNAPSHOT

Fluency Instruction in a Third-Grade Classroom

When Carol Richards went through her undergraduate teaching program, little was said about fluency instruction. In her 10 years of teaching, Carol frequently conducted choral readings in her classroom; however, she did not have a comprehensive plan for fluency instruction. A workshop at her state reading conference sparked Carol's interest. Since that time, she has attended workshops on fluency and has read quite a bit about fluency instruction. Carol has worked with her grade-level team to develop a plan for regular fluency instruction.

Carol begins the year with IRIs for all of her 25 students. Carol reads aloud to her students daily to model fluent reading. All 25 students are engaged in shared readings and choral readings as part the regular reading program. All students participate in the AR program. Carol starts CWPT for the whole class during the first grading period. For students who need sustained support, Carol continues CWPT thoughout the year. Carol has five students who need extra support in fluency. She has trained a paraprofessional to work individually with these students with repeated readings, and to track their performance during sessions three times a week.

CONTINUING TO DEVELOP STUDENT READING AND WRITING PROFILES

Use Part VII of the Student Reading and Writing Profile (Form 7.1) to record outcomes for fluency assessment and to plan appropriate levels of instruction. As part of your planning, remember that some students will require more frequent assessments of fluency than others. Students who are fluent readers can be monitored less frequently than students who are struggling.

CHAPTER SUMMARY

Fluency is the ability to read text accurately and quickly with intonation and expression while constructing meaning of what is read. Poor readers are often characterized by a lack of fluency. Helping children read quickly, accurately, and smoothly helps improve reading comprehension. Fluency involves other factors as well. Although it is generally associated with oral reading, fluency is actually also a factor in silent reading, since it appears to be indirectly related to silent reading comprehension. Moreover, researchers believe that fast, accurate word recognition skills should lead to fluent reading and that the more sight words a student knows, the more likely he or she will be to exhibit fluent reading. Although identified as an important component of proficient reading, fluency is often neglected in reading instruction. Many teachers have students who read at various levels and who are in different stages of fluency development, and these teachers are looking for the best way to use assessment and to improve their instruction. The good news is that this is not an impossible task. In order to design effective fluency instruction, teachers should perform regular and systematic fluency assessment that can aid them in planning appropriate instructional goals and strategies. Various reliable formal and informal assessment measures are available for accurate assessment and monitoring of fluency. Furthermore, there are many research-based instructional strategies that teachers can use to develop fluency and comprehension. Teachers should thus strive to make fluency an instructional goal, particularly for struggling readers.

KEY TERMS AND CONCEPTS

Accelerated reader
Antiphonal reading
Audiobooks/books on tape
Choral reading
Classwide peer tutoring (CWPT)
Echo reading
Errors
Fluency
Inflection
Juncture
Miscues
Neurological impress method (NIM)
Phrasing
Pitch
Prosody
Reading aloud
Reading rate
Repeated listening
Repeated reading
Shared reading
Sustained silent reading (SSR)
Tone
Words correct per minute (wcpm)
Words per minute (wpm)

REFLECTION AND ACTION

1. We all sound different when we read aloud. You may sound different from a colleague or student. What do you notice when you read aloud? What aspects of reading do you monitor while reading? Write a half-page reflection on what you are doing and thinking as you read aloud.
2. How is silent reading different from reading aloud? Do you monitor your reading differently when you read silently? Write a half-page reflection on what you do to pay attention to your own reading when reading silently.
3. From reading this chapter (and perhaps other professional literature), what do you know about fluency? What strategies will you implement in your classroom or school? Write three goals concerning the fluency of your students that you would like to accomplish. Include one or two sentences (or bullet points) stating how you can reach each goal.
4. What materials will you need to meet the goals you have just listed? Create a "wish list" of materials that would help you become a better teacher of fluency. You might include ways to secure the funding to obtain these materials.

READ ON!

Allington, R. (2006). *What really matters for struggling readers* (2nd ed.). Boston: Pearson/Allyn & Bacon.

Allington reviews research and discusses strategies that work with struggling readers.

Chall, J. S., Bissex, G., Conard, S., & Harris-Sharples, S. (1996). *Qualitative assessment of text difficulty: A practical guide for teachers and authors.* Cambridge, MA: Brookline Books.

This book will help you assess and select text appropriate for your students.

Johns, J., & Berglund, R. (2002). *Fluency: Questions, answers, evidence-based strategies.* Dubuque, IA: Kendall/Hunt.

This is a great resource for classroom teachers to use for building fluency.

Saenz, L. (2002). Examining the reading difficulty of secondary students with learning disabilities. *Remedial and Special Education*, *23*(1), 31–42.

Although this was a study involving secondary education, the article is still worth reading. It describes a research study of 111 high school students with LDs and their ability to read expository and narrative text. Students read two expository and two narrative reading passages. Fluency was measured by counting words read correctly in two minutes. Students then completed 10 comprehension questions. It was found that these students with LDs had a harder time comprehending expository passages than narrative passages. Specific strategies to increase reading fluency are discussed (repeated reading, previewing).

Samuels, J. (1979). The method of repeated readings. *The Reading Teacher*, *50*(5), 376–382.

How to use repeated readings in the classroom is outlined in this article. Research is reported on using repeated readings with developmentally disabled students.

SHARPENING YOUR SKILLS: SUGGESTIONS FOR PROFESSIONAL DEVELOPMENT

1. Write a definition for *fluency* and keep it in a visible place. Refer to it often, for your benefit and for the benefit of your students.
2. Frequently review the National Reading Panel's standards, as well as your state standards. Making sure that you are aware of expectations is a big step toward meeting these standards.
3. Visit websites on reading instruction frequently. Stay up-to-date by reading newly published articles.
4. Consider starting a book club at your school for teachers who want to read professional literature on teaching reading, or specifically on fluency.
5. Talk to your department/grade-level chair about discussing one element of teaching reading at each meeting. For example, you might discuss phonological awareness one month, phonics the next, fluency the following month, then vocabulary, and finally comprehension. This will allow you to share strategies and research with colleagues who are teaching students from the same population as you.

RESOURCES FOR ASSESSMENT AND INSTRUCTION

Allen, J. (1995). *It's never too late: Leading adolescents to lifelong literacy*. Portsmouth, NH: Heinemann.

A teacher-researcher writes on helping at-risk high school students with a balanced literacy program in this great book.

Allen, J. (2000). *Yellow brick roads: Shared and guided paths to independent reading 4–12*. Portland, ME: Stenhouse.

Another great book by Janet Allen that outlines research and instructional strategies for shared, independent, and guided reading.

Allen, J. (2002). *On the same page: Shared reading beyond the primary grades*. Portland, ME: Stenhouse.

This is an excellent resource for shared and guided reading research and strategies for students of all grades.

Allen, J., & Gonzalez, K. (1998). *There's room for me here: Literacy workshop in the middle school*. Portland, ME: Stenhouse.

This is a fantastic example of how to set up and organize a literacy workshop classroom in your school. It describes the literacy project in one middle school and contains great ready-to-use pages in the appendix.

Fountas, I. C., & Pinnell, G. S. (1999). *Matching books to readers: Using leveled books in guided reading, K–3*. Portsmouth, NH: Heinemann.

This directory lists more than 7,000 books for students in grades K–3. Included is information on how to use, acquire, and level books.

Pavalak, S. (1985). *Classroom activities for correcting specific reading problems*. New York: Parker.

Games and activities are shared to build phonic analysis, oral reading, comprehension, and structural analysis skills.

Rasinski, T. (2003). *The fluent reader: Oral reading strategies for building word recognition, fluency, and comprehension*. New York: Scholastic.

This is a great how to guide for teaching is how and why to include time for read alouds and repeated readings. There is a good chapter on oral reading across the curriculum.

Shanker, J. L., & Ekwall, E. (2003). *Locating and correcting reading difficulties*. Upper Saddle River, NJ: Merrill/Prentice Hall.

Strategies are provided for teachers to locate and remediate reading difficulties.

Strickland, D. S., Ganske, K., & Monroe, J. K. (2002). *Supporting struggling readers and writers: Strategies for classroom interventions, 3–6*. Portland, ME: Stenhouse.

This book offers research-based practices for improving students' reading and writing skills.

Trelease, J. (2001). *The read-aloud handbook* (5th ed.). New York: Penguin.

This is a terrific resource for techniques for reading aloud, as well as fabulous selections to read aloud to your students. Titles and brief summaries are provided by grade level.

RECOMMENDED WEBSITES

Dynamic Indicators of Basic Early Literacy Skills (DIBELS)
http://dibels.uoregon.edu

A great assessment website that provides access to free downloads of the DIBELS measures designed to assess phonological awareness, the alphabetic principle, and fluency with connected text. The site also contains a separate fee-based service, the DIBELS Data System, which allows you to enter students' DIBELS data online and generate automated reports for a fee of $1 per student per year. Assessment targets students in grades K–3.

University of Oregon: Institute for the Development of Educational Achievement (IDEA)
http://idea.uoregon.edu/assessment/analysis_results/assess_results_erc_flu.html

This website is an excellent resource that provides different lists of assessments for use as screening, diagnosis, progress monitoring, or outcome instruments to assess fluency in grades K–3.

FORM 7.1. Student Reading and Writing Profile (Part VII)

Student Reading and Writing Profile

Part VII: Fluency

Fluency

Name of test	Date	Score

Student strengths in fluency ______________________________

____

Student areas for improvement in fluency ______________________________

____

____

Instructional recommendations ______________________________

____

____

Plan for monitoring fluency ______________________________

____

____

EIGHT

Once upon a Time

Comprehending Narrative Text

Adriana L. Medina
Paola Pilonieta

VIGNETTE

It's three weeks into the school year. As Meg Gardner, a first-year teacher at an urban elementary school, drives home, she finds herself replaying these weeks' events in her head. Meg has assumed that the majority of her second-grade students will be reading at grade level. Unfortunately, this is not the case. Instead, she has found that some of her students can decode the words in the text, but they don't comprehend what they have read. More specifically, they cannot succinctly retell a story; when she asks them to retell what happened in the story they just read, they get lost in the details and tend to ramble on about seemingly unrelated events. As she tries to reconcile what she has learned in her teacher education program with suggestions from more seasoned teachers in her school, Meg is faced with a puzzling plethora of strategies, ideas, and questions she can't quite begin to sort out. How and when does she begin to assess her students? How does she know which strategy is best for each reading difficulty? And what about her students who are English-language learners (ELLs)?

ANTICIPATION QUESTIONS

- What are some reasons why the act of reading comprehension is so complex?
- What are key principles guiding reading comprehension strategy instruction?
- How are narrative and expository texts different?
- What are some formal and informal measures that can be used to assess comprehension?
- What are appropriate strategies to use during each part of a reading lesson for narrative text?
- How do you provide more intensive instruction for students who need extra help?

INTRODUCTION

In the preceding chapters, you have already read about instruction in decoding and fluency. These elements are all essential parts of comprehension (Pressley, 2002a). If children cannot decode words, comprehension will not occur. If children cannot read fluently, comprehension will be impaired. Comprehension instruction is not just asking children questions while they read a story. Instruction in comprehension consists of teaching students strategies that they can use to help them understand texts, and teaching them what to do when comprehension is interrupted. As Meg has found, there seem to be so many strategies out there, but deciding which strategies to use can be confusing.

The present chapter and Chapter 9 are companion chapters. This chapter begins with an overview of research and background information about reading comprehension instruction in general, including a section on why students have difficulties in text comprehension. Strategy instruction is an important component of comprehending both narrative and expository text; thus an overview of strategy instruction is presented. Differences between the nature of comprehension of narrative and expository text are then discussed. The remainder of the chapter focuses on general comprehension assessment, followed by assessment and instruction in comprehension of narrative text. Chapter 9 provides additional strategies for assessment and instruction in comprehension of expository text.

READING COMPREHENSION

Dolores Durkin (1980) wrote, "If there is no comprehension, there is no reading" (p. 191). Indeed, decoding means little if the reader cannot grasp, interpret, and evaluate an author's message. The comprehension process involves an understanding of words and how those words are used to create meaning. It involves contextualizing, analyzing, synthesizing, and evaluating words, phrases, sentences, and longer passages during reading. It involves integrating prior experiences and knowledge of the world to construct meaning. The process also involves the ability to remember (short-term or long-term) what was read, for purposes of discussion or taking a test.

Various definitions of reading comprehension have emerged over the years. As early as 1917, Thorndike argued that reading is more than sound–symbol relationships; rather, Thorndike identified reading as reasoning. Later, Johnston (1984) suggested, "Reading comprehension is viewed as the process of using one's own prior knowledge and the writer's cues to infer the author's intended message" (p. 16). Mosenthal (1984) developed this notion further when he proposed the "context" pyramid that expanded Johnston's definition to include specific contexts and their interaction: reader, text, task, setting, and situation. Thus the definition of reading comprehension began to take on a sociocultural tone. Irwin's (1991) definition added even more specificity to the definition and outlined a model for assessment and instruction:

> Comprehension can be seen as the process of using one's own prior experiences and the writer's cues to construct a set of meanings that are useful to the individual reader reading in a specific context. This process can involve understanding and selectively recalling ideas in individual sentences (microprocesses), inferring relationships between clauses and sentences (integrative processes), organizing ideas around summarizing ideas (microprocessors), and making inferences not necessarily intended by the author (elaborative processes). These processes

> work together (interactive hypothesis) and can be controlled and adjusted by the reader as required by the reader's goals (metacognitive processes) and the total situation in which comprehension is occurring (situational context). When the reader consciously selects a process for a specific purpose, that process can be called a reading strategy. (p. 9)

In 2002, the Rand Reading Study Group simplified the definition of reading comprehension, but maintained the complexity of the concept by stating, "We define reading comprehension as the process of simultaneously extracting and constructing meaning" (Sweet & Snow, 2003, p. 1). In other words, reading comprehension is more than simply reading the words.

As educated adults, we seldom think about why or how we comprehend what we read—we just do it! However, it is important for us as educators to be in touch with the complexity of the reading comprehension process, and to help students learn what to do when comprehension breaks down.

What Does Research Say about Reading Comprehension?

The research on reading comprehension instruction is vast and well documented. Major reviews of reading comprehension research provide insights about how to structure comprehension instruction (e.g., Dole, Duffy, Roehler, & Pearson, 1991; Mastropieri & Scruggs, 1997; Pearson & Fielding, 1991). Common conclusions in these reviews of the literature are that techniques for comprehending can be taught, that comprehension requires active thinking and involvement with text, and that it takes time to teach comprehension. In recent years, two major research reviews have provided guidelines for reading comprehension instruction: the National Reading Panel (2000a) report and the Rand report (Sweet & Snow, 2003).

RESEARCH BRIEF ✐ Durkin's Classic Work

Dolores Durkin's two classic studies conducted in the late 1970s and early 1980s had a strong influence on reading research and instruction. The first investigation (Durkin, 1978–1979) was an observational study conducted in elementary classrooms during reading and social studies periods. Her goal was to document reading comprehension instruction in reading classes and the transfer of strategies learned to content area reading during social studies. Her findings indicated that very little explicit comprehension instruction occurred. The most common activities were "read the passage, answer the question" routines, with little direct instruction about how to read and learn from text. Social studies instruction emphasized content coverage, with little emphasis on how to read to learn.

A second study (Durkin, 1981) was a content analysis of reading comprehension instruction in five different basal readers (K–6). In this study Durkin wanted to learn if the instructional guidelines provided in commercial reading texts mirrored the type of instruction observed in the previous investigation. The analysis revealed that teachers were provided with few tools for explicit instruction of reading comprehension. The basals emphasized student independent practice, rather than teacher modeling, demonstration, and strategy instruction. While questioning in the basal readers was the primary assessment tool, explanations for how answers were derived were visibly absent from the text.

Taken together, these studies launched years of research. Researchers at the Center for the Study of Reading at the University of Illinois (Champaign–Urbana) led the way in examining how best to help improve the quality of reading comprehension instruction. As a result, teachers have more tools (including basal readers) to help struggling readers.

One of the major areas covered in the National Reading Panel (2000a) report was reading comprehension. The Panel found that reading comprehension could be improved by teaching students to use cognitive strategies. Such strategies help students become self-regulated readers and give students options to consider when they encounter barriers to comprehension. Teaching cognitive comprehension strategies can lead to increased retention and understanding of text. The National Reading Panel found that eight kinds of instruction appear to be effective and most promising for classroom use:

- Comprehension monitoring
- Cooperative learning
- Graphic and semantic organizers
- Story structures
- Question-answering strategies
- Question generation
- Summarization
- Multiple-strategy teaching

Along with determining the status of research-based comprehension instruction, it was important to develop a focused research agenda to guide future investigations in reading comprehension. In 1999, the U.S. Department of Education's Office of Educational Research and Improvement asked the Rand Reading Study Group to examine existing research literature and create a research agenda. This group found three areas in urgent need of more research (Snow, 2002). First, in terms of the teaching of comprehension, we have more to learn about the optimal time for instruction and about how best to integrate reading strategy instruction in the content areas. Second, the report recommends that research on how best to prepare teachers to teach comprehension needs to be ongoing. Third, the area of assessment of reading comprehension needs continued exploration. This is particularly true in regard to both a seamless merger of assessment and instruction, and continued development of reliable and valid measures. So while we have learned a great deal, there is still much to learn.

Why Do Students Have Trouble with Reading Comprehension?

The Rand report outlined four elements that must interact dynamically for reading comprehension to occur: the reader, the text, the activity, and the context. These elements can provide insight into why students have trouble with the comprehension process.

The Reader

Chapter 2 has outlined general reader-based factors that influence reading achievement. Certainly any one or a combination of these factors can cause a breakdown in the ability to comprehend. Other chapters in this book highlight important academic precursors to reading comprehension (e.g., decoding, reading fluency, and vocabulary). In addition, another factor has a strong impact: facility in reading comprehension processes.

READING COMPREHENSION PROCESSES

Chapter 5 has described Marilyn Adams's (1990) model of the reading process. Adams's model has four processing components: phonological, orthographic, meaning, and contextual. You have already read about phonological and orthographic processing in previous chapters. *Meaning processing* refers to the reader's use of prior knowledge or background knowledge, as well as the reader's knowledge of vocabulary. *Contextual processing* refers to the reader's ongoing efforts to use contextual clues to make sense of the author's message and to interpret and evaluate the message. Judith Irwin's (1991) model of reading comprehension processes provides even more depth to aid in the understanding of meaning and context processing.

Irwin's model (see Figure 8.1) provides a structure for understanding the components of the reading comprehension process: *microprocesses* (understanding sentences), *integrative processes* (connecting segments of text), *macroprocesses* (understanding narrative and expository text structures), *elaborative processes* (working beyond the text to

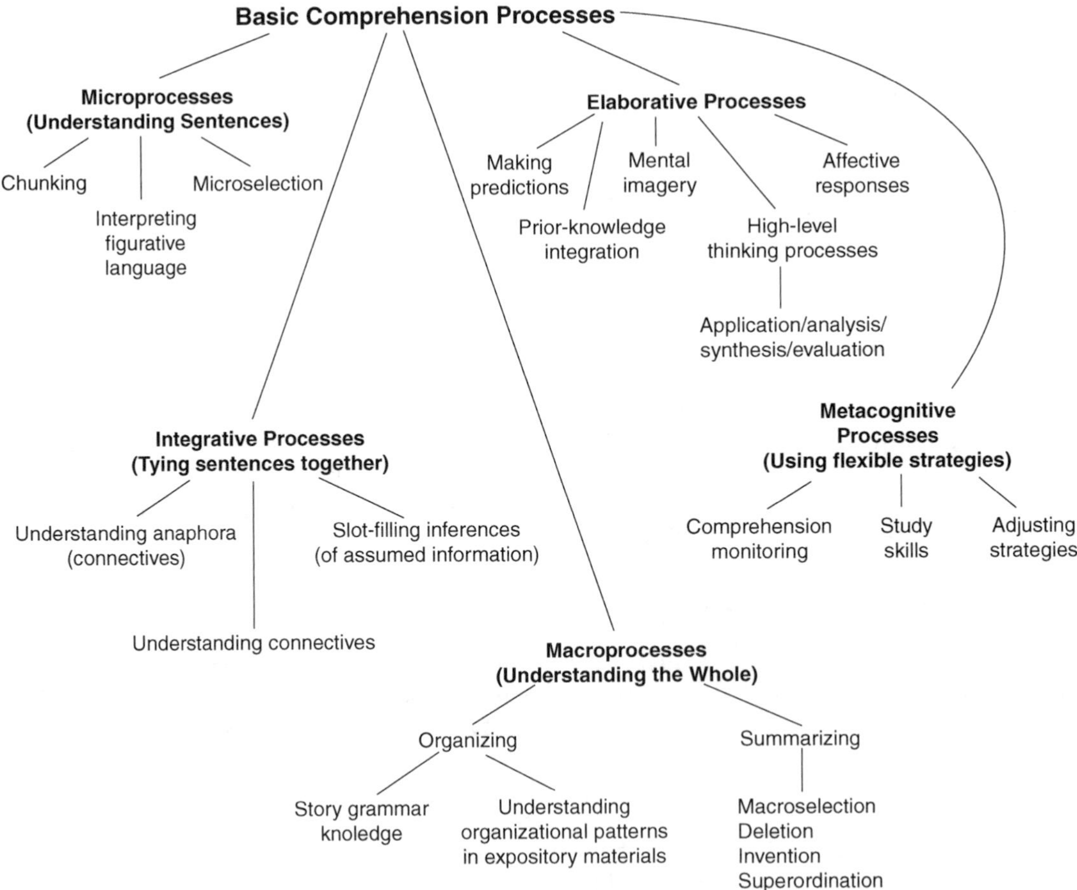

FIGURE 8.1. Irwin and Baker's model of reading comprehension. From Irwin and Baker (1989). Copyright 1989 by Prentice-Hall. Reprinted by permission.

make meaningful connections), and *metacognitive processes* (monitoring comprehension and retaining information for future use). When all of these processes are working together, comprehension occurs. Disruption at any of the process points can have an impact other processes and comprehension as a whole. Similarly, inability to coordinate the processes and use them smoothly can interrupt comprehension. Throughout this chapter and Chapter 9, we'll make references to these processes and provide suggestions for assessment and instruction. Two aspects of the model that are particularly salient to reading comprehension are prior knowledge and metacognition.

Prior Knowledge. Schema theory is important to the understanding of reading comprehension. *Schemata* (the plural of *schema*) are also referred to collectively as *prior knowledge* or *background knowledge.* "Schema theory attempts to explain how knowledge is represented in the mind and how these representations facilitate comprehension and learning" (Harris & Sipay, 1990, p. 559). A schema is the framework in the mind that houses what you know about a particular concept. These same frameworks are what you use to store information learned. Schemata provide frameworks to organize text information by making connections between what is known and the new information in the text (Rumelhart, 1976). By attaching new information to existing information, comprehension is achieved. Schemata provide the prior knowledge students need to understand what they are reading. Students cannot be expected to comprehend a text when they lack sufficient prior knowledge.

Schema processing is a top-down procedure. First you think about a big idea—let's say, winter—and then you think about the details: cold weather, snow, snowman, and hot cocoa. Think of your mind as a filing cabinet. You already have a "file folder" for the big idea—winter. Inside the folder are all the details you already know about winter. Every time you learn something about winter, it's easier for you to understand it, because you already have a file for that concept. When your students are reading a story for which they don't have any prior knowledge or file folders, it is necessary for you to supply your students with this background knowledge, so that they can create the file folders, and the new information they read about has a place to go. As you increase your knowledge, you enlarge your schemata, and as you enlarge your schemata, you can learn more information and create new folders.

Research has found the following:

- Readers with more prior knowledge understand and remember more (Brown, Bransford, Ferrara, & Campione, 1983).
- To improve comprehension, prior knowledge must be activated (Bransford & Johnson, 1972).
- Poor readers and younger readers often fail to activate their prior knowledge (Paris & Lindauer, 1976).
- Good readers revise prior knowledge that is not consistent with what they are reading if they are convinced by the author's argument. In turn, ideas in the text may be rejected when they clash with a reader's prior knowledge (Pressley, 2000).

The role of prior knowledge of topic and genre is vital for understanding student difficulties with text. This is particularly true for students who have limited experiences beyond their own neighborhoods, or students whose backgrounds differ from mainstream culture.

RESEARCH BRIEF Schemata and Culture

Steffenson, Joag-dev, and Anderson's (1979) classic study demonstrates the importance of cultural background and content schemata in comprehending texts. Two passages of equivalent readability were given to a group of American adults and a group of Indian adults. One passage was about traditional American wedding customs, and the other was about traditional Indian wedding customs. After reading, when asked to recall the texts, the groups recalled more information from the passages that aligned with their cultural content schemata and judged those passages easier to read. That is, Americans recalled more details and judged the passage about American weddings easier to read than the passage about Indian wedding customs, and vice versa for the Indians. This important finding from this study points to individual knowledge of content as a source of differences in text comprehension.

Metacognition. Baker and Brown (1984) define *metacognition* as "the knowledge and control the child has over his or her own thinking and learning activities, including reading" (p. 353). Jacobs and Paris (1987) simply define it as "thinking about thinking." Reflect about your own reading. When you are reading a chapter and you don't understand what you have read, you might reread the passage, look a word up in a glossary, read ahead to see if some clues further along in the text might help, or ask someone for help. Proficient readers monitor their understanding of text and use adjustment or fix-up mechanisms as necessary. Students who are less successful in reading may not engage in such active reading strategies, may blame the task or others for not being able to comprehend, or may just avoid reading altogether (Paris, Wasik, & Turner, 1991). Some students may pick up self-regulating strategies on their own; some may do so with practice in classroom activities designed to promote metacognition; and still others may require explicit and intensive instruction.

The Text

As you will read further in Chapter 9, texts may be the source of reading difficulty for several reasons. First, the readability level may be too high for the reader. Readability levels are gauged with formulas based on word difficulty (vocabulary) and sentence length. In general, the more advanced the words and the longer the sentences, the more difficult the text (Dale & Chall, 1948; Fry, 1989). Second, text may be difficult because it does not include features that make it considerate or user-friendly to the reader (Armbruster & Anderson, 1984). For example, texts that highlight key vocabulary, have boxes to summarize key points, and have introductions and summaries are more user-friendly to readers than texts that do not include such features. Finally, student interest and prior knowledge of both the topic of the text and the genre of the text can have an impact on the level of difficulty, as can a student's ability to sustain concentration and learn from the material (Baldwin, Peleg-Bruckner, & McClintock, 1985).

The Activity

A reading activity can be either externally imposed (e.g., by a teacher or through an assignment), or it can be internally imposed (i.e., when one is seeking knowledge, information, or entertainment for one's own use). The activity and the reader's perception of the purpose of the activity can have a strong effect on whether or not attention to the task, persistence with the task, and ultimately comprehension can occur. For students with learning disabilities or attention disorders, lack of task persistence can be extremely potent (Gersten, Fuchs, Williams, & Baker, 2001). Activities that promote engagement with the text, such as applying specific strategies for learning and memory, assist in the comprehension process.

The Context

Sociocultural theory (Vygotsky, 1978) has highlighted the importance of understanding context and how context influences learning. Community, home, school, and classroom contexts can all have an influence on individual students and groups of students. For example, fifth-grade students who have been tracked in a low reading group for their entire academic career may react in negative ways to reading assignments. Or a kindergarten student who did not attend preschool and comes from a home where parents cannot afford books and magazines may be at a disadvantage when peers discuss books and nursery rhymes. In assessing student strengths and areas for improvement, it is important to keep context in mind.

Reading Comprehension Strategies

Many skills and strategies are necessary for comprehension to occur; however, before we begin, it is important to make a distinction between *skills* and *strategies*. According to Dole and colleagues (1991), skills are automatic and routine, are associated with lower levels of thinking and learning, and are rigid. Strategies, on the other hand, are controlled by the reader, are metacognitive, are intentional, are flexible, and emphasize reasoning. Strategy utilization takes an active reader—one who interacts with the text. Some students are active readers by nature; others are not. Fortunately, students can be taught how to interact with text, thus helping them become active readers. The emphasis in this book is on the teaching of reading strategies.

Dole (2003) defines comprehension strategies as a "set of routines or procedures that help readers become active processors to achieve the goal of comprehension." If our goal is to develop readers who are independent, know how to select appropriate strategies and how to use them, and know how to monitor the effectiveness of strategies and their own learning, then we need to teach student-centered reading strategies that will lead to that goal. Dole also explains that there is sometimes a difference between student-centered comprehension strategies that students control to monitor their comprehension and teacher-centered strategies that help students comprehend. There is also some overlap—especially when teachers model comprehension strategies. The important thing is to keep the goal in mind: active student engagement in systematic, independent learning.

Several basic principles guide strategy instruction:

1. Strategy instruction should be explicit. Dole (2003) provides a sequence for strategy instruction: (a) Introduce the strategy and its purpose, (b) explain and model the strategy, (c) provide guided practice with feedback, and (d) provide independent practice.
2. Strategy selection should be purposeful. When you select a strategy to teach to your students, think about why you want to select that particular strategy (as opposed to others), how it fits with other strategies your students already know, and how you are going to explain the purpose of the strategy to your students.
3. Strategy instruction should provide opportunities for students to become profi-

cient in the use of the strategy. Teachers often introduce a vast array of strategies without giving students the opportunity to develop a high level of skill with each one. There are levels of strategy learning: (a) general awareness, (b) basic proficiency, (c) advanced proficiency, and (d) in-depth understanding of when to use the strategy and why.

4. Strategy instruction should be connected. When students learn strategies in isolation, they may not realize how to put them together to read and learn from text. In this chapter and the next, you'll read about multiple strategies that provide practice in helping students read text and prepare for tests and class discussions. Think about the model of reading comprehension introduced earlier in this chapter. Multiple strategies help students weave together various components of comprehension processing, and help them to become more adept and facile in their use.

5. Strategy instruction should be coordinated at a schoolwide level. Some students learn one set of strategies in primary grades, another in intermediate grades, still others in resource settings—and who knows what happens when they go to middle school? Such random instruction leads to strategy confusion. Students don't know what to do and when to do it. Well-intentioned teachers have been trying, but the lack of a coherent plan confuses students—particularly the students who are the least strategic learners.

6. Strategy instruction should be fun. In general, students like "tricks" for learning. If presented as such, strategy instruction can be enjoyable.

7. Strategy instruction should be evaluated. Students should have an opportunity to reflect about the strategy, how it helped them learn, and why. When asked, students often have definite opinions about the utility of strategies and good suggestions for improvement.

PARENT POINTER ☞ Engaging Parents in Strategy Instruction

If you want strategy instruction to have a full impact, parents should be brought into the process. Develop a mini-handbook of three to five strategies that your students have learned. Introduce the handbook to parents at a parents' night. Then design home learning activities that can help the students practice strategies at home.

Most studies on comprehension have been conducted with children in the intermediate grades. In fact, it is often assumed that primary-grade students, who are focusing on decoding skills, are not ready to tackle the task of learning comprehension strategies. Pearson and Duke (2002) take the position that not only is it beneficial for primary-grade students to learn comprehension strategies, but there is research to support this claim. They make three points:

1. When teachers provide explicit instruction in comprehension strategies, comprehension improves.
2. When activities are designed and implemented to enhance the understanding of text, comprehension improves.
3. Reading instruction in the primary grades can focus on both decoding and comprehension.

Although more research is still needed in this area, Pearson and Duke illustrate that many comprehension strategies—such as story structure, retelling, multiple-strategy instruction programs (e.g., reciprocal teaching), and repeated readings—improve comprehension and are suitable for primary students.

Comparing Narrative and Expository Text

Pappas and Pettegrew (1998) define *genre* as the "different ways in which language patterns are realized in written texts to meet various social, [and] communicative goals" (p. 36). Stamboltzis and Pumfrey (2000) elaborate on this definition and state that genre includes two aspects: the purpose for which the text was written, which has an effect on the second aspect, the structure of the text, which is the way the words for the text are chosen and arranged. Because narrative and information books serve different purposes, different textual patterns and linguistic registers are used to communicate their meaning (Pappas, 1993). As a result, different genres require different mental stances in order to read and process information.

There are many different genres in literature, but in this chapter we are discussing *narratives*, or stories. Narrative texts have characters, have a plot and setting, are temporally ordered, and are goal-based (Yopp & Yopp, 2000). Pappas (1991) adds that narratives use coreferentiality, mental and everyday words, and past verb tenses. *Coreferentiality* refers to the way a character is introduced and how an author uses referent words like *he, him*, or *the* throughout the book to refer to the same character. Mental words, like *thought* or *refused*, are used in narratives to show the intentions of characters for solving their problems. Narratives typically use everyday, common-sense vocabulary. Finally, narratives are usually written in the past tense.

While reading narratives for aesthetic purposes, readers focus on living through what the characters are experiencing. Furthermore, while reading narratives, readers participate in an activity that the poet Samuel Taylor Coleridge (1817/1907) termed "willing suspension of disbelief" (p. 6). This allows the readers to accept that although events in narratives may be impossible, in the world of narrative they are not only plausible, but acceptable as well. Narratives include stories, fairy tales, folk tales, mysteries, science fiction, and historical fiction. Biographies are both narrative and expository, because they recount actual events but are often written in a narrative format.

As you will read in Chapter 9, *expository* texts are designed to inform. Expository texts include textbooks, manuals, and trade books that are informational in nature (e.g., travel guides, how-to books, cookbooks). Informational texts are not about specific characters and their goals. Instead, they make general and specific statements about topics. Moreover, expository texts have very different structures from narrative text and typically introduce a large amount of technical knowledge.

While assessment and instruction of narrative and expository texts differ, there are some commonalities. We'll begin with a general discussion of formal and informal reading comprehension. Specific assessment and instruction techniques for narrative text follow. Specifics for expository text are covered in Chapter 9.

What Are Formal Assessments of Reading Comprehension?

Anyone who has taken the Scholastic Aptitude Test (SAT) or Graduate Record Examination (GRE) is familiar with the traditional "read the story, answer the question" format of reading comprehension tests. Most comprehension tests still follow that format and include multiple-choice questions of various types (e.g., detail, main idea, inference). This includes group administered high-stakes tests used for state and district accountability purposes. Some more recent tests include multiple-choice questions about reading processes and elicit written responses to questions based on passages. Traditional tests typically include both narrative and expository passages, although the percentage of each varies widely from measure to measure.

Some standardized tests use a modified *cloze* or *maze* format, in which words are deleted from a sentence or passage. The reader is required to choose from a list of three or four words that would most make sense in the passage.

Test of Reading Comprehension–3

The Test of Reading Comprehension–3 (TORC-3; Brown, Hammill, & Wiederholt, 1995) is a 30-minute standardized test that can be administered by a teacher or reading specialist individually or to a group of students ranging from ages 7 to 17. The test is composed of eight subtests (General Vocabulary, Syntactic Similarities, Paragraph Reading, Sentence Sequencing, Mathematics Vocabulary, Social Studies Vocabulary, Science Vocabulary, Reading the Directions of Schoolwork) derived from core tests of general vocabulary, syntactic similarities, paragraph reading, and sentence sequencing, and it generates a Reading Comprehension Quotient. The TORC-3 yields information about a student's strengths and weaknesses in each of the comprehension components it tests.

Woodcock–Johnson III Diagnostic Reading Battery

The Woodcock–Johnson III Diagnostic Reading Battery (Woodcock, Mather, & Schrank, 2004) is an individually administered measure used to diagnosis student strengths and areas for instruction. It includes a Brief Reading screening subtest, as well as subtests in Reading Comprehension, Phonics Knowledge, and Oral Language Comprehension. The Broad Reading subtest is a combination of fluency and comprehension. The Basic Reading subtest is a combination of vocabulary and phonics. The test is appropriate for students in grades K–16.9.

Gates–MacGinitie Reading Tests

The Gates–MacGinitie Reading Tests (GMRT; MacGinitie, MacGinitie, Maria, & Dreyer, 2000) is a norm-referenced, group-administered instrument that has been scientifically researched and is effective in helping teachers screen K–12 students and adults. The GMRT not only helps teachers understand student reading instructional needs, but can calculate a *lexile score*. A lexile score is a calculation of the level of comprehension a students will have with a text. If a student has the same lexile score as the lexile level of the text, then it is estimated that the student will comprehend that text with at least 75% accuracy. Software enables the generation of a list of appropriate books for a student, based on the GMRT score.

Degrees of Reading Power

The Degrees of Reading Power (DRP; Koslin, Zeno, & Koslin, 1987) is an example of a standardized test that uses a maze (or modified cloze) format. Students are given passages with missing words and (under untimed conditions) are required to determine the best missing word in a multiple-choice format. Both primary and standard levels are available, with a total range of grades 1–12. In addition to reporting standardized test scores, DRP scores can be used to match students with books of appropriate reading levels.

What Are General Informal Assessments of Reading Comprehension?

Informal Reading Inventories

Informal reading inventories (IRIs) include graded reading passages and comprehension questions that can be used for several purposes (see Appendix B for more details). First, the passages can be used to gauge oral reading comprehension. Students read passages aloud and then answer questions posed orally. Second, the passages can be used to assess silent reading comprehension. Students read the passage silently and answer questions orally. Third, the passages can be read aloud by an administrator to test a student's listening comprehension. The administrator reads the passage; the student answers the questions orally.

IRIs can include sets of both narrative and expository passages. In addition, some IRIs include narrative and expository retelling checklists. Still others now incorporate prior knowledge questions for each passage.

Regular Student Observations

Here are some ways to recognize a student who has a reading comprehension problem:

- Can the student answer questions on the materials read?
- Can the student retell the material read?
- Can the student answer literal, interpretive/inference, application, and discussion questions?
- What is the student's level of participation during discussion?
- Observe the student's written work in reference to the materials read.
- Observe the student's drawings in reference to the materials read.

Teacher-Made and Textbook Assessments

Informal measures that you construct or that are available through textbooks, teacher resource manuals, and online can be used as informal assessments. Or you can use Form 8.1 to record student mastery of various reading comprehension processes.

RESEARCH BRIEF ✎ Comprehension and Fluency

Comprehension is a process that builds on word recognition, vocabulary, and fluency. As word recognition and fluency improve and vocabulary grows, cognitive resources can be released and focused on comprehension. Jenkins, Fuchs, van den Broek, Espin, and Deno (2003) studied 113 fourth graders while they read a passage from a folk tale (words in context) and a list of words from the same folk tale (context-free words), in order to analyze the relationship between comprehension and fluency. Overall, they found that the speed in which students read the passage, or the fluency of context reading, predicted reading comprehension more effectively than did the fluency of context-free reading. More specifically, they found that skill in reading a word list made a larger contribution to fluency for less fluent readers, whereas for more fluent readers, fluency depended on their comprehension process. Their findings have three major applications in the classroom:

(1) You can use fluency to estimate overall reading comprehension; (2) slow reading speeds are a result of poor word identification skills; and (3) fluent reading reflects comprehension processes as well as word identification skill.

What Are Informal Assessments of Comprehension of Narrative Text?

Comprehension Checklist for Narrative Text

A comprehension checklist for narrative text can be used to informally assess a single student at a time. Determine what aspects of narrative comprehension you are going to assess. Divide those items into before reading, during reading, and after reading. Then use those items to create a comprehension checklist. You can use the checklist (see Form 8.2 for an example) during different settings for one student or multiple students. (Figure 8.2 is a filled-in example.) Although several skills are listed for each part of the reading lesson, modify the ones you use, so that they are those that you have taught and those that are age-appropriate for your students.

Comprehension Self-Assessment

After an independent reading session, provide each student with a list of comprehension strategies (see Form 8.3). Then ask each student to identify which strategies were used to help understand the text while reading. Ask the student to give an example of how the strategy was used.

Assessing Prior Knowledge

Prior knowledge can be assessed during prereading discussions and through prewriting assignments. The research reviews of Holmes and Roser (1987) and Valencia and Stallman (1989) yield a number of ways to assess prior knowledge. Students can be asked to define key words and concepts either orally or in writing, complete multiple-choice tests before reading, and make predictions of content based on key words from the story.

Story Retelling

Story retelling can be used as an assessment technique to prove you with information about a student's short-term retention, ability to note important details, and use of text structure to aid in recall. To use retelling as an assessment, prepare an outline of the events of the story the student will read. Have the student read the story silently. Then have the student retell as much of what was remembered. Check off the events and details the student recalls, and then follow up with prompts to elicit additional information the student might have missed. Form 8.4 is a generic assessment form for story retellings.

Metacomprehension Strategy Index

The Metacomprehension Strategy Index (MSI; Schmitt, 1990) is an informal instrument that you can use to assess metacognition. The survey instrument contains 25 items divided among three areas: before, during, and after reading (Form 8.5). The MSI is spe-

Comprehension Checklist for Narrative Text

Legend — Indicates first time skill is observed.

+ Indicates second time skill is observed.

* Indicates third time skill is observed and that the student has accomplished the skill.

Note: Although several skills are listed for each part of the reading lesson, modify the ones you use so that they are those that you have taught and those that are age-appropriate for your students.

Student names:	John	Michael	Maria	Jamal	Anna
Before reading					
Uses titles, pictures, captions to predict	—			+	
Uses background knowledge to predict		+			—
Is intrinsically motivated to engage in reading			*		
During reading					
Is aware when text does not make sense	+				—
Asks for help when comprehension is difficult		—	—		
Uses preceding text to predict				*	
Makes inferences					
After reading					
Can discuss elements of the story					
Recalls important information	—				
Can summarize or retell the story		+		*	
Can identify literary elements (setting, character, theme, etc.)			*		
Refers back to the text for support for conclusions					+
Compares and contrasts characters and events in text					
Can make connections between story read, other texts, and personal experiences				*	

FIGURE 8.2. Comprehension Checklist for Narrative Text (filled-in example).

cifically designed to tap metacognition while students are reading narrative text. Questions relate to the following strategies: predicting, previewing, purpose setting, prior knowledge, summarizing, and fix-up strategies.

TECH TIP Retelling Artifacts

Make an audio- or videotape of each student's story retellings at the beginning, middle, and end of the school year. Make sure the retelling is of a story each student really enjoyed. Parents and students will enjoy seeing the progress the students have made.

How Do You Provide Differentiated Instruction in Comprehension of Narrative Text?

Level 1: High-Quality Core Instruction

Narrative comprehension lessons have three parts: *prereading*, *during reading*, and *postreading*. Teachers can imbed instruction in the various components of the reading comprehension process model within the framework of the "before, during, and after the story" sequence. Lessons may begin with a preteaching of a specific process and then attending to that process at the appropriate time during the story. Keep in mind that prereading, during-reading, and postreading strategies can be used with teacher read-aloud sessions as well as with student oral or silent reading.

Prereading strategies occur before reading the story. This is when teachers need to help students activate their own background knowledge (schema or schemata) on the topic(s) of the story and/or to provide background information to promote successful comprehension. During-reading strategies are used to help students become active readers—that is, to help them engage with the story. Teachers should model what good readers do to comprehend and should monitor the comprehension of their students. During the postreading phase of reading instruction, teachers help students summarize what they have read and assess comprehension. In order to ensure comprehension of any text, it is important that lessons include all three phases of reading instruction. Initially, it is wise to model the three phases in teacher-led whole-class or small-group lessons. Eventually, students should be provided with opportunities to work through the phases in small groups and independently

PREREADING

The purpose of prereading strategies is to prepare students for reading. To do this, it is important to activate the students' schema or schemata on the topic(s) of the story, and, if necessary, to build background knowledge that will help students get the most from the narrative text they are reading. Teachers can help activate students' existing prior knowledge about a topic by having them think about what they already know about the topic before they read about it. Before reading the story, help students think about what they already know about the genre of the story, the setting, and some key concepts or themes included in the selection.

Some or all of your students may not have the necessary background knowledge to fully comprehend a narrative text you have selected. This may be particularly true for students with diverse cultural and linguistic experiences. If so, spending a little bit of time preteaching a few key concepts may enable students to get more from the story.

Prereading can also include *prediction* activities. Having students predict from its title what a story will be about, and make predictions while reading the story, helps the students become active and engaged readers. Think about when you watch a movie or television show. It's actually fun to anticipate what's going to happen as the story unfolds. As Slaughter (1993) points out, when students make predictions about stories, they are more likely to be attentive and involved. A study examining the effectiveness of predictions made by poor readers before reading found that students who made predictions performed significantly better on weekly tests of higher-level comprehension than those who did not (McCormick & Hill, 1984).

In addition to activating and building background knowledge, predicting story events and outcomes, and motivating students to read, preteaching of vocabulary can enhance comprehension (as you will read in Chapter 10). Other suggestions for prereading activities follow.

Word Maps. Word maps can be used to activate and build students' prior knowledge (Schwartz & Raphael, 1985). Before reading the story with the class, the teacher picks a concept related to the story and writes it on the board. For example, when reading Eric Carle's (1971) *The Very Hungry Caterpillar*, the concept might be caterpillars. The teacher then asks the students what comes to mind when they think of caterpillars and writes these ideas on the board (see Figure 8.3). Having various members of the class participate in this activity can extend students' knowledge of caterpillars. This type of activity also helps remedial students relate information to their background knowledge more effectively (McCormick, 1999).

Previewing. Research has shown that *previewing* can increase the comprehension of text (Graves, Cooke, & Laberge, 1983). The purpose of previewing is to create interest in the story and to help students link the story to something familiar in their prior knowledge. To preview the story, the teacher prepares a written preview of the story and gives a copy to each student. The first part of the preview consists of statements and questions to

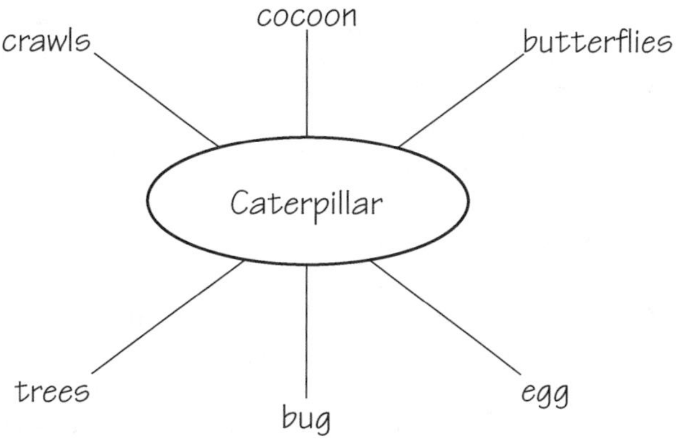

FIGURE 8.3. Sample word map.

arouse students' interest. The teacher reads them aloud and then leads a short discussion about the story's topic. The teacher then reads a short summary of the story that includes the setting, a description of the characters, and general information about the plot up to the ending. Next the teacher reads a statement about the characters written on the board. The students now read the final portion of the preview, where three or four difficult words are defined. The students are now ready to read the story silently.

This strategy is more in-depth than what basal readers recommend, yet it only takes approximately 10 minutes to implement and has proved to be quite effective. In one study, students' recall of facts was 13% higher when using the preview strategy, and higher-level comprehension increased by 38% (Graves et al., 1983). When recall was tested several days later, students who used the written preview scored higher than those who did not. In addition, students reported liking the strategy, which is very important when helping reluctant or unmotivated readers.

Picture Walk. Illustrations stimulate children's interest in books by enticing them to read and interact with text. Illustrations may also play an important role in the comprehension process, especially with young children. Fang (1996) found that children could identify more easily with experiences presented in pictures than with those presented in text because children are more familiar with pictures. More importantly, pictures provide mental images for children, so that they can more easily understand text and remember it longer.

Picture walks are a good way for young students to preview a story. Picture walks can be used to make predictions and develop vocabulary (Cunningham & Allington, 2003). When conducting a picture walk, the teacher reads the title of the story and shows the cover of the book to the students. Based on the title and the cover, the teacher asks the students what they think the book will be about. Next, the students look through the illustrations as the teacher asks questions such as "Who is this story about?", "Where do you think the story takes place?", and "What do you think this story is about?" After looking through the book, talking about what is happening, and using the knowledge to develop vocabulary, the children are ready to read the story.

Going beyond the Printed Page. Instructional activities for building background knowledge and motivating students to read can and should go beyond the printed page. This is particularly true for students who are struggling readers. Peregoy and Boyle (2001) emphasize the importance of using materials and experiences beyond the book to promote comprehension among ELLs. Using maps, globes, films, simulation games, role playing, and field experiences can not only stimulate interest in reading, but help students appreciate and remember what they have read.

Setting the Mood. Your own enthusiasm for reading a story can serve as the best catalyst to motivate students to read. As Tompkins and McGee (1993) point out, there are a number of ways that teachers can set the mood for reading and can promote engagement. One way is to have students develop identification with a character's problem or situation in a story. This can be accomplished in class discussion or through reflective writing. Thinking about how they might react to a character's dilemmas can foster focus. Another way is to read the first few lines of the story in an animated way to get students moving.

DURING READING

Think-Alouds. Think-alouds are used to activate an awareness of the thinking process and are important in teaching processes. Think-alouds consist of thinking about the text as you are reading it and of the comprehension strategies you are using (Pressley, 2002b). The goal of think-alouds and of metacognition is to help students work toward controlling their thinking before, during, and after reading. Think-alouds can be used by the teacher to model strategies that students are being introduced to, or by the students when teachers want an insight into their comprehension process.

Teacher think-alouds can be used while generating predictions, relating what is read to prior knowledge, integrating new knowledge, or solving problems when the text becomes confusing or when unknown words are encountered. As a matter of fact, think-alouds can be used to model any of the reading comprehension processes. For example, a teacher might notice during the reading of a story that a character, Tom, is also referred to as *he*, *him*, *stepson*, *freckle-faced kid*, and *pest*. Teachers can think aloud about this use of *anaphora* (using words or phrases to replace each other) in the story, and think through how the different words and phrases relate to Tom.

Imagery. When you read a story, you see images in your mind's eye related to the events you are reading in the story. These images assist with comprehension and recall. Research has found that poor readers do not form visual images that relate to the text. Before reading a story, inform your students that as they read, they should be forming pictures in their minds' eyes of the events occurring in the story. So try this: Ask your students to close their eyes and listen to you as you read the first part of a descriptive story (if it's a picture book, don't show the pictures or the cover). Stop and have your students illustrate what they saw in their minds' eyes. Then have your students get into groups and discuss their pictures. The pictures should give you an indication of the students' visualization development.

AFTER READING

Literature Circles. Literature circles are small discussion groups made up of four to six students who have read the same piece of literature. Students choose what group they want to participate in, based on their interest in the novel or short story. These groups are not based on ability level. Each student prepares for the discussion by taking on different jobs and completing different tasks. For example, the discussion leader leads the discussion by generating thought-provoking questions; the vocabulary manager picks out difficult or unknown words in the selection; the illustrator draws a sketch of a pertinent passage of the chapters read; and the connector links the selection to a prior experience he or she may have had. Assignment sheets can be used that help each student fulfill the assigned role in the circle. Different literature circles can have different roles; for example, you can have one circle summarize passages read and another track the movement of the characters.

Literature circles provide scaffolds to participation in story discussions and are especially helpful for poor readers, who have difficulty engaging in these types of activities. In literature circles, the students' roles provide structure for the conversation and act as scaffolds. In most classroom discussions, the teacher is the one to take the lead, while the students respond to the teacher's probes. In literature circles, the students, not the teacher, are the ones who "set the agenda and determine what is of value in the reading, responding from the tasks associated with the assigned reader role" (Blum, Lipsett, & Yocom, 2002, p. 101).

Story Maps and Frames. Having a sense of a story's structure aids in comprehension and recall, so teachers should not only teach the elements of a story but have students map out those story elements as well. There are various elements in a story. The most common are character(s), setting (time and place), problem(s), and resolution. Depending on the age of the students being taught, different elements can be added, such as theme, chain of events, episodes, the different types of plots, the five parts of a linear plot (introduction, rising action, climax, falling action, and conclusion), and so forth. *Story maps* (see Form 8.6) create a visual and graphic organizer for the story elements. A story map helps the students visualize the relationships between the elements in the story. The students then use the story map to build schemata and make sense of the story. The teacher can use story maps to plan instruction, generate questions, and foresee possible comprehension problems related to the story. A story map can be handed out to the students so that they can fill it out as they read the story. Students can also be asked to create a story map after they have read the story. Story maps lead to better comprehension (Beck, Omanso, & McKeown, 1982; Idol, 1987).

Story frames are variations of story maps and function in much the same way (see Form 8.7). Story frames provide more scaffolding for the student. Their aim is to focus students' attention on specific elements or aspects of a story.

Retellings. Retellings can be oral or written. They are free recalls of what a student remembers from a text read or heard. Retellings provide insight into students' comprehension, as well as their ability to use the text's structure to organize and retain information (Moss, 2004). Retelling is a more natural process for children than summarizing is. Even as early as kindergarten, children can retell stories they have heard or read. Retelling is a strategy that children need to be familiar with before they are ready to summarize. Students can present their retellings to the whole class and then get suggestions for improving the retellings in the future.

PARENT POINTER ☞ Say It Again

Story retellings are a "natural" for home–school collaboration. For a home learning assignment, have students read a book with their parent and then submit a video or audio recording of a joint retelling. You can also plan reading events (some schools have parent–child pajama parties) where joint reading and retelling of stories is a main event.

MULTIPLE-STRATEGY INSTRUCTION

One important principle of strategy instruction is to help students connect strategies. Following are examples of multiple strategies.

Guided Reading. Guided reading is a multistep, scaffolded reading experience that is teacher-led. Fountas and Pinnell (1996, 1999) initially designed guided reading for students in the primary grade, but older readers can benefit from the procedure as well (Tierney & Readence, 2004). Teachers work with individual students or small groups (no more than six students per group) to guide their reading through a text that is at a comfortable reading level. Teachers group students with similar reading levels and select books at or near their instructional reading level. Each student has an individual copy of a leveled text to follow along during the guided reading session. Group composition is dynamic, based on teachers' ongoing assessment of students' needs. Guided reading sessions follow a "before, during, and after reading" framework, with activities based on the needs of individual readers in the group.

Cooper (2006) views guided reading as an essential component of reading instruction, in that it enables students to work toward independence in reading. Cooper sees the road to independence as one that begins with maximum teacher modeling and support and ends in independent reading. The five components of reading instruction as defined by Cooper include (1) teacher read-alouds (teacher reading and providing think-alouds and question generation), (2) shared reading (teachers and students share in the reading and responding experience with the same book), (3) guided reading (teachers work with small, homogeneous groups of students and guide them through reading of a comfortable text), (4) cooperative reading (students work in cooperative learning groups to provide support), and (5) independent reading (students read and respond on their own). Cooper goes on to explain that similar scaffolded steps can occur with writing instruction.

Directed Reading–Thinking Activity. The *directed reading–thinking activity* (DR-TA) developed by Stauffer (1969) is designed to assist students in setting a purpose for reading; making, justifying, and verifying predictions; and coming to conclusions. To do DR-TA, have students survey the text to be read. Students should then make predictions based on the survey. It is important to have students justify their predictions, or give a reason why they think their predictions make sense. Then set a purpose for reading by having students read to find out if their predictions are correct. Students begin by reading silently up to a predetermined section of the text. Have students confirm or alter their predictions based on the new information read and create new predictions. Have students read the next section and continue with confirming or altering and creating new predictions until the reading is complete. A useful trick during DR-TA is to have students cover up the sections they are not reading, to prevent reading ahead or skimming and scanning for upcoming information. You should ask various questions at each stopping point, but remember to vary the level and the type of questions asked.

Reciprocal Teaching. Reciprocal teaching is a cooperative learning strategy developed by Palinscar (1984) to help students who have adequate decoding skills but have difficulty with comprehension. In reciprocal teaching, the teacher and students engage in a discussion about a segment of text, structured by four strategies:

- Predicting—making hypothesis about what will happen next in the story.
- Question generating—making up questions based on prior knowledge and information from the text.
- Clarifying—discussing parts of the text that are difficult to understand, discovering why they are confusing, and restoring meaning.
- Summarizing—identifying the main idea of a paragraph or of the story up to a given point.

Initially the teacher models each strategy individually for the students. Once the students are proficient with the strategies, the students take turns leading the discussion about each segment of text. The strategy relies on the teacher, or the student who is acting as the leader, to model and scaffold the strategies for the rest of the group. As students gain proficiency in the strategy, the leader's role is reduced, thereby removing the scaffolds gradually.

To introduce students to reciprocal teaching, the teacher can provide them with a short story. The teacher reads the title and has students predict what the story will be about. Next the students read a brief portion of the story, to gain an idea of what they will be reading. The teacher tells the children, "Today I will act as the leader of the discussion, but in a couple of days you will take turns being the leader of the discussion."

During the second step, the teacher models each of the four comprehension strategies, using the material that has been given to the children. It is important that when modeling the strategies, the teacher make his or her thought process overt and explicit.

The third step prepares students to assume the role of the leader. While generating questions, the teacher might ask the students, "What question would you ask?" The teacher might also remind the students how to do the strategy: "Remember that summarizing doesn't include a lot of details, just the most important parts." During this part, the teacher's scaffolding is slowly reduced.

Guiding students as they assume the teacher's role is the fourth step. Once the students are comfortable with the four comprehension strategies and with the group discussion, the teacher chooses a student to take the role of the leader. As this is being done, the teacher provides feedback and praise to the group—for example, "That question really makes you think," or "Another way of summarizing the section would have been to . . ."

The process continues for each section of the text, followed by discussion led by a different student. Reciprocal teaching is suitable for all age groups (Dougherty Stahl, 2004). Research shows that reciprocal teaching results in increased comprehension monitoring and comprehension (Paris, Wixson, & Palinscar, 1986). Reciprocal teaching can also be used in a peer tutoring setting.

The example in Figure 8.4 uses the short story "She," by Rosa Guy (1984). In this example, reciprocal teaching has been introduced, but the students are not doing it independently just yet. The teacher is working with one small group of students at a time.

Level 2: Supplemental Instruction

MODIFICATIONS OF STRATEGIES

All of the strategies provided in this chapter can be taught to all students, including ELLs and children with reading difficulties or disabilities. However, for students not proficient in English and for divergent learners, modifications must be made. Techniques commonly used to assist ELLs—such as providing hands-on experience, using nonverbal means (e.g., gestures), utilizing visuals to accompany oral and written materials, modifying vocabulary, speaking slowly, and utilizing repetition, to name a few—should be incorporated into all lessons (Garcia, 2003). Story maps are most frequently mentioned in the literature as being beneficial for ELLs (Fitzgerald & Graves, 2004) and for students with learning disabilities (Idol, 1987) in reading narrative text.

When you are planning for these special populations, use more teacher and student modeling, more small-group and individual lessons, and more opportunities for guided practice and independent practice. These same adaptations will benefit all learners in

TEACHER: Read up to where I have drawn a black dot. Please do not read beyond the black dot until I tell you to read the next section. (*The teacher allows students enough time to read the section.*)

> "Just where do you think you're going?" she said.
> "To the bathroom," I said.
> "No, you're not," she said. "Not before you wash up these dishes."
> "This is a matter of urgent necessity," I said. I hated that even my going to the bathroom had to be questioned.
> "Don't want to hear," she said. "I'm sick and tired of emergency, emergency every night after dinner. Get to the sink."
> "I'll wash the dishes," Linda said. She got up and started to clear off the table. I slipped out of the kitchen. The angry voice followed me down the hall:
> "Linda, don't keep letting your sister get away with everything."
> "I don't mind—really, Dorine," Linda said.
> "That girl's just too lazy . . . " I shut the bathroom door to muffle the sounds of her grievances against me. She didn't like me. She never had. And I didn't care. Stepmothers . . .!

TEACHER: Recall that during the last couple of times, I have led the discussion. Today I will begin the discussion, and then you all will ask and answer questions. In a couple of days, you will begin taking turns at leading the discussion. Remember we are focusing on the four strategies I've written on the board: predicting, generating questions, clarifying, and summarizing. Let's begin. The first thing we do is make predictions. Based on what I've read, I predict that there is going to be more conflict between the main character and her stepmother, because they obviously don't get along. Who else has a prediction?

MARIE: I predict this is a story about a girl who doesn't get along with her stepmother.

TINISHA: I predict they are going to keep arguing.

CHRIS: I predict the sister is going to stop picking up her sister's slack.

TEACHER: Any other predictions? OK, who has questions about what we just read?

SYLVIA: Who is the older of the two?

TEACHER: Does anyone have an answer?

CAROLINE: The author hasn't said it yet.

TEACHER: Another question?

TINISHA: What's the main character's name?

CHRIS: It hasn't been given yet.

MARIE: Why don't they get along?

SYLVIA: What if she really needed to go to the bathroom?

CAROLINE: But it says here she did this every night after dinner. It's an excuse.

CHRIS: Yeah, she doesn't want to do her chores. I don't always like doing my chores.

TINISHA: Why does the sister, Linda, do it?

SYLVIA: Maybe she feels bad for the stepmother.

CAROLINE: Or for her sister.

MARIE: How about the dad? Where is he?

TEACHER: Does anyone need anything clarified?

CHRIS: What does the word *grievances* mean?

(cont.)

FIGURE 8.4. Example of a reciprocal teaching script.

TINISHA: *Grievances* sounds like *grief*. It means to be sad.

TEACHER: Good connection, but not exactly. Look at the sentence before it. Look at what the stepmother said: "That girl's just too lazy." Does that give you a clue?

SYLVIA: Maybe it means *insults*?

TEACHER: Yes, a grievance is like an insult. A complaint. Good. You all are following the strategies well. Keep it up! Good job! What's the next strategy that we use?

MARIE: Summarizing.

TEACHER: Good. Anyone have a summary to make?

CAROLINE: A girl is at dinner and goes to the bathroom instead of washing the dishes, and her sister does it for her, and then she gets into a fight with her stepmother.

TEACHER: That's pretty good. Can we make it a bit shorter?

CHRIS: A girl is fighting with her stepmother because she doesn't want to do the dishes.

TEACHER: Good. Let's read up to the next marker.

FIGURE 8.4. *(cont.)*

your classroom. Assess who your students are and what their needs are, so that you can plan effectively and appropriately.

In addition, some of the supplemental strategies described in Chapter 7 on fluency can also apply to supplemental instruction for narrative text. Classwide peer tutoring (CWPT; Greenwood & Delquadri, 1995; Mathes, Fuchs, Fuchs, Henley, & Sanders, 1994) was designed initially for use with narrative text. CWPT includes a retelling component that will provide students with peer-supported practice in retelling stories. Repeated reading activities have the dual benefit of improving fluency and comprehension (Samuels, 1979). Audiobooks can provide fluent models and can enhance comprehension for students who need a boost.

GUIDED RETELLINGS

For students who have difficulty with story retellings, provide prompts to help them develop a sense of the components of a solid retelling. Turn the components of the retelling checklist into questions to prompt student responses. For example, you might ask, "What is the setting of the story?" If you get no response, you may need to use further prompts: "Where did the story take place?" "When did the story take place?"

In addition, for students with limited independent reading skills, provide opportunities for them to practice retellings of stories they have heard or viewed. This will give them practice in retelling that they can later transfer to retellings of stories they have read.

Level 3: Intensive Support

Because narrative text is so prevalent on television and in the primary grades, whole-group instruction with some supplementation is sufficient for most students. For students who need intensive support in reading stories, you may need to dig deeper in terms of assessment. If the problem is with narrative structure, providing individual assistance is appropriate, as is increased exposure to stories through viewing and listening. If the problem is an underlying comprehension process (i.e., microprocessing, integrative processing), then explicit, direct instruction and practice need to occur in those areas. In Chapter 9 you'll read more about how to help students with microprocessing and integrative processing.

SNAPSHOT

Narrative Comprehension Instruction in a Second-Grade Classroom

Cesar Martinez teaches second grade. Cesar immigrated to the United States during his teens. During college he worked in a summer camp and found that working with young children was extremely fulfilling to him. Cesar changed his major from communication to elementary education.

His children's literature and reading classes were an eye-opener for Cesar. Cesar was not familiar with many of the children's stories everyone in his classes seemed to know from childhood. He got hooked on books and has developed a rather substantial library of children's books—particularly those that represent multicultural perspectives.

Cesar has learned to balance strategy instruction for his second graders with the love of reading. He teaches prereading, during-reading, and after-reading strategies to all of his children, with lots of think-alouds and modeling. He is selective about the strategies he uses and has lots of repetition, so that the strategies fade and comprehension and enjoyment bubble up. For students who need additional help, Cesar has started an after-school reading club that involves both children and their parents.

FURTHER DEVELOPING STUDENT READING AND WRITING PROFILES

Use Part VIII of the Student Reading and Writing Profile (Form 8.8) to record student assessment results, strengths, and areas for improvement in overall comprehension and narrative comprehension. For more detailed information, you may want to use Form 8.1 to assist with your planning and instruction.

CHAPTER SUMMARY

Instruction in comprehension is a lot more than just asking questions after students read a passage. Teaching reading comprehension requires choosing the most appropriate strategy to teach your students, offering a rationale for learning the strategy, modeling the strategy, providing explicit and clear instruction in doing the strategy, and giving students guided and independent practice with the strategy in an authentic context. It is vital to use proper strategies from each stage of a reading lesson to facilitate comprehension. Don't be intimidated by strategies with multiple components. Although they are a bit more difficult to implement, they are well worth the effort in the end and can lead your students to independence in learning.

Teaching students strategies for reading narrative text can give them a gift for life. Helping students learn how to become immersed in a book and to share what was experienced with a family member or friend is one of the most important things we can do as teachers. For students who have struggles in learning to comprehend, provide support through strategies, and provide encouragement and motivation with oral stories and stories on film.

KEY TERMS AND CONCEPTS

Anaphora
Cloze
Directed reading–thinking activity (DR-TA)
During reading
Elaborative processes
Guided reading
Imagery
Integrative processes
Literature circles
Macroprocesses
Metacognitive processes
Microprocesses
Narratives
Picture walks
Postreading
Predicting
Previewing
Reciprocal teaching
Retellings
Schema (plural: schemata)
Story maps and frames
Think-alouds
Word maps

REFLECTION AND ACTION

1. Write your own definition of *reading comprehension*. How does your definition compare with those mentioned in the text and others you find in the literature?
2. Although proficient readers have many comprehension strategies in their repertoire, they don't often think about the strategies they use while they read, because these strategies have become automatic. Think of the strategies you have learned about in this chapter. Reflect on your reading of this chapter or other appropriate material. Make a list of the strategies you used, when you used them, and how you used them.
3. Look through the teacher's manual of a reading basal. Reflect on the principles that should be used in teaching a comprehension strategy. Analyze how the teacher's manual of a basal reader meets these criteria.
4. Choose a strategy for teaching one aspect of reading. Using the key principles for teaching a strategy, plan a lesson and teach that lesson to your classmates. Have your classmates evaluate you on whether you achieved all six key principles.
5. First, create a whole-class lesson plan for predicting, summarizing, or imagery. Second, modify your lesson plan with the purpose of providing supplemental instruction to a small group of students. Third, modify your lesson plan again with the purpose of providing individualized instruction.
6. Examine the Plan Sheet for Assessment Measures Related to the Comprehension Model (Form 8.9). Think about how the components of the reading comprehension model align with your state or district reading standards. Then identify assessment measures in this book, in your basal reader, or other professional resources that can help you develop a comprehensive assessment plan for comprehension. You may want to work with a grade level team to complete this task.

READ ON!

Block, C. C., & Pressley, M. (2003). Best practices in comprehension instruction. In L. M. Morrow, L. B. Gambrell, & M. Pressley (Eds.), *Best practices in literacy instruction* (2nd ed., pp. 111–126). New York: Guilford Press.

Presents an update on the theory and research of comprehension instruction, the word-level and vocabulary processes that affect comprehension, and the processes that are used to teach comprehension.

Dole, J. A., Duffy, G. G., Roehler, L. R., & Pearson, P. D. (1991). Moving from the old to the new:

Research on reading comprehension instruction. *Review of Educational Research*, *61*(2), 239–264.

Discusses the history of current comprehension instruction, and proposes an alternate curriculum focusing on five strategies and how they should be taught.

Farstrup, A. E., & Samuels, S. J. (Eds.). (2002). *What research has to say about reading instruction* (3rd ed.). Newark, DE: International Reading Association.

Leaders in the field of reading provide a collection of compositions related to various aspects of the reading process and based on theory and research.

Fitzgerald, J., & Graves, M. F. (2004). *Scaffolding reading experiences for English-language learners.* Norwood, MA: Christopher-Gordon.

Provides a comprehensive guide to scaffolded instruction in before, during, and after reading for ELLs.

Hickman, P., Pollard-Durodola, S., & Vaughn, S. (2004). Storybook reading: Improving vocabulary and comprehension for English-language learners. *The Reading Teacher*, *57*(8), 720–730.

Offers a strategy that can be used to enhance the vocabulary and comprehension skills of ELLs in the primary grades through the use of read-alouds.

Pressley, M., Rankin, J., & Yokoi, L. (1996). A survey of instructional practices of primary teachers nominated as effective in promoting literacy. *Elementary School Journal*, *96*(4), 363–384.

Kindergarten through second-grade teachers who were nominated as effective teachers were asked to complete a survey regarding the instructional practices that they used in their classrooms. The article describes practices used by these teachers that promote and impair literacy development.

SHARPENING YOUR SKILLS: SUGGESTIONS FOR PROFESSIONAL DEVELOPMENT

1. Develop a personal collection of children's books for your favorite narrative lessons. Once friends and family members know that you are a collector, books will pour in.
2. Join a book club—either in person or online. Book clubs have become increasingly popular, because people are learning about the social connections they can make through the enjoyment of the written word.

RESOURCES FOR ASSESSMENT AND INSTRUCTION

Benson, V., & Cummins, C. (2000). *The power of retelling.* Desoto, TX: Wright Group/McGraw-Hill.

This professional development book describes the *developmental retelling* model. This model guides students through four stages of retelling: pretelling, guided reading, story map reading, and written retelling. Resources for assessment and instruction are provided.

Dougherty Stahl, K. A. (2004). Proof, practice, and promise: Comprehension strategy instruction in the primary grades. *The Reading Teacher*, *57*(7), 598–609.

The article reviews the research on comprehension strategies appropriate for the primary grades and separates them into those that are strongly supported by research and those that currently lack a research base in the primary grades. The article further divides each category into strategies that are often used by teachers and those that are not.

Irwin, J. W., & Baker, I. (1989). *Promoting active reading comprehension strategies: A resource book for teachers.* Englewood Cliffs, NJ: Prentice-Hall.

Provides a thorough explanation of the comprehension processes. For each process, comprehension strategies are provided that can be used for assessment as well as remediation.

Oczkus, L. D. (2003). *Reciprocal teaching at work: Strategies for improving comprehension.* Newark, DE: International Reading Association.

This monograph is a valuable tool for implementing reciprocal teaching. It includes recommendations for whole-class, small-group (teacher-led), and literature circle grouping patterns. Rubrics for student observation and student self-assessment are included as well.

Rhodes, L. K. (Ed.). (1993). *Literary assessment: A handbook of instruments.* Portsmouth, NH: Heinemann.

A companion book to *Windows into Literacy* (see below), this book contains assessment instruments to gather data on a student's literacy proficiency.

Rhodes, L. K., & Shanklin, N. L. (1993). *Windows into literacy: Assessing learners, K–8.* Portsmouth, NH: Heinemann.

Provides information about the aspects of reading and writing that can be assessed to assist teachers in planning for instruction.

RECOMMENDED WEBSITES

Center for the Improvement of Early Reading Achievement
www.ciera.org

This site provides access to reports, articles, and conference presentation focusing on all aspects of early reading. It also includes hyperlinks to other research organizations and resources.

Library of Graphic Organizers
curry.edschool.virginia.edu/go/edis771/notes/graphicorganizers/graphic/

This site maintains a page of 24 graphic organizers. There are organizers for analogies, sequencing, decision making, comparison/contrast, and more. The graphic organizers are ready to print and use.

Reading Comprehension Strategies Toolbox
www.manatee.k12.fl.us/sites/elementary/palmasola/rcompindex.htm

This site supports the curriculum for Manatee County, Florida. It provides links for many areas of reading—phonemic awareness, phonics, word study skills, vocabulary, and reading comprehension. Each link provides standards and benchmarks, as well as activities, practice sheets, and quizzes.

Reading Rainbow
http://gpn.unl.edu/rainbow/default.asp

This site, which accompanies the PBS-TV series, offers lesson plans, discussion topics, curricular activities, and themes that can be used along with the series or independently.

Starfall.com
www.starfall.com

Although primarily a website geared toward decoding, Starfall.com gives children from kindergarten to second grade an opportunity to read simple texts online. The website offers plenty of short, animated stories focusing on a particular sound. As children read the story, they can click on any word, and the computer will read the word for them.

What Works Clearinghouse
www.w-w-c.org

This website was developed by the U.S. Department of Education's Institute of Education Science to provide educators, policymakers, and researchers with a place to locate scientific evidence for what works in education. It presents a database of user-friendly reports that review the effectiveness of educational interventions.

FORM 8.1. Comprehension Checklist Based on the Comprehension Model

Comprehension Checklist Based on the Comprehension Model

Legend – Indicates first time skill is observed.

\+ Indicates second time skill is observed.

* Indicates third time skill is observed and that the student has accomplished the skill.

Note: Although several skills are listed for each part of the reading lesson, modify the ones you use so that they are those that you have taught and those that are age-appropriate for your students.

Student names:					
Microprocesses					
Phrase reading					
Sentence reduction					
Integrative processes					
Anaphora					
Connectives					
Slot-filling inferences					
Macroprocesses					
Story structure					
Retellings					
Expository patterns					
Summarizing					
Elaborative processes					
Predictions					
Prior-knowledge structures					
Imagery					
Higher-level questions					
Affective responses					
Critical thinking					
Metacognitive processes					
Comprehension monitoring					
Reading-related study skills					
Fix-up strategies					

FORM 8.2. Comprehension Checklist for Narrative Text

Comprehension Checklist for Narrative Text

Legend – Indicates first time skill is observed.

\+ Indicates second time skill is observed.

* Indicates third time skill is observed and that the student has accomplished the skill.

Note: Although several skills are listed for each part of the reading lesson, modify the ones you use so that they are those that you have taught and those that are age-appropriate for your students.

Student names:					
Before reading					
Uses titles, pictures, captions to predict					
Uses background knowledge to predict					
Is intrinsically motivated to engage in reading					
During reading					
Is aware when text does not make sense					
Asks for help when comprehension is difficult					
Uses preceding text to predict					
Makes inferences					
After reading					
Can discuss elements of the story					
Recalls important information					
Can summarize or retell the story					
Can identify literary elements (setting, character, theme, etc.)					
Refers back to the text for support for conclusions					
Compares and contrasts characters and events in text					
Can make connections between story read, other texts, and personal experiences					

FORM 8.3. Comprehension Self-Assessment

Comprehension Self-Assessment

Name ______________________________ Title of text ________________ Date ________

A. Indicate which strategy you used during reading time to help you understand what you were reading.

1. ____ I made a prediction.
2. ____ I went back and reread what I did not understand.
3. ____ I created a picture of what I was reading with my mind's eye.
4. ____ I asked a friend to explain something I did not understand.
5. ____ I discussed the story with a friend.

B. Provide an example of one of the strategies you indicated above.

____

____

____

____

____

____

____

____

____

____

____

____

____

____

____

____

FORM 8.4. Story Retelling Checklist

Story Retelling Checklist

Name ________________________________ Date ________________

Story read ____

Readability level of text ____________________

Story heard ____________________

(if retelling of a story read aloud to student)

Story component	**Student initiates response**	**Responds to prompt**	**Observations**
Names title of story			
Names author of story			
Names illustrator of story, if appropriate			
Names primary characters			
Names secondary characters			
Describes setting/place			
Describes setting/time in history			
Describes setting/duration			
States problem posed in story			
States sequence of actions			
States resolution of problem			
Describes personal reaction to story in terms of affective response			
Provides a critique of story			

Overall evaluation of retelling:

Recommendations for instruction:

FORM 8.5. Metacomprehension Strategy Index

Metacomprehension Strategy Index

Directions: Think about what kinds of things you can do to help you understand a story better before, during, and after you read it. Read each of the lists of four statements and decide which one of them would help you the most. There are no right answers. It is just what you think would help the most. Circle the letter of the statement you choose.

I. In each set of four, choose the one statement, that tells a good thing to so to help you understand a story better *before* you read it.

1. Before I begin reading, it's a good idea to:
   A. See how many pages are in the story.
   B. Look up all of the big words in the dictionary.
   C. Make some guesses about what I think will happen in the story.
   D. Think about what has happened so far in the story.
2. Before I begin reading, it's a good idea to:
   A. Look at the pictures to see what the story is about.
   B. Decide how long it will take me to read the story.
   C. Sound out the words I don't know.
   D. Check to see if the story is making sense.
3. Before I begin reading, it's a good idea to:
   A. Ask someone to read the story to me.
   B. Read the title to see what the story is about.
   C. Check to see if most of the words have a long or short vowel in them.
   D. Check to see if the pictures are in order and make sense.
4. Before I begin reading, it's a good idea to:
   A. Check to see that no pages are missing,
   B. Make a list of the words I'm not sure about.
   C. Use the title and pictures to help me make guesses about what will happen in the story.
   D. Read the last sentence so I will know how the story ends.
5. Before I begin reading, it's a good idea to:
   A. Decide on why I am going to read the story.
   B. Use the difficult words to help me make guesses about what will happen in the story.
   C. Reread some parts to see if I can figure out what is happening if things aren't making sense.
   D. Ask for help with the difficult words.
6. Before I begin reading, it's a good idea to:
   A. Retell all of the main points that have happened so far.
   B. Use the difficult words to help me make guesses about what will happen in the story.
   C. Reread some parts to see if I can figure out what is happening if things aren't making sense.
   D. Ask for help with the difficult words.
7. Before I begin reading, it's a good idea to:
   A. Check to see if I have read this story before.
   B. Use my questions and guesses as a reason for reading the story.
   C. Make sure I can pronounce all of the words before I start.
   D. Think of a better title for the story.

(cont.)

8. Before I begin reading, it's a good idea to:
   <u>A.</u> Think of what I already know about the things I see in the pictures.
   B. See how many pages are in the story.
   C. Choose the best part of the story to read again.
   D. Read the story aloud to someone.
9. Before I begin reading, it's a good idea to:
   A. Practice reading the story aloud.
   B. Retell all of the main points to make sure I can remember the story.
   <u>C.</u> Think of what the people in the story might be like.
   D. Decide if I have enough time to read the story.
10. Before I begin reading, it's a good idea to:
    A. Check to see if I am understanding the story so far.
    B. Check to see if the words have more than one meaning.
    <u>C.</u> Think about where the story might be taking place.
    D. List all of the important details.

II. In each set of four, choose the one statement that tells a good thing to so to help you understand a story better *while* you read it.

11. While I am reading, it's a good idea to:
    A. Read the story very slowly so that I will not miss any important parts.
    B. Read the title to see what the story is about.
    C. Check to see if the pictures have anything missing.
    <u>D.</u> Check to see if the story is making sense by seeing if I can tell what's happening so far.
12. While I am reading, it's a good idea to:
    <u>A.</u> Stop to retell the main points to see if I am understanding what has happened so far.
    B. Read the story quickly so that I can find out what happened.
    C. Read only the beginning and the end of the story to find out what it is about.
    D. Skip the parts that are too difficult for me.
13. While I am reading, it's a good idea to:
    A. Look all of the big words up in the dictionary.
    B. Put the book away and find another one if things aren't making sense.
    <u>C.</u> Keep thinking about the title and the pictures to help me decide what is going to happen next.
    D. Keep track of how many pages I have left to read.
14. While I am reading, it's a good idea to:
    A. Keep track of how long it is taking me to read the story.
    <u>B.</u> Check to see if I can answer any of the questions I asked before I started reading.
    C. Read the title to see what the story is going to be about.
    D. Add the missing details to the pictures.
15. While I am reading, it's a good idea to:
    A. Have someone read the story aloud to me.
    B. Keep track of how many pages I have read.
    C. List the story's main character.
    <u>D.</u> Check to see if my guesses are right or wrong.
16. While I am reading, it's a good idea to:
    A. Check to see that the characters are real.
    <u>B.</u> Make a lot of guesses about what is going to happen next.
    C. Not look at the pictures because they might confuse me.
    D. Read the story aloud to someone.
17. While I am reading, it's a good idea to:
    <u>A.</u> Try to answer the questions I asked myself.
    B. Try not to confuse what I already know with what I'm reading about.
    C. Read the story silently.
    D. Check to see if I am saying the new vocabulary words correctly.
18. While I am reading, it's a good idea to:
    <u>A.</u> Try to see if my guesses are going to be right or wrong.
    B. Reread to be sure I haven't missed any of the words.

(cont.)

Underlined responses indicate metacomprehension strategy awareness.

C. Decide on why I am reading the story.
D. List what happened first, second, third and so on.

19. While I am reading, it's a good idea to:
A. See if I can recognize the new vocabulary words.
B. Be careful not to skip any parts of the story.
C. Check to see how many of the words I already know.
D. Keep thinking of what I already know about the things and ideas in the story to help me decide what is going to happen.

20. While I am reading, it's a good idea to:
A. Reread some parts or read ahead to see if I can figure out what is happening if things aren't making sense.
B. Take my time reading so that I can be sure I understand what is happening.
C. Change the ending so that it makes sense.
D. Check to see if there are enough pictures to help make the story ideas clear.

III. In each set of four, choose the one statement that tells a good thing to so to help you understand a story better *after* you read it.

21. After I've read a story, it's a good idea to:
A. Count how many pages I have read with no mistakes.
B. Check to see if there were enough pictures to go with the story to make it interesting.
C. Check to see if I met my purpose for reading the story.
D. Underline the causes and effects.

22. After I've read a story, it's a good idea to:
A. Underline the main idea.
B. Retell the main points of the whole story so that I can check to see if I understood it.
C. Read the story again to be sure I said all of the words right.
D. Practice reading the story aloud.

23. After I've read a story, it's a good idea to:
A. Read the title and look over the story to see what it is about.
B. Check to see if I skipped any of the vocabulary words.
C. Think about what made me make good or bad predictions.
D. Make a guess about what will happen next in the story.

24. After I've read a story, it's a good idea to:
A. Look up all of the big words in the dictionary.
B. Read the best parts aloud.
C. Have someone read the story aloud to me.
D. Think about how the story was like things I already know about before I started reading.

25. After I've read a story, it's a good idea to:
A. Think about how I would have acted if I were the main character in the story.
B. Practice reading the story silently for practice of good reading.
C. Look over the story title and pictures to see what will happen.
D. Make a list of the things I understood the most.

Underlined responses indicate metacomprehension strategy awareness.

FORM 8.6. Story Map

Story Map

Characters:

Setting (time and place):

Problem(s):

Resolution:

FORM 8.7. Story Frame

Story Frame

____________________ (title of the story) by ________________ (author) takes place ______________. ____________ (character) is the main character of the story, who ______________ . ____________ (character) is another character, who ________________.
A problem occurs when ______________________. Next, ____________________________.
After that, _________________________. Finally, _____________________________.
The problem is resolved ______________________. The story ends ____________________.

FORM 8.8. Student Reading and Writing Profile (Part VIII)

Student Reading and Writing Profile

Part VIII: General and Narrative Reading Comprehension

General Comprehension

Name of test	Date	Score

Student strengths in general comprehension ______________________________

____

Student areas for improvement in general comprehension ______________________________

____

Instructional recommendations ______________________________

____

Narrative Comprehension

Name of test	Date	Score

Student strengths in narrative comprehension ______________________________

____

Student areas for improvement in narrative comprehension ______________________________

____

Instructional recommendations ______________________________

____

FORM 8.9. Plan Sheet for Informal Assessment Measures Related to the Comprehension Model

Plan Sheet for Informal Assessment Measures Related to the Comprehension Model

Reading comprehension processes	Informal assessment measures
Microprocesses Phrase reading Sentence reduction (most important idea in a sentence)	
Integrative processes Anaphora Connectives Slot-filling inferences	
Macroprocesses Story structure Retelling Expository patterns Summarizing	

(cont.)

Elaborative processes Predictions Prior-knowledge integration Imagery Higher-level questions Affective responses Critical thinking	
Metacognitive processes Comprehension monitoring Reading-related study skills Fix-up strategies	

NINE

Making Sense of Knowledge

Comprehending Expository Text

MICHELE MITS CASH
JEANNE SHAY SCHUMM

VIGNETTE

Renée is nearing the end of fourth grade. Her teacher, Karen Rose, considers Renée to be an excellent student. She participates in class discussions, completes homework and assignments on time, and seems anxious to do well. However, Karen is concerned because when it comes time for taking teacher-made tests or the tests that accompany the basal reader, Renée's performance falls. She also seems to have difficulty in taking science and social studies tests based on text material, even though she seems to be knowledgeable about the material in class discussions.

Renée likes to read children's literature and can typically be found reading a book when she completes daily assignments. Her parents confirm that she is an avid reader at home; they can't seem to keep her in books. They are baffled by her grades—especially since Renée was a solid student in the primary grades.

However, Karen is concerned that Renée's high-stakes assessment test scores may not be sufficient for her to progress to fifth grade. Moreover, she is concerned that Renée will have a tough time succeeding in the upper elementary grades and middle school, when reading and learning from text become emphasized more.

ANTICIPATION QUESTIONS

- Why is reading expository text difficult for some students—even when they have few problems with reading narrative text?
- What are some common expository text patterns? When should those patterns be introduced to students?
- What assessment tools can be used as a starting point for planning classroom instruction for expository reading comprehension? At the phrase and sentence levels? At the paragraph level? At the passage level?

- How can students link what they have read in content area textbooks with material presented in class? How can students prepare for teacher-made tests based on expository material?

INTRODUCTION

As you have read in Chapter 8, reading comprehension is a complex task that involves processing information at the word, sentence, paragraph, and passage or book levels. It involves active engagement of the reader before, during, and after reading as the reader takes in the author's message, interprets the message, responds to the message, and (if required) retains the message for a variety of different purposes (discussions, tests, personal information). The reading of both narrative and expository text entails most aspects of Irwin's (1991) model of basic reading comprehension processes (see Figure 8.1 in Chapter 8). Where they differ is primarily in the area of macroprocessing. Narratives rely on story patterns or story grammar; expository patterns have very different organizational types.

Until recently, children tended not to be introduced to informational text in any form (including media such as television or film) until later in the elementary years. The consequence is that students often find expository text difficult to read and basically uninteresting. Once students have passed the "learning to read" stage, they enter the phase of "reading to learn." The bulk of their reading in school is done to gain information or enhance their understanding of particular topics. Reading expository text is not only important for school-related tasks and high-stakes tests; it is important for daily living (e.g., reading legal documents, manuals, and reports). Therefore, it is essential that teachers assist students in learning how to identify the different types of expository patterns, as well as in developing proficiency in strategies to help in the understanding and retention of complex concepts. Indeed, exposure to strategies for comprehending expository text should begin as early as kindergarten (Snow, 2002).

This chapter begins with a discussion of expository text patterns. Next informal measures of expository text are presented, followed by suggestions for differentiated instruction of expository text, including instruction of reading-related study and research skills. As noted in Chapter 8, the assessment and instructional sections of this chapter provide suggestions not only for teaching expository text patterns, but for helping students who have comprehension problems that seem to go beyond narrative or expository text structure. For these students, you'll need to dig deeper to provide the foundation they need to read and understand text.

EXPOSITORY TEXT COMPREHENSION

Informational texts are not about specific characters and their goals. Instead, they make general and specific statements about a topic. Pappas (1991) explains that informational texts have six elements: topic presentation; description of the attributes of the topic; characteristic events or processes of the topic; category comparison (compares different elements of the topic); final summary; and an afterword, which adds extra information about the topic. Of the six elements, only the first three are mandatory. Instead of coreferentiality in narrative text, informational material uses *coclassification.*

Coclassification refers, for example, to how authors may use the word *their* and the plural form of a noun to refer to a class of animals, like dogs, and not a specific dog. Informational texts also use more technical words and they are written in the present tense. Informational texts use several expository patterns or text structures to organize the topic.

Expository text patterns are the ways in which information is organized in expository text. The patterns might be in a single sentence, paragraph, series of paragraphs, or in a larger unit of text. Tonjes and Zintz (1987) list 11 patterns; we've added a 12th, enumeration (see examples in Table 9.1).

TABLE 9.1. Expository Text Patterns

Pattern	Example
Introductory	This chapter begins with a discussion of the sources of pollution and continues with the impact of pollution on the environment.
Definition	Photographic memory is the uncanny ability to remember visual images in minute detail.
Transactional	We began with a description of the causes of the Civil War. Next, an overview of the major turning points of the war will be presented.
Illustrative	Each of the 50 states has a nickname. For example, Florida is the Sunshine State, California is the Golden State, and Connecticut is the Constitution State.
Summary	This section has presented the roots of early jazz. Jazz is a melting pot of African rhythms, European harmonies, and folk music from the United States.
Main idea and/or supporting details	There are nine planets. Each planet is a body that revolves around the sun. The names of the planets are Mercury, Venus, Earth, Mars, Jupiter, Saturn, Uranus, Neptune, and Pluto.
Chronological order	Some hurricanes cause so much damage that their names are retired. These include Camille (1969), David (1979), and Alicia (1983).
Compare/contrast	A biography and an autobiography are both stories of a person's life. When the author is someone other than the person being described, it is a biography. An autobiography is a personal account of one's own life.
Cause and effect	Because President Thomas Jefferson wanted to make sure that people in the United States could navigate the Mississippi without problems, he purchased the Louisiana Territory from France.
Problem and solution	Some children watch too much television. To help children change their habits, some parents are turning off the television and encouraging their children to get engaged in sports, games, and other play activities.
Descriptive	The dermis and epidermis are the two layers of human skin. The dermis is the inner layer, and the epidermis is the outer layer that consists of multiple, integrated sublayers.
Enumeration	There are four basic instrument families: (1) wind, (2) stringed, (3) percussion, and (4) keyboard.

1. Introductory
2. Definition
3. Transactional (transition from one pattern to another)
4. Illustrative
5. Summary
6. Main idea and/or supporting details
7. Chronological ordering
8. Compare/contrast
9. Cause and effect
10. Problem and solution
11. Descriptive
12. Enumeration

Knowledge of expository text patterns not only can assist students in their ongoing comprehension of informational material; it can also help them organize ideas in preparing for tests and for class discussions. Moreover, knowledge of the expository text patterns can assist students in structuring their own writing.

Why Do Students Have Trouble Comprehending Expository Text?

In this chapter's vignette you have read about Renée, who has a history of success in reading narrative text, but less success in reading expository text. As national assessments indicate, a *fourth-grade slump* in reading achievement is not unusual (Chall, Jacobs, & Baldwin, 1990). There are a number of theories about why this occurs. Lack of reading fluency and understanding of technical vocabulary may cause this slump. Duke (2000) suggests that the slump may occur because students do not have sufficient exposure to informational text. Assessment to determine if students have difficulty with expository patterns per se or if their difficulties are due to underlying processes is vital.

RESEARCH BRIEF ✎ Expository Texts in Primary Classrooms

How much time do primary students spend reading informational text? Duke (2000) investigated this question in an observational study of 20 classrooms in an urban setting (10 low-socioeconomic-status [low-SES] classes, 10 high-SES classes). Overall, she found a paucity of informational texts in these classrooms, with fewer such texts in the lower-SES classrooms. The title of her investigation was "3.6 Minutes a Day: The Scarcity of Informational Texts in First Grade." Duke recommended the inclusion of informational text reading in state standards, as well as increased time in reading expository materials in the primary grades. She cautioned, however, that reading of expository text should not take the place of narrative text reading.

What Are Informal Assessments of Expository Reading Comprehension?

Chapter 8 has included suggestions for formal and informal general assessment of reading comprehension, as well as more specific assessments for narrative text. Some assessments of narrative text comprehension can be adapted for expository text as well. In addition, the following informal assessments can help you learn more about how your students understand informational text.

Expository Textbook Awareness

To assess students' knowledge about expository textbook features, conduct a small-group or individual interview, using the checklist in Form 9.1. You can use variations of this checklist throughout the elementary years. Don't assume that intermediate students are aware of textbook parts and how those parts can help them learn.

K-W-L

One of the most popular approaches teachers use to assess student's topic knowledge of expository text information is known as *K-W-L* (Ogle, 1986). The procedure is quite simple, thus its popularity. In a three-column format (see Form 9.2), students record K (what they know about a topic), W (what they want to learn about a topic), and L (what they learned about the topic and still need to learn). The first two steps (K and W) are prereading strategies to tap prior knowledge and encourage students to make predictions. The final step occurs after reading, when students reflect about what they have read and what new information and facts they have learned.

K-W-L was originally designed as a reading comprehension strategy to help guide student reading of content area texts. However, using K-W-L as an assessment tool can provide teachers with insights about students' processing of expository text before and after reading.

Cloze

Cloze is a procedure that requires the reader to read a sentence and fill in a missing word or words. The original purpose of the cloze procedure was to measure the readability of a passage (Taylor, 1953). However, cloze can also be used to gauge students' comprehension, particularly in terms of microprocessing. Cloze can give you an idea of how students are processing the semantics and syntactic of language at the sentence level. Cloze can also be used with different expository patterns to see how well students process various patterns.

To create a cloze test, choose a passage with 250 words. Leave the first sentence intact. Beginning with the second sentence, remove every 5th word. Leave the final sentence intact. If the 250th word is in the middle of a sentence, write down the rest of the sentence. Do not leave the final sentence of the cloze passage in midstream. Only the exact replacement word is scored as correct. Misspellings are allowed. Calculate the number of blanks the student filled in correctly, and divide by the number of total blanks to get a percentage. Passages can be created representing a range of readability levels, as well as representing both expository and narrative text.

Below 40%, the reading passage is too difficult for the student and the passage is at the student's frustration level. Scores ranging between 40% and 59% indicate that the reading passage is appropriate for the student if help is provided. The reading is at the student's instructional level. Scores 60% or above indicate that the reading passage is easy enough for the student to read without teacher support and is at the student's independent reading level.

Maze is a variation of the cloze procedure. With a maze test, rather than filling in a blank, students are given a choice of words that can complete the sentence. In other words, maze is a multiple-choice variation of cloze. Constructing a maze text can become elaborate. For example, the choices can be the correct answer; a distractor that is semantically correct, but syntactically incorrect; and a distractor that is syntactically correct, but semantically incorrect. The criteria for grading maze passages is more stringent than for open-ended cloze tests.

Online resources are available to help teachers construct cloze passages for narrative and expository text (*www.edhelper.com/cloze.htm* and *www.schoolhousetech.com*).

Propositions Recalled

Moss (2004) points out that sometimes there is confusion about the difference between a *summary* and a *retelling*. A summary is a condensed recap of text that highlights only the main ideas. A retelling is a more elaborate recount of what was heard or read. The expository parallel to story retelling is *propositions recalled*. The purpose is to see how well students retain key information. The procedure is as follows:

1. Select an expository passage at a student's independent reading level.
2. Identify key points in the passage.
3. Have the student read the passage and then identify key points first without prompts or look-backs, and then with prompts or look-backs.
4. Try the same procedure with the student at an instructional reading level.

This procedure can be conducted in an individual session or as a group session where students read and then write key ideas from recall. In addition, Moss (2004) also suggests developing a rating scale for evaluating expository text retellings. Highest scores would be for cohesive, well-sequenced accounts that reflect an awareness of the expository text pattern and relate the information to prior knowledge and to real life.

Textbook Reading/Study Strategies Inventory

Although it was originally designed for college students, the Textbook Reading/Study Strategies Inventory (TRSSI; Saumell, Schumm, & Post, 1993) can be used to help students in the intermediate grades reflect about their reading/study skills needs and work with you to set goals for meeting those needs (see Form 9.3). Use the TRSSI at the beginning and end of the year to have students see their progress in reading and learning from text.

How Do You Provide Differentiated Instruction in Expository Reading Comprehension?

Level 1: High-Quality Core Instruction

Traditionally, most basal readers relied primarily on narrative text in the elementary grades. Most recently published basal readers include expository text passages and strategies for comprehension of informational text. While you can take the lead for lesson planning from a basal reader, high-quality core instruction in expository text requires explicit instruction in expository text patterns, guided reading, and multiple strategies. To prepare for high-stakes tests and to strengthen their proficiency in reading comprehension, students should have opportunities for practice of reading comprehension at their independent, instructional, and grade levels. In addition, explicit instruction in how to combine text reading with class notes to prepare for class discussions and tests should be included. High-quality core instruction also includes direct instruction in research skills; Appendix E provides guidelines for helping elementary students learn research skills in the elementary grades.

EXPLICIT INSTRUCTION IN EXPOSITORY TEXT PATTERNS

Explicit instruction in various expository patterns is typically included in basal reading programs. When you are teaching the 12 patterns, several guidelines apply:

1. Make certain that you find a sample passage that provides a clear example of the pattern being taught.
2. Provide opportunities for students to examine pattern features and to discuss how the pattern is alike or different from other patterns.
3. Connect reading and writing. Have students write sentences, paragraphs, or larger passages using the pattern of focus. You will read more about reading–writing connections in Chapter 12.

GUIDED READING

Guided reading is a good approach to helping all students with comprehension—not only during the reading/language arts block, but also during content area instruction in science, social studies, and health. If you are using shared reading and read-alouds each day and still have students who are not fluent readers, or who are reading at a speed that you believe hinders their comprehension, you should work with these students in small guided reading groups. Guided reading has usually been associated with young emergent readers, but can also benefit older readers if you have time to work with students in small groups (Allen, 2000). Some consider guided reading the heart of a balanced reading program (Fountas & Pinnell, 1996). You must have appropriate materials, though, as reading at the instructional level is a critical part of guided reading (Burns, 2001).

In guided reading, the teacher meets with a small group of students and supplies reading materials. (Students should be grouped intentionally, based on their reading/fluency needs.) The students read the selected material silently. The teacher stops the students periodically to make time for questioning, predicting, using strategies, making connections, and reinforcement. The teacher guides the students through the reading process as they are reading, making sure that they are able to read and understand the material. Seeing the students read silently, observing how long it takes each student to read the selected passage, and assessing their reading and comprehension strategies will provide a good indication of the various areas in which each student is struggling. It is important to take the time to create guided reading groups in order to gain this valuable insight. What the students are taught during guided reading time should then transfer into their bank of independent reading strategies.

MULTIPLE STRATEGIES

The National Reading Panel (2000a) has recommended the use of multiple or combined strategies for reading comprehension. Using multiple strategies as part of the curriculum helps students to see how reading comprehension processes work together to learn from text. The use of such strategies puts students on the road to independence.

PARENT POINTER ☞ Selecting Multiple Strategies

Sometimes teachers use so many comprehension strategies that students and parents get mixed up. They become confused by multiple strategies and terms, and end up using nothing. Select multiple strategies carefully. Provide students with ample opportunity to use the strategies both at school and in home learning. If parents learn the language of strategy instruction, they can reinforce on the home front what you are doing in school.

Collaborative Strategic Reading. Collaborative strategic reading (CSR) is a set of comprehension strategies that have been put together in a "system" to assist students who may be at different levels, who have learning disabilities, or who may be English-language learners (ELLs). Students work together in cooperative learning groups to understand expository information (Klingner, Vaughn, Dimino, Schumm, & Bryant, 2002; Klingner, Vaughn, & Schumm, 1998). CSR incorporates four specific comprehension strategies that are explicitly taught to students. These strategies are all based on previous research and include (1) the *preview*, (2) *click and clunk*, (3) *get the gist*, and (4) *wrap-up*. A CSR learning log can be used to help individual students follow along with the process (see Form 9.4).

During the preview stage, students activate background knowledge while building the skill to intrinsically generate interest and motivation to study a particular topic *before* they begin to read a selection. Students learn to scan material, looking for clues to identify what they will be reading about. They will make informed predictions and, as they become more sophisticated in the use of the strategy, develop questions that will set a purpose for reading the material. The preview involves taking an overview of the entire reading assignment for the day. The next two strategies occur *during* reading. Students read through one paragraph or subsection of the text at a time, and then pause to click and clunk and to get the gist.

Click and clunk is a self-monitoring strategy that students implement during reading. The students are clicking if as they are reading they understand the material and can extend their understanding beyond the text they are reading. Students are clunking when they encounter words or concepts they do not understand. Students write down clunk words and phrases as they come across them, and discuss their clunks with the group to develop their understanding of key words and concepts.

During reading, students get the gist by focusing on one paragraph or subsection of text at a time and identify the main idea in 10 words or less. Getting the gist is actually a summarization strategy. *Summarizing* is the identification of the most important idea(s) in the passage or text; it is brief and to the point (Moss, 2004). Retelling and finding the main idea are precursors to summarizing. Summarizing a lengthy text requires identifying and recalling the main idea of several paragraphs or passages and then combining that information into a summary of the entire selection. Brown and Day (1983) created some rules for teaching students to summarize:

1. Teach students to omit insignificant information and redundant information.
2. Teach students how to create general labels for specifics.
3. Teach students to identify explicit main ideas.
4. Teach students how to express implicit main ideas.

Be sure your students can find the main idea and recall important information from the text before you ask them to summarize.

The final strategy is the wrap-up and happens after reading the assigned text material. The wrap-up allows students the opportunity to demonstrate what they have learned by generating "teacher"-type questions about the material they just read. This strategy, like getting the gist, helps students to summarize the main ideas of the selection; it also aids them in understanding and determining what should be remembered for future learning.

CSR is first taught to the students as a whole class, one strategy at a time. Once students have mastered the individual strategies, the teacher organizes students into small, heterogeneous groups where each student has a role (e.g., leader, clunk expert, reporter). Each role is well defined and is interdependent with other group roles.

ReQuest. Research has found that students who generate their own questions improve their comprehension more than students who merely answer teachers' questions (Dole, Duffy, Roehler, & Pearson, 1991). ReQuest (Manzo, 1969) is a procedure whereby both the students and the teacher ask and answer questions. ReQuest is used to assist students with predicting, creating questions, and comprehension monitoring. When a passage is introduced, the teacher and the students read the title and first sentence of the story together. Then they examine the illustrations related to the title and first page. Next, the students are encouraged to ask the teacher as many questions as they can generate in reference to the title, first sentence, and illustrations. After the teacher responds to the questions, the students are asked questions about the title, first sentence, and illustrations. The teacher's goal at this point is to focus the class on the purpose for reading and on the author's purpose. Together, the teacher and students read more of the passage up to a predetermined point. Again, the students are encouraged to ask the teacher as many questions as they can generate in reference to the section read. Then the teacher takes a turn to ask questions. The goal here is identifying important points, clarifying information, and summarizing. This cycle continues for at least 10 minutes, depending on the number of reading segments the teacher identifies. The teacher's questions need to model the types of questions the students need to learn to create and ask—both lower-level (main idea, detail) and higher-level (inference, drawing conclusions, making judgments). Then the students and the teacher read the rest of the passage silently. In culmination, the teacher asks the students if they read for the correct purpose, and asks the students various other comprehension questions. The teacher needs to make sure to help students identify and summarize the most important ideas in the story read. ReQuest can be used with the whole class, with small groups, with individuals, and with ELLs.

Question–Answer Relationships. Question–answer relationships (QARs) assist students in understanding the demands of questions and in learning how to use information sources to respond to questions (Raphael, 1982, 1986). There are four QAR categories: *factual* (Right There), *interpretive* (Think and Search), *applicative* (Author and You), and *transactive* (On My Own). Right There indicates that the answer is "right there" or directly stated in the text. The factual information is explicitly stated and requires the student either to recall it or to locate it in the text. Think and Search indicates that the student must "think and search" the text for the answer. The student needs to interpret and read between the lines in order to put the information read together and draw a conclusion to answer the question. Author and You indicates that the student must think about the information the author has provided in the text and must use prior knowledge to draw an inference in order to answer the question, because the answer is not in the text. On My Own indicates that the student must create an answer based on prior knowledge. The answer is not in the text, and the text information may not even be necessary to answer the question. (See Table 9.2 for the QAR categories and examples of questions for each.)

When teaching QARs, the teacher needs to first introduce the four QAR categories to the students. Second, he or she must model types of questions from each category, using a reading passage the class has read and is familiar with. Next the teacher has students practice identifying and answering each type of QAR. Finally, the students need to apply QARs to class readings.

Questioning the Author. Questioning the author (QtA; Beck, McKeown, Hamilton, & Kucan, 1997) is an approach designed to promote active engagement with text through a close examination of the author's message and intent. Students are taught to examine not only the content of the message, but also the way the message is conveyed. Particular attention is focused on the author's inclusion of considerate or friendly text features (headings, subheadings, introductions, summaries, etc.).

The following questions are used to guide students through QtA:

1. What is the author trying to tell you?
2. Why is the author telling you that?
3. Does the author say it clearly?
4. How could the author have said things more clearly?
5. What would you say instead?

QtA helps students realize that comprehension problems are sometimes caused because the author's language and style is not reader-friendly. It also helps students learn how to tackle difficult text in reading and create more reader-friendly messages in their own writing.

TABLE 9.2. Types of Question–Answer Relationships (QARs) and Examples of Questions

Type of QAR	Example of question
Factual/Right There: The answer is in the text.	What is a peninsula?
Interpretive/Think and Search: The reader must read in different portions of text or between the lines to gather the information and interpret the text. The answer to the question is not explicitly stated in one single part of the text.	How are a peninsula and an island alike and different?
Applicative/Author and You: The reader must put together the information the author has provided in the text with personal background knowledge to answer the question.	The author provides several examples of peninsulas and islands. What are other examples of these land forms? Use your own experience and an atlas to answer this question.
Transactive/On My Own: The answer is not stated in text, nor can it be found in the text.	What do you think it would be like to live on an island, such as Oahu in Hawaii? What would be some advantages and disadvantages of living on an island?

Note. Adapted from Raphael, Taffy E. (1986). Teaching question–answer relationships, revisited. *The Reading Teacher*, *39*(6), 516–522. Copyright 1986 by the International Reading Association. Adapted by permission.

TECH TIP Use WebQuests to Enhance Comprehension

Whether teachers want it or not, the computer has become a fixture in today's classroom. If it is going to be there, why not use it? The *WebQuest*, developed by Bernie Dodge at San Diego State University, was designed as a type of computer-based tool for teachers to use to enhance students' understanding of complex topics. A WebQuest develops the "higher-order" thinking skills that have become a national focus in education. Using a constructivist perspective, the WebQuest strategy promotes student motivation in a particular subject, allows students to work in cooperative groups, and scaffolds background knowledge with new information, allowing students to develop deeper schemata on a particular subject. Because multiple cooperative groups are looking at the same central question, students learn that viable solutions can differ—sometimes considerably. When WebQuests are connected to previous and subsequent activities and topics covered in the class, they become an integrated part of the curriculum and classroom instruction. In addition, and most importantly, students develop the cognitive skills required to guide and monitor their own learning situations. Several sites exist that explain WebQuests and show how to develop your own. But, if you (like most teachers) have limited time, there are also many existing WebQuests that can be implemented as written or modified to meet your needs. Check out the following websites for more in-depth information on WebQuests.

The WebQuest Page, San Diego State University
webquest.sdsu.edu

Bernie Dodge created this site to serve as a resource for individuals using the WebQuest model to teach with the Web.

WebQuests and More
www.ozline.com/learning/index.htm

Tom March has worked with Bernie Dodge since early 1995. This website assists individuals in effectively integrating the Web into classroom instruction, and offers many suggestions and useful links.

Kathy Schrock's Guide for Educators—WebQuests
http://school.discovery.com/schrockguide/webquest/webquest.html

Along with varied WebQuests, this site provides a 16-slide PowerPoint presentation based on the information found at The WebQuest Page site.

Teach-nology WebQuest Generator
www.teach-nology.com/web_tools/web_quest

This site helps individuals create their own WebQuests through the WebQuest Generator, using a step-by-step process. Note that if the complete link does not take you to the site, go to *www.teach-nology.com* and search for Web tools.

ReadingQuests.Org
http://curry.edschool.virginia.edu/go/readquest

This is a website designed for social studies teachers who wish to engage their students more effectively with the content in their classes. ReadingQuests include comprehension strategy instruction and practice materials.

PRACTICE FOR HIGH-STAKES TESTING

High-stakes testing is a reality of elementary and secondary education in today's schools. Parents, teachers, and in some cases students have argued that an overemphasis on test preparation (so-called "teaching to the test") can detract from the curriculum—

particularly from the joy of reading and writing. For the most part, test preparation should be embedded within high-quality reading comprehension instruction, and should use genuine text and motivating contexts. The multiple strategies described earlier can serve as vehicles for test preparation by including the types of questions and genres included in the high-stakes tests. Figure 9.1 lists questions you should ask about the high-stakes test administered to your grade at your school; the answers can inform your approach to instruction.

As McCabe (2003) has pointed out, both good and poor readers can lack a sense of self-efficacy for taking high-stakes tests. Many teachers prepare students by giving them practice passages that are similar to those in the state or district assessment. While this may help some students, others can get frustrated with the length, readability level, and time conditions inherent in the sample passages. Although teachers may want to include practice passages for guided test strategy sessions, practice should also be provided for students at "comfortable" reading levels.

McCabe (2003) suggests ways that teachers can gradually build self-efficacy through providing structured practice opportunities and developing a "can-do" atmosphere in the classroom. Here are some suggestions for making this happen:

1. Schedule some time each week for a reading lab period.
2. Collect materials that are multileveled (e.g., SRA/McGraw Hill, Jamestown Publishing) and that focus on multiple skills and specific skills. Many multileveled materials come with placement tests than can assist you in making individual assignments.
3. Collect materials that will provide students with opportunities to practice basic reading comprehension processes (microprocesses, integrative processes, macroprocesses, elaborative processes, metacognitive processes), based on individual needs and at comfortable reading levels.
4. Give students assignments to complete that are individualized. Start any assignment at a student's independent reading level (see Form 9.5). Give students the opportunity to have initial success.
5. As students complete assignments, grade them immediately so that the students

---

1. What is the readability level of the test?
2. What is the length of text passages?
3. What percentage of the passages are narrative text? Expository text?
4. What types of questions are typical of the test?
5. What subtests does the test include? Decoding? Vocabulary? Comprehension?
6. What are the timing conditions of the test?
7. How are students expected to respond to reading passages? Multiple-choice responses? Written responses to a prompt?
8. What accommodations are made possible for students with disabilities?
9. What accommodations are made possible for ELLs?
10. What scores are generated, and how are those scores interpreted to parents?

FIGURE 9.1. Questions to ask about the high-stakes test for your grade at your school.

can get feedback. If you have a volunteer or paraprofessional in the classroom during reading lab, you can have the volunteer grade the students' work. However, you need to be the one to give students feedback.

6. When students are achieving 90% or higher on assignments, move to a higher grade level. If students are earning a 60% or lower, move to a lower grade level. If students are earning between 61% and 89%, have then redo any mistakes to learn from their errors and then remain at the same grade level for the time being.
7. Gradually add timed conditions.

We have found that reading lab time is engaging for students. They can see their progress as they gradually move up grade levels. Tracking their progress helps them to see what they have achieved. Moreover, students build confidence through day-by-day success.

We have also found that teachers find reading lab to be an opportunity for ongoing, informal assessment. Students' strengths and challenge become readily apparent. The lab format gives teachers the opportunity to pull students for mini-lessons and modeling as needed.

TWO-COLUMN NOTE TAKING

Most students benefit from systematic instruction in taking notes. This includes taking notes while reading text, as well as taking notes from lectures. Instruction in taking notes can begin as early as third grade. Schumm and Lopate (1989) offer these suggestions for teaching note-taking skills:

1. Set a purpose. Discuss why note-taking skills are important in school and in daily life.
2. Set classroom norms. Develop a set of guideline for taking notes. Think about what needs to be done before, during, and after reading or hearing a lecture.
3. Provide a model. Using an overhead projector, show how to take notes. You can use a videotape of a lecture or presentation to assist.
4. Set up practice sessions. Give ample opportunities for practice, and give frequent feedback so that students can make improvements.
5. Give open-note tests from time to time, so that you can assess students' mastery of note-taking skills.

The two-column note-taking system (Pauk, 1962) is one of the more common styles of note taking (see Form 9.6). In the recall column, students keep a running record of the lecture or key ideas from the text. Students should be encouraged to write one idea per line, omit unnecessary words, and put a star by important ideas. Later, key terms and phrases are placed in the cue column as prompts. The students can then use the notes as a study guide, covering up the recall column and using the ideas in the cue column to prompt remembering of information.

Tom Roberts introduced note-taking skills to his sixth graders at the beginning of the school year. He was teaching a unit on famous explorers. First, Tom introduced note-taking guidelines in a whole-class session, using the two-column format. Next, he modeled note taking as the group watched a video on Ponce de León (see Figure 9.2). Teams of students then prepared an oral report on one explorer. Before listening to the group report, Tom assigned the students to read the relevant section of the textbook and take notes on their reading, using the two-column procedure. When the groups gave their

Two-Column Note Taking

Lecture: Juan Ponce de León	Date: 11/9/04
Cue column	Recall column
Life span	Born around 1460? in Spain Died 1521 in Cuba
First expedition	1512, commissioned by King Ferdinand of Spain to find "Bimini" —explored Bahamas —landed in Fla.
What did he name the land he claimed?	Fla. – in Sp. "La Florida" or flower
Whom did he battle?	Calusa Indians
Where did his crew make a base?	Near Fort Myers

Summary ____

____

____

____

____

____

FIGURE 9.2. Two-Column Note Taking (filled-in example).

reports, the other students took notes on the lecture. Students then worked in cooperative learning groups to discuss what they had read and heard, and to combine their notes to prepare for a test. At the end of the unit, Tom gave the students an open-note test on explorers to gauge their progress in taking notes. At the beginning and end of the unit, Tom also had the students write a reflection about their note-taking skills.

Level 2: Supplemental Instruction

EXPOSITORY TEXT WEBS

Expository text webs can be used as a postreading activity or as a prewriting activity for students who need additional instruction in patterns. Using different visual configurations can help students think about the structure of the text and retain the information (see Figure 9.3). As a postreading activity, students can write key ideas from the text, using a form that you provide—or one that they create themselves. As a prewriting activity, students can use a text web to plan paragraphs and essays that correspond to different patterns.

FLIP

Students who are less strategic readers can benefit from direct instruction in how to analyze an expository reading assignment and make a plan for reading. *FLIP* is an acronym for helping students do just that (Schumm & Mangrum, 1991). The students go through five steps. Steps 2–5 require students to rate four aspects of text on a 1 (low) to 5 (high) scale: Friendliness, Language, Interest, and Prior Knowledge.

1. Preview the reading assignment, looking at headings, subheadings, captions, and so on. Read the introduction and summary if included.
2. Rate the friendliness of the assignment. Does it include many friendly text features (e.g., margin notes, headings, study questions, words in color)?
3. Rate the language of the assignment. Does it have many new words and long, complicated sentences?
4. Rate your interest in the assignment topic. Does it seem very interesting to you?
5. Rate your prior knowledge of the topic. Are you familiar with the material being presented?

Better study guides formulate questions in such a way that they prompt strategic reading and focus on one or more aspects of basic reading comprehension processes.

STUDY GUIDES

Study guides (Wood, Lapp, & Flood, 1992) provide road maps for students as they navigate through a reading assignment. Unlike end-of-chapter questions, study guides are meant to have students become active readers as they read and reflect on different portions of text. Good study guides not only focus on the content of what is being read, but also provide scaffolding for use of reading comprehension processes as students read.

Readence, Bean, and Baldwin (2000) recommend three steps for constructing a study guide:

1. Identify the key ideas that you want students to learn from the passage.
2. Develop questions that focus on multiple levels of understanding (you can use Irwin's [1991] model as a guide to doing so).
3. Follow up reading and completion of the study guide with class discussion.

PARENT POINTER ☞ Study Guides

Parents are often perplexed about how to help their children prepare for science and social studies tests based on textbook material. Such texts are typically dense in terms of new vocabulary and new concepts. Student guides not only can guide students as they read and prepare for tests, but

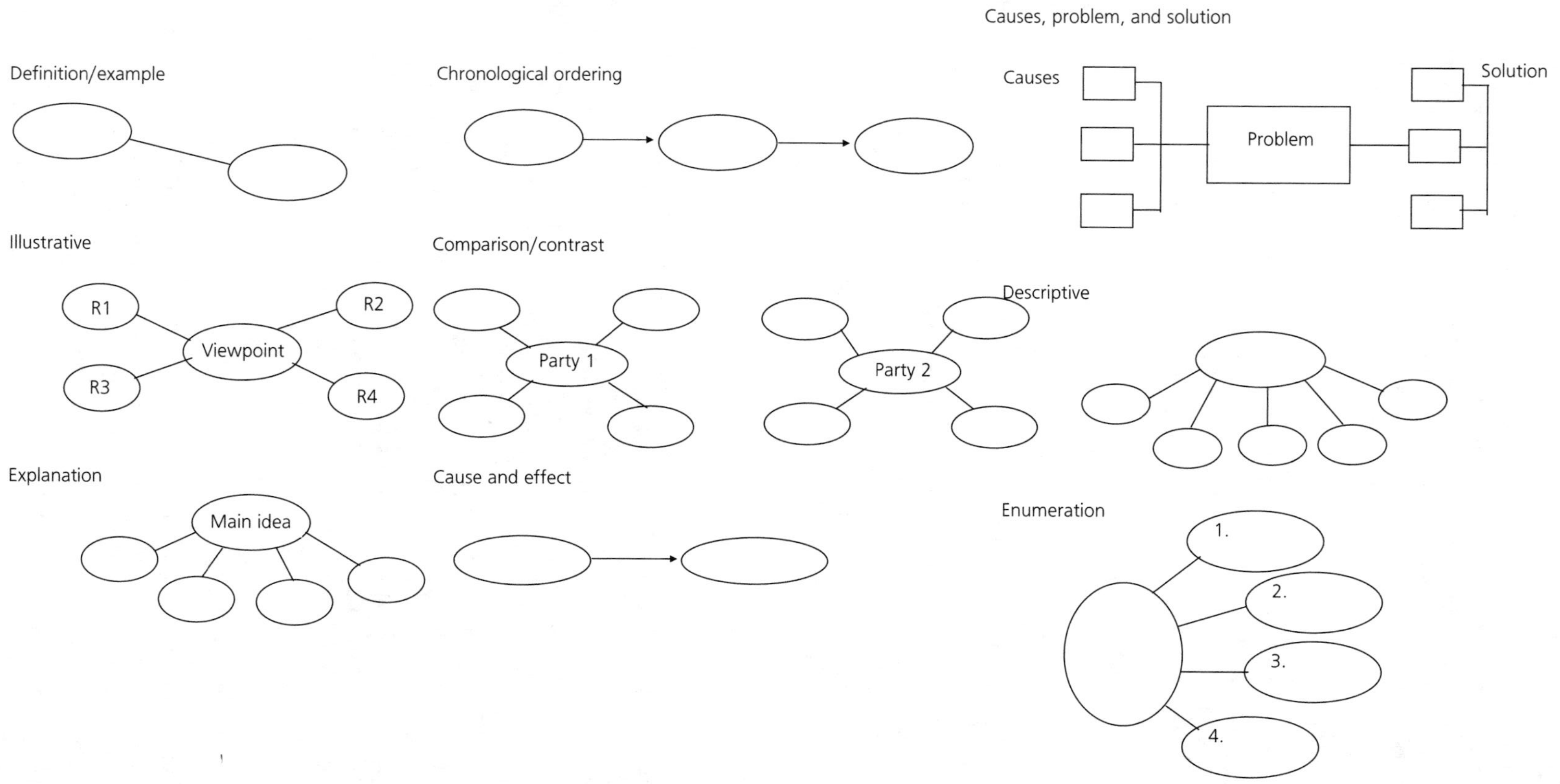

FIGURE 9.3. Expository text webs.

can also provide parents with a structure that helps them understand what their child will be expected to know. As you prepare study guides, think about including parent pointers to let parents know how best they can assist with home learning.

EXPOSITORY TEXT RETELLINGS

Like story retellings, expository text retellings can be used to assess student comprehension and to instruct students about expository text patterns (Moss, 2004). Moss recommends using teacher modeling to start instruction in expository text retellings. Students can work in collaborative learning groups or in small teacher-led groups to participate in retelling sessions. Form 9.7 can be used as a template for teacher, self, and peer review of expository text retellings.

PARAPHRASING FOR COMPREHENSION

Writing a summary can be a daunting task for some students. Fisk and Hurst (2003) provide a sequence for scaffolding instruction for students who need extra support in this area. First, students read a passage, followed by a whole-class or small-group discussion. Second, students read the passage a second time, taking notes along the way. Third, students write a paraphrase or summary in their own words. Finally, students share their paraphrase with a partner and compare how they are alike and different. Form 9.7 can also be used to help students evaluate their own paraphrase or that of a partner.

Level 3: Intensive Support

RESEARCH BRIEF Making Textbook Adaptations

What do classroom teachers think about making textbook adaptations for students with reading and other learning disabilities? To answer this question, Schumm and Vaughn (1991) asked elementary and secondary teachers to rate adaptations recommended in the literature in terms of their desirability (how desirable the adaptation was for student learning) and feasibility (how feasible the adaptation was, given the reality of the classroom condition). In general, most adaptations were recommended as desirable, but feasibility ratings were lower. Clearly, making adaptations is effortful for teachers and takes some planning. However, it is worth the effort. In a later survey of students' perceptions of textbook adaptations, Schumm, Vaughn, and Saumell (1992) found that students of varying grade and achievement levels appreciated such adaptations and preferred teachers who were willing to make them.

READING COMPREHENSION PROCESSES

For some students, expository or narrative text patterns are not the source of reading comprehension problems. Rather, problems are due to underlying processes at the sentence or intersentential levels. Table 9.3 provides instructional activities that can give such students more intensive instruction in microprocessing (sentence level) and integrative processing (connecting sentences).

TABLE 9.3. Instructional Activities for Microprocessing and Integrative Processing

Student difficulties	Instructional suggestions
Student uses word-by-word reading and does not cluster words in meaningful units.	• Work on fluency (see Chapter 7), with an emphasis on echo reading at the sentence level. • Develop a set of flashcards that break sentences apart into meaningful clusters. Have the student read clusters separately and then more fluidly as a sentence. • Have the student use word phrase manipulatives, such as reading rods (ETA/Cuisenaire), to practice reading of phrases.
Student cannot detect the key idea in each sentence.	• Practice *sentence shrinking*—removing one word at a time that is unnecessary until the key idea emerges. • Use commercial materials such as Reading for Understanding that focus on sentence-level processing for guided and independent practice.
Student has limited knowledge of anaphora.	• Select children's books that have clear examples of anaphora. Have the student identify when multiple terms are used to refer to the same person or thing. • During Writers' Workshop, demonstrate how to use anaphora to make writing less repetitive and more interesting.
Student does not know common connecting words.	• Use maze activities. Construct sentences with missing connecting words. Have student select from two or three possible words to complete the sentence. • Show how connecting words are used in different expository patterns.
Student has difficulty "filling in the blanks" when making inferences at the sentence level.	• Use teacher think-alouds to model sentence-to-sentence inferencing.
Student has difficulty remembering ideas at the sentence level and connecting ideas in larger pieces of text.	• Have the student tape-record key ideas while reading. • Teach annotation and note-taking skills.

MULTIPASS

In working with students with disabilities, Schumaker, Deshler, Alley, Warner, and Denton (1984) developed *multipass*, a three-step approach for systematic rereading of expository text. First, students read an assignment to get an overview of the topic and to detect the organization of the text. Second, students read comprehension questions, guess an answer based on their reading of the text and then confirm their guess with a rereading of the passage. Third, students prepare for tests by quizzing themselves on comprehension questions. The multipass strategy is introduced step by step, with lots of teacher modeling and guided practice.

HIGH-INTEREST, LOW-VOCABULARY BOOKS

Students who are struggling with informational text may do so because topics are dry and the readability level of the text is too difficult. High-interest, low-vocabulary books can help reluctant intermediate-grade students to get engaged in reading. Fortunately, the number of such books is increasing rapidly, offering teachers and students more choices.

HIGHLIGHTED TEXTS

Teachers can provide students with highlighted texts that emphasize key ideas important for tests and classroom discussions. The teacher's highlighting serves as a model for students. Teachers can provide explicit instruction on how to highlight, annotate, and take notes from text, to lead students toward independence.

AUDIOTAPES

For students with more severe reading problems, audiotaping of science and social studies texts may be necessary for the students to participate in learning from content area texts. Volunteers and students from higher grade levels can participate in preparing audiotapes for these students to hear in a listening center or at home.

SNAPSHOTS

Expository Reading Comprehension Instruction in a Fifth-Grade Classroom

Tabitha Scott tries to allocate as much time as possible for reading comprehension instruction and practice for her fifth graders. Here's how. Tabitha's reading/language arts block is 90 minutes long. While she is working with one of her three basal reading groups, providing guided reading and lessons in comprehension processes, students work on individualized reading assignments in a reading lab setting. Tabitha works with Marcia Hennings, a paraprofessional, who grades reading lab assignments. Tabitha reviews student lab work daily and makes new assignments for the next day. She also makes note of any mini-lessons she may need to provide for individual students or for groups of students she may pull on a temporary basis.

Students who finish assignments early during the day are allowed to read independently in a self-selected book or continue to work on individual lab assignments.

At the beginning of the year, part of the reading/language arts block is spent on whole-class strategy instruction on the components of CSR. Once students have mastered the strategies, Tabitha plans CSR sessions three times a week during science and social studies lessons. She balances CSR sessions with hands-on activities and projects on alternate days. She also has adapted CSR to assist students in reading of math word problems in cooperative learning groups.

Finally, Tabitha begins and ends each day with a teacher read-aloud. She alternates between narrative and expository texts, with read-alouds to model fluent reading in a variety of genres.

Expository Reading Comprehension Instruction in an Elementary Resource Setting

Paul Winfield is a special educator working with intermediate students with varying exceptionalities. His students are fourth and fifth graders with learning disabilities and behavior disorders. Paul's students are mainstreamed for most of the school day, but they come to a resource room for additional work in reading, writing, and mathematics.

Paul makes every effort to align the strategies for reading comprehension with those used in the general education setting. All teachers in the school have been trained in using CSR, so Paul uses the four strategies with his students in teacher-led reading comprehension strategy sessions. Paul has found that these students can become strategic learners, but that it takes more time and practice.

CONTINUING TO DEVELOP STUDENT READING AND WRITING PROFILES

Part IX of the Student Reading and Writing Profile (Form 9.8) can be used to record your students' assessment results for formal and informal measures of expository text comprehension.

CHAPTER SUMMARY

Comprehension starts with a basic understanding of words, phrases, sentences, and syntax, but it ends in our minds, where our thoughts are—where we mull things over and make decisions. Comprehension is the mechanism through which we decide what to do and believe. Success in reading and learning from expository text involves the reader's motivation, interest, and background knowledge in the subject; familiarity with the conventions of expository text structure; and knowledge of how strategies are used to control and direct meaning making. Good readers have a clear purpose for why they are reading. They also regulate their reading rate and slow down when new and difficult concepts are introduced, and they have well-defined fix-up strategies to overcome trouble spots in the text.

Once students have passed the "learning to read" stage, the bulk of their reading in school centers on gaining information and enhancing knowledge of particular topics. This continues beyond the elementary grades and into adulthood. Therefore, it is important as early as kindergarten for teachers to assist students in identifying different types of expository formats, mastering strategies for comprehending expository text in regular classroom instruction, reading informational trade books on a personal level, and learning how to take high-stakes tests.

KEY TERMS AND CONCEPTS

Cloze
Collaborative strategic reading (CSR)
Expository text patterns
Expository text webs
FLIP
Fourth-grade slump
Guided reading
K-W-L
Multipass
Propositions recalled
Question–answer relationships (QARs)
Questioning the author (QtA)
ReQuest
Study guides
Two-column note taking
WebQuest

REFLECTION AND ACTION

1. Background knowledge is a critical component to comprehension. Choose a topic in a content area, and think about what you know about that specific subject. Write a two-page paper that describes how you acquired that specific knowledge (firsthand experience, reading about it, seeing a movie/video about it, etc.) and how you might incorporate those methods into a comprehension lesson/activity.
2. Choose some content material that is difficult for you to understand. As you read the material, think about which comprehension strategies you use to assist in your understanding of the mate-

rial. Apply those strategies to the text material, and think about how your students might do the same with content material that might be difficult for them to comprehend. Remember, you must be proficient at using a strategy before you can effectively support your students' use of the same strategy.
3. Now that you have read the material and you have applied comprehension strategies to help you understand it, think about which reflection strategies would support long-term retention of the information. Once you have decided on a strategy (i.e., guided reading, CSR, QARs, QtA, and WebQuests, etc.), do it. As you are completing the reflection strategy of your choice, think about how your students would apply the same strategy. Is there a different strategy that might work better? Would different students benefit more using other reflection strategies? Why did you choose the one you did? How can you help students choose the most appropriate strategy for the task/activity?
4. Think about how you would put the previous tasks together to create a study system that would support student learning and preparation for testing. Which strategy or strategies would you use, and why? How would you help your students choose the best strategies to meet their learning needs?
5. Examine the Partner Paraphrasing Form (Form 9.7). How could you modify that checklist for students in the primary grades?

READ ON!

Barrentine, S. J., & Stokes, S. M. (Ed.). (2005). *Reading assessment: Principles and practices for elementary teachers* (2nd ed.). Newark, DE: International Reading Association.

A collection of articles from *The Reading Teacher*, with practical suggestions and instruments for classroom use. Includes an appendix written by a panel of experts in reading assessment discussing the pros and cons of high-stakes tests.

Block, C. C., & Pressley M. (2002). *Comprehension instruction: Research-based best practices.* New York: Guilford Press.

Excellent resource for finding and implementing research-based reading comprehension practices.

Dougherty Stahl, K. A. (2004). Proof, practice, and promise: Comprehension strategy instruction In the primary grades. *The Reading Teacher*, *57*, 598–609.

Dougherty Stahl reviews the research on reading comprehension instruction in the primary grades. She identifies research-based practices that teachers use more and less frequently. She also identifies practices with a limited research based that frequently used.

Gersten, R. M., & Jimenez, R. T. (1998). *Promoting learning for culturally and linguistically diverse students*. Belmont, CA: Wadsworth.

The chapter on comprehension will help teachers understand the needs of diverse students.

Klingner, J. K., & Vaughn, S. (1999). Promoting reading comprehension, content learning and English acquisition through collaborative strategic reading. *The Reading Teacher*, *52*, 738–747.

Klingner, J. K., Vaughn, S., & Schumm, J. D. (1998). Collaborative strategic reading in heterogeneous classrooms. *Elementary School Journal*, *99*, 3–21.

These two articles discuss research on CSR and provide detailed instructions on how to implement CSR in the classroom setting.

National Reading Panel. (2000). *Teaching children to read: An evidence-based assessment of the scientific research literature on reading and its implications for reading instruction.* Rockville, MD: National Institute of Child Health and Human Development.

Chapter 4 specifically deals with comprehension and provides information about best practices, as well as providing references for follow-up. This chapter can also be downloaded from a website (*www.nichd.nih.gov/publications/nrp/report.htm*).

Pearson, P. D., & Johnson, D. D. (1978). *Teaching reading comprehension.* New York: Holt, Rinehart & Winston.

This classic book is a landmark text linking theory to practice in the teaching of reading comprehension.

Pearson, P. D., Roehler, L. R., Dole, J. A., & Duffy, G. G. (1992). Developing expertise in reading comprehension. In S. J. Samuel & A. E. Farstrup (Eds.), *What research has to say about reading instruction* (pp. 145–199). Newark, DE: International Reading Association.

Excellent review and summary of comprehension strategies. Describes how teaching comprehension strategies is different from teaching skills.

Readence, J. E., Bean, T. W., & Baldwin, R. S. (2000). *Content area literacy: An integrated approach* (8th ed.). Dubuque, IA: Kendall/Hunt.

An excellent guide for teachers, providing instructional suggestions for teaching expository text reading, writing, and related study skills.

Sweet, A. P., & Snow, C. E. (2003). *Rethinking reading comprehension.* New York: Guilford Press.

This book, a collection of research articles, addresses comprehension from different perspectives and summarizes findings of the Rand Reading Study Group.

SHARPENING YOUR SKILLS: SUGGESTIONS FOR PROFESSIONAL DEVELOPMENT

1. The National Reading Panel report (see "Read On!") described 20 years of research supporting the use of reading strategies to promote comprehension. Choose five research-based comprehension strategies and become proficient in their use. Make a plan to assist your students in becoming proficient at matching each strategy to text and applying the strategy to learning tasks.
2. Visit colleagues as they model different comprehension strategies in their classroom. Incorporate effective techniques into your own instructional style. Have a colleague observe you as you model a comprehension strategy for your students.
3. The International Reading Association publishes modules for teacher literacy study groups. The modules include a text, selected articles, lesson plans, and a module study guide. Modules on vocabulary, reading comprehension, struggling readers, and ELLs are available. Have your study group make use of these modules.

RESOURCES FOR ASSESSMENT AND INSTRUCTION

Duke, N. K., & Bennett-Armistead, V. S. (2003). *Reading and writing informational text in the primary grades: Research-based practices.* New York: Scholastic.

This book describes the need form informational text in the primary grades and discusses how to integrate research-based practices into classroom activities.

Hoyt, L. (2003). *Navigating informational texts: Easy and explicit strategies, K–5* [Videotapes]. Portsmouth, NH: Heinemann.

This set of three videos demonstrate research-based instructional practices for students including ELL students.

Klingner, J. K., Vaughn, S., Dimino, J., Schumm, J. S., & Bryant, D. (2002). *From clunk to click: Collaborative strategic reading.* Longmont, CO: Sopris West.

This book on CSR contains lessons for all four strategies and includes sample teacher–student dialogues, suggestions for whole-class activities, and reproducible materials.

Kristo, J., & Bamford, R. (2004). *Nonfiction in focus: A comprehensive framework for helping students become independent readers and writers of nonfiction, K–6.* New York: Scholastic.

This book provides a step-by-step approach to developing a curriculum for teaching expository text. Provides plentiful strategies and classroom examples.

McLaughlin, M., & DeVoogd, G. (2004). *Critical literacy: Enhancing students' comprehension of text.* New York: Scholastic.

Here is a guide for teaching critical reading. It provides suggestions and strategies for helping students to become more analytic readers and to express their own opinions and responses to a variety of texts.

Pearson, P. D., & Harvey, S. (2004). *Nonfiction reading and writing workshops.* Washington, DC: National Geographic Society.

This set of modules provides guidelines and materials for teaching 15 different expository text patterns and formats (e.g., compare/contrast, biographical sketch, informational article). Includes suggestions for modeling.

Readence, J. R., Moore, D. W., & Rickelman, R. J. (2000). *Prereading activities for content area reading and learning* (3rd ed.). Newark, DE: International Reading Association.

This collection of prereading activities will help you get students engaged in text.

Schumm, J. S. (2001). *School power* (2nd ed.). Minneapolis, MN: Free Spirit.

Originally designed for middle school students, this handbook is equally appropriate for intermediate-grade elementary students. Written for students, this book provides study skill guidelines written in "kid-appropriate" language.

Strichert, S. S., & Mangrum, C. T. (2001). *Teaching study skills and strategies to students with learning disabilities, attention deficit disorder, or special needs* (3rd ed.). Boston: Allyn & Bacon.

A step-by-step guide to teaching note taking, test taking, and other reading-related study skills to students with special needs.

Wood, K. D., Lapp, D., & Flood, J. (1992). *Guiding readers through text: A review of study guides.* Newark, DE: International Reading Association.

This monograph is a collection of sample study guides. Descriptions of how to construct and implement study guides are included.

RECOMMENDED WEBSITES

Center for the Improvement of Early Reading Achievement (CIERA)
www.ciera.org

This is the site for a federally funded research group focused on research-based practices for early reading. The site includes a library of center-generated resources, as well as links to other sites related to reading.

Center for the Study of Reading
www.ed.uiuc.edu/BER

Founded in 1976 at the University of Illinois, the faculty at this research center has led the way in comprehension research. The site includes summaries of center-generated research.

LD Online
ldonline.org

LD Online provides resources for parents and teachers in working with students with disabilities. It includes references to research findings and specific in-depth instructional strategies in reading.

Reading Quest
http://curry.edschool.virginia.edu/go/readquest/strat

This site has an excellent collection of reading strategies for use in content area instruction. The site offers downloadable handouts for many of the strategies.

Step by Step
www.csrclearinghouse.org

Step by Step is an online resource for instructional practices sponsored by the National Clearinghouse for School Reform. The site has links to training modules and other resources for improving the quality of reading comprehension instruction.

FORM 9.1. Textbook Awareness Checklist

Textbook Awareness Checklist

Questions to pose about text features	Check if correct	Verbatim response if incorrect
1. Show me the title page. What information is usually included in a title page?		
2. Show me the table of contents. How do you use the table of contents?		
3. Show me the index. How do you use an index?		
4. Show me the glossary. What information is included in a glossary?		
5. Show me the bibliography. What is the purpose of a bibliography?		
6. Show me the appendix. What is the purpose of an appendix?		
7. Look in Chapter 1. What special features does this book have in the chapter that can help you learn?		

FORM 9.2. K-W-L Strategy Sheet

K-W-L Strategy Sheet

K—What we know	W—What we want to find out	L—What we learned and still need to learn

FORM 9.3. Textbook Reading/Study Strategies Inventory

Textbook Reading/Study Strategies Inventory (TRSSI)

Directions: The purpose of this scale is to learn more about your perceptions of various reading and study strategies. We are interested in knowing how familiar you are with different strategies, how effective you feel the strategies are in helping you learn, and how often you use the strategies to read and study for tests.

For example, you may be very familiar with how to outline textbook chapters, so your familiarity rating might be a 5. However, because outlining is very time-consuming, you use that strategy only rarely, so your *use* rating might be a 2.

Rate each of the strategies below on a 1–5 scale (1 = low; 5 = high) in terms of familiarity and use. Circle the number of your rating for each strategy in the appropriate column.

Strategy	Familiarity					Actual use				
1. Identify prefixes and suffixes to pronounce words or get the meaning of words.	1	2	3	4	5	1	2	3	4	5
2. Use context clues to get the meaning of words.	1	2	3	4	5	1	2	3	4	5
3. Use the glossary or dictionary to define words in textbooks.	1	2	3	4	5	1	2	3	4	5
4. Conduct a chapter preview before you read.	1	2	3	4	5	1	2	3	4	5
5. Read chapter introduction and summary before reading the whole chapter.	1	2	3	4	5	1	2	3	4	5
6. Underline key concepts in the textbook.	1	2	3	4	5	1	2	3	4	5
7. Make notes on key concepts presented in the textbook.	1	2	3	4	5	1	2	3	4	5
8. Take notes on key concepts presented in the textbook.	1	2	3	4	5	1	2	3	4	5
9. Outline textbook information.	1	2	3	4	5	1	2	3	4	5
10. Create tables or charts of textbook information.	1	2	3	4	5	1	2	3	4	5
11. Draw semantic maps of textbook information.	1	2	3	4	5	1	2	3	4	5

(cont.)

Adapted from Saumell, L., Schumm, J., & Post, S. (1993). *College Students' Perceptions of the Feasibility of Reading and Study Strategies*. Paper presented at the College Reading Association Conference, Richmond, VA. Reprinted in *Reading Assessment and Instruction for All Learners*, edited by Jeanne Shay Schumm.

Strategy	Familiarity					Actual use				
12. Use study questions presented in the textbook to guide your reading or review of a chapter.	1	2	3	4	5	1	2	3	4	5
13. Develop flashcards of key textbook information.	1	2	3	4	5	1	2	3	4	5
14. Reread chapters to prepare for tests.	1	2	3	4	5	1	2	3	4	5
15. Use chapter headings and subheadings to guide reading and study.	1	2	3	4	5	1	2	3	4	5
16. Monitor your understanding while you read, and take action to use "fix-up" strategies when you don't understand.	1	2	3	4	5	1	2	3	4	5
17. Identify main ideas of paragraphs as you read.	1	2	3	4	5	1	2	3	4	5
18. Identify most important details as you read.	1	2	3	4	5	1	2	3	4	5
19. Use paragraph organization (such as cause and effect or problem and solution) to help you understand as you read.	1	2	3	4	5	1	2	3	4	5
20. Use punctuation clues to help you understand difficult sentences.	1	2	3	4	5	1	2	3	4	5
21. Use typographic aids such as boldface type and italics to help identify key information.	1	2	3	4	5	1	2	3	4	5
22. Use multistep reading strategies such as SQ3R.	1	2	3	4	5	1	2	3	4	5
23. Relate new information to what you already know.	1	2	3	4	5	1	2	3	4	5
24. Create mental pictures or images to envision what you are reading.	1	2	3	4	5	1	2	3	4	5
25. Anticipate or predict what the author will say next as you read.	1	2	3	4	5	1	2	3	4	5
26. Predict questions teachers might ask on tests.	1	2	3	4	5	1	2	3	4	5
27. Write summaries to reflect on key information in chapters.	1	2	3	4	5	1	2	3	4	5

(cont.)

Strategy	Familiarity					Actual use				
28. Adjust your reading rate to your purpose for reading and the level of difficulty of the material.	1	2	3	4	5	1	2	3	4	5
29. Practice for tests using rehearsal or recitation strategies.	1	2	3	4	5	1	2	3	4	5
30. Use mnemonic or memory systems to remember information for tests.	1	2	3	4	5	1	2	3	4	5
31. Read chapter before taking notes on the topic in class.	1	2	3	4	5	1	2	3	4	5
32. Review lecture notes within 24 hours after taking the notes.	1	2	3	4	5	1	2	3	4	5
33. Rewrite lecture notes.	1	2	3	4	5	1	2	3	4	5
34. Examine author's ideas to judge the use and value of the reading assignment.	1	2	3	4	5	1	2	3	4	5
35. Identify facts and opinions as you read.	1	2	3	4	5	1	2	3	4	5
36. Set goals and schedule for study sessions.	1	2	3	4	5	1	2	3	4	5
37. Use specific strategies to study for different kinds of tests (e.g., multiple-choice, essay, identification).	1	2	3	4	5	1	2	3	4	5
38. Use performances on first test in a class to adjust study strategies for subsequent tests.	1	2	3	4	5	1	2	3	4	5
39. Prepare for tests by meeting with a study partner or study group.	1	2	3	4	5	1	2	3	4	5

My goals for improving my reading and study strategies this semester are:

1. ______________________________
2. ______________________________
3. ______________________________

FORM 9.4. Collaborative Strategic Reading (CSR) Recording Sheet

Collaborative Strategic Reading (CSR) Recording Sheet

Name ______________________________

Date ______________________________

Group name ______________________________

Assignment ______________________________

Step 1: Preview
- Write what you know.
- Write what you want to learn.

Step 2: Click and clunk
- Read one section.
- Record your clunks.
- Fix up the clunks and write your answers.

Step 3: Get the gist
- Think about the section you just read.
- What is the most important who or what?
- What is the most important idea about who or what?

Step 4: Wrap-up
- After reading all sections for today's assignment, think about what you just read.
- Write the big ideas about what you learned.
- Write some questions that ask about the most important information.

What I know [Step 1: Preview]	What I want to learn [Step 1: Preview]	What I learned [Step 4: Wrap-up]

Step 2: Clicks and clunks
Step 3: Get the gist

Section 1 ______________________________

Clunks ______________________________

____

____

Gist ______________________________

____

____

Section 2 ______________________________

Clunks ______________________________

____

____

Gist ______________________________

____

____

Section 3 ______________________________

Clunks ______________________________

____

____

Gist ______________________________

____

____

Section 4 ______________________________

Clunks ______________________________

____

____

Gist ______________________________

____

____

Section 5 ______________________________

Clunks ______________________________

____

____

Gist ______________________________

____

____

Step 4: Wrap-Up
Test questions:

____

____

____

____

FORM 9.5. Daily Reading Assignments

Daily Reading Assignments

Name ____

Title of material __________ Title of material ______________ Title of material ______________

Date assigned	Date completed	Exercise #	# Right 1st try	# Total possible	% Right 1st try	% Right 2nd try	Level	Comments	Date assigned	Date completed	Exercise #	# Right 1st try	# Total possible	% Right 1st try	% Right 2nd try	Level	Comments	Date assigned	Date completed	Exercise #	# Right 1st try	# Total possible	% Right 1st try	% Right 2nd try	Level
1									1									1							
2									2									2							
3									3									3							
4									4									4							
5									5									5							
6									6									6							
7									7									7							
8									8									8							
9									9									9							
10									10									10							
11									11									11							
12									12									12							

Your instructor will (1) initial every assignment (you never write on this sheet); (2) move you up when you make 90% or more; (3) move you down when you make 60% or below; (4) take off an assignment when you reach 12th-grade level in that material with a 90% average; and (5) encourage you to do one assignment from all nine columns before doing a second assignment in any.

FORM 9.6. Two-Column Note Taking

Two-Column Note Taking

Lecture: <u>Cue column</u>	Date: <u>Recall column</u>

Summary ____

FORM 9.7. Partner Paraphrasing

Partner Paraphrasing

Partner 1 ______________________________ Partner 2 ______________________________

Step One: Examine your own paraphrase.	Yes	Sometimes	No
1. Did I write the paraphrase in mostly my own words?			
2. Did I write in all the important ideas?			
3. Did I remove unnecessary details?			

Step Two: Examine your partner's paraphrase, and then discuss.	Yes	Sometimes	No
1. Did my partner write the paraphrase in mostly his or her own words?			
2. Did my partner keep in all the important ideas?			
3. Did my partner remove unnecessary details?			
4. How was my partner's paraphrase like mine?			
5. How was my partner's paraphrase different from mine?			
6. What are some ideas for making our paraphrases better next time?			

FORM 9.8. Student Reading and Writing Profile (Part IX)

Student Reading and Writing Profile

Part IX: Expository Reading Comprehension

Expository Comprehension

Name of test	Date	Score

Student strengths in expository comprehension ______________________________

____

____

Student areas for improvement in expository comprehension ______________________

____

____

Instructional recommendations ______________________________________

____

____

TEN

The Wonder of Words

Learning and Expanding Vocabulary

LINA LOPEZ CHIAPPONE

VIGNETTE

'Twas brillig, and the slithy toves
Did gyre and gimble in the wabe:
All mimsy were the borogoves,
And the mome raths outgrabe.
"Beware the Jabberwock, my son!
The jaws that bite, the claws that catch!
Beware the Jubjub bird, and shun
The frumious Bandersnatch!" . . .

[As Alice put it,] "It seems very pretty," she said when she had finished it, "but it's *rather* hard to understand!" (You see she didn't like to confess, even to herself, that she couldn't make it out at all.) "Somehow it seems to fill my head with ideas—only I don't exactly know what they are!"

(Lewis Carroll, from *Through the Looking-Glass and What Alice Found There*, 1872/1996)

As Pat Simmons reads the beginning of the poem "Jabberwocky" to her fourth graders, Alice's lament over not understanding what she read rings loud and clear for this language arts teacher. Her students began the school year excited about the units of study Pat had planned. But now all that seems to be changing, and the transition to a new grade has not been easy. While the students are able to read near or on grade level and are able to keep up with the work in general, the material seems to be getting harder and harder for them to understand. At times, it seems that every other word on the page confuses the students. Blank stares from students are common after they finish reading a passage. And like the fictitious Alice, they feel that their heads are filled with ideas, but they don't know exactly what these are.

From discussions with her colleagues at school, Pat realizes that while in previous years her students were diligent about completing assigned schoolwork, they never grew beyond that to develop the reading habit, and the lack of this habit has contributed to their limited vocabulary. Although at one time the students used to enjoy reading, their subsequent attempts to embrace reading for pleasure have been sporadic. Now that the reading task has become more arduous, Pat has noticed that the students are growing increasingly reluctant to read the assigned work or to read for enjoyment.

Pat has determined that the students are able to decode words well, but that their comprehension is hampered because the students lack a wide vocabulary to understand what they read. When they read, they are merely word calling. Pat teaches some vocabulary words, particularly those specifically related to the content areas. But she is also aware that direct instruction does not account for all vocabulary learning. So she also needs to engage her students in effective instructional techniques and strategies, to help them learn how to learn new words on their own. Now that Pat Simmons has identified her main goals for vocabulary instruction, how can she best achieve them?

ANTICIPATION QUESTIONS

- How does background knowledge relate to word learning, and how can teachers assist students in developing such knowledge?
- What strategies are effective for encouraging independent word learning?
- How do you decide what words to teach?
- How can teachers address the special needs of students with learning disabilities or students who are English-language learners (ELLs)?
- How can teachers use both formal and informal assessment to determine students' needs?
- What vocabulary-learning strategies are most useful for before, during, and after reading?
- What is the most effective way to incorporate dictionary use?
- What strategies and materials can be used to stimulate students' interest in language?

INTRODUCTION

While people may list many characteristics when asked to define what it means to be an "educated person," having command of a rich vocabulary is one of the most obvious traits essential to this definition. Our vocabulary identifies us in a variety of ways. For example, the use of some words might place us in certain socioeconomic categories or as being from a particular region of the country. The connection between a rich and varied vocabulary and school achievement has been long recognized. Research supports that such a vocabulary is needed to excel in school, because of the extent to which it relates to successful reading comprehension. Vocabulary knowledge is closely connected and critical to the comprehension and understanding of text, as the poem "Jabberwocky" demonstrates (Stahl, Hare, Sinatra, & Gregory, 1991; Stahl & Jacobson, 1986).

Nagy and Herman (1987) estimated that there are 88,500 distinct word families in the printed English used in grades 3–9. Even systematic, explicit teaching of vocabulary would not enable teachers and students to meet this goal. Nagy and Herman also estimated that each year through grade 12, the average child learns about eight words per day. But what about children who are not average? Consider students who are ELLs, or those who have reading difficulties. While some students might learn as many as eight or more words in one day, many others are learning significantly fewer than that, perhaps even none (Shefelbine, 1990; White, Graves, & Slater, 1990). Furthermore, in today's Information Age, where we talk of "multiliteracies" and "information as a source of power," the ability to learn new vocabulary efficiently and independently is more important than ever.

VOCABULARY DEVELOPMENT

How do students learn new words? What factors contribute to rich vocabulary development? How can teachers meet the needs of learners of diverse abilities or backgrounds? Studies have shown that no one method of vocabulary instruction is superior in all circumstances and for all purposes (Harris & Sipay, 1990). Therefore, developing a systematic vocabulary program that encompasses a variety of approaches is one way teachers can begin to answer these questions and begin to devise a master plan for instructing students in vocabulary—a plan that they hope will help mold students into lifelong word learners and word lovers.

What Does Research Say about Vocabulary Instruction?

The importance of developing students' vocabulary is a commonly held goal among reading teachers. However, while classroom teachers often talk about the importance of word study, most are unable to specifically define the role and relevance of a well-developed vocabulary program that supports reading comprehension, particularly for students in grades 1–3. *Preventing Reading Difficulties in Young Children* (edited by Snow, Burns, & Griffin, 1998) examined the effectiveness of interventions for young children who are at risk of problems in learning to read; it found that important sources of word knowledge are exposure to print and independent reading, as well as direct instruction using strategies that focus in particular on knowledge in the content areas.

The committee that researched and prepared the Snow and colleagues (1998) report for the U.S. Department of Education and the U.S. Department of Health and Human Services included some of the most respected researchers in literacy and cognition, including Marilyn Jager Adams, Edward Kame'enui, Keith Stanovich, and Elizabeth Sulzby. The committee's review of research found that vocabulary study, which includes having full and precise understanding of the meanings of words, promotes comprehension. The implications for the classroom include the use of strategies that not only teach specific vocabulary but encourage wide reading—by far the most important source for learning new vocabulary in authentic contexts, especially since no vocabulary teaching program alone can produce the vocabulary growth that is necessary to become a proficient reader.

Vocabulary instruction was also examined as part of the National Reading Panel (2000a) report. While the number of studies that met the Panel's criteria was too small for a formal meta-analysis, 50 studies were identified to examine trends and to glean suggestions for instruction and future research. The Panel endorsed direct and indirect vocabulary instruction, teaching of vocabulary in context, and the use of technology in the teaching of vocabulary. The Panel also concluded that current research does not indicate which specific instructional approaches or combinations of approaches best promote vocabulary learning, and that more research is needed. However, it did encourage the use of multiple approaches, both direct and indirect.

Wide Reading

Wide reading is often mentioned as an important quality of effective vocabulary instruction (Blachowicz & Lee, 1991; Nagy, 1998). Time spent engaged in independent reading can have positive effects upon children's reading proficiency, including incidental learning of words and acquiring higher levels of word mastery through practice, which improves automaticity. As students learn new words well, opportunities for learning other words dramatically increase. By reading a variety of genres, students not only are exposed to new vocabulary, but experience known words in new contexts to foster deeper levels of word knowledge (Cunningham, Moore, Cunningham, & Moore, 2000). This type of incidental learning of vocabulary does not have a significant effect in the short run; rather, there appear to be cumulative and long-term effects on general knowledge and the understanding of broad topics, which support reading comprehension (Harris & Sipay, 1990). For the effects of wide reading to be most influential, several factors need to be considered: text difficulty, number of words unknown to the reader, contextual support, and the child's ability to infer meaning from context or morphology. A dynamic program of classroom vocabulary teaching and learning addresses these issues and provides direct instruction in these skills, so that students are able to transfer this knowledge to their independent reading.

Direct Teaching of Words

A well-rounded vocabulary program also includes direct teaching of words–in particular, content-specific words—which is further enhanced by repeated exposure to words through reading. The more children read, the more new and partially known words they will encounter, and the more word knowledge they will acquire. By developing in young children the skills that will help them successfully learn new words, teachers are also teaching them how to be independent learners whose vocabularies will continue to expand outside the classroom.

The direct teaching of vocabulary seems to be particularly important for students with learning disabilities (Jitendra, Edwards, Sacks, & Jacobson, 2004). Vocabulary acquisition through wide reading can be stilted if students have difficulty decoding or are not inclined to participate in independent reading on a regular basis. In their review of research on vocabulary instruction for students with learning disabilities, Jitendra et al. concluded that direct instruction coupled with systematic practice were important for vocabulary development among students with language-based disabilities.

Cognates and the Vocabulary Learning of ELLs

For ELLs, the use of *cognates* is a valuable source of information that can be used to support reading comprehension. Cognates are words in two or more languages that share phonological and/or orthographic form, and that may be related semantically. Psycholinguists explain early vocabulary development of ELLs through the *parasitic hypothesis*. This notion in part explains the use of cognates by stating that on initial exposure to a word in the new language (L2), ELLs automatically resort to linking the new word to an existing one in the native language (L1) or the L2 by detecting phonological and orthographic forms (Hall, 2002). The new word latches on, in a sense, to existing knowledge of language forms.

One study showed that among ELLs whose L1 was Spanish and who had equal English vocabulary knowledge, Spanish vocabulary knowledge and the ability to recognize cognates predicted English reading comprehension; this indicated that students used positive transfer of cognate relationships in their English reading (Nagy, Garcia, Durgunoglu, & Hancin-Bhatt, 1993). However, some studies confirm that less fluent bilingual individuals who have a greater uncertainty about the new language may more quickly assume that two similar words are cognates. Similarly, fully fluent bilingual individuals are sometimes confused by *false cognates*, or words that are similar in appearance, however vastly differing in meaning (Hall, 2002).

By viewing students' L1 skills as an asset, teachers can capitalize on that linguistic knowledge to facilitate acquisition of vocabulary in the L2. Instruction in root words, both of Latin and of Germanic origin, needs to be part of a reading program serving ELLs. Even novice learners will recognize cognates easily when they begin to realize how many English words they do know, based on their similarity to words in their native language (Rodriguez, 2001). Interestingly, Spanish-speaking ELLs often know many words that native speakers of English do not know or rarely use, such as *culpable* (*guilty*) and *penultimate* (*second to last*). Finally, because cognates are more easily recognized during reading than during listening, independent reading of a wide selection of topics and genres needs to be modeled, encouraged, and supported.

RESEARCH BRIEF Addressing the Vocabulary Needs of ELLs

One reading intervention with fifth-grade Hispanic ELLs and native English speakers (Carlo et al., 2004) tested the impact of a 15-week English vocabulary enrichment intervention that combined direct word instruction with word-learning strategies. During the study, 12–15 words were directly taught each week during 30- to 45-minute daily sessions, with a review of previous words being done every five weeks. Words to be taught during the intervention were general-purpose academic words selected according to Beck, McKeown, and Kucan's (2002) method (described later in this chapter), as well as those words that had meaning depth potential and that could be used to teach cognates.

Researchers found that a challenging curriculum that focused on teaching academic words, awareness of polysemy, strategies for inferring word meaning from context, and tools for analyzing morphological and cross-linguistic aspects of word meaning did improve the performance of both ELLs and native speakers of English to equal degrees. An improvement in comprehension was also noted, even though the study did not focus specifically on teaching comprehension. Researchers suggested that teachers should introduce novel words in the context of engaging texts, design many activities such as charades that allow learners to manipulate and analyze word meaning, heighten attention to words in general, ensure that students write and spell the target words several times, ensure repeated exposures to the novel words, and help children note how the word meaning varies as a function of context. Furthermore, Carlo and colleagues (2004) reported that teaching children strategies for inferring the meaning of unknown words is effective with both ELLs and native English speakers, if it builds on well-verified procedures such as teaching how to use context cues, teaching morphological analysis, and teaching about cognates.

Seven Principles of Vocabulary Instruction

The best way to teach vocabulary has been a topic of debate among reading researchers for decades (Blachowicz & Fisher, 2000). Research examining the various perspectives on a general theory of vocabulary instruction reveals seven common principles to guide instruction (see Figure 10.1). While there are distinctions between students with language

Principle 1: Develop awareness of stages of word knowledge.
Principle 2: Build experiential background for students.
Principle 3: Make word learning related to students' backgrounds.
Principle 4: Develop depth of meaning through multiple sources and repeated exposures.
Principle 5: Foster appreciation and enthusiasm for word learning.
Principle 6: Teach strategies to build independent word learning.
Principle 7: Teach words in context.

FIGURE 10.1. Seven principles of vocabulary instruction.

differences (ELLs) and students with language disorders, the principles apply to both groups as well as to the vocabulary learning of all students.

PRINCIPLE 1: DEVELOP AWARENESS OF STAGES OF WORD KNOWLEDGE

Knowing word meanings is not a destination, but rather a journey. Growth in acquiring word meanings occurs along a continuum. No one learns the full meaning of a new word, along with all the shades of meaning it carries, in a single exposure. Dale and O'Rourke (1971) list four stages of word knowledge:

1. I never saw it before.
2. I've heard of it, but I don't know what it means.
3. I recognize it in context—it has something to do with . . .
4. I know it.

The progression from never having seen a word to possessing a deep understanding of it requires explicit instruction, use of meaningful context, and a variety of opportunities to experience the word. Beck, McKeown, and Omanson (1987) have suggested that the continuum of word knowledge includes the following points:

1. No knowledge.
2. A general sense—such as knowing that the word *chubby* has a more positive connotation than the word *fat* does.
3. Narrow, context-bound knowledge—such as knowing that a *radiant* bride is a beautifully smiling and happy one, but being unable to describe an individual in a different context as *radiant.*
4. Having knowledge of a word, but not being able to recall it readily enough to use it in appropriate situations.
5. Rich, decontextualized knowledge of a word's meaning, its relationship to other words, and its extension to metaphorical uses—such as understanding what someone is doing when he or she is *picking your brain.*

PRINCIPLE 2: BUILD EXPERIENTIAL BACKGROUND FOR STUDENTS

Students who are equally actively involved in rich experiences in and out of the classroom have the potential to build equally rich vocabularies. However, even in the rare event that all of the students in your classroom come from similar backgrounds (e.g., culturally, linguistically, economically), not all of them will have comparable levels of experiences to draw upon. A crucial part of building your students' vocabularies is to provide rich experiences, even if this is done indirectly through videos, computer simulations, or other media. Then it is important to talk about these experiences and begin to incorporate new words that arise from the active learning. By discussing the activity, students can concretize it and commit it to memory. Consider this important point: It is no coincidence that childhood memories generally begin to be recalled at about age two, when an explosion of language occurs for most children. The ability to express with language what children have experienced routes the experience into their memory banks (Wells, 2004).

PRINCIPLE 3: MAKE WORD LEARNING RELATED TO STUDENTS' BACKGROUNDS

When students can personalize word learning and connect it to their backgrounds, they become actively engaged in making connections between and among words. Personalization can occur when students devise mnemonic strategies for remembering words or when they are involved in the selection of words for study (Beck & McKeown, 1983; Blachowicz & Fisher, 2000; Carr, 1985; Gipe, 1979–1980; Pressley, Levin, & Delaney, 1982). Activities that require students to develop a personal clue for each new word help deepen comprehension of meaning. Students who self-select words for instruction not only tend to choose words at or above grade level, but retain knowledge of their meanings. Furthermore, vocabulary strategies used as part of reciprocal teaching tend to have positive effects on reading comprehension as well (Rosenshine & Meister, 1994). Personalization of vocabulary instruction is also effective for establishing relationships among new and previously learned words and for boosting retention of meaning.

PRINCIPLE 4: DEVELOP DEPTH OF MEANING THROUGH MULTIPLE SOURCES AND REPEATED EXPOSURES

To acquire new word meanings, students need accurate and enriched instruction. Superficially defining a word does not provide the necessary context for acquiring shades of meanings for words. Similarly, preteaching vocabulary using meaning alone is ineffective. Students need to experience a newly learned word in a variety of contexts and through multiple exposures. Teachers should activate a variety of learning modalities to develop depth of meaning, such as CD-ROM dictionaries, labeled pictures and diagrams for technical vocabulary, reference books, dramatizations, read-alouds, videotapes, and computer simulations. Although students may develop only a vague notion of a word's meaning after one exposure, repeated exposures (even incidentally) help clarify meaning. Using various modalities is an especially important consideration for students with reading disabilities or students who are ELLs.

PRINCIPLE 5: FOSTER APPRECIATION AND ENTHUSIASM FOR WORD LEARNING

One of the most important jobs of a teacher is to help foster students' love of language, interest in the musicality of language, and curiosity and eagerness to discover new words beyond the classroom walls. First, the teacher's interest in language and vocabulary must be genuine. This is often easier said than done, as most of us probably had less than memorable vocabulary instruction while in school. However, we can probably recall a few teachers in our past who seemed to brim with anticipation and excitement when encountering new words—teachers whose enthusiasm for language was infectious. To have an engaging and effective vocabulary program, we ourselves have to demonstrate that level of excitement. For many of us, it might mean becoming students again and learning about words, word histories, functions and uses of words, and the like in order to compensate for an incomplete vocabulary education. Incorporating riddles, puns, "word of the day" activities, dictionary activities, and other forms of word play in the classroom can help students experience the academic effervescence that can lead them to becoming lifelong word lovers, or *logophiles* (Johnson, 2001).

PRINCIPLE 6: TEACH STRATEGIES TO BUILD INDEPENDENT WORD LEARNING

Once the fire of interest in word learning has been lit, teachers need to show students how to learn new words and build independence in doing this. Even in a well-designed program of vocabulary instruction, only about 400 words per year can be well taught through direct instruction (Beck et al., 1987). But students need to know thousands of words to achieve academic success, so direct teaching of strategies to be used for independent word learning needs to be a focus of a solid program of vocabulary instruction (Kame'enui, Dixon, & Carnine, 1987). Such instruction needs to incorporate independent strategies because a great deal of word learning occurs incidentally. Together with wide reading of a variety of texts, these strategies support independent learning for growth in word learning.

PRINCIPLE 7: TEACH WORDS IN CONTEXT

While it is important for teachers to have a formal plan in place for teaching new vocabulary, direct instruction alone does not account for the large numbers of words that students must, and do, learn throughout their academic careers. In one estimate, students learn just over 40,000 words from the time they enter first grade until high school graduation—an average of 3,000 words per year (Nagy & Anderson, 1984). In addition to direct instruction, research has shown that gains in vocabulary are linked to incidental learning of new words in context, particularly when students listen to repeated reading of stories.

RESEARCH BRIEF Learning New Words in Context

Brett, Rothlein, and Hurley (1996) examined vocabulary acquisition under practical conditions in elementary classrooms, in which trade books were read by a teacher to a class (a chapter or section each day). The purpose of the study was to compare the effects of three conditions on fourth graders' vocabulary acquisition: listening to stories, with a brief explanation of the meaning of unfamiliar target words as they were encountered within the context of the stories; listening to stories, with no explanation of the words; and having no systematic exposure to the stories or vocabulary. One hundred seventy-five students in two urban schools in Miami, Florida, took part in the study, with the schools' populations being predominantly African American and Hispanic.

Results of the study indicate that fourth graders can acquire new vocabulary from listening to stories if there is a brief explanation of new words as students encounter them within a meaningful context of an authentic piece of children's literature. Students in this study who heard the stories along with explanations of words learned the meanings of an average of three new words for each of the two books, and remembered the meanings of an average of six new words six weeks later. Findings also suggest that repeated readings of the same story may not be necessary for vocabulary acquisition if new words are explained in context. The study provides further evidence of the value of reading to children. Reading aloud, accompanied by explanations of unfamiliar words as they occur in the story, appears to be an effective method of teaching children the meanings of new words. Additional research is needed, however, to find out whether students are able to internalize the new words and use them as part of their written and spoken vocabulary.

Why Do Some Students Have Trouble with Vocabulary Learning?

Children vary greatly in the rates at which they acquire new words. Differences in vocabulary knowledge are clearly evident among learners of varying socioeconomic status (SES), linguistic backgrounds, and language abilities.

Studies have shown that first-grade children from higher-SES groups knew about twice as many words as lower-SES children (Graves, Brunetti, & Slater, 1982; Graves & Slater, 1987; Juel, 1996). Children from homes with limited economic resources may not have access to concrete experiences, print (books, newspapers, magazines), and technological resources that can broaden vocabulary knowledge.

Similarly, for students whose first language is not English, the inability to develop vocabulary skills comparable to those of native English-speaking peers is strongly linked with low academic performance (Freeman & Freeman, 2000). One persistent area of concern for educators is the large gap between the reading performance of white non-Hispanic and Hispanic children on national assessments in the United States. This gap contributes to inequalities not only in school performance, but also later on in the work force, as jobs are contingent upon school success. One major determinant of poor reading comprehension for Hispanics and other struggling readers is poor knowledge of vocabulary, particularly "academic" words encountered in middle and secondary school texts. Therefore, elementary teachers face the added challenge of teaching these students strategies for expanding vocabularies.

While vocabulary knowledge in the primary language develops generally rapidly from preschool to adulthood, children vary greatly in the rates at which they acquire new vocabulary (Ruddell, 1999). For students with communication disorders or delays, students with learning disabilities, or students with limited intellectual functioning, vocabulary may grow at a slower rate (Vaughn, Bos, & Schumm, 2003). Students with language-related disabilities may have not only more limited vocabulary, but also difficulties with pronunciation, appropriate word usage, word retrieval, and interpretation of figurative language.

Research has found that because there are such notable differences in vocabulary size among children at all levels of development, intellectual ability must account in part for these variations (Harris & Sipay, 1990). Intelligence has a profound effect on vocabulary size and the rate at which new word meanings are acquired (Anderson & Freebody, 1985). Low levels of intelligence result in delayed language development or limited language altogether. Furthermore, these students have particular difficulty in acquiring or understanding vocabulary as it relates to abstract or complex ideas. Students with low intellectual capacity also have trouble benefiting from instruction and using context clues to derive meaning. These struggling readers also fall victim to the *Matthew effect*: More proficient readers will read more than low-ability readers, for whom the reading task is arduous (Stanovich, 1986). The more the students read, the more vocabulary they are exposed to in varied contexts, the more fluent they become as readers, and the more they want to read. Conversely, low-ability readers who struggle with text are usually not avid readers, therefore limiting their exposure to new words or familiar words in novel contexts that could potentially help to deepen the meaning of the words they do know.

Vocabulary knowledge is indisputably regarded as critical to children's successful reading comprehension. Children with well-developed vocabularies have a sort of "word sense" and are able to make connections among words and note new semantic and conceptual relationships; these abilities have a positive impact on comprehension (Anderson & Freebody, 1981; Beck & McKeown, 1991a; Beck, Perfetti, & McKeown, 1982). It is interesting to note that despite the recognized importance of vocabulary for reading comprehension, research has found that vocabulary instruction plays a very small part in elementary reading programs (Durkin, 1978–1979; Graves, 1986).

Limited vocabulary is thus both a cause and an effect of poor achievement in reading. While students learn new words from family, friends, TV and radio, class discussions, and other sources, reading is a major source of new words. However, poor readers tend to read less than more proficient peers, further limiting their exposure to new words. Also, poor readers have smaller vocabularies than more proficient peers, and they have a more restricted knowledge of the words they do know. Cumulative vocabulary differences don't begin to interfere with students' learning until about grade 4, when content area texts are used more heavily and the vocabulary becomes more abstract and more technical. Most troubling, however, is the fact that these differences are often difficult to remediate.

What Are Formal Assessments of Vocabulary?

While literacy experts do not dispute the importance of teaching strategies for acquiring vocabulary, the issue of how to assess vocabulary knowledge is fertile ground for debate. Assessment of vocabulary is a complex task that raises more questions than it does answers. Furthermore, the current assess-for-accountability trend has made the interpretation and use of assessment outcomes doubly controversial. The dilemmas regarding assessments of vocabulary and the instructional implications that flow from these assessments require thought and planning, in order for them to be effective and useful for classroom purposes.

Why is assessing vocabulary such a challenge? Johnson (1981) identified three main problems in assessing vocabulary. First is the decision regarding which words to assess. Should the words come from the curriculum you teach? Should you consider student-selected words? Do you focus on high-frequency words, or words of high interest to students, but perhaps of limited frequency in school texts? What about district- or state-generated lists of words for mastery?

Second, defining what it means to *know* a word is tricky. Does knowing mean being able to recognize it in print and pronounce it? Or recognize it when spoken? Does it mean being able to define the word with one or perhaps more plausible definitions? What about knowing related words or special functions of the word? Finally, what is your method for actually testing knowledge of a word? Will students write dictionary-type definitions for the word? Or synonyms and antonyms? Will the students have to demonstrate or illustrate the word's meaning? It is important to note that every type of test format will yield somewhat different information. A study examining vocabulary test format effects with more than 800 elementary students found that children "knew" a word when tested one way, but didn't "know" the same word when tested another way (Johnson, 2001).

Standardized measures, such as norm-referenced and criterion-referenced tests, relate performance to some standard measure of performance; they try to be objective; and they draw conclusions from a sample of performance that is assumed to be a valid and reliable predictor of general performance (Blachowicz & Fisher, 1996). Most standardized reading tests include subtests of vocabulary and comprehension, with the total reading score usually being a composite of the two. When using standardized or criterion-referenced tests, teachers should read test manuals carefully. Technical data, particularly the information about validity, reliability, and the demographics of the norming population samples, can help teachers make informed classroom decisions. Teachers also need to be alert to some other possible trouble spots (Blachowicz & Fisher, 1996; Johnson, 2001):

- Test dependence on language development
- Inappropriate or outdated content
- Multiple "correct" answers
- Ambiguity of directions and items
- Inability to provide for partial understanding
- Cultural and linguistic bias toward the dominant middle class
- Lack of diagnostic value

Most reputable test makers take great pains to produce well-constructed tests that measure what they say they do. Teachers need to be aware of how useful a particular test is to their teaching context. According to Blachowicz and Fisher (1996), teachers should be conscious of the following as well:

- Vocabulary tests are measures of prior knowledge, experience, and culture. Regional differences in language use need to be taken into account. Tests of oral vocabulary using pictures are often confusing, because they are ambiguous or culture-bound.
- Vocabulary tests are measures of decoding. Weak decoders will score poorly on written assessments even when the words exist in their oral vocabularies.
- Vocabulary tests often measure superficial aspects of word learning, not the ability to use a word in a rich context. For this reason, standardized measures can overestimate or underestimate vocabulary that ELLs know in their new language.

Some common formats for standardized measures include selecting the word that doesn't belong from a group of words; choosing the word that best fits the sentence; choosing the word closest in meaning to another word from a group of words; providing synonyms and antonyms; and putting words in the right categories (Johnson, 2001). When the school district mandates use of standardized measures for vocabulary assessment, ask yourself the following:

1. Where do the test words come from?
2. Why have these words been selected and not others?
3. What assumptions does the test author seem to make about what it means to know a word?
4. What test format is used? Why this format and not others?
5. What do these results really mean?

A well-designed vocabulary program must also take into account the use of these mandated measures and should strive to prepare students for such assessments; it would be pedagogically negligent not to. Standardized assessments measure test-taking skills as well as content (Blachowicz & Fisher, 1996). While teachers cannot (and should not!) focus on teaching students the exact words that will be on the test, teachers can expose students to various testing formats during the course of the school year in routine classroom assessments. Some of the vocabulary teachers choose to focus on can be assessed using formats similar to standardized ones, in order to build familiarity with the format and reduce test anxiety—particularly for students new to the U.S. school system, who may not be familiar with these types of assessments.

The vocabulary sections of certain individual intelligence tests, such as the various versions of the Wechsler Intelligence Scale for Children and the Stanford–Binet Intelligence Scales, also can be useful in assessing oral vocabulary. Other standardized tests you will read about in this book also include vocabulary subtests (see Appendix C). For disabled readers, however, standardized tests do not provide the best measure of their knowledge of word meanings, because many such readers are not able to identify or pronounce the words on the test.

Peabody Picture Vocabulary Test–III

One standardized measure routinely used to assess receptive vocabulary and the comprehension of spoken English is the Peabody Picture Vocabulary Test–III (PPVT-III), an orally administered, norm-referenced test designed for use with standard-English-speaking individuals ages 2½ to 90+ years (Dunn & Dunn, 1997). The test format is an easel with stimulus items consisting of large, clear, black-and-white drawings, with four pictures per page. The test administrator shows four pictures and reads a word. The test subject must point to the picture most closely depicting the word or state the number of the correct picture. Each form has 204 items that are grouped into 17 sets of 12 items each. For each set, the three easiest items are placed first, the six most difficult ones are randomly placed in the middle, and three relatively easy ones conclude each item set (Bessai, 1998).

The test authors caution that the PPVT-III measures only listening vocabulary, which is a more restricted aspect of overall linguistic and cognitive functioning. Further caution is needed in interpreting results, as students with impaired vision, hearing loss, or limited ability in English were not included in the standardization sample used for developing norms. However, development of test items included a review by a panel to determine if any of the items contained racial, ethnic, or gender biases.

What Are Informal Assessments of Vocabulary?

Formal measures, while having merit for comparing students to peers nationwide and providing a baseline for assessment, yield little practical information for planning classroom instruction. Therefore, informal classroom assessments are needed to provide a complete picture of a child's abilities. When a student is struggling in reading, and more specifically in vocabulary, you'll want to do an individual diagnosis to help plan instruction accordingly.

A commonly used informal diagnostic measure used by teachers is an informal reading inventory (IRI), perhaps because of the advantages of being able to observe a child in the act of reading and to record a host of varied data. Most commercially available IRIs consist of passages for oral and silent reading, passages to measure listening comprehension, and graded word lists used for decoding assessment. For vocabulary assessment using an IRI, students read a passage and are asked questions that involve interpretation of preselected words or are sometimes asked direct questions about the meaning of a word in the passage context. The appeal of the IRI lies in the teacher's ability to probe student responses because of the one-on-one format. Underlying difficulties in acquiring vocabulary and developing comprehension can be diagnosed through this process. (For further discussion of IRIs, see Appendix B.)

Bader Reading and Language Inventory

The Bader Reading and Language Inventory (Bader, 2005) is a diagnostic battery of tests for levels from preprimer to grade 12, providing procedures for individual, in-depth assessment in seven areas: Emergent Reading, Word Identification and Phonics, Comprehension, Spelling, English as a Second Language, Writing, and Oral Processing. Unique to this inventory is an arithmetic screening test, so reading and language skills can be compared with math skills for better overall assessment. Visual and auditory discrimination screening is also included.

According to the author, this inventory was developed for teachers and specialists who need a diagnostic battery that encompasses vital areas of evaluation based on research and practice, is efficient in administration and interpretation, and is relatively inexpensive to use. Included is a case study as an example of a diagnostician's reasoning as he or she plans and carries out an assessment and makes recommendations for instruction.

Ekwall–Shanker Reading Inventory

The Ekwall–Shanker Reading Inventory (ESRI; Shanker & Ekwall, 1999) provides flexible assessment to match the needs of the individuals who will use it. The ESRI contains instruments for assessing students' knowledge of letters, basic sight vocabulary, phonics, structural analysis, and contractions from preprimer levels to grade 9. It also includes a form for assessing student interests. The ESRI may be used as a quick screening device, for placement of students in groups or classes, for a brief assessment, or for comprehensive individual diagnosis. Specific directions guide the teacher in conducting the kinds of diagnosis appropriate for each setting.

The ESRI provides clear, easy-to-follow instructions that tell the examiner exactly how to go about conducting and interpreting the diagnosis. The instructions for both administering the test and formulating a diagnosis have been refined in this edition to make them more user-friendly.

Qualitative Reading Inventory–3

The Qualitative Reading Inventory–3 (QRI-3; Leslie & Caldwell, 2000) is based on the latest research and includes narrative and expository passages at each level from preprimer to grade 12. The QRI-3 helps analyze abilities such as word identification, fluency, and comprehension, while providing concrete suggestions for intervention.

The book features passages with pictures for early reading levels, simplified directions for usage, and a description of the assessment process with questions to be answered by the examiner, as well as reconstructed methods for assessing prior knowledge.

Reading Inventory for the Classroom

The Reading Inventory for the Classroom (Flynt & Cooter, 2003) includes a protocol for determining if a reader's focus is on word recognition or on comprehension. Through the use of this inventory, teachers can determine how to (1) provide students with appropriate reading/instructional materials, and (2) place them into appropriate basal reading programs. They'll also acquire insight into reading development, learn to plan collaborative learning activities, and be able to determine which non-negotiable skills require further development. A miscue analysis form after each miscue grid helps to identify the specific reading skills each pupil needs to develop, and offers ideas for appropriate intervention strategies.

This measure includes a variety of reading passages—both long and short, and all on topics of high interest for elementary and secondary students, from prekindergarten to grade 12. It also features story grammar analysis and expository text grammars.

Classroom Reading Inventory

The majority of stories included in the latest edition of the Classroom Reading Inventory (CRI; Silvaroli & Wheelock, 2004) are new and reflect contemporary and multicultural themes. The authors indicate that this diagnostic tool can efficiently be used in classrooms because of the short time needed to administer it (about 15 minutes). The subskills section enables a teacher to evaluate a student's ability to decode words in and out of context, and to evaluate the student's ability to answer factual/literal, vocabulary, and inference questions. The reader response section is designed around the predicting and retelling of stories. Included with the book is a CD-ROM featuring two complete testing of two children. The CRI can be used from elementary to adult levels.

Other Measures for Classroom Use

In addition to using commercially available IRIs, some of the best opportunities to informally assess students' vocabulary arise naturally in classrooms (Forgan, 1977; Johnson, 2001). General student observation can be very informative when you know what to look and listen for. Here are some suggestions:

1. Listen to students talk. Notice those students who use many words, as compared to those who have a limited speaking vocabulary. The speaking vocabulary is generally larger than the reading vocabulary at young ages.
2. Read graded selections to students, and then check their listening comprehension to see if students comprehend at least 75% of what they have heard.
3. Develop simple IRIs using classroom texts, particularly content area materials. Ask questions such as these:
   a. What does ___________ mean in the passage?
   b. Can you use ___________ in a sentence?
   c. What is another word for ___________?
   d. What is the opposite of ___________?
4. Other quick activities to test word knowledge include the following:
   a. Read the word and circle a picture of it.
   b. Look at a picture and circle the word for it.
   c. Read the word and circle a definition.
   d. Read the word and circle a synonym.

e. Read the word and circle an antonym.
f. Read the word in context and circle a definition, synonym, or antonym.
g. Read a sentence and write the missing word.
h. Read a sentence and supply the missing word orally.
i. Read the word and draw a picture or tell about it.
j. Read the word and put it in a category.
k. Find the word in a category in which it does not belong.

When a student's comprehension appears to be affected by lack of vocabulary, you can use a combination of standardized and informal measures to create a complete picture of the learner (Blachowicz & Fisher, 1996). Developing a vocabulary diagnostic profile with a variety of measures is useful for balancing information gathered from both standardized and informal assessments. While standard measures are able to provide comparisons with an external norming group, the informal measures help put this information in a meaningful context that is useful for planning classroom instruction specifically tailored to student needs.

How Do You Provide Differentiated Instruction in Vocabulary?

Once you've decided to share your love of language with students so that they too will become lifelong word lovers, it is time to develop a well-planned, systematic, continuous program of vocabulary instruction in order to reach your goal. No one method of instruction is superior in all circumstances and for all purposes with all students. While explicit instruction is more effective for the acquisition of specific vocabulary, a combination of incidental learning and direct instruction is likely to be more effective in increasing overall vocabulary knowledge than is relying on either approach alone. Following the principles of vocabulary instruction outlined earlier in this chapter, you need to decide what words to teach. Then you need to decide which techniques of instruction are most beneficial to the students in your particular teaching context. But first, you need to spark in your students the fire of curiosity regarding words.

Building and Maintaining Student Interest

This chapter has addressed the fact that both teachers and students need to actively enjoy word learning in order to maximize instruction and have the benefits extend beyond the classroom. For teachers, this may mean building their own personal word knowledge. For students, this means that a program of vocabulary instruction needs to be rich and lively in order for them to become interested and enthusiastic about words; Beck and colleagues (2002) refer to such a program as *robust instruction*. Actively engaging learners in word study that has meaningful use is the cornerstone to this type of instruction. (See the Resources for Instruction, at the end of this chapter, for books that can be used to stimulate interest in vocabulary.)

TECH TIP Using CD-ROM Storybooks

One effective way for classroom teachers to support vocabulary development and integrate technology is to use CD-ROM storybooks to support the teaching of reading, particularly for struggling readers requiring extra scaffolding during independent reading practice. Once considered ancillary materials to a basal series, CD-ROMs now often form part of the main instruction related to the text. Furthermore, school media centers routinely purchase a wide variety of CD-ROM materials, making them ubiquitous in classrooms. CD-ROMs designed to support reading often include glossed text; in other words, electronic dictionary support is available while students are reading. This digital support comes in the form of pronunciations, definitions, and illustrations, which help the reader understand the material. In addition to aiding with automaticity and fluency, digital dictionary support is a useful tool for ELLs. The digital supports help explain difficult vocabulary, develop a relevant context, and in some cases provide background knowledge for students from a nonmainstream culture. Collateral benefits include anonymity of use and unlimited requests for assistance for a struggling reader, who might otherwise be self-conscious about seeking help (Chiappone, 2003). With proper modeling from the teacher, students can learn to maximize their use of the digital dictionary supports while reading.

Active learning ensures mental engagement in the process and also builds high interest in vocabulary study (Scott & Nagy, 1997). Instruction that uses active mental processing encourages students to reason with words and to integrate new information into their background knowledge. Compare this to the classroom mainstay of looking up definitions (often ill-fitting ones) in the dictionary for the purpose of passing a quiz! Students passively involved with instruction will tune out. For vocabulary instruction to have lasting effectiveness, students must become actively engaged so that generative thinking can occur. Therefore, teachers must constantly search for learning activities that make generative thinking about words a reality (Reutzel & Cooter, 1999).

Active involvement should include word reasoning (Ruddell, 1999). First, a new word needs to be developed and understood in the meaning context in which it is found (Blachowicz & Lee, 1991). Text that presents new vocabulary in a reading-friendly manner provides some sort of definition of the word and follows up with an example to illustrate the meaning. When text does not provide this contextual support, the teacher must guide children in formulating a definition through use of the text or glossary and through discussion. In addition, new words need to be semantically related to similar words and word groups through comparison and contrast, and through new and varied contexts to refine, connect, and integrate meanings (Kibby, 1995). Recognizing the interconnectedness of words begins to develop in students a curiosity about word meanings, which, when coupled with developing conceptual links to other words, is a hallmark of those individuals who develop large vocabularies (Beck et al., 2002). Caution must be taken, however, about relying solely on context to teach vocabulary. Many naturally occurring contexts do not provide sufficient support for developing word meanings, because most authors, while being good communicators and storytellers, do not write with developing context in mind.

Determining What Words Should Be Taught

Language is fluid and dynamic; for this reason, new words are continuously being added to the English *lexicon*, or collection of words. Consider the following ways of developing new words (Johnson, 2001, p. 5):

- Forming derivatives and compounds (e.g., *childlike*, *tugboat*).
- Blending and clipping (e.g., *television* + *marathon* = *telethon*).
- Adding words from science and technology (e.g., *liposuction*).
- Allowing abbreviations to take on meaning (e.g., *ATM*, *CD*).

- Creating new slang and everyday expressions (e.g., *downsize*).
- Coining words to take the place of words (e.g., *thingamabob*, *doohickey*, *gizmo*).

With the fields of science and technology in particular continuously adding new words, you must decide which words will be the focus of active instruction. You need to consider not only which words will be taught, but if they will be taught before, during, or after reading a selection.

To get an idea of the kinds of words that need instructional attention, Beck and McKeown (1985, p. 15) identified a literate individual's vocabulary as comprising three tiers:

Tier 1: Includes most basic words (e.g., *clock*, *baby*, *happy*) that rarely require direct instruction.
Tier 2: Contains words that are of high frequency for mature language users and are found across a variety of domains, such as *coincidence*, *absurd*, and *fortunate.* Rich knowledge of these words has a direct impact on verbal functioning. Instruction with these words is the most productive.
Tier 3: Contains low-frequency words that are often limited to specific domains and are not of high utility for most students. These words are learned for a specific need (e.g., terms for land forms before a geography lesson).

To identify Tier 2 words, first think of words that would be useful additions to students' repertoires. Also consider if the students already have ways to express the concepts represented by the words. The new words should not merely be synonyms of known words, but should provide a deeper or more precise meaning of known words.

Because students must learn vocabulary in language arts, science, social studies, and other academic areas, it is important to have a rationale for selecting or excluding words from instruction. Beck and colleagues (2002) offer these tips for identifying Tier 2 words:

- *Importance and utility*: Words that are characteristic of mature language users and appear frequently across a variety of domains.
- *Instructional potential*: Words that can be worked with in a variety of ways, so that students can build rich representations of them and of their connections to other words and concepts.
- *Conceptual understanding*: Words for which students understand the general concept, but that provide precision and specificity in describing the concept.

Bear in mind, however, that many words will not fit the criteria for Tier 2, yet their meanings will need to be developed in order to understand a particular text. In addition to these words, it is appropriate to select words that, while they do not appear in a text, are conceptually related to the text and useful to the learner in general. This is especially important in working with young children, whose reading selections might include only a limited number of words. This is a wonderful opportunity to introduce more complex words that relate to the text.

When selecting words for study, you also need to consider your students' grade and age, their language and academic proficiencies, and the difficulty and relatedness of the words to be taught. Students can be involved in the selection process as well. They can select words that they themselves want to learn, or words that they would like to contribute to the class list. In one variation, students can nominate words for study, with the teacher selecting from this list of nominees. Involving students in the process naturally emphasizes choice and ownership as the students are invested in their own learning.

Building upon Prior Knowledge

Once you've identified the words that you will be actively instructing, it is important to develop *prior knowledge* or build upon students' experiences in order for the instruction to be meaningful. Prior knowledge is the bridge to new knowledge, so maximizing its use is an indispensable part of developing word knowledge. During classroom instruction, prior knowledge can be activated by using the following techniques:

- *Brainstorming*. This is usually a first step when exploring a new topic. Students generate a variety of ideas related to the concept at hand. This can be done orally or in written form.
- *Questioning*. The act of posing questions activates prior knowledge, as students recall information on a topic in order to develop appropriate questions.
- *Predicting*. This is effective as a knowledge activation strategy, because students must relate what is known to them to new, undeveloped concepts. Confirming or revising predictions further taps preexisting knowledge.
- *Writing*. Students who write brief entries on a topic before investigating it tap into previous knowledge and prepare themselves for new learning.
- *Discussing*. In this free-flowing exchange of ideas on a topic, students engage with the teacher in a give-and-take dialogue that addresses issues related to the topic to be studied. This prepares the students for assimilating new information into what is already known.

Determining When to Teach Words

One of the most important decisions a teacher makes is to determine when vocabulary instruction will take place. Before reading a selection, the teacher can present unfamiliar words that are crucial to understanding the passage but are not explained well in it. The remainder of the words can be taught following reading. After reading a passage, students will probably have at least a vague notion of what the remaining words mean. At the very least, they have the general context of the story to frame their understanding. Table 10.1 shows which contexts lend themselves to vocabulary instruction before, during, or after reading.

Teachers often talk about capitalizing on "teachable moments"—those times when a situation presents itself as an authentic moment in time to learn about something. While this cannot be disregarded as an excellent technique to pique student interest in a topic, teachers need to beware of overdoing teachable moments to the point that enjoyment of a text or discussion topic is impeded. Take cues from your students and know when to maximize those teachable moments related to vocabulary instruction.

Classroom Challenge: Using Dictionaries

The use of dictionaries in the classroom is one of those common practices that tends to exist because it has always existed. While the value of being able to use dictionaries is unquestioned, more often than not the method for instructing students in their use has

TABLE 10.1. When to Introduce and Develop New Words

Context conditions	Before reading	During reading	After reading
The words are essential for children's comprehension of the selection.	×		
Student background knowledge is not sufficient for independent understanding.	×		
The words are potential barriers to comprehension.	×		
The words appear in unfriendly text in which the context is not useful.	×	×	
The children do not already know the words.	×	×	
A goal of instruction is to develop abilities to understand new words independently.		×	
A goal of instruction is to develop abilities to use reference resources in the classroom.		×	
Students will understand the words on the basis of personal prior knowledge or friendly text.		×	
Students can determine meaning from context.		×	×
Small-group discussion is needed to connect new meanings to prior learning.			×
A goal of instruction is to deepen and enrich vocabulary learning.			×
Elaborated discussion is needed for long-term acquisition of vocabulary.			×

Note. From Robert Ruddell, *Teaching Children to Read and Write* (3rd ed.). Published by Allyn and Bacon, Boston, MA. Copyright 2002 by Pearson Education. Reprinted by permission of the publisher.

been given little thought. Furthermore, classroom activities related to dictionaries are usually limited to locating definitions, and students receive little if any direct instruction in how to do this. It is often taken for granted that once students are comfortable with alphabetical order, then they should be able to work with dictionaries. However, familiarity with alphabetical order is only the first step in learning how to use a dictionary. Once students are able to locate the words, many more skills are needed to use a dictionary properly. Without direct instruction and practice in their use, dictionaries can become a source of frustration for students.

Miller and Gildea (1987) examined the results of having children look up definitions of new words and write them in their own sentences; they concluded that the errors children made were so serious and frequent as to make the task instructionally useless. However, children need to be taught how to use a dictionary, to know when use of a dictionary is warranted, and to understand the information that is found in the dictionary. The key is to model dictionary skills through functional use, rather than isolated drills. By modeling the "dictionary habit," teachers can potentially motivate students to use this wonderful tool spontaneously and independently.

Some specific skills need to be modeled, and ample practice in these skills needs to be given, before students can work comfortably and efficiently with dictionaries (Alvermann & Phelps, 2001; Gunning, 2002). These skills include the following:

- Locating words in alphabetical order.
- Locating and understanding entries, including the use of abbreviations, synonyms, illustrations, and phrases or sentences with the word. Word histories, or etymologies, often form part of a dictionary entry as well.
- Matching dictionary entries with the proper context for the target words.
- Selecting among homographs, which are often listed as separate entries.
- Pronouncing the unfamiliar words by using the diacritical marks.
- Finding variant parts of speech. For example, *incredulity* would appear as part of the entry for *incredulous*.

Developing Interest in Language

One of the most useful ways to stimulate or sustain the natural interest in language that children exhibit practically from birth is to incorporate word and language play as part of a rich verbal environment in the classroom (Beck et al., 2002; Johnson, 2001). It is impossible for teachers to teach children all the words they need to succeed in school; therefore, students must discover words on their own. The impulse to do this arises out of a personal interest in words and language.

To create this type of environment, teachers are encouraged to capitalize on any opportunities to surround students with words that have already been taught, as well as with unfamiliar words that students can slowly begin to understand and incorporate into their own vocabularies. Some activities that help support this goal are described below.

WORD WIZARD

The *Word Wizard* activity establishes the importance of paying attention to words in and out of school. Beck and colleagues (2002) describe this activity as an effective way of extending classroom word instruction to contexts outside of school.

1. To build interest in the activity before beginning it in your classroom, design an advertising campaign about the opportunity to become a Word Wizard. For example, you can design leaflets called "You Can Be a Word Wizard!" that describe the different categories students can achieve, such as Word Wildcat, Word Whirlwind, Word Winner, Word Worker, and Word Watcher; the highest category, of course, is Word Wizard. The leaflet can also describe the scoring system.
2. Create a chart titled "Word Wizard" with your students' names listed on it.
3. Provide a space to add tally marks as students report sightings or uses of words that have been introduced in class.
4. Points are given for words heard on television, on the radio, on the street, or at home.
5. Students must tell you where they heard or saw the word and how it was used.
6. Points are tallied every few weeks, and students receive certificates based on their totals. The certificates can be designed around the different categories.

WORD OF THE DAY

Direct teaching of a word a day is effective for motivating students to use "big words" in their speaking and writing.

- Select words that are useful, but that students might not encounter in their materials.
- Say each word, define it, use it in a meaningful context, and ask students to provide synonyms, antonyms, examples, and nonexamples.
- Tell students that you will use the word during the day and they must catch you using it.
- Students can keep a log on a blank calendar of the daily words. Students can also record instances when they hear the word on TV or the radio, for example. To encourage independent study of the words, use the words as bonus questions on a test.
- Post a list of the daily words, and encourage students to use them in their writing.

TECH TIP A Word a Day

In order for students to become active and independent learners of vocabulary, they need to be actively exposed to the nuances of language—their own, as well as foreign ones. A simple way to introduce new words to students is for teachers to learn new words themselves, as through the use of the website A Word A Day (*www.wordsmith.org/awad*). Once you subscribe, you'll receive a new word via email each day. The creators of the site tout the "music and magic of words" that you'll experience when you join this online community of over half a million subscribers in 200 countries eager to explore the world of words. For teachers, the best use for this site is to develop personal knowledge of words—knowledge that can then be used to enhance word lessons. In addition to providing definitions, the entries include citations from popular media where the words appear, as well as etymologies (which can be the source of interesting class discussions, particularly with older learners). The words are often linked by themes, such as words borrowed from African languages. The site maintains an archive of all the words sent since it began in 1994. The Theme List link is useful when teachers are searching for words for a particular unit of study.

WORD WALK

A *word walk* works effectively with ELLs, as well as younger students who are learning about words. Students observe, study, and record any environmental print. This can be done as a homework assignment. Have students check off the words they can read. As a group, ask questions related to the lists:

- What's the longest word on your list? The longest word anybody found?
- Find words that begin with the same sound or letter.
- Did you see a word everyone else missed?
- Can you make a picture dictionary from some of your words? (This can be a group activity.)
- How about writing a story about the word walk, using lots of the words we found?
- Get together with a friend and see if you can find out about some of the words on your list that you did not check off.

PARENT POINTER Using the Newspaper to Develop Vocabulary

Newspapers provide a vast amount of material for developing many reading skills (Cheney, 1984). Incorporating the use of newspapers in the classroom and at home is an inexpensive way of providing ample amounts of reading material for students on diverse and timely topics. Hold a Newspapers in Education night as a parent event. Your local newspaper might be willing to be a cosponsor to supply newspapers for each parent for the event. Some possible activities with newspapers include the following:

- Cut out newspaper photos, and write descriptive words that appear to fit the personalities of the people in the pictures.
- Students can keep track in a log of new words that they learn while reading the newspaper. At the end of the week, they can share one with the class.
- Write four different categories across the top of a sheet of paper: countries, cities, people in the news, problems. Down the left side of the paper, spell out a word such as NEWS. The students try to find words for each category from their study of the newspaper; the words must start with the letters in the word NEWS. After each word, they put the page number and column from the newspaper in which they found the word. The person with the most correct words at the end of a given time is declared a winner. The game can be varied by using only one category and changing the word in the left-hand column.
- Have ELLs find pictures related to a topic, such as furniture. They are to find pictures in the newspaper, cut them out, glue them on a piece of paper, and label them. They can then use this "pictionary" when they write in class.

THE ALLURE OF LONG WORDS

Most teachers and parents will agree that an area of fascination for children is the challenge of long words. Because they are distinctive, long words are often easier for children to remember than shorter words. This is especially true for students for whom word recognition is difficult, and who often rely on the visual shapes of words to recall them (compare the plain-looking *car* to *automobile*, with its tall letters interspersed in the word).

Teachers often build interest in these challenging words by calling them "50-cent words" or "dollar words" (compared to "nickel words," let's say). Dale and O'Rourke (1971) suggested calling them "*sesquipedalian* words," from the Latin *sesqui* (*one and one-half*) and *ped* (*foot*), to imply their substantial length. Combined with an activity such as Word Wizard (described above), students can be encouraged to collect long and interesting words to add to a personal dictionary or word log, or perhaps even a class bulletin board for everyone to enjoy. As an extension activity, students in the class can use the dictionary to determine correct pronunciations.

Level 1: High-Quality Core Instruction

Strategies selected for whole-group instruction will generally tend to focus on the seven principles of vocabulary instruction identified earlier in this chapter. In particular, high-quality core instruction links new knowledge to prior knowledge and, most importantly, models strategies for independent learning. Independent learning in turn helps to develop a general knowledge about words, or word sense. This word sense acts as a background for strategy use and provides internal context for expanding personal vocabulary. Independent word-learning strategies are really metacognitive processes and should be the ultimate goal of any vocabulary program.

All techniques work to some degree. However, some techniques work better than others, and some are effective in some situations but not others. In choosing a technique, consider three factors:

- What is the nature of the word? Is it abstract or concrete? Common or rare? Is it a technical word? Does it have many meanings?
- What background will students bring to this word? Will this be a word with which they are vaguely familiar? Do they have the conceptual background but lack the label? Do they lack the conceptual background but have the label? Do they lack both the label and the conceptual background?
- How will the students use this word? Is it essential to the meaning of a story they are about to read? Is it a high-utility word that will appear again and again in this and other selections? Do you simply expect them to recognize it when they hear it? Will they be required to use it in their writing or speaking?

CONTEXTUAL ANALYSIS

The goal of *contextual analysis* is for students to derive the meaning of a word by examining the context in which the unknown word appears. However, research has shown that contextual clues in publications occur only about one-third of the time, and readers will use the context successfully only between 5% and 20% of the time. Explicit instruction in this procedure and time for practice are essential for it to be effective. Classroom instruction on the use of context clues should begin in the early grades, with the hope that over time, students will use the skill naturally. Sternberg and Powell (1983) identified a three-step cognitive process in using context clues:

1. *Selective encoding.* Students select only relevant information that will help them arrive at the meaning of an unknown word.
2. *Selective combination.* Students combine clues into a tentative definition.
3. *Selective comparison.* Students use their background experience to determine the meaning of a word.

SEMANTIC MAPPING

The use of a graphic organizer is good for students who need a visual aid to organize information and see relationships. A *semantic map* is a graphic organizer that uses lines and circles to organize information according to categories.

1. Select a word that represents the concept, term, or topic you want students to understand in great depth.
2. Discuss briefly, and/or use pictures and other vicarious experiences related to the word.
3. Have students write down as many words as possible that they think have some relationship to the word.
4. Share the word associations while guiding the categorizing and mapping of the words on the board.
5. Have the children create a title for each category and add more words to each category.

6. As students discover new information on the concept, term, or topic, they can add additional words to the chart.

KNOWLEDGE RATING SCALE

The Knowledge Rating Scale (Blachowicz, 1986) is a prereading activity designed to introduce a list of potentially unknown content words to students. As students complete the survey and participate in class discussion, they become aware of how much they already know about the subject to which the words are related. The scale activates students' existing background knowledge and helps them begin to forge links with the new vocabulary concepts.

1. Select a list of important vocabulary words from a new unit or a chapter of text. Prepare a handout for your students that lists the vocabulary words, followed by three columns labeled *Know It Well, Have Heard/Seen It*, and *No Clue.*
2. Divide the class into mixed-ability groups of three or four students with opportunities to share their diverse background knowledge.
3. Have each student consider individual words on the Knowledge Rating Scale and place an × in the appropriate column next to the words.
4. After students have completed the scale, ask them to write definitions in their own words for the words they know.
5. Lead the class in a discussion about the words for which students have definitions. As students read the chapter in the following days, direct them to add definitions for unknown words and confirm (or, if appropriate, change) the definitions they have written.

LIST–GROUP–LABEL

List–group–label (LGL; Taba, 1967) is based on the notion that categorizing words can help students organize new concepts and experiences in relation to previously learned concepts. LGL is an easy-to-implement three-part strategy:

1. *Listing.* The teacher decides on a one- or two-word topic to serve as a stimulus for listing words. Topics are drawn from the materials students are reading. Students are asked to brainstorm any words or expressions related to the topic. Responses are recorded. About 25 responses should be adequate.
2. *Grouping.* After the teacher reads all the responses aloud, students are instructed to make smaller lists of words related to the topic, using only words from the large list that the class has generated. These smaller groupings should consist of words that have something in common with one another, and each grouping should have at least three words. Words from the large list may be used in more than one smaller group, as long as the groupings are different. Students are also told that they must give their group of words a label or title indicating the words' shared relationship.
3. *Labeling.* Using another part of the board or piece of paper, the teacher solicits and records categories of words and their labels from the students, one grouping at a time. After a category is recorded, the student offering the group must state why the words have been categorized in this particular way. This will enable all

students to see category possibilities that may not have occurred to them. This is an excellent strategy for review of a chapter in a content area text.

CONTEXTUAL REDEFINITION

In *contextual redefinition*, students contrast definitions from words in isolation and words in context. The use of context clues is emphasized, and dictionary skills are reinforced.

1. Pick words that are important to the understanding of the focal text and which may pose problems for students.
2. Words are presented in isolation on the board. Student volunteers are asked to pronounce the words out loud and define them. Because the words are out of context, students must rely solely on morphemic analysis to determine word meanings and explain how they arrived at them. Students will probably have incorrect meanings for some words; however, encourage students to agree on one meaning for each word.
3. The same words are then presented in context, preferably using the context in which they appear. If not, the teacher can create the sentences. Students must again provide the meanings of vocabulary words and their rationale for arriving at them. Students must agree on a meaning for each word.
4. The dictionary is then consulted to verify possible meanings. The group chooses the most appropriate definition for each word.

Level 2: Supplemental Instruction

For students who struggle with retaining meaning and who are not developing this word sense, small-group instruction is warranted. The goals of this type of instruction are to increase exposure to words, to aid in making connections among words, and to deepen existing meaning of known words.

MODELING CONTEXT USE IN THE CLASSROOM

C(2)QU is a technique for modeling context use in the classroom (Blachowicz, 1993). It involves students in the process of making hypotheses about meaning from what they already know or from their first look at a contextualized word, and then cross-checking these hypotheses with other information. Words suitable for the C(2)QU process are any that appear in reading material in a context that provides some information for hypothesizing. Most productive are new labels for already known concepts or partially known words, for which the context adds a new twist or further rich information. This process is not suitable for vocabulary that represents totally new concepts. The steps in C(2)QU are as follows:

- C1. Give the word in a broad but meaningful context (e.g., "My new *stepmother* moved into our house after the wedding"). For postreading vocabulary work, this can be a usage selected from a story or chapter. Ask students to form hypotheses about the word's meaning; to give attributes, ideas, or associations; and to "think aloud" to explain to the group the source of their hypotheses.
- C2. Provide more explicit context with some definitional information (e.g., "When

my father got married again, his new wife became my *stepmother*"). Ask students to reflect back on their initial ideas and to reaffirm or refine them again in a "think-aloud" mode.

Q. Ask a question that involves semantic interpretation of the word (e.g., "Can a person have a mother and a *stepmother* at the same time?"). At this point you can also ask for a definition or give one if necessary. Discuss as needed with group members, using each other's cues and explanations as more data.

U. Ask students to use the word in meaningful sentences. Go back into the loop as needed.

POSSIBLE SENTENCES

Possible sentences (Moore & Moore, 1992) is an activity designed to enable students to determine independently the meanings and relationships of unfamiliar words in text-reading assignments. This is a five-part lesson and consists of the following steps:

1. The teacher lists vocabulary central to the major concepts to be encountered in the text. The words must be adequately defined by the text.
2. Students are asked to use at least two words from the list and make a sentence—one they think might possibly be in the text. The sentences are recorded on the board exactly as the students dictate them.
3. Students read the text to check the accuracy of the sentences generated.
4. A discussion ensues as each sentence is evaluated. This calls for careful reading, since students must define judgments of the accuracy of sentences. Sentences are deleted or refined.
5. New sentences are generated to further extend understanding of the words.

SEMANTIC FEATURE ANALYSIS

Semantic feature analysis (Johnson & Pearson, 1984) helps students visualize relationships among concepts. While this strategy is most commonly used with nonfiction texts related to science and social studies topics, it can also be used to build understanding of central characters in literature.

1. Select a topic or category from your text that you want your students to analyze in some depth. Write the name of the topic on the board—for example, *vegetables*.
2. List terms related to the topic down the left side of the grid—for example, *tomatoes, lettuce, potatoes, carrots, peppers*.
3. List features or properties related to the topic across the top of the grid—for example, *grows under the ground, grows on a vine or bush, shaped like a sphere, leafy*.
4. Discuss each topic word and feature word as you read it aloud.
5. Guide your students through the matrix. Ask them to decide how each topic word relates to each feature on the top of the matrix. Students place a plus (+) on the grid if the feature relates to the topic word, a minus (–) if it does not, or a question mark if they are unsure.
6. After completing the chart, direct students to read the appropriate chapter in

their textbooks. As they do, they will expand their vocabulary related to the subject and build their background knowledge.

7. Discuss the selection with the class, and add students' suggestions to the appropriate areas of the grid.

CAPSULE VOCABULARY

Capsule vocabulary (Carr & Wixson, 1986) encourages vocabulary learning by involving listening, speaking, reading, and writing.

1. Students are presented with a list of words related to a topic of interest being studied in class.
2. Working in pairs, students take turns discussing the topic for five minutes, using the given words.
3. After each partner has had a turn, each student writes a summary of the topic, using the words on the list.

PREDICT-O-GRAM

Predict-o-gram (Blachowicz & Fisher, 1996) is a strategy used with fictional stories to predict which vocabulary words will be used to describe the elements of a story. The teacher selects key words from the story. The goal of this activity is to make connections between the vocabulary and the story, and among the vocabulary words.

1. An overview of the words is provided for the students, to make sure that students have at least an idea about the meaning of the words.
2. The teacher begins to ask the students which words will be used to describe the setting, the characters, the story problem, the plot, and the resolution.
3. Once all the words have been sorted, students can be asked to predict what will happen in the story.
4. Predictions should be revised after the students read the story.

DRAMATIZATION

In order to provide context and meaning for target vocabulary words, direct experience is not always an option. One way to develop word meanings through direct experience is to dramatize vocabulary words, either singly or in groups of related words (Herrell & Jordan, 2004). Through simple skits, words are brought to life for both the performers and the audience by activating several learning modalities to help students commit the target word or words to memory. A variation of this activity is to present hints about the target words during dramatization for the audience to guess.

Level 3: Intensive Support

The students for whom vocabulary learning provides the most challenge will benefit from one-on-one instruction that focuses on linking newly learned words to prior knowledge and developing a core set of strategies to support vocabulary learning. For these students, teachers should activate several learning modalities for learning to support cognition. In addition to direct instruction using paper and pencil or the board, teachers should consider the building of experiential background, even if through videos or simulations, the use of kinesthetic approaches, and various other media (e.g., digital storybooks, CD-ROM dictionaries, or interactive games).

GIPE'S FOUR-STEP PROCEDURE

Gipe's (1978–1979) four-step procedure is a way to help students contextualize new vocabulary words.

1. Students are given a passage in which the first sentence uses the new word appropriately, thereby providing valuable syntactic and semantic information. The context is composed of familiar words and situations.
2. The second sentence of the passage describes some of the attributes of the new word.
3. The third sentence defines the new word, with care being taken to use familiar concepts.
4. The last sentence gives the students an opportunity to relate the new word to their own lives by asking them to write an answer to a question about the word's meaning, or to complete an open-ended statement that requires application of the word's meaning.

Here is an example of all four steps:

> The boys who wanted to sing together formed a *quintet*. There were five boys singing in the *quintet*. *Quintet* means a group of five, and this group usually sings or plays music. If you were in a *quintet*, what instrument would you want to play?

THINK-ALOUD

The goal of the *think-aloud* procedure is to make explicit the mental processes occurring when good readers encounter new vocabulary words that must be learned (Harmon, 1998). For struggling readers, many of the strategies for word acquisition are not obvious. Therefore, the mental processes at work during strategy use must be verbalized in order to make them clear for these struggling readers.

When students are stumped by a difficult word, the teacher can offer a series of prompts to encourage students to explain their thinking processes, such as "Tell me what you are thinking when you see that word. What else can you tell me?" Once the teacher determines the processes each student is using to identify the unknown word, the teacher can use the think-aloud procedure to instruct the students on how to integrate effective strategies for word learning. By providing a type of external scaffold to word learning, the teacher begins to develop students' confidence with word analysis.

VOCABULARY SELF-COLLECTION STRATEGY

The goal of the *vocabulary self-collection strategy* (Haggard, 1980) is to develop in students an awareness of words and an interest in learning about them. This activity is best done after careful reading of a text, so students are aware of which words are important to what they are reading.

1. Each student picks one word to learn. The word should be one that is important for the whole class to learn.
2. Students write the sentence in which the word appeared or the context in which they heard it, if the word is not from a classroom text.
3. Students must be able to justify to the class why the group at large should learn their chosen words.
4. The students write down words selected on study sheets. The teacher can model use of context to derive word meaning, as well as use of the dictionary to verify correct meaning and pronunciation of the word.
5. As students become conscious of words around them while considering word candidates, the rate of acquiring new vocabulary increases.
6. Vocabulary logs or journals can be incorporated with this activity, in order for students to track their progress in learning new words and to review them frequently for use in school assignments.

CONCEPT LADDER

A *concept ladder* (Gillet & Temple, 1982) is a type of graphic organizer that expands word knowledge by showing students how multiple concepts are related to other words and concepts they already know, creating a semantic network for each term. The graphic organizer develops concepts as follows:

Concept:
Also called?
Kind of?
Replaces or replaced by?
Made of?
Parts are?
Made (used) for?
Looks like?

TOTAL PHYSICAL RESPONSE

Total physical response (TPR) is a systemized approach to the use of commands developed by psychologist John Asher (1982, 2005). TPR is based on the premise that the human brain has a biological program for acquiring any natural language on earth—including the sign language of the deaf. The process is commonly seen in babies internalizing their first language. For example, a parent says, "Look at Mommy," and the infant automatically follows the command. Asher developed his technique following the notion that babies don't learn language by memorizing lists of words, so why should children and adults learning a new language. In TPR, teachers interact with students by delivering commands, and students demonstrate comprehension through physical response—imagine a game of Charades, but in reverse. The teacher would say and model commands that could easily be executed in a classroom setting. TPR can be used to teach new vocabulary and grammar, so that students immediately understand the target language in chunks rather than word by word. Students are not expected to respond orally until they feel ready; therefore, this strategy involves little or no pressure to speak.

- Students respond to verbal commands, but because little emphasis is given to speech production, the level of anxiety is low.
- Incidental learning of a great deal of vocabulary takes place this way.

CONTEXTUALIZED STRATEGY

Harmon's (1998) *contextualized strategy* for vocabulary development allows a teacher to use a new term and then elaborate and extend its meaning immediately:

- "Let's start *recounting* the events of the story. *We will tell about the beginning, the middle, and the end.*"
- "This is an *excerpt—one tiny piece.*"

In a strategy described by Nagy and colleagues (1993), teachers point out cognates students can use from their native language. For example, words such as *general* and *transform* are similar in Spanish. Students should also be taught to be wary of false cognates such as *actual*, which means *nowadays* in Spanish, and *dime*, which means *tell me* in Spanish. Providing or extending prior knowledge is doubly crucial for ELLs.

Many ELLs—and native speakers of English as well—have trouble understanding common English expressions, or *idioms*, because of the use of figurative language. The teaching of idioms is beneficial to both native and non-native speakers of a language, because it taps into nuances of language use that help deepen meaning for students. For all students, the following should be helpful:

- Teach a new idiom each week to expose students to figurative language.
- Read the idiom out loud. Clarify any unknown words, such as *belfry* (as in *bats in the belfry*).
- Ask students if they can guess what the meaning is. Prompt as needed.
- Clarify what the saying means. Have students illustrate the literal meaning and write an explanation of the true meaning.
- Post the idioms around the class. Model their use in conversation.
- Encourage independent learning, using the books by Terban listed under Resources for Instruction.

Students struggling with vocabulary will undoubtedly have difficulty handling content area texts, and therefore will require instruction regarding the specialized vocabulary in science and social studies, for example. Specialized vocabulary usually includes labels for important concepts being discussed in the text. Some words will not be new to pronounce but will have a new meaning, such as *mouth* used to describe a part of a river. Other words will address completely new concepts and should be taught as such, using some of the techniques for concept development explained above.

Research has not found a superior time for presentation of specialized vocabulary (before, during, or after reading). However, students need direct strategy instruction with specialized vocabulary. Looking words up in a glossary is not sufficient for word mastery. In the content areas, labeled diagrams should be used whenever possible, as many technical terms can often be illustrated and appear as such in textbooks and similar materials. Labeled diagrams provide a starting point for discussion of relationships among words. Furthermore, when the information is coded in both pictures and words, retention of the information in memory is enhanced.

SNAPSHOT

Vocabulary Instruction in a Fifth-Grade Classroom

Sam Turner remembers how vocabulary was taught when he was in elementary school. Each week his teacher gave him a list of 20 words to learn. Monday night, for homework, he looked the meanings up in a dictionary. Tuesday night he wrote the words in sentences. Wednesday night he finished a worksheet on the words. Thursday night he studied for a vocabulary test. Friday he took the test. He never remembers his teachers actually discussing the meanings of the words in class. Sam admits that perhaps something might have rubbed off; he always performed well on standardized tests of verbal ability. However, when Sam made the decision to become an elementary school teacher, he decided that he would try to instill the love of words in a different way.

Sam teaches in an urban school that has many students with limited vocabularies—at least in terms of academic language. His goal each year is to get his students excited about learning new words. He begins each day with a word of the day. Sam introduces the word in the morning and tries to infuse the word in as many contexts as he can throughout the day. His goal with the word of the day is to teach general vocabulary.

Sam also teaches technical vocabulary in the content areas of science and social studies. He uses a variety of strategies and gets feedback from his students about which strategies are fun, which strategies help them learn new words, and which strategies are boring or useless.

Finally, Sam keeps a bank of five-minute lessons for vocabulary learning. There are always times when there are gaps in the day. Rather than losing valuable instructional time, Sam pulls an activity from his "Vocab Bank" for a five-minute activity related to learning new words.

FURTHER DEVELOPING STUDENT READING AND WRITING PROFILES

You can add results from formal and informal tests of vocabulary knowledge to Part X of the Student Reading and Writing Profile (Form 10.1). You can also make note of any language differences or language disorders or delays you observe among your students that may have an impact on their vocabulary learning.

CHAPTER SUMMARY

A large vocabulary is necessary for successful reading, and thus for successful schooling in general. A classroom vocabulary program should be systematic and encompass a variety of approaches, including opportunities for direct instruction, incidental learning, and independent strategy practice. Students must have repeated exposure to new words in authentic contexts whenever possible, in order for word learning to take place. Ideally, vocabulary instruction should relate new vocabulary to what students already know; it should develop broader understanding of word knowledge in a variety of contexts; it should actively involve students in learning new words; and it should develop strategies for independent vocabulary acquisition. The overarching goal of a successful vocabulary program is for students to become lifelong word lovers, so they will continue to discover the wonder of words beyond classroom walls.

KEY TERMS AND CONCEPTS

Cognates
False cognates
Idioms
Mnemonic strategies
Parasitic hypothesis
Prior knowledge
Robust instruction
Semantic mapping
Total physical response (TPR)

REFLECTION AND ACTION

1. Observe in a classroom to identify components of the teacher's vocabulary teaching plan. What aspects are noteworthy? Can you make suggestions for improvement?
2. Develop your classroom vocabulary teaching plan. Include a "mission statement" or statement of purpose; identify the main vocabulary goals for the group of students you have; determine how you will select words for direct teaching; and address how you will build a vocabulary rich environment.
3. Develop mini-lessons for a flexible-ability group with a particular vocabulary-related challenge.
4. Take a critical look at a classroom curriculum, and identify ways to infuse vocabulary instruction across all academic areas.
5. Look through a teacher's guide for a basal reading program. Identify what strategies are suggested to teach or expand vocabulary knowledge. Does there appear to be a wide variety of strategies offered? Or is the selection limited to a few basic ones? How are the vocabulary needs of special learners addressed?

READ ON!

Beck, I. L., McKeown, M. G., & Kucan, L. (2002). *Bringing words to life: Robust vocabulary instruction*. New York: Guilford Press.

This engaging book provides a research-based framework and practical strategies for vocabulary development. Includes concrete examples, sample classroom dialogues, and exercises for teachers to incorporate the material in their classrooms.

Baumann, J. F., & Kame'enui, E. J. (Eds.). (2004). *Vocabulary instruction: Research to practice*. New York: Guilford Press.

An excellent resource for learning about the teaching of vocabulary with research-based practices. Includes ideas for teaching structural analysis, contextual analysis, and word-learning strategies.

Johnson, D. (2001). *Vocabulary in the elementary and middle school*. Boston: Allyn & Bacon.

Research-based yet highly readable, this book is a great resource for developing a vocabulary teaching plan. Of note is the chapter on word games and language play activities to stimulate student interest in language. A great choice for teachers who need to supplement their own knowledge of vocabulary.

Lively, T., August, D., Snow, C. E., & Carlo, M. S. (2003). *Vocabulary improvement program for English language learners and their classmates*. Baltimore: Brookes.

This vocabulary curriculum, available for fourth, fifth, and sixth graders, provides students with daily vocabulary practice in just 20–30 minutes per day. The lessons in this 18-week curriculum include step-by-step instructions and a wide range of activities to develop vocabulary in the classroom and reinforce it outside of school. This research-based curriculum has been proven equally effective for ELLs and for native speakers of English.

Terban, M., & Brace, E. (2003). *Building your vocabulary*. New York: Scholastic.

Chapters focus on prefixes, roots, and suffixes; word families; homonyms and homographs; understanding the meaning of words by using context clues; how to use a dictionary and thesaurus; and how to increase one's vocabulary by using techniques such as games. Also includes interesting information on the longest words in the English language and how words change in meaning and usage over time. This book is written for students, but it would be interesting to use it for quick read-alouds in the classroom to stimulate interest in language.

Terban, M., & Devore, J. (1998). *Dictionary of idioms*. New York: Scholastic.

The authors explain the meanings and origins (if known) of more than 600 idioms and proverbs in this intriguing book. Included are idioms from Native American and African American speech, as well as from the Bible, Aesop, and Shakespeare. This book is a must-have for teaching students how to use figurative language

SHARPENING YOUR SKILLS: SUGGESTIONS FOR PROFESSIONAL DEVELOPMENT

1. One of the ways to encourage your students to develop word radar is to model your own interest in learning new words. You can do this informally, by sharing words you've picked up from television or your own reading.
2. Sharpen your research skills by taking a close look at different vocabulary methods you use. Pretest students on target words before teaching, and posttest afterward. Also, elicit students' reflections about each vocabulary method and how it helped or hindered their own learning. This can help you make data-based decisions about whether or not to continue the use of the method, refine the method, or leave it out of your repertoire.
3. Develop a set of five-minute lessons for in-between times at the beginning, middle, or end of the day. Time in school is precious—use it.

RESOURCES FOR INSTRUCTION

Graham-Barber, L., & Lehman, B. (1995). *A chartreuse leotard in a magenta limousine: And other words named after people and places*. New York: Hyperion.

This collection of *eponyms* and *toponyms*—words derived from people and places, respectively—is a great resource for making the study of word origins come to life. Because the explanations draw on the fields of history, geography, and so forth, this is a great way to attract students into nonfiction reading.

Gwynne, F. (1987). *The sixteen-hand horse*. New York: Prentice Hall.
Gwynne, F. (1988a). *A chocolate moose for dinner*. New York: Aladdin.
Gwynne, F. (1988b). *The king who rained*. New York: Aladdin.
Gwynne, F. (1990). *A little pigeon toad*. New York: Aladdin.

These books by the late Fred Gwynne (the actor from *The Munsters* and *My Cousin Vinny*) are easy to read and grandly illustrated with large pictures. Working with homophones and other tricky forms of language, these books use comic illustrations to depict figurative forms of the English language in a memorable way. The topic and design of the books make them appealing to children of all ages, particularly for those who are unfamiliar or who struggle with the nuances of language.

Terban, M. (1982). *Eight ate: A feast of homonym riddles.* New York: Clarion Books.
Terban, M. (1983). *In a pickle and other funny idioms.* New York: Clarion Books.
Terban, M. (1984). *I think I thought and other tricky verbs.* New York: Clarion Books.
Terban, M. (1985). *Too hot to hoot: Funny palindrome riddles.* New York: Clarion Books.
Terban, M. (1986). *Your foot's on my feet: And other tricky nouns.* New York: Clarion Books.
Terban, M. (1987). *Mad as a wet hen! And other funny idioms.* New York: Clarion Books.
Terban, M. (1988). *Guppies in tuxedos: Funny eponyms.* New York: Clarion Books.
Terban, M. (1990). *Punching the clock: Funny action idioms.* New York: Clarion Books.
Terban, M. (1993). *It figures! Funny figures of speech.* New York: Clarion Books.

These books by Marvin Terban address the colorful aspects of language that make language learning fun for students of all ages. With such topics as homonyms, idioms, eponyms, and palindromes, the books use funny illustrations to motivate and encourage word play. These books could be an effective addition not only to a vocabulary program but also to a writing program, to spice up students' personal word banks and enrich their speaking and writing abilities.

RECOMMENDED WEBSITES

About English as 2nd Language
http://esl.about.com

This site provides a wealth of information related to the needs of students learning English as a second language. There are vocabulary lists, worksheets, games, and songs, as well as general information. While the site has a bit of a hodge-podge feel, the information is useful for learners of all ages and grade levels. The site is part of the About network, which uses professionals and experts in a variety of fields as guides for collecting Internet resources on a host of topics.

Dave's ESL Cafe
www.eslcafe.com

This comprehensive site for teachers and students involved in learning English as a second language offers a treasure trove of useful information. In addition to information on language use, quizzes, idioms, slang, and the like, there are special forums for teachers and students to connect with others interested in English as a second language.

Interesting Things for ESL Students
www.manythings.org

This website is for ELLs. There are quizzes, word games, word puzzles, proverbs, slang expressions, anagrams, a random-sentence generator, and other computer-assisted language-learning activities. This site is a great way to introduce or reinforce some of the more difficult aspects of vocabulary, such as idioms and slang.

Language Center
http://langcent.man.ac.uk/ill/vocab.htm

This website offers independent learners various strategies for learning new vocabulary. It offers hints on what to do when encountering new words, as well as ways of remembering and using new words.

LD Online
www.ldonline.org/ld_indepth/teaching_techniques/ellis_clarifying.html

This site is geared for teachers and parents of students who have learning disabilities. Among the myriad activities, articles, and suggestions, this particular page outlines an elaboration technique useful for helping students learning new vocabulary by developing meaningful context.

Ohio ESL
www.ohiou.edu/esl/teacher/vocabulary.html

This web page is a resource page, listing several great websites for additional vocabulary resources, vocabulary research, and teaching materials and plans. Some very useful resources this page offers include graded word lists for ELLs, vocabulary resources for ELLs, and L2 vocabulary learning strategies.

One Stop English
www.onestopenglish.com

This website provides valuable support in vocabulary instruction, as well addresses many other topics related to teaching ELLs. From the home page, click the Grammar and Vocab link to find resources for teachers of ELLs, such as a grammar reference section, grammar teaching approaches, vocabulary lesson plans (including theme-based lesson plans for American and British English), metaphor lesson plans that examine the roots of English, and a series of articles with lesson plans.

Resource Room
www.resourceroom.net/comprehension/vocabactivities.asp

This site provides teachers with some guidelines for teaching vocabulary. It offers detailed suggestions, which include having structure and organization behind the words teachers present, incorporating multisensory learning when possible, modeling activities first, and going beyond the definitions of words. From the guidelines page, there is a link to a page of vocabulary lessons with Greek and Latin roots.

Tower of English
http://towerofenglish.com/vocabulary.html

This website contains links for other vocabulary websites, such as 1000 Most Common Words, Anagram Hall of Fame, Daily Buzzword, OxymoronList.com, and many more! For each link, there is a brief description of the website (as well as a definition and activity, if applicable), then the link.

Vocabulary in Beginning Reading
http://reading.uoregon.edu/voc/voc_teach.php

This site offers an understanding of why building vocabulary in beginning reading is important, why teaching vocabulary is important, how to teach vocabulary, and how to assess vocabulary.

Vocabulary University
www.vocabulary.com

Started by a word lover and his educator wife, this website offers a collection of vocabulary activities, puzzles, and educational games. Many activities are grouped by themes, so they can be easily incorporated into existing classroom curricula. This site supports the notion of word play and its relation to becoming a lifelong learner of language. The site is free of access charges; its creators say that the pleasure they derive from the project rewards them with "psychic income."

FORM 10.1. Student Reading and Writing Profile (Part X)

Student Reading and Writing Profile

Part X: Vocabulary

Vocabulary

Name of test	Date	Score

Student strengths in vocabulary ________________________________

Student areas for improvement in vocabulary ________________________

Instructional recommendations ________________________________

ELEVEN

The Magic of Literature

Trade Books in the Classroom

JEANNE BERGERON

VIGNETTE

A few years ago, Lainey finished third grade in a new suburban school. She had good grades and could read above grade level, but she did not like to read. On a family car trip that summer, her Aunt Dede pulled out a copy of the second Harry Potter book, *Harry Potter and the Chamber of Secrets* (Rowling, 1999), as a surprise for her niece. But the surprise came when Lainey took one look at the book, rolled her eyes, and moaned, "Borrrring!"

Aunt Dede, a teacher in another state, had read *Harry Potter and the Chamber of Secrets* the previous year to the students in her K–5 gifted language arts class, and they had loved it. Even the youngest children in the class were captivated by the story. They listened intently, then enthusiastically participated in grand conversations about Harry's adventures.

"How can you say it's boring? Have you read it?" probed Aunt Dede.

"No, and I don't want to read it. It's too long and it doesn't have any pictures," whined Lainey.

"Oh, that's where you are wrong; there are lots of pictures. Every page is full of pictures; you just have to read the words to see them. It's like magic."

"Nice try, Aunt Dede," Lainey replied sourly from the back seat of the minivan.

Another try was in order. "Well, if you don't want to read it, give it back. Maybe your mom would enjoy hearing the story while we drive." The book sailed through the air and landed on the dashboard. Aunt Dede picked it up and began to read aloud. By the end of the first chapter, requests were coming from the back seat: "Speak up," and "Please read a little louder."

Lainey is an example of a reluctant reader. As demonstrated in this vignette, Lainey can become excited about reading when she is presented with literature on topics that interest her, and when the people around her model engagement in the reading process.

ANTICIPATION QUESTIONS

- What is *children's literature*?
- Why is children's literature valuable?

- How does experiencing children's literature contribute to students' personal, emotional, social, and academic development?
- What are the characteristics of the various literary genres (e.g., picture books, traditional literature, modern fantasy, poetry, contemporary realistic fiction, historical fiction, multicultural literature, nonfiction)?
- What is the value of each genre in a classroom setting?
- How can children's literature be meshed with assessment and instruction?

INTRODUCTION

Teachers, especially those with struggling readers in their classes, may wonder how they can possibly pack more reading into their day. They are already busy following the district reading program; they are using their basal readers and workbooks according to the teacher's manuals for these; and they are incorporating the prescribed reading strategies to improve scores on state-mandated tests. However, these activities and materials are designed to teach children how to read effectively, not to develop the "joy" of reading. Both emergent and struggling readers need more than just reading instruction to become successful readers; they also need to develop a love of reading. The best way to build enthusiasm for reading is by reading good books.

As we have just seen in the vignette, Lainey started the vacation as a reluctant reader; she was able to read, but did not select reading as a pastime. Although her development as a reader was at a higher level than that of most struggling readers at her grade level, she was at a consequential transition point. In order for struggling readers or reluctant readers like Lainey to independently recognize the value and personal enjoyment that come from reading, several elements must be present. First, they need to discover that books are a bridge into themselves. Whether people are reading about facts and figures or science fiction, books have an impact on their readers. When people share the impact books have had on them (e.g., how books educated them, expanded their imaginations, changed their perspective on a particular topic, caused them to experience specific emotions), they in turn share with others the importance of reading. In addition, when people choose literature from different genres and sample a variety of authors, they discover that the impact of reading can take many forms and be far-reaching. Second, strong readers need access to high-quality literature. Third, by listening to stories read aloud and participating in discussions about these stories, readers become more engaged in the reading process. This chapter discusses how to make your classroom rich in the elements necessary to make reading an enjoyable activity your students will seek out.

Cramer (2004) makes this analogy: "A fisherman needs a lure, a hook, and skill to reel in a catch. Good books read aloud are the lure, thoughtful discussions the hook, and independent reading the catch" (p. 316). He goes on to say that in order to reel in emerging, reluctant, or struggling readers, good books need to be readily available—a lot of good books. However, how do we teachers determine if a book is good?

The chapter begins with descriptions of the literary genres that are typically part of an elementary school curriculum, along with the potential benefits of each genre. It continues with measures that can be used to assess what students know about children's literature, as well as their interest in a variety of genres. Suggestions for using children's literature as a form of authentic assessment are also provided. The chapter concludes with ideas for incorporating children's literature in the classroom, including ideas for students who are reluctant readers.

DEFINING CHILDREN'S LITERATURE

Children's literature, most simply defined, is the collection of fiction, nonfiction, and poetry that is intended for children. Gangi (2004) expands the definition to include specific identifying characteristics within each division. She notes that children are usually the protagonists in fictional prose narratives; that nonfiction is well researched, has a clear and informative style, and pleasing artwork; and that the poetry written for children centers on subjects that interest children, such as swings, friendship, or a thumb sucker's thumb. These definitions sort children's books into three broad groups, but do little to help us identify the magical quality, or lure, that will capture a child's attention and spark a desire to read. Stoodt-Hill and Amspaugh-Corson (2001) offer this definition: "Children's literature is literature to which children respond; it relates to their experiences and is told in language they understand. The major contrast between children's literature and adult literature takes into account the more limited life experience of the audience, because readers use their experiences to understand text" (p. 5). In short, children's literature is writing that appeals to the interests of children and that they find enjoyable.

It is important to remember that *basal readers* and *textbooks* are instructional books that are written on various grade levels and are marketed to school districts. These books are typically not found in libraries. In contrast, *trade books* are any children's books that are marketed to libraries, wholesale booksellers, retail bookstores, and book clubs (Anderson, 2002). There are over 50,000 children's stories and informational books already in print in the United States, and that number is growing by an additional 5,000 books a year (Cramer, 2004).

With so much to choose from, how can teachers help their students find high-quality children's books? One method of identifying and selecting books is to turn to those titles that are considered classics and have stood the test of time. A *classic* is any book that is praised by one generation and enjoyed by another or multiple generations (Jordan, 1974). These classics are probably among the books that teachers themselves found enjoyable as children.

Selecting children's books that have received an award from an organization concerned with literacy is an even more effective method of identifying high-quality children's literature. Three of the best-known and the most prestigious awards given to children's books each year are the Newbery Medal, the Caldecott Medal, and the Coretta Scott King Award. The American Library Association (ALA) awards the Newbery Medal, named for the 18th-century children's book publisher John Newbery, to the most distinguished American children's book published the previous year. The ALA employs specific criteria in the selection of Newbery winners. These criteria include the following elements: (1) interpretation of the theme or concept; (2) presentation of information, including accuracy, clarity, and organization; (3) development of plot; (4) delineation of characters; (5) delineation of setting; and (6) appropriateness of style. These standards are also applied to the runner-up books, which are designated as Newbery Honor winners. Teachers should consider the same guidelines when they select books for their students.

The Caldecott Medal, named for the 19th-century illustrator Randolph Caldecott, is awarded annually by the Association for Library Service to Children (a branch of the ALA) to the artist of the most distinguished American picture book for children (*www.ala.org*). The winner of this award is the illustrator, who may also be the author. For instance, the 2002 Caldecott winner was David Wiesner (2001) for his book *The Three Pigs*; he was both the author and the illustrator. The 2001 winner was David Small, the illustrator of Judith St. George's *So You Want to Be President* (2000). Caldecott Medal and the runner-up Caldecott Honor winners must meet the following criteria: (1) excellence of execution in the artistic technique employed; (2) excellence of pictorial interpretation of story, theme, or concept; (3) appropriateness of style of illustration to the story, theme, or concept; and (4) delineation of plot, theme, characters, setting, mood, or information through the pictures.

The Coretta Scott King Award is named in honor of the work for peace and social justice of the late Dr. Martin Luther King and his recently departed wife, Coretta Scott King. The award is given to writers and illustrators of African American lineage. Awards are given to emerging writers, as well as more established authors and illustrators in the field. A seven-member panel judges entries for the competition. Award-winning books include biographies (e.g., *Ray Charles* by Sharon Bell Mathis, G. Ford, and G. C. Ford in 1974) as well as fiction (e.g., *The People Could Fly: American Black Folktales* by Virginia Hamilton in 1986).

Whereas the Newbery, Caldecott, and King awards do not include a book's popularity as a factor in selecting the winners, the Children's Choice Awards use popularity as the main criterion. The winners of these awards are the results of a poll conducted by the International Reading Association and the Children's Book Council. Publishers select books from those published the previous year to be included in the contest. The books are then read to or by roughly 10,000 children around the country, who vote on their favorites. The top 100 books are announced at the annual convention of the International Reading Association, and the list is then published in the October issue of *The Reading Teacher* (Anderson, 2002). In addition, recognizing the growing interest in nonfiction trade books, many organizations include nonfiction books as a target for their awards programs (e.g., the Society of School Librarians, the National Book Foundation). The National Council of Teachers of English sponsors the Orbis Pictus Nonfiction Award. Two recent winners were Pam Ryan's (2002) *When Marian Sang: The True Recital of Marian Anderson* and Rhoda Blumberg's (2004) *York's Adventures with Lewis and Clark: An African-American's Part in the Great Expedition.*

THE VALUE OF CHILDREN'S LITERATURE

Children's literature contributes to the personal enjoyment, cultural knowledge, and educational growth of youngsters. First and foremost, the value of children's literature comes from the personal enjoyment that reading a good book brings to the reader. By reading high-quality children's literature, a child can be transported to exotic lands, travel through time, solve mysteries with a favorite character, discover methods for dealing with growing pains, and view examples of outstanding artwork. Spending quiet time with a good book offers a special type of enjoyment unlike any other and can lead to a lifelong love of reading. Through repeated enjoyable interactions with a good book, even struggling readers can have positive experiences, which lead to positive attitudes that foster the desire to spend more time reading. Reading a good book aloud can build a bond between the reader and the listeners and can create an interest in books. Part of the universal experience that links us to our culture is children's literature. From one generation to the next, books transmit information that gives us a common core of knowledge known as our *literary heritage* (Cramer, 2004; Norton & Norton, 2003).

Literature also contributes to the academic growth of children. It builds their linguistic knowledge enabling them to communicate more effectively with others (Cramer, 2004). Through reading, children are exposed to new and expanded vocabulary, along with concepts that they may not encounter otherwise. Books build background knowledge about the topic, help construct concepts of story structure, expository text structure, increase vocabulary, develop syntax, expand ideas, and aid in the development of imagination and higher-order thinking skills (Huck & Kiefer, 2004).

Reading to and with children from a wide variety of children's books can have a positive influence on struggling readers in particular. Even though a child may not yet be able to read a book independently, the child can still participate in and benefit from the experience, and participate in thoughtful conversations about a book he or she has enjoyed aloud. Furthermore, reading aloud encourages attentive listening skills.

Allington (2006) reinforces the notion that the way struggling readers become fluent readers is by reading and talking about good books—a lot of good books. The old adage "Practice makes perfect" applies to struggling readers as well. It cannot be overemphasized: Struggling readers need to practice reading over and again, and the practice needs to be conducted with the rich vocabulary, beautiful illustrations, entertaining story lines, and fascinating characters that are found in high-quality children's literature. Additional benefits of various literary genres follow.

LITERARY GENRES

Children's books are grouped into categories according to their content or characteristics. These categories are called *genres*. The conventional genres of children's literature include picture books, traditional literature, modern fantasy, contemporary realistic fiction, historical fiction, multicultural literature, poetry, nonfiction, biographies, and award winners. The boundaries of each genre are not fixed; it is possible for one book to be included in several genres. In fact, prose, poetry, picture books, multicultural literature, and award winners can and often do cross the borders of several genres. For example, the Newbery Medal winner in 1998, *Out of the Dust* by Karen Hesse (1997), tells the story of a young girl's struggle during the Dust Bowl of the 1930s. This historical fiction is written in free verse, a form of poetry. Therefore, *Out of the Dust* can be classified as an award winner, as historical fiction, and as poetry. Each of the major genres can also be divided further into smaller groups called *subgenres*. For example, ABC books are a subgenre of picture books, and science fiction stories are a subgenre of modren fantasy.

Teachers must be familiar with the tremendous variety of literature available if they are going to provide appropriate reading materials for their students. Therefore, the characteristics of each genre are described in the following sections. In addition, examples of books from each genre are given.

RESEARCH BRIEF Genre: The Home–School Connection

Whether it's found in books, package labels, or mail, children are confronted with a variety of print in the home. But what's the overlap between genres children experience in the home and genres children experience at school? In particular, what is the overlap for low-socioeconomic-status (low-SES) children, who may not have access to a wide array of children's literature in the home? To explore this issue, Duke and Purcell-Gates (2003) conducted a series of observations of low-SES children in home and school settings. They discovered that some genres were unique to the home (e.g., lottery tickets, menus), some were unique to the school (e.g., word walls, pledges), and there were some areas of overlap (e.g., calendars, newspapers). The authors encourage teachers to be aware of genres that may go beyond what students have experienced in the home, and to provide additional orientation and instruction when necessary. They also suggest that teachers bring genres from the home into the classroom to create home–school connections, when appropriate. Building such bridges can help students see the importance of literacy and applications in their daily lives.

Picture Books

Visual and graphic stimuli and the information they carry have a constant impact on our lives. From the time we get up in the morning until we go to bed at night, we are busy receiving and processing visual images (Tunnell & Jacobs, 2000). Even when we are sleeping, the visual images in our dreams can cause us to awaken and sit bolt upright! The information that pictures convey is powerful.

The format of picture books, rather than their content, creates the genre. Picture books are usually larger in size than other books, to allow more surface area for illustrations. On these larger pages, picture books offer children the opportunity to experience and interact with beautiful art (Tunnell & Jacobs, 2000). Furthermore, by interacting with picture books, children have the opportunity to develop a skill known as *visual literacy*. Visual literacy is the ability to interpret graphic stimuli and is an important component of the language arts.

The illustrations in picture books expose children to the visual elements of line, shape, color, texture, and composition. In addition, through picture books, children experience an extraordinary array of artistic styles, including realism, surrealism, expressionism, impressionism, abstract art, and naive art. The illustrations in children's books utilize numerous painterly and graphic media. *Painterly media* comprise artwork that is applied directly to a surface and include paint (oil, acrylic, watercolor, gouache, and tempera), pencil (charcoal, graphite, colored pencil, crayon, pastels), and pen and ink. In *graphic media*, the artwork is created elsewhere first. Graphic media that can be seen in picture books include woodcuts, linoleum cuts, collage, stone lithography, photography, and computer-generated art (Tunnell & Jacobs, 2000). Artists may use one or a combination of these techniques within the pages of a single picture book.

Tunnell and Jacobs (2000) summarize the important function of artwork in picture books: "Through the beautifully crafted picture books available today, young readers not only may become aware of the variety of artistic styles, media, and techniques that artists employ but also may develop a sense for judging quality" (p. 34).

The illustrations in picture books not only expose children to art; they also aid in the development of literacy skills. In most picture books, the pictures work in tandem with the text to tell the story and convey the message of the book. There is usually a balance between the illustrations and text, as in the book *My Friend Rabbit* by Eric Rohmann (2002). Illustrations are used to develop and support the plot by communicating information about the characters, mood, time, and setting, as done by Robert McCloskey in *Make Way for Ducklings* (1941). The pictures also have the ability to set the tone of the story and evoke emotions. The pictures invite active participation in their viewing, unlike so many of the random images that are flashed in front of us each day. To get the full measure of meaning and fulfillment from a good picture book, the reader must attend carefully to both the pictures and the text (Kiefer, 1995).

Picture books such as *No David* by David Shannon (1998) allow students to conceptualize the words and find themselves in context with others through the visual representation of the text. Pictures develop an understanding of characters, setting, and mood that can evoke a personal response. Reading picture books aloud gives children the opportunity to experience books that they may not be able to read on their own and to use their imagination. Furthermore, picture books expand concepts of locations, people, and circumstances that children might not have the chance to learn about otherwise.

In wordless picture books, however, the illustrations do all of the work. The entire story is told through pictures. Wordless books help children develop observational skills, encourage the use of descriptive vocabulary, and foster the ability to create stories by observing a logical sequence (Tunnell & Jacobs, 2000). *Frog Goes to Dinner* by Mercer Mayer (1977) and *Tuesday* by David Wiesner (1991) are examples of classic and contemporary wordless picture books.

Concept books, alphabet books, and counting books are other subgenres of picture books. These books are intended for the very young, but can also be enjoyed by older children. These books are often in the form of board books and are constructed with rounded corners and glossy cardboard pages that are difficult to tear and can be wiped clean. They usually have one illustration per page, and the pictures carry the meaning. Since these books rely heavily on visual information to convey messages, they are an excellent resource for struggling readers.

Benefits for Readers

- The illustrations in picture books expose children to art.
- Pictures aid in the development of literacy skills.
- The pictures can give needed practice in obtaining meaning from books.
- Picture books incorporate language that is simple enough for a struggling reader to understand.
- Since all of the other genres are represented in picture books, reading picture books exposes readers to literary genres that may be out of their reach otherwise.

Traditional Literature

Traditional literature comprises stories, wise sayings, and rhymes that have been passed down over the generations by storytellers. Traditional literature stands out from other forms of children's literature, in that its authorship is always unknown (Norton & Norton, 2003). These works came from the oral tradition and were not originally intended for children. However, over time children began to share in the storytelling; with the advent of the printing press, the tales were captured in print, and they became part of children's literature.

Since traditional literature evolved from an oral tradition, multiple versions of the same story may exist across various cultures. Each culture's version reflects its own dialect, setting, clothing, and values (Galda & Cullinan, 2002). These original stories are copyright-free and continue to evolve and change as new adaptations are published (Anderson, 2002).

Folk Tales

Most traditional literature falls under the heading of *folk tales*. There are many different types of folk tales. The uniting trait of folk tales is that they are stories from the "folk" or people and they originated from an oral tradition.

Fairy Tales

Fairy tales are the best-known type of traditional literature. The conventional introduction of "Once upon a time" and the optimistic conclusion of "And they lived happily ever after" can identify a fairy tale. The settings are vague, but often include a castle or kingdom. The stereotyped characters reflect qualities of good and evil; they usually include a beautiful daughter, a handsome prince, an evil stepmother, and an ogre or a witch. Fairy tales also usually contain an element of enchantment or a magical object, as well as information about a culture's past and current values. Numerous versions, at different reading levels, of *Cinderella*, *Sleeping Beauty*, *Rumpelstiltskin*, *Jack and the Beanstalk*, and *Little Red Riding Hood* are all examples of traditional fairy tales.

Cumulative Tales

Cumulative tales have repeated actions and a rhythmic refrain. The events in the plot repeat and accumulate, making it easy for the storyteller to remember the story as he or she works toward a surprise ending. *There Was an Old Lady Who Swallowed a Fly* by Simms Taback (1997) and *Chicken Little* by Steven Kellogg (1987) are familiar cumulative tales.

Pourquoi Tales

Pourquoi means *why* in French, and *pourquoi tales* explain why natural phenomena occur. *Why Mosquitoes Buzz in People's Ears* by Verna Aardema (1978) and the classic *How the Camel Got His Hump* by Rudyard Kipling (2001) are excellent example of pourquoi tales.

Noodlehead Tales

Noodlehead tales show good-hearted characters acting foolishly and making ridiculous decisions. *The Squire's Bride* by Peter Asbjornsen and Jorgen Moe (1983), *It's Too Noisy* by Joanna Cole (1989), *and The Three Sillies* by Steven Kellogg (1999) would fall into this subgenre.

Animal Tales

Animal tales depict animals with human qualities. This category includes classics such as *Puss in Boots* by Charles Perrault (1999), *The Three Little Pigs* by Paul Galdone (1984), and *The Three Billy Goats Gruff* by Janet Stevens (1995).

Myths

Myths are ancient stories that attempt to explain unexplainable events, such as the creation of the world, religious beliefs, or the mysteries of life. There is usually a hero who confronts the gods or goddesses. Myths are often long and complex, so they work well with more advanced readers. Examples include *Cupid and Psyche* by M. Charlotte Craft (1996) or a collection of myths such as *Greek Myths* by Geraldine McCaughrean (1993).

Fables

Fables are straightforward short stories designed to entertain and teach a lesson. The "moral to the story," a universal truth, is expressly stated at the end of each fable. Fables usually have animal characters that have human qualities. Many European fables are attributed to a Greek slave, Aesop. Arnold Lobel, Heide Holder, and Mitsumasa Manno have all written adaptations of Aesop's fables.

Legends

Legends combine history and mythology. The characters are based on real people from history; however, the truth is stretched and their accomplishments are exaggerated. Legends include stories about Johnny Appleseed, Davy Crockett, and Daniel Boone.

Tall Tales

Tall tales are humorous stories based on both real and imaginary characters from the American frontier. The characters are exaggerated and are often composites of characteristics that reflect people's occupations during the settling of the West. For instance, Steven Kellogg's (1992) *Pecos Bill* is a cowboy, and Kellogg's (1985) *Paul Bunyan* represents lumberjacks. In Julius Lester's (1994) *John Henry*, a railroad worker is portrayed.

Rhymes

Mother Goose poems and other nursery rhymes constitute one of the best-known forms of folk literature. Even very young children can appreciate the musical language, humor, and entertaining incidents that are represented in nursery rhymes (Anderson, 2002).

Benefits for Readers

- Traditional literature leads to an understanding of the traditions of different cultures.
- It introduces children to times before recorded history from all parts of the world.
- It helps children understand the world and identify with universal human struggles.
- It provides examples of story structure.

Modern Fantasy

Modern fantasy incorporates the same story lines as traditional literature. However, the principal difference between these two genres is that modern fantasy has known authors, while traditional literature is anonymous. Modern fantasy is characterized by stories with at least one impossible or magical element. Even though there is an element in the story that is impossible, the plot, characters, and setting may be believable. "Suspending disbelief" is the topmost requirement for modern fantasy (Norton & Norton, 2003). If you are among the many who have cried when Charlotte dies in E. B. White's (1974) *Charlotte's Web*, or cheered as J. K. Rowling's Harry Potter prevails over evil, then you have experienced the essence of modern fantasy.

Modern Fairy Tales

Modern fairy tales have the same characteristics as those from the oral tradition. The difference between these fairy tales and those of traditional literature is authorship. Hans Christian Andersen is credited with writing the first modern fairy tales. Classics such as *Peter Pan* by James M. Barrie (2003) and *The Adventures of Alice in Wonderland* by Lewis Carroll (1999) are also included in this genre. *In the Night Kitchen* by Maurice Sendak (1996), as well as Chris Van Allsburg's (1981) *Jumanji*, are picture books that are also modern fairy tales.

High Fantasy

In *high fantasy*, the main character is heroic and embarks on a purposeful quest. All of the characters are credible in their setting, and the world they live in is believable. Values such as courage, justice, and wisdom are part of high fantasy. J. R. R. Tolkien's (1986) *Lord of the Rings*, as well as J. K. Rowling's *Harry Potter* stories and *The Chronicles of Narnia* by C. S. Lewis (1994), are all excellent examples.

Modern Animal Tales

The characters in *modern animal tales* are anthropomorphic animals. That is, they talk, think, and act like people. *Click, Clack, Moo: Cows That Type* by Doreen Cronin (2000), William Steig's (1987) *Sylvester and the Magic Pebble*, and E. B. White's (1974) *Charlotte's Web* are examples of modern animal fantasies.

Science Fiction

In *science fiction*, technology (real or imagined) replaces magic. Lois Lowry incorporates science fiction in both *The Giver* (1993) and *Gathering Blue* (2002), as does Madeleine L'Engle in her trilogy *A Wrinkle in Time* (1998), *A Swiftly Tilting Planet* (1981), and *A Wind in the Door* (1974).

Benefits for Readers

- Modern fantasy allows reader to enter imaginative realms of possibility.
- It helps children expand their curiosity and become observers of life.
- It assists children dealing in dealing with real-world problems.
- It helps children become able to differentiate between fantasy and reality.

Contemporary Realistic Fiction

The books included in contemporary realistic fiction tell realistic stories about contemporary life. The main characters are credible, common people, usually about the same age as the intended audience (Anderson, 2002). The common threads that tie all contemporary realistic fiction together are the contemporary time frame in which the story takes place and its believability. There is no magic in realistic fiction—just the persistence, creativity, and struggle of the characters to come to terms with their personal situations. Contemporary realistic fiction is frequently narrated in the first person by the main character, which makes the story even more believable.

The plots found in this genre can deal with familiar everyday situations, such as school, family life, love, friendship, sports, and pets. *Vera's First Day of School* by Vera Rosenberry (1999), *Paperboy* by Dave Pilkey (1999), and *There's a Girl in My Hammerlock* by Jerry Spinelli (1993) are examples of this type of contemporary realistic fiction. However, more serious life issues, such as divorce, death, illness, war, poverty, drugs, survival, and special needs, can also be the focus. *When Sophie Gets Angry—Really, Really Angry* by Molly Bang (1999), *Walk Two Moons* by Sharon Creech (1994), and *Summer of the Swans* by Betsy Byars (1996) present less than perfect, but realistic, pictures of life.

Benefits for Readers

- Contemporary realistic fiction helps readers discover that the dilemmas and longings of their lives are not unique.
- It shows new and different ways to look at and deal with conflicts.
- It expands readers' horizons by broadening their interests.
- It enables readers to experience adventures vicariously through books.
- Contemporary realistic fiction gives readers alternative ways to handle their own problems.
- It helps them to empathize with viewpoints that may be different from their own.

Historical Fiction

Historical fiction is a collection of realistic stories that are set in the past. This definition raises the question "When is the past?" For youngsters born in the 1990s, the events and attitudes of the 1980s can seem like ancient history! There isn't one hard-and-fast cutoff date for the stories that are included in the historical fiction genre. Norton and Norton (2003) use the end of World War II as the dividing point between historical and contemporary fiction. Gangi (2004) and Mitchell (2003) divide the two genres after the events and turmoil of the civil rights movement of the 1960s. However, Anderson (2002) is very specific about the division point between the contemporary and historical fiction genres, giving the year 1964 as this point. In any case, the marker that separates contemporary and historic fiction is sure to move with time, as it has in the past. Alcott's (2004) *Little Women* debuted in the 19th century as contemporary realistic fiction, but with the passing of time is now viewed as an example of historical fiction (Galda & Cullinan, 2002).

Although the chronological boundary for historical fiction may seem fuzzy, the characteristics of this genre are easy to recognize. As stated earlier, the stories have realistic characters and take place any time in the past. The backdrop can be anywhere in the world—ancient Egypt (*Mara, Daughter of the Nile* by Eloise Jarvis McGraw, 1990; *Pharaoh's Daughter* by Julius Lester, 2000); a village in the Middle Ages (*Crispin: The Cross of Lead* by Avi, 2002); the countryside of 12th-century Korea (*A Single Shard* by Linda Sue Park, 2001); or war-torn Connecticut during the American Revolution (*My Brother Sam is Dead* by James and Christopher Collier, 1989)—as long as the story is believable and grounded in the facts of history. The stories must reflect the time period accurately or recreate a historical event. Even though historical fiction can portray actual people and events, these elements are often just a vehicle to carry a fictional tale (Galda & Cullinan, 2002).

Benefits for Readers

- Historical fiction helps readers understand why past or present problems exist and how they came about.
- It allows readers to gain knowledge about the people, values, beliefs, hardships, and physical surroundings common to various time periods.
- It brings history to life.
- Historical fiction increases understanding of a people's or character's heritage.
- It teaches children that throughout history people have depended upon one another and shared similar needs.

RESEARCH BRIEF Literature for All Students

Children's literature has evolved to include children from all minority cultures since Nancy Larrick (1965) first published her landmark study, "The All-White World of Children's Literature." This article focused attention on the problem of underrepresentation of children of color in children's books published in the United States. Larrick examined more than 5,000 children's books published between 1962 and 1964, and found only 40 books (0.8%) that contained illustrations or text representing contemporary African American children. Larrick's article had a strong impact on publishers and the public, resulting in an increased focus on ethnic diversity and equity in children's literature.

Multicultural Literature

As you have read in Chapter 3, the population in U.S. schools is becoming increasingly diverse. Therefore, "American children need to develop a world view that appreciates the richness of other cultures while at the same time preserving and celebrating their uniqueness" (Rothlein & Meinbach, 1996, p. 246). Teachers can use *multicultural literature* as one tool to create a culturally responsive climate in the classroom (Montgomery, 2001).

All books come from the perspective of a particular culture and can be read from many points of view (Schmidt, 1999). However, because America's literary roots were in European-dominated culture, early literature written for children did not make room for other voices. Rudine Sims Bishop (1997) points out that children's literature has the power to function as a mirror in which children can see themselves, or as a window through which they can view other people. Bishop argues that too often children's literature only functions as a mirror for white children, while children of color are marginalized and only able to look through the window, never seeing themselves in the mirror of literature. This mirror must reflect all children—children from different ethnic groups, races, genders, and sexual orientations, as well as those with disabilities.

Multicultural literature is a term used to describe works "that represent any distinct group through accurate portrayal and rich detail" (Hancock, 2000, p. 168). Multicultural literature is a relatively new genre that has been created to includes books by and about peoples from all cultures. Each book reflects various elements of a culture, including its way of life, values, beliefs, and patterns of thinking. Rothlein and Meinbach (1996) and McNair (2003) summarize Bishop's classification system for multicultural literature. *Socially conscious literature* is written to encourage children from the majority culture to develop empathy, understanding, and tolerance for other cultures. *Melting-pot literature* presents America as a homogeneous culture and ignores racial differences among children, except for physical ones such as skin color. *Culturally conscious literature* is free of cultural stereotyping and presents the authentic perspectives of the cultures about which it is written; most authors are native to the cultures being described.

High-quality multicultural children's literature can be a valuable tool in today's classrooms. This collection of books can help our students learn about the world beyond their neighborhoods and understand social change (Asselin, 2003). Multicultural children's literature is an excellent vehicle to address the topic of diversity and to encourage discussion about issues of diversity in elementary classrooms (Ballentine & Hill, 2000; Duren, 2000). It builds knowledge about places and cultures, while helping students develop an understanding and respect for diverse people, cultures, and geographic regions of the world. Perhaps most importantly, as Bishop (1997) pointed out, multicultural children's literature can function as a mirror that allows all children to see where they fit into the world and help them develop a sense of pride for their own cultural heritage.

When you are selecting multicultural children's literature, look for books that avoid stereotypes and that give positive three-dimensional portrayals of the characters, with a variety of personalities, virtues, faults, skills, and interests (Lowery, 2003). Since illustrations can have a strong impact on children, make sure that the illustrations are authentic to the culture being represented and that they function to enhance the story. The dialogue in multicultural literature should reflect the dialect and speech rhythms of the language portrayed. Finally, look for pluralistic themes that foster a belief in the value of cultural diversity as a national asset (Pang, Colvin, Tran, & Barba, 1992).

Examples of high-quality children's multicultural literature include *Cousins* (1993) and *M. C. Higgins, the Great* (1999) by Virginia Hamilton; *Bud, Not Buddy* (1999) and *The Watsons Go to Birmingham* (1995) by Christopher Paul Curtis; *Dragon's Gate* (1993) and *Thief of Hearts: Golden Mountain Chronicles* (1995) by Laurence Yep; *My Name Is SEEPEETZA* by Shirley Sterling (1992); and *Esperanza Rising* by Pam Munoz Ryan (2000). For younger or struggling readers, you might select *Grandfather's Journey* by Allen Say (1993), *Uncle Jed's Barbershop* by Margaree King Mitchell (1993), *The Lotus Seed* by Sherry Garland (1993), and *Tar Beach* by Faith Ringgold (1996).

Benefits for Readers

- Multicultural literature builds respect across cultures.
- It sharpens all readers' sensitivity to others, and improves the self-esteem of members of racial and ethnic minority groups.
- It encourages children to accept and be sensitive to diversity.
- It develops understanding of and respect for universal human rights and fundamental freedom.
- Children learn to respect the values and contributions of minority groups in the United States.
- Children broaden their understanding of history, geography, and natural history.

Poetry

Poetry takes the ordinary word and makes it extraordinary. Poetry also expresses feelings and ideas quickly and memorably, and usually taps into strong emotions (Anderson, 2002). The words in poems are not only selected to create striking impressions; they are chosen for their sounds. Poems are multidimensional: They can tell a story, describe an object, recount a life experience, or just make the reader laugh. Poetry is a broad genre that includes songs and raps, word pictures, and novels in the form of free verse.

According to Tompkins (2002), poetry books for children are published in three formats. The first format is a *picture book version of a single poem*. In these books, the illustrations on each page portray an individual line or stanza of the poem. Edward Lear's (1998) *The Owl and the Pussycat* (1998) and Clement Moore's (2002) *The Night Before Christmas* are examples of picture books that present a single poem. Another category for poetry books is the *specialized collection*. In this group, either a single poet or a single topic is represented. Shel Silverstein's *The Light in the Attic* (1981) and *Where the Sidewalk Ends* (1974) are both examples of a collection of works by a single poet. *Blast Off! Poems about Space* by Lee Bennett Hopkins (1996) is an example of a book of poems on a single topic. *Comprehensive anthologies* are the third type of children's poetry book. These books often have a theme and present different types of poems by various authors. *The Random House Book of Poetry for Children*, compiled by well-known children's writer Jack Prelutsky (1983) and illustrated by Arnold Lobel, is an excellent anthology.

Poetry is best enjoyed when it is read aloud, so that the music of the words can be emphasized. Poetry is a good reading choice for struggling readers, because the images in poems are strong, and poetry plays with words and ideas (Strickland, Galda, & Cullinan, 2004). Poetry also provides a vehicle for teaching figurative language (see Figure 11.1); this is of particular importance to students who are English-language learners (ELLs). Moreover, poetry represents a wide variety of topics, which makes it easy to match a child to a poem. Poems are often short with plenty of white space on the page, which makes the poem look less daunting to a struggling reader than a full page of text. Poetry lends itself to choral reading and other repeated reading activities that also support struggling readers. Finally, as Tompkins (2002) points out, most children already have some background knowledge and exposure to poetry from their playground jump-rope chants and clapping games, as well as from the words of popular songs.

Figurative language makes reading and writing more interesting. The acronym SHAMPOO can help students identify and remember the different types of figurative language used in children's literature.

S—simile: A stated comparison that uses the connective words *like* or *as* (e.g., *The silence pours in like water filling a hole*).

H—hyperbole: Exaggeration not meant to be taken seriously (e.g., *older than dirt*).

A—alliteration: The repetition of initial sounds in neighboring words or stressed syllables (e.g., *Betty bought a bit of bitter butter*).

M—metaphor: An implied comparison in which a word or phrase ordinarily used for one thing is applied to another (e.g., *All the world's a stage*).

P—personification: A figure of speech in which a thing, quality, or idea has human characteristics (e.g., *The trees whispered my name*).

O—onomatopoeia: The use of sound words to make writing more vivid (e.g., *hiss, slurp, bang*).

O—oxymoron: A figure of speech that combines contradictory ideas or terms (e.g., *thunderous silence, sweet sorrow*).

FIGURE 11.1. Figurative language.

Some poems tell a story; others have strong rhythm and rhyming patterns; in still other poems, the words and sentences follow specific guidelines of length and meter. A few different types of poems are as follows:

- *Narrative poems* tell a story with a definite beginning, middle, and end.
- *Limericks* are humorous poems that follow a prescribed pattern of five lines of verse with an AABBA rhyming scheme. Here is an example:

  A fly and a flea in a flue
  Were imprisoned, so what could they do?
  Said the fly, "Let us flee!"
  "Let us fly," said the flea.
  So they flew through a flaw in the flue.

- *Haiku* is a form of Japanese poetry that consists of 17 syllables arranged in three lines of 5, 7, and 5 syllables. The topic of a haiku usually involves nature or the seasons. Here is an example:

  Wind ventriloquist
  Announcing presence and strength
  Wind chimes move in spring. (Jeanne Bergeron, 2004)

- *Free verse* includes poems with irregular rhythmic patterns and line lengths. It may be rhymed, but is usually unrhymed. *Love That Dog* by Sharon Creech (2001) is an example of contemporary realistic fiction written in free verse and therefore is also classified as poetry.

Benefits for Readers

- Poetry leaves a strong or beautiful impression with a limited number of words.
- It has a musical quality that attracts children and appeals to their emotions.
- It suggests new and interesting images that can enhance topics being discussed in class.
- It can create delightful word plays.
- It introduces children to a new way of writing and thinking.
- Poetry encourages children to play with and discover the power of words.
- It suggests something different every time it is read.
- It provides children with knowledge about concepts in the world around them.
- It encourages children to appreciate language and expand their vocabulary.

Nonfiction

For many years, the term *informational books* was used to delineate the nonfiction genre. Now there is a trend in children's literature toward using the general term *nonfiction* to describe trade books that have a primary purpose of informing the reader with in-depth explanations and illustrations about factual material. As Colman (1999) points out, the label *informational book* triggers thoughts of encyclopedias and textbooks, instead of the rich, well-written, beautifully illustrated, and engaging collection of nonfiction available for children today.

In an observational study of classroom libraries and time spent in elementary classrooms spent on reading nonfiction, Duke (2000) noted the paucity of informational books present and the minimal time (3.6 minutes a day) devoted to reading informational text. Duke noted that many difficulties students in intermediate grades have in reading expository text may be attributed to lack of exposure to genres other than narrative forms.

Moss (2004) cites two reasons for increased interest in expository text in the elementary grades: (1) the need to help students cope with the demands of an information age, and (2) the fact that high-stakes tests usually include expository material. The interest in expository text is high. Fortunately, nonfiction trade books can be as engaging and entertaining as fiction, and the number of high-quality nonfiction books for children grows daily.

No matter what you call it—informational books or nonfiction—this genre is packed with variety. True, encyclopedias are a part of this group, but there is so much more. Nonfiction includes real-life adventures as depicted in *Shipwreck at the Bottom of the World* by Jennifer Armstrong (1999), and history as depicted in *The Middle Passage: White Ships/Black Cargo* by Tom Feelings (1995), *The Wigwam and the Longhouse* by Charlotte and David Yues (2000), and *Inside the Alamo* by Jim Murphy (2003).

Science can also come to life when children's nonfiction literature is used to expand knowledge. Seymour Simon has written hundreds of nonfiction books that are appropriate for struggling readers. Simon covers topics such as *Storms* (1992), *The Brain* (1997), *Planets around the Sun* (2003), *Cool Cars* (2004), and *Crocodiles and Alligators* (1999). Photographic essays can present specific information in a journalistic style; *Fiesta U.S.A.* by George Ancona (1995) is an example of this subgenre. Craft and how-to books, including cookbooks, share directions for projects, activities, and favorite foods. First-person narratives such as *Orphan Train Rider: One Boy's True Story* by Andrea Warren (1996) are still another subgenre of the nonfiction trade books that are being published in record numbers (Huck & Kiefer, 2004).

Ganske, Monroe, and Strickland (2003) believe that some nonfiction books are better than fiction at "hooking and holding" readers. The students, however, need to be taught how to navigate the special features associated with this genre, such as matching captions to illustrations and interpreting graphs and charts.

Benefits for Readers

- Nonfiction text is supported by illustrations.
- Detailed visual design adds to children's understanding of facts.
- Nonfiction encourages children to look at the world in new ways, and to discover laws of nature and society.
- It provides high adventure and drama.
- It helps children acquire vocabulary, syntax, story/text structures, ideas, and concepts.

Biographies

A *biography* is a nonfiction work in which an author describes the life, or part of the life, of a real historical or contemporary individual. (A special type of biography, an *autobiography*, is written by a person sharing his or her own life story.) A well-written biography can give readers a peek into the real lives, locations, and times of a person, making his or her experiences come alive for the reader. Biographies can help children understand that people and their actions form history (Galda & Cullinan, 2002). As with all people, the characters in a biography work through their real-life struggles to accomplish their goals, which are attained through persistence and hard work. Biographies can feature famous people, such as sports figures and entertainers, political and social leaders, or even children's favorite authors or illustrators. Biographies can also share the life or accomplishments of lesser-known people (Anderson, 2002).

An *authentic biography* is a well-documented and carefully researched account of a person's life or an event in a person's life. The information shared in an authentic biography is verifiable, and any dialogue that is included has been substantiated by reliable personal recollections or by historical documents such as letters and diaries (Anderson, 2002). *Anne Frank Beyond the Diary* by Ruud van der Rol and Rian Verhoeven (1993) and *Franklin Delano Roosevelt* by Russell Freedman (1992) are examples of authentic biographies.

A *fictionalized biography* is also grounded in research, but the narrative (which carries the story) is dramatized, and the dialogue is invented. An important aspect of a fictionalized biography is that the events, personality, and mannerisms of the person who is being depicted are generally revealed accurately, rather than that every word is absolutely true. Fictionalized biographies, with their real-life characters, can function as a bridge between historical fiction and nonfiction. However, the trend in today's market is toward authenticity and accuracy (Huck & Kiefer, 2004). Children should have the opportunity to read both authentic and fictionalized biographies, and to discuss the similarities and differences among presentations.

While most biographies focus on a single person, a *collective biography* tells the story of two or more people whose lives are intertwined in some way. Collective biographies can share the story of people who have done something together, such as *The Wright Brothers: How They Invented the Airplane* by Russell Freedman (1991). Collective biographies can also be linked by a theme or a common experience, ethnicity, gender, or occupation; for instance, they can describe children who survived the Holocaust, African American baseball players, or women authors.

Struggling readers may find simplified or "easy-reader" biographies or picture book biographies, such as *A Picture Book of Thomas Jefferson* by David Adler (1991), enjoyable. These books use a straightforward writing style with simple language supported by illustrations or photographs. In a picture book biography, the illustrations add information about the setting or events that is not conveyed by the words alone. This can assist the student in building background knowledge that clarifies and extends concepts.

Benefits for Readers

- Biographies provide real information, details, and insight into the lives of individuals.
- They help children develop an understanding of how events and choices affect one's life.
- They provide models for the future.
- They reveal the processes needed to accomplish life goals.
- Biographies demonstrate that each person has a unique life.
- They develop sensitivity to and awareness of people representing many cultures.
- They offer the special satisfaction of knowing that the people and events described are true and accurate.

LINKING CHILDREN'S LITERATURE WITH ASSESSMENT AND INSTRUCTION

As we have seen throughout this text, assessment is the first step of instruction. Without careful and thorough assessment, it is not possible to tailor our teaching to meet the needs of our students. Assessment is an ongoing process that is used to determine children's strengths as well as their needs. Knowing what each child can do, or is interested in, gives us a starting point on which to build and expand; understanding each child's needs tells us where performance requires improvement. Guiding instruction is the ultimate purpose of all assessment, and this assessment–instruction paradigm holds true for children's literature too. As assessment relates to children's literature, it is conducted to determine the reading habits, topics, and/or types of books that children are interested in and therefore most likely to read.

Assessment can be linked to children's literature in three ways. First, we can use assessment to estimate what grade-level books might be appropriate for students. Second, we can assess what students know about children's literature and their interest in a variety of genres. Third, we can use children's literature as text for reading assessment.

What Are Informal Assessments of Knowledge of Children's Literature?

Scholastic Reading Inventory

The Scholastic Reading Inventory (SRI; Scholastic, Inc., 2005) is a computer-based, interactive comprehension test that can be used to place students in books that are appropriate in terms of both reading level and interest level. A print version of the SRI is available as well. The SRI is designed for students in grades 1–12 and generates both norm- and criterion-based scores. The assessment includes both narrative and expository text. With the computer version, a student selects an interest area, takes a test within that area, and then receives a list of trade books that should be within the student's reading range. Because the SRI has a brief administration time (about 20 minutes), scores can be used to monitor student progress in reading on an ongoing basis.

In addition to percentile ranks and stanine scores, the SRI also provides a *lexile score*. A lexile score is based on a framework that estimates level of difficulty of text. A student's lexile score on the SRI is then matched with books with similar lexile scores. Lexile scores range from 200L (beginning readers) to 1700L (advanced readers).

Title Recognition Tests

Title recognition tests (TRTs) are a quick way to get an idea of students' familiarity with children's literature. They are lists of actual children's books, mixed in with *foils*, or made-up names of books. The task is to have students check off which titles are real books. The score is the total number of correct titles minus the total number of foils identified as real books.

Cunningham and Stanovich (1991) developed the original TRT, designed for students in grades 4–6 (see Figure 11.2). Later, McDowell, Schumm, and Vaughn (1993) developed a primary version, the TRT-P (see Figure 11.3). You may want to try one of these versions with your students or create your own. Either way, you can get an idea of which students have had more exposure to children's literature and which students have had less.

TITLE RECOGNITION QUESTIONNAIRE

Name ______________________________ Grade ____________

Date ______________

Below you will see a list of book titles. Some of the titles are names of actual books and some are not. You are to read the names and put a check mark next to the names of those that you know are books. Do not guess, but only check those that you know are actual books. Remember, some of the titles are not those of popular books, so guessing can easily be detected.

____ 1. *A Light in the Attic*
____ 2. *Joanne*
____ 3. *How to Eat Fried Worms*
____ 4. *It's My Room*
____ 5. *Call of the Wild*
____ 6. *Hot Top*
____ 7. *The Chosen*
____ 8. *Tales of a Fourth-Grade Nothing*
____ 9. *Don't Go Away*
____ 10. *The Missing Letter*
____ 11. *The Polar Express*
____ 12. *The Indian in the Cupboard*
____ 13. *The Rollaway*
____ 14. *The Civil War*
____ 15. *Sadie Goes to Hollywood*
____ 16. *Homer Price*
____ 17. *Heidi*
____ 18. *Freedom Train*
____ 19. *The Schoolhouse*
____ 20. *James and the Giant Peach*
____ 21. *By the Shores of Silver Lake*
____ 22. *Superfudge*
____ 23. *He's Your Little Brother!*
____ 24. *Dr. Dolittle*
____ 25. *From the Mixed-up Files of Mrs. Basil E. Frankweiler*
____ 26. *Island of the Blue Dolphins*
____ 27. *Ethan Allen*
____ 28. *Ramona the Pest*
____ 29. *The Great Brain*
____ 30. *Misty of Chincoteague*
____ 31. *The Lost Shoe*
____ 32. *Henry and the Clubhouse*
____ 33. *Tales of a Fourth-Grade Nothing*
____ 34. *Dear Mr. Henshaw*
____ 35. *Searching the Wilds*
____ 36. *Harriet the Spy*
____ 37. *The Lion, the Witch and the Wardrobe*
____ 38. *Iggie's House*

FIGURE 11.2. Title Recognition Questionnaire. From Cunningham, A. E., & Stanovich, K. E. (1991). Tracking the unique effects of print exposure in children. *Journal of Educational Psychology, 83*, 264–274. Copyright 1991 by the American Psychological Association. Reprinted by permission.

TITLE RECOGNITION TEST—PRIMARY (TRT-P)

Title

____ 1. *Jimmy and Fat Joe Find a Ghost*
____ 2. *The Magic School Bus inside the Earth*
____ 3. *Zak and the Dream Machine*
____ 4. *Miss Nelson Is Missing*
____ 5. *The Adventure of Barney the Pig*
____ 6. *The Very Hungry Caterpillar*
____ 7. *The Cut-Ups*
____ 8. *In a Dark, Dark Room*
____ 9. *"No, No, No!" Cried the Babysitter*
____ 10. *The Evil Witch's Spell*
____ 11. *No Room for Turtles*
____ 12. *Amelia Bedelia and the Surprise Shower*
____ 13. *Are You My Mother?*
____ 14. *Dancing Shoes for Darla*
____ 15. *Chicka-Chicka Boom Boom*
____ 16. *The Polar Express*
____ 17. *Hot Air Henry*
____ 18. *The Berenstein Bears and the Spooky Old Tree*
____ 19. *Corduroy*
____ 20. *Whose Room Is It Anyway?*
____ 21. *Hop on Pop*
____ 22. *Madeline*
____ 23. *Brown Bear, Brown Bear, What Do You See?*
____ 24. *The Napping House*
____ 25. *The Baby Blue Cat Who Said No*
____ 26. *Prince Trillium*
____ 27. *Jack and Jake*
____ 28. *Ira Says Goodbye*
____ 29. *The Kid in the Red Jacket*
____ 30. *The Haunted Hallway*
____ 31. *The Playground Wars*
____ 32. *Seven Diving Ducks*
____ 33. *Princess Furball*
____ 34. *The Terrible Trouble on Terwilliger Street*
____ 35. *The Stupids*
____ 36. *A Mouse in My House*
____ 37. *Nate the Great*
____ 38. *The Magic Penny*
____ 39. *My Mother Lost Her Job Today*
____ 40. *Good Hunting Blue Sky*
____ 41. *The Mystery of the Lost Umbrella*
____ 42. *The Great Submarine Sandwich Race*
____ 43. *The Bears' Picnic*
____ 44. *Put Me in the Zoo*
____ 45. *Babar*
____ 46. *Arthur's Tooth*
____ 47. *My Brother the Pest*
____ 48. *Encyclopedia Brown and the Case of the Treasure Hunt*

FIGURE 11.3. Title Recognition Test—Primary (TRT-P). From McDowell, J. A., Schumm, J. S., & Vaughn, S. (1993). Assessing exposure to print: Development of a measure for primary children. In D. J. Leu & C. K. Kinzer (Eds.), *Examining Central Issues in Literacy Research, Theory, and Practice* (pp. 101–107). Chicago: National Reading Conference. Copyright 1993 by the National Reading Conference. Reprinted by permission.

RESEARCH BRIEF The Original Title Recognition Test

Cunningham and Stanovich (1991) developed the original TRT to estimate the free reading of students in intermediate grades. Titles that are typically popular with students in grades 4–6 were chosen for the measure, but books and stories that were part of the regular school curriculum were not. The goal was to construct a measure of out-of-school, independent reading. The measure has several advantages over other methods used to assess free reading, such as interviews and journals: It's easy to administer, it has a mechanism to detect guessing, and it does not pull for social desirability. The researchers found that performance on the measure is predictive of word recognition and spelling in particular, but also of vocabulary.

Elementary Reading Attitude Survey

The Elementary Reading Attitude Survey (ERAS; McKenna & Kear, 1990), also known as The Garfield Scale, is a measure of students' attitude toward reading (see Figure 11.4). Items fall into two categories: attitudes about reading at home, and attitudes about reading at school. The 20-item measure is a Likert-type scale, except that instead of using words to describe Likert categories, each item has 4 "Garfields" ranging from a very happy Garfield to a very grumpy Garfield. For primary children, you can read the items aloud and have them circle the items. Older children can typically complete the scale independently.

Reading Interest Inventory

Interest and background knowledge about a topic can provide the means for students to read material that would otherwise be considered too difficult or above their reading level. As support for this notion, Ganske and colleagues (2003) point out that interest fosters persistence and a desire to understand, while topic knowledge supports children's word identification and comprehension because they can draw on what they already know. When the text being read builds on students' interests and knowledge, the combination of knowing a lot about the topic and being able to talk with others about this knowledge supports literacy.

A systematic way of determining what topics or genres might capture a child's attention is a *reading interest inventory*. A reading interest inventory is an informal assessment device that may be administered individually or to a group. It is usually a series of open-ended questions teachers can use to glean specific information in order to help the children find reading materials that they will read and enjoy.

A reading interest inventory can also give insight into a child's reading habits. For example, it can reveal how much time the child spends reading, whether there are books available in the home, and whether the child has access to a public or school library. Furthermore, a reading interest inventory can identify activities that the child might select instead of reading. It can shed light on the type of television shows the child watches, along with the amount of time spent watching television or playing video games. The inventory can also identify extracurricular activities such as sports, hobbies, music, or art that the child is involved or interested in. Having this type of information about a student's interests and habits can help teachers guide students' selection of reading materials. As you might imagine, commercial informal reading inventories (IRIs) include interest inventories. Form 11.1 includes sample questions that can be used to construct a reading interest inventory.

ELEMENTARY READING ATTITUDE SURVEY

School__________ Grade___ Name______________________

1. How do you feel when you read a book on a rainy Saturday?

JIM DAVIS

2. How do you feel when you read a book in school during free time?

3. How do you feel about reading for fun at home?

4. How do you feel about getting a book for a present?

FIGURE 11.4. Elementary Reading Attitude Survey. Reprinted from Kear, Coffman, McKenna, and Ambrosio (2000). Garfield copyright by Paws, Inc. Reprinted by permission.

2

5. How do you feel about spending free time reading?

6. How do you feel about starting a new book?

7. How do you feel about reading during summer vacation?

8. How do you feel about reading instead of playing?

FIGURE 11.4. *(cont.)*

3

9. How do you feel about going to a bookstore?

10. How do you feel about reading different kinds of books?

11. How do you feel when the teacher asks you questions about what you read?

12. How do you feel about doing reading workbook pages and worksheets?

FIGURE 11.4. *(cont.)*

4

13. How do you feel about reading in school?

14. How do you feel about reading your school books?

15. How do you feel about learning from a book?

16. How do you feel when it's time for reading class?

FIGURE 11.4. *(cont.)*

5

17. How do you feel about the stories you read in reading class?

18. How do you feel when you read out loud in class?

19. How do you feel about using a dictionary?

20. How do you feel about taking a reading test?

FIGURE 11.4. *(cont.)*

Finding the Right Book

There are several techniques for finding and matching the right book to the child. The simplest method of assessment is "kid watching." Kid watching includes observing what books the child selects during library time, listening to the child when he or she is talking with friends, and engaging the child in conversations about hobbies or personal activities.

Once a topic or genre of interest to the child has been identified—either by kid watching, by chatting informally, or by administering a reading interest inventory—then the reading level of the book can be evaluated to determine if the book is at the child's independent reading level. Readability formulas can be used to estimate the level of a book. However, many word-processing programs now include readability estimates if you type in a 100-word sample from the book.

Another way to determine if a book is the right "fit" for a child is the five-finger method. In this simple strategy, the child is asked to select and read a page of text from the book. As the child reads the page, he or she holds up one finger each time an unknown word is located on that page. If there are more than five unknown words on a single page, the book may be too difficult for the child to read independently.

What Are Informal Assessments using Children's Literature?

Running Records

Marie Clay of New Zealand devised a way to use tradebooks as a vehicle for analyzing student oral reading (Clay, 1985). Keeping *running records* of student reading is the heart of Clay's Reading Recovery program for struggling readers in the early grades. However, running records can be adapted for use with older readers as well. One benefit of running records is that they tap students' understanding of genuine text and provide teachers with information about how students are processing authentic literature. Another benefit is that running records provide an excellent way to demonstrate reading performance to parents. Here are steps for conducting a running record:

1. Choose a passage approximately 100 words in length for primary children or struggling readers, or 200 words in length for intermediate children.
2. Use a Running Record Observation Form (Form 11.2) to record student responses (you can also use a photocopy of the passage and record responses in a manner similar to an IRI).
3. As the student reads, mark a check for each word read correctly. Make verbatim notes of substitutions, insertions, omissions, reversals, and self-corrections. Remember to be sensitive to the student's dialect, and do not count dialect differences as substitutions (i.e., mispronunciations). (See sample in Figure 11.5.)
4. Record a total number of miscues (do not count self-corrections).
5. Calculate the percentage of words accurate by dividing total words correct by total words in the passage.
6. Determine student reading level based on the following: 95–100% accuracy = independent level; 90–94% accuracy = instructional level; below 90% = frustration level.
7. Make note of any miscues that alter the meaning of the text.
8. Record observations that provide insights about both the student's processing of text and indicators of frustration.
9. Determine an action plan for appropriate instruction based on student performance.

Running Record Observation Form

Name Rick Date 4/24

Text The Tale of Peter Rabbit

Readability level of text ________ Number of words in text 100

Check one: ____ New text X Familiar text

Page	Running record	S	I	O	R	SC	T
6	✓ ✓ ✓ ✓ ✓ ✓ ✓ ✓						6
	✓ ✓ ✓ ✓ ✓ ✓ ✓ ✓ ✓ ✓						
	✓ ✓ ✓ ✓ ✓ ✓ ✓ sandbank	1					
	sandbox						
8	✓ ✓ ✓ ✓ ✓ very ✓ ✓ ✓			1			
	✓ ✓ ✓ ✓ ✓ ✓ ✓ ✓ into ✓		1				
	lane ✓ ✓ ✓ ✓ ✓ ✓ ✓	1					
	line						
	✓ ✓ ✓ ✓ accident ✓ ✓ ✓ ✓	1					
	accent						
	✓ ✓ ✓ ✓ ✓ ✓						
9	✓ ✓ ✓ ✓ ✓ ✓ ✓ mischief	1					
	mistake						
	✓ ✓ ✓ ✓						
10	✓ ✓ ✓ ✓ ✓ ✓ ✓ ✓ ✓						
	umbrella ✓ ✓					1	
	umbrella						

Code: S (substitutions), I (insertions), O (omissions), R (reversals), SC (self-corrections), T (total miscues).

Total words in passage 100

Total miscues 6

Total correct 94

Percent accuracy 94 (Total correct/Total words)

Level (check one):

Independent ______ 95%–100% accuracy

Instructional 94 90%–94% accuracy

Frustration ______ Below 90%

(cont.)

FIGURE 11.5. Running Record Observation Form (filled-in example).

Miscues affecting meaning:

sandbank	lane	accident	mischief
sandbox	line	accent	mistake

Observations:

Rick read with some hesitation. He struggled with multisyllable words. Used picture clues to self-correct "umbrella."

FIGURE 11.5. *(cont.)*

Because running records are conducted on a one-to-one basis, even though individual sessions are short, administration of running records can be time-consuming when you consider class sizes of 25 students and up. Reading Recovery lessons include daily administration of running records. Obviously this is possible in a resource setting, but it is impractical in general education settings unless a coteacher is involved. Some students need closer monitoring of their reading than others. Based on an initial running record and other measures of reading performance, develop a running record calendar. Determine which students you need to monitor by semester, monthly, weekly, and (with resources) daily.

Benchmark Books

Another way to assess student progress is through the use of *benchmark books*. Benchmark books are leveled trade books, both narrative and expository text. Periodically during the year (every grading period), you can assess if students have met a certain *benchmark*—in other words, if students can read a targeted book level at 95% word recognition accuracy and with satisfactory retelling or answering of text-based questions. Commercial sets of benchmark books are available, along with corresponding assessments including online assessments.

Retellings

You can follow up a running record session by having the student do a retelling to assess comprehension. Chapters 8 (narrative text comprehension) and 9 (expository text comprehension) describe procedures for children's retellings. These can be used for reading of material from basal readers and trade books as well.

How Do You Provide Differentiated Instruction in Children's Literature?

Level 1: High-Quality Core Instruction

In elementary classrooms, children's literature is not typically taught as a separate subject, but rather is integrated throughout the curriculum. References to the incorporation of children's literature in assessment and instruction are sprinkled throughout this book. Providing instruction in genres, developing affective responses to literature, and motivating students to develop a lifelong reading habit should be regular parts of basal reader and supplemental reading programs. In Chapter 14, you'll read about creating a print-rich environment in your classroom and about planning and organizing schoolwide reading programs. Here are some activities that can highlight children's literature in your classroom.

SUSTAINED SILENT READING

For the past 30 years, students have been participating in the learning activity of *sustained silent reading* (SSR) or *drop everything and read* (DEAR). SSR or DEAR is a period in the school day when everyone in the classroom, including the teacher, reads without interruption (McCracken & McCracken, 1977). The theoretical framework for this activity contains three components: (1) self-selection of the reading material, either for pleasure or for information; (2) teacher modeling of the reading behavior; and (3) nonaccountability—that is, the reading is not graded or logged (Yoon, 2002). The time spent on SSR varies from grade level to grade level; it is shorter for younger students and longer for older students. At the beginning of the year, it is advisable to start with short periods of reading and gradually move to longer periods of time—as much as 20 minutes for older students.

The purpose of SSR or DEAR is to help students develop a love of reading by providing them with opportunities to read books. Morrow, O'Connor, and Smith (1990) found that children's attitudes toward reading were improved by reading children's literature. What better place to practice reading high-quality children's books than the classroom?

While the National Reading Panel did not find experimental research supporting SSR and DEAR, this does not mean that it doesn't have a place in the reading curriculum. Allington (2002, p. 229) responded to the Panel's report by saying,

> It can't be that science proves that Sustained Silent Reading isn't reading instruction, because in 1985 the National Academy of Science's *Becoming A Nation of Readers* recommended the practice enthusiastically. Research suggests that the amount of independent, silent reading children do in school is significantly related to gains in reading achievement.

Recently, Yoon (2002) conducted a meta-analysis of three decades of research on the effects of SSR on attitudes toward reading, and found that providing a fixed time for children to read self-selected books helped their attitude toward reading. Accordingly, Yoon recommended SSR as a classroom practice. If the ultimate goal of reading instruction is to produce not only readers, but effective readers who receive personal rewards from the reading process, then we need to provide independent practice with a variety of high-quality children's books. Without SSR as part of the daily routine, some children will not have an opportunity to interact with children's literature.

In the spirit of "balanced" literacy, throwing out SSR may be throwing out the baby with the bath water. Structured reading activities are important, but student-centered activities such as SSR are equally important. Key to the success of SSR is helping students select the right books. Yes, self-selection is important, but some students have a tough time with book selection (just watch your reluctant readers during library time). If you can assist students with finding engaging books, and if you model reading yourself (rather than grading papers during SSR), SSR can be a rich and rewarding experience for you and your students.

READING ALOUD TO STUDENTS

Reading aloud to students is a vital part of the reading curriculum. The work of Jim Trelease (2001) has triggered enthusiasm for reading aloud among parents, grandparents, and teachers. Regularly scheduled read-alouds in the classroom can provide you with opportunities to motivate students to read and to expose students to children's literature. The benefits of reading aloud include the following:

- Exposing students to a wide range of authors, titles, and genres.
- Introducing new concepts and vocabulary.
- Modeling fluent reading.
- Introducing reading comprehension strategies through listening comprehension.
- Getting students excited about reading.

Cooper (2006) identifies two kinds of read-alouds: *general read-alouds* and *instructional read-alouds*. General read-alouds are intended to provide motivation to read and model fluent reading. Teachers can conduct read-alouds, but paraprofessionals, administrators, parents, and members of the community can also get involved in classroom read-alouds (see Chapter 14).

Instructional read-alouds are similar to guided reading lessons (see Chapter 8), with an emphasis on development of listening comprehension strategies. Instructional read-alouds can be used to teach a specific comprehension strategy or to model the implementation of multiple strategies. Tiffany Reed, a fourth-grade teacher, uses read-alouds to introduce reading comprehension strategies. Tiffany says, "Learning a reading comprehension strategy and focusing on decoding can be tough for some of my students. I use listening comprehension to introduce and model a strategy, and then have students apply the strategy in their own reading."

While classroom read-alouds are important, it is also important to provide strategies and suggestions for parents to read aloud in the home. At parent gatherings or through class newsletters, you can provide parents with pointers for effective read-aloud sessions and suggest books that are appropriate for their children. Parents who are more comfortable in a language other than English should be encouraged to read aloud to their children in books written in their native tongue. Whether the language of the book is English or otherwise, the benefits of modeling fluent reading, generating motivation to read, and concept learning still occur.

RESPONSE TO BOOKS

Louise Rosenblatt's (1938, 1978) *reader response theory* highlights the importance of personal interpretation of literature. Reader response theory describes reading as a transaction between the reader and author. How the reader interprets and responds to text is largely dependent on prior experience and knowledge. Two readers will not necessarily interpret a text in the same way. Students need opportunities to share their responses to text—both intellectual and affective—and to engage in conversation with others to learn about different points of view.

Oprah Winfrey tapped a nerve with the public when she began her Oprah's Book Club. Apparently many members of the American public were "hungry" to share their intellectual and affective responses to literature. Sharing books is one of the most exciting opportunities in the life of elementary classrooms. Monthly book reports may have their place. Similarly, using programs such as Accelerated Reader to assess student comprehension of trade books may also have a place in the curriculum. However, children need opportunities for the joy of reading. Chapter 8 has provided suggestions for literature circles. Literature circles can be equally effective with fiction and nonfiction trade books. Beyond literature circles, the options for book sharing are limitless (see Figure 11.6)—so here's your opportunity as a teacher to be creative!

TECH TIP Sharing Reflections about Books via Email

Email provides opportunities for students to share their reflections about books with fellow students around the country and world. Instead of pen pals, students become *keypals*. For example, one school in Miami with a large Bahamian American student population partnered with a school in the Bahamas to provide email exchanges. Another example is that a university professor of a children's literature course partnered each of her college students with a keypal at a local elementary school.

An alternative is to work through a keypals service such as Mighty Media Keypals Club (*www.mightymedia.com/keypals*) or Intercultural E-mail Classroom Connections (*www.iecc.org*).

BOOK LOGS

Students enjoy keeping a record of books they have read throughout the year in school and out. The Book Log (Form 11.3) can be used to keep a record of books read, as well as an informal assessment of whether or not the student would recommend each book to a friend.

Level 2: Supplemental Instruction

DIALOGUE JOURNALS

Students who have difficulty in responding to text may need additional modeling to get them started. One way to provide such modeling is with *dialogue journals*. A dialogue journal is a journal shared by a child with an adult or older child (Gambrell, 1985; Schumm, Leavell, Gordon, & Murfin, 1993). A student can be paired with a classroom teacher, a parent, a classroom volunteer, or an older child from another class.

When partners are assigned together, they get a bound notebook to share. The journal begins with the child writing an "all about me" letter to the partner. The partner writes back with an "all about me" response. After the entries are written, each person reads the other's entry.

At a second session, the pair works together to set "rules" for the journal. The child should be encouraged to develop the rules. There can be rules like "We write in ink, not pencil," or "Spelling doesn't count," or "Write neatly so my partner can read what I wrote."

Subsequent sessions are structured in a regular routine. An individual dialogue journal event begins with a shared reading of a book, short story, newspaper article, or magazine article. After reading, the child writes a letter to the partner describing reactions to the passage. The partner's dialogue response consists of two parts—encouraging feedback about the child's response, and a personal reaction to the reading. Then partners take turns reading their responses aloud.

1. List ten characters in the book.
2. List five characters and next to each name, write the character's occupation.
3. How old do you think the main character is? Why? Name three things the character does that match that age.
4. If you could meet one of the characters, who would it be? List five questions you'd like to ask him or her. What answers do you think you'd receive?
5. Choose a character who made an important decision. Describe the incident.
6. Describe the foods and drinks that one character might have for lunch.
7. List five characters from the book. Give each a nickname and tell why you chose it.
8. Find an example of stress or frustration. Tell about it. How did the character resolve it?
9. Do you think the main character would like a job at a local fast food restaurant? Why or why not?
10. Would you choose the main character as your best friend? Why or why not?
11. Pick your favorite character. Give at least three reasons for your choice.
12. Pick your favorite and least favorite characters in the book. Give reasons why these characters could or could not be your friends.
13. Write a letter of advice to one of the characters.
14. Dress up as one of the characters or make a mask of the character.
15. Bring in props mentioned in the book and out on a play.
16. Your favorite character has just been granted three wishes. (None of the wishes may be for more wishes.) Tell what those wishes would be.
17. It's your favorite character's birthday. What gifts would you bring to the party?
18. Your favorite character just bought a T-shirt. Draw a picture of the T-shirt. Explain the picture.
19. One of the characters has a problem. Describe it and tell how it was solved.
20. Make a diary entry that your favorite character might write.
21. Act out various scenes in the book.
22. Make a video about one of the scenes in the book. You may have friends and family help with this assignment.
23. Pick seven events that happen in the book and write them on a time line or draw them in a cartoon strip.
24. List five events that happen in the book in chronological order.
25. Write a follow-up chapter for the book.
26. In what season does the book take place? Give supporting statements.
27. Would you like to live in the setting (time and place) of this book? Why or why not?
28. List different kinds of transportation mentioned in the book.
29. Use a blank world or U.S. map to locate settings in the book.
30. Compare or contrast objects found in the book to what we have today.
31. Find examples of feelings in the book–love, guilt, honesty, trust, loneliness.
32. Find an example of humor in the book.
33. Survey ten students from your class. Ask them two opinion questions about the book. Record your results.
34. Write a poem about the book.
35. Write a rap about the book.
36. Write a song about the book.

(cont.)

FIGURE 11.6. Fifty fantastic ideas for book sharing. From Schumm, Jeanne Shay, and Schumm, Gerald E., Jr. (1999). *The Reading Tutor's Handbook: A Commonsense Guide to Helping Students Read and Write*. Minneapolis, MN: Free Spirit. Copyright 1999 by Jeanne Shay Schumm. Reprinted by permission.

37. Read your favorite part as if you were a radio announcer. Tape-record your reading.
38. If your book were made into a movie, who would you choose to play various roles? You may pick friends or famous people.
39. Read a selection from the book to two friends and one family member. Write about their reactions.
40. Make up a dozen questions and answers about the book. Make a board game using the questions.
41. Make up three essay questions that would be good for the end of the book test.
42. Tell the book's publisher or author what you think about the book.
43. Make up ten interview questions you'd like to ask the author.
44. Make up a new title for the book. Why did you choose it?
45. Make up a title for each chapter.
46. Look up the author in a reference book. Tell five things you learned about this person.
47. Keep a Wonderful Word List. When you come to a new word or a nifty saying or phrase, write it down.
48. Find three examples of onomatopoeia (words that resemble sound, like *moo, hiss, cluck, slam*).
49. Draw a picture of the house (or other dwelling) where the main character lives.
50. Come up with your own activity.

FIGURE 11.6. *(cont.)*

Dialogue journals give struggling readers the opportunity to see fluent models of reading and writing. The spelling of the child should not be corrected, but the partner can model correct spelling of the same word in the response. More importantly, the dialogue journal format provides students with a intimate way to learn how to express responses to a variety of genres.

INCREASING ACCESS TO PRINT

Some children may have limited access to books in their homes. To respond to this need, many schools have tried to extend school library hours so that students will have access not only to books, but also to computers. Blum (1995) and colleagues developed a book bag program to give students more opportunities to read at home. Teachers created book bags, each one containing a read-aloud book, a recording of the book on tape, and a parent letter with directions in English and Spanish. The letter outlined three activities that the parent and student could complete with each other. A 19-week study resulted in high levels of satisfaction for both parents and students.

Level 3: Intensive Support

As you get to know your students, you'll learn that some need more support than others in becoming engaged in children's literature. This will be true not only for struggling readers, but for proficient readers as well. You need to be prepared for individual differences in attitudes about reading and the motivation to read, and to think creatively about providing the support students need. The following four categories and student profiles can prompt your thinking about how to respond to individual differences. The student profiles and teacher responses are meant to be exemplary, not exhaustive—be prepared for variations in your own classroom.

CHILDREN WHO CAN READ AND WILL

At first glance, having students who can read and will seems like no problem at all; however, it can be. Think about Ricardo. Ricardo would read anything—as long as it was science fiction. He kept a book with him at all times, including when he goes to the lunchroom. The problem was twofold. First, his teacher, Mary Yoder, couldn't get him to stop reading long enough to finish his assignments in any subject area. Second, she couldn't get him interested in even trying any other genres. He was stuck, and his grades were suffering.

Mary held a conference with Ricardo and his parents. They worked out a plan and made a contract. Ricardo would keep his current sci-fi book in his desk. When assignments were completed—including assignments that related to other forms of literature—he could take his book out. If he stuck to the plan, he was rewarded with an hour of uninterrupted reading time in the library each week. Mary also highlighted Ricardo as the classroom sci-fi expert and provided opportunities for him to share his expertise with other students in the class.

CHILDREN WHO CAN READ AND WON'T

Students who are fluent readers and refuse to read are sometimes called *aliterate*. In such cases an old adage applies: "You can lead a horse to water, but you can't make him drink—unless you have some salt. Greg needed some salt." Greg learned to read sort of naturally. When asked how he learned to read, he said that he learned by watching *Sesame Street* and programs from football games. He'd look at the pictures of players (he knew their faces from TV) and then learned how to decode their names. Greg performed well on standardized tests, but would do anything to get out of a reading assignment. Greg's fifth-grade teacher, Martina Gates, got out the salt shaker. First, she administered the class a reading interest inventory. She found that sports were Greg's thing. Next, a university student volunteer who was also a student-athlete (Mark Taber) was assigned as a partner with Greg. Together they started a dialogue journal and got engaged in active written and oral discussions about sports magazine articles and books. Meeting with a university student was a booster for Greg, because Mark was able to convince him that as a student, "sometimes you read what you want, and sometimes you read what you are assigned. It's part of life in school."

CHILDREN WHO CAN'T READ AND WILL

Some struggling readers want to read, but just don't know how. Patrice was a fourth grader who was reading at a preprimer level. She qualified for exceptional student education services because of a diagnosed learning disability. Patrice was placed in a fourth-grade inclusion classroom and received services from a special educator (Diane Burke) during the reading and language arts block. Sometimes Patrice sat in the reading corner and flipped through books—longing to read, but unable to do so.

Diane wanted to encourage Patrice to maintain her desire to read, even though the process was grueling for her. Diane put together a three-pronged plan to make this happen. First, Diane found that Patrice loved listening to and telling stories. She encouraged any opportunity for Patrice to share her love of stories through the oral mode. Second, Diane set up a listening center in the general education classroom for Patrice to listen and read along to taped books. Third, Diane sent home book bags to encourage listening and responding to books as a home learning activity.

CHILDREN WHO CAN'T READ AND WON'T

Children who can't read and won't are the toughest. They are children who are victims of the *Matthew effect*: They've tried, failed, and given up. Tomas was a fifth grader who had lived in the United States for two years. He did not have the opportunity to attend school regularly in his home country, so he did not have the benefit of reading and writing instruction in his first language, Spanish. The challenges of learning a new language and learning to read and write were daunting for Tomas. It seemed that everyone around him was doing so well, and he was still assigned "baby books."

Tomas might have given up, but his teacher, Megan Richards, did not. Because Tomas had a great sense of humor, Megan got him hooked on reading books of jokes and riddles. The jokes and riddles were filled with figurative language that was new and interesting to him. Although Tomas was still working with his spoken English, he wasn't shy. Megan decided to involve Tomas in the reading of short plays. She taped the dialogue for Tomas and then provided him with opportunities to do readings and rereadings of the plays. Bit by bit, Megan worked on Tomas's self-confidence and got him over the day-to-day hurdles of learning to read in English. In addition, Megan encouraged Tomas's parents to read to him at home in Spanish. When parents read to children in their first language, it helps them learn about many aspects of reading comprehension, genres, and response to literature.

PARENT POINTER ☞ Reading Aloud: Suggestions for Parents

Anderson (2002) provides the following read-aloud suggestions for parents:

1. Read to and with your child every day! Reading together builds a special bond with your child.
2. Select books appropriate for the child's developmental age.
3. Seat the child close to you, and hold the book so that the child can easily see the pictures.
4. Help your child link the story to his or her own experience through discussion after reading.
5. Encourage your child to act out the story. Drama will increase the child's understanding of the story and increase interest.
6. Read in a lively, storytelling manner.
7. Children are never too young to be read to. Children are never too old to be read to.
8. Take your child to the library, and let him or her select books for reading aloud.
9. When reading poetry, read a bit slower than with prose. Use your natural voice, but with a tone that suits the poem.
10. Remember to be enthusiastic and have fun while sharing books with your child.

SNAPSHOT

The International Reading Association's (2003) *Standards for Reading Professionals* document emphasizes the importance of creating a literate environment. One of the best ways teachers can achieve this goal is by having a variety of high-quality books available for students. These books need to be accessible, on shelves or in baskets, and teachers need to let students know that they value and enjoy sharing them. This message can be modeled by incorporating the books from classroom collections into every aspect of the curriculum, not just during language arts. As teachers build their classroom libraries, they need to consider their students' interests and preferences in children's literature.

Over the past 30 years, quilts have made their way into numerous classrooms in the form of "class quilts." In the classroom, quilting and all it entails can be used to extend literature by giving the students a new medium with which to visually represent their understanding of concepts. A class quilt can be the centerpiece of a thematic unit, and at the same time can be a vehicle to develop new skills, enhance self-confidence, and integrate learning across the curriculum.

In the Children's Literature classes at the University of Miami, preservice teachers create individual quilts that visually represent high-quality children's books. Then each teacher combines the activity with service learning by donating their quilt and its companion book to a needy child. This assignment introduces future teachers to a time-honored craft that lends itself to a unique method of extending children's literature in their classrooms.

Jen Gerber participated in the quilt-making process while enrolled in Children's Literature at the University of Miami. Here, she shares a classroom story about the magic of children's literature.

"For many of us, there are certain landmarks that bring to mind images of specific cities. One can hardly think of the Eiffel Tower without thinking of Paris, and although they no longer stand, the Twin Towers will forever be a symbol of New York. These landmarks, like the cities they represent, have a rich and colorful history. In *The Man Who Walked between the Towers*, Mordicai Gerstein (2003) chronicles the story of Philippe Petit, a young Frenchman who walked on a tightrope between the Twin Towers in 1974. This beautifully written book had a profound impact on one of the struggling readers I had the pleasure of teaching during my student teaching experience.

"I was making a class quilt with my students as a culminating activity to a science unit on butterflies. I invited one of my university professors to my class to talk about quilts and quilt making. Dr. Bergeron had taught us how to expand children's literature by making quilts based on children's books. When Dr. Bergeron arrived at my class, she read *The Man Who Walked between the Towers* to my students, and showed them the quilt she had made to accompany the book. The students were all amazed by the quilt, and were surprised to learn that a quilt could be made based on a book. The students colored in their own quilt squares as Dr. Bergeron read. After her initial reading came requests for her to read the story again. One of the students making the request was José. I must admit that I was pleasantly surprised, as José did not have a history of engaging in reading activities, and was reading below grade level. The students were as captivated with the second reading as they had been with the first. Dr. Bergeron encouraged the students to go home and look for information on Philippe Petit on the Internet. José was the only student in the class who brought me information the next day. Something in that book had definitely touched José, and made a student who was not well known for doing his homework do some extra work.

"When our class quilt was placed in a show at a local museum of art, the students in our class took a field trip to see their quilt and the other quilts. José went straight over to Dr. Bergeron and asked where the Philippe Petit quilt was. He stood and stared at it, and then told Dr. Bergeron that it was his favorite quilt in the show. When Dr. Bergeron realized how much José had been affected by the story of Philippe Petit, she decided that she would give the quilt and the book to him. She and I went to José's parents' Cuban restaurant to present the book to him. José was shocked to receive the quilt, but the most shocking part of the evening was when José opened the book and started reading it out loud. In the classroom, José only read when instructed to do so, and never took the initiative to read on his own. As José read, his mother watched him and spoke about how much he liked the story. José's mother does not speak English, and was unable to understand what her son was reading; still, his expressions and actions told her that he was reading a book that he truly enjoyed.

"José spoke about Philippe Petit and how brave he had been to walk between the towers. Dr. Bergeron used José's admiration of Philippe Petit to link the story to his own life. She told José that she thought that, just like Philippe Petit, he too was brave. She talked about his bravery when he came to the United States from Cuba in a small boat, where the passengers could feel the sharks bumping against the bottom. José had never considered himself brave, yet hearing someone else tell him that he was like his newfound hero, he began to believe it.

"*The Man Who Walked between the Towers* touched José, a struggling reader, in so many ways. Yet the most important thing it did for him is give him the desire to pick up a book without pressure from an adult, and read, simply for the sake of the story."

CONTINUING TO DEVELOP STUDENT READING AND WRITING PROFILES

Use Part XI of the Student Reading and Writing Profile (Form 11.4) to record data about students' knowledge of literature and motivation to read. After conducting an initial running record, make a plan for how frequently you need to monitor each student's reading using running records.

CHAPTER SUMMARY

As Jen Gerber's experience illustrates, children's literature can elicit strong personal responses—even among young children or struggling readers. Keeping the "magic of literature" alive is particularly important when an emphasis on accountability and assessment seems to overshadow instruction. Fortunately, with some creativity, teachers can spark students' imaginations by using a variety of literary genres and formats for responding to literature. Literature can also be used as a vehicle for authentic assessment in the classroom. The best way for you to help your children become familiar with and enjoy children's literature is to do so yourself. You'll find it is easy to get hooked on children's books.

KEY TERMS AND CONCEPTS

American Library Association (ALA)
Benchmark books
Biographies
Caldecott Medal
Contemporary realistic fiction
Coretta Scott King Award
Dialogue journals
General read-alouds
Genres
Historical fiction
Instructional read-alouds
Modern fantasy
Multicultural literature
Newbery Medal
Nonfiction
Orbis Pictus Award
Picture books
Poetry
Reader response theory
Reading interest inventory
Running records
Sustained silent reading
Title recognition tests
Traditional literature
Visual literacy

REFLECTION AND ACTION

1. Reflect about your own journey as a reader. What children's books had the most impact on you and why? What classroom-based and out-of-classroom experiences had an impact on your concept of children's literature?
2. If you are teaching or student-teaching, make a list of the stories you read in class during the school year. Do a content analysis of the books you have read. Are you emphasizing one genre over another? Are you including multicultural literature? Have you sought out new books to include? Make notes about how you might make changes in your book reading the following year.

READ ON!

Forgan, J. W., & Gonzalez-DeHass, A. (2004). How to infuse social skills training into literacy instruction. *Teaching Exceptional Children*, *36*, 24–30.

This article describes three ways to merge social skills training with children's literature: bibliotherapy (using books for models of problem solving), folk literature, and experiential learning. While targeted for students with mild disabilities, this article has implications for all elementary students.

Meir, T. (2003). "Why can't she remember that?": The importance of storybook reading in multilingual, multicultural classrooms. *The Reading Teacher*, *57*(3), 242–252.

Meir clearly explains possible cultural influences on reading comprehension and makes a strong case for understanding students' backgrounds.

Rosenblatt, L. M. (1978). *The reader, the text, the poem: The transactional theory of the literary work.* Carbondale: Southern Illinois University Press.

This classic book has shaped the thinking of many in the language arts community. The book provides the rationale for reader response theory.

Vasquez, V., Muise, M. R., Adamson, S. C., Heffernan, L., Chiola-Nakai, D., & Shear, J. (2003). *Setting the context: A critical take on using books in the classroom.* Newark, DE: International Reading Association.

This book poses important questions about using children's books to address issues of critical literacy and social justice. The book includes classroom examples of how to initiate powerful discussions and responses to children's literature among elementary-grade children.

SHARPENING YOUR SKILLS: SUGGESTIONS FOR PROFESSIONAL DEVELOPMENT

1. Taking running records is a bit intimidating at first, but with practice it can be an efficient way to conduct ongoing informal assessment. Practice administration of running records to students who are both fluent readers and struggling readers. Try practicing with familiar and unfamiliar passages for each student to detect any differences.
2. Keeping up with the mass of new children's books published each year can be a full-time job. To assist teachers, *The Reading Teacher* publishes two book lists annually that can help keep you up to date. The Children's Choices book list is published in the October issue of this journal. More than 2,000 participate in this selection process, which is cosponsored by the International Reading Association and the Children's Book Council. In November, a second list, Teachers' Choices, is published in *The Reading Teacher.* A panel of teachers selects book that they have

found to be most helpful in planning curriculum. Both sets can be used to help you recommend books to parents, grandparents, and other caregivers.

3. Examine your classroom library to make certain that you have books reflecting the cultures of all students in your classroom. You might also want to develop a network of guest speakers from your community who are of the same backgrounds as students in your class. Ask the speakers to select from a few books that you have preselected to read. Having guest speakers will help students develop a sense of belonging in the classroom and will give you an opportunity to learn more about your students' backgrounds.

RESOURCES FOR ASSESSMENT AND INSTRUCTION

Deem, D., Feely, L., Fullmer, C., Lienemann, D., & Moore, K. (2002). *Ready-to-go management kit for teaching genre: Dozens of engaging response activities to use with any book that help kids explore 10 genres independently.* New York: Scholastic.

This book provides activities, reproducibles, and resources to help students learn about literary genres. It includes a list of related books that represents different student interests and reading levels.

Gambrell, L. B., Palmer, B. M., & Mazzoni, S. A. (1996). Assessing motivation to read. *The Reading Teacher, 49,* 518–533.

This article describes a measure entitled the Motivation to Read Profile. The profile includes 20 multiple-choice items about perceptions of reading and of oneself as a reader. It is followed with more open-ended questions about perceptions of narrative and expository text.

Gerke, P. (1996). *Multicultural plays for children: Vol. 1 (grades 1–3) and Vol. 2 (grades 4–6).* Lyme, NH: Smith & Kraus.

Students look forward to the one or two plays that are included in their basal readers. Plays are fun and provide students with opportunities to participate through drama. This collection of plays is focused on folk tales from around the world.

Kletzien, S. B., & Dreher, M. J. (2004). *Informational text in K–3 classrooms: Helping children read and write.* Newark, DE: International Reading Association.

This valuable resource provides ways to use informational text in teaching all aspects of reading and language arts. Of particular interest are suggestions for teaching in general education classrooms, inclusion classrooms, and resource settings.

McElveen, S. A., & Dierking, C. C. (2001). Children's books as models to teach writing skills. *The Reading Teacher, 54,* 362–364.

Reading–writing connections are a powerful way to promote literacy. Sometimes children do not always see those connections. This article provides a list of children's books that can be used to model different writing styles and techniques (e.g., vivid verbs, questions as leads, similes).

Moss, B. (2003). *Exploring the literature of fact: Children's nonfiction trade books in the elementary classroom.* New York: Guilford Press.

This book provides practical suggestions for linking nonfiction trade books with regular classroom instruction. Specific suggestions for teaching content area material, developing research skills, and making writing connections are provided.

Reutzel, D. R., & Fawson, P. C. (2002). *Your classroom library: New ways to give it more teaching power: Great teacher-tested and research-based strategies for organizing and using your library.* New York: Scholastic.

Your classroom library is an important way to say to your students that reading is important. This book not only presents ideas for selecting and displaying books; it also provides suggestions for making the classroom library a focal point for reading lesions.

Rothlein, L., & Meinbach, A. M. (1996). *Legacies: Using children's literature in the classroom.* New York: HarperCollins.

Liz Rothlein and colleagues have created a series of books that bring children's books alive with lots of practical applications. This book with Anita Meinbach provides a great overview of children's literature instruction. This team, along with Anthony Fredericks, has also written books on thematic units in the classroom. Rothlein's *Read It Again* series targets more specific areas, such as multicultural books, Native American books, and books that can be used to prepare students for inclusion classrooms.

Trelease, J. (2001). *The read-aloud handbook* (5th ed.). New York: Penguin.

This is a popular how-to book for teachers and parents. The book provides a rationale for read-alouds, strategies for implementation, and suggestions for age-appropriate books for read-aloud sessions.

Young, T. A. (Ed.). (2004). *Happily ever after: Sharing folk literature with elementary and middle school students.* Newark, DE: International Reading Association.

This edited book provides rich information about the genre of folk tales. The book includes general background information, makes multicultural connections, and provides instructional suggestions to implement folk tales in the classroom.

RECOMMENDED WEBSITES

American Library Association (ALA)
www.ala.org/alsc

The ALA link for children's literature and more. The official site for the Newbery and Caldecott Medals. Has activities related to children and books. Although the site can be difficult to navigate, it has a lot of information to offer.

BookMuse
www.bookmuse.com

BookMuse offers in-depth Muse Notes for readers of all ages, including a special KidMuse section. Contains questions to spark discussion, thoughtful commentaries, author biographies, leader's tips, and suggestions for further reading. There is a $35/year membership fee.

Lexile Framework for Reading
www.lexile.com

This website provides detailed information about lexile scores, with a particularly helpful section on Frequently Asked Questions.

New York Times
www.nytimes.com/learning

Offers teachers, students, and parents a lot of resources. Includes daily lesson plans, lesson plan archives, education news, and suggestions on how to use the daily news in the classroom. Free registration required.

Northwest Regional Education Laboratory
www.nwrel.org/sky

This site is the Northwest Regional Education Laboratory's Library in the Sky. Appealing to teachers, who can find information through the search, or by department, or by materials. Offers resources in many subject areas for teachers, students, parents, and librarians. This site is well organized and easy to navigate.

Reading Is Fundamental
www.rif.org

This is the website for the Reading Is Fundamental nonprofit organization. The site includes excellent ideas for reading aloud to students that you can use in your classroom and share with parents.

Rosetta Project
www.childrensbooksonline.org/library.htm

The Rosetta Project's collection currently contains about 2,000 antique children's books published in the 19th and early 20th centuries. This site provides classic children's books online, complete with illustrations and in various languages.

University of Virginia
www.lib.virginia.edu/education

The education library of the University of Virginia contains search engines and databases.

University of Wisconsin/Madison
www.soemadison.wisc.edu/ccbc

This website contains book lists from the Children's Book Cooperative. Included is a list of multicultural literature entitled *Thirty Books That Every Child Should Know.*

FORM 11.1. Reading Interest Inventory

Reading Interest Inventory

Do you enjoy being read to?

What kinds of stories do you like to listen to?

Who reads aloud to you?

Do you like to read?

Where do you like to read?

What time of the day/night do you like to read?

What books have you read lately?

Who is your favorite author?

Who is your favorite illustrator?

What is your favorite book?

What book or books did you *not* enjoy? Why?

What does reading mean to you?

How often do you read?

Outside of school, how much time do you spend reading each day?

Do you read on weekends?

Do you like getting books as gifts?

Do you have a collection of books at home?

How many books do you think you own?

Do you have a library card?

How often do you go to the library?

Can you always find a book at the library that you want to check out?

Circle the topics that you like or might like to read about.

Adventure	Animals	Art/drawing	Biographies
Detective stories	Fantasies	Fairy tales	Folk tales
History	How-to-do-it books	Humor	Mysteries
Novels	Picture books	Plays	Poetry
Science fiction	Sports	Travel	War stories

(cont.)

FORM 11.1. *(page 2 of 2)*

Do you like to read the newspaper?

What section of the newspaper do you like to read first?

Do you like magazines?

What is your favorite magazine?

Which television shows do you like?

How many television shows do you watch every day?

Do you like to watch videos?

What is your favorite video?

Do you like to play video games?

How much time do you spend playing video games each day?

Do you use the Internet?

What is your favorite Internet site?

Do you have a hobby? What?

What is your favorite movie?

Do you read the book before or after the movie comes out?

Who is your favorite entertainer?

Say anything you would like about reading.

FORM 11.2. Running Record Observation Form

Running Record Observation Form

Name ______________________________ Date ____________

Text ______________________________

Readability level of text ____________ Number of words in text ____________

Check one: ____ New text ____ Familiar text

Page	Running record	S	I	O	R	SC	T

Code: S (substitutions), I (insertions), O (omissions), R (reversals), SC (self-corrections), T (total miscues).

Total words in passage ______

Total miscues ______

Total correct ______

Percent accuracy ______ (Total correct/Total words)

Level (check one):

Independent ______ 95%–100% accuracy

Instructional ______ 90%–94% accuracy

Frustration ______ Below 90%

(cont.)

FORM 11.2. *(page 2 of 2)*

Miscues affecting meaning:

Observations:

FORM 11.3. Book Log

Book Log

Student's name ______________________________ Grade ____________

Rating scale:

1 = I would recommend this book to anyone.
2 = Maybe I would recommend this book.
3 = I would not recommend this book to anyone.

Title of the book I read	Author of the book	Date finished	Rating	Comments about the book

FORM 11.4. Student Reading and Writing Profile (Part XI)

Student Reading and Writing Profile

Part XI: Children's Literature

Children's Literature

Name of test	Date	Score

Student primary interests in genres ______________________________

____

____

Student areas for improvement in interest and motivation to read trade books ____________

____

____

Instructional recommendations for interest and motivation in trade book reading __________

____

____

Instructional recommendations for genres in children's literature ____________________

____

____

TWELVE

The Parallel Bar

Writing Assessment and Instruction

ADRIANA L. MEDINA

VIGNETTE

In recent years, writing instruction has moved away from a product approach and toward a process approach. How the writing occurs is as important as what the final written product is. Teaching a process approach to writing may require a paradigm shift for some teachers, because it requires that teachers provide their students with time to write; give up some control over treasured assignments; give students control over their writing; and have faith in the writing process, in themselves, and in their students.

I am Adriana Medina, the author of this chapter. Like many other teachers, I was taught to write under a product approach to writing, and I began my teaching of writing that way too. However, when I went back to school, I first learned about the process approach to teaching writing. One class activity I was assigned was to do a self-reflection of my teaching of writing. As I thought of how I taught writing and of the writing my students produced, I realized I was dissatisfied with the written products I was getting from my students. However, I thought the problem was with them, not necessarily with *my* teaching of writing. I sat through the course and tried to keep an open mind, even though inside I often thought, "That's not gonna work with my students," "That doesn't go with my teaching style," and so forth.

Part of the coursework required that we work through the writing process to produce a final piece of writing. Interestingly enough, I realized that although I *thought* the process approach to writing did not "go" with my teaching style or was not going to work with my students, it did "work" with me as a writer. The process approach to writing was how I wrote. It then made perfect sense. At the end of that course, after I had been presented with a great deal of evidence and testimony, I decided that I would implement a process approach to writing in my class during the next school year. I used my summer vacation to prepare my lessons; I read additional books suggested in class on the topic; and I promised myself that I would give this process approach an honest try. I have not regretted it since. I have evidence of my own now that the process approach produces better writers and better-written products. I hope you're willing to keep an open mind and give the approaches described in this chapter a try too.

ANTICIPATION QUESTIONS

- How were you taught to write?
- How have you been taught to teach children to write?
- What are some of the challenges teachers face in teaching writing?
- What is a workshop approach to teaching writing?
- What is the teacher's role in assessing students' writing?

INTRODUCTION

One of the most exciting parts of elementary education is teaching students how to become writers. Helping students learn how to express their ideas through the written word is a lifelong skill that has both personal and professional implications. As computers become more prevalent, sharing thoughts and ideas via the written word is becoming more and more a part of our daily lives. Thus helping students learn that writing is a process and learn how to work through that process is one of the most valuable gifts educators can provide.

This chapter begins with a description of the process approach to writing instruction and a discussion of why some students have difficulty with learning to write. Then there is a section on how writing is assessed, with information on formal and informal writing assessments. The section on instruction includes suggestions for how to apply reading instruction to writing instruction, and how to make modifications for teaching writing to special populations. It also contains a detailed description of a Writers' Workshop as one way to put the process approach to teaching writing into practice. Included in this description are ways to get started implementing Writers' Workshop; answers to frequently asked questions about putting Writers' Workshop into practice; a day-by-day scripted overview lesson plan; and suggested mini-lessons, projects, and products for use during Writers' Workshop.

THE WRITING PROCESS

Farnan and Dahl (2003) describe the writing process as follows: "Writing is process, or rather set of mental processes writers use when they write. . . . We speculate that the term *process writing* was coined as a reaction to the days when writing instruction consisted of three components: assign, write, assess" (p. 995). The work of Janet Emig (1971) and Donald Graves (1978, 1983, 1994) has been largely responsible for the shift from product to process in writing instruction. The work of Graves and his colleagues emphasizes the development of writers from early, legitimate phases of writing (such as scribbling) to more mature writing of various types for different purposes—both personal and academic. Moreover, the writing of individual pieces is viewed as a series of interrelated stages that lead from the initial decision on a topic to planning of the topic development and format based on knowledge of an intended audience; drafting; revising and editing; and finally publication.

The stages of the writing process were drawn from observation and reflection about what writers actually do when developing a written piece (Dyson & Freedman, 1991). While different authors may offer variations in the terminology used to describe stages of the writing process, most agree that the process is more than composition. In this chapter I use the following terms to refer to the stages of the writing process:

- *Prewriting*—determining genre, topic, audience, and format.
- *Drafting*—writing an initial draft.
- *Rewriting*—editing, including revising (attention to meaning and how the message is communicated) and proofreading (attention to spelling and mechanics).
- *Postwriting*—sharing the final written piece with the intended audience.

The stages of the writing process should not be thought of as lockstep and linear; rather, the stages are fluid and recursive (Emig, 1971; Flower & Hayes, 1980, 1981). In other words, during any stage of the writing process, students may engage mental processes in a previous or successive stage. For example, when rewriting, a student may find it necessary to rethink audience or format. In addition, different stages of the writing process may take more or less time due to students' level of familiarity with the genre, topic, audience, and format, as well as students' general fluency in writing

A writing process view of writing instruction creates very different roles and responsibilities for students and teachers (Calkins, 1991). Students are viewed as "authors" in the writing process—authors who have ideas and language that are worthy of expression. Teachers are viewed as "mentors" who nurture authors through the various stages of their own writing development and in the stages of writing an individual piece. Rather than waiting for a final draft to get feedback, students receive feedback from teachers and their peers during all stages of the writing process. In addition, teachers are responsible for developing a community of authors within the classroom and beyond—through the development of a writing-rich environment; through helping students learn how to support each other while writing; and through the identification of audiences for student writing in the school, home, and community.

In a synthesis of research on teaching composition, Cotton (2001) concluded that process writing instruction does lead to positive academic outcomes. "Recognizing that writing is a complex, recursive, dynamic nonlinear process, experts in the field of composition have developed and tested instructional methods more in keeping with the true nature of writing" (p. 4). More recently, Unger and Fleischman (2004) observed that while many small-scale studies (including case studies) have been conducted to determine the effectiveness of writing process, few large-scale studies exist. Evidence from the 1992 and 1998 administrations of the writing subtest of the National Assessment of Educational Progress (NAEP) do shed some light on the promise of writing process (National Center for Education Statistics, 1998). Students who participated in NAEP also completed surveys about the nature of writing instruction in their schools. In both cases, there was a clear association between higher scores on the writing subtest and engagement in writing process as part of the regular curriculum. While Unger and Fleischman (2004) presented their observations with caveats, they did say that current research offers "cautious support for process writing instruction" (p. 2).

Similarly, in a meta-analysis of 11 studies of the teaching of writing to students with learning disabilities, Gersten and Baker (1999) found that the explicit teaching of various stages of the writing process resulted in positive outcomes in the writing of these students. In addition to explicit teaching, Gersten and Baker also emphasized the importance of teacher demonstration, providing examples, and giving specific, regular feedback.

Teaching the writing process is also recommended for students who are English-language learners (ELLs) (Kroll, 1990; Myles, 2002; Peregoy & Boyle, 2001) even though lack of fluency in a second language can pose challenges. Writing is a form of expressive language. Many ELL students have higher competency in receptive language (i.e., listening and reading) than in expressive language (i.e., speaking and writing). In a review of research on the writing process and ELL students, Myles (2002) concluded that teachers need to continue to motivate students to take risks with their writing; provide frequent feedback, so that errors in use of English language do not get "fossilized"; and provide clear models of written products, as well as teacher think-alouds to demonstrate the thinking that is associated with composition. It is also important to remember that while engaged in the writing process, students are engaged in learning strategy and expressing their ideas in writing at the same time. Therefore, ELL students may need a great deal of modeling and support from teachers and their peers.

Why Do Some Students Have Trouble with the Writing Process?

Because producing a written product is complex, there are multiple reasons why students may experience difficulty. Think about what it requires to write a business letter, research paper, grocery list, or invitation to a New Year's Eve party. It's important for teachers to sort out whether any troubles students may experience in writing are due to linguistic or cultural differences, cognitive or language disorders, opportunities for home and school experiences, or motivation. Here are some typical "trouble spots" in writing.

First, writing tasks require planning. Planning includes not only knowledge of the writing genre (e.g., letter, list, etc.) but also knowledge and/or ability to research the content. Students may have difficulty with planning if they have not had exposure to such genres or if they have cognitive disorders that inhibit their organizational skills (Englert & Raphael, 1988).

Second, writing tasks require a facile use of language. Using appropriate vocabulary and constructing coherent sentences, paragraphs, and larger units of text require a great deal of language dexterity. ELLs, students with communication disorders, and students with limited exposure to print may face difficulty in writing because of their less developed expressive language in English (Bos & Vaughn, 2002).

Third, writing tasks require an understanding of the conventions of standard English text. Knowledge of conventions such as spelling, grammar, and mechanics (e.g., capitalization, punctuation, etc.) is important in most writing tasks (Fearn & Farnan, 1998).

Fourth, writing tasks require either handwriting or keyboarding skills. Students who have difficulty in forming letters or who are not fluent in handwriting will have difficulty completing writing assignments. Students with extreme writing problems may be diagnosed with *dysgraphia*, a learning disability characterized by severe problems in size, shape, and spacing of letters despite adequate instruction (Hallahan, Lloyd, Kauffman, Weiss, & Martinez, 2005). More and more, using a keyboard is becoming important in the writing process (Cotton, 2001). Students who have not learned keyboarding skills may be at a disadvantage in completing writing assignments, particularly in the upper grades.

Fifth, writing tasks require students to be positive, persistent, and patient. Writing is a process. Without a positive attitude, without the determination to keep going, and without the ability to understand that there is an end to the process, writing can be difficult. In addition, students need to learn to be patient when giving feedback to peers and receiving feedback about their own writing from teachers and peers. Thus the classroom climate the teacher sets is vital—not only in terms of the academic aspects of writing, but in terms of the social and motivational aspects as well.

RESEARCH BRIEF ✎ The Reading–Writing Connection

Communication involves both receptive language (listening and reading) and productive language (speaking and writing). Because reading and writing are both productive language acts, many scholars hypothesize that they involve similar cognitive strategies. For example, in their composing model of reading, Tierney and Pearson (1984) suggest that reading and writing both involve planning, revising, aligning, drafting (i.e., schema activation), and ongoing monitoring. It is not surprising that many of the strategies used to teach reading have applications to written communication as well. Despite the similarities, Shanahan (1988) cautions that there are differences as well. Not all good readers are good writers, and the opposite is true as well. Teachers cannot assume that what is taught in writing will automatically transfer to reading, or vice versa.

What Are Formal Assessments of Writing?

When our students ask us whether a class topic will be on the test, they express the view that if we value it, we will assess it (White, 1996). When people think about assessment, they think about tests (Holland, Bloome, & Solsken, 1994). Although historically not much attention has been paid to writing assessment, more recently "the assessment of writing stands at the center of new educational directions being pursued as a result both of growing dissatisfaction with traditional testing practices and of changing views of the learning process" (Wolcott, 1998, p. 1). According to Trimbur (1996), the ability to write is being "called on to provide a common means of communication in a divided culture, to promote national economic recovery, and to explain the success or failure of individuals in a class society" (p. 48). Most Americans believe that students need to acquire some level of writing ability (Brossell, 1996), but there is much debate as to what that ability level should be.

Traditionally, and even presently in some settings, students' knowledge of writing was (and is) assessed via multiple-choice questions on grammar and usage (Brossell, 1996). Yet much has been learned about the writing process (prewriting, drafting, rewriting, and postwriting) from how authors actually write. Additionally, assessment of writing is complex because writing itself is a complex act. According to Odell (1999), writing is an act of discovery, of constructing meaning, of communicating, of thinking—and thinking is complex. Due to this complexity, a finished written text does not reflect all the thinking processes that went into creating it (Odell, 1999). Yet it is possible to find in a finished text some evidence of the strategies that went into completing the text. Therefore, the goal in writing assessment is to reflect that knowledge. Ideally, modern-day writing assessment should be able to balance the process with the product.

Many states are now including a test of writing as part of their high-stakes testing programs. For example, the state of Florida administers the Florida Comprehensive Assessment Test (Writing) to students in elementary and secondary grades. During the test, students are given a writing prompt and asked to produce a response to that prompt under timed conditions (45 minutes). The prompts are designed to elicit either a narrative, expository, or persuasive response. Trained raters evaluate student writing based on focus, organization, support (i.e., examples and details), and conventions (i.e., spelling, grammar, and mechanics). While student writing with the state assessment does focus on the written product, teachers are encouraged to use a writing process approach beginning in kindergarten to build student proficiency in writing and to prepare for state assessments.

Direct or Indirect Assessment?

There is some debate about whether assessments of writing should be direct or indirect. Writing on demand and impromptu writing are examples of direct methods of assessing writing. With direct assessments, the topic, the context, and the resources can be controlled so as to prevent cheating and reveal each student's ability. They can also be used to control for statistical measurement. Although this method has the advantage of moving toward authentic assessment, it is still criticized on many points.

CRITICISMS OF DIRECT WRITING ASSESSMENTS

For one, direct writing assessments still focus on the product, not the process. Direct methods are criticized for lack of authenticity: There is no ownership of the writing, and it is out of context. Due to the differences among the various modes of writing and how these can affect the writer and the scorer, the modes of writing a student can use are limited (Wolcott, 1998). They are limited for statistical purposes as well. Time constraints are artificial, even though more time does not guarantee better writing. However, the focus on time may cause anxiety and limit prewriting, revising, and proofreading. Another point of criticism is that one sample of a student's writing is inadequate; it may not give the entire picture. Still another problem is that for statistical purposes, a topic is usually given, and it is difficult to find topics that all students (regardless of background) can relate to. If a topic prompt is given, the accessibility of the topic—how readily the student can grasp the topic and think of something to say—is a concern (Wolcott, 1998). Personal experience topics are often used, since they are easily accessible, yet they lead to other problems. A personal experience writing piece may lead to problems in evaluation. The scorer may become subjective when asked to evaluate a personal response, due to its personal nature. Personal experience prompts may also cause the writer to relive the experience, thereby diverting the writer from the craft of writing (Wolcott, 1998). These are the major criticisms of direct assessments.

CRITICISMS OF INDIRECT WRITING ASSESSMENTS

Indirect assessments are also criticized. Indirect assessments such as standardized norm-referenced tests are considered fragmented, decontextualized, and intrusive. As noted earlier, these tests have traditionally taken the form of multiple-choice tests on the mechanics and usage of writing. A point of criticism is that being able to capitalize (for example) does not necessarily indicate that a student can compose a sentence. White (1996) believes that indirect assessments drive the curriculum away from the entire writing process, because they focus on editing only.

According to Murphy (1999), new views of writing include a focus on the process students are using to write. Acknowledged as well is the fact that different modes and purposes draw on different knowledge and skills. Writing assessment needs to incorporate these new views.

Because of these concerns about indirect assessments, the majority of standardized tests in use today employ direct assessment methods and either holistic or analytic scoring scales. Below are just a few examples.

Test of Written Expression

The Test of Written Expression (McGhee, Bryant, Larsen, & Rivera, 1995) is used to identify students with writing difficulties, to reveal writing strengths and weaknesses, to document student writing process, and to aid in writing research. It has basal and ceiling levels, and the scores are interpreted based on the age of students. It is designed for students ages 6 to 14. A student's writing sample is scored according to an analytic rubric that determines the presence or absence of a characteristic.

Integrated Writing Test

The Integrated Writing Test (Beery, 1993) is designed to evaluate "good writing." Students have 15 minutes to respond to a teacher-generated prompt. The total test score is a composite of three or more subtests out of the six dimensions: Legibility (number of words judged as illegible in a five-line sample), productivity (number of words in a five-line sample—usually lines 10–14), Clarity (a rating of 1–6 for the entire story), Punctuation (number of errors in a five-line sample), Spelling (number of errors in a five-line sample), or Vocabulary (number of words of seven letters or more in a five-line sample). An examiner is allowed to score the entire writing sample or to score only five lines of the sample for all subtests except the Clarity subtest. The test is designed for students in grades 2–12.

Comprehensive Assessment Program

The Comprehensive Assessment Program's Assessment of Writing (Wick, Gatta, & Valentine, 1991) measures students' writing abilities through essays. It is scored according to a 6-point holistic scale and a diagnostic scoring system for content, organization, usage, sentence structure, and mechanics. It is designed for students in grades 3–12.

CTB Writing Assessment System

The CTB Writing Assessment System (CTB/McGraw-Hill, 2004) includes writing measures to aid educators in evaluating writing programs and students' writing abilities. Students write to prompts that are self-standing or associated with the reading of a passage. It is scored both holistically and analytically. Scoring procedures are made available to the administrator, although student writing can be submitted to the publisher for scoring. This assessment has four levels and is appropriate for students in grades 2–12.

Writing Process Test

The Writing Process Test (Warden & Hutchinson, 2004) is actually a measure of both writing product and process. Analytic scoring includes evaluation of how the student develops a piece of writing (planning and revising), as well as evaluation of the final product in terms of content and mechanics. This test is designed for students in grades 2–12.

Further Comments

Formal writing assessments face many concerns. Research indicates that writing is a recursive process and that what should be evaluated is the process, but what is actually evaluated is still the product. Evaluating the written product is important, but it should not be the only thing being evaluated. Although different forms of evaluation such as portfolios are more comprehensive and more aligned with present theories of writing, it is understandable that due to limited resources of human power and time, portfolios are not used at the standardized test level.

As with all forms of assessment, writing assessment suffers from issues of reliability and validity. It is difficult to ensure that every evaluator is reliable in his or her method of evaluating student writing. Equally difficult is interrater reliability. Validity also comes into question. What do evaluations of student writing really say about student writing? How generalizable is the evaluation process? Standards of reliability and validity are monitored for experiments and for large-scale assessments such as state tests, but they are not monitored or controlled in everyday evaluations. Generating reliable and generalizable writing assessments is difficult because writing is complex (Shals, 1996).

Assessment takes place on many levels—internationally, nationally, socially/politically, and at the school/classroom level. It is a valuable tool to monitor learning, to gauge the effectiveness of teaching strategies and to guide instructional decision making (Isaacson, 1999). It can be both formative and summative. Assessment can promote and facilitate learning, or it can prevent and inhibit learning (Little, 1990). Of course, whatever method is used to assess writing and evaluate it will ripple down to instructional programs (Wolcott, 1998). Although teachers speak disparagingly of "teaching to the test," they have no choice but to do so. "Writing assessment not only sets out to measure the effectiveness of a writing teacher's work, but defines the content of their work" (White, 1996, p. 11). Writing assessment and evaluation have come a long way, but they still have a long way to go.

What Are Informal Assessments of Writing?

Implementation of a process writing approach provides you with the opportunity for ongoing informal assessment of your students' work. As you observe your students' writing, think about the "trouble spots" mentioned earlier in this chapter: (1) planning, (2) language, (3) conventions, (4) handwriting/keyboarding, and (5) motivation. Descriptions of some additional informal assessments follow.

Writing Attitude Survey

The Writing Attitude Survey (Kear, Coffman, McKenna, & Ambrosio, 2000) is useful in providing insight into a student's attitude toward writing (see Figure 12.1). It is administered to a whole class and takes about 15–25 minutes. There are 28 questions that focus on writing, each followed by four pictures of Garfield depicting four different emotional states—very happy, somewhat happy, somewhat upset, and very upset.

Writer Self-Perception Scale

The Writer Self-Perception Scale (Bottomley, Henk, & Melnick, 1997) can be used to assess students' feelings about their efficacy as writers (see Form 12.1). The scale includes several dimensions, including perceptions of general performance, specific progress, observational comparison, social feedback, and physiological states. The instrument can be used to help you work with students to set goals for their writing.

In-Class Informal Writing Assessment

- Have lined and unlined paper available, and have different types of writing utensils available.
- Tell the students that they can pick whatever type of paper they like and whatever type of writing utensil they like, and ask them to write whatever they want.

Name ______________________________ School ____________________ Grade ________

1. How would you feel writing a letter to the author of a book you read?
2. How would you feel if you wrote about something you have seen or heard?
3. How would you feel writing a letter to a store asking about something you might buy there?
4. How would you feel telling in writing why something happened?
5. How would you feel writing to someone to change their opinion?
6. How would you feel keeping a diary?

(cont.)

FIGURE 12.1. Writing Attitude Survey. From Kear, Dennis, J., Coffman, Gerry A., McKenna, Michael C., and Ambrosio, Anthony L. (2000, September). Writing Attitude Survey. *The Reading Teacher*, *54*(1), 16–23. Garfield copyright by Paws, Inc. Reprinted by permission.

7. How would you feel writing poetry for fun?

8. How would you feel writing a letter stating your opinion about a topic?

9. How would you feel if you were an author who writes books?

10. How would you feel if you had a job as a writer for a newspaper or magazine?

11. How would you feel about becoming an even better writer than you already are?

12. How would you feel about writing a story instead of doing homework?

(cont.)

FIGURE 12.1. *(cont.)*

13. How would you feel about writing a story instead of watching TV?

14. How would you feel writing about something you did in science?

15. How would you feel writing about something you did in social studies?

16. How would you feel if you could write more in school?

17. How would you feel about writing down the important things your teacher says about a new topic?

18. How would you feel writing a long story or report at school?

(cont.)

FIGURE 12.1. *(cont.)*

19. How would you feel writing answers to questions in science or social studies?

20. How would you feel if your teacher asked you to go back and change some of your writing?

21. How would you feel if your classmates talked to you about making your writing better?

22. How would you feel writing an advertisement for something people can buy?

23. How would you feel keeping a journal for class?

24. How would you feel writing about things that have happened in your life?

(cont.)

FIGURE 12.1. *(cont.)*

FIGURE 12.1. *(cont.)*

- Tell them that you will collect it and look over it, but that you will not grade the papers.
- Give the students about 15 minutes to write.
- Collect the papers and look over them, making notes to yourself as to where each student is and where the students are as a class.

Do not be surprised at what you find. Remember that you gave no guidelines, so accept what you have and work from there. For example, you may find that Abel chose lined paper and a pencil and wrote the times tables ($5 \times 1 = 5$, $5 \times 2 = 10$, etc.). This may indicate that Abel likes math or that he is working on memorizing his times table. You may need to press Abel to "write" something else to get an idea of his writing ability. He may tell you that his favorite subject is math and that he doesn't like to write. Then you'll know what you'll need to work on with Abel. Or you may find that Carmen chose unlined paper and a colored pencil and drew pictures. You may have to work with Carmen on putting her drawings into writing. For the most part, however, you will find out what aspects of the writing craft you will need to focus on for the entire class (capitalization, punctuation, complete sentences, transitions, spelling, etc.). You can do this again at midyear, to informally assess how the students have progressed and what you may need to focus on next.

Timed Writing to Prompts

If your state has a high-stakes writing test that requires students to write to a prompt, it is a good idea to give students practice in writing to a prompt under timed conditions consistent with state guidelines. Use the state scoring rubrics to evaluate student work and to set goals to work on during daily process writing time. Find out if some of your students qualify for extended time due to a diagnosed learning disability.

How Do You Provide Differentiated Instruction Using the Writing Process?

Level 1: High-Quality Core Instruction

The process approach to writing is beneficial for all learners, including ELLs. It allows all students to write from their own experiences; it helps others get to know them; they benefit from the collaborative nature of the process; and there are opportunities for drawing, listening, and talking (Peregoy & Boyle, 2001). High-quality core instruction includes specific instruction in the components of the writing process. This section on Level 1 begins with instructional suggestions for the stages of the writing process and continues with methods for evaluating student writing in the writing process, followed by suggestions for Writer's Workshop, a format for implementing writing process instruction for all learners. The section concludes with additional suggestions for writing activities for all students in your class.

TEACHING THE WRITING PROCESS

As noted at the beginning of this chapter, the writing process has four stages: prewriting, drafting, rewriting, and postwriting. The different parts of the writing process go by many names, depending on the resource you are using. Choose the ones that make sense for you to teach and are most appropriate for your students. You can indicate to them that there is more than one name for each of the processes, but the most important thing to teach your students is that the writing process is recursive. You can jump in anywhere at any time. When teaching the writing process, first teach each part separately as a minilesson. Do not attempt to teach the entire process at one time. The students will learn the writing process as they write and move through it to their finished writing piece. Figure 12.2 provides one way of presenting the writing process to your students.

PREWRITING STAGE

All parts of the writing process take time, but prewriting takes a great deal of time because it is the part of the writing process where the writer makes decisions about genre, topic, audience, and format. The less familiar your students are with genre, topic, audience, and format, the more time prewriting will take. These decisions may be altered and amended along the way, due to the recursive nature of the writing process. Nonetheless, prewriting serves as an important initial planning stage.

1. Prewriting (getting it out)
   - Putting words/ideas on paper
   - Brainstorming
   - Generating ideas
   - Making plans
   - Doodles
   - Deciding who is the audience, and what is my purpose
   - Asking myself: How will I choose a topic?
2. Drafting (getting it down)
   - Developing fluency (flow)
   - Developing coherence (relating and making sense)
   - Asking myself: How can I capture my audience's attention?
   - Sharing my writing with others
3. Rewriting (getting it right)
   - Revise
   - Organize
   - Clarify
   - Edit
   - Peer-edit
   - Proofread
   - Polish
   - Asking myself: Which words can I change to make my writing more vivid?
   - Asking myself: How can I improve my writing?
4. Postwriting (going public)
   - Final copy
   - Asking myself: Is my final copy neat?
   - Asking myself: How would I like to share my writing with others?

FIGURE 12.2. The writing process.

Several strategies are provided below, and I suggest you try them all. Try anything that will help your students generate ideas for writing. Students need to develop a collection of prewriting strategies, because not every strategy will generate a good idea every time. Some of these prewriting strategies will be useful for any type of genre, but some can be used to elicit a particular type of outcome. For example, the prewriting strategy of continuing the story may best be used to generate a piece of fiction, whereas the prewriting strategy of using a Venn diagram may generate a comparison/contrast paper. Remember that the purpose of prewriting is for students to get their ideas out of their heads and onto paper, but using the appropriate prewriting technique can help produce a desired product.

Listing Topics. Ask your students to list 20 topics they could write about. Go around the class and ask each person to share one item on his or her list. Tell the students, "If someone mentions a topic you have on your list, then you check it off. If someone mentions a topic you don't have on your list, you add that topic to your list." Keep going around the class until all the topics have been mentioned.

If a topic is mentioned—for example, writing about a pet puppy—and some students say, "I don't have a pet puppy," tell them to write it down anyway because they can always make up a story about a pet puppy.

Ask the students to keep this list in their writing folder as a reference they can always turn to when they need to find something to write about.

Freewrites. Have your students each take out a blank piece of paper, and take one out for yourself. Then tell your students the following:

> "I am going to give us five minutes to write about whatever comes into our minds. I am not going to collect this, nor is anyone going to read it. Don't worry about spelling or grammar; just write. The purpose of a freewrite is to get your 'writing juices' flowing. Try not to stop and think about what your brains are thinking about, but rather just write down what your brains are thinking about. I will take any questions now, but after I start the timer, no more questions—just writing."

Set the timer for 5 minutes, and write.

Continuing the Story. Another strategy has the students start by writing down the beginning of a story. They write until the teacher says to stop. Then they each pass their paper to another student (the teacher can decide if they pass the paper back, forward, to their right, or to their left). The next student reads what has been written and continues the story until the teacher says to stop. The paper is passed to another student again. The next student reads what has been written and continues the story. The story is passed along until the teacher says that at the next pass, the student will finish the story. Then the paper is handed back to the story's originator. The students are given time to read how their initial stories turned out. This activity usually surprises most students and gives them lots of laughs.

Story Starters. Have accessible sentences or paragraphs of story starters for your students to use. You can purchase books of story starters, find them on the Internet, or create them yourself. Story starters can be as simple as the following examples:

> Write about your favorite animal.
> I get upset when . . .
> What if there was no such thing as plastic?

Or they can be a bit more complex, like this one:

> I had finished making my sandwich, just the way I like it, and had sat down at the kitchen counter to eat it when I heard a strange noise in the backyard. I thought it was probably that annoying, yappy dog of ours, and grabbed my sandwich. Then I realized that our yappy dog wasn't yapping at the noise. That was strange. I put my sandwich down and went over to the sliding glass door. I moved back the curtains and witnessed . . .

Graphic Organizers. Any graphic organizer used during reading to understand the structure of a genre can be used for structuring the student's writing of that genre. Story maps are used to "plot the plot" of stories read, but they can also be used to "plot the plot" of stories to be written. Have your students use story maps to develop the stories they would like to write. If you have your students use a Venn diagram to help them deconstruct a contrast essay or a comparison/contrast piece, you can have them use a

Venn diagram as a prewriting strategy for creating a contrast or a comparison/contrast piece of writing.

Drawing. For young writers, drawing may be the best way for them to create a story. For older students, drawing can be a way to help reluctant writers begin writing, and it can also be a way for students to develop their writing ideas. When you ask your students to draw as a prewriting strategy, remind them that the drawing does not have to be a perfect creation of art, but just a sketch to help them put on paper what they are thinking about writing. You can use the drawing strategy in conjunction with another prewriting strategy. For example, after you have your students continue a story starter and they are finding themselves not knowing where the story is going to go next, ask them to draw what they've written thus far. As they are drawing or after they have finished drawing, they may have a better idea of what is going to happen next. For young writers, you may have to write down the text for the stories they have drawn.

Responding to Music. Teachers often leave drawing to the art teacher and music to the music teacher, but these disciplines belong in the writing classroom as well. Have your students listen to a piece of instrumental music (classical, jazz, etc.). Enlist the expertise of the music teacher to provide you with pieces of music that will produce the desired outcome. Do this prewriting strategy more than once, using a different type of music each time. Have students use their five senses and jot down smells, tastes, textures, colors, and sounds they sense as the music is played. Using the words they have written, have them create sentences or short paragraphs about the images the music conjures up in their minds' eyes (Jordan & Wright, 2004).

Responding to Literature. Have students respond in writing to literature pieces read. You can ask them to respond to any part of the literature read. Students can respond to the setting, the characters, their actions, the outcome, the theme, etc. Remember to tailor your prewriting strategy to the product desired. If you'd like the final product that stemmed from literature to be a persuasive letter, for example, then asking your students to determine their position on the subject might be how you would like to initiate the prewriting.

DRAFTING STAGE

In the drafting process, students are concerned with getting all initial ideas down on the paper in such a manner that the ideas flow and make sense. A writer needs to continue to refine the aim of the written piece and concentrate on the writing genre. The writer also needs to continue to think of the intended audience and tailor the piece to that audience. Since writers are immersed in writing and may not be able to see the forest for the trees, they need to share writing drafts with others. During drafting, the focus should be on format and on conveying a coherent message. Attention to matters related to editing can occur at the rewriting stage.

One obstacle to overcome with younger, less experienced, and/or reluctant writers is that a first draft is not a last draft. Encourage students to think about the ideas they want to share, and let them know that they will have time and support to refine their work at another time.

Below are some strategies that can be used during this stage in the writing process.

Keeping It Flowing. Composing can be tough for some students. If a student has a hard time getting started, provide an opening sentence. If a student gets stuck on a word or an idea, have him or her write in a space or question mark and keep rolling. Remember the importance of teacher modeling. Demonstrate how you keep your writing flowing during the drafting stage, using an overhead projector and a teacher think-aloud procedure.

Aims and Genres. Teach your students that writing has several aims: Writing can be used to inform, to persuade, to express oneself, and/or to create a literary work. Provide your students with examples such as the ones in Table 12.1.

These aims can take the form of various genres of writing. Each writing genre is characterized by the writing style, format, or content used. Educate your students on the different types of writing genres. Fill your classroom with various examples of these genres, so that your students have a variety of options when creating their writing pieces. Table 12.2 lists several genres that can be used for writing projects and written products.

Focus on Audience. As students are writing, have them think about their target audience to make certain that they are communicating clearly to their intended readers. Questions to promote thinking about the audience include the following:

- Who are the people in my intended audience?
- What can I assume that they already know about the topic?
- What does my intended audience need to learn?
- Is my language friendly to the intended audience?

REWRITING STAGE

The rewriting stage is when writers edit their own work and get feedback from others to refine a written piece. Rewriting is an editing process that focuses on revising (attending to meaning and how the message is communicated) and proofreading (focusing on spelling and mechanics).

Teaching students to edit their own work and that of others is challenging. Students must learn to be critical readers, to give feedback to others in constructive ways, and to receive feedback about their own work. Also, students can get overwhelmed and frus-

TABLE 12.1. Aims of Writing

Aim	Example
Inform	Hey, Liz, Patty's having a slumber party this weekend! You going?
Persuade	It's not as if we are cheating. You're just helping out your best friend this one time by indicating the best choice! A, B, or C! Come on, I won't think less of you. I won't tell, either.
Allow self-expression	I think this class is ___________.
Create literary work	Roses are red, Violets are blue. I didn't do my homework. Did you?

TABLE 12.2. Genres for Projects and Products

Advertisements/commercials	Memoirs
Allegories	Memos
Alphabet books	Menus
Anecdotes	Monologues
Arguments	Narratives
Articles (sports, beauty)	News report
Autobiographies	Notes
Ballads	Novellas
Biographies	Obituaries
Cards	Observations
Cartoons	Odes
Catalogs	Parables
Commentaries	Plays (drama, comedy, satires)
Critiques	Poems
Debates	Posters, signs
Descriptions	Prayers
Dialogues	Profiles
Diaries	Proposals
Dictation	Proverbs
Dictionaries (words and/or pictures)	Puzzles
Directions	Questions
Dreams	Raps
Editorials	Recipes
Epics	Reports (books, research)
Epistles	Resumes
Epitaphs	Reviews (films, books)
Essays	Riddles
Eulogies	Sermons
Fables	Skits
Film scripts	Slogans (election, sales)
Folk tales, fairy tales, tall tales, legends, myths	Soliloquies
Gift books	Songs
Hero tales	Sonnets
Histories	Speeches
Hymns	Stories (detective, mystery fantasy, sci-fi, romance, horror)
Instructions (how-to)	Summaries
Interviews	Thesaurus
Jingles	Vignettes
Joke books	Web pages
Journals	
Laws, rules	
Letters (fan, business, complaint, friendly, thank you, to the editor)	

trated if too many aspects of revising and proofreading are provided at one time. Focus on one or two aspects of rewriting at a time, to avoid bombarding your students.

By sitting with your students individually during your conference time and by working on their papers with them, you will also be teaching them the skills of editing. If you teach your students how to peer-edit each other's work, and ask them that before they come to you they should have had at least two or three other students read and comment on their writing pieces, it will help them become better editors themselves. Sample questions for self, peer, and teacher editing are included in Form 12.2.

Myles (2002) cautions that the rewriting stage can be the most difficult for ELLs who are not fluent in English vocabulary, spelling, or grammatical conventions. More time needs to be allotted for ELLs during this critical period, so that they can get the scaffolding they need to develop writing proficiency.

Clock Editing. One of the most useful strategies for helping my students during the rewriting stage has been *clock editing* (Carroll & Wilson, 1993). Clock editing takes place on the day that the final draft is due. The script in Figure 12.3 can be used to guide students through the clock editing process. A clock editing sheet is included in Figure 12.4.

Clock editing makes reading and grading easier, because students have caught many (although not all) of the errors. It is a big help! It's not a problem for a student who has prepared the first draft of the paper on time and participated in the clock editing process to take that paper home, make additional corrections, and turn it in the next day. (Besides, if the student is making the paper better, then that will facilitate the grading process.) Also, having the initials of the person who checked for a particular step in the clock editing is very useful. When you are grading the paper, keep the clock editing sheet handy. If you find several misspelled words, make it a point to call upon the author and the peer editor whose initials appear next to spelling and usage and have a conference with both of them. Ultimately, it is the author's duty to do the final proofreading and catch personal errors, but the peer editor can be responsible too. Peer editing should be taken seriously. (If the author added the misspelled words after the clock editing, then the peer editor is "off the hook.") If a spelling lesson needs to be taught or retaught, you can teach it to both of them, using the author's writing piece.

POSTWRITING STAGE

After a piece is finished, it should be shared. Publication is part of sharing. It does not have to be a formal publication; it could mean making the students' work available for others to read in an Authors' Center. It could also mean creating a class book or individual book; sharing their writing with other classes or students; or presenting their writing to teachers, administrators, or family members. Yet formal publication is possible too (see Figure 12.5 for a list of publications that accept student work). Publication is important, because students will be motivated when they know they are writing for others (Szedeli, 1993). When students have authentic opportunities to share their writing with their intended audience, they begin to feel like "writers" and are more anxious to engage in writing in the future.

PARENT POINTER ☞ How Parents Can Help with Writing

Parents are a child's first teachers of writing, and they can do many things to help develop writing skills and a love of writing in their child. Here are some of these things:

- Provide writing materials.
- Provide opportunities to write.
- Celebrate and support their child's writing attempts and completed pieces.
- Provide high-quality literature as models of high-quality writing.
- Talk to their child about writing.
- Allow their child to help them with writing tasks at home (making grocery lists, creating to do lists, writing letters to family members or for business matters, writing cards, taking telephone messages for other family members, creating invitations, etc.).

TEACHER: Any student who is not ready to turn in his or her final draft, please take your writing piece and sit over there [or outside, or at the computer, etc.]. Since you are not ready, you will not have the benefit of clock editing, and your grade will go down one letter grade for every day this writing piece is late.

Everyone else, take out your final piece, all your drafts for that piece, and a blank piece of paper.

Put all your drafts in order, and put your final draft on top. (*Teacher hands out jumbo paper clamps, and each student clips his or her entire stack together.*) On the blank piece of paper, write at the top today's date and *This paper belongs to [your name].* Take your stack of drafts and your sheet of paper and a pen, and let's get into two rows. (*Teacher organizes the desks into two rows that face each other.*) You are going to exchange writing pieces with the person in front of you. One row will rotate, and the other will not. The row that rotates, everyone moves one seat down, and the last person comes to the first seat. When you rotate, you take whatever writing piece you have with you. Do not hand it back to the person you got it from. Now, on your sheet of paper, draw a line, write the number 1, and write *Process*. (*Teacher writes it on the board as well. See Figure 12.4 for a sample format.*) Now swap paper stacks with the person in front of you. Look over the writing piece you have received. Is there prewriting? Are there multiple drafts? Are they labeled as such? Is there a final draft? If so, put a smiley face next to *Process*, and put your initials on the line before the number 1. If not, put a sad face next to *Process*, and write your initials on the line.

Now the row that's rotating, clock over one. Take that piece with you. On the sheet of paper, draw a line, write the number 2, and write *Format*. Swap the paper with the new person in front of you. Is the final draft typed? Is it neat? Is there a cover page? Is there a title? If yes to all of the above, put a smiley face and your initials; if not, put a sad face and your initials.

Now the row that's rotating, clock over one. Take that piece with you. On the sheet of paper, draw a line, write the number 3, and write *Title* and *Lead*. Swap the paper with the new person in front of you. Is the title catchy? Is the lead catchy? If yes, put a smiley face and your initials; if not, put a sad face and your initials.

Now the row that's rotating, clock over one. Take that piece with you. On the sheet of paper, draw a line, write the number 4, and write *Grammar*. Swap the paper with the new person in front of you. Read the entire final draft, looking only for errors in grammar. When you spot an error, do not write on the person's paper; write the error and page number on the clock editing sheet. When you finish, initial on the line.

The row that's rotating, clock over one. Number 5 is *Spelling and usage*. Swap papers and read the entire final draft, looking only for errors in spelling and usage. When you spot an error, do not mark on the person's final draft; instead, write the page number and error on the clock editing sheet. When you finish, initial on the line.

(*Teacher continues to do the same for whatever other mini-lessons have been taught. The last step is for the reader to provide some possible improvements and positive comments.*)

Hand back the stack to the person it belongs to. Writer, read over the comments on your clock editing sheet. Write on the bottom [or back, in some cases] of your clock editing sheet the following: *I have read the above. I will take into consideration the suggestions made, and I will make the necessary corrections*. And then sign your name.

Now consider whether the corrections you need to make are minor ones that could be taken care of with some correction fluid, or if they are major ones that would require retyping or writing another draft. If they are minor, take care of them right now. Now, if your paper is ready to hand in right now, today, I'll take it. If you need to make the minor corrections and it's ready to hand in today, I'll take it. If your paper needs work, then take it home and correct your errors, and I'll take your paper on Monday—no letter grade down, no penalties, nothing. But after Monday, it will be one letter grade down for every day it's late.

FIGURE 12.3. Teacher script for clock editing process.

CLOCK EDITING SHEET

This paper belongs to (name) ______________________ Date ____________

____ 1. Process (prewriting, drafts, final)
____ 2. Format (typed, neat, cover page, title, double-spaced)
____ 3. a. Title—catchy? b. Lead—catchy?
____ 4. Grammar
____ 5. Spelling and usage
____ 6. Dialogue
____ 7. Transitions
____ 8. Vibrant verbs
____ 9. Possible improvements
____ 10. Positive comments

I have read the above. I will take into consideration the suggestions made, and I will make the necessary corrections. ______________________
(Signature of author)

FIGURE 12.4. Sample clock editing sheet.

Cricket Magazine Group
Carus Publishing Company
P.O. Box 9307
LaSalle, IL 61301
www.cricketmag.com

Writing! (A Weekly Reader Publication)
Weekly Reader Subscriber Services
3001 Cindel Drive
Delran, NJ 08075
www.weeklyreader.com

The 21st Century
P.O. Box 30
Newton, MA 02461
www.teenink.com
editor@teenink.com

Merlyn's Pen
4 King Street
P.O. Box 910
East Greenwich, NJ 02818
www.merlynspen.org

Stone Soup
P.O. Box 83
Santa Cruz, CA 95063
www.stonesoup.com

FIGURE 12.5. Publications that accept student work.

METHODS FOR EVALUATING STUDENT WRITING IN THE WRITING PROCESS

Writing teachers know that writing and the teaching of writing are complex. Also complex is evaluating student writing. According to White (1996), many writing teachers are attached to their own form of evaluation—be it the red pen marking in the margins, the proofreading abbreviations, or the grade and comments at the end of the paper. Yet there are many different forms of evaluating writing. Student writing can be evaluated by using portfolios, holistic measures, analytic scales, or other methods. All of these have advantages and disadvantages.

Portfolios. Portfolios can help bring writing assessment practices more in line with current theories of writing (Murphy, 1999; Soodak, 2000; Speck, 2000). While some believe that one essay is a one-item test yielding one data point, others believe that students' writing should not be judged on the basis of one piece of writing, but rather on several pieces (Camp, 1996; Murphy, 1999). *Portfolios* are collections of students' work. They are very versatile and can take on many forms. Portfolios can be composed of final drafts or a combination of rough drafts and finished pieces. They allow insight into students' performance on different tasks, revealing the students' areas of strength and areas for growth (Murphy, 1999). With a portfolio, the aspects of writing a student has under control and those he or she needs more work on are evident. Portfolios provide information on the writing process and on students' versatility in ways that holistic and analytic measures do not (Murphy, 1999). Portfolios provide samples of how students have addressed a variety of audiences and have written for a variety of purposes. They provide evidence of students' knowledge of the writing process and of writing strategies. Portfolios also allow for creativity. With portfolios, you can assess your students' use of the writing process. You might compare their rough drafts with their final drafts and give grades for prewriting, revision, and final drafts.

For students, portfolios decrease the pressure of grades. Through portfolios, the students are empowered. Their voices are heard, and they can become part of the assessment process by choosing what is included in their portfolios, as well as by helping create the criteria for evaluation (Townsend, Fu, & Lamme, 1997). For students who need constant feedback, however, portfolios will not be enough. Portfolios are evaluated in increments, not daily or weekly. Although portfolios give teachers a great deal of information about their students' growth as writers, portfolios also increase the paper load. Teachers will be evaluating four or five papers for each student at grading time, rather than one at a time over the grading period (Bratcher, 1994). In addition, evaluating portfolios can be problematic, because it can conflict with other evaluation systems (Speck, 2000).

TECH TIP Using Computers in Writing Evaluation and Instruction

- Use the computer to write your comments about your students' writing pieces. In this way, you will always retain a record of the comments you've made to the students in reference to their writing, and you will also be respecting your students' ownership of their written pieces by not writing on them.
- Instead of pen pals, try *keypals* (pen pals via email). Your students' keypals don't have to be across the continent; they could be in another class in your own school or district.

Holistic Methods. Holistic grading works under the premise that the whole is worth more than the parts (Wolcott, 1998). The success of the whole piece of writing is evaluated by using a point scale (Bratcher, 1994; Wolcott, 1998). Holistic evaluation is a single-score assessment (Murphy, 1999). It examines the writing for generalized features such as organization, idea development, usage, and mechanics, to name a few. Murphy (1999) notes that holistic rubrics are not useful for guiding the growth of a writer. However, for placement and grading purposes, holistic measures are useful (Isaacson, 1999). With holistic measures, large numbers of essays can be scored quickly.

There are various types of holistic measures. At the extreme of holistic measurement is *impressionistic grading*. This type of evaluation is highly subjective, because the value for the grading is not made explicit (Bratcher, 1994). It is evaluated just as its name suggests—by the impression it makes on the scorer. This type of measure is most useful in the primary grades.

Analytic Methods. Analytic grading is more useful in diagnosing a student's strengths and areas for growth (Isaacson, 1999). Analytic scales break writing into components. This type of approach assumes that the quality of the piece of writing is the sum of each part. A disadvantage of analytic evaluation is that it is time-consuming. It is sometimes difficult to identify the appropriate categories or the appropriate rating.

In response to the limitations of holistic scoring, *primary trait evaluation* was developed (Wolcott, 1998). In primary trait evaluation, the writing is evaluated against a small list of criteria (Bratcher, 1994). The student receives feedback on this small number of items, although other important criteria may be neglected.

Assorted Methods. Although classroom teachers can use holistic and analytic methods, there are other methods as well. *Dimensional scoring* is one way to evaluate portfolios in particular. It allows the scorer to look at the portfolio in its entirety, as well as across different writing conditions (Murphy, 1999).

Writing conferences are becoming very common. One advantage is that the student can talk and give his or her input. Conferences allow for on-the-spot teaching with immediate explanations. The disadvantage of conferences is that they are time-consuming and on occasion can become confrontational. Tape-recorded teacher assessment of a writing piece is a little less time-consuming than conferences, but the student does not get a chance to give his or her input.

The most common type of response to student writing is a written one. This can be done in longhand, on a computer, or on a grade sheet. With written responses, the concern is that editing marks rob the student of ownership, and often the responses focus on the negative. (See the "hot dog" method in Figure 12.6 for commenting on students' papers.)

PUTTING THE WRITING PROCESS TO WORK: USING WRITERS' WORKSHOP

One way to put the process approach to teaching writing into practice is through a *Writers' Workshop*. The purpose of a Writers' Workshop is to provide students with the opportunity to engage in writing. Using a Writers' Workshop approach to teaching writing allows a teacher to diagnose and remediate writing on a continuous basis. Through writing, students can communicate their thoughts and express their ideas, as well as improve their writing skills. Students want to write, but they need a purpose and a safe environment for experimenting. The teacher needs to create an environment in his or her

Use the **hot dog** to make comments on students' papers!

- Start with positive remarks.
- Provide the "meaty" comments related to one or two aspects of writing (no more than two) the student needs to work on.
- End with an encouraging note.

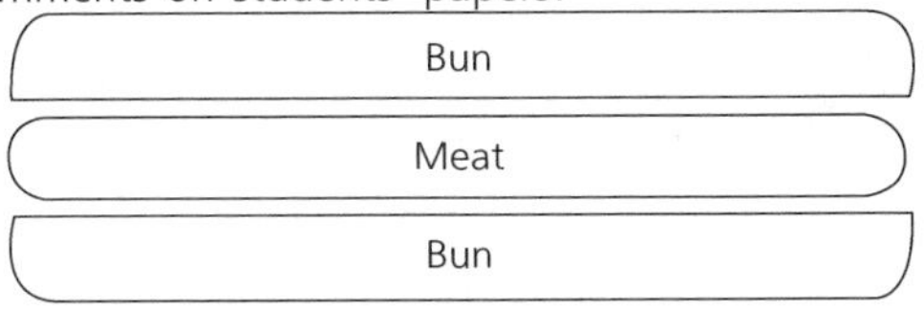

For example: Tomas, I enjoyed reading about how you got your first puppy. It reminds me of how I felt when I got my first pet. Your piece would benefit from some more description of the puppy. Don't just tell the reader about the puppy, but help the reader *feel* the puppy (describe his fur and wet nose, for example). What did the puppy smell like? What did the puppy do when you held him? What noises did the puppy make? I look forward to reading your revised piece and getting to know your puppy, Rocco, better. Will I meet him at the school's Pet-Walk-A-Thon?

Another example: Paul, it is obvious that you did extensive research on both sides of the myth for this research paper. We need to sit down and work on the comparison/contrast organization of this paper. Start working with the attached graphic organizer. In order to help the reader better distinguish which version you are referring to, you need to add some transitional words and phrases, too. (See the points I've indicated in the text.) Revising this piece will make it more suitable for the "Fact or Fiction" column of the school newspaper.

FIGURE 12.6. The "hot dog" method for commenting on students' papers.

classroom where students can feel free to express themselves and learn from their mistakes. This can be accomplished in the form of a Writers' Workshop. According to Nancie Atwell (1987, p. 18),

> a workshop approach benefits adolescents by affording them the responsibility and autonomy they're ready to begin assuming as they approach adulthood. . . . [It] provides a structure that keeps them on track, and an authoritative adult model with whom they can discover the sense of reading and writing.

In addition, the very structure of Writers' Workshop ensures that the teacher is addressing the entire class, working with small groups, and providing individualized instruction.

There is the misconception that if a teacher simply gives students time to write, the teacher is incorporating a Writers' Workshop approach. However, Writers' Workshop has specific components. A Writers' Workshop has five parts: a *mini-lesson*, *writing time*, *status of the class*, *conference time*, and *sharing time* (Atwell, 1987).

Mini-Lesson. Every Writers' Workshop day starts with a mini-lesson. This mini-lesson, as the name implies, should be brief (anywhere from 10 to 20 minutes). The topic of the lesson can range from grammar to the craft of writing to publishing. Figure 12.7 is a sample mini-lesson on creating a title. Figure 12.8 is a list of mini-lesson topics. Figure 12.9 is a list of suggested mini-lessons to be taught with different writing genres.

Writing Time. Ideally, writing time should occur daily. If not every day, Writers' Workshop should be held at least three to four times a week. Thirty minutes should be the minimal amount of writing time. Students need time to write, and writing takes time. As your students grow as writers, so will their need for more time, so do not despair if at first 30 minutes seem like too much time. Eventually students will anticipate that they

TITLES

Speak with the class in reference to the importance of a title.

Ask what a title is supposed to offer to the reader. (Short, sweet, not supposed to tell the reader the contents of the story, enticing, catchy.)

Group sharing: Go around the room and have each student read his or her title.

Class decides whether each one is catchy or not.

(If no title, or a boring title, no one will want to read the piece.)

Have each student come up with two or three alternative titles.

Ask each student to share his or her piece with two peers and tell them the title options. Peers can offer advice.

Each student then decides on the best title.

Group sharing: Go around and have each student read his or her current title. The class members will give their opinions on its potential.

FIGURE 12.7. Sample mini-lesson.

Topic choice
Dialogue
Different writing genres
Guideline for formal papers and manuscripts
Organization of ideas
Library skills/reference materials
Transitional words and phrases
Friendly letters, business letters, and thank-you notes
Fiction notes and fiction vocabulary
Vibrant verbs
Sentence combining
How to correct sentence errors
Dead words/overused words
Using punctuation as a way of getting meaning
Peer response
Proofreading
Spelling rules
Descriptions
Names
Sentence errors (run-ons, sentence fragments, comma splices)
Occupations
Writing introductions or lead-ins
Using quotation marks
Characterization
Titles
Types of writing
Vocabulary skills
Paragraph organization patterns
Addressing an envelope
Point of view
Showing instead of telling
Demand writing
Main idea and topic sentence
Homophones and homographs
Glossary for writers
Where to get ideas
Parts of speech
Contests
Idiosyncrasies
Places

FIGURE 12.8. Possible topics for mini-lessons. (These are not in any particular order, nor is this a complete list.)

Descriptive writing

Examples—Description of an event or thing, comparison/contrast of two things or events
Mini-lessons—Writing descriptions, collecting sensory details, using precise language, using spatial order, describing a thing, describing an event, describing a person, vivid verbs, showing instead of telling, varied sentences, language mechanics

Narrative writing

Examples—Personal experience, point of view, biography, autobiography, legend, log, journal, diary, fantasy, eulogy, myth, fable, report of an event
Mini-lessons—Using chronological order, dialogue, news story, historical event, characterization, varied sentences, language mechanics

Expository writing

Examples—Explanations, directions, definitions, recipes
Mini-lessons—Main idea, conveying information, structuring an explanation, comparison/contrast, answering questions, researching topics, outlining, varied sentences, language mechanics

Persuasive writing

Examples—Opinion, advertisement, commercial, letter to the editor, editorial, campaign speech, book or movie review
Mini-lessons—Writing persuasively, determining a position, evaluating evidence, developing a strategy, strengthening your argument, varied sentences, precise language, language mechanics

Essay writing

Examples—Criticism, judgment, etc.
Mini-lessons—Introduction, thesis statement, body, conclusion, organization of ideas, unified paragraphs, varied sentences, language mechanics

Research paper writing

Mini-lessons—Selecting topic, narrowing down topic to one idea, investigating a topic, using the library to find resources, using the Internet to find resources, writing sources in correct bibliographic format on source cards, recording information on note cards, organizing note cards according to how information will be presented, making an outline from notes, writing the report, proofreading, varied sentences, language mechanics

Letter writing

Examples (*friendly letters*)—News, informal invitation and reply, formal invitation and reply, thank you and appreciation, sympathy, get well, congratulations
Examples (*business letters*)—Placing an order, applying for a job, reporting errors, making an inquiry or request
Mini-lessons—Contents of a letter, format of a letter, contents of address on an envelope, format of address on an envelope, varied sentences, language mechanics

Poetry writing

Examples—Concrete poem, haiku, tanka, cinquain, diamante, free verse, limerick, narrative poem
Mini-lessons—Formulas for poems, language mechanics

FIGURE 12.9. Suggested mini-lessons to be taught with different writing genres.

have to write, and as the day goes by and events happen in their lives, they will make a mental note of something they want to write about during Writers' Workshop. Students will begin to see life through the eyes of a writer. This is what Lucy Calkins terms "living the writerly life" (Calkins, 1994). The teacher's role during writing time is to model, model, model. As with other subjects, if a teacher loves his or her subject, that enthusiasm can often be passed on to the students. During Writers' Workshop, students need control of topic choice. If they choose what they want to write about, they are likely to do a better job.

Status of the Class. The purpose of the status of the class is to know where each student is in the writing process. It takes only three to five minutes to take the status of the class, and after the first couple of weeks, a student can do it for you. The procedure is to have each student tell you where he or she is in the writing process. (Obviously, the writing process needs to have been a previously taught mini-lesson.)

On a status-of-the-class form, next to each student's name, the teacher indicates the writing piece the student is working on and at what stage he or she is in reference to that piece. This is very useful information for accountability purposes. If at the end of the week, you look at the status of the class and notice that Juan has been on the first draft of the same piece, you can confer with Juan and ask him if he needs help in order to move along on his draft. Maybe Juan hasn't been using his writing time wisely. If at the end of the week you look at the status of the class and realize that on Monday Maria was working on a first draft about her cat, on Tuesday she was on a first draft about her pure-bred Labrador retriever, and on Wednesday she was on a first draft of a piece about her first time horseback riding, then maybe you need to confer with Maria about elaborating on one topic or writing a larger piece that can include all the animals she loves.

Conference Time. Conferences are critical to successful implementation of the writing process. Conferences provide writers with the opportunity to get feedback from their peers, as well as from the teacher. They can occur during any stage of the writing process. There are two kinds of conferences: student–teacher and student–student.

In a student–teacher conference, your role is to serve as a guide. You can choose the students you will be meeting with on a given day, or the students can sign up to confer with you. For all conferences, you should keep a record of what was discussed. The conferences should last anywhere from five to seven minutes per student. These conferences are most beneficial, because you can devote one-on-one attention to each student as you work on some aspect of writing with that student. If you meet with at least three children a day, in two weeks you will have given each child in the class individualized attention and direct instruction.

Student–student conferences help students learn how to listen to others. It is important to remember that the author is to request help and that the author makes the final decision on his or her own piece. If as the teacher you need more accountability of what happens during the student conferences, you can require a peer conference record form where the writer indicates on the paper what he or she needs help with, and the responder indicates on the same paper his or her questions and responses to the writing piece. This way you have a record of what was said and decided upon during the student–student conference.

Three strategies to teach your students are *say back*, *highlighting*, and *pointing* (Carroll & Wilson, 1993). These can be done in pairs or small groups of four or five.

Say back consists of the following steps (Carroll & Wilson, 1993, p. 157):

1. Writers read the whole piece, pause, and then read it again.
2. Listeners listen. Upon the second reading, listeners jot down two things:
   a. What they liked.
   b. What they want to know more about.
3. Listeners say these back to the writer.

Highlighting has four steps (Carroll & Wilson, 1993, p. 154):

1. Writers read the whole piece, pause, and then read it again.
2. Listeners listen. Upon the second reading, listeners write down the images they liked.
3. After the reading, listeners repeat back these images.
4. Writers highlight these images on their papers.

Pointing has three steps (Carroll & Wilson, 1993, p. 151):

1. Writers read the whole piece, pause, and then read it again.
2. Listeners listen. Upon the second reading, listeners jot down words, phrases, and images, in order to keep track of what they heard.
3. After each reading, listeners point out what they liked (i.e., they keep it positive).

Student–teacher conferences serve a different purpose, as noted above. During these conferences, you work with each student at the stage he or she has reached in the writing process. For example, if the student is revising and editing, you will be guiding the student in grammar and the mechanics of writing, rather than focusing on penmanship. Such conferences with students may require a mini-lesson or reinforcement of a previously taught skill. However, if the student is working on the final draft and is close to publishing, then maybe penmanship will be the focus of the conference.

Sharing Time. Sharing is an important part of a Writers' Workshop. It allows the students the opportunity to ask for help, as well as the opportunity to present their work to an audience. This is important, because students need feedback on what they write from someone other than the teacher. Sharing time can be structured as group sharing or pair sharing. Group sharing allows the students to hear what others are writing about, as well as supplying the students with a pool of ideas for future writing pieces. (Let's not forget that the teacher needs to share with the students what he or she has written, too!)

How to Get Started with Writers' Workshop

- Create a schedule for teaching writing, and stick to it. Start small, and then expand as needed. Make sure to provide your students with ample time and plenty of opportunities to write.
- Prepare your mini-lessons ahead of time. Often you won't really know what lessons need to be taught until you informally assess your students, confer with the students, read some of their writing pieces, and see what their needs are. Some lessons will be taught to the whole class, others to small groups, and still others individually.
- Use good literature as examples and as inspiration. This includes the basal readers and trade books the students are reading for class; selected children's literature and young adult literature books in the classroom library; and writing and literary magazines. Have a large and varied classroom library.

• Have various supplies and resources handy. Different writers like to use different types of paper, different writing utensils, and so on. Have staplers, highlighters, tape, dictionary, thesaurus, and other writing supplies available for use as well. If it is all easily available, students will have no excuses for not being able to get started writing. Figure 12.10 contains a list of suggested materials.

• Organization is a must. Since everyone in class is at a different stage in the writing process, a classroom management plan must be in place. In addition, there is a need for Writers' Workshop rules. Either have these rules posted or have the students write them down. Atwell (1987) has suggested some possibilities:

- *No erasing*. If you change your mind, draw a line through it. Save all records of your thinking and how it has changed.
- *Save everything*. You will be creating a history of yourself as a writer this year, and what you decide against is as much a part of your writing as what you decide to keep—so hold on to all your false starts and ideas that don't work out (any notes, doodles, and drafts).
- *Write on one side of the paper only*. This will be helpful in case you need to cut and paste later.
- *Label everything*. Put your name, the date, and the draft number on all your writings.
- *Speak quietly*. Writing is thinking, and you can't think if your thoughts are interrupted by someone else's chatter. When you are given the time for conversing about your writing, you must do so quietly as well.

• Faith, patience, and perseverance are essential. Have faith in the process, in yourself, and in your students. Be patient with the process, with yourself, and your students. Do not give up.

Paper (different sizes, colors, and textures): Lined paper, construction paper, drawing paper, etc.
Writing utensils (different types and colors): Pencils, pens, crayons, markers, etc.
Erasers
Correction fluid
Staplers
Staple removers
Paper clips
Scissors
Glue
Transparent tape
Hole punchers
Overhead projector, transparencies, and markers
Typewriter and/or computer with word-processing program and printer
Reference materials (dictionary, grammar books, spellers, handbooks, etc.)
Resource materials (anthologies, basals, paperback books, magazines, etc.)
File folders
Good and varied literature

FIGURE 12.10. Suggested materials for classroom writing.

• Model, model, model. Whenever you ask your students to write, you sit down and write too. You may not write as long as you ask them to write, but write nonetheless. By the time your last period rolls around, you'll have written plenty. Remember to have rules in place, so that discipline is not your main concern during writing time. When you ask your students to share, don't forget to share your writing as well. Submit your writing pieces for publication in teacher journals. The value of modeling cannot be underestimated. Talk often to your students about writing, and celebrate writing.

• Pursue continuing education. Grow as a writer and as a teacher of writing—attend writing classes, workshops, and institutes.

Frequently Asked Questions about Writers' Workshop

✎ *What about spelling?* All students are at different stages in spelling. Inventive spelling has a place in rough drafts, because a rough draft is mainly concerned with content and with ideas. Besides, it is just that—a rough draft. Students use words they need, and they may or may not know how to spell the words they need to express themselves. If they only use the words they can spell, their writing will be dull. If they can't make mistakes because they're afraid of getting a bad grade, then they'll "play it safe" and won't grow as writers or spellers. Make spelling rules the topics of mini-lessons. Teach students to circle the words of whose spelling they aren't sure. Allow students to consult with peers and the dictionary for the spelling of words. However, correct spelling should be expected in the final draft.

✎ *What modifications can I make to teach the process approach in my primary class?* For kindergartners, prewriting in the form of shared doodles and drawings is probably the farthest you'll get in teaching the process. Allow your kindergartners to enjoy writing and make connections about letter–sound relationships. For first graders, prewriting and sharing will also be the focus—but you can introduce certain aspects of grammar (such as capital letters and end punctuation), as well as other skills taught at that grade level (such as penmanship).

✎ *What if I give up control of the topic, and the topics students choose to write about are inappropriate?* You need to set up rules for Writers' Workshop, and those rules need to correspond to your school's and district's rules. Do not be afraid to inform your students of your rules. If you do not allow foul language in your classroom, do not allow it in students' writing pieces. Tell your students that you will read everything they write, and make sure to do so. If you read anything about violence to themselves or others, for example, inform your students that you have a responsibility to confront them about what they have written and take appropriate action. This should be the case for any topics that are of concern for teachers—from child abuse, to students' hurting others, to students' hurting themselves. Tell your students that you care about them and that you take their writing seriously; that is why you will privately consult with them whenever you read something that concerns you. You will have to ascertain whether what they are writing is fiction, nonfiction, or fiction based on facts. When students are given the opportunity to express themselves openly through writing, you will get to know a great deal about your students, and not all of it may be pretty. Students are complex individuals with complex experiences. Fortunately for them, the classroom is a safe environment in which to learn about themselves, others, and the world.

✎ *To prepare my students for standardized writing tests, I give them topic prompts. How do I balance Writers' Workshop with the demands of standardized tests?* Learning to write in response to a topic prompt is a very important skill not only for standardized tests in elementary school, high school, and college, but also for job applications. Writing on demand is a very useful skill, and one that you should incorporate into your mini-lessons. Teach students how to dissect a topic prompt. Teach them how to identify what they are being asked to do, and how to respond to the prompt accordingly. Then teach them how to pace themselves in a timed situation, and how to divide their time into prewriting, writing, and proofreading.

✐ *If I use Writers' Workshop in my classroom, does that mean that I forsake teaching grammar or writing conventions?* On the contrary, you will find that many of your mini-lessons and conferences with students will focus on grammar and conventions of writing. Lessons on grammar and writing conventions will become more relevant to the students, because they will be taught in the context of the students' own writing pieces.

✐ *Is there a way that I can manage all the papers I need to take home to grade?* A strategy to facilitate reading and grading papers is staggering their due dates. If you teach in a departmentalized setting, either stagger the dates by class periods (first period's final draft is due on Monday, second period's final draft is due on Wednesday, and third period's final draft is due on Friday, and then these are rotated for each writing piece), or stagger the due dates for each class alphabetically by students' last names (A–H due Monday, I–P due Wednesday, Q–Z due Friday). If you are an elementary school teachers, stagger the due dates for your class alphabetically.

✐ *What are some challenges to starting a Writers' Workshop in my class?* The higher the grade you teach, the more you'll find that the largest challenge is changing students' perceptions of what writing is. If the teachers before you did not incorporate a Writers' Workshop approach to writing, then students are used to being handed a writing topic and not used to coming up with their own topics. This then leads to another challenge—getting students to stick to one topic and develop it. Students who have not previously had a Writers' Workshop approach are used to finishing a draft and not looking at it again, whereas in Writers' Workshop students revisit their drafts several times to get to a better finished product. They stick with one topic and develop it. A challenge at a different level is that of curriculum and support. You need to plan ahead of time and provide concrete documentation to your school's administrators assuring them that in your Writers' Workshop you will be covering your subject and grade curriculum. By doing that, you will begin to get their support. It may also be difficult to get the support of parents because, like their children, they may not have been exposed to a Writers' Workshop approach. Explain to your students' parents what Writers' Workshop is, how you will conduct your classes, what types of writing their children will produce, how they can help, and what to expect, so that you can begin to gain their support as well. Believe it or not, you may also experience a challenge in gaining support from your fellow teachers if you teach in the upper elementary grades. You will need their support if your school is interested in having a coherent writing program. It is difficult for students to improve their writing if writing is done one way in your class and a different way in other classes. Work with your fellow teachers.

If you teach in a departmentalized setting, tell your fellow teachers that you will work with the students you share. For example, if the social studies teacher is having his or her students work on persuasive speeches, tell that teacher that in your class that week you will do a mini-lesson on persuasive writing, and that you will allow the students to work on their speeches during Writers' Workshop. When the speeches are due, you and the social studies teacher can share in the grading. The social studies teacher can grade the oral speech and the written copy for her objectives, and you can read the speeches afterwards and grade them for your objectives. This is one way to offer a coherent writing program, and a way to begin to gain support from your fellow teachers.

Another challenging point is getting around to reading and grading all the writing pieces. This has always been a challenge for teachers of writing. As explained above, clock editing and staggering due dates are two ways to facilitate the reading and grading.

✎ *What are some benefits to incorporating Writers' Workshop in my classroom?* What students learn about themselves and about reading and writing is the best benefit of Writers' Workshop. In addition, the students produce an amazing variety of styles and writing pieces! Figure 12.11 provides a day-by-day sequence for implementing Writers' Workshop.

ADDITIONAL ACTIVITIES FOR HIGH-QUALITY WRITING INSTRUCTION

Journal Writing. Daily journal writing can be an important part of writing instruction for all students. Journal writing can begin as early as kindergarten, when students may mix drawings with the written word. Many teachers have definite opinions about the role of journal writing. Some believe that journals should be "safe writing," where students have to worry less about mechanics and can concentrate more on self-expression. Some believe that journals, like diaries, should remain confidential. Others see journal writing as part of the curriculum and thus as writing to be graded, like any other piece of work. However, most teachers agree that journals are a terrific way to get to know students and to evaluate their progress in writing.

If you decide to include journal writing, you need to make several decisions:

- Is the journal for personal expression only and not part of a "grade"?
- Who will read the journal? The student only? Parents? Peers? You?
- Will you respond to students' writing? How often? In what format?
- Will students be provided with a daily prompt to generate ideas?
- Will students have the option to respond to a prompt or generate their own ideas?

In addition to journal writing, students can write *learning logs*. Learning logs are reflections about what was learned during content area instruction. Three prompts can be used to structure learning log entries:

- What did I learn today?
- What was confusing to me?
- What would I like to learn more about?

Handwriting and Keyboarding. Although computers are part of our daily lives, legible handwriting is still important for academic success and functioning in today's world. Systematic instruction in printing in the primary grades and cursive writing in the intermediate grades is important. There is some debate about whether handwriting should be taught as a whole-class activity or as part of individual composition activities. If your school or district does not have guidelines for how to organize handwriting instruction, you'll need to have a plan in mind.

Similarly, keyboarding instruction is an important part of computer literacy. Some schools organize keyboarding instruction in computer lab sessions; others leave it up to individual classroom teachers or parents. Systematic instruction in keyboarding during school hours is particularly important for students who do not have access to home computers. The Resources for Assessment and Instruction section of this chapter includes resources for teaching handwriting and keyboarding.

Day 1

Introduction to Writers' Workshop, rules, expected behavior; distribution of folders, set-up of classroom.

Day 2

The writing process, generating ideas, control of topic, end-of-year portfolio, and class anthology.

Days 3–6

Mini-lessons: Choose your mini-lesson based on the needs of your students (topic choice, sentence combining, vibrant verbs, sentence errors).
Writing time: Writing.
Status-of-the-class.
Sharing.

Day 7

Mini-lesson: Listening and responding to one another (maybe using TAG):
<u>T</u>ell what you liked.
<u>A</u>sk questions.
<u>G</u>ive ideas.
Writing time: Writing.
Conferencing: Teacher goes around the class to at least five or six students to see where they are in their writing and to offer guidance. Teacher takes notes on each student, the date, skills used correctly, and skills taught. No more than two or three skills should be taught at any one time.
Status of the class.
Sharing (use TAG).

Day 8

Mini-lesson: Leads and introductions.
Writing time: Writing.
Conferencing: Teacher goes around the class to at least five or six other students. The Day 7 procedure is followed with these other students.
Status of the class.
Sharing: Of leads only.

Days 9–19

Teacher continues like this for a few days, adding mini-lessons as suggested by the conferences (usually on grammar, dialogue, vivid verbs, etc.). About **Day 10**, teacher asks students to pick one piece on one topic that they would like to stick with and take through the writing process. From then onward, they need to work solely on that piece. Some students change again, and that's OK, but they will have more work to do in a shorter period of time. About **Day 15**, students turn toward a final product. For the sake of this example, let's say Day 15 is a Friday.

TEACHER: Boys and girls, a week from today, next Friday, your first writing piece is due. I realize that some of you are still on your first drafts, others are on your third or fourth drafts, and some of you are already conferring with your peers. Yet, by Friday, you must be ready to turn in a final piece. This will require more work from you at home on the writing piece. Your homework is to make time for writing every night, so that you can finalize your piece by Friday. You have this weekend and all of next week until Thursday. *Do not* leave it for Thursday night, or you will not have the final piece you want. You already know that writing takes time; do not procrastinate.

Starting on Monday, **Day 16**, the mini-lessons will be on coming up with a catchy title, conferencing skills (highlighting, say back, pointing), format for a final paper (typing, neatness, cover page, etc.).

Day 20

Clock editing.

FIGURE 12.11. Day-by-day sequence for implementing Writers' Workshop.

Level 2: Supplemental Instruction

Using process writing and a Writers' Workshop approach, you can provide supplemental instruction to all students based on ongoing assessment of individual writing products. The flexibility of Writers' Workshop enables teachers to provide mini-lessons, reteaching, and additional practice as needed in any of the critical areas of the writing process: (1) planning, (2) language, (3) conventions, (4) handwriting/keyboarding, or (5) motivation.

In addition, for students who need supplemental support, you can use many of the same modes of scaffolding reading to scaffold writing. (Think about reading and writing as mirror images.) Some of these modes are as follows:

- *Writing aloud.* The teacher writes something and thinks aloud for students, in order to model the thinking that occurs during the writing process. This strategy is useful at all stages for teaching students how to use a particular type of writing mode.
- *Shared writing.* The students and the teacher write a common piece. Both the students and the teacher do the actual writing. When only the students write the words, even though the teacher has participated in the brainstorming of the writing, this becomes interactive writing.
- *Guided writing.* The students work on their individual pieces of writing. The teacher models, coaches, and serves as editor.
- *Cooperative/collaborative writing.* Two students work as partners on developing a single product. The students take turns writing. Both students contribute to the final product. This is a useful strategy for students who dislike writing.
- *Independent writing.* Students write on their own.

Reading	Writing
Reading aloud	Writing aloud
Shared reading	Shared writing
Guided reading	Guided writing
Cooperative reading	Cooperative/collaborative writing
Independent reading	Independent writing

Level 3: Intensive Support

Just as in reading instruction, adaptations must be made for students with difficulties in writing.

PROVIDE SUPPORT WITH WORD RETRIEVAL AND SPELLING

Students often have ideas about what they want to say, but they lack the vocabulary or they have difficulty with spelling. For such a student, you can provide a *personal word bank or word wall.* Have the student tell you what he or she wants to say, and then write down the words you know the student may have difficulties with. It's always important to provide a print-rich environment; thus utilize word walls and personal word banks in your classroom.

BREAK DOWN A TASK INTO MANAGEABLE UNITS

For students with writing problems or limited attention spans, writing a whole story or essay may be a daunting task. In these cases, have students write parts rather than the whole thing at once (have them write the introduction one day, the body the next, etc.).

Writing takes different amounts of time depending on the genre and the student. If you feel a student needs more time to work on a writing piece, accept the piece in parts as opposed to its entirety. For example, if a completed draft is due Friday, have Tanya turn in the introduction to her piece on Monday. You will have some product to evaluate and on which to begin to base a grade, and you will still be providing Tanya with the time she needs to finish her writing piece.

Scott and Vitale (2003) suggest identifying one or two skill areas at a time and teaching those skills before identifying other areas that need improvement. Scott and Vitale provide students with a *writing wheel*, which is the stages of the writing process on a wheel. The wheel has a cover with a pie slice cut out, so that the student can focus on only one part of the writing process at a time. Using the wheel prevents the student from being overwhelmed by all the steps of the writing process and allows the tasks to be broken into smaller chunks.

RESEARCH BRIEF Accommodations for ELL Students

Wolfersberger (2003) examined what first-language (L1) composing processes and strategies writers with lower-second-language (L2) proficiency transferred to L2 writing. The findings suggested that if L2 writers faced writing tasks that required an L2 proficiency level above that which they possessed, the writers did not transfer L1 strategies to the L2 writing process. According to the author, L2 writers faced with challenging writing tasks need to be taught compensating strategies. Some compensating strategies suggested in the article are (1) breaking writing tasks down into smaller chunks; (2) using L1 during the brainstorming and idea organization stages of the writing process; and (3) recognizing that errors and vagueness in the L2 during the drafting stages are temporary and can be corrected later. For students with lower L2 proficiency, writing instruction needs to be tied to language instruction.

PROVIDE ADDITIONAL RESOURCES

Your classroom will probably be equipped with a dictionary and a thesaurus, but you should perhaps give your struggling writers their own resource copies. Also, provide a writing buddy for each struggling writer. This student should be a more capable writer who can serve to assist in answering some basic questions about punctuation, spelling, and ideas.

PARENT POINTER Family Response Journals

In this day and age, children have a lot more to say, but sometimes few opportunities to share it with family members. Hence family response journals can give children and their families a means to discuss unsaid things in a nonthreatening way. These journals can also be used to develop and maintain communication among a child, a parent, and a teacher (Kyle, McIntyre, Miller, & Moore, 2002). When maintained for an extended period of time, the journal can help children understand new concepts by writing about them. Finally, writing for a purpose and for an authentic audience helps children do their best writing.

PROVIDE FREQUENT FEEDBACK

Provide multiple methods of conveying feedback to a struggling writer. A struggling writer may also be a struggling reader. Thus this student may not be able to make sense of the feedback you are providing, and therefore will not grow as a writer. Having a writing conference with this student and providing the feedback orally with concrete references that tie to writing will be most beneficial. In addition, when providing feedback on the writing pieces, limit the number of skills or areas that you focus on. Giving feedback on too many areas may just confuse and frustrate the student.

PROVIDE GRAPHIC ORGANIZERS

Provide an appropriate graphic organizer (comparison/contrast, problem and solution, time/order sequence, fishbone, cluster or web, Venn diagram, etc.), depending on the type of writing piece the student is working on. For example, for a student writing a story, provide a graphic organizer of story text structure to facilitate idea development and sequential writing skills (see Figure 12.12).

Research has found that students with learning disabilities may lack a story schema (Montague, Maddux, & Dereshiwsky, 1990). Therefore, when asked to write narrative stories, these students will encounter difficulties with the task. A story frame or planner during the prewriting stage can provide necessary support. The story frame you provide for writing can be the same one that you use during reading to analyze the structure of a narrative text. Have a student fill in the characters, parts of the plot, events, and outcomes for the narrative story being planned. Providing this scaffold for the student with a learning disability (or even for an average learner) should assist the student with both understanding the structure of narrative texts and writing narrative stories.

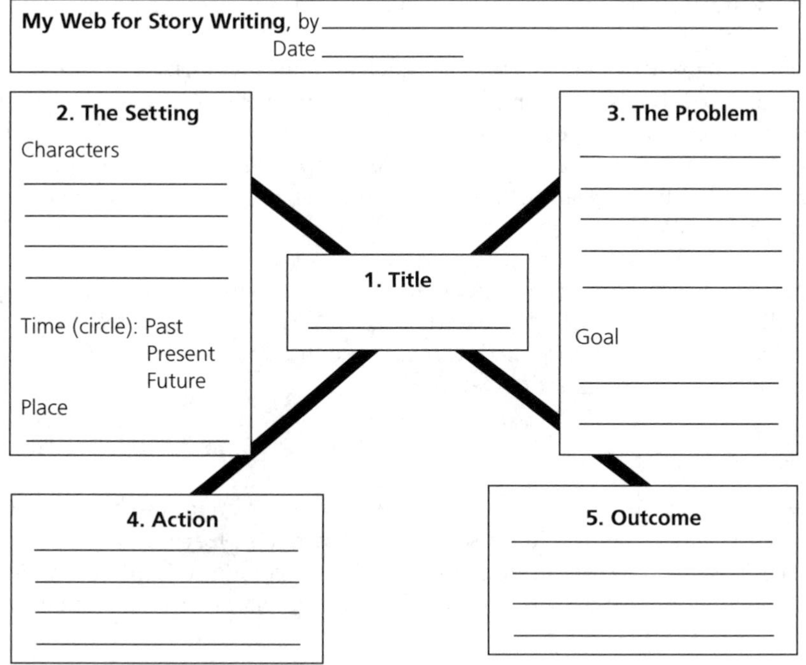

FIGURE 12.12. Story Web. From Zipprich, M. (1995). Teaching web making as a guided planning tool to improve student narrative writing. *Remedial and Special Education*, *16*(1), 3–15, 52. Copyright 1995 by PRO-ED, Inc. Reprinted by permission.

TEACH SPECIFIC STRATEGIES

COPS. Use the COPS mnemonic technique to remind students to check their writing pieces for the following:

C—Capitalization
O—Organization
P—Punctuation and paragraph indentation
S—Spelling and complete sentences

Self-Regulated Strategy Development. Self-regulated strategy development (SRSD) is a six-step process (Mason, Harris, & Graham, 2002). It is effective in improving student performance in writing narrative products. During step 1, the teacher introduces two strategies: *WWW, What = 2, How = 2* and *POW.*

WWW, What = 2, How = 2 is a seven-step planning strategy for writing stories, and the planning questions are as follows:

Who is the main character?
When does the story take place?
Where does the story take place?
What does the main character do or want to do? What do other characters do?
What happens then? What happens with other characters?
How does the story end?
How does the main character feel; how do other characters feel?

The POW strategy prompts students to Pick an idea, Organize notes, and Write and say more.

During step 2 of SRSD, the teacher has each student memorize the strategies. During step 3, the teacher models the complete planning and writing process, making sure to think aloud throughout the steps. The teacher also has the students develop their own personal self-instructions (their own think-aloud steps). Step 4 is collaborative practice, and step 5 is guided practice in SRSD. Step 6 focuses on students' independent writing performance using SRSD.

PLAN. PLAN is a strategy for providing students with support in writing expository pieces (Englert, Raphael, & Anderson, 1989). A PLAN Think Sheet (see Form 12.3) gives students a structure for organizing their thoughts for different expository patterns (e.g., compare/contrast, explanation, etc.).

TEACH SENTENCE COMBINING

Students with language difficulties and differences tend to write in short sentences. One research-based practice for providing scaffolded practice in learning to write more complex sentences is *sentence combining* (Cotton, 2001). Provide students with pairs of simple, related sentences, and have them combine the sentences to form a new one.

PROVIDE ADDITIONAL TIME

Some students may need additional time to complete a written product. Concentrate on fewer assignments, to give students adequate time. In particular, during the revising and editing stage, allow students more time to revise and edit their writing pieces.

PROVIDE ENCOURAGEMENT

Although a student may have a writing problem, you still need to value the student's ideas. This is a very important first step in developing the student's writing ability. Ask your student to read to you what has been written. Much as in a language experience approach, you may even write down what the student is dictating. Begin to work from this point as you would with a beginning or primary writer. Depending on the level of writing difficulty your student has, you may need to encourage your struggling writer to record a few letters that represent his or her message, even if he or she begins by copying your letters. Another idea is to have your student record his or her writing idea on tape, and then work with the student to get that idea on paper.

SNAPSHOT

A Glimpse into My Classroom

The very structure of Writers' Workshop allows the learner to work at an individual level and allows the teacher to work with students as a whole class, in small groups, and individually. For example, mini-lessons can be taught to a whole class. Supplemental lessons can be taught to a small group and to an individual. If my mini-lesson for the day is dialogue, I first teach it to the entire class. All students are to incorporate dialogue into their writing pieces. As I go around and read my students' drafts and examine their use of dialogue, I create a list of students who need me to give the lesson again. For this small group of students, I supplement the initial mini-lesson with another mini-lesson on dialogue, and with more examples and opportunities for practice. I use their writing pieces as authentic examples for the lesson. I may provide worksheets for practice as well. The next day, I review my students' writing pieces. I note which of my students still do not "get it." I then decide if I need another small-group lesson or if individual lessons are needed. If I feel that individual lessons would be best, then I meet with each student individually and work with him or her on the dialogue in the student's writing piece. Whenever possible, I allow my ELLs to use words in their native language in their rough drafts. Eventually, those words or concepts are translated into English, but I don't want to let their limited English proficiency get in the way of their ideas and what they want to say.

FURTHER DEVELOPING STUDENT READING AND WRITING PROFILES

Use Part XII of the Student Reading and Writing Profile (Form 12.4) to record student overall needs in terms of the writing process. In addition, keep several samples of student written products at the beginning and end of the school year to demonstrate progress to parents. As part of each student's writing portfolio, keep weekly and daily accounts of ongoing informal assessment.

CHAPTER SUMMARY

Like the writing process, the teaching of writing is in itself a process—one that may take longer to master than the one year a student is in your class. Yet the earlier writing is taught as a process, the sooner students will master the process. Do not be apprehensive about attempting to teach writing as a process. Begin with one aspect of the writing process at a time; try some of the strategies and techniques offered in this chapter. Then teach the entire process and go through the process with your students. It may take you longer than a year to master teaching writing as a process, but at least you'll have taken the first step.

KEY TERMS AND CONCEPTS

Analytic grading
Clock editing
Cooperative/collaborative writing
Conference time
Direct writing
Drafting
Emulation
Guided writing
Holistic grading
Indirect writing
Individual writing
Loose modeling
Mini-lesson
Modeling
Portfolios
Postwriting
Prewriting
Rewriting
Shared writing
Sharing time
Spinoff modeling
Status of the class
Structural modeling
Style modeling
Writers' Workshop
Writing aloud
Writing conferences
Writing process
Writing time

REFLECTION AND ACTION

1. Pick a stage in the writing process. First, create a whole-class mini-lesson plan for any aspect of the writing craft at that stage. Second, modify your mini-lesson with the purpose of providing supplemental instruction to a small group of students. Third, modify your mini-lesson again with the purpose of providing individualized instruction.
2. Find the writing standards for your state. Pick a grade level. Choose three standards or benchmarks for that grade level. Create a matrix that has the standards; then describe how you plan to teach those standards, and how you would evaluate your students' progress toward attainment of those three standards.
3. Think about the books you use with your students. Create some writing activities your students could do in response to the literature you use in your class. Tailor those writing activities to specific genres you'd like to see as products of the writing task.

READ ON!

Atwell, N. (1998). *In the middle: New understandings about writing, reading, and learning* (2nd ed.). Portsmouth, NH: Heinemann.

More for the middle school teacher, this book provides practical information on teaching both reading and writing.

Calkins, L. M. (1994). *The art of teaching writing.* Portsmouth, NH: Heinemann.

The foundations of the Writers' Workshop are provided in this book.

Fletcher, R., & Portalupi, J. (2001). *Writing workshop: The essential guide.* Portsmouth, NH: Heinemann.

Provides teachers with an overview of the Writers' Workshop, key components, and a systematic approach to getting the workshop up and running in the classroom.

Graves, D. H. (2003). *Writing: Teachers and children at work* (20th anniversary ed.). Portsmouth, NH: Heinemann.

This classic book was written by one of the originators of the process writing movement, Donald Graves.

Hubbard, R. S., & Shorey, V. (2003). Worlds beneath the words: Writing workshop with second language learners. *Language Arts*, *81*(1), 52–61.

This article provides findings that indicate that for ELLs, reading and writing in the primary language must continue for academic concepts and English language to develop.

Kern, D., Andre, W., Schilke, R., Barton, J., & McGuire, M. C. (2003). Less is more: Preparing students for state writing assessments. *The Reading Teacher*, *56*(8), 816–826.

This article's premise is that best practices in writing instruction aligned with state literacy standards will lead to improved writing instruction. The article outlines six basic principles of writing that are highly student-centered. According to the authors, less test preparation and more emphasis on the process of writing will better prepare students for high-stakes assessments.

Olness, R. (2005). *Using literature to enhance writing instruction.* Newark, DE: International Reading Association.

This book helps teachers make explicit connections between literature and writing. It provides specific suggestions for teaching idea organization, voice, fluency, genre, and even editing.

SHARPENING YOUR SKILLS: SUGGESTIONS FOR PROFESSIONAL DEVELOPMENT

1. Consider taking some writing courses or workshops. Look into local and national programs such as the New Jersey Writing Project, Columbia University Teachers College Reading and Writing Project Institute, the Bay Area Writing Project (San Francisco), or the Zelda Glazer Writing Institute (Miami).
2. Practice what you preach. Write as much as you ask your students to write. Keep a journal of your experience as a teacher. Take a risk and send something you've written to a contest or to a publication. Share your writing experience and publication experience (even rejection letters!) with your students.

RESOURCES FOR ASSESSMENT AND INSTRUCTION

Carroll, J. A., & Wilson, E. E. (1993). *Acts of teaching: How to teach writing.* Englewood, CO: Teacher Ideas Press.

Provides a plethora of strategies and techniques to use in teaching writing as a process.

Dahlstrom, L. M. (2000). *Writing down the days: 365 creative journaling ideas for young people.* Minneapolis, MN: Free Spirit.

If you need ideas for keeping journal writing exciting for your students, here's your resource. This book is chock-full of activities to motivate success.

Harris, K., & Graham, S. (1996). *Making the writing process work: Strategies for composition and self-regulation* (2nd ed.). Cambridge, MA: Brookline Books.

This book is an outgrowth of Harris and Graham's research on the writing of students with learning disabilities. It provides cognitive strategy instruction to help students learn to plan and organize their writing assignments. It includes many samples of student writing.

Mavis Beacon Teaches Typing (*www.mavisbeacon.com*).

This software package is highly interactive and provides students with gentle feedback about their keyboarding errors. Students like the jokes, riddles, and rhymes that are included with the sound components of the package.

Read, Write, and Type (*www.readwritetype.com*).

This is a software package that makes links among reading, writing, and typing. It provides specific suggestions for students with learning disabilities and ELLs.

Scott-Simmons, D., Barker, J., & Cherry, N. (2003). Integrating research and story writing. *The Reading Teacher*, *56*(8), 742–745.

This article presents a four-week unit that requires students to conduct research using the Internet and to incorporate the information they find into a creative story of fact and fiction. At the end of the unit, the story is presented to the entire class.

RECOMMENDED WEBSITES

Chateau Meddybemps
www.meddybemps.com/9.700.html

This site provides story starters. Children can create a story and, if capable of doing so, can write it down themselves. If not, an adult can write the story a student creates.

Kent State University
www.kent.k12.wa.us/curriculum/writing

This site offers online resources for teaching writing to both elementary and secondary students.

Kinder Korner
www.kinderkorner.com/starters.html

This site provides story starters for primary grades, but the story starters can be adapted for use by any age group.

National Writing Project
www.writingproject.org

The National Writing Project is committed to improving writing instruction in the United States. Its website features publications and resources related to writing research and instruction, as well as information about programs and summer institutes.

ProTeacher
www.proteacher.com

This site offers writing ideas and even some mini-lessons on writing.

University of Connecticut
www.literacy.uconn.edu/writing.htm

This site is part of the literacy web at the University of Connecticut. It has an annotated list of writing websites for educators.

FORM 12.1. Writer Self-Perception Scale

Writer Self-Perception Scale

Listed below are statements about writing. Please read each statement carefully and circle the letters that show how much you agree or disagree with the statement. Use the following scale:

SA = Strongly Agree
A = Agree
U = Undecided
D = Disagree
SD = Strongly Disagree

Example: I think Batman is the greatest superhero. SA A U D SD

If you are *really* positive that Batman is the greatest, circle SA (Strongly Agree).
If you *think* that Batman is good, but maybe not great, circle A (Agree).
If you can't decide whether or not Batman is the greatest, circle U (Undecided).
If you *think* that Batman is not all that great, circle D (Disagree).
If you are *really* positive that Batman is not the greatest, circle SD (Strongly Disagree).

(OC)	1.	I write better than other kids in my class.	SA A U D SD
(PS)	2.	I like how writing makes me feel inside.	SA A U D SD
(GPR)	3.	Writing is easier for me than it used to be.	SA A U D SD
(OC)	4.	When I write, my organization is better than the other kids in my class.	SA A U D SD
(SF)	5.	People in my family think I am a good writer.	SA A U D SD
(GPR)	6.	I am getting better at writing.	SA A U D SD
(PS)	7.	When I write, I feel calm.	SA A U D SD
(OC)	8.	My writing is more interesting than my classmates' writing.	SA A U D SD
(SF)	9.	My teacher thinks my writing is fine.	SA A U D SD
(SF)	10.	Other kids think I am a good writer.	SA A U D SD
(OC)	11.	My sentences and paragraphs fit together as well as my classmates' sentences and paragraphs.	SA A U D SD
(GPR)	12.	I need less help to write well than I used to.	SA A U D SD
(SF)	13.	People in my family think I write pretty well.	SA A U D SD
(GPR)	14.	I write better now than I could before.	SA A U D SD
(GEN)	15.	I think I am a good writer.	SA A U D SD

(cont.)

(OC)	16. I put my sentences in a better order than the other kids.	SA A U D SD
(GPR)	17. My writing has improved.	SA A U D SD
(GPR)	18. My writing is better than before.	SA A U D SD
(GPR)	19. It's easier to write well now than it used to be.	SA A U D SD
(GPR)	20. The organization of my writing has really improved.	SA A U D SD
(OC)	21. The sentences I use in my writing stick to the topic more than the ones the other kids use.	SA A U D SD
(SPR)	22. The words I use in my writing are better than the words I used before.	SA A U D SD
(OC)	23. I write more often than other kids.	SA A U D SD
(PS)	24. I am relaxed when I write.	SA A U D SD
(SPR)	25. My descriptions are more interesting than before.	SA A U D SD
(OC)	26. The words I use in my writing are better than the ones other kids use.	SA A U D SD
(PS)	27. I feel comfortable when I write.	SA A U D SD
(SF)	28. My teacher thinks I am a good water.	SA A U D SD
(SPR)	29. My sentences stick to the topic better now.	SA A U D SD
(OC)	30. My writing seems to be more clear than my classmates' writing.	SA A U D SD
(SPR)	31. When I write, the sentences and paragraphs fit together better than they used to.	SA A U D SD
(PS)	32. Writing makes me feel good.	SA A U D SD
(SF)	33. I can tell that my teacher thinks my writing is fine.	SA A U D SD
(SPR)	34. The order of my sentences makes better sense now.	SA A U D SD
(PS)	35. I enjoy writing.	SA A U D SD
(SPR)	36. My writing is more clear than it used to be.	SA A U D SD
(SF)	37. My classmates would say I write well.	SA A U D SD
(SPR)	38. I choose the words I use in my writing more carefully now.	SA A U D SD

(cont.)

Writer Self-Perception Scale Scoring Sheet

Student name ______________________________

Teacher ______________________________

Grade ______________ Date ______________

Scoring key:
5 = Strongly Agree (SA)
4 = Agree (A)
3 = Undecided (U)
2 = Disagree (D)
1 = Strongly Disagree (SD)

Scales

General Progress (GPR)	Specific Progress (SPR)	Observational Progress (OC)	Social Feedback (SF)	Physiological States (PS)
3.____	22.____	1.____	5.____	2.____
6.____	25.____	4.____	9.____	7.____
12.____	29.____	8.____	10.____	24.____
14.____	31.____	11.____	13.____	27.____
17.____	34.____	16.____	28.____	32.____
18.____	36.____	21.____	33.____	35.____
19.____	38.____	23.____	37.____	
20.____		26.____		
		30.____		

Raw Scores

____ of 40	____ of 35	____ of 45	____ of 35	____ of 30

Score interpretation	GPR	SPR	OC	SF	PS
High	39+	34+	37+	32+	28+
Average	35	29	20	27	22
Low	30	24	23	22	16

(cont.)

FORM 12.1. *(page 4 of 4)*

Writer Self-Perception Scale: Directions for Administration, Scoring, and Interpretation

The Writer Self-Perception Scale (WSPS) provides an estimate of how children feel about themselves as writers. The scale consists of 38 items that assess self-perception along five dimensions of self-efficacy (General Process, Specific Process, Observational Comparison, Social Feedback and Physiological States). Children are asked to indicate how strongly they agree or disagree with each statement, using a 5-point scale ranging from Strongly Agree (5) to Strongly Disagree (1). The information yielded by this scale can be used to devise ways of enhancing children's self-esteem in writing and, ideally, to increase their motivation for writing. The following directions explain specifically what you are to do.

Administration

To ensure useful results, the children must (a) understand exactly what they are to do, (b) have sufficient time to complete all items, and (c) respond honestly and thoughtfully. Briefly explain to the children that they are being asked to complete a questionnaire about writing. Emphasize that it is not a test and that there are no right or wrong answers. Tell them that they should be as honest as possible because their responses will be confidential. Ask children to fill in their names, grade levels, and classrooms as appropriate. Read the directions aloud and work through the example with the students as a group. Discuss the response options and make sure that all children understand the rating scale before moving on. The children should be instructed to raise their hands to ask questions about any words or ideas that are unfamiliar.

The children should then read each item and circle their response to the statement. They should work at their own pace. Remind the children that they should be sure to respond to all items. When all items are completed, the children should stop, put their pencils down, and wait for further instructions. Care should be taken that children who work more slowly are not disturbed by classmates who have already finished.

Scoring

To score the WSPS, enter the following point values for each response on the WSPS scoring sheet (Strongly Agree = 5, Agree = 4, Undecided = 3, Disagree = 2, Strongly Disagree = 1) for each item number under the appropriate scale. Sum each column to obtain a raw score for each of the five specific scales.

Interpretation

Each scale is interpreted in relation to its total possible score. For example, because the WSPS uses a 5-point scale and the General Progress scale consists of 8 items, the highest total score is 40 (8 × 5 = 40). Therefore, a score that would fall approximately at the average or mean score (35) would indicate that the child's perception of her- or himself as a writer falls in the average range with respect to General Progress. Note that each remaining scale has a different possible maximum raw score (Specific Progress = 35, Observational Comparison = 45, Social Feedback = 35 and Physiological States = 30) and should be interpreted accordingly, using the high, average, and low designations on the scoring sheet.

FORM 12.2. Sample Questions for Editing

Sample Questions for Editing

Sample Questions for First Grade

MOK (Is the meaning OK?)
1. Did I say what I wanted to say?
2. Does it make sense?
3. Are my facts correct?

SOK (Is each sentence OK?)
1. Is there a period or question mark at the end of each sentence?
2. Is the first word capitalized?
3. Does each sentence make sense?

WOK (Is each word OK?)
1. Is each word spelled correctly?
2. Are the names of people capitalized?

NOK (Is the neatness OK?)
1. Are the size and shape of each letter OK?
2. Are words and letters spaced correctly?
3. Are the margins even?
4. Is the heading correct?

Sample Questions for Third Grade

MOK (Is the meaning OK?)
1. Did I say what I wanted to say?
2. Does it make sense?
3. Are my facts correct?

SOK (Is each sentence OK?)
1. Is there a period, question mark, or exclamation point at the end of each sentence?
2. Is the first word capitalized?
3. Does each sentence make sense?
4. Does each sentence express a complete thought?
5. Is the sentence too long or too short?

POK (Is each paragraph OK?)
1. Is each paragraph indented?
2. Are paragraphs made up with sentences related to one topic sentence?

(cont.)

WOK (Is each word OK?)
1. Is each word spelled correctly?
2. Is each word capitalized correctly?
3. Is each word correct the way it is used in the sentence?

NOK (Is the neatness OK?)
1. Are the size and shape of each letter OK?
2. Are words and letters spaced correctly?
3. Are the margins even?
4. Is the heading correct?

Sample Questions for Sixth Grade

MOK (Is the meaning OK?)
1. Are ideas expressed clearly?
2. Are ideas expressed concisely?
3. Are ideas expressed completely?
4. Are ideas expressed correctly?

SOK (Is each sentence OK?)
1. Is there a period, question mark, or exclamation point at the end of each sentence?
2. Is the first word capitalized?
3. Does each sentence make sense?
4. Does each sentence express a complete thought?
5. Is the sentence too long or too short?

POK (Is each paragraph OK?)
1. Is each paragraph indented?
2. Do paragraphs consist of sentences related to one topic sentence?
3. Is each paragraph connected logically with paragraphs that come before and after?

WOK (Is each word OK?)
1. Is each word spelled correctly?
2. Is each word capitalized correctly?
3. Is each word correct the way it is used in the sentence?
4. Are pronoun referents clear?
5. Are any words overused?
6. Is each word the *best* word, or could a more effective synonym be substituted?

NOK (Is the neatness OK?)
1. Are the size, shape, and slant of each letter OK?
2. Are words and letters spaced correctly?
3. Are the margins even?
4. Is the heading correct?

FORM 12.3. PLAN Think Sheet

PLAN Think Sheet

Name ______________________________ Date ____________

Topic: ______________________________

Who: Who am I writing for?

____

____

Why: Why am I writing this?

____

____

What: What do I know? (Brainstorm)

1. ______________________________
2. ______________________________
3. ______________________________
4. ______________________________
5. ______________________________
6. ______________________________
7. ______________________________
8. ______________________________

How: How can I group my ideas?

[ ]	[ ]
______________	______________
______________	______________
[ ]	[ ]
______________	______________
______________	______________

How will I organize my ideas?

_______Comparison/contrast _______Problem/solution

_______ Explanation _______Other

FORM 12.4. Student Reading and Writing Profile (Part XII)

Student Reading and Writing Profile

Part XII: Writing Process

Writing Process

Name of test	Date	Score

Student strengths in writing process ____________________

Student areas for improvement in writing process ____________________

Instructional recommendations ____________________

III

FOCUS ON CONNECTIONS

THIRTEEN

The Digital Connection

An Exploration of Computer-Mediated Reading Instruction

William E. Blanton
Rita M. Menendez

VIGNETTE

In a small, crowded fourth-grade classroom located in the old part of a recently renovated large urban public school, a student sits at one of six personal computers. Surrounding him at five other computers are the other members of his group. These students are intently focused on the computer monitors in front of them, as each one reads along with the text that appears on the screen. Each student is at a different point in the computer-mediated reading program. Some students read along as the text flashes on the screen; others almost simultaneously stand up and shout words into the microphone on the top of the monitor, as the screen gives them cues to record their spelling words. The students are working with a compact disc (CD) from Read 180, a computer-mediated/teacher-mediated program that provides reading instruction to students at their current reading levels, according to scores obtained with the Scholastic Reading Inventory (SRI). The students take the SRI on the computer every nine weeks to monitor their progress.

In another area of the room, the six members of an independent reading group are mostly sprawled on the floor across four beanbags. With four beanbags and six students per group, sharing the reading space can be tricky, but today two of the group's members are opting to do modeled reading with a tape recorder—an alternative to independent reading. The books that students read during independent and modeled reading are aligned with the CD that corresponds to their independent reading level. The Read 180 program also generates a list of books each student can read that accompanies the program. The list may change every nine weeks when students retake the SRI.

The third group of six sits at a medium-sized, kidney-shaped table with the teacher. The students are working in the school-issued language arts practice books. Today's objectives include differentiating between fact and opinion in a reading passage. At this moment the students work independently, although they typically receive teacher-directed instruction during the 20-minute period. Instruction in the fifth-grade textbooks and practice materials is required by the state department of education and local district standards. The teacher has integrated the materials into the Read 180 curriculum, although there is little room for modification in the original structure of the Read 180 program.

While a few of the students described above are labeled as having learning disabilities, the majority are English-language learners (ELLs) who fall below the 25th percentile on a standardized measure of reading achievement. The Read 180 program is used as a special intervention for students who are experiencing difficulty in learning to read. The program is an integrated system that mixes teacher-mediated and computer-mediated reading instruction. In essence, students participate in a rotation of learning activities that include computer-mediated reading instruction aimed at their weaknesses in decoding, word meaning, and comprehension; guided independent reading and reading–listening activities with reading materials on their instructional and independent reading levels; and small-group teacher-mediated instruction.

ANTICIPATION QUESTIONS

- What is a reasonable view for teachers to take on computer-mediated instruction?
- What does the research evidence reveal about the application of computer-mediated instruction to learning how to read? How effective are the computer-mediated reading instruction programs currently being marketed?
- Will just seating a student in front of a computer that provides practice on reading skills be a desirable environment for learning to read?
- How effective is reading instruction organized around educational and computer games on reading instruction?

INTRODUCTION

The focus of beginning reading instruction is generally on the mastery of basic knowledge about reading, such as phonemic awareness, and basic reading skills, such as phonics, vocabulary development, comprehension, and reading fluency. Research indicates that students who do not master these basics during beginning reading instruction fall behind early and rarely catch up with their more successful peers. After third grade, the focus of reading instruction turns to learning by reading and emphasizes the application of reading skill to subject matter texts. Students who enter middle school as poor readers usually begin a pattern of academic failure that persists through secondary school. At the middle school level and beyond, struggling readers are more likely to receive remedial instruction on basic reading skills in pull-out programs (Irvin, 1990). Consequently, struggling readers often participate at the periphery of instruction that focuses on comprehending, interpreting, evaluating, and applying the information obtained by reading subject matter texts.

Providing differential instruction to struggling readers has profound implications for their lives (Allington, 2001; Greenleaf, Jimenez, & Roller, 2002; Kohn, 2000; Kohn & Henkin, 2002; Murphy, 1998). It is important for schools to explore, adopt, and implement alternative reading instruction early and continuously, so that struggling readers can master the knowledge and skills leading to accomplished reading ability. The interventions adopted must engage students with instruction in age-appropriate materials, at their instructional level. Although there is no single method or approach to "fixing" struggling readers (Buly & Valencia, 2002), research findings suggest that their reading ability can be substantially improved through instruction that is organized around computers and educational software. Thus schools are turning to *computer-mediated reading instruction* as an intervention of choice to meet the needs of struggling readers. Unfortunately the programs being adopted generally include extensive drill and practice components (Becker & Anderson, 2000). Therefore, struggling readers are likely to be engaged in pull-out drill and practice, and to continue participating at the periphery of subject matter instruction (Wenglinsky, 1998).

Scenes such as the vignette at the beginning of this chapter are typical moments in the lives of the teacher and students in that classroom. It is becoming more common for schools to turn to the use of computer-mediated instruction as an intervention. There are at least two motivations for this turn. First, the public seems to believe that the computer is a tool of choice to solve many of the teaching–learning problems confronting schools. Second, the social, political, and professional climate created by mandated statewide testing programs, the public grading of schools, and the No Child Left Behind Act (NCLB) are forcing schools to look for innovations.

The purposes of this chapter are to present information on computer-mediated reading instruction, and to provide a discussion of the research evidence demonstrating the effectiveness of computer-mediated reading instruction and learning. The chapter begins with a discussion of computer applications to reading instruction, followed by an overview of research on computer applications in the teaching of reading. The chapter continues with a discussion of *integrated learning systems* (ILSs), as well as research on the effectiveness of ILSs. The last section provides information about application of computer games for reading instruction and related research.

THE APPLICATION OF COMPUTERS TO READING INSTRUCTION

The application of computers to reading instruction has a relatively short history. The earliest published study (Atkinson & Hansen, 1966–1967) arranged for students to access reading lessons on a mainframe computer located at Stanford University. By today's standards, the hardware used was big and bulky. The software presented instructional frames similar to traditional worksheets. However, the results of this "proof of concept" study demonstrated that it was possible for students to learn reading skills through computer-mediated instruction. Desktop and laptop computers, sophisticated software, immediate access to instruction at different levels of difficulty through digital technology, Google.com, Microsoft Word, Windows XP, digital databases, and notes and reference systems were generations away. Today, *computer applications* are used to engage students in an array of computer-mediated reading instruction that ranges from drill and practice to ILSs.

The latest information available indicates that on average, there is approximately one computer for every five students in a U.S. classroom (Cuban, 2001; Market Data Retrieval, 2002). We can expect every student in school to be engaged in some form of computer-mediated reading instruction. This may be aimed at providing students with introductory reading instruction, augmenting the reading instruction of the classroom teacher, providing practice on reading skills, engaging students in remedial reading instruction, or (in some special cases) engaging students with computers to provide cognitive coaching to enhance basic reading processes.

Combining our thinking with that of others (e.g., Becker, Ravitz, & Wong, 1999; Foshay, 2000), we have developed the seven categories below to describe how computer technology is currently applied to reading instruction:

1. *Game applications*, such as Reader Rabbit, Missing Link, and Reading Blaster, are designed to supplement reading instruction or to provide students with practice on specific reading skills. Students learn skills such as phonics, following written directions, and comprehension. Software of this kind is available either off the shelf or from vendors who handle educational software.

2. *Generative applications*, such as Microsoft Word, PowerPoint, Hyperstudio, Kid Pix, and Story Book Weaver, enable students to develop representations of their responses to reading that can be published in their classrooms and shared with parents. Applications of this kind also engage students in cognitively processing information obtained by reading more deeply.

3. *Access applications*, such as Google, Microsoft Explorer, Netscape, and Yahooligans, provide access to information. Students access the Internet to find, read, and evaluate information for the purpose of developing a product—for example, answers to questions raised by a group, a digital story, or an essay. When used in goal-oriented activity, these applications provide students with opportunities to engage in authentic reading tasks.

4. *Tutoring applications*, such as Watch Me Read, act as stand-in teachers to meet the individual needs of students, provide learning assistance, and give immediate feedback. The computer takes over a number of teaching functions and engages students in interactive dialogue to ensure that they understand what they are learning.

5. *Thinking and problem-solving applications*, such as Oregon Trail, SimCity, SimEarth, and Zoombinis Island Odyssey, engage students in learning activity that integrates reading, listening, viewing, writing, and thinking.

6. *Communication applications*, such as email and online discussion spaces, give students opportunities to think about their responses to text and to formulate and communicate their thoughts to others. The key to organizing instruction around these applications is to arrange for students to have a meaningful purpose for communicating with others.

7. *Integrated learning systems* (ILSs), such as the Waterford Early Reading Program, Fast ForWord, and Read 180, are applications that manage multiple components (including computers, software, reading curriculum, and diagnostic information) and learning activities that support both teacher-mediated and computer-mediated reading instruction. Many publishers imply that ILSs are *stand-in* programs that can replace classroom teachers, since ILSs can diagnose instructional needs, prescribe instruction, measure and evaluate the effects of instruction, make necessary adjustments to instruction, generate data for program evaluation, and create reports faster than classroom teachers can (Heuston, 1996).

These applications may also be characterized according to their focus on the scope and sequence of reading instruction and its curricular strands (e.g., phonemic awareness, phonic skills, vocabulary, comprehension, and reading fluency); the instructional approach and learning interactions promoted; the level of student engagement expected; and the amount of professional development that is required of teachers to implement and manage the application.

The scope and sequence of instruction vary widely among applications, depending on the particular reading curriculum to which applications are aligned. For example, many published reading programs emphasize phonemic awareness and vocabulary development during the early stages of reading instruction, while others emphasize phonics and comprehension. Applications aligned with reform publications such as the National Reading Panel (2000a) report, or aligned with different national and statewide assessments, will also emphasize different scopes and sequences.

Applications may also differ in terms of instructional approaches and the kinds of learning interactions they promote. One application may promote students' engagement in independent computer-mediated learning activity, while another promotes group activity organized around the computer. Some applications may target initial instruction in reading skills and support practice, some supplemental reading instruction, and some remedial reading instruction.

The amount of engaged learning time students are expected to spend actively engaged in instruction with an application to attain reading outcomes also varies from one application to another. For example, some applications expect students to be engaged at the computer 15–20 minutes every day. Others expect students to be engaged every other day for 20–30 minutes. Still other applications leave decisions about the amount of engaged learning time to the discretion of the classroom teacher.

Finally, the key to understanding and sustaining effective computer-mediated reading instruction is the provision of sufficient professional development and support to the classroom teacher—and this varies tremendously across applications. Some publishers provide teachers with little more than a scanty manual or a one-shot introduction to the application. Others provide teachers with in-depth professional development and follow-up. Variability in the amount of professional development provided does not appear to be correlated with the knowledge and skill teachers need in order to implement an application.

RESEARCH ON THE APPLICATION OF COMPUTERS TO READING INSTRUCTION

Early research on the application of computers to reading instruction was concerned with answering general questions, such as whether or not computers could be used to teach selected reading skills and how efficacious computers were at measuring reading ability. The early research was followed by research designed to determine the effects of engaging students in more extensive learning with computers (e.g., learning to read and comprehend longer narrative and expository text). With the results of previous research in hand, researchers and developers have turned to designing ILSs consisting of computers and software packages to deliver and manage a complete reading curriculum—including instruction programs; diagnostic and prescriptive instruction; and management, evaluation, and reporting tools that can organize school data to meet the demographic reporting requirements of the NCLB legislation. We discuss ILSs separately later in the chapter. Here, we present a summary of the findings of the general research.

To summarize the general research on applying computers to reading instruction, we first consulted the meta-analyses of research published between 1975 and 2000 designed to determine the effects of computer-mediated reading instruction on the reading development of students (e.g., Blok, Oostdam, Otter, & Overmatt, 2002; Kulik, 1994; Kulik & Kulik, 1991; Murphy et al., 2002; Niemiec & Walberg, 1985; Ouyang, 1993; Ryan, 1991). Next we reviewed selected studies that made the largest contribution to the results of the meta-analyses and that were most relevant to classroom reading instruction. Then we reviewed the published research on the effects of ILSs designed to provide reading instruction. Finally, we read the research exploring the effects of engaging students in playing educational computer games on learning to read.

From the earliest to the most recent meta-analysis of research on computer-mediated reading instruction, the effects that have been obtained are significant. From our reading of the literature, it seems safe to conclude that participation in computer-mediated instruction has a positive effect on prekindergarten through middle school students' learning of basic reading skills and development of thinking skills that are essential to reading comprehension. The research also indicates that computer-mediated instruction increases the reading achievement of low-achieving students, ELLs, and students with learning disabilities. Computers also seem to motivate students to access and read information on topics that increase their general world knowledge.

Based on the individual studies that made significant contributions to the meta-analyses, we believe that the following conclusions are warranted.

- Beginning readers
  - Teaching phonological awareness through computer-mediated instruction has a significant effect on beginning reading achievement (Barker & Torgesen, 1995; Foster, Erickson, Foster, Brinkman, & Torgesen, 1994; Mioduser, Tur-Kaspa, & Leitner, 2000; Mitchell & Fox, 2001; Torgesen & Barker, 1995).
  - Using computer-mediated instruction to provide beginning readers with independent practice on learning reading skills improves their reading performance (Davidson, Coles, Noyes, & Terrell, 1991; Mioduser et al., 2000; Reitsma, 1988).
- Upper elementary and middle school students
  - When compared to traditional reading instruction, computer-mediated reading instruction is beneficial for older students and may yield higher reading gains than traditional reading instruction (Weller, Carpenter, & Holmes, 1998).
- English-language learners
  - Use of multimedia, electronic dictionaries, and electronic glossaries appears to have a significant effect on ELLs' acquisition of word meaning and improves their performance on measures of comprehension (Chun & Plass, 1966; Knight, 1994; Leffa, 1992; Plass, Chun, Mayer, & Leutner, 1998).
- At-risk learners
  - Computer-mediated reading instruction appears has a positive impact on at-risk students' learning of early reading skills, such as phonological awareness, letter naming, and word recognition (Mioduser et al., 2000).

PARENT POINTER ☞ Creating a Home–School Connection via the Internet

An invaluable resource for classroom teachers and parents alike is the home–school connection. The Internet now offers a unique way to link parents with classroom activity through the use of a classroom–home web page. This web page can hold vital information that pertains to regular classroom activities, home learning assignments, suggestions for independent reading, links that can help with current concepts or assignments, and a link to communicate with the classroom teacher.

For more information on how to create a classroom–home web page, visit the following site: A Beginner's Guide to HTML (*www.ncsa.uiuc.edu/General/Internet*).

THE APPLICATION OF INTEGRATED LEARNING SYSTEMS TO READING INSTRUCTION

As we have noted earlier, it is argued that ILSs have the potential to replace classroom teachers. Therefore, we consider it especially important to review research on the effects of ILSs on learning to read. In this section we begin with a brief description of three ILSs to demonstrate how ILSs are used, followed by a listing and brief description of ILSs that market research identifies as widely used in classrooms. Then we provide a matrix of information for comparing ILSs. This is followed by a section summarizing the research on the effectiveness of ILSs to teach reading.

Examples of ILSs

There are two main ways that ILSs are used. When an ILS is *pushed into* a classroom, students do not leave the classroom for instruction; rather, the ILS is embedded in the classroom. The computers may have a variety of educational software loaded onto their hard drives and may be connected to a local network for accessing software and accessing the Internet. Additionally, teachers may have free-standing software that can be installed or used on an as-needed basis throughout the school day. The classroom teacher decides how the computers are integrated into the classroom. In contrast, some schools *pull out* students who go to a special resource room (e.g., a room where ELLs or students with learning disabilities receive special instruction, or a technology lab where large numbers of students can receive reading instruction with computers).

Read 180

Read 180 is an ILS often used to provide reading instruction in grades 3–12. (See Figure 13.1 for an example of how Read 180 can be used in within-class, push-in instruction.) With Read 180, reading instruction is both computer-mediated and teacher-mediated. Students who are usually selected to participate in the program include students with learning disabilities, ELLs, and struggling readers. However, it is important that students who are selected be proficient in phonemic awareness and basic phonics skills.

The Read 180 program allows students to be engaged in two brief whole-group activities with the classroom teacher prior to and after their engagement with computers and with other teacher-mediated activities. Student participation is managed with three small-group rotations that include face-to-face instruction with the teacher, independent reading, modeled reading, and computer instruction. Instruction is based on the Read 180 texts that students read during independent reading or the texts of the local district's reading program. All of the reading materials contain content appropriate to the interest and developmental levels of students. As they enter the program, students take the SRI. Their SRI scores are used by the management system to match their reading levels with leveled texts of the program. Students choose from these texts for their independent reading.

Topical CDs are provided for students to use during computer instruction. The topical CDs provide students with background knowledge through full-motion video before they read text presented by the computer. Next students read and respond to passages based on the video. After viewing the video and reading the passages, students interact with three instructional sections on the CD: Word Zone, Spelling Zone, and Success

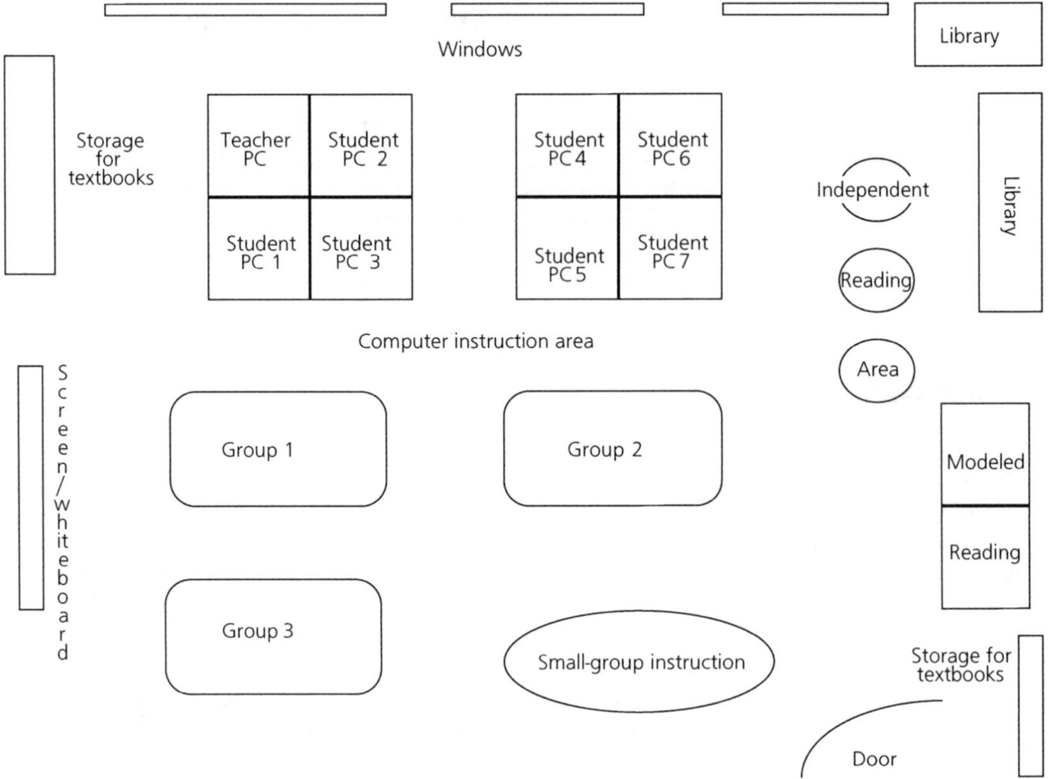

FIGURE 13.1. Example of how a classroom can be set up for Read 180.

Zone. These three components are designed to build students' basic reading skills through using the vocabulary words and comprehension probes based on previously read passage. The Word Zone presents instruction for developing basic decoding skills and the ability to use structural analysis with the vocabulary words from the reading passages. The Spelling Zone provides instruction on the acquisition and transfer of spelling patterns and sounds related to the vocabulary found in the reading passages. Finally, in the Success Zone, students are assessed on word recognition, comprehension, and fluency.

Read 180 management components use a number of measures to obtain information for making instructional decisions. Students take the SRI comprehension test to determine their placement in the program and their readiness to move on to a new level. Quick-Writes, completed by students while reading text, are also used. Informal assessments, students' journals, and home learning assignments are also considered by the teacher in periodic evaluations of student progress.

The Read 180 manual recommends a class size of 15–20 students, who are organized in three small groups for rotations through computer-mediated instruction, teacher-mediated instruction, and independent reading. The Read 180 classroom should be large enough for at least six personal computers and should have a comfortable and spacious area for the classroom library and independent reading. Also needed are a printer, seating in the reading area for six students, tape recorders for modeled reading, and a table that seats six students for small-group instruction with the classroom teacher.

Fast ForWord

Fast ForWord is generally used to provide reading instruction to students who are pulled out for instruction in a technology lab. The lab can vary in size, depending on the school's needs, the number of computers available, and space. (See Figure 13.2 for an example of a lab arranged to use Fast ForWord.) Students who typically participate in this program are those at the prereading level or those who need instruction on basic language skills essential for learning to read, such as phonemic awareness and basic phonics skills.

Students come to the lab daily from their classroom during time allocated for reading and language arts instruction, and spend roughly 90 minutes engaged with language exercises. Along with the lab teacher, the classroom provides support and technical assistance. Students sit at computers, listen to instruction through headphones, and use the computer mouse to interact with the Fast ForWord program. The program adjusts to individual student needs by prescribing specific learning activities. The instructional components emphasize phonological awareness sustained focus and attention, listening comprehension, and language structures.

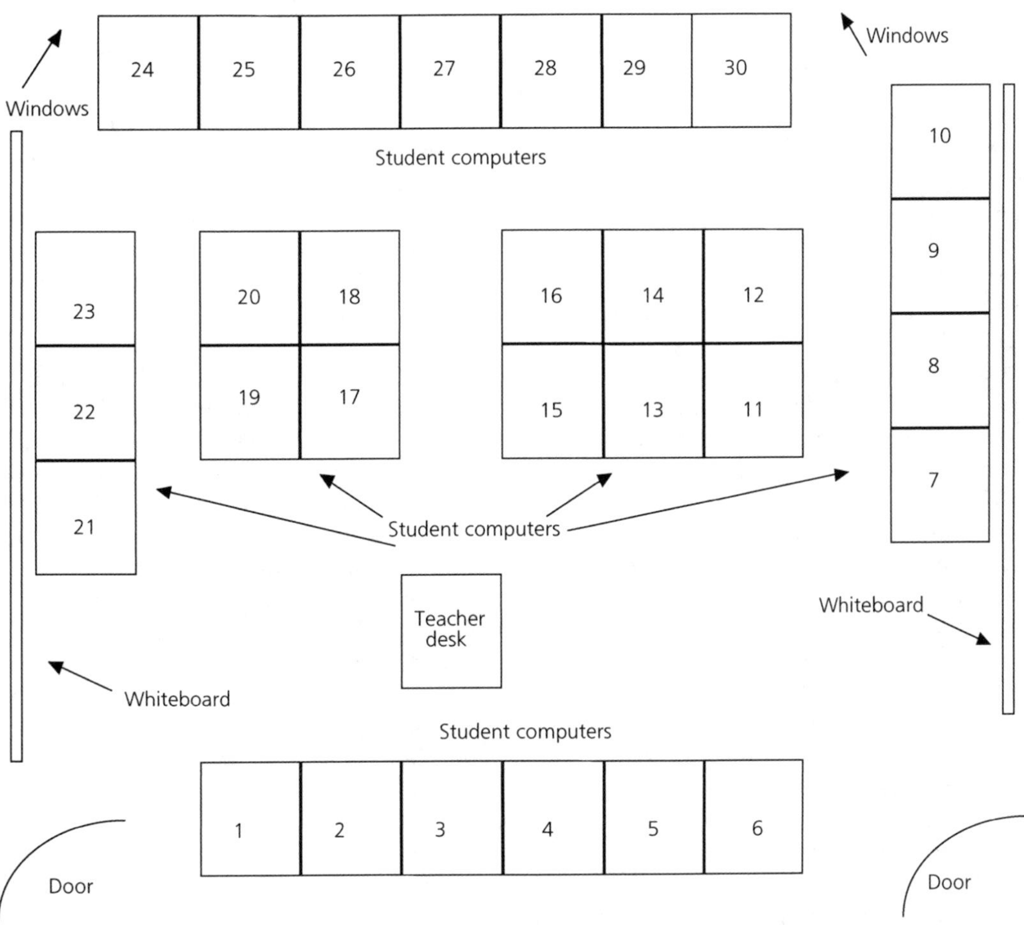

FIGURE 13.2. Example of how a technology laboratory can be set up for Fast ForWord.

Examples of Fast ForWord learning exercises include the following:

- Phonic Words. To improve sound processing and word recognition skills, students listen to pronounced words and identify the word that matches a picture.
- Language Comprehension Builder. Students build language comprehension skills by viewing pictures depicting action and then matching a spoken sentence with the correct picture.
- Circus Sequence. Students engage in exercises designed to increase their ability to differentiate between short tones and to improve the sequencing, sound-processing, and working memory skills crucial for fluent reading.

Students may participate in the program in one of three intensive schedules: 90–100 minutes a day, five days a week, for 4–8 weeks; 75 minutes a day, five days a week, for 6–10 weeks; or 50 minutes a day, five days a week, for 8–12 weeks. Student progress is recorded and analyzed with a management system called the Fast ForWord Progress Tracker, a Web-based monitoring tool that connects directly to the publisher's server; a teacher can access this system at any point in time to determine if any adjustments need to be made to a specific student's instruction.

Waterford Early Reading Program

The Waterford Early Reading Program (WERP) is often used as a push-in program. (See Figure 13.3 for an example of how the WERP can be used for push-in instruction.) The WERP is used for 15–20 minutes per day, one student at a time, to provide supplemental early reading instruction in a regular education classroom. Students have access to a set of 52 related books that they may take home to read. An additional set of the same 52 books is kept at each computer station for students' use. The classroom teacher uses the program to monitor student progress and to generate weekly progress reports that are sent home to parents.

Before beginning the program, each student has a digital picture taken. The pictures are entered into a database, along with names. When it is a student's turn to come to the computer, his or her picture appears on the screen. The student currently at the computer is instructed by the computer to call the next student for his or her instructional time. Students watch computer-animated short stories, play educational games to reinforce reading skills, and print out storybooks and certificates of achievement to share with parents. The content of each book closely resembles the content found within the WERP software program. The books are taken home, and students are encouraged to share them with their families. Each student also receives four educational videos to view at home.

The WERP contains three levels of instruction for emergent, beginning, and fluent readers. The three levels combined provide a minimum of 225 hours of individualized reading instruction. Level One is designed to teach emergent literacy skills. Instruction enables students to become successful readers, regardless of their reading level or primary language. This level concentrates on building emergent skills, such as phonological awareness, automatic letter recognition and sound recognition. In addition, Level One provides (a) practice in mastering basic print concepts; (b) experiences with oral and written language through stories, songs, and rhymes; and (c) expanding vocabulary.

Level Two is designed to increase reading ability by solidifying skills in (a) phonemic awareness; (b) blending letter sounds to make words; (c) decoding word patterns quickly; (d) recognizing sight words automatically; (e) applying comprehension strate-

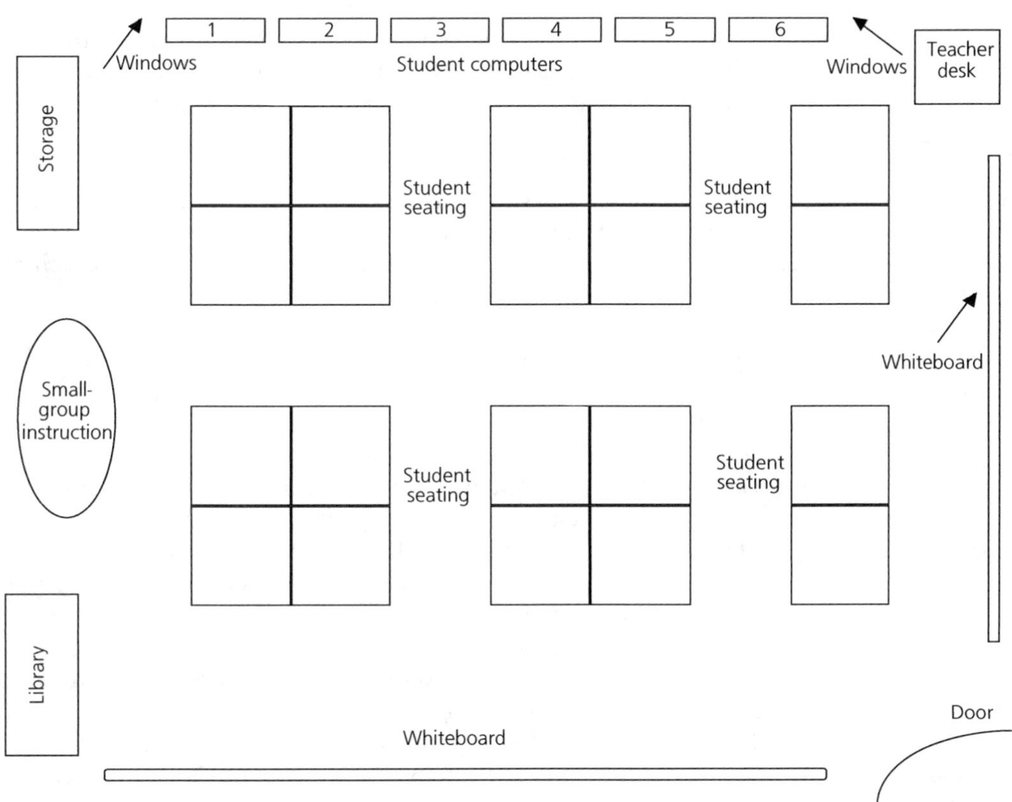

FIGURE 13.3. Example of how the Waterford Early Reading Program (WERP) can be used in class instruction.

gies; (f) reading and listening to a variety of literature and text; (g) expressing ideas in writing; (h) understanding basic grammar, punctuation, and language rules; and (i) expanding vocabulary building.

Level Three is designed to build on the foundation of skills learned in the preceding two levels, leading to full fluency and reading independence. The objectives of this level are for students to gain experience in (a) analyzing word structure and patterns; (b) utilizing a variety of comprehension strategies; (c) extending reading skills to other content areas; (d) understanding the steps in the writing process; (e) understanding grammar, punctuation, and language usage; (f) working with spelling patterns and deciphering sight words accurately; (g) expanding vocabulary; (h) reading aloud fluently and expressively; and (i) using a word processor for writing.

Comparing ILSs

At this writing, the ILSs listed below appear to be the most widely used in U.S. schools:

1. The Academy of Reading is an ILS designed to provide reading instruction to struggling readers by meeting individual needs. It can be used as a supplement to a balanced reading program.

2. Accelerated Reader is an ILS that contains leveled texts coded according to level of reading difficulty. Three different types of assessment provide data on students' reading development, instructional needs, texts read, and performance on assignments based on the leveled texts.

3. Breakthrough to Literacy is an ILS that provides individualized reading instruction to students on phonemic awareness, phonics instruction, and comprehension skills. Students read books accompanying the program as often as they like and can record their retelling of the stories they read. Students also receive instant feedback on their learning. A management system is provided to assist teachers in monitoring student work and progress.

4. DaisyQuest, more a stand-alone program than an ILS, is limited to providing students with instruction and practice in phonemic awareness, blending, segmenting, rhyming, and beginning and ending sounds.

5. Destination Reading is an ILS that provides explicit instruction on phonics and comprehension skills, using fiction and nonfiction texts to create a meaningful context. The management system assists the teacher in determining areas of reading in which students need instruction. The curriculum is aligned with many state standards.

6. Fast ForWord, as described above, is an ILS consisting of a set of computer-based exercises designed to develop oral language, listening, and comprehension skills essential to learning to reading. Students work independently at computers.

7. Headsprout Early Reading is a Web-based online ILS that can be accessed from anywhere with an Internet connection. The program provides instruction on phonemic awareness, phonics, vocabulary, comprehension, and reading fluency. Skills lessons are 30 minutes in length and can be adapted to meet individual needs. Print materials accompanying the program include duplication masters and flashcards.

8. KnowledgeBox is an ILS that utilizes multimedia. The curriculum is aligned to state and national standards. Students have access to hundreds of movies, software activities, Internet links, and print resources.

9. Leaptrack Assessment and Instruction System is an ILS that provides instruction across a broad curriculum. An assessment component gives teachers instant assess to student data for monitoring student progress. Instruction utilizes skill card activities that are assigned to students to meet their individual needs.

10. Little Planet uses anchored instruction by providing a story to develop background knowledge with which to connect instruction and engage students in learning tasks provided by the program. Students can record themselves reading stories and have the opportunity to retell the stories. The teacher has access to a management suite that allows for individualized skills lessons.

11. PLATO Focus is an ILS that uses a combination of teacher-directed lessons, interactive computer-based instruction, and daily practice to teach a total reading curriculum. Accompanying print materials provide further exposure to the skills developed with the computer.

12. Project Listen is an ILS that uses an automated Reading Tutor to assist, instruct, and monitor students. Students can choose texts to read from a list of high-interest stories. The system also uses a speech recognizer to analyze students' oral reading. The Reading Tutor steps in when the reader makes an error, is stuck in the text, clicks for help, or reaches a point in a text that is too difficult to read.

13. Read 180, as described above, is an ILS reading program organized around three phases of instruction that students rotate through. Students spend equal amounts of time engaged in computer-mediated instruction at computers, small-group teacher-

mediated instruction, independent reading, and modeled reading. The program uses a set of videos to provide students with prior knowledge relevant to computer instruction that focuses on decoding skills, vocabulary, and comprehension. The teacher-mediated small-group instruction is used to align ILS instruction with the local reading curriculum and to meet the individual needs of students.

14. Read, Write, & Type! Learning System uses regularly spelled words that follow rules to enable students to establish a strong pattern of letter–sound associations. The system integrates phonemic awareness, phonics, reading, writing, spelling, and keyboarding.

15. SuccessMaker is an ILS that uses literature-based activities that include instruction on phonics, vocabulary, comprehension and writing skills. The program also includes an online portfolio-writing tool.

16. The Watch-Me!-Read program is a speech-recognition reading program designed to help students in grades K–2 develop a strong foundation in reading. When using Watch-Me!-Read, students read aloud from books accompanying the program. Teachers can also scan other texts into the program. In addition, stories composed by students can be scanned and read by students. As students read, they are followed by a computerized "pal" who provides assistance, as needed, throughout a reading session. The "pal" recognizes errors and asks students to repeat words that were misread, reading the words back correctly if needed. The program stores the words that students misread and makes them available for further study and practice. At any time during reading, students can play back what they have just read. Students create multimedia presentations that can be shared with peers and others.

17. The WERP, as described earlier, is an ILS with a three-level design that teaches the five components identified by the National Reading Panel's report on reading. Each level provides one year of instructional activities and a take-home set of books for each student. The length of time students are expected to be engaged with the program is about 15 minutes per day for Level One and 30 minutes per day for Levels Two and Three.

18. WiggleWorks is an ILS that supports instruction with a variety of texts, graphics, speech, and sound. Multimedia are used, and inclusion strategies are also provided.

Table 13.1 presents a matrix of information for making comparisons among the above-listed ILSs. The dimensions we believe to be most important for making comparisons include grade level, reading components, assessment, and amount of research conducted on program effectiveness. As can be seen, the ILSs vary greatly in grade level, reading curriculum, measurement, and research evidence attesting to the effectiveness of each program. Five of the ILSs focus on scope and sequence of all the major reading curriculum strands, such as phonics, vocabulary, comprehension, and fluency. Six focus on early reading instruction. Surprisingly, only seven of the programs have a reasonable amount of evidence obtained through rigorous research attesting to their effectiveness. The research evidence for another eight of the ILSs is limited to research conducted during their development as prototypes, and the remaining two depend on informal school-based evaluation to demonstrate their effectiveness. Many publishers of ILSs post the results of their program evaluations on their home pages; however, one cannot put any confidence in the results of research funded or conducted by companies on their programs. Moreover, research and evaluation published on the Internet have not been peer-reviewed—a significant criterion of scientific research.

TABLE 13.1. Comparing Integrated Learning Systems

Name	Grade level	Reading components[a]	Assessment	Type of research[b]	Publisher	Web address
Academy of Reading	3rd–8th	1, 2, 3, 5	Yes	a	AutoSkill International Inc.	*www.autoskill.com*
Accelerated Reader	K–11th	5	Yes	c	Renaissance Learning, Inc.	*www.renlearn.com*
Breakthrough to Literacy	PreK–1st	1,2, 3, 4, 5	Yes	a	Wright Group/McGraw-Hill	*www.earlyliteracy.com*
DaisyQuest	PreK–K	1, 2	No	c	Metiri Group	*www.metiri.com/Solutions/DaisyQuest.htm*
Destination Reading	PreK–3rd	1, 2, 3, 5	Yes	a	Riverdeep, Inc.	*www.riverdeep.net/products/language_arts/destination_reading_intro.jhtml*
Fast ForWord	K–8th	1, 2, 3	Yes	b	Scientific Learning Corporation	*www.scilearn.com*
Headsprout Early Reading	PreK–2nd	1, 2, 3, 5	Yes	c	Headsprout	*www.headsprout.com*
KnowledgeBox	K–6th	1 ,2, 5	No	a	Pearson Digital Learning	*www.knowledgebox.com*
Leaptrack	K–5th	1, 4, 5	Yes	a	Leapfrog Enterprises, Inc.	*www.leapfrogschoolhouse.com/Products/LeapTrack.asp*
Little Planet	K–1st	1, 2 , 5	Yes	a	Sunburst Technology	*www.sunburst.com/littleplanet/research/index.shtml*
PLATO Focus	K–12th	1, 4	Yes	a	PLATO Learning, Inc.	*www.plato.com/k12/instructional/focus.asp*
Project Listen	2nd–5th	4, 5	No	c	Carnegie-Mellon University	*www-2.cs.cmu.edu/~listen*
Read 180	3rd–6th	3, 4, 5	Yes	b	Scholastic, Inc.	*http://teacher.scholastic.com/read180*
Read, Write, & Type! Learning System	K–5th	1, 2, 3, 4, 5	Yes	c	Talking Fingers, Inc.	*www.readwritetype.com*
SuccessMaker	K–8th	2, 4, 5	Yes	a	NCS Learns	*www.successmaker.com*
Watch Me! Read	PreK–2nd	3, 5	Yes	a	IBM	*www.ibm.com/ibm/ibmgives/grant/education/programs/reinventing/watch.shtml*
Waterford Early Reading Program (WERP)	K–1st	1, 2, 3, 4, 5	Yes	c	Pearson Digital Learning	*www.pearsondigital.com/waterfordearlyreading*
WiggleWorks	K–2nd	2, 5	Yes	c	Scholastic, Inc.	*teacher.scholastic.com/products/wiggleworks/index.htm*

[a] Reading components: 1, phonemic awareness; 2, phonics; 3, fluency; 4, vocabulary; 5, comprehension.
[b] Type of research: a, limited to prototype; b, limited to school evaluation; c, experimental.

TECH TIP Coordinating Computer Learning at Home and School

Many students are now learning about computers outside of school. Unless there is some integration between the subject matter students are learning in school and what they are learning about computers outside of school, schools will have little impact on how students come to value the potentially "good" uses of computers as primary learning tools. The key to solving this problem is to arrange learning activities that make using computers subservient to the task of accomplishing a meaningful learning goal. One way to do this and integrate computer use with subject matter, reading, thinking, and critically analyzing information is through WebQuest searches. To learn what you need to know and how to implement this strategy, visit the WebQuest Page (*http://webquest.sdsu.edu*).

RESEARCH ON INTEGRATED LEARNING SYSTEMS

Research on ILSs is scarce. Research on DaisyQuest (Barker & Torgesen, 1995; Foster et al., 1994; Mioduser et al., 2000; Mitchell & Fox, 2001; Torgesen & Barker, 1995) consistently demonstrates positive effects for beginning reading instruction. The available research on the other programs is very limited, and the results are mixed. For example, one set of studies reports that participation in ILSs such as the WERP and Accelerated Reader significantly improves students' reading performance (e.g., Pavonetti, Brimmer, & Cipelewski, 2003; Peak & Dewalt, 1994; Topping & Paul, 1999); another set of studies reports results indicating that effects can probably be attributed more to the classroom teacher than to the ILS (e.g., Patterson, Jacobs Henry, O'Quin, Ceprano, & Blue, 2003). In other words, the effectiveness of reading instruction provided with ILSs is determined by the knowledge of reading instruction possessed by teachers, their ability to make appropriate use of the technology, and their ability to manage classroom instruction that is organized around an ILS.

THE APPLICATION OF COMPUTER GAMES TO READING INSTRUCTION

Computer technology provides an opportunity for classroom teachers to use a different set of learning principles to supplement their classroom reading instruction with *basic reading activity*, as opposed to instruction in basic reading skills. Basic reading activity is organized around a mix of computer games and board games to enable students to learn skills that are necessary for reading. Students get exposure to and practice with reading skills in the context of meaningful activities, not separately from them. They learn and practice the reading skills needed to accomplish tasks in which they have a personal interest.

In basic reading activity, the reading skills students learn are embedded in and subservient to accomplishing tasks important to accomplishing a personal goal, such as being able to play a computer game as well as it can be played. As an illustration, students enter the activity of playing a reading game with limited reading ability. In the beginning, they may not be able to focus on comprehending written directions, because they must direct their attention to decoding and word meaning. However, while engaging in game play with a more knowledgeable classmate or volunteer, who provides help with both recognizing words and following written directions, students learn how to use word recognition strategies and how to follow written directions in order to have fun or to play the game. In doing so, they come to develop an understanding of the importance of following written directions that goes beyond the level of understanding reached through the completion of worksheet exercises.

The classroom teacher uses a set of core learning principles to orchestrate basic reading activity. Core principles are used in considering the choices available for making instructional decisions. The resulting learning activity goes further than simply providing the procedural steps of learning and following scripted lessons.

Core Principles

We have found the following core principles helpful in organizing basic reading activity arranged around computers and educational games.

1. Two heads are better than one. Human beings learn more through participating in a conversation than they do listening to the same conversation (Clark, 1992). When students engage in collaborative activity around a computer, their level of skill development improves, and they are more likely to transfer the skills learned to new situations (Cassell & Ryokai, 2001; Roschelle, 1991; Strommen, 1993).

2. Writing is important in basic reading activity. Having students formulate and explain what they have learned about reading and the strategies they used contributes to their understanding of what they learn. For example, when students summarize what they learn and how, and place it in a journal, it can help them to "see" their thoughts and make explicit the relations between the key elements of what they know. This helps students uncover elements they thought to be clear that were not, and to formulate explanations that lead to a richer and deeper understanding of what they are learning. Communicating with others about what one is learning affects inferential thinking and thus extends learning.

3. Computer work should be included in the creation of the common knowledge of the classroom. Through discussions with the collective classroom, students should be encouraged to talk about (a) what is important to know about playing a game they played; (b) how they know when they are playing a game well; (c) how they figured out what to do when playing a game; (d) how a game is organized; (e) how a game is like another game they have played; and (f) what they learned about word recognition, word meaning, and comprehension that they did not know before playing a game. When computer work is included as an important topic of classroom discussion, students who engage in it have a share in the collective understanding of practices, such as reading, its purposes, the knowledge and skills used, and why, and the diversity of responses to the reading of text. Thus class discussions of what all students are doing provides an opportunity for all to bring what they are learning to the center of classroom activity, rather than keeping it on the periphery.

4. Basic reading activity depends on a student getting help from a more accomplished peer or volunteer to carry him or her through accomplishing a task with a computer or other tool before being able to carry it out independently.

5. Working cooperatively with others in basic reading activity assures that students will acquire the metalanguage necessary for framing reading tasks, becoming skillful at the self-regulation necessary for reading and studying, and engaging with others in social activity.

Arranging Basic Reading Activity with Computer Games

Arranging basic reading activity around computers and computer games is not difficult. To begin, take a piece of cardboard or corkboard and create a board similar to the board used to play Monopoly. As can be seen in Figure 13.4, divide the board into 10 or so places. Randomly or purposefully put the names of reading games, such as Reading Blaster and Word Muncher, that meet the needs of students; other computer games, such as Tetris and Weltris; and a few board games, such as Othello and Battleship, in each place. Be creative and group games together, or make themed rows of places (such as Phonics Row, Vexing Vocabulary, etc.). Depending on how many games you have available, put four to six games in each place. Label one place on the board as "Begin Here," one as "Move to Any Place," and one as "Go Back Two Places."

Create a Basic Reading Activity Log (see Form 13.1) to keep a record of student progress and to note where students are on the board when their game-playing session ends. Then create a Hints Book and develop sheets for students to enter hints others might use in playing each game; doing so enables students to complete a writing obligation (see Form 13.2). Of course, each teacher will develop a set of rules that students must follow in order for the games to be integrated with other classroom activity. These rules may include (1) procedures for when and who plays a game and for how long; (2) responsibilities of partners or buddies if they are used as helpers; (3) how to consult the Hints Book to find strategies for playing a game; and/or (4) responsibilities for maintaining equipment and record keeping.

Next, and most important, develop a Basic Reading Activity Card (BRAC) (see Figure 13.5 for an example). A BRAC should be available for each game to help students and helpers get started, and to provide necessary information for playing the game. It is designed to encourage students to think about the activity of playing the game, and to bring the game and learning reading skills together. The quality of the BRAC plays a *big* role in how well students learn from playing the games. Each BRAC also provides a writing obligation that must be completed before a student moves on to play the next game. All obligations require reflection; they include writing to others, writing in a personal journal, and putting information in the Hints Book.

A BRAC has three levels. The levels differ in the degree of proficiency required, so that students of various reading levels and degrees of expertise can play and enjoy the games. The levels of the BRAC are as follows:

1. *Beginner level.* During this level, a student should begin to explore the game's variables, tools, and goals. If there is no apparent goal, break the game up into smaller pieces, and identify goals and key concepts.
2. *Good level.* During this level, a student should begin to acquire and test different strategies that may help in increasing skills and knowledge for playing the game.
3. *Expert level.* At this level, a student should be able to demonstrate the strategies required for playing at increasing levels of complexity. Students should also show mastery of the game's rules and concepts, and should be able to communicate their knowledge to others.

As noted earlier, a BRAC also provides a writing obligation that must be completed before a student moves to the next place on the board. The writing task generally involves writing in a personal journal, writing to parents, or putting information in the Hints Book that will help another student play the game. Again, the purpose of the Hints

Place 4	**Place 3**	**Place 2**	**Place 1**	**Begin Here**
Reader Rabbit: 3 Interactive Reading Journey First Phonics	Dr. Quandary Math Munchers Deluxe	Carmen Sandiego: Think Quick Clue Finders 6th	Reading Blaster 6–9 Clue Finders 4th	Carmen Sandiego: Space Reader Rabbit: Math
Place 5 Carmen Sandiego: Time Reader Rabbit: Math Journey Carmen Sandiego: World Magic School Bus: Ocean		Basic Reading Activity Board		**Place 11** Storybook Weaver Reader Rabbit: 2 Magic School Bus: Dinosaurs Reading Blaster
Place 6 Reader Rabbit: 1 Magic School Bus: Explore the Human Body Carmen Sandiego: Word Detective Math Blaster Boogle	**Place 7** Word Munchers Reader Rabbit: 1 Math Mansions Math Blaster Mystery Othello	**Place 8** ***Go Back Two Places or Play These Games*** Super Solvers: Reading Knowledge Munchers Deluxe Math Balster 4th Magic School Bus: Inside the Earth	**Place 9** Dr. Bain: Mind Adventure Ace Detective Reader Rabbit: Reading Library Reader Rabbit: K Mastermind	**Place 10** ***Move to Any Place or Play These Games*** Clue Finders 3rd Magic School Bus: Solar System Number Munchers Troggle Trouble Math

FIGURE 13.4. Basic Reading Activity Board.

SAFARI SEARCH

Safari Search consists of 12 search games. In 6 of the games you search for one animal, and in 6 you search for two animals. The animals hide in a box. Each box contains a clue, which you uncover with a magnifying glass tool. You use the review button to bring up all the clues and help you find the animals. Remember that you only have one chance to catch each animal, and a bunch of chances to gather clues.

As you embark on this safari search, your goal is to find as many animals as you can.

BEGINNER LEVEL

Choose "Intuit the Iguana" from the Game List. Choose different boxes on the grid, using the magnifying glass tool, and try to find the iguana. Keep on clicking on the grids until you "Intuit the Iguana." Use the review tool to show you all of the clues you have gathered. It might help you to write down the clues that show up on the monitor. After you find the iguana, go on and search for the flamingo and the seal. The instructions are very similar. Once you have mastered these games, go on to the Good level and search for the rest of the safari animals. Stop here, and you can stay in this place or move ahead one place.

GOOD LEVEL

At this level, play "Discover the Dragon," "Locate the Loon," "Catch the Kittens," and "Sight the Snails." In "Catch the Kittens" and "Sight the Snails," you have to locate both animals hidden in the grid. Keep a record of how many clues it takes you to find each animal. You can also take turns with your helper and see who can find the animal with the least number of clues. Once you feel comfortable with these games, move on to the Expert level. Stop here, and you can stay in this place, move ahead one place, or move back one place.

EXPERT LEVEL

You made it to the Expert level! Congratulations!!! In this level you will play "Detect the Donkey," "Round up the Rhinos," "Collect the Kangaroos," "Locate the Llamas," and "Capture the Cats." These animals really know how to hide. It will be harder to find them–*read the instructions carefully*! To be an Expert, you have to find all the animals. When you become an expert, you can stay in this place, move ahead two places, or move back two places.

Remember! Write in the Hints Book before moving to your next place to play a game!

FIGURE 13.5. Example of a Basic Reading Activity Card (BRAC).

Book is to create an archive of information on each game played so that other students can access it (see Form 13.2 for an example of a Hints Book page). We have found that students are equally interested in writing in a journal, the Hints Book, or a letter to parents.

The teacher may either assign games for students to play or let students begin at the "Begin Here" place. The determination of which place or places to travel to next, or how long a student stays in a place, is related to the level of mastery attained in playing the current game. The rules can be as follows: Beginner level = stay in the same place, move forward one place, or move backward one place; Good level = stay in the same place, move forward one place, or move backward one place; Expert level = stay in the same place or move to any place on the board. (A classroom teacher may decide to use a different set of rules for levels of game play.) How long a student stays in a place is determined by the level of mastery he or she attains at playing a game.

An accomplished classmate or volunteer is assigned to assist a student in setting goals for playing a game and figuring out strategies to attain higher levels of performance on a game. The Basic Reading Activity Log (see Form 13.1) is used to record each student's progress around the board. Students are encouraged to set the level at which they will learn to play the game. Students move around the board by playing the games in each place on the board and reaching different levels of mastery.

RESEARCH BRIEF Playing: A Way to Improve Literacy Skills

Barab, Thomas, Dodge, Carteaux, and Tuzun (2003) describe a framework of learning that applies Vygotskian principles of learning and development to construct a computer-mediated and multimedia-mediated environment. Through participation in this environment, students engage in inquiry learning that integrates reading, thinking, evaluating information, and writing. Most students do not perceive themselves as doing schoolwork when engaged in this kind of activity.

Quest Atlantis (QA), developed with funds from the National Science Foundation, is a Web-based, community-driven metagame mediated by computers, multimedia, and 3D technologies. It combines elements of education, play, role playing, and adventure to engage students in activities that extend their reading, writing, critical thinking, reflective, and communicative abilities. Students enter QA through a virtual portal and meet the citizens of the lost continent of Atlantis. They learn that Atlantis is facing impending disaster, created by a loss of values and corrupt leadership. The only way that Atlantis can be saved is to rebuild its lost wisdom. The Atlantian Council has created a series of WebQuests that students are invited to complete and help save Atlantis. The completion of each Quest provides a piece of the knowledge Atlantis needs for survival.

To complete a Quest, students must visit a diverse set of World Wide Web sites to access and read information. They must evaluate and synthesize the material they read, write a brief report, and submit it to the Atlantian Council. Among the academic tasks students engage in are conducting environmental studies, researching other cultures, analyzing newspaper articles, calculating frequency distributions, and developing action plans. The Council evaluates the work completed to fulfill a Quest according to a rubric, and students receive points for their work.

Along with its fascinating design, Quest activities meet state and local curriculum standards head on. There are over 500 Quests and seven unit plans students can complete. Students can accumulate points for their Quests and exchange them for trading cards, T-shirts, and comic books. Students can also develop their personal home pages. In addition, there is a protected chat space that students can enter, clothed in the virtual personae they develop, to meet and interact with other QA students from around the world.

The classroom teacher is able to control participation in the QA program through a virtual teacher space. Here the teacher manages student activity online by assigning, monitoring, and evaluating the Quests students complete. With a click of a computer key, the teacher has immediate access to the progress of students. In addition, teachers can work with students to develop portfolios of their activity. The virtual space for teachers also provides a place where teachers can interact with other teachers, along with submitting Quests they develop to the QA program to be shared.

The QA program has been field-tested with students around the world. The evidence to date indicates that it is an effective program for developing literacy skills. The research on QA continues,and revisions are made based on the research results. Take a peek at the program by visiting its website (*www.questatlantis.org*).

RESEARCH ON BASIC READING ACTIVITY ORGANIZED AROUND COMPUTER GAMES

The results of research we have obtained on the effects of playing reading computer games are compelling, even though the educational technology has mainly involved using off-the-shelf computer games and low-tech computers. First, our research has demonstrated that students spend a greater amount of time in learning activity related to basic skills and acquire proficiency in using computers in the process of game play (see Mayer, Schustack, & Blanton, 1999, for an elaborated discussion of findings). Second, when students participating in basic reading activity are compared with their counterparts in control groups, significant effects are found for participation in basic reading activity on measures of near transfer, such as reading, comprehending, and following written directions (Blanton, Menendez, Moorman, & Pacifici, 2003), as well as on statewide measures of reading achievement (Blanton, Moorman, & Hayes, 1998).

TECH TIP Computers and Graphic Organizers

There is an abundance of scientific evidence demonstrating that visual displays and graphic organizers, such as semantic maps, text pattern guides, concept charts, flow charts, and other kinds of diagrams, significantly increase children's learning from text. Unfortunately, many teachers do not have the time or tools to create these aids. Blue-line masters rarely fit the text a teacher wants to use.

If you are such a teacher, explore the software program Inspiration. This program makes the task of creating graphic organizers and displays easy for teachers and is available both for PCs and Macintosh computers. Kidspiration, a spinoff of Inspiration, is available for children to use when making visual displays of information, and helps children develop the same kinds of displays that teachers use. Inspiration can be downloaded and examined during a 30-day free demo period (*www.inspiration.com*). Also read Anderson-Inman and Horney (1996–1997).

CHAPTER SUMMARY

In this chapter, we have discussed a number of approaches to computer-mediated reading instruction, as well as the results of research attesting to their effectiveness. At this writing, most computer-mediated reading instruction is based more on one-shot feasibility studies than on programmatic research exploring a possible scope and sequence for delivering a reading curriculum with computer technology. The body of published research reported fails to meet standards of scientific research (e.g., Shavelson & Towne, 2002). As an illustration, the National Reading Panel (2000a) identified 350 studies on the application of computers to reading instruction. However, the panel found that a scant 21 met the standards of scientific research. The concerns about the quality of research are echoed by other research reviews. For example, other researchers (e.g., Murphy et al., 2002) excluded the majority of studies they selected to review because they failed to meet scientific standards (Blok et al., 2002).

Although research on computer reading instruction has obtained positive results, conclusions should be drawn with caution. The most positive and convincing evidence has been obtained for the application of computer-mediated instruction to the teaching of phonemic awareness, and the application of computers and computer games to create basic reading activities. We lack important information about (1) what effects different computer programs and software have on students' learning when programs are used for different purposes, at different grade levels, and for different students; (2) how to integrate and sustain computer-based reading instruction in classrooms; (3) what the proper mix of teacher-mediated and computer-mediated reading instruction is; (4) how the characteristics of effective programs interact with the characteristics of regular and special-needs students; and (5) how computer-mediated reading instruction should be organized.

Surprisingly, most computer-based reading instruction programs that enter classrooms have barely been field-tested as prototypes. There is virtually no scientific research evidence available on the effectiveness of ILSs on reading achievement, although publishers and their representatives make creative sales pitches claiming that research evidence does exist. As a matter of fact, the What Works Clearinghouse, created with federal funding in 2002, includes virtually no evidence on the effects of ILSs. However, such evidence will be available in 2006, when the findings of a large set of studies are due to be reported.

KEY TERMS AND CONCEPTS

Basic reading activity
Computer application
Computer-mediated reading instruction
Integrated learning system (ILS)
Teacher-mediated reading instruction

REFLECTION AND ACTION

1. Now that you have an overview of computer-mediated instruction and how it can be arranged, stop and think about how you could orchestrate computer-mediated instruction in your own classroom. How might your reading instruction appear to an outsider who is looking into your classroom?
2. Would you rather implement computer-mediated instruction with two or more students around a computer, or individual students engaged with a computer? Why?
3. For what purposes do you think computer-mediated instruction should be used in a classroom (e.g., drill and practice, basic reading activity, introductory instruction)? Why?

READ ON!

Cuban, L. (2001). *Oversold and underused: Computers in the classroom.* Cambridge, MA: Harvard University Press.

Written by an expert in school reform, this book provides a critical look at how computers are used in the classroom.

Gee, J. P. (2003). *What video games have to teach us about learning and literacy.* New York: Paulgrave Macmillan.

Can video games promote learning in a positive and productive way? James Paul Gee examines video games as tools for both academic and ethical learning.

Provenzo, E. F., Brett, A., & McCloskey, G. N. (2005). *Computers, curriculum, and cultural change: An introduction for teachers* (2nd ed.). Mahwah, NJ: Erlbaum.

This book not only provides practical suggestions for using technology to enhance professional development as a teacher, but covers issues related to the use of technology as a catalyst for change in contemporary society.

SHARPENING YOUR SKILLS: SUGGESTIONS FOR PROFESSIONAL DEVELOPMENT

1. Join the Society for Information Technology and Teacher Education (SITE; *www.aace.org/site/default.html*). The SITE is an international association of individual teacher educators who have an interest in the creation and dissemination of knowledge about the use of technology in teacher education and faculty/staff development.
2. Participate in *Reading Online* (*www.readingonline.org*), an online journal of the International Reading Association. Although *Reading Online* is organized with a number of departments that present information, four departments are particularly important to teachers who have an interest in the application of computers to reading instruction. First, the Articles section offers peer-reviewed articles and other writings that often deal with computers and reading. Second, the Electronic Classroom section is a valuable resource for ideas and information about technology and literacy instruction. Next, the New Literacies section is an archive of articles and features on media literacy, critical literacy, digital literacy, visual literacy, and other emerging literacies necessary for central participation in a society. Finally, one may also join the Online Communities listserv for the purpose of exploring topics such as computer-mediated reading instruction with other classroom teachers, researchers, developers, and authors of instructional materials.
3. Take a university course in computer-mediated reading instruction that is applicable to certification renewal, a new certification, or a graduate degree. If such a course is not available in your area, consider a college or university course delivered through distance learning.
4. Another alternative is to take advantage of commercial training such as Scholastic Red (*www.scholasticred.com*). Scholastic Red is a comprehensive professional development website whose purpose is to improve teacher practices and ultimately to raise student achievement in reading. The content targets (a) improving student reading achievement, (b) improving teachers' reading instruction, and (c) using scientific-research-based instruction that is tightly aligned to the NCLB legislation. Available options through the website are online reading courses to develop the reading background of educators, reading workshops on specific strategies for K–1 settings, literacy training for administrative personnel, and customized professional development.

RESOURCES FOR ASSESSMENT AND INSTRUCTION

Grabe, M., & Grabe, C. (2004). *Integrating technology for meaningful learning* (4th ed.). New York: Houghton Mifflin.

This book provides teachers with a comprehensive look at theory and practice in the use of technology. Emphasis is placed on using technology to promote critical thinking.

Leu, D. J., Leu, D. D., & Coiro, J. (2004). *Teaching with the Internet K–12: New literacies for new times* (4th ed.). Norwood, MA: Christopher-Gordon.

This practical guide provides teachers with ways to use the Internet in all subject areas. Chapters on communicating via the Internet and using the Internet to support multicultural education are also included.

Robyler, M. D. (2003). *Integrating educational technology into teaching* (3rd ed.). Upper Saddle River, NJ: Merrill/Prentice Hall.

This teacher-friendly book provides practical suggestions for integrating technology in a wide range of subject areas. It is suitable for teachers with limited technology background, as well for those with more advanced skills.

RECOMMENDED WEBSITES

Websites Supporting Computer-Mediated Literacy Learning

Children's Literature Web Guide
www.ucalgary.ca/~dkbrown

A resource for children's literature on the Internet. It includes discussions about books, pages where authors discuss their books, and links to many related sites.

Cultures of the World
www.ala.org/parentspage/greatsites/people.html#b

This website is the American Library Association's contribution to cyberspace and children everywhere. It provides numerous literacy links and connections to websites that are suitable, educational, and appropriate for children. This website even allows its users to add new links when the pages are in keeping with approved criteria.

K–5 CyberTrail: Multicultural Curriculum Resources
www.wmht.org/trail/explor02.htm

Multicultural resources and links abound on this site. The ability to join an email exchange group is also available. This website provides equal amounts of resources to children and teachers on topics such as African Information for K–12 Education, American History Archive, American Immigration Home Page, Christmas Traditions around the World, Embassy Page, Holocaust Museum, Japan Home Page, Global Village, Native American Information, Rev. Dr. Martin Luther King Jr. Home Page, St. Patrick's Day—Irish Resources, and a Multicultural Pavilion.

Kidlink
www.kidlink.org/english/general/intro.html

Kidlink is a noncommercial, user-owned organization based in Norway and focused on empowering children with free educational programs. Its activities help them collaborate with peers around the world (individually or through classrooms). This website also strives to create social networks that allow users to engage in appropriate social interactions. The Kidlink site has resources for children and teachers alike. According to the information on this site, children from

162 countries have participated since 1990. There exist over 100 public and private virtual conferencing communities. Information is available in over 30 languages. Only enrolled participants can access the private chat areas. Some 500 volunteers in over 50 countries support the Kidlink knowledge network.

Wonderful Tales
www.angelfire.com/ma3/mythology/introduction.html

The creators of this website have attempted to duplicate on the website what the elders of each nation have done throughout the centuries. Explorers of this site will find a collection of various stories from many countries, found in libraries, national archives, museums, and art collections. The website also accepts stories from users who wish to add information about their own home country's myths and folklore.

Search Engines

Ask Jeeves for Kids
www.ajkids.com

A directory and a search engine based on natural language. This means that a child simply types in a question, and Ask Jeeves for Kids finds the best site with the answer.

KidsClick!
http://sunsite.berkeley.edu/KidsClick!

KidsClick! was created by a group of librarians at the Ramapo Catskill (New York) Library System, to address concerns about the role of public libraries in guiding their young users to valuable and age-appropriate websites.

Yahooligans
www.yahooligans.com

Contains an extensive collection of resources for young children. It screens sites for appropriateness and child safety issues.

Software Companies

Name	Telephone	Web address
Broderbund Software, Inc.	1-415-382-4683	*www.broderbund.com*
Davidson & Associates, Inc.	1-800-545-7677	*www.education.com*
Edmark Corporation	1-800-426-0856	*www.edmark.com*
Forest Technologies	1-800-544-3356	*www.foresttech.com*
The Learning Company	1-800-685-6322	*www.learningco.com*
Optimum Resources, Inc.	1-800-327-1473	*www.stickybear.com*
Sunburst Communications	1-800-321-7511	*www.sunburstonline.com*
Tom Snyder Productions	1-800-342-0236	*www.TeachTSP.com*

FORM 13.1. Basic Reading Activity Log

Basic Reading Activity Log

Name:		Classroom:		
Place number	Game played	Level reached	Helper	Notes

FORM 13.2. Hints Book Page for Basic Reading Activity

Hints Book Page

Game: ____

Name of player: ____

What is important to know to play this game well?

How did you figure out how to play this game?

How is this game like another game you have played?

What did you like most about this game?

What did you dislike most about this game?

FOURTEEN

Putting It All Together in Classroom and Resource Settings

Organizational Frameworks for Differentiated Instruction

JEANNE SHAY SCHUMM

VIGNETTE

My journey as a teacher started when I taught sixth grade in the South. At 21 years of age, I had not yet graduated from college (I had one more class to take) and was given a temporary certificate to teach school. I was not a teacher educator, but a religion major. It was a good thing because I needed lots of prayers.

My class was composed of 40 students. The students were all low-achieving, with standardized test scores in reading of stanines 1, 2, and 3. One student was considered to be too old for special education (she was 15), so she was assigned to my class as well. There was no set curriculum for teaching reading and language arts. In addition to the challenges of teaching struggling readers and writers with virtually no training, no professional development, and no curriculum, there were social challenges as well. It was the first year of school desegregation in the district where I taught. Many of my students were children of poverty—children who came to school hungry and tired. Like most first-year teachers, I felt alone and afraid to ask for help.

At the end of the school year, I did some serious self-reflection. My students deserved better. I deserved better. I left teaching temporarily and went on to get professional training as an elementary school teacher and as a reading specialist. The training made a difference for the students I have taught since that very first group. My journey continues now that I am a researcher and teacher educator. All the way along my journey, I have kept my first group of students in mind—they have been my inspiration. All of our students deserve the best education we can possibly provide.

ANTICIPATION QUESTIONS

- What roles and responsibilities do professional educators have in teaching reading in elementary settings?
- How can professionals in the school plan and evaluate schoolwide reading programs?

- What are ways that classroom teachers and resource teachers can communicate and collaborate effectively?
- How can teachers in coteaching arrangements work with each other most effectively?
- How can parents and caregivers become engaged in literacy activities that promote student motivation to read and student achievement?
- How can you get involved in continuous improvement in planning, organizing, and implementing differentiated instruction?

INTRODUCTION

Chapter 1 has described the challenges teachers and administrators face in providing high-quality literacy programs: accountability, changing classrooms, and controversy about how reading should be taught. The chapter also presents five resources for meeting the challenge. Two of those resources, assessment and evidence-based instruction, have been emphasized throughout this book. This chapter focuses on professional networking, parents and students, and self-reflection. The chapter begins with a discussion of professional networking and how teachers can work in an interdisciplinary way to provide optimal instruction. Next, schoolwide and classroom reading programs that involve parents and students are discussed. The chapter ends with a section on self-reflection that includes reflection on how to plan and organize your classroom for differentiated instruction, whether you work in a general education, inclusion, or resource setting.

PROFESSIONAL NETWORKING

In a speech at the White House Conference on Preparing Tomorrow's Teachers, Edward Kame'enui urged the professional community and community at large to move "beyond vulgar dichotomies" (*www.ed.gov/admis/tchrqual/learn/preparingteachersconference/kameenui.html*). By the "vulgar dichotomies," Kame'enui was referring to the "reading wars" (see Chapter 1); he recommended that we look to research to continue learning ways to teach all students. The same "vulgar dichotomies" could apply to the fields of reading, special education, and teaching English to speakers of other languages (TESOL). For the good of research, and of linking research to teacher professional development and to the actual teaching of students, we need to learn from each other's expertise and work together.

All too often, at national, state, district, and school levels, general education teachers, reading specialists, educators of exceptional students, teachers of gifted students, and bilingual educators have worked autonomously. Students have suffered from duplication of efforts, gaps in efforts, and strategy instruction that leaves them more confused than ever. Coherent reading programs demand consistent collaboration among all professionals involved.

Risko and Bromley (2001) describe collaboration as a problem-solving process that is dynamic and involves an ongoing dialogue among key stakeholders as they plan, develop, and evaluate schoolwide reading programs. Clearly, as professionals break out of isolation and work more closely with each other (as well as with parents and community members), the best ways to work together need to be explored. While collaboration and networking are not without pitfalls, the benefits of working with colleagues who have different areas of expertise can result in comprehensive plans that foster success for diverse learners.

Planning and Evaluating Schoolwide Reading and Writing Programs

Even when state and district standards and curricula for reading and writing instruction are well defined, a great deal of planning must still occur for the implementation of successful schoolwide reading programs. The leadership for such planning may be the principal, assistant principal, reading coach, or planning team. Our own experience in working with our university-related *Professional Development Schools*, and in conducting large-scale evaluations of reading programs for the South Florida Annenberg Challenge, have led us to conclude that schoolwide planning is of vital importance.

Over a decade ago, we (Vaughn & Schumm, 1995) developed a set of guidelines for what we termed "responsible inclusion." At the time, few research-based models for the inclusion of students with disabilities existed; many school districts and schools were "shooting from the hip" in meeting mandates for inclusion implementation. Our experience tells us that these principles apply to schoolwide planning for reading and writing programs as well (see Figure 14.1).

To assist schools in self-evaluation of literacy programs and in setting goals for program improvement, Kame'enui and Simmons (2000, 2003) have developed a planning and evaluation tool. The instrument items evaluate most of the components of *responsible reading and writing programs*, including goals, assessment, instructional practices and materials, instructional time, differentiated instruction/grouping, administration/organization/communication, and professional development. The instrument is available online (*www.idea.uoregon.edu.*)

As you can imagine from the tone of this book, we advocate involvement of interdisciplinary teams in the planning of schoolwide programs. We also advocate strong principal involvement, using the administrative guidelines presented in the International Reading Association's (2003) guidelines for reading professionals. The role of the principal as an instructional leader is imperative to school reform efforts (Bessell, Schumm, Lee, Liftin, & Walsh, 2003). In addition, we endorse the genuine and substantive participation of parents and community groups in program planning.

Reading Coaches

Many school districts and individual schools have begun to hire *reading coaches* to coordinate the planning and implementation of schoolwide reading programs (Bean, 2004; Walpole & McKenna, 2004). The roles and responsibilities of reading coaches (sometimes referred to as *literacy coaches*), and the professional preparation they receive for their role, vary considerably. Some coaches work among different schools; others are assigned to work with one particular school. In general, coaches provide professional development in instruction and assessment, and provide leadership in helping teachers implement high-quality reading practices.

The International Reading Association has developed a position statement related to this important role. It defines reading coaching "as a means of providing professional development for teachers in schools" (2003, p. 1). The Association recognizes that the one-shot, "spray and pray" workshops so typical of professional development in education will not work if substantial improvement is going to be made in the quality of reading and writing and instruction. Teachers are often isolated and on their own in the implementation of new practices. The coaches can provide teachers with the scaffolding they need to be successful. Reading coaches can provide support by modeling practices in

Responsible Inclusion

Student first
The first thing is the extent to which the student with disabilities is making academic and/or social progress in the general education classroom. Ongoing assessment, monitoring, and placement consideration are critical to success.

Adequate resources are considered and provided for inclusive classrooms
Personnel understand that for inclusion to be successful, considerable resources, related to both personnel and material, are required to develop and maintain effective inclusive classrooms.

Models are developed and implemented at the school-based level
School site personnel develop inclusive models that are implemented and evaluated to meet the need of students and families in their community.

A continuum of services is maintained
A range of education programs is available to meet the needs of students with learning disabilities. It is not expected that the needs of all students will be met with full-time placement in the general education classroom.

Service delivery model is evaluated on an ongoing basis
The success of the service delivery model is considered and fine-tuned in light of the nature of the students with learning disabilities and with consideration to the extent to which it meets their academic and social needs.

Ongoing professional development
Personnel realize that for teachers and others to be effective at inclusion, ongoing professional development at the school site level is required.

Responsible reading/writing programs

Student first
The first thing is the extent to which each student is making satisfactory academic progress in reading and writing and feels self-confidence as a reader and as a writer. Ongoing assessment, monitoring, and placement consideration are critical to success.

Adequate resources are considered and provided for reading and writing instruction
Personnel understand that for reading and writing instruction to be successful for all learners, considerable resources, related to both personnel and material, are required to develop and maintain high-quality literacy programs.

Models are developed and implemented at the school-based level
School site personnel develop reading and writing models that are implemented and evaluated to meet the needs of students and families in their community.

A continuum of services is maintained
A range of reading/writing services is available to meet the needs of all students. It is not expected that the needs of all students will be met with full-time placement in the general education classroom.

Service delivery model is evaluated on an ongoing basis
The success of the reading/writing program is considered and fine-tuned in the light of the needs of all students and with consideration to the extent to which it meets their academic and social needs.

Ongoing professional development
Personnel realize that for teachers, principals, paraprofessionals, and reading leaders to be effective at reading and writing instruction, ongoing professional development at the school site level is required.

(cont.)

FIGURE 14.1. Parallels between responsible inclusion and responsible reading/writing programs. Adapted by permission of Sage Publications Ltd. from Vaughn, S., and Schumm, J. S. (1995). Responsible inclusion for students with learning disabilities. *Journal of Learning Disabilities*, *28*, 264–270, 290. Copyright 1995 by Sage Publications.

Teachers and other key personnel discuss and develop their own philosophy on inclusion This philosophy on inclusion guides practice at the school and sets a tone of acceptance for all students.	**Teachers and other key personnel discuss and develop their own philosophy on reading and writing instruction** This philosophy on reading and writing instruction guides practice at the school and sets a tone of high expectations and acceptance for all students.
Curricula and instruction that meet the needs of all students are developed and refined Successful inclusion provides for curricula and instructional practices that meet the needs of all students.	**Curricula and instruction that meets the needs of all students are developed and refined** Successful reading and writing instruction provides for curricula and instructional practices that meet the needs of all students.

FIGURE 14.1. *(cont.)*

the classroom, demonstrating how to administer assessments, leading study groups, and developing curricula.

The International Reading Association (2003) recommends that reading coaches have advanced professional development in literacy theory and practice as outlined in its *Standards for Reading Professionals,* and that they have the experience, leadership skills, and presentation skills to coach colleagues. Given that the need for coaches is great and that professional development for coaches may not be readily available, the organization recommends that coaches set personal professional preparation goals and work closely with someone at the district or state level who has such credentials.

Schoolwide Grouping for Reading Instruction

Throughout this book, we have discussed various models of in-class grouping for reading instruction. One of the most fundamental decisions in planning and implementing schoolwide programs is the decision of how to group students for reading instruction. Decisions about student grouping at the schoolwide level have strong implications for the assignment of personnel and for the roles and responsibilities they will play. No one schoolwide reading model has been empirically demonstrated as the most effective in terms of yielding positive student academic and social outcomes (Barr, 1995). Therefore, it is important that careful decisions are made at the school level, based on student population and available resources.

In our travels among schools, we are often amazed at the number of variations created on a few basic models (see Figure 14.2). Obviously, there are pros and cons to each model. The best model is one that best meets the needs of students, parents, and teachers at the local level.

The Classroom–Resource Setting Connection

Many schools have resource or pull-out settings to meet the diverse needs of students. These can include resource settings for students with disabilities, English-language learners (ELLs), or gifted students, as well as Title I programs in reading. Advocates of resource or pull-out programs maintain that the individual needs of students with similar needs can be addressed in an efficient manner. Critics of such programs point out that many are ill coordinated with instruction in general education classrooms, and that valuable instructional time is lost when students move from room to room (Johnston & Allington, 1991; McGill-Franzen, 1994). Obviously, to avoid curricular fragmentation and to maximize instructional time, collaboration is vital.

We have already discussed the importance of well-designed schoolwide programs and grouping patterns. This up-front planning can go a long way toward easing collaboration. However, ongoing communication about curricula and the needs of individual students takes time and energy. Recommendations follow:

- Communicate about logistics in terms of scheduling, efficient movement of students from setting to setting, and monitoring of students during "shifts."
- Monitor procedures for logistics on an ongoing basis, to make sure the system works.
- Find out who is responsible for taking the lead in collaboration among general education and resource teachers.
- Advocate for regular times for classroom–resource planning and communication.
- Hold parent conferences in which both types of professionals are involved.
- Take the opportunity for joint professional development, so that both resource and classroom teachers learn about strategies that can be reinforced from setting to setting.

Coteaching

Coteaching occurs when there are two certified teachers in one classroom. Some refer to coteaching primarily with general education–special education teaching pairs in classrooms that include students with disabilities (e.g., Cook & Friend, 1995). However, coteaching can also apply when a general educator works in the same classroom with a Title I teacher, TESOL specialist, or gifted education teacher. The key is that there are

---

Grade-level grouping—Students are placed in classrooms with students in the same grade. When students are of similar reading levels in the same grade, they are grouped *homogeneously*. When students are of differing reading levels in the same grade, they are grouped *heterogeneously*.

Cross-grade grouping—Students of similar reading level, but different grade levels, are placed in the same classroom during the reading period. This is also known as the *Joplin plan*.

Pull-out programs—Students are pulled out of the general education classroom into resource rooms for regular or supplemental reading instruction. Resource teachers may be reading specialists or special educators.

Inclusion or push-in programs—Students eligible for special services in reading through the Individuals with Disabilities Education Act (IDEA) or Title I are provided support in the general education classroom. Reading specialists or special educators work with the general education teacher to provide regular or supplemental reading instruction.

FIGURE 14.2. Models for schoolwide grouping for reading instruction.

two professionals in the classroom, each of whom is actively engaged in maximizing learning time and ensuring that individual needs of students are being met.

The drawbacks and benefits of coteaching have been debated. Clearly, some teachers would prefer working independently; others enjoy the synergy of planning and teaching with a partner.

RESEARCH BRIEF ✎ The Pros and Cons of Coteaching

To learn more about general and special education teachers' perceptions of coteaching, researchers at the University of Miami conducted surveys and focus group interviews with teachers throughout the state of Florida (Arguelles, Vaughn, & Schumm, 1996; Schumm, Hughes, & Arguelles, 2001). Overall, the teachers' perceptions were positive and reflected their enthusiasm about learning from colleagues with a different perspective and different professional training. General education teachers respected the strategy knowledge of special educators. Special educators recognized the general educators as content specialists. However, participants did register concerns. Lack of planning time was troublesome. Some special educators felt that they were performing as teacher aides rather than as professional teachers. When teachers had well-defined roles and responsibilities, where there was administrative support for planning time, and when teachers made a pact to be "flexible," the coteaching experience was rewarding.

So what do teachers recommend for successful coteaching? First, there must be time for teachers to develop rapport and talk about common expectations. Second, adequate time is necessary for both long-term and daily planning. Third, ongoing communication is vital; some days communication may be via email, but daily conversations are a must. Fourth, coteaching is often like coparenting, and students can "play games" and create wedges. Coteachers must anticipate how they plan to work together to present a united front. Finally, because the real benefit of coteaching is that students have two trained professionals in the classroom, the coteachers should take turns taking the lead so that this message is conveyed to students.

PARENT POINTER ☞ Coteaching: Bringing Parents into the Loop

Parents need to know that coteaching is a joint effort, and that coteachers plan to work collaboratively to help all students do their best. There are several ways to communicate the message:

- Put the names of both teachers at the front door of the classroom.
- Send home joint parent letters.
- Hold joint parent conferences.
- Communicate roles and responsibilities early on, and let parents know when changes are made.
- Be supportive of each other in conversations with parents.

There are several models of coteaching (see Figure 14.3). Sometimes models are determined at the school level; sometimes teachers work out models together. No one "research-based" model has been shown to be most effective. Therefore, it is important to work together to find what seems to work best to improve students' learning and what is feasible for teachers to implement.

One teach, one observe—One teacher manages the instruction of the entire group while the other gathers data on one student, a small group of students, or even the entire class.

One teach, one assist—One teacher manages the instruction of the entire group of students, while the other professional is circulating among the students providing assistance.

Parallel teaching—Two professionals split the group of students in half and simultaneously provide the same instruction.

Station teaching—The teachers divide instruction into two, three, or even more nonsequential components, and each is addressed in a separate area of the room, with each student participating in each station.

Alternative teaching—A teacher pulls aside a small group of students to the side of the room for instruction.

Teaming—Professionals, who have built a strong collaborative relationship and have complementary teaching styles, fluidly share the instructional responsibilities of the entire student group.

FIGURE 14.3. Models of coteaching. From Marilyn Friend and William D. Bursuck, *Including Students with Special Needs: A Practical Guide for Classroom Teachers* (3rd ed.). Published by Allyn and Bacon, Boston, MA. Copyright 2005 by Pearson Education. Reprinted by permission of the publisher.

Partnering with Paraprofessionals, Volunteers, and New Professionals

With so much to be done, most teachers relish having an extra pair of hands in the classroom—even for limited periods of time. Paraprofessionals (paid teacher assistants), volunteers (unpaid adults or students from local high schools or colleges), and new professionals (college students with field experience or student teaching assignments) vary considerably in terms of their own training to teach reading and writing and the time commitments they can make. While some schools offer systematic training for individuals in supporting roles, often it is a teacher who provides that training. Here are some general pointers for working with individuals in supporting roles:

- Be welcoming. The initial meeting sets the tone: You care about your students, you need help, and you are happy to have support.
- Spend time interviewing the individual. Ask why the person is spending time in the schools, what his or her interests are, how much time the person has available, and what strengths he or she can bring to the classroom.
- Explain school guidelines. To protect students, schools have sign-in procedures, require most school visitors to wear name tags, and may require fingerprinting in some cases.
- Arrange for a school tour. It's helpful to become oriented to the physical plant and to understand schedules and routines.
- Decide how best to engage the support person to maximize student learning. While making photocopies may help, there may be some more substantive ways you can involve the person in helping students learn to read and write.
- Provide training. Teachers know their students, know their curriculum, and know their routines. The time spent in training is critical for a coordinated effort.

- Set expectations, but be prepared to troubleshoot when things do not work out. Your students come first.
- Recognize the individual's efforts. Everyone likes to be patted on the back. A kind word from the teacher or thank-you notes from students can go a long way in building morale.

Paraprofessionals and Paid Tutors

Unlike others in supportive roles, *paraprofessionals* are paid. Similarly, many schools pay part-time *tutors* to assist with supplemental instruction. One of the largest programs is the America Reads tutorial program, which provides federal funding for college students to tutor in public schools (see the Research Brief on the Miami Reads Tutorial Program, below). Consequently, there is more leverage for accountability in terms of attendance, responsibilities, and training. Discussions with paraprofessionals and paid tutors indicate that they prefer working in classrooms where expectations are explicit, where roles and responsibilities are clear, and where they are treated with respect. Although paraprofessionals and paid tutors may or may not have college degrees, many of the principles of coteaching apply—particularly in terms of classroom management and in how their role is interpreted to students.

RESEARCH BRIEF The Miami Reads Tutorial Program

In 1996, President Clinton launched the America Reads Challenge. The fundamental purpose of the America Reads Challenge was to hire college work–study students to tutor in high-needs schools. The Miami Reads Tutorial Program was a collaborative effort among Miami–Dade County Public Schools, Miami–Dade College, University of Miami, Florida International University, and Barry University (Young, Bolla, Schumm, Moreyra, & Exley, 2001). Together, the group developed a common curriculum for tutoring and organized systematic training for administrators, teachers, and tutors. Surveys and focus group interviews of key stakeholders involved in the program indicate that the quality of the curricular materials and the rigor of the tutor training were essential to the ongoing success of Miami Reads (Cramer, Schumm, Moreyra, & Young, 2005). Miami Reads provided tutors with a systematic way to supplement ongoing reading programs.

The International Reading Association (2003) has set guidelines for paraprofessionals involved in reading and writing programs. Having another adult in a classroom is an asset too valuable to squander. Paraprofessionals can and should learn how to read aloud to students, monitor students' reading and writing, help students select appropriate books, and assist teachers with assessment and instruction.

It is the administration's and teachers' responsibility to provide professional development and guidance for paraprofessionals. With such professional development, paraprofessionals can work with individual students or small groups of students to provide Level 2 or 3 instruction. The time providing paraprofessionals with basic reading assessment vocabulary, concepts, and procedures is time well spent. Here are some examples.

Marie Jeanne Pierre works as a paraprofessional in three elementary classrooms in a school that has a large Haitian American population. Marie's roles vary from class to class. However, the three teachers have worked together to develop core instructional strategies that are consistent from room to room and have provided Marie with professional development in those strategies. Marie has been trained in how to guide repeated readings of stories and to monitor student fluency in repeated readings. She assists students who need more individual attention in sight words with flashcard sessions. Marie also provides support for teachers during parent conferences when translation is necessary.

Catherine Holt is a retired elementary school teacher. She works as a paraprofessional three mornings a week to assist during the reading/language arts block. Catherine does not want to work with entire classrooms; she no longer wants the responsibility of whole-class management. However, she enjoys working with small groups of students. Catherine and Tabitha Marlow, the classroom teacher, have weekly planning meetings to coordinate small-group instructional time. Catherine also assists during Writers' Workshop. She is assigned 10 students with whom she has conferences about their writing projects.

Volunteers

Volunteers for reading and writing programs can offer their services for one-shot efforts or for sustained, ongoing programs. Volunteers may be parents, grandparents, or other family members of students. Volunteers can also include service–learning groups from high schools or colleges, business partners from local companies, or faith-based groups from the religious community. The plus of volunteers is that caring individuals are there to help; the minus is that their efforts can be fragmented and not focused on the reading and writing mission of the school. We (Radencich, Beers, & Schumm, 1993) recommend that school-based volunteer programs include systematic plans for the enlistment, training, placement, and monitoring of volunteers. Ongoing program evaluation from the perspective of all participants is necessary for program improvement. We also recommend that plans be in place for the recognition of volunteer efforts both large and small.

In many schools, involvement of volunteers has gone beyond making bulletin boards and clerical tasks to more active involvement in working with reading and writing instruction. The blossoming of volunteer tutoring programs in recent years has helped educators get a better idea of what works and what doesn't work. Wasik (1998) examined volunteer tutoring programs throughout one county and developed the following guidelines for high-quality programs: (1) a program coordinator to train and oversee tutors, (2) well-structured lessons, (3) tutors who provide support and scaffolding for students as they learn, and (4) tutors who model reading strategies. Similarly, Elbaum, Vaughn, Hughes, and Moody's (2000) meta-analysis of over 29 studies that involved a tutoring component indicated that tutor training is essential for positive student achievement outcomes.

New Professionals

As part of their professional development, preservice teachers or *teacher candidates* are required to put in a given number of hours in schools. The field placements may be short-term and associated with a particular class, or more long-term with a 10- to 15-week associate teaching or student teaching experience. The support that teachers provide young professionals in the school is an important part of the young persons' growth as teachers; frankly, it can "make or break" their future as educators. However, the needs of K–6 students in the classroom come first. Our work in the University of Miami's Professional Development Schools has helped us understand that there is a great deal you can do as a classroom teacher to simultaneously support new professionals and assure that the instructional needs of students are being met.

In addition to the guidelines for support individuals mentioned earlier, make certain that a teacher candidate is aware of dress code conventions for the school, and that you have procedures set in place for any deviations to the set schedule. If the teacher candidate is sick, explain how you want to be informed (phone, email, etc.). You don't want to be in a position of depending on a college student to teach a lesson and then be left in the lurch. Attendance and professional responsibility are part of every teacher candidate's professional development.

Take the time to explain your reading and writing program. This is a golden opportunity for the teacher candidate to learn from an experienced professional. The more they can learn from you and other teachers in classroom and resource settings how to organize and implement instruction, the more they will bring to their own teaching.

For a short-term assignment, arrange a time to meet with the teacher candidate to find out the nature of his or her assignment. You need to determine the duration of the assignment and what activities the teacher candidate needs to complete (e.g., observations, teaching a small-group lesson, teaching a whole-class lesson). Ask to see any observation forms, and especially preview lesson plans. Your are responsible for what happens in your classroom and need to make certain that lessons are consistent with what you are trying to accomplish.

For long-term placements, teacher candidates may be responsible for overall lesson planning and implementation for a stretch of time. You still need to be very involved, however, to ensure that lessons are consistent with state and local standards as well as with the school and classroom reading and writing program. Work together with the teacher candidate to determine how best to use your individual and combined talents and time. When whole-class instruction was the norm, teacher candidates were required to "take over" the classroom. Now, with the emphasis on coteaching, differentiated instruction, and high-stakes testing, many colleges and universities are more flexible about that requirement. Classroom and resource teachers can take advantage of having another adult in the classroom to work with small groups and individual students in need of assistance. Work with the student candidate and the college supervisor to determine an effective arrangement for all involved—particularly for your students.

PARENTS AND STUDENTS

While much is written about the importance of parent engagement in public education, administrators and teachers often struggle for ways to develop such involvement. Efforts to involve parents can be challenging, but they can be rewarding as well. It is important to be sensitive to family needs, responsibilities, and customs in enlisting family involvement. It is also important to realize that parents may be involved in a variety of ways, depending on their needs and interests. Epstein (1995) has described multiple levels of parent involvement ranging from parenting to school and community activism. Two general areas for parent involvement are special reading programs and home learning.

Special Reading Programs

Motivational Reading Programs

Special programs at the school or classroom level can help students become motivated to read and write, and can communicate to parents the importance of becoming partners in literacy. *Motivational reading programs* cannot take the place of high-quality reading programs, but they can ignite energy and enthusiasm. You've heard about principals sitting on the roof of the school or getting "slimed" when students reach a goal of reading *X* number of books. While this may seem extreme, elementary students get the picture that learning to read and write is important.

When a motivational reading program is being developed at the school or classroom level, administrative support is crucial. School principals can play key roles in setting the programs as a priority, articulating program goals to the school and community at large, and garnering resources for the program. A planning committee is recommended that consists of teachers, parents, and students. Organization is key for program success. Assurances need to be made to make certain that all parents and students have the opportunity to participate and that communication about program activities is clear. Figure 14.4 provides a list of ideas for motivational reading programs. Some examples follow.

To promote motivation to read, Pine Acres Elementary School holds two read-aloud events a year: Parents' and Grandparents' Day, and Community Leaders' Day. The letter of invitation gives each reader the option to bring a book to read or to come to the media center early on the day of the reading to get a book. The letter also provides pointers about effective read-alouds. Adults are dispersed to classrooms, where they spend about 30 minutes reading and discussing the book. The program has spawned an interest in reading aloud at home. Volunteers also return on a regular basis to provide read-aloud support while teachers are working with small groups during instructional reading time.

Each year, the fifth-grade classes at Citrus Elementary School plan a Living Library. The planning committee is composed of the media specialist, fifth-grade teachers, parents, and students. Each fifth grader selects a character from literature, puts together a costume to represent that character, and prepares a one-minute overview of the character and the book. During the day of the Living Library, the fifth graders are placed strategically around the media center, standing like statues. Parents who are "guest librarians" escort groups of students from other grade levels on tours of the Living Library. When the "guest librarians" touch a character, that character comes alive and explains the character and book he or she represents. Because the younger students "look up" to the fifth graders, they are motivated to explore new books. The younger students talk about the books and characters, and start anticipating what character they will be when they are in fifth grade.

In some cases, motivational programs can go beyond the boundaries of one school and reach to an entire school district. One such program, the Dallas Reading Plan (Cooter et al., 1999), encouraged the entire community to become involved in an effort to put all students on grade level by the end of third grade. Using sustained silent reading, summer reading programs, reading backpacks, and availability of a public access cable television channel on which popular Public Broadcasting System (PBS) reading programs were aired, the reading initiative helped children improve their reading skills.

Family Literacy Programs

For most children, their first encounters with print are in the home. The importance of parents, caregivers, and siblings in reading and writing development cannot be underestimated. *Family literacy* has received more and more attention in recent years. The Barbara Bush Literacy Foundation has provided leadership in launching family literacy as a national theme. While no one definition of family literacy is accepted uniformly, in general the International Reading Association discourages "deficit" definitions that define family literacy as only academically related events. In a report of the Association's Commission on Family Literacy, Morrow and Paratore (1993) encourage definitions that

TWENTY SUGGESTIONS FOR SCHOOLWIDE LITERACY ACTIVITIES THAT GIVE EVERYONE A CHANCE TO PARTICIPATE

1. Reading sleepovers.
2. Read-alouds by high-profile community members.
3. Peer or cross-age reading programs.
4. "Write to Your Favorite Author."
5. Character dress-up days.
6. Used book sales or exchange programs.
7. Student book sales or exchange programs.
8. Student book reviews in school newsletter or pockets in school library books.
9. Audiotaping of books for younger children.
10. Reading of student-authored pieces on school television.
11. Book fairs.
12. Family folk tale storytelling "bees."
13. Storybook/author door-decorating activities.
14. Special days (Comic Book Day, Celebrate a Book Day, etc.).
15. "Literacy clubs" that meet before or after school or at lunch.
16. Monthly contests (designing a book, slogan, T-shirt, etc.).
17. Lotteries in which faculty and students earn entries for every book read (Lubell, 1991).
18. Children's or young adults' author of the month.
19. Student-authored section in the school media center.
20. "I Read to the Principal Today" programs, in which children whose names are drawn at random read to the principal and are rewarded with a button or a snapshot on a bulletin board.

BUSINESSES AND NONPROFIT GROUPS THAT SPONSOR LITERACY PROGRAMS

AutoZone
www.autozone.com

Bank of America
www.bankofamerica.com/foundation

Barbara Bush Foundation for Family Literacy
www.barbarabushfoundation.com/nga.html

MS Read-a-Thon
www.ms-readathon.org

Pizza Hut Book-It!
www.bookitprogram.com

Reading Is Fundamental
www.rif.org

Staples Foundation for Learning
www.staplesfoundation.org

Verizon Foundation
http://foundation.verizon.com

FIGURE 14.4. Ideas for motivational reading programs.

"support literacy as part of the fabric of everyday life. This viewpoint suggests that rather than accomplishing academically defined skills and activities, literacy occurs as family members go about their daily lives" (p. 196). More inclusive definitions can help bridge home and school literacy activities and genres (Duke & Purcell-Gates, 2003).

Family literacy programs can occur in home, in school, or at community centers. They can be focused on adults or can take place as intergenerational events. In an examination of successful family literacy programs, Newman, Caperelli, and Kee (1998) found that the programs had several characteristics in common. First, programs engaged the target participants in all aspects of planning, recruitment, and evaluation. The community and context were kept in mind, and the language and culture of target populations were respected (Auerbach, 1989). Second, the needs of participants in terms of transportation, child care, and scheduling were accommodated. Third, adults had opportunities not only to nurture their children's academic needs, but to pursue opportunities for personal and professional growth on their own. Here are two examples.

At Palmer Elementary School, the school's reading leader developed a parent advisory committee for home–school connections. Palmer is located in a high-poverty area in a large urban community and had a history of low parent involvement. The school principal and advisory committee knew that they could do better. The committee decided on topics that would be potentially appealing to parents, and planned once-a-month parent meetings. A parent from the community was hired on an hourly basis as a home–school coordinator and put the committee's decisions into action. Topics have included tips for selecting books, read-aloud pointers, and using recipes to teach reading and measurement skills. Some programs are intergenerational; others provide parallel activities for children and adults. Parents and caregivers can earn "Palmer Dollars" for attending these events and for volunteering in classrooms during the day. Once a year, the school holds a "Palmer Shopping Spree" where parents can exchange Palmer Dollars for small appliances, furniture, and other housewares (some new, some used) donated by local businesses and charitable organizations. As a result, parents have learned some valuable ways to promote reading and writing in the home, and have shared with each other tips and suggestions for improving home learning.

Fairview Elementary School's family literacy program has focused on computer literacy. Through a small grant, Fairview's principal was able to hire a computer technician who repaired and retooled donated computers. Parents could acquire a computer for home use by attending a 12-hour series of training sessions in computer basics and becoming familiar with reading educational software appropriate for their children and installed on the computer. This highly successful program has benefited children, in that they have access to computers in their homes and can spend more time on reading software related to what they are learning in school. Parents have learned new skills that benefit them both at home and on the job.

Home Learning

The area where parents most typically get engaged with the school is with homework—or, as some school districts call it, *home learning*. Harris Cooper (1989), one of the nation's experts in the area of homework and related research, defines homework as "tasks assigned to students by school teachers that are meant to be done during non-school hours" (p. 7). There are various reasons to assign homework in reading and writing:

- To provide independent practice of skills and concepts presented in class.
- To enrich or expand on material learned in class.
- To develop study habits and personal discipline for learning.
- To prepare for tests and class discussions.

Based on his analysis of the research, Cooper endorses homework as having a positive impact on student achievement—under certain conditions. First, there should not be too much homework. For students in grades 1–3, Cooper recommends only one to three assignments that should not take more than 15 minutes to complete. For students in grades 4–6, Cooper recommends two to four assignments that can be completed in 45 minutes or less. The goal of homework should not be to burn parents and students out.

Second, homework needs to be purposeful. The rationale for homework assignments needs to be clearly articulated to students. If the homework is seen as "busy work," student motivation diminishes, along with parental support.

Third, school districts, schools, and individual teachers need to have clear homework policies that are clearly articulated to parents and to students. We (Schumm & Radencich, 1984) recommend that as a classroom teacher, you take a three-pronged approach to developing a homework policy: (1) Explain what you expect of the child, (2) explain what you expect of the parent, and (3) explain what the parent and child can expect of you. Homework Perspectives: A Toolkit for Reflection (*www.goenc.com*) is an excellent website that guides teachers through a reflection process about their own homework policies and procedures.

Micki Ellsworth teaches fourth grade in a school with a large Haitian American population. Micki begins the school year with a parent meeting to explain homework policies. Written guidelines for students, for parents, and for herself are given in English and in Haitian Creole. A translator is present to explain the procedures and to answer parents' questions. Micki develops monthly homework calendars for students to take home. These are translated into Haitian Creole. The calendars take some time and advance planning, but Micki has found that she is able to circumvent many problems.

While Cooper's pointers apply to all students, students with disabilities may need accommodations for homework. Warger (2001) suggests that homework assignments for students with disabilities should consist of activities that they can complete successfully, in a timely way, and with minimal frustration. Students with disabilities may need additional help in organizing themselves to complete their homework. So be prepared to "teach" organizational skills before homework is sent home.

SELF-REFLECTION

Reflection about Your Planning for Differentiated Instruction

Getting the Big Picture

THE PHYSICAL SPACE

When administrators, parents, and students walk into your classroom, the classroom should speak for itself: "Reading and writing are important here." The importance of creating a *print-rich environment* is well documented in the literature (see Morrow, 2001, for a review). However, some teachers get carried away; they place so much print around that it is overwhelming and potentially distracting. Children spend most of their waking hours in the classroom. Creation of physical space that not only is inviting, but also conveys an academic message, is a basic and important part of instructional planning.

Jamie DeFraites is a kindergarten teacher. She inherited a classroom that was chock-full of resources, but not organized the way she would have liked. She enlisted a parent who was an interior decorator to help her take a look at the flow and design of her classroom. Another parent made curtains to carry forward a "primary color" scheme that Jamie used for plastic storage bins and bulletin board backgrounds. Having two additional pairs of eyes helped her to see where she could make changes with minimal cost. The time she spent reflecting by herself and with others resulted in a classroom space that enhanced learning for her kindergartners.

Recognizing the impact of classroom environment on the literacy development of young readers, Wolfersberger, Reutzel, Sudweeks, and Fawson (2004) developed a rating scale to help teachers, administrators, and researchers plan and evaluate literacy classrooms. The Classroom Literacy Environmental Profile (CLEP) went through an extensive development procedure that included a literature review, focus group interviews with teachers, classroom observations, "expert" reviews, and tests for interrater reliability in administering the profile. The 33-item CLEP contains two subscales. The first addresses materials and tools housed in the classroom; the second focuses on the physical arrangement and appeal of classroom organization.

A second instrument, TEX-IN3 (Hoffman, Sailors, Duffy, & Beretvas, 2004), takes the evaluation of classroom literacy environments one step further and makes a link between literacy environment and student outcomes. Developed primarily in Texas (TEX), the instrument has three parts (IN3). The first part involves an inventory of print and nonprint materials included in the physical space of a classroom. The second part is a classroom observation intended to gauge the "richness" of the classroom environment for teaching reading. The third part involves structured interviews with teachers and students to tap their knowledge of literacy materials included in the classrooms and how to use those materials.

Here are some basic dos and don'ts to guide your thinking about the physical space you create for your students' learning.

Do:

- Include a wide variety of reading and writing materials that represent a wide range of student interests and reading levels, and that are sensitive to the cultural backgrounds of students.
- Plan for physical accommodations for students with disabilities or special needs.
- Have flexible space for a variety of groupings.
- Use print to enhance classroom management (e.g., message boards, attendance charts, calendars, daily routines).
- Label objects in the room to help primary children and older students who are learning English.
- Create a reading corner that is both comfortable and well stocked.
- Have a writing center that is well organized and will avoid forcing students to run around for supplies.
- Develop learning centers that are purposeful and designed for independent learning.
- Have a combination of permanent learning centers that are refreshed regularly and ad hoc centers that change throughout the year.
- Get students engaged in planning bulletin boards and displays of student work.

Don't:

- Hang print so high that it is beyond students' eye level.
- Forget to rotate books on display.
- Let clutter build up—get students involved in regular cleanup as part of being classroom citizens.
- Limit yourself to books only—think about a variety of print sources (magazines, menus, newspapers, etc.).
- Neglect to create a workspace for coteachers, paraprofessionals, and volunteers.
- Get carried away to the point that the classroom goes beyond being print-rich and just an eyesore.

IN-CLASS GROUPING

After considering the schoolwide grouping plan, thinking about what adult support you'll have, and conducting initial screening and assessment of your students, you'll need to think about how to group your students for reading instruction. Throughout this book, you have read about a variety of grouping patterns (e.g., peer tutoring, small teacher-led groups, cooperative learning groups). While grouping students at similar skill levels in reading and writing may be necessary at some points, same-ability grouping should be part of an overall plan that includes a variety of grouping formats. In addition, student placement in same-ability groups should be monitored carefully with ongoing assessment and adjusted as necessary.

In-class grouping patterns differ on three dimensions: size, composition, and leadership. These dimensions hold in general education and resource settings. Group size may be whole-group or whole-class, small-group, student pairs, or individual students. Group composition can be *homogeneous* (same) or *heterogeneous* (mixed). The homo- or heterogeneity can be determined by overall reading level, skill needs, interest levels, English-language proficiency, or special needs. In regard to leadership, groups can be teacher-led, support-personnel-led, or student-led. The decisions you make about size, composition, and leadership should be flexible and dependent on your instructional goals and available resources.

"WHAT DO I DO WITH THE REST OF THE CLASS?"

You will have students reading at a variety of levels and therefore needing different levels of assistance. If you need to work with students in small groups or in one-on-one situations, you will have to decide what to do with the rest of the class. Here are some guidelines for facilitating this:

1. Spend time making certain that students are familiar with routines and procedures for activities. Think about Maria Montessori: Before students are allowed to use particular materials or learning centers in the Montessori method, they must be fully trained in their use. This is solid practice. You may want to consider having students earn a "certificate" to use certain materials or centers. The certificate can be suspended or revoked if a center or material is not used properly.
2. Set clear rules and consequences for times when you are engaged with a small group. In particular, discuss your policy for interrupting you while you are teaching a small group.

3. Make certain that activities have an "accountability" component (e.g., written product, checklist, oral report, etc.).
4. If at all possible, plan small-group instructional time when another adult is in the classroom.

Consider the following options for the remainder of your class.

Centers. Students can be divided into small groups where they each work on different tasks. Creating activities that incorporate aspects of a balanced literacy program are best (those that involve reading, writing, grammar, etc.). A few ideas for centers are editing or revising papers, independent reading, spelling and vocabulary games, books on tape, and peer conferences.

Independent Reading. If your students are able to read text independently without your assistance, then it may be useful to give them time for independent reading. Consider it "lab time" to improve fluency or to work on particular areas that need improvement (see Chapter 9).

Final Drafts. If you have a writing workshop as part of your language arts curriculum, then consider having students hold conferences with each other and complete final drafts of writing during this time.

Research. If you are fortunate enough to have access to technology, then having students work in groups to do research may be useful while you are working with individuals. If you do not have access to computers, you can consider other types of research—finding new vocabulary words, adding words to the word wall, word games, or researching an author they might like to read next.

Regardless of what you have the rest of the class doing, the activity should be one that does not require your full attention. Having students continue something you already started with them is much wiser than giving them either a new activity to do or "busy work" (e.g., worksheets).

THE WEEKLY PLAN

For the most part, elementary students respond well to routine. They like predictable schedules so that they can anticipate what's next. Deviations from the schedule can provide a break from time to time, but for the most part, having a weekly plan that is systematic and regular provides a solid framework for learning.

Most school districts plan a 90- to 120-minute daily reading and language arts block. Teachers may or may not have autonomy in terms of how that time is allocated. If you do have that autonomy, here are some questions to guide your reflection in developing the weekly plan. Have you allotted sufficient time for the following:

1. All aspects of the "big five" areas identified by the National Reading Panel?
2. Guided and independent practice in reading?
3. Daily engagement in Writers' Workshop?
4. Self-selected and recreational reading and writing?
5. Reteaching and additional support for students who need assistance?
6. Explaining home learning activities in adequate detail?

Esther Parks teaches first graders. She has 20 students and a part-time paraprofessional, Sara Gibson, for one hour of her reading/language arts block. Esther saves her teacher-led reading group time for when Sara is in the classroom. Sara is responsible for monitoring learning centers while Esther is teaching small groups. Esther and Sara have developed a monitoring checklist that helps her gather information about student behavior during center activities, but also about their instructional needs that Esther can address at a later time. Esther's schedule can be found in Figure 14.5.

Becky Randall and Eric Sanchez coteach in a fourth-grade classroom in a Title I school. Eric (the Title I reading specialist) is in Becky's classroom during the 120-minute reading and language arts block. At the beginning of the school year, they developed the weekly plan shown in Figure 14.6. While some minor tweaking was necessary, for the most part the schedule has held up. As Becky put it, "The time we spent up front in developing our weekly plan was worth it. We drafted an initial plan after we had spent the first two weeks giving informal reading inventories. We really critiqued our plan trying to anticipate pitfalls."

The Lesson Plan

Planning individual lessons for differentiated instruction requires a high level of professional expertise. It requires teachers to pull together all they know about individual student needs, the classroom climate, instructional practices, and assessment. To assist teachers in this complex task, we (Schumm, Vaughn, & Leavell, 1994) developed the *Planning Pyramid*. Initially developed for planning multilevel content area lessons in science and social studies, the Pyramid can be used to plan reading and writing lessons as well. It can also be used for collaborative lesson planning in coteaching situations (Schumm, Vaughn, & Harris, 1997).

The Planning Pyramid is based on the basic premise that all students can learn. However, not all students will learn at the same rate, nor do all students bring the same prior knowledge and skills to the table. In planning a lesson, teachers need to examine the content and to decide what are the essential skills or concepts that all children should learn. These critical concepts should be taught, and appropriate accommodations should be made for individual students or groups of students if necessary (see Figure 14.7). The base of the Pyramid is what all students will learn. The middle portion of the Pyramid extends learning to broaden and extend the base concepts; it represents skills and concepts that most students will learn. Finally, the top of the Pyramid includes information that some, but not all, students will learn. This represents more detailed or complex information that some children will be more ready to learn than others. We encourage teachers not to "lock" students into levels, but to think about individual student needs on a lesson-by-lesson basis.

The Planning Pyramid has gone through multiple phases of refinement. The Lesson Plan form (Form 14.1) is designed specifically for reading lessons, and the rubric presented in Table 14.1 facilitates development of and reflection on a plan. Both the form and the rubric begin with reference to local of state standards and objectives. Agenda and procedures for the teacher and student before, during, and after reading come next. The form also includes spaces to identify instructional strategies, evaluation/assessment, resources (including technological resources), home learning, and reflection. A space for identifying accommodations for students with disabilities or ELL students is included as well (again, Figure 14.7 lists possible adaptations). A sample lesson plan for teaching how to use research tools is presented in Figure 14.8. While it is not likely that such a

Time	Focus	Monday	Tuesday	Wednesday	Thursday	Friday
9–9:30 A.M.	Whole-class activities	Journal writing Teacher read-aloud	Making words	Journal writing Teacher read-aloud	Making words	Journal writing Teacher read-aloud
9:30–9:50 A.M.	Center activities	**Group A** Teacher-led guided reading of basal reader **Group B** Reading center **Group C** Writing center **Group D** Computer center	**Group C** Teacher-led guided reading of basal reader **Group A** Basal reader follow-up activities **Group B** Reading center **Group D** Writing center	**Group A** Teacher-led guided reading of basal reader **Group B** Reading center **Group C** Writing center **Group D** Computer center	**Group C** Teacher-led guided reading of basal readers **Group A** Basal reader follow-up activities **Group B** Reading center **Group D** Writing center	Open centers Reteaching of basal reading objectives—pull individuals or small groups as needed
9:50–10:10 A.M.	Center activities	**Group B** Teacher-led guided reading of basal reader **Group A** Basal reader follow-up activities **Group C** Reading center **Group D** Writing center	**Group D** Teacher-led guided reading of basal reader **Group C** Basal reader follow-up activities **Group B** Writing center **Group A** Computer center	**Group B** Teacher-led guided reading of basal reader **Group A** Basal reader follow-up activities **Group C** Reading center **Group D** Writing center	**Group D** Teacher-led guided reading of basal reader **Group C** Basal reader follow-up activities **Group B** Writing center **Group A** Computer center	Open centers Reteaching of basal reading objectives—pull individual or small groups as needed
10:10–10:30 A.M.	Center activities	**Group B** Basal reader follow-up activities **Group D** Teacher-led phonological awareness **Group A** Writing center **Group C** Computer center	**Group D** Basal reader follow-up activities **Group C** Teacher-led phonological awareness **Group A** Reading center **Group B** Computer center	**Group B** Basal reader follow-up activities **Group D** Teacher-led phonological awareness **Group A** Writing center **Group C** Computer center	**Group D** Basal reader follow-up activities **Group C** Teacher-led phonological awareness **Group A** Reading center **Group B** Computer center	Open centers Reteaching of phonological awareness objectives—pull individual or small groups as needed
10:30–11:00 A.M.	Whole-class activities	Introduce spelling words	Language arts mini-lesson and follow-up activities	Spelling mini-lesson	Language arts mini-lesson and follow-up activities	Spelling test Language arts test

FIGURE 14.5. Esther Park's weekly schedule for her first-grade reading/language arts block.

Monday		
Whole class	9:00–9:30 A.M.	Journal writing Classwide peer tutoring
Reading groups	9:30–10:00 A.M.	Introduction to spelling and basal vocabulary words
	10:00–10:15 A.M.	Discussion: Making predictions about basal story
	10:15–11:00 A.M.	Teacher-directed reading of basal story
Tuesday		
Whole class	9:00–9:30 A.M.	Journal writing Self-selected reading
	9:30–10:00 A.M.	Silent reading of basal story
Reading groups	10:00–10:30 A.M.	Discussion of basal story Group activity related to story
Centers	10:30–11:00 A.M.	Activities providing applications and practice of spelling, vocabulary, and grammar skill of the week
Wednesday		
Whole class	9:00–9:30 A.M.	Journal writing Classwide peer tutoring
Reading groups	9:30–10:00 A.M.	Continued discussion of basal story
	10:00–10:30 A.M.	Teacher-directed grammar skill lesson
Literature circle	10:30–11:00 A.M.	Heterogeneous groups of students discuss trade book selected for whole class
Thursday		
Whole class	9:00–9:30 A.M.	Completion of unfinished workbook questions Self-selected reading
	9:30–10:00 A.M.	Discussion on completed workbook questions
Small groups	10:00–11:00 A.M.	Review grammar skill and basal story
Centers	10:00–11:00 A.M.	Writing centers: Prompts provided related to basal story
Friday		
Whole group	9:00–9:30 A.M.	Classwide peer tutoring Study for spelling test
	9:30–10:15 A.M.	Spelling test Basal comprehension test
Reading groups	10:15–10:30 A.M.	Reteaching skills in small groups
Literature circle	10:30–11:00 A.M.	Heterogeneous groups of students discuss trade book selected for whole class
Centers	10:15–11:00 A.M.	Retelling of story through dramatic play, different art forms, etc.

FIGURE 14.6. Becky Randall and Eric Sanchez's weekly schedule. (Becky and Eric each work with one reading group. There are 22 students in the class. Becky has 15 students; Eric has 7 students who are reading below grade level.)

detailed form will be used for every lesson, we have found the Lesson Plan form to be helpful for beginning teachers and teachers new to planning for differentiated instruction.

The Individual Plan

THE INDIVIDUALIZED EDUCATIONAL PROGRAM

Federal law (IDEA) requires an *individualized education program* (IEP) for all students who receive special education services. While the format for an IEP differs from state to state (and even among districts within states), several components of the IEP are common and indeed mandated by law. These components include current levels of student performance, measurable short-term and long-term goals, and plans for the student's interaction with general education peers (Bos & Vaughn, 2002). Special and general education

Lesson plan code	**Adaptation**
E1	Centers for active listening
E2	Audiotapes and dialogues
E3	Visual aids
E4	Hands-on activities (experiments, etc.)
E5	Computer programs and the Internet
E6	Peer teacher or student tutors
E7	After-school homework buddy system
E8	Peer tutor
E9	Cooperative learning groups
E10	Simplified worksheets for ELL students
E11	Simplify grammatical structures–avoid long words; use familiar words, short sentences
E12	Evaluate constantly, ask questions, observe students
E13	Incorporate prompts, cues, facial expressions, body language, and concrete objects
E14	Give short, concise directions, one step at a time
E15	Teach essential vocabulary and provide a word bank
E16	Reinforce language learning along with content
E17	Check for meaning–make sure students know what is expected of them
E18	Use clear, simple vocabulary
E19	Clarify multiple-meaning words as they appear in the text
E20	Go over vocabulary before the lesson
E21	Encourage ELL student to use English

FIGURE 14.7. Possible adaptations to a lesson plan (insert codes in section for adaptation strategies at lower right of Form 14.1). Adapted from the work of Jeanne Bergeron by permission.

TABLE 14.1. Lesson Plan Rubric

Elements	1 point	1 point	1 point	1 point	1 point	1 point	Total
Learning goals	Consistent with state and local standards	Stated in terms of learning outcomes rather than activity	Broad statements of long-range learning outcomes	Reflect learning outcomes of total plan rather than specific lessons	Attainable within the given time frame	Based on learners' mastery of learning objectives	
Lesson objectives	Referenced to goals	Clear statements of specific and observable learner outcomes	Logical sequence	Evidence of mastery by learners so as to accomplish broader goals	Sufficient variety of objectives to accommodate individual differences (Pyramid)	Adaptations for linguistically diverse students are provided	
In-class activities: Agenda and procedures	Include combinations of teacher-directed and teacher-assisted activities	Include a variety of teaching methods, instructional strategies, learning tasks, and grouping structures	Provide learners with multiple opportunities to engage in activities that reflect lesson objectives	Reflect a logical order of teaching and learning, including methods for identifying students' prior knowledge	Enable the development of thinking skills among all learners	Supplemental activities are planned as needed	
Time frame	Consideration is given to the amount of time expected for each activity implemented	Estimate time to be spent on teaching/learning tasks and grouping structures	Amount of time allocated for each segment of learning is specified	Logical order in which knowledge will be learned is a part of the plan	Sufficient breadth and depth of content and learning activities are included	Analysis of possible problems that will affect time frame	

Materials	Planned use of *aids* (items used by teacher) logically sequenced as needed	Planned use of *materials* (items used by the students) logically sequenced as needed	Materials accommodate the range of individual differences among learners	Identification of websites and/or software to support learning objectives	Resources for learning enable the development of thinking skills among learners	Identification of trade books to support lesson
Assessment and evaluation	Informal assessment (procedures measure learning goals/objectives)	Formal assessment (procedures measure learning goals/objectives with grading criteria)	Formative assessment (ongoing information for improvement and growth)	Summative evaluation (judgment relative to a standard)	Alternative assessment (for diverse learners with grading criteria)	Hard copy of assessment instrument, including grading criteria
Home learning	Frequency and quantity comply with grade-level guidelines	Practice—reinforces newly acquired learning	Preparation—prerequisite for new learning	Extension and application—learners go beyond completed learning tasks and extend knowledge	Reflects the range of learners' characteristics and levels	Activities included for monitoring home learning and providing feedback
Reflection	Based on assessment results, were the learning objectives met?	Did lesson adaptations support students' diversity?	Discuss students' on-task behavior and engagement throughout the lesson	Discuss time management and organization in relation to the lesson plan	Describe your procedures for postlearning reflections with students	What would you do differently if you were to reteach this lesson?
						Total for all categories:

Note. Adapted from the work of Jeanne Bergeron, by permission.

Lesson Plan

Subject area: Language arts Grade 4 Date(s) 2/15 & 2/16

<table>
<tr><td colspan="2">State curricular standard
Standard 16.3</td><td>Theme/topic
Research tools</td></tr>
<tr><td colspan="3">Lesson objective
Student will locate research tools and identify purpose for each.</td></tr>
<tr><td>Agenda and procedures (what the teacher will do)
2/15 Administer pretest
2/16 PowerPoint lecture
1. Definition of research
2. Purpose of research
3. Research tools and purpose of each
4. Citing resources
Observe during library scavenger hunt
Explain home learning Assignment re: scenarios</td><td colspan="2">In-class activity/assignment (what the students will do)
2/15 Complete pretest
2/16 Take notes during lecture
Participate with cooperative learning group in library scavenger hunt to locate research tools
Take notes of location of research tools—hard copy and websites</td></tr>
<tr><td>Instructional strategies
☒ Lecture
☐ Discussion
☒ Demonstration
☒ Cooperative learning
☐ Group work
☐ Peer tutoring
☐ Learning or interest centers
☐ Simulation or role play
☐ Learning games
☐ Guided independent study
☒ Other: Media center visit</td><td colspan="2">Evaluation/assessment Details
☐ Observation of final product
☐ Interview with student
☐ Group assessment (critique)
☒ Observation of process (student working)
☐ Self-assessment by student
☐ Teacher-generated assignment
☒ Written product Scenarios
☒ Test/quiz Pretest
☒ Other: Class notes quiz</td></tr>
<tr><td>Aids (teacher)
Sample research tools
Vocabulary: Plagiarism
Related literature: See language arts text, Chapter 15
Supporting technology: PowerPoint</td><td>Materials (students)
Notebooks
Scavenger hunt lists
Related literature:
Supporting technology:
Internet access in media center</td><td rowspan="2">Planning pyramid
Some will learn:
How to cite each type of research tool
Most will learn:
Research tools
• Location of online versions
All will learn:
Research tools
• Location of hard copy
• Purpose of each</td></tr>
<tr><td colspan="2" rowspan="2">Home learning
List of research tools and 10 scenarios (research tasks). Student will match scenarios to research tools.</td></tr>
<tr><td>Adaptations strategies [lesson plan code]
Cooperative learning groups to assist with locating tools and taking notes</td></tr>
<tr><td colspan="3">Reflection
Max, Peter, and Pam need reteaching on purposes. Media specialist will meet with them to do a follow-up.</td></tr>
</table>

FIGURE 14.8. Lesson Plan form (filled-in example). Adapted from the work of Jeanne Bergeron, by permission.

teachers, as well as parents (and, if appropriate, the individual student), are required to participate in IEP meetings.

IEPs are important—not only from a legal standpoint, but even more so for monitoring the individual progress of students with special needs. Therefore, general and special education collaboration and communication are vital. Special education teachers need to provide within-school forums and discussions for keeping general education colleagues up to date about laws, procedures, and district expectations for general education participation. When general education teachers are informed about the formats for necessary paperwork, as well as about salient deadlines, they are more likely to cooperate.

General education teachers need to recognize that working with children with special needs is a shared responsibility. If professional development opportunities are not provided, then general education teachers need to meet with their special education colleagues to ask what is required. Communication needs to be a two-way street. When teachers are all on the "same page," meetings with parents go more smoothly, and ongoing monitoring and instruction of students are more seamless.

OTHER INDIVIDUAL PLANS

Developing individual plans for students is common for teachers planning instruction in pull-out or resource settings. Due to the mandates of No Child Left Behind, individual plans are mandated for students in general education classrooms who are at risk or who have not passed high-stakes assessment tests. While many districts have their own planning templates, the complete Student Reading and Writing Profile (Appendix A) provides a template for planning for individual student needs in reading and writing. In addition, Avalos (2003) has developed a Profile Assessment Record and Instructional Reflection Log, which provides a more streamlined way to summarize assessment and instructional plans for individual students (Form 14.2).

SNAPSHOT

Miami Stars

How can the community work together to promote high-quality reading instruction? This is an awesome task, and collaboration is the key. Miami Stars is an example of a growing collaborative effort to bring research-based practices into the schools. Miami Stars is an afterschool tutorial program for elementary children who are tutored by graduate students in the University of Miami's Reading and Learning Disabilities master's program. Two of the University of Miami's Professional Development Schools serve as off-campus sites for Miami Stars. University faculty members and doctoral students supervise the tutoring sessions. The faculty members share research-based practices from the literature and from their own research in urban settings, and master's students are required to implement and reflect about the impact of these practices on student learning. Master's students are required to communicate with the parents and teachers of the elementary students they tutor, to learn about students' strengths and challenges, report assessment results, and work together to forge home–school–tutoring connections. At one school site, while students are tutored, parents engage in seminars designed to enhance literacy activities in the home.

The master's students and the classroom teachers at the Professional Development Schools participate in a two-week summer institute to learn more about research-based reading practices and make plans for implementing those practices in their own classrooms. The institute is cosponsored by the school district. Reading leaders from the district also attend the institute and are prepared to give participants support at their school sites for implementing practices. Preservice teachers from the university obtain field experiences in the classrooms of these teachers, so they can see in action the research-based practices they learn about on campus.

Miami Stars is a win–win situation for all involved.

CHAPTER SUMMARY

My personal journey as a literacy teacher had a rough start. Like many young teachers, I found the responsibility of teaching reading and writing to all students an awesome task. And like many young teachers, I felt isolated in my classroom and tried to do it alone. With professional development and years of experience, I learned that taking the risk to seek advice and support from other professionals and from professional organizations is well worth the effort.

To best serve the needs of our students, classroom and resource teachers need to continue to build the knowledge, skills, and confidence we need. As teachers we are the hub for students, parents and caregivers, and the community at large. We need to develop expertise in the use of technology and the information coming from educational research to fulfill our role. We also need to engage in ongoing reflection about how to make our classrooms and schools a better place to promote reading and writing.

In its position statement *What is Evidence-Based Reading Instruction?*, the International Reading Association recognizes the important role of the teacher. In reflecting about years of educational research beginning with the seminal work of Bond and Dykstra (1967), IRA states, "Time and again, research has confirmed that regardless of the quality of a program, resource, or strategy, it is the teacher and learning situation that make the difference" (2002, p. 1). You make the difference. I wish you peace and joy in your journey.

KEY TERMS AND CONCEPTS

Cooperative learning groups
Coteaching
Family literacy
Heterogeneous grouping
Home learning
Homogeneous grouping
Individualized educational programs (IEPs)
Joplin plan
Motivational reading programs
Paid tutors
Paraprofessionals
Planning Pyramid
Print-rich environments
Professional Development Schools
Pull-out programs
Reading coaches
Reading specialists
Resource settings
Responsible reading and writing programs
Teacher candidates
Volunteers

REFLECTION AND ACTION

1. Examine the models for schoolwide grouping in Figure 14.2. Think about the pros and cons of each. If you were to set up a schoolwide grouping model for reading and writing instruction, what would be your plan?

2. What are the potential barriers to developing schoolwide reading programs that involve parents and caregivers? How can teachers work to overcome those barriers?
3. Use Form 14.1 (the Lesson Plan form based on the Planning Pyramid) to develop a multilevel lesson plan for teaching a reading lesson. Use the rubric in Table 14.1 to reflect about your plan before and after implementing the lesson.

READ ON!

Bean, R. M. (2004). *The reading specialist: Leadership for the classroom, school, and community.* New York: Guilford Press.

This book provides clear guidelines for professional in the reading specialist role. Specific suggestions for planning schoolwide reading programs and professional development at the school level are included.

Edwards, P. A. (2004). *Children's literacy development: Making it happen through school, family, and community involvement.* Boston: Allyn & Bacon.

Patricia Edwards provides a "curriculum" for family involvement in reading and writing. Grounded in theory, research, and history, this is a one-of-a-kind book that can guide planning of parent involvement initiatives.

Fashola, O. S. (2002). *Building effective after-school programs.* Thousand Oaks, CA: Corwin Press.

The author takes a close look at a variety of after-school programs, draws conclusions, and makes recommendation about best practice.

Friend, M., & Cook, L. (2002). *Interactions: Collaboration skills for school professionals* (4th ed.). Boston: Allyn & Bacon.

The authors of this popular text provide specific guidelines for how school professionals can work together most effectively. It includes valuable information on working with parents.

Gregory, G. H., & Chapman, C. (2001). *Differentiated instructional strategies: One size doesn't fit all.* Thousand Oaks, CA: Corwin Press.

This book links assessment with instruction to accommodate individual learning needs in the classroom.

McAndrew, D. A. (2005). *Literacy leadership: Six strategies for peoplework.* Newark, DE: International Reading Association.

This monograph provides a theoretical discussion of leadership, but also includes specific strategies for leadership in the classroom and beyond.

Morrow, L. M. (2001). *Literacy development in the early years: Helping children read and write* (4th ed.). Boston: Allyn & Bacon.

Overall this is an excellent resource for planning and implementing reading programs for younger students. Chapters on family literacy, motivating readers and writers, and preparing the physical environment are particularly strong and provide wonderful suggestions.

Nagel, G. K. (2001). *Effective grouping for literacy instruction.* Boston: Allyn & Bacon.

This book provides a theoretical framework for grouping and gives examples to link this theory with practice.

Risko, V. J., & Bromley, K. (Eds.). (2001). *Collaboration for diverse learners: Viewpoints and practices*. Newark, DE: International Reading Association.

The editors of this book take a broad look at collaboration. They build a strong case for the importance of collaboration, and individual authors provide specific examples of promising practices in collaborative work.

Walpole, S., & McKenna, M. C. (2004). *The literacy coach's handbook: A guide to research-based practice*. New York: Guilford Press.

The authors of this book work closely with literacy coaches in the state of Georgia and beyond. The book is a comprehensive guide to planning schoolwide reading programs and to giving classroom teachers the support they need to be effective teachers of reading.

SHARPENING YOUR SKILLS: SUGGESTIONS FOR PROFESSIONAL DEVELOPMENT

1. Reexamine the International Reading Association's (2003) *Standards for Reading Professionals*. Create a professional development plan for your own growth as a teacher of reading and writing.
2. One good way to learn more about reading curricula is to volunteer to review textbooks at the school or district level. Comparing and contrasting textbooks from a variety of publishers helps the reviewer think about what is valued most in curricular and instructional support materials.

RESOURCES FOR ASSESSMENT AND INSTRUCTION

Boult, B., & Walberg, H. (1999). *176 ways to involve parents*. Glenview, IL: SkyLight.

Making parents welcome is a good start. This book leads teachers and administrators beyond the welcome and toward regular and sustained involvement of parents in substantive ways.

Finney, S. (2003). *Independent reading activities that keep kids learning . . . while you teach small groups (grades 3–6)*. New York: Scholastic.

This handy resource gives ideas for meaningful reading and writing activities that students can do with minimal teacher direction.

Hoffman, J. V., Sailors, M., Duffy, G., & Beretvas, S. N. (2004). The effective elementary classroom literacy environment: Examining the validity of the TEX-IN3 observation system. *Journal of Literacy Research*, *36*, 303–334.

A tool for planning and evaluating classroom literacy environments, using multiple data sources: materials inventory, classroom observations, and interviews with teachers and students.

Kame'enui, E. J., & Simmons, D. C. (2003). *Consumer's guide to evaluating a core reading program grades K–3: A critical elements analysis*. Retrieved from *www.idea.uoregon.edu*

Marriott, D., Kupperstein, J., Connelly, G., & Williams, C. (1997). *What are the other kids doing while you teach small groups?* Huntington Beach, CA: Creative Teaching Press.

This book addresses one of the most commonly posed classroom management questions. Particular emphasis is placed on students' accountability while working independently or in groups.

Pierangelo, R., & Crane, R. (2000). *The special education yellow pages*. Upper Saddle River, NJ: Prentice Hall.

This is a fantastic resource for general and special education teachers and for parents. It is indeed a "yellow pages" of resources and contact information to help the reader work through a maze of definitions, laws, and helpful contacts.

Schumm, J. S. (2004). *How to help your child with homework* (3rd ed.). Minneapolis, MN: Free Spirit.

This book is written for parents. However, teachers can use the book to give specific suggestions for helping their child with home learning.

Schumm, J. S., & Schumm, G. E. (1999). *The reading tutor's handbook: A commonsense guide to helping students read and write.* Minneapolis, MN: Free Spirit.

This manual can be used to prepare volunteer tutors for working in elementary classrooms and after-school programs.

Tyner, B. (2004). *Small-group reading instruction: A differentiated teaching model for beginning and struggling readers.* Newark, DE: International Reading Association.

Tyner poses a developmental model of early reading, and gives step-by-step guidelines for systematic reading instruction based on this model.

Wolfersberger, M. E., Reutzel, D. R., Sudweeks, R., & Fawson, P. C. (2004). Developing and validating the Classroom Literacy Environmental Profile (CLEP): A tool for examining the "print richness" of early childhood and elementary classrooms. *Journal of Literacy Research*, *36*, 211–272.

Describes the procedures for development and validation of an instrument that can be used to plan and evaluate literacy classrooms. A copy of the 33-item inventory is included in the article.

RECOMMENDED WEBSITES

Colorin Colorado!
www.colorincolorado.org

This is a helpful website filled with parent pointers for reading and writing in two languages: English and Spanish.

Compact for Reading
www.ed.gov/pubs/CompactforReading/index.html

This website provides resources for planning a schoolwide reading program that involves parents and caregivers, teachers, administrators, and students.

4Teachers.org
www.4teachers.org

This website has a number of interactive tools to help the busy teacher. The Onlinequizzes and Rubistar features help generate tests and rubrics. Casa Notes generates notes for parents in English and Spanish.

Four Blocks Literacy Model
www.four-blocks.com

Patricia Cunningham and Dorothy Hall have developed a model for schoolwide and in-class reading and writing programs. The website includes instructional materials, as well as information about research that led to Four Blocks development.

ReadbyGrade3.com
www.readbygrade3.com

This website provides valuable information for parents, teachers, and administrators.

Reading Rockets
www.readingrockets.org

The Reading Rockets initiative is a multimedia effort initially funded with a federal grant to WETA, a PBS television station. Updated daily, the site provides resources for parents and teachers.

FORM 14.1. Lesson Plan

Subject area: ________________________ Grade _______ Date(s) ____________________

State curricular standard

Theme/topic

Lesson objective

Agenda and procedures (what the teacher will do)

In-class activity/assignment (what the students will do)

Instructional strategies

- ☐ Lecture
- ☐ Discussion
- ☐ Demonstration
- ☐ Cooperative learning
- ☐ Group work
- ☐ Peer tutoring
- ☐ Learning or interest centers
- ☐ Simulation or role play
- ☐ Learning games
- ☐ Guided independent study
- ☐ Other:

Evaluation/assessment

- ☐ Observation of final product
- ☐ Interview with student
- ☐ Group assessment (critique)
- ☐ Observation of process (student working)
- ☐ Self-assessment by student
- ☐ Teacher-generated assignment
- ☐ Written product
- ☐ Test/quiz
- ☐ Other:

Details

Aids (teacher)

Vocabulary:

Related literature:

Supporting technology:

Materials (students)

Related literature:

Supporting technology:

Planning pyramid

Some will learn:

Most will learn:

All will learn:

Home learning

Adaptation strategies [lesson plan code]

Reflection

FORM 14.2. Profile Assessment Record and Instructional Reflection Log

Profile Assessment Record and Instructional Reflection Log

Student name ____________________ Grade ________ Teacher ____________________

Assessments:	Strengths:	Instructional needs:	Goals:	Objectives:	Instructional plan:	Parent participation:	Progress made or objective met:
List assessments used to determine the strengths and needs of the students. Include test name, date of administration, and results.	List the strengths this student brings to the reading process.	List the student's instructional needs.	Based on the student's instructional needs, choose learning goals from the state standards.	Based on the goals, choose an objective for each instructional need from the school district's grade-level benchmarks.	Identify strategies and methods you will use to meet each objective.	Identify how you will engage and/or empower the parents to help the student meet instructional objectives.	List assessments used to determine progress made and/or objectives met. (Assess on an ongoing basis.)

Adapted from the work of Mary A. Avalos, by permission. Reprinted in *Reading Assessment and Instruction for All Learners*, edited by Jeanne Shay Schumm.

APPENDICES

APPENDIX A

Student Reading and Writing Profile

Student Reading and Writing Profile
Part I: Getting to Know Your Student

Student's name ______________________________

School ______________________ Grade _______ Age _______

Teacher's name ______________________________

Summary Data from Parents/Guardians

Student strengths in reading and writing ______________________

Student areas for improvement in reading and writing ______________________

Possible reasons for difficulties ______________________

Parent/guardian goals for student improvement in reading and writing ______________________

Summary Data from Student

Student strengths in reading and writing ______________________

Student areas for improvement in reading and writing ______________________

Possible reasons for difficulties ______________________

Student goals for improvement in reading and writing ______________________

(cont.)

Part II: Gathering Existing Data

Summary Data from Cumulative Records

Retentions (grades) ____________________

Special education placements or referrals ____________________

Remedial placements ____________________

Academic grades in reading and language arts

Grade	K	1	2	3	4	5	6	7	8	9	10	11	12
Reading													
Language arts													

Scores on high-stakes tests

Grade	K	1	2	3	4	5	6	7	8	9	10	11	12
Reading													
Language arts													

Other previous testing

Name of test	Date	Score

Recommendations from previous teachers in cumulative folders

Student strengths in reading and writing ____________________

Student areas for improvement in reading and writing ____________________

Possible reasons for difficulties (cognitive/neurological, physical, educational, language, personality, family) ____________________

Part III: Data Pertaining to English Language Learners

Summary Data from Cumulative Records

Previous placements in English as a second language or bilingual programs ____________________

____

____

(cont.)

Previous language testing

Name of test	Date	Score

Recommendations from previous teachers in cumulative folders

Student strengths in language learning ______________________________

____

Student areas for improvement in language learning ______________________________

____

Possible reasons for difficulties ______________________________

Part IV: Emergent Literacy

Environmental Print Awareness

Name of test	Date	Score

Student strengths in environmental print ______________________________

____

Student areas for improvement in environmental print ______________________________

____

Instructional recommendations ______________________________

____

(cont.)

Book Awareness

(Book awareness areas: book holding, page turning, front and back of book)

Name of test	Date	Score

Student strengths in book awareness ______________________________

____

Student areas for improvement in book awareness ______________________________

____

Instructional recommendations ______________________________

Print Awareness

(Print awareness areas: letter names, left-to-right orientation, knowledge of "word")

Name of test	Date	Score

Student strengths in print awareness ______________________________

____

Student areas for improvement in print awareness ______________________________

____

Instructional recommendations ______________________________

____

Phonological Awareness

(Phonological awareness areas: onset, rhyme, isolating, counting, segmentation, blending)

Name of test	Date	Score

(cont.)

Student strengths in phonological awareness ______________________________

____

Student areas for improvement in phonological awareness ____________________

____

Instructional recommendations ______________________________________

____

Part V: Word Recognition

Alphabet Knowledge

(Alphabet knowledge areas: letter recognition, identification, formation)

Name of test	Date	Score

Student strengths in alphabet knowledge ________________________________

____

Student areas for improvement in alphabet knowledge ______________________

____

Instructional recommendations ______________________________________

____

Phonics

(Phonics areas: see Form 5.3, Phonics Elements Profile)

Name of test	Date	Score

(cont.)

Student strengths in phonics ______________________________

____

Student areas for improvement in phonics ______________________________

____

Instructional recommendations ______________________________

____

Spelling

Name of test	Date	Score

Student strengths in spelling ______________________________

____

Student areas for improvement in spelling ______________________________

____

Instructional recommendations ______________________________

____

Part VI: Sight Words and Structural Analysis

Sight Words

Name of test	Date	Score

Student strengths in sight words ______________________________

____

Student areas for improvement in sight words ______________________________

____

Instructional recommendations ______________________________

____

(cont.)

Structural Analysis

Name of test	Date	Score

Student strengths in structural analysis ______________________________

____

Student areas for improvement in structural analysis ______________________________

____

Instructional recommendations ______________________________

____

Part VII: Fluency

Fluency

Name of test	Date	Score

Student strengths in fluency ______________________________

____

Student areas for improvement in fluency ______________________________

____

Instructional recommendations ______________________________

____

Plan for monitoring fluency ______________________________

____

(cont.)

Part VIII: General and Narrative Reading Comprehension

General Comprehension

Name of test	Date	Score
____________________________	____________	____________
____________________________	____________	____________
____________________________	____________	____________
____________________________	____________	____________
____________________________	____________	____________
____________________________	____________	____________

Student strengths in general comprehension ________________________________

____

Student areas for improvement in general comprehension ________________________

____

Instructional recommendations ____

____

Narrative Comprehension

Name of test	Date	Score
____________________________	____________	____________
____________________________	____________	____________
____________________________	____________	____________
____________________________	____________	____________
____________________________	____________	____________
____________________________	____________	____________

Student strengths in narrative comprehension _______________________________

____

Student areas for improvement in narrative comprehension _______________________

____

Instructional recommendations ____

____

(cont.)

Part IX: Expository Reading Comprehension

Expository Comprehension

Name of test	Date	Score

Student strengths in expository comprehension ______________________

____

Student areas for improvement in expository comprehension ______________________

____

Instructional recommendations ______________________

____

Part X: Vocabulary

Vocabulary

Name of test	Date	Score

Student strengths in vocabulary ______________________

____

Student areas for improvement in vocabulary ______________________

____

Instructional recommendations ______________________

____

(cont.)

Part XI: Children's Literature

Children's Literature

Name of test	Date	Score

Student primary interests in genres ______________________________

____

Student areas for improvement in interest and motivation to read trade books ______________

____

Instructional recommendations for interest and motivation in trade book reading ______________

____

Instructional recommendations for genres in children's literature ______________________________

____

Part XII: Writing Process

Writing Process

Name of test	Date	Score

Student strengths in writing process ______________________________

____

Student areas for improvement in writing process ______________________________

____

Instructional recommendations ______________________________

____

(cont.)

Summary Report for Parents

Student's name ____

School ____________________________ Grade ______ Age ______

Teacher's name ____

Key assessments:

Name of test	Date	Score

Student strengths in reading and writing ________________________

____

Student areas for improvement in reading and writing ________________

____

Recommendations for additional assessment ______________________

____

Recommendations for instruction ______________________________

____

____

Time of next review ______________________________________

APPENDIX B

Frequently Asked Questions about Informal Reading Inventories—Revisited

In 2003, Paris and Carpenter wrote an article in *The Reading Teacher* entitled "FAQs about IRIs" (see "For Additional Reading," below). Although this article is helpful, our work with graduate and undergraduate students has led us to believe that more questions exist than Paris and Carpenter suggested. Thus we have revisited their questions and have added more.

What is the purpose of an informal reading inventory (IRI)?

An IRI is an individually administered informal assessment used to determine a student's reading level. Knowledge of a student's reading level can assist teachers in placing students in reading groups, assigning reading materials at an appropriate level for the students, and determining needs for additional assessment in specific areas.

There are many IRIs on the market. What is the "best" IRI to use?

You are right—there are many IRIs on the market. Appendix C provides a list of commercial IRIs. In addition, many basal reading series include their own IRIs with passages drawn from the basal readers. Which one is best? It really depends on your purpose—what you want to know about your students' reading. If your school does not require a particular IRI, examine a variety of IRIs to decide which will provide you with the information you need and will use.

What are the different components of an IRI?

While IRIs do differ, they do have two basic components in common: *graded word lists* and *graded passages*. Typically, IRIs have more than one set of graded passages—at least one form for oral reading of passages; and one form for silent reading of passages. Graded passages also include a series of reading comprehension questions. The type (e.g., literal, inferential) and number of questions vary. Questions are typically open-ended rather than multiple choice. Also, some IRIs include a measure of student prior knowledge of a topic before reading a passage. Still others include story retellings as an additional measure of reading comprehension.

Many commercial IRIs also include supplemental measures to add to an assessment portfolio or to serve as a follow-up. Supplemental measures can include student interviews, interest inventories, or tests of a range of specific areas of reading instruction (e.g., sight words, phonics, structural analysis, etc.).

What data can be collected with an IRI?

IRIs have subtests that enable teachers to determine independent, instructional, and frustration levels for the following:

- Word identification in isolation (graded word lists).
- Word identification in context (oral reading of graded passages).
- Oral reading comprehension (answering questions based on graded passage).
- Silent reading comprehension (answering questions based on graded passages).
- Listening comprehension (answering questions based on administrator-read passages).

Criteria for determining independent, instructional, and frustration levels can vary slightly among IRIs. Make certain that you read the administration manual carefully.

What training do I need to administer an IRI?

While formal training is not required to administer an IRI, it can be tricky. If you are not enrolled in a class to learn how to administer an IRI, make certain that you read the administration directions carefully. If at all possible, observe someone experienced in using an IRI during several administrations. Some experts recommend 10–15 practice administrations to develop fluency in administration. Many IRIs now come with training videotapes or CDs to provide such demonstrations. Finally, if you are a novice in using an IRI, practice. Get permission from the parents of several children to do practice administrations. Explain to each child's parents that the administration is just that—a practice administration—and that you are learning to use the tool.

What do I need to do to prepare for an administration of an IRI?

To administer an IRI, you need materials for the student to read (the word lists and graded passages) and teacher recording/scoring sheets. The student materials are not consumable—they can be used over and over again. The graded word lists can be presented to student as a word list or on individual flashcards. The passages can be kept in a three-ring binder in plastic sleeves to keep them clean. The teacher materials needed are an examiner word list to record word identification on the graded word lists, and examiner copies of graded passages and reading comprehension questions. Prepare photocopies of the teacher materials in advance, and keep these on a clipboard during administration. You may also want to have a stopwatch to time the student's silent reading of passages.

How do I establish rapport with a student before administering an IRI?

Individual testing situations are a new experience for many children and can be stress-producing. Rapport needs to be established before, during, and after the administration of an IRI. Before the IRI, spend a little time talking with the student about his or her interests, and then briefly explain the assessment procedure. Include in your explanation a statement that some words and passages will be easier than others, and tell the student to "just try the best you can." Also, explain that you are interested in learning about the student's reading, so you will be taking notes along the way. Give the student time to ask any questions before you begin.

During the administration, continue to bolster the student. When difficult words or questions come along, encourage the student to try, but also give the option to say "pass" or "skip" if appropriate. If the child seems to be getting fatigued, take a break or schedule a second session.

After the administration, thank the student and explain that you will use the information gathered to plan instruction.

IRIs have graded word lists and graded passages. How do I know where to start and where to stop?

Graded word lists are used to assess a student's word recognition in isolation and to help determine a starting point for reading passages. The rule of thumb is to start the word lists two years below a student's grade placement. You stop when independent, instructional, and frustration reading levels have been determined.

The starting point for oral passages is the student's highest independent level on the graded word lists. The stopping point is when independent, instructional, and frustration reading levels have been determined for both word recognition in context and oral reading comprehension.

The starting point for silent passages is the student's highest independent level on oral reading comprehension. The stopping point is when independent, instructional, and frustration reading levels have determined.

How do I administer graded word lists?

When administering the graded word lists, you are looking for how quickly and accurately a student reads words in isolation. Some IRIs have separate scoring systems for timed and untimed word reading. Present word lists one at a time to the student. Start two grade levels below the student's current grade placement, or at preprimer. If the student reads the word correctly, put a + on the scoring sheet. If the student misreads the word, write down the pronunciation for future analysis. Do not count dialect differences as miscues.

How do I administer graded reading passages read orally?

This is probably the most intricate part of administering the IRI. While the student is reading the passages out loud, the examiner needs to record student miscues. A *miscue* is any deviation from the printed text in the student's reading. Goodman (1965) suggested that *miscue* is a more appropriate term than *mistake* or *error*. A careful examination of the types of miscues that students make can offer rich information about how students are trying to use various cue systems to make sense of text. Different commercial IRIs call for different marking systems and scoring systems for oral reading miscues. Read the directions carefully to make certain that your marking and scoring are consistent with the particular IRI that you are using.

Miscues can be of several types:

- *Substitutions*—when a word is substituted for what is on the printed page.
- *Insertions*—when a word is added.
- *Omissions*—when a word printed in text is left out during oral reading.
- *Reversals*—when a letter is turned about (b for p) or when letters within a word are turned about (*was* for *saw*).

How do I administer graded reading passages read silently?

Present a passage to the student and ask the student to read the passage silently. Some IRIs provide the option of having the administrator time the silent reading to determine a silent reading rate. After the student reads the passage, ask the comprehension questions. The student answers the questions orally. Most IRIs provide scoring guidelines for full or partial credit for student answers.

Do I let students look back in a passage to find answers to reading comprehension questions?

For most IRIs, scoring of reading comprehension questions is based on students' *not* looking back into the passage to find answers. Check the manual carefully for administration guidelines. When a student does not look back, you get a sense of what a student can read and keep in short-term memory. However, after you have recorded the student's responses without look-backs, you may want to "test the limits" and have the student find the correct answer. If the student cannot find the answer even with looking back, it gives you another piece of information about how the student comprehends.

Should I audiotape the assessment session?

When you are first administering an IRI, it is useful to audiotape the administration sessions—particularly the student's oral reading of graded word lists and passages. Trying to "tune in" to student miscues is somewhat difficult at first. Audiotaping and rescoring after the administration can help you become a better listener and more attentive to each student's reading patterns.

How do you determine a student's reading level?

After completing the IRI administration, you should have independent, instructional, and frustration reading levels for (1) words in isolation, (2) words in context, (3) oral comprehension, and (4) silent comprehension. In collapsing these ratings, you are getting an "estimate" of a student's overall reading level. This is not a perfect science. Sometimes scores are consistent across the four areas, sometimes not. Particularly for decisions about placement in instructional materials, a conservative estimate (with ongoing monitoring of student performance) is best.

What student behaviors should I observe while administering an IRI?

During the administration of the IRI, look for signs and symptoms of anxiety and frustration. Mangrum and Forgan (1979) listed the following signs of frustration:

- Abnormal voice
- Word-by-word reading
- Disregarding punctuation
- Lip movements or vocalization during silent reading
- Finger pointing
- Requests for aid
- Refusal to read

If it appears that a student is overly frustrated, stop the administration and try again at another time.

Should I assist students when they run into problems reading the word lists or passages?

The purpose of the IRI is to determine what a student can do independently. Avoid assisting the student if at all possible. If you do assist, make a note of it.

Can an IRI be used as a group-administered assessment?

Some commercial IRIs do have directions for group administration. However, group-administered IRIs can tap only silent reading comprehension, so they are of limited use.

Are there any special considerations I need to make when administering an IRI to English-language learners (ELLs)?

Yes, there are special considerations to make when you are administering an IRI to ELLs. For example, if you are not familiar with the speech sounds of the ELL student that you will be assessing, make sure to set aside a few minutes before the assessment begins to have a conversation about a familiar topic. During the conversation, it is important to become familiar with the student's accent, in order not to confuse a strongly accented word with a reading error. Also, be sure that the passages in the IRI are not culturally biased, as this may interfere with the results of an ELL student's IRI score. If you are not sure whether a passage is biased, you can survey the student and find out if he or she is familiar with the topic of the passage. Also, whenever possible, you should try to use an IRI that includes story retellings, as this is a technique that works well for assessing reading comprehension of ELL students.

Are there any special considerations I need to make when administering an IRI to students with diagnosed learning disabilities, attention disorders, or severe reading problems?

Students who have a history of difficulty in learning to read may exhibit a great deal of anxiety with an individually administered assessment. Take more time in establishing rapport and putting such a student at ease. Be prepared to repeat directions more than once, and to be patient if the student needs assistance in understanding the format for the IRI. If the student has attention problems, you may want to break the assessment into several sessions to get a better idea of student strengths and areas for improvement. Finally, keep encouraging the student to do his or her best along the way, and say that it's OK if some parts of the test are too difficult.

Administration of IRIs can be time-consuming, particularly for students in upper grades. How do I administer IRIs to all students in my class when I have 25 students to monitor?

Some schools provide resources to teachers to make this happen. For example, reading coaches and special education teachers may assist with administration. Paraprofessionals may be assigned to the classroom while teachers are administering IRIs. If such resources are not available, conduct a San Diego Quick Assessment with all students (see Form 6.1); next administer full-blown IRIs with students who appear to have more distinct reading needs first; and then gradually conduct IRIs with other students.

FOR ADDITIONAL READING

Mangrum, C. T., & Forgan, H. W. (1979). *Developing competencies in teaching reading*. Columbus, OH: Merrill.

Paris, S. G., & Carpenter, R. D. (2003). FAQs about IRIs. *The Reading Teacher*, *56*, 579–581.

APPENDIX C

Assessment References

COMMERCIALLY PUBLISHED ASSESSMENTS

Beery, K. E. (1993). *Integrated Writing Test.* Redding, CA: Golden Educational Center.

Brown, V., Hammill, D., & Wiederholt, J. L. (1995). *Test of reading comprehension–3.* Austin, TX: PRO-ED.

CTB McGraw Hill. (2002). *Fox in a Box: An adventure in literacy.* Monterey, CA: Author.

CTB/McGraw-Hill. (2004). *The CTB writing assessment system.* Monterey, CA: Author.

Dunn, L., & Dunn, L. (1997). *Peabody Picture Vocabulary Test–III.* Circle Pines, MN: American Guidance Service.

Good, R. H., & Kaminski, R. A. (2002). *Official DIBELS Home Page.* Retrieved from *http://dibels.uoregon.edu/index.php*

Hoover, H. D., Dunbar, S. B., & Frisbie, D. A. (2001). *Iowa Tests of Basic Skills, Form A.* Itasca, IL: Riverside.

Karlsen, B., & Gardner, E. F. (1995). *Stanford Diagnostic Reading Test* (4th ed.). San Antonio, TX: Harcourt.

Koslin, B. L., Zeno, C. S., & Koslin, S. (1987). *The Degrees of Reading Power: An effective measure of reading.* New York: College Entrance Examination Board.

Larsen, S., Hammill, D., & Moats, L. (1999). *Test of Written Spelling–4.* Austin, TX: PRO-ED.

MacGinitie, W. H., MacGinitie, R. K., Maria, K., & Dreyer, L. G. (2000). *Gates–MacGinitie Reading Tests* (4th ed.). Itasca, IL: Riverside.

Markwart, F.C. (1996). *Peabody Individual Achievement Test—Revised.* Circle Pines, MN: American Guidance Service.

Mather, N., Hammill, D. D., Allen, E. A., & Roberts, R. (2004). *Test of Silent Word Reading Fluency.* Austin, TX: PRO-ED.

McGhee, R., Bryant, B. R., Larsen, S. C., & Rivera, D. M. (1995). *Test of Written Expression.* Austin, TX: PRO-ED.

Reid, D. K., Hresko, W. P., & Hammill, D. D. (2001). *Test of Early Reading Ability–3.* Austin, TX: PRO-ED.

Richardson, E., & DiBenedetto, B. (1985). *The Decoding Skills Test.* Los Angeles: Western Psychological Services.

Roswell, F., & Chall, J. (1997). *Roswell–Chall Diagnostic Reading Test.* Cambridge, MA: Educators Publishing Service.

Scholastic, Inc. (2005). *Scholastic Reading Inventory.* Retrieved from *http://teacher.scholastic.com/products/sri/overview/faq.htm*

Slosson, R. L., & Nicholson, C. L. (1994). *Slosson Oral Reading Test.* New York: Slosson Educational Publications.

STAR Early Literacy. (2001). Wisconsin Rapids, WI: Renaissance Learning, Inc.

Torgesen, J. K., & Bryant, B. R. (2004). *Test of Phonological Awareness—Second Edition: Plus.* Austin, TX: PRO-ED.

Warden, M. R., & Hutchinson, T. A. (2004). *Writing Process Test.* Austin, TX: PRO-ED.

Wick, J. W., Gatta, L. A., & Valentine, T. (1991). *The Comprehensive Assessment Program.* Iowa City, IA: American College Testing Program.

Wiederholt, J. L., & Bryant, B. R. (2001). *Gray Oral Reading Tests–4.* Austin, TX: PRO-ED.

Wilkinson, G. S. (1993). *Wide Range Achievement Test—3.* Wilmington, DE: Wide Range, Inc.

Woodcock, R. W., Mather, N., & Schrank, K. (2004). *Woodcock–Johnson III Diagnostic Reading Battery.* Itasca, IL: Riverside.

Woodcock, R. W., Muñoz-Sandoval, A. F., Alvarado, C., & Ruef, M. (2001). *Woodcock–Muñoz Language Survey.* Itasca, IL: Riverside.

COMMERCIAL INFORMAL READING INVENTORIES

Bader, L. (2005). *Bader Reading and Language Inventory* (5th ed.). Upper Saddle River, NJ: Prentice Hall.

Flynt, S. E., & Cooter, R. B. (2003). *Reading Inventory for the Classroom* (5th ed.). Upper Saddle River, NJ: Prentice Hall.

Johns, J. (2001). *Basic Reading Inventory: Pre-primer–grade twelve and early literacy assessments.* Dubuque, IA: Kendall/Hunt.

Leslie, L., & Caldwell, J. (2000). *Qualitative Reading Inventory–3.* New York: Longman.

Shanker, J. L., & Ekwall, E. E. (1999). *Ekwall–Shanker Reading Inventory* (4th ed.). Needham Heights, MA: Allyn & Bacon.

Silvaroli, N. J., & Wheelock, W. H. (2003). *Classroom Reading Inventory* (10th ed.). New York: McGraw-Hill.

Stieglitz, E. L. (2001). *The Stieglitz Informal Reading Inventory: Assessing reading behaviors from emergent to advanced levels* (3rd ed.). Needham Heights, MA: Allyn & Bacon.

Woods, M. L., & Moe, A. J. (2003). *Analytic Reading Inventory.* Upper Saddle River, NJ: Prentice Hall.

OTHER ASSESSMENTS

Bottomley, D. M., Henk, W. A., & Melnick, S. A. (1997). Assessing children's views about themselves as writers using the Writer Self-Perception Scale. *The Reading Teacher, 51,* 286–296.

Bruce, D. (1964). An analysis of word sounds by young children. *British Journal of Educational Psychology, 34,* 158–170.

Cunningham, P. (1990). The Names Test: A quick assessment of decoding ability. *The Reading Teacher, 44,* 124–129.

Cunningham, A. E., & Stanovich, K. E. (1991). Tracking the unique effects of print exposure in children. *Journal of Educational Psychology, 83,* 264–274.

Fry, E. B., Kress, J. E., & Fountoukidis, D. L. (2000). *The reading teacher's book of lists* (4th ed.). Paramus, NJ: Prentice Hall.

Gentry, J. R. (1985, May). You can analyze developmental spelling—and here's how to do it! *Teaching K–8,* pp. 44–45.

Kear, D. J., Coffman, G. A., McKenna, M. C., & Ambrosio, A. L. (2000). Writing Attitude Survey. *The Reading Teacher, 54*(1), 16–23.

Kottmeyer, W. (1959). *Teacher's guide for remedial reading.* St. Louis, MO: Webster.

LaPray, M. H., & Ross, R. R. (1969). The graded word list: Quick gauge of reading ability. *Journal of Reading, 12,* 305–307.

McDowell, J. A., Schumm, J. S., & Vaughn, S. (1993). Assessing exposure to print: Development of a measure for primary children. In C. K. Kinzer & D. J. Leu (Eds.), *Examining central issues in literacy research, theory, and practice* (pp. 101–107). Chicago: National Reading Conference.

Saumell, L., Schumm, J. S., & Post, S. (1993). *College students' perceptions of the feasibility of reading and study strategies.* Paper presented at the College Reading Association Conference, Richmond, VA.

Schmitt, M. C. (1990). A questionnaire to measure children's awareness of strategic reading processes.*The Reading Teacher, 43,* 454–461.

Scholastic, Inc. (2002). *CORE Phonics Survey.* New York: Author.

Yopp, H. K. (1995). A test for assessing phonemic awareness in young children. *The Reading Teacher, 49*(1), 20–29.

APPENDIX D

Children's Literature References

Aardema, V. (1978). *Why mosquitoes buzz in people's ears.* New York: Puffin.
Adler, D. (1991). *A picture book of Thomas Jefferson.* New York: Holiday House.
Alcott, L. M. (2004). *Little women.* New York: Signet Classics.
Ancona, G. (1995). *Fiesta U.S.A.* New York: Lodestar.
Armstrong, J. (1999). *Shipwreck at the bottom of the world.* New York: Crown.
Asbjornsen, P., & Moe, J. (1983). *The squire's bride.* New York: Simon & Schuster.
Avi. (2002). *Crispin: The cross of lead.* New York: Hyperion.
Bang, M. (1999). *When Sophie gets angry—really, really angry.* New York: Scholastic.
Barrie, J. M. (2003). *Peter Pan.* New York: HarperFestival.
Base, G. (1987). *Animalia.* New York: Harry N. Abrams.
Battaglia, A. (1973). *Mother goose.* New York: Random House.
Blumberg, R. (2004). *York's adventures with Lewis and Clark: An African-American's part in the great expedition.* New York: HarperCollins.
Brown, M. W. (1984). Goodnight moon. New York: Harper & Row.
Butler, A., & Neville, P. (1987). *May I stay home today?* Crystal Lake, IL: Rigby.
Byars, B. (1996). *Summer of the swans.* New York: Puffin.
Carle, E. (1971). *The very hungry caterpillar.* New York: Penguin.
Carroll, L. (1999). *The adventures of Alice in Wonderland.* Cambridge, MA: Candlewick.
Cole, J. (1989). *It's too noisy.* New York: Crowell.
Collier, J., & Collier, C. (1989). *My brother Sam is dead.* New York: Scholastic.
Cowley, J. (1990). *Dan the flying man.* Bothell, WA: Wright Group.
Craft, M. C. (1996). *Cupid and Psyche.* New York: Morrow.
Crane, C. (2000). *S is for sunshine: A Florida alphabet.* (M. G. Monroe, Illus.). Chelsea, MI: Sleeping Bear Press.
Creech, S. (1994). *Walk two moons.* New York: HarperCollins.
Creech, S. (2001). *Love that dog.* New York: HarperCollins.
Cronin, D. (2000). *Click, clack, moo: Cows that type.* New York: Simon & Schuster.
Curtis, C. P. (1995). *The Watsons go to Birmingham.* New York: Delacorte.
Curtis, C. P. (1999). *Bud, not Buddy.* New York: Delacorte.
Dahl, R. (1996). *The magic finger.* New York: Viking.
Dahl, R. (2004). *Fantastic Mr. Fox.* New York: HarperCollins.
Dragonwood, C., & Aruego, J. (1992). *Alligator arrived with apples: A potluck alphabet feast* (A. Dewey, Illus.). New York: Simon & Schuster.
Ernst, L. C. (2004). *The turn-around, upside-down alphabet book.* New York: Simon & Schuster.
Feelings, T. (1995). *The middle passage: White ships/black cargo.* New York: Dial.
Freedman, R. (1991). *The Wright brothers: How they invented the airplane.* New York: Holiday House.
Freedman, R. (1992). *Franklin Delano Roosevelt.* New York: Clarion.
Galdone, P. (1984). *The three little pigs.* New York: Clarion.
Garland, S. (1993). *The lotus seed.* New York: Harcourt Brace Jovanovich.

Gerstein, M. (2003). *The man who walked between the towers.* Brookfield, CT: Millbrook.
Graham-Barber, L., & Lehman, B. (1995). *A chartreuse leotard in a magenta limousine: And other words named after people and places.* New York: Hyperion.
Guy, R. (1984). She. In D. R. Gallo (Ed.), *Sixteen: Short stories by outstanding writers for young adults* (pp. 147–153). New York: Dell.
Gwynne, F. (1987). *The sixteen-hand horse.* New York: Aladdin.
Gwynne, F. (1988a). *A chocolate moose for dinner.* New York: Aladdin.
Gwynne, F. (1988b). *The king who rained.* New York: Aladdin.
Gwynne, F. (1990). *A little pigeon toad.* New York: Aladdin.
Hamilton, V. (1986). *The people could fly: American black folktales.* New York: Knopf.
Hamilton, V. (1993). *Cousins.* New York: Scholastic.
Hamilton, V. (1999). *M. C. Higgins, the great.* New York: Simon.
Hesse, K. (1997). *Out of the dust.* New York: Scholastic.
Hopkins, L. B. (1996). *Blast off! Poems about space.* New York: HarperCollins.
Kellogg, S. (1985). *Paul Bunyan.* New York: Morrow.
Kellogg, S. (1987). *Chicken Little.* New York: HarperTrophy
Kellogg, S. (1992). *Pecos Bill.* New York: HarperTrophy.
Kellogg, S. (1999). *The three sillies.* New York: Walker.
Kipling, R. (2001). *How the camel got his hump.* New York: Michael Neugebauer.
Lear, E. (1998). *The owl and the pussycat.* New York: HarperCollins.
L'Engle, M. (1974). *A wind in the door.* New York: Yearling.
L'Engle, M. (1981). *A swiftly tilting planet.* New York: Yearling.
L'Engle, M. (1998). *A wrinkle in time.* New York: Yearling.
Lester, J. (1994). *John Henry.* New York: Dial.
Lester, J. (2000). *Pharaoh's daughter: A novel of ancient Egypt.* New York: Harcourt Brace.
Lewis, C. S. (1994). *The chronicles of Narnia.* New York: HarperCollins.
Lowry, L. (1993). *The giver.* Boston: Houghton Mifflin.
Lowry, L. (2002). *Gathering blue.* New York: Laurel Leaf.
Martin, B. (1996). *Brown bear, brown bear, what do you see?* New York: Holt.
Martin, B., & Archambault, J. (1989). *Chicka-chicka boom boom.* New York: Simon & Schuster.
Mathis, S. B., Ford, G., & Ford, G. C. (2000). *Ray Charles.* New York: Lee & Low Books.
Mayer, M. (1977). *Frog goes to dinner.* New York: Puffin.
McCaughrean, G. (1993). *Greek myths.* New York: Margaret K. McElderry.
McCloskey, R. (1941). *Make way for ducklings.* New York: Viking.
McGraw, E. J. (1990). *Mara, daughter of the Nile.* New York: Puffin.
Mitchell, M. K. (1993). *Uncle Jed's barbershop.* New York: Simon & Schuster.
Moore, C. (2002). *The night before Christmas.* New York: Simon & Schuster.
Murphy, J. (2003). *Inside the Alamo.* New York: Delacorte.
Musgrove, M. (1980). *Ashanti to Zulu: African traditions.* New York: Puffin Books.
Pallota, J. (1987). *The icky bug alphabet book.* Watertown, MA: Charlesbridge.
Patrick, G. (1974). A bug in a jug. New York: Scholastic.
Park, L. S. (2001). *A single shard.* New York: Clarion.
Perrault, C. (1999). *Puss in boots.* New York: North South.
Pilkey, D. (1999). *Paperboy.* New York: Orchard.
Prelutsky, J. (Ed.). (1983). *The Random House book of poetry for children.* New York: Random House.
Ringgold, F. (1996). *Tar beach.* New York: Dragonfly.
Rohmann, E. (2002). *My friend rabbit.* Brookfield, CT: Roaring Brook.
Rosenberry, V. (1999). *Vera's first day of school.* New York: Holt.
Rowling, J. K. (1999). *Harry Potter and the chamber of secrets.* New York: Scholastic.
Ryan, P. M. (2000). *Esperanza rising.* New York: Scholastic.
Ryan, P. M. (2002). *When Marian sang: The true recital of Marian Anderson.* New York: Scholastic.
St. George, J. (2000). *So you want to be president?* New York: Philomel.
Say, A. (1993). *Grandfather's journey.* Boston: Houghton Mifflin.
Sendak, M. (1996). *In the night kitchen.* New York: HarperCollins.
Seuss, Dr. [Geisel, T.] (1957). *The cat in the hat.* New York: Random House.
Shannon, D. (1998). *No David.* New York: Scholastic.

Shannon, G. (1999). *Tomorrow's alphabet* (D. Crews, Illus.). New York: Morrow.
Silverstein, S. (1974). *Where the sidewalk ends*. New York: HarperCollins.
Silverstein, S. (1981). *A light in the attic*. New York: HarperCollins.
Simon, S. (1992). *Storms*. New York: HarperTrophy.
Simon, S. (1997). *The brain: our nervous system*. New York: Morrow.
Simon, S. (1999). *Crocodiles and Alligators*. New York: HarperCollins.
Simon, S. (2003). *Planets around the sun*. Minneapolis, MN: Sagebrush.
Simon, S. (2004). *Cool Cars*. New York: Seastar.
Spinelli, J. (1993). *There's a girl in my hammerlock*. Minneapolis, MN: Aladdin.
Steig, W. (1987). *Sylvester and the magic pebble*. Minneapolis, MN: Aladdin.
Sterling, S. (1992). *My name is SEEPEETZA*. Vancouver: Douglas & McIntyre.
Stevens, J. (1995). *The three billy goats gruff*. New York: Harcourt.
Taback, S. (1997). *There was an old lady who swallowed a fly*. New York: Viking.
Terban, M. (1982). *Eight ate: A feast of homonym riddles*. New York: Clarion Books.
Terban, M. (1983). *In a pickle and other funny idioms*. New York: Clarion Books.
Terban, M. (1984). *I think I thought and other tricky verbs*. New York: Clarion Books.
Terban, M. (1985). *Too hot to hoot: Funny palindrome riddles*. New York: Clarion Books.
Terban, M. (1986). *Your foot's on my feet: And other tricky nouns*. New York: Clarion Books.
Terban, M. (1987). *Mad as a wet hen! And other funny idioms*. New York: Clarion Books.
Terban, M. (1988). *Guppies in tuxedos: Funny eponyms*. New York: Clarion Books.
Terban, M. (1990). *Punching the clock: Funny action idioms*. New York: Clarion Books.
Terban, M. (1993). *It figures! Funny figures of speech*. New York: Clarion Books.
Tolkien, J. R. R. (1986). *The lord of the rings*. New York: Del Rey.
Van Allsburg, C. (1981). *Jumanji*. Boston: Houghton Mifflin.
van der Rol, R., & Verhoeven, R. (1993). *Anne Frank beyond the diary*. New York: Viking.
Warren, A. (1996). *Orphan train rider: One boy's true story*. Boston: Houghton Mifflin.
White, E. B. (1974). *Charlotte's web*. New York: HarperTrophy.
Wiesner, D. (1991). *Tuesday*. New York: Clarion.
Wiesner, D. (2001). *The three pigs*. New York: Clarion.
Wood, A. (2001). *Alphabet adventure* (B. R. Wood, Illus.). New York: Scholastic.
Yep, L. (1993). *Dragon's gate*. New York: HarperCollins.
Yep, L. (1995). *Thief of hearts: Golden mountain chronicles*. New York: HarperCollins.
Yue, C., & Yue, D. (2000). *The wigwam and the longhouse*. Boston: Houghton Mifflin.

APPENDIX E

Research Skills

Students in the elementary grades can begin to learn how to use research tools and how to summarize information they have gathered for oral and written reports. Explicit teaching of research skills helps to build a foundation for academic research in the middle grades and above. It also provides valuable skills that students can use for personal activities, such as comparative shopping and planning vacations. Teaching research skills early in the school year will help students succeed in assignments and projects throughout the school year.

For students in the elementary grades, research involves investigating a topic by collecting information and summarizing that information in a clear and concise way. When you are introducing research skills, begin with a discussion of what research is and the purposes of research at home and at school.

CHOOSING AND USING RESEARCH TOOLS

Elementary students need to become familiar with a variety of research tools, both online and in hard copy. Some high-stakes tests include a subtest on research skills. A typical subtest includes identification of a variety of research tools, their purposes, and their use. Typical research tools for elementary students include the following:

- Reference books
  - Almanacs
  - Atlases
  - Dictionaries
  - Encyclopedias
  - Thesauruses
  - Directories
  - Manuals
- Periodicals
  - Newspapers
  - Journals
  - Magazines
- Books/trade books
  - Textbooks
  - Biographies
  - Autobiographies

Thanks to Rodney Rouzzard for his assistance in preparing this Appendix.

- Electronic sources
  - The Internet
  - Videos/DVDs
  - Cassettes/CDs

You can use the pretest in Figure E.1 to test your students' knowledge of information sources. It is important for students to understand what research tools are appropriate for what purposes and how to use those tools. It is also important for students to use a variety of resources and not overrely on a single website, encyclopedia article, or other source. In assigning a research project, you may want to designate a certain number and type of sources for students to include. Your media specialist can assist you with locating these tools in the library and on the Internet, and with demonstrating the use of each tool.

One skill that poses a challenge for many students is citing sources. You may want to suggest to your faculty colleagues that the school identify a single citation format for use throughout the grades, so that students can get consistent practice. Teach your students to cite sources whenever they quote, paraphrase, summarize, or otherwise refer to the work of another. It's never too early to learn about plagiarism and the consequences of presenting another's work or ideas as your own.

Learning to evaluate and think critically about information gathered is important for you to teach and model. This is particularly true in evaluating information obtained via the Internet. Almost anyone can put information on the World Wide Web; however, it is sometimes hard to know what the exact source of the information is, the source's reputation, or the qualifications of the author. To some people, the Web is a place to voice opinions and not necessarily to report facts. It is difficult to tell if the sources are objective or qualified. The following questions and guidelines can be used to help your students evaluate their sources:

1. What person or organization is the source of this information?
2. What do you know about him, her, or it?
3. How could you check the source's reliability?

SOURCES OF INFORMATION

Directions: Match each term with the correct definition.

1. Almanac	a. A daily/weekly publication
2. Atlas	b. A book of words and their meanings
3. Dictionary	c. A set of volumes packed with information–can also be found in electronic versions
4. Directory	d. A book of synonyms
5. Encyclopedia	e. A book of "how to" information
6. Internet	f. A book of specific lists, charts, and tables
7. Journal	g. A book or listing of names and addresses
8. Magazine	h. A periodical presenting articles on a specific subject
9. Manual	i. A book of geography, mostly maps
10. Newspaper	j. A periodical containing a collection of articles, stories, pictures, etc.
11. Periodical	k. A huge computer network used to access the World Wide Web for information
12. Thesaurus	l. A publication issued at intervals

FIGURE E.1. Pretest on knowledge of information sources.

4. How current is the information? Is any of it out of date?
5. Why is the person writing this piece? Is it for information, entertainment, opinion, or marketing/advertisement purposes? If for information, is the writer objective?
6. How does the information compare with information in other sources? Read through written sources you find for answers to one question at a time. Pause carefully and to take notes when you find an answer. Then continue reading for additional information that answers the question.
7. Keep track of where you found the information. Write down the author, title, publisher, place and date of publication, and pages on which you found answers to a question.
8. Prepare for interviews, whether you meet with the person or speak by telephone. Think of questions in advance. Listen carefully. Take notes or use a tape recorder. Follow up with the interviewee if necessary.
9. When making observations, remember that your own background, experience, and emotions affect what you observe and how you see it. Test what you observed by examining other evidence. Compare your observations with those of others.
10. Before using information you've found, evaluate each source you've consulted.
11. Review the information you've gathered. Have you found answers to all your questions? Ask new questions if necessary. Gather additional information if you need it.

PREPARING RESEARCH REPORTS

The experiencing of gathering, organizing, and interpreting information can be a satisfying and exciting educational experience. Developing an oral or written research report provides students with a forum for presenting the results of their investigation of a selected topic. However, most students—including high-achieving students—need structure and support for preparing research reports. Many students have never read or seen a research report. Even those who have some experience in writing research reports may not be clear about the format and style that you have in mind.

Schumm and Radencich (1984) suggest that in the elementary grades, a three-step method can be used for a series of workshops on writing research reports. The first workshop is a whole-class research report written with a great deal of teacher direction. The second workshop is a report written by committees of five or six students. The third workshop is an individual report. The Research Paper Checklist (Figure E.2) can serve as a framework for various phases of the workshops.

RESEARCH PAPER CHECKLIST

Assignment: To write a term paper on ______________________________

Due date: ______________

Requirements

My paper will need:	It should be:
_______ Title page	_______ Typed
_______ Table of contents	_______ Double-spaced
_______ Bibliography	_______ Handwritten OK
_______ Graphics	

What kind of graphics? ______________________________

	Steps	**Date due**	**Date done**
____	1. Choose a topic.	_______	_______
____	2. Write a thesis sentence. Have it approved by the teacher.	_______	_______
____	3. Do library research. *Sources:*	_______	_______
____	4. Contact community resources for information. *Names of resources:*	_______	_______
____	5. Write letter or email to request information from national sources. *Wrote letter or email to*:	_______	_______
____	6. Take notes *Took notes from these resources:*	_______	_______
____	7. Make a writing plan.	_______	_______
____	8. Write a rough draft.	_______	_______
____	9. Revise and edit rough draft; make corrections.	_______	_______
____	10. Write the final draft.	_______	_______
____	11. Turn the final draft in on time.	_______	_______

FIGURE E.2. Research Paper Checklist. From Schumm, Jeanne Shay. *School Power*. Minneapolis, MN: Free Spirit. Copyright 2000 by Free Spirit. Reprinted by permission.

Glossary

Academic language proficiency (ALP) or cognitive academic language proficiency (CALP)—Advanced literacy, or understanding of low-frequency words (not commonly used in everyday language) that appear in content area or technical texts.

Accelerated Reader (AR)—Computerized reading program that logs which books a student reads and records performance on quizzes taken on each text.

Adequate yearly progress (AYP)—The No Child Left Behind Act (NCLB; see below) requires states to define criteria for students' AYP in reading. Based on individual state standards, each state is required to document how subgroups of students are making progress in achieving state target levels in reading by the year 2014. Criteria vary considerably from state to state.

Affix—A prefix or suffix that changes the meaning or part of speech of a word when attached to a root word (e.g., *un-* in *unhappy*, *-ment* in *enjoyment*).

Alphabetic principle—The idea that there is a systematic relationship between speech sounds and words in print.

American Library Association (ALA)—Professional organization of public and private librarians that gives annual awards for outstanding children's literature.

Analytic grading—Scales used to evaluate student written work, based on an evaluation of preidentified components of the written product.

Analytic phonics—An approach to teaching phonics that emphasizes whole-to-part-to-whole. Students begin by learning whole words, analyzing the parts of words, and then generalizing those parts to the learning of new words.

Anaphora—The substitution of one word for another. Anaphora can take many forms, including substitution of a pronoun for a noun (*he* for *David*) or a noun for another noun (*father* for *David*).

Assessment—The process of collecting, interpreting, and reporting data from both formal and informal measures. Data can be used for screening, diagnosis, progress monitoring, program evaluation, and accountability to key stakeholders.

Audiobooks/books on tape—Books on tape that match the text. Students should listen to the tape while their eyes follow the words on the page.

Automatic alphabetic phase—The mature phase of reading development, where the reader recognizes most words in text automatically by sight. The reader also routinely uses a variety of strategies and cue systems to decode unknown words.

Automaticity—The ability to recognize words rapidly and without pausing. Automaticity of word recognition enables the reader to focus more on comprehension of text.

Balanced instruction—A perspective on the teaching of reading that draws on both the systematic teaching of skills and literature-based instruction.

Base word—A root or stem to which affixes (prefixes and suffixes) can be attached to change a word's meaning or part of speech (e.g., *-able-* in *disabled*, *ability*).

Basic interpersonal conversational skills (BICS)—Oral proficiency in a language, indicated by commonly used words and conversational skills.

Basic reading activity—Instructional activity organized around a mix of computer games and board games, to enable students to learn skills that are necessary for reading.

Benchmark books—Leveled trade books, both narrative and expository, used periodically during the school year to determine if students have reached a predetermined level of reading accuracy and retelling proficiency.

Biography—A nonfiction work in which an author describes the life, or part of the life, of a real historical or contemporary individual.

Blending—Combining separate phonemes to form words.

Bottom-up perspective—A perspective of reading instruction that is based on reading as a process of breaking the code. Bottom-up advocates see rapid, context-free word recognition as the hallmark of a proficient reader.

Caldecott Medal—American Library Association annual award for outstanding illustrator of children's books.

Children's rights to read—The International Reading Association has designated 10 rights of individual children in their journey as readers (see Figure 1.2).

Choral reading—Students reading along as a group with teacher or another fluent adult reader. Students must be able to see the same text that the teacher or adult reader is reading. Patterned or predictable books are best for this, since their repetitive design invites students to join in.

Clock editing—A process for engaging students in self-editing of written work at the time a final draft is due.

Cloze—A procedure to gauge student understanding of syntactic and semantic cues in text. Cloze passages have systematically deleted words that students insert.

Cognates—Words derived from the same ancestral language (e.g., *international* and *internacional*). There are *true* or *friendly cognates* that have the same or similar meaning (e.g., *edificio* and *edifice*), and *false* or *unfriendly cognates* that sound the same, but do not share similar meanings (e.g., *embarrassed* in English is a false cognate of the Spanish word *embarazado* [pregnant]).

Collaborative strategic reading (CSR)—A multiple comprehension strategy designed to provide students support in comprehending expository text. Students work in collaborative learning groups to read and engage in four strategies: *preview*, *click and clunk*, *get the gist*, and *wrap-up*.

Comprehensible input—Making content understandable for ELLs by using visuals, a slower rate of speech (with modified tones), gestures, and context clues while relating instruction to students' experiences.

Computer applications—Computers can be applied to reading instruction in the following ways: games, generative, access, tutoring, thinking and problem solving, communication, and integrated learning systems (ILSs; see below).

Computer-mediated reading instruction—The use of computers to teach reading, with a variety of possible applications.

Cooperative/collaborative writing—Students working in pairs or small groups to develop a written piece.

Cooperative learning groups—Groups of four to six students working together to achieve a common learning goal. Successful cooperative learning groups set standards for both individual and group accountability.

Conference time—In Writers' Workshop, individual conferences that enable teachers and students to review progress in development of a written product.

Consolidated alphabetic phase—The fourth of four phases of word recognition, where students begin to notice patterns in words such as consonant clusters, common word endings, or vowel patterns.

Consonant blends—Consonant patterns where two or three consonants appear together. These consonants retain their sounds when the blend is pronounced.

Consonant digraphs—A combination of two consonants that make a new sound (e.g., ph, th, sh).

Contemporary realistic fiction—Realistic yet fictional stories about contemporary life.

Contextual processing—The ability of readers to use syntactic and semantic context clues to glean meaning from text, and to decode or get the meaning of individual words within text.

Coretta Scott King Award—Annual award for outstanding children's books for authors of African American lineage.

Coteaching—Teaching that occurs when there are two certified teachers in one classroom. Can apply when a general educators works in the same classroom with a special educator, Title I teacher, specialist in teaching English to speakers of other languages (TESOL), or gifted education teacher.

Criterion-referenced tests—Tests that assess student performance on particular instructional standards or learning goals. Students' scores on the test are compared to predetermined criteria and are used for instructional planning and/or to determine if students have mastered designated standards.

Culturally relevant—Meaningful or relevant to the learner, based on the learner's cultural experiences and background.

Derivational affix—A prefix or suffix that is added to a root or stem to form another word. An example is *un-* as in *unlike*, or *-ness* as in *likeness*.

Diagnostic instruments—Reading and writing assessments designed to identify individual student strengths and areas of difficulty.

Dialogue journals—A journal shared by a child with an adult or older child. Partners respond to each other's journal entries. Students benefit from modeling of fluent writing.

Differentiated instruction—The practice of planning instructional activities to meet the instructional needs of individual students in resource or classroom settings. Differentiation can occur with variations in grouping, instructional materials and strategies, instructors, instructional time, and type of practice.

Direct writing—A method of writing assessment in which the student writes an impromptu piece on demand. With direct writing assessments, the topic, the context, and the resources can be controlled.

Directed reading–thinking activity (DR-TA)—A teacher-directed activity designed to help students in setting a purpose for reading; making, justifying, and verifying predictions; and drawing conclusions.

Discourse patterns—Interactive conversational patterns that vary depending upon socioeconomic status, audience, purpose, and environment.

Dolch Basic List—A list of 220 basic sight words identified as the most common words in beginning reading.

Drafting—Stage of writing process when writers compose an initial draft.

Dyslexia—A learning disability that is manifested in moderate to severe difficulties in learning to read and spell. Students with dyslexia frequently have difficulty with phonological awareness; this leads to difficulties with word recognition, fluency, and comprehension.

Echo reading:—An activity where a skilled reader reads a text one sentence at a time, as the learner follows along, pointing to the words of the sentence passage as it is being read. The learner then echoes or imitates the skilled reader.

Elaborative processes—Reading comprehension processes that go beyond literal meaning of text and encourage higher-order thinking processes.

Emergent literacy—The idea that children are learning about language, reading, and writing in natural stages before beginning formal instruction in school.

English-language learners (ELLs)—Children with a first language other than English who are learning English.

Environmental print—Print that surrounds children each day on items such as cereal boxes, restaurant signs, food labels, cleaners, magazines, street signs, and stores. This type of print is often a child's first exposure to print.

Evidence-based instruction—Instructional programs and practices that are based on objective, valid, reliable, systematic, and refereed data.

Expository text patterns—Expository or information text is designed to teach and inform. Paragraph patterns are the ways in which information is organized in expository text.

False cognates—Words in different languages that are similar in spelling but not similar in meaning (see *cognates*, above).

Family literacy—While there is no one uniformly recognized definition of *family literacy*, in general definitions that are not deficit-oriented and that endorse reading as a lifelong activity embedded in daily, culturally relevant literacy routines are preferred.

FLIP—A procedure for students to use to estimate the difficulty level of text and to develop a reading plan to read and learn from text. The acronym stands for Friendliness, Language, Interest, and Prior Knowledge.

Fluency—The ability to read connected text with speed, accuracy, and expression, in order to gain meaning from what is read.

Fourth-grade slump—Situation when students who were successful in reading achievement during primary grades fall behind or hit a plateau in the intermediated years. Believed to be caused by lack of transition from "learning to read" to "reading to learn."

Frustration reading level—The level at which reading simply becomes too difficult, and the child can only decode 90% or less of the words accurately while comprehending only 50% or less of the material.

Full alphabetic phase—The third of four phases of word recognition, in which students remember how to read specific words by forming connections between the written letters they see in the text and the phonemes present in the pronunciation of the word.

General read-alouds—Reading aloud to students in informal ways, to generate appreciation for literature and to model fluent reading. Teachers, parents, community members, or older students can conduct read-alouds.

Grapheme–phoneme correspondence—The relationship between written letters (*graphemes*) and the spoken sound (*phonemes*) they represent.

Guided reading—Students reading in small groups with a teacher as a facilitator. The students each read silently, and the teacher asks guiding questions.

Guided writing—Students working on their own to develop a written product, with a teacher available to model, coach, and serve as an editor.

Heterogeneous grouping—Grouping of students at varied achievement levels and/or with diverse instructional needs for reading and/or writing instruction.

High-stakes tests—Statewide tests that are used to determine student promotion and eligibility for high school graduation. Test scores are also used to hold teachers and administrators accountable to the general public.

Historical fiction—Realistic stories set in the past.

Holistic grading—Use of a point scale to evaluate student writing. Writing is examined for organization, idea development, usage, and mechanics.

Home learning—Teacher-assigned activities designed to provide practice with skills and concepts learned in school, to extend and enrich material learned in school, to develop study habits, and to help students prepare for tests and class discussions. Homework.

Homogeneous grouping—Grouping of students at similar achievement levels and/or with similar instructional needs for reading and/or writing instruction.

Idiom—A figure of speech when the meaning of a word or phrase differs from the literal meaning. Usually culture-specific.

Imagery—Mental images that are created in relation to the events and topics read in text.

Independent reading level—The level at which a student reads independently, without help or assistance from others. Generally defined as the level at which a child can accurately pronounce or decode 99% of the words without any assistance from the teacher.

Indirect writing —Writing assessments that use indirect techniques (e.g., multiple-choice tests on the mechanics and usage of writing) to gauge student understanding of writing.

Individualized education program (IEP)—A program required for every student who is eligible for special education services. It is an individualized plan based on diagnosed needs.

Inflection—The bend or slide in the voice used in good reading and speaking.

Inflectional suffix—A suffix that changes the part of speech of a word; changes the tense of verbs; or expresses plurality, possession, or adjective/adverb comparison.

Informal reading inventory (IRI)—Observation or informal procedure to diagnose or evaluate reading proficiency or reading problems, and to determine independent, instructional, and frustration reading levels.

Instructional read-alouds—Read-aloud events designed for a specific instructional purpose, such as highlighting a particular literary device, reading comprehension strategy, or other educational objective.

Instructional reading level—The level at which a child can accurately decode at least 95% of the words.

Integrated learning systems (ILSs)—Computer applications that manage multiple components, including computers, software, reading curriculum, diagnostic information, and learning activities that support both teacher-mediated and computer-mediated instruction.

Integrative processes—Reading comprehension processes that connect segments of text to enable the reader to derive a coherent message from text.

Interactive–compensatory model—A theory of the reading process that recognizes rapid, context-free word recognition as the hallmark of a proficient reader. The theory also indicates that good readers are facile in their use of a variety of cue systems (e.g., semantic, syntactic, phonological) and can use one cue system to compensate when another cue system doesn't work.

Isolating—The ability to set apart a specific phoneme in a word.

Joplin plan—Cross-grade grouping for reading instruction, where students of similar reading achievement levels are placed together regardless of grade placement.

Juncture—The ability to pause appropriately when reading (slight pauses between words, longer pauses between phrases, and even longer pauses between sentences).

K-W-L—A procedure to engage students in active reading. Students first record what they Know about a topic, what they Want to learn, and (after reading) what they Learned and what they still need to learn.

L1—First, native, or primary language spoken.

L2—Second language learned, acquired, or spoken.

Least restrictive environment—Students who qualify for special education services are required to be placed in an educational environment that will best meet their individual needs and will also give them an opportunity to interact with general education peers. Students with disabilities can receive services in inclusion classrooms, part-time resource settings, self-contained classrooms, or special schools, based on their IEPs.

Levels of intensity—A plan for differentiated instruction that includes high-quality core instruction, supplemental instruction, and intensive support, depending on individual students' needs.

Lexile score—A score based on a framework that estimates the difficulty level of text. A student's lexile score on the Scholastic Reading Inventory (SRI) can be matched with books with similar lexile scores. Lexile scores range from 200L (beginning readers) to 1700L (advanced readers).

Linguistic phonics—An approach to phonics that is a variation of the analytic approach. Beginning instruction usually focuses on word patterns or word families.

Literature circles—Cooperative learning groups that focus on discussion of stories in basal readers or trade books.

Macroprocesses—Reading comprehension processes that support readers in their comprehension of narrative and expository text structures.

Matthew effect—The idea that when children get off to the wrong start in learning to read and write (for whatever reason or combination of reasons), their problems escalate and compound. Children who do not have a successful start in learning to reading and write are likely to stay behind their peers in academic tasks.

Meaning processing—The ability of readers to use prior knowledge and information in text to derive meaning from the printed page.

Metacognitive processes—Reading comprehension processes that enable the reader to monitor comprehension, to use fix-up strategies when comprehension does not occur, and to retain information for future use.

Microprocesses—Reading comprehension processes that enable the reader to understand text at the sentence level.

Mini-lesson—Brief, targeted lessons (especially within Writers' Workshop) to assist students with a variety of writing techniques, from topic selection to grammar to preparing a piece for publishing.

Miscues—The errors a student makes while reading.

Mnemonic strategies—Memory strategies that can be used to learn new vocabulary and key concepts.

Modeling—Teacher demonstration of reading and writing strategies.

Modern fantasy—Literature that incorporates the same story lines as traditional literature, but is penned by contemporary authors. Even though modern fantasy includes magical or impossible events, the plot, characters, and setting may be believable.

Morpheme—The smallest unit of meaning in a word.

Morphological analysis—An analysis of the structure of words, including word origins, inflection, and compound words.

Motivational reading programs—Schoolwide, classroom-based, or community programs to encourage the reading habit.

Multicultural literature—Literature of various genres that includes accounts of peoples from all cultures and reflects various elements of each culture, including its way of life, values, beliefs, and patterns of thinking.

Narratives—Stories that have characters, a plot, and a setting; are temporally ordered; and are goal-based.

National Assessment of Educational Progress (NAEP)—A standardized test that is used to provide a global picture of reading and writing achievement for students in grades 4, 8, and 12. Known as the "Nation's Report Card." Data are based on a sample representative of the student population in the United States.

National Board for Professional Teaching Standards—A nonprofit organization that has created standards to guide teachers in systematic professional development. These standards are used to guide applicants for National Board certification.

Newbery Medal—American Library Association annual award for outstanding author of children's books.

No Child Left Behind Act (NCLB)—The U.S. government's 2001 reauthorization of the Elementary and Secondary Education Act. The NCLB is based on four themes: accountability; choices for parents and students; flexibility for states, school districts, and schools; and putting reading first. It requires that states conduct statewide assessments in basic skills.

Nonfiction—Books with the primary purpose of informing the reader through in-depth explanations and illustrations of factual matter.

Norm-referenced tests—Individual or group-administered standardized tests that compare an individual student's performance with that of a sample or norming population of students. Most offer standard, percentile, stanine, and sometimes grade equivalent scores.

Onset—The initial part of a syllable that occurs prior to the vowel.

Orbis Pictus Award—An annual award for nonfiction children's books, sponsored by the National Council of Teachers of English.

Orthographic processing—In reading, the process of identifying letters in isolation, in individual words, and in running text.

Outcome measures—Assessments that are used to make judgments about student grades, promotion, and placement.

Paid tutors—Individuals who are hired either part- or full-time to tutor students in reading and writing. Paid tutors can be hired privately (by parents or other family members) or in school settings. The training of paid tutors varies considerably.

Paraprofessionals—Paid teacher assistants who provide support for certified teachers. The International Reading Association has outlined standards for the professional preparation for paraprofessionals in reading.

Parasitic hypothesis—The idea that ELLs automatically resort to linking new words in their second language to words in their native language.

Partial alphabetic phase—The second of four phases of word recognition, in which children begin to recognize more words and usually learn these words by recognizing and connecting with one or more of the actual letters in the word.

Phoneme deletion—Isolating one sound in a word and blending the remaining sounds.

Phonemic awareness—The ability to notice, think about, and work with the individual sounds (*phonemes*) in spoken words.

Phonetic stage—Stage of spelling development when students are aware of the alphabetic principle and use letters to spell words based on the sounds they hear.

Phonics—One aspect of word recognition instruction. Phonics instruction emphasizes the teaching of sound/symbol relationships and patterns. The teaching of phonics is highly related to spelling instruction.

Phonological awareness—The ability to detect and manipulate the speech sounds in language. Components of phonological awareness include onset, rhyme, segmentation, blending, and phoneme manipulation.

Phrasing—Applying the stress and intonation patterns of spoken language when reading, to make it sound like spoken language.

Picture books—Children's books that focus primarily on the visual message. The format of picture books, rather than their content, creates the genre.

Planning Pyramid—A framework for planning multilevel unit and lesson plans.

Poetry—Literary genre that expresses feelings and ideas quickly and memorably, and usually taps into strong emotions. A broad genre that includes rhymes, free verse, songs and raps, word pictures, and novels in the form of free verse.

Portfolios—Samples of student work and records of student progress in reading and writing that can be used to help students monitor their own progress and to report this progress to parents, guardians, and administrators.

Postwriting—Stage of the writing process when writers share the final written piece with the intended audience.

Prealphabetic phase—The first of four phases of word recognition, in which children remember how to read words by connecting visual cues in the word.

Precommunication stage—The stage of spelling development when students have not yet mastered the alphabetic principle.

Prefix—A word part (affix) attached to the beginning of a root or base word that alters the meaning of the word.

Prereading—Reading comprehension strategies used to ignite students' interest and motivation to read, and to activate prior knowledge of the topic to be read. The purpose of prereading is to prepare students for reading.

Prewriting—Stage of the writing process when writers determine genre, topic, audience, and format.

Print-rich environments—School or home environments that provide students with a rich array of reading materials representing a variety of genres, and writing materials that can be used to compose a variety of products.

Prior knowledge—Knowledge and experiences students already have that provide a foundation for learning and retaining new information.

Professional Development Schools—Public or private schools in partnership with a college or university. Professional Development School personnel work in collaboration with university faculty and staff to provide hands-on experiences for teacher candidates.

Progress-monitoring measures—Measures used to gauge ongoing progress of students. Data can be used to inform instruction and provide insights about adjustments to instruction that may be necessary.

Prosody—Reading in meaningful phrases.

Pull-out programs—Special services designed to meet the individual needs of students in reading. Students are pulled out of the general education classroom to receive these services. Students placed in pull-out programs can be students with disabilities, ELLs, gifted students, or designated students in Title I programs.

Question–answer relationships (QARs)—A reading comprehension strategy that assists students in understanding different types of comprehension questions.

Questioning the author (QtA)—A reading comprehension strategy designed to promote active engagement with text through a close examination of the author's message and intent.

Read 180—A computer program developed by Scholastic, Inc., to improve reading

Reader response theory—Louise Rosenblatt's theory undergirding the importance of personal interpretation of literature. Describes reading as a transaction between the reader and author.

Reading aloud—Activity in which the teacher reads aloud and the students merely listen. They may or may not have a copy of the text.

Reading rate—The speed with which a person reads, usually gauged in words per minute (wpm).

Reading coaches—School-based instructional leaders who plan and implement schoolwide reading programs, provide professional development for colleagues, and coach colleagues in the implementation of assessment and instructional practices.

Reading specialists—Teachers with advanced professional development in reading, who meet International Reading Association professional standards for reading specialists.

Reciprocal teaching—A multiple strategy that includes predicting, question generating, clarifying, and summarizing.

Repeated readings—Reading and rereading a text as a form of practice.

ReQuest—A procedure in which both the students and the teacher ask and answer questions. Used to teach predicting, creating questions, and comprehension monitoring.

Resource settings—Settings other than regular classrooms, in which student receive *pull-out programs* (see above). Again, students placed in resource settings to receive these services can be students with disabilities, ELLs, gifted students, or designated students in Title I programs.

Responsible reading and writing programs—A set of guidelines for planning and evaluation of schoolwide reading and writing programs.

Retellings—Students' oral or written recountings of narrative or expository text, which can be used to assess student comprehension of text. Retellings can also be used to help students organize information read and retain that information.

Rewriting—Stage of the writing process when writers edit their work, including revising (attention to meaning and how the message is communicated) and proofreading (attention to spelling and mechanics).

Rhyme—The remaining portion of a syllable after the initial part, beginning with the vowel.

Robust instruction—Vocabulary instruction that is engaging, is intense, and stimulates student interest in learning new words.

Running record—An assessment tool used to tap student processing and understanding of text, using authentic reading materials.

Root—Also known as a *base word* (see above), a root forms the core meaning of a word. Roots can be altered by adding affixes or through compounding.

Scaffolding—Providing support for students in their learning, and then gradually diminishing the support as students become more independent. There are several forms of scaffolding: teacher/peer, content, task, and material scaffolding.

Schema—A mental framework that houses what is known about a particular concept. *Schemata* (the plural of *schema*), also known collectively as *prior knowledge* (see above), provide the basis for enabling readers to make sense of new information.

Schwa—A vowel in an unstressed or unaccented syllable.

Screening measures—Assessment tools that are brief and easy to administer. Screening measures can be used to make initial instructional plans, to group students for instruction, and to identify needs for additional assessment.

Semantic mapping—Graphic organizers that use lines and circles or squares to organize information in categories.

Semiphonetic stage—Stage of spelling development where students may use letters to represent whole words and are beginning to form letters.

Segmenting—Recognizing and separating the distinct sounds in a word.

Self-reflection—Regular and systematic reflection about professional development and instruction. The goal of self-reflection is to improve teaching, student learning, and professional advancement.

Shared reading—Activity in which the teacher reads aloud as the students follow along with a copy of the text.

Shared writing—The composition of a common written product by students and teachers.

Sharing time—In Writers' Workshop, group time for students to share written products with the teacher and peers. Students receive feedback and ideas for future pieces.

Sight word—A word that is recognized instantly and does not require decoding.

Standards for Reading Professionals—A set of standards approved by the International Reading Association's Board of Directors in 2003. Standards for professional practice of paraprofessionals, classroom teachers, reading specialists, administrators, and teacher educators are included.

Status of the class—A three- to five-minute check-in to determine where each student is in the process of developing a written product.

Structural analysis—An examination of multisyllable words, using knowledge of root words, prefixes, suffixes, and compound words to derive word meaning.

Study guides—Teacher-made guides to help students become actively engaged before, during, and after reading.

Suffix—An affix attached to the end of a base, root, or stem that changes the meaning or grammatical function of a word.

Sustained silent reading (SSR)—Regularly scheduled period of time during the school day when students read self-selected books without interruption.

Synthetic phonics—An approach to teaching phonics that emphasizes first letter sounds and then blending those sounds into words.

Teacher candidates—Teachers in preservice or inservice professional development programs who are candidates for an undergraduate or graduate degree in education.

Teacher-mediated instruction—Teacher intervention at an individual, small-group, or class level to provide support in learning.

Think-aloud—A procedure that involves verbalizing thought processes while reading or writing. Teachers, students, or teachers and students together can engage in think-alouds.

Title recognition tests—Assessment tools consisting of lists of real and imaginary book titles; used to tap student knowledge of children's literature.

Tone—The type of voice used when speaking.

Top-down perspective—A perspective of reading instruction that is based on reading as a process of making meaning. Top-down advocates see reading as a psycholinguistic process, with emphasis on the use of personally relevant and authentic reading material.

Total physical response (TPR)—A communicative approach that can be used to assist students in vocabulary learning during initial stages of second-language learning. With TPR, students respond physically rather than orally to verbal commands.

Traditional literature—Stories, wise sayings, and rhymes that have been passed down over the generations by storytellers from diverse cultures. Examples of traditional literature include folk tales, fairy tales, fables, and myths.

Transitional stage—The stage of spelling development where students are making the transition to conventional spelling. Vowels are used appropriately, and writers are beginning to apply systematic rules to their spelling.

Two-column note taking—A system for helping students structure notes from lectures or from text they have read. Consists of a cue column where key words and concepts are listed, and a recall column where definitions and further elaborations are recorded.

Visual literacy—The ability to interpret and glean a message from graphic stimuli. Particularly important in deriving a message from picture books.

Volunteers—Unpaid adults or students from local high schools or colleges who assist in reading instruction, either during school or in after-school programs.

Vowel digraphs—Vowel combinations that work together to represent a single sound (e.g., *-eigh* in *weigh*, *-ay* in *pay*).

Vowel diphthongs—Vowel combinations that form new sounds (e.g., *-oi-* in *boil*, *-ou-* in *bout*).

Vowel patterns—Also called *spelling or syllable patterns*, *word families*, or *phonograms*; groupings of vowels in words or syllables that are decoded according to the position of the vowels and the consonants surrounding them. There are six different types of vowel patterns that appear in 85%–88% of all English-language words (Moats, 2000).

WebQuest—Computer activities that involve use of the Internet to conduct research and solve problems.

Word maps—Graphic organizers used to detail word meanings and relationships with other words and concepts.

Word-to-word matching—The ability to isolate a sound in the same position in two distinct words and compare the sound.

Words per minute (wpm)—The number of words read in one minute's time.

Writers' Workshop—Regularly scheduled class time when students have the opportunity to engage in the writing process, working on both individual and collaborative pieces. Writers' Workshop includes mini-lessons, designated writing time, status of the class, conference time, and sharing time.

Writing process—A series of fluid and recursive stages that writers go through in developing a product. The stages can be applied to writing instruction for students and include prewriting, drafting, rewriting, and postwriting.

Writing time—Regularly scheduled classroom time designated for development of written products.

Young adult literature—Books written with adolescents in mind as an audience.

References

For references for assessment instruments, see Appendix C. For children's literature references, see Appendix D.

Adams, M. J. (1990). *Beginning to read: Thinking and learning about print.* Cambridge, MA: MIT Press.

Adams, M. J., Foorman, B., Lundberg, I., & Beeler, C. (1998). *Phonemic awareness in young children: A classroom curriculum.* Baltimore: Brookes.

Afflerbach, P. (2004). *National Reading Conference policy brief: High stakes testing and reading assessment.* Chicago: National Reading Conference.

Ager, S. (1998). *Omniglot: A guide to writing systems—Cherokee Syllabary.* Retrieved from *www.omniglot.com/writing/cherokee.htm*

Allen, J. (1995). *It's never too late: Leading adolescents to lifelong literacy.* Portsmouth, NH: Heinemann.

Allen, J. (2000). *Yellow brick roads: Shared and guided paths to independent reading 4–12.* Portland, ME: Stenhouse.

Allen, J. (2002). *On the same page: Shared reading beyond the primary grades.* Portland, ME: Stenhouse.

Allen, J., & Gonzalez, K. (1998). *There's room for me here: Literacy workshop in the middle school.* Portland, ME: Stenhouse.

Allington, R. L. (1983). Fluency: The neglected goal. *The Reading Teacher, 36*(6), 556–561.

Allington, R. L. (2001). *What really matters for struggling readers.* New York: Longman.

Allington, R. L. (2002). *Big Brother and the national reading curriculum: How ideology trumped evidence.* Portsmouth, NH: Heinemann.

Allington, R. L. (2006). *What really matters for struggling readers* (2nd ed.). Boston: Pearson/Allyn & Bacon.

Alvermann, D. E., & Phelps, S. F. (2001). *Content reading and literacy: Succeeding in today's diverse classrooms.* Boston: Allyn & Bacon.

American Library Association. (1987). *Terms and criteria: Randolph Caldecott Medal.* Retrieved December 2, 2005, from *www.ala.org*

Anderson, N. A. (2002). *Elementary children's literature: The basics for teachers and parents.* Boston: Allyn and Bacon.

Anderson, R. C., & Freebody, P. (1981). Vocabulary knowledge. In J. T. Guthrie (Ed.), *Comprehension and teaching: Research reviews* (pp. 77–117). Newark, DE: International Reading Association.

Anderson, R. C., & Freebody, P. (1985). Vocabulary knowledge. In H. Singer & R. B. Ruddell (Eds.), *Theoretical models and processes of reading* (3rd ed., pp. 343–371). Newark, DE: International Reading Association.

Anderson, V., & Roit, M. (1998). Reading as a gateway to language proficiency for language minority students in the elementary grades. In R. M. Gersten & R. T. Jiménez (Eds.), *Promoting learning for culturally and linguistically diverse students* (pp. 42–54). Belmont, CA: Wadsworth.

Anderson-Inman, L., & Horney, M. (1996–1997). Computer-based concept mapping: Enhancing literacy with tools for visual thinking. *Journal of Adolescent and Adult Literacy, 40*(4), 302–306.

Asher, J. J. (2005). *Total physical response.* Retrieved November 28, 2005, from *www.tpr-world.com*

Arguelles, M. E., Morris, P. B., & Ross, J. (2003). *Meeting the needs of struggling readers: A resource for secondary English language arts teachers.* Austin: University of Texas/Texas Education Agency.

Arguelles, M. E., Vaughn, S., & Schumm, J. S. (1996). Executive summaries for ESE/FEFP pilot program. Tallahassee, FL. Report submitted to Florida Department of Education. Strategy for middle school students. *Dissertation Abstracts International, 40,* 5369A.

Armbruster, B. B., & Anderson, T. H. (1984). *Producing "considerate" expository text or easy reading is damned hard writing* (Reading Education Report No. 46). Champaign: Center for the Study of Reading, University of Illinois.

Arnoff, M. (1994). Morphology. In A. C. Purves, L. Papa, & S. Jordan (Eds.), *Encyclopedia of English studies and language arts* (Vol. 2, pp. 820–821). New York: Scholastic.

Asher, J. J. (1982). The total physical response approach. In R. W. Blair (Ed.), *Innovative approaches to language teaching* (pp. 54–66). Rowley, MA: Newbury House.

Asselin, M. (2003). Literacy and diversity: Working with the grain. *Teacher Librarian, 30*(4), 53–54.

Atkinson, R., & Hansen, D. (1966–1967). Computer-assisted instruction in initial reading. The Stanford Project. *Reading Research Quarterly, 2,* 5–26.

Atwell, N. (1987). *In the middle: Writing, reading, and learning with adolescents.* Portsmouth, NH: Boynton/Cook.

Atwell, N. (1998). *In the middle: New understandings about writing, reading, and learning* (2nd ed.). Portsmouth, NH: Heinemann.

Au, K. H. (1993). *Literacy instruction in multicultural settings.* Orlando, FL: Harcourt Brace.

Au, K. H. (2002). Multicultural factors and effective instruction of students of diverse backgrounds. In A. Farstrup & S. J. Samuels (Eds.). *What research says about reading instruction* (pp. 392–413). Newark, DE: International Reading Association.

Auerbach, E. R. (1989). Toward a socio-contextual approach to family literacy. *Harvard Educational Review, 59,* 165–181.

August, D. (2003, December). Overview. In T. Shanahan (Chair), *National Literacy Panel on Language Minority Children and Youth: Findings from the Panel's research synthesis.* Symposium conducted at the 53rd annual meeting of the National Reading Conference, Scottsdale, AZ.

Avalos, M. A. (2003). Effective second-language reading transition: From learner-specific to generic instructional models. *Bilingual Research Journal, 27*(2), 171–199.

Bader, L. A. (2005). *Bader Reading and Language Inventory* (5th ed.). Upper Saddle River, NJ: Prentice Hall.

Baker, S., Linan-Thompson, S., & Arguelles, M. E. (2003). *Oregon Reading First and English language learners: An overview of key concepts and principles.* Eugene: Oregon Reading First Center.

Baker, L., & Brown, A. L. (1984). Metacognitive skills and reading. In P. D. Pearson, R. Barr, M. Kamil, & P. Mosenthal (Eds.), *Handbook of reading research* (Vol. 1, pp. 353–394). New York: Longman.

Baldwin, R. S., Peleg-Bruckner, Z., & McClintock, A. (1985). Effects of topic interest and prior knowledge on reading comprehension. *Reading Research Quarterly, 20,* 497–504.

Ball, E. W., & Blachman, B. A. (1991). Does phonemic awareness training in kindergarten make a difference in early word recognition and developmental spelling? *Reading Research Quarterly, 26,* 49–66.

Ballentine, D., & Hill, L. (2000). Teaching beyond once upon a time. *Language Arts, 78,* 11–20.

Barab, S. A., Thomas, M., Dodge, T., Carteaux, R., & Tuzun, H. (2003). *Making learning fun: Quest Atlantis, a game without guns.* Retrieved from *http://inkido.indiana.edu/research/onlinemanu/papers/QA_ETRD.pdf*

Barker, T. A., & Torgesen, J. K. (1995). An evaluation of computer-assisted instruction in phonological awareness with below average readers. *Journal of Educational Computing Research, 13,* 89–103.

Barr, R. (1995). What research says about grouping in the past and present and what it suggests about the future. In M. C. Radencich & L. J. MacKay (Eds.), *Flexible grouping for literacy in the elementary grades* (pp. 1–24). Boston: Allyn & Bacon.

Barrentine, S. J. (Ed.). (1999). *Reading assessment: Principles and practices for elementary teachers.* Newark, DE: International Reading Association.

Barrera, R. (1983). Bilingual reading in the primary grades: Some questions about questionable views and practices. In T. H. Escobedo (Ed.), *Early childhood bilingual education: A Hispanic perspective* (pp. 164–183). New York: Teachers College Press.

Baumann, J. F., Edwards, E. C., Font, G., Tereshinski, C. A., Kame'enui, E. J., & Olejnik, S. (2002). Teaching morphemic and contextual analysis to fifth-grade students. *Reading Research Quarterly*, *37*(2), 150–176.

Baumann, J. F., & Kame'enui, E. J. (Eds.). (2004). *Vocabulary instruction: Research to practice*. New York: Guilford Press.

Bean, R. M. (2004). *The reading specialist: Leadership for the classroom, school, and community*. New York: Guilford Press.

Bear, D. R., Invernizzi, M., Templeton, S., & Johnson, F. (2000). *Words their way: Word study for phonics, vocabulary, and spelling instruction* (2nd ed.). Upper Saddle River, NJ: Merrill.

Bear, D. R., & Templeton, S. (1998). Explorations in developmental spelling: Foundations for learning and teaching phonics, spelling, and vocabulary. *The Reading Teacher*, *52*, 222–242.

Beck, I. L., & McKeown, M. G. (1983). Learning words well: A program to enhance vocabulary and comprehension. *The Reading Teacher*, *36*, 622–625.

Beck, I. L., & McKeown, M. G. (1991). Conditions of vocabulary acquisition. In R. Barr, M. L. Kamil, P. Mosenthal, & P. D. Pearson (Eds.), *Handbook of reading research*(Vol. 2, pp. 789–814). White Plains, NY: Longman.

Beck, I. L., & McKeown, M. G., Hamilton, R. L., & Kucan, L. (1997). *Questioning the author: An approach for enhancing student engagement with text*. Newark, DE: International Reading Association.

Beck, I. L., McKeown, M. G., & Kucan, L. (2002). *Bringing words to life: Robust vocabulary instruction*. New York: Guilford Press.

Beck, I. L., McKeown, M. G., & Omanson, R. C. (1987). The effects and uses of diverse vocabulary instructional techniques. In M. G. McKeown & M E. Curtis (Eds.), *The nature of vocabulary acquisition* (pp. 147–163). Hillsdale, NJ: Erlbaum.

Beck, I. L., Omanso, R. C., & McKeown, M. G. (1982). An instructional redesign of reading lessons: Effects on comprehension. *Reading Research Quarterly*, *17*, 462–481.

Beck, I. L., Perfetti, C. A., & McKeown, M. G. (1982). The effects of long-term vocabulary instructional techniques. *Journal of Educational Psychology*, *74*, 506–521.

Becker, H. J., & Anderson, R. (2000). *Subject and teacher objectives for computer using classes by school socio-economic status*. Irvine and Minneapolis: Center for Research on Information Technology and Organizations, University of California–Irvine and University of Minnesota.

Becker, H. J., Ravitz, J. L., & Wong, Y. (1999). *Teacher and teacher-directed student use of computers and software* (Vol. 2000). Irvine and Minneapolis: Center for Research on Information Technology and Organizations, University of California–Irvine and University of Minnesota.

Benson, V., & Cummins, C. (2000). *The power of retelling*. Desoto, TX: Wright Group/McGraw-Hill.

Bergeron, B. (1990). What does the term whole language mean?: Constructing a definition from the literature. *Journal of Reading Behavior*, *22*, 301–329.

Bermúdez, A., & Márquez, J. (1998, June–July). Gifted and talented students. *Intercultural Development Research Association Newsletter*. Retrieved from *www.idra.org/Newslttr/1998/jun/Andrea.htm*

Bernhardt, E. B. (1991). *Reading development in a second language: Theoretical, empirical, and classroom perspectives*. Norwood, NJ: Ablex.

Bessai, F. (1998). *Peabody Picture Vocabulary Test—III* [Review]. Retrieved July 14, 2004, from *http://gateway2.ovid.com/ovidweb.cgi*

Bessell, A. G., Schumm, J. S., Lee, O., Liftin, E., & Walsh, S. (2003). Beyond standardized test scores: Using case studies to evaluate a reform strategy. In W. Simmons & M. Grady (Eds.), *Research perspectives on school reform: Lessons from the Annenberg Challenge* (pp. 117–132). Providence, RI: Brown University.

Betts, E. A. (1946). *Foundations of reading instruction*. New York: American Book.

Betts, E. A. (1957). *Foundations of reading instruction* (4th ed.). New York: American Book.

Bhat, P., Griffin, C. C., & Sindelar, P. T. (2003). Phonological awareness instruction for middle school students with learning disabilities. *Learning Disabilities Quarterly*, *21*, 73–87.

Birch, B. M. (2002). *English L2 reading: Getting to the bottom*. Mahwah, NJ: Erlbaum.

Bishop, R. S. (1997). Selecting literature for a multicultural curriculum. In V. J. Harris (Ed.), *Using multiethnic literature in the K–8 classroom*. Norwood, MA: Christopher-Gordon.

Blachman, B. A. (1988). The futile search for a theory of learning disabilities. *Journal of Learning Disabilities*, *21*, 286–288.

Blachman, B., Ball, E. W., Black, R., & Tangel, D. (1999). *Road to the code: A phonological awareness program for young children.* Baltimore: Brookes.

Blachowicz, C. (1986). Making connections: Alternatives to the vocabulary notebook. *Journal of Reading, 29*, 543–549.

Blachowicz, C. (1993). Modeling C(2)QU: Modeling context use in the classroom. *The Reading Teacher, 47*, 268–269.

Blachowicz, C., & Fisher, P. (1996). *Teaching vocabulary in all classrooms.* Columbus, OH: Merrill.

Blachowicz, C., & Fisher, P. (2000). Vocabulary instruction. In M. L. Kamil, P. B. Mosenthal, P. D. Pearson, & R. Barr (Eds.), *Handbook of reading research* (Vol. 3, pp. 503–523). Mahwah, NJ: Erlbaum.

Blachowicz, C., & Lee, J. (1991). Vocabulary development in the whole literacy classroom. *The Reading Teacher, 45*, 188–195.

Blanton, W., Menendez, R., Moorman, G., & Pacifici, L. (2003). Learning to comprehend written directions through participation in a mixed activity system. *Early Education and Development, 14*(3), 313–333.

Blanton, W., Moorman, G., & Hayes, B. (1998). Effects of participation in the Fifth Dimension on far transfer. *Journal of Computing Research, 16*, 371–396.

Blevins, W. (1997). *Phonemic awareness activities for early reading success.* New York: Scholastic.

Blevins, W. (2001). *Teaching phonics and word study in the intermediate grades: A complete sourcebook.* New York: Scholastic.

Block, C. C., & Pressley, M. (2002). *Comprehension instruction: Research-based best practices.* New York: Guilford Press.

Block, C. C., & Pressley, M. (2003). Best practices in comprehension instruction. In L. M. Morrow, L. B. Gambrell, & M. Pressley (Eds.), *Best practices in literacy instruction* (2nd ed., pp. 111–126). New York: Guilford Press.

Blok, H., Oostdam, R., Otter, M., & Overmatt, M. (2002). Computer-assisted instruction in support of beginning reading instruction: A review. *Review of Educational Research, 72*(1), 101–130.

Bloomfield, L., & Barnhart, C. L. (1961). *Let's read: A linguistic approach.* Detroit, MI: Wayne State University Press.

Blum, I. H. (1995). Using audiotaped books to extend classroom literacy instruction into the homes of second language learners. *Journal of Reading Behavior, 27*, 535–563.

Blum, H. T., Lipsett, L. R., & Yocom, D. J. (2002). Literature circles. *Remedial and Special Education, 23*, 99–108.

Bond, G., & Dykstra, R. (1967). The cooperative research program in first-grade reading instruction. *Reading Research Quarterly, 2*, 5–142.

Bos, C. S., & Vaughn, S. (2002). *Strategies for teaching students with learning problems* (5th ed.). Boston: Allyn & Bacon.

Boult, B., & Walberg, H. (1999). *176 ways to involve parents.* Glenview, IL: SkyLight.

Bowman, M., & Treiman, R. (2002). Relating print and speech: The effects of letter names and word position on reading spelling performance. *Journal of Experimental Child Psychology, 82*, 305–340.

Bradley, L., & Bryant, P. (1983). Categorizing sounds and learning to read: A causal connection. *Nature, 301*, 419–421.

Bransford, J. D., & Johnson, M. K. (1972). Contextual prerequisites for understanding: Some investigations of comprehension and recall. *Journal of Verbal Learning and Verbal Behavior, 11*, 717–726.

Bratcher, S. (1994). *Evaluating children's writing: A handbook of communication choices for classroom teachers.* New York: St. Martin's Press.

Brett, A., Rothlein, L., & Hurley, M. (1996). Vocabulary acquisition from listening to stories and explanations of target words. *Elementary School Journal, 96*, 415–422.

Brossell, G. (1996). Writing assessment in Florida: Reminiscence. In E. M. White, W. D. Lutz, & S. Kamusikiri (Eds.), *Assessment of writing: Politics, policies, practices* (pp. 25–32). New York: Modern Language Association of America.

Brown, A. L., Bransford, J. D., Ferrar, R. A., & Campione, J. C. (1983). Learning, remembering, and understanding. In J. H. Flavell & E. M. Markmans (Eds.), *Handbook of child psychology* (4th ed., Vol. 3, pp. 515–529). New York: Wiley.

Brown, A. L., & Day, J. D. (1983). The development of plans for summarizing texts. *Child Development, 54*, 968–979.

Brown, A. L., & Palincsar, A. (1989). Guided, cooperative learning and individual knowledge acquisition. In L. B. Resnick (Ed.), *Knowing, learning, and instruction: Essays in honor of Robert Glaser* (pp. 393–451). Hillsdale, NJ: Erlbaum.

Brown, K. J. (2000). What kind of text—for whom and when? *The Reading Teacher, 53*, 292–307.

Brown, K. J. (2003). What do I say when they get stuck on a word?: Aligning teachers' prompts with students' development. *The Reading Teacher, 56*(8), 720–733.

Bruce, D. (1964). An analysis of word sounds by young children. *British Journal of Educational Psychology, 34*, 158–170.

Bryant, P., & Bradley, L. (1985). *Children's reading problems: Psychology and education*. Oxford: Blackwell.

Bryant, P., MacLean, M., Bradley, L., & Crossland, J. (1990). Rhyme and alliteration, phoneme detection and learning to read. *Developmental Psychology, 26*, 429–438.

Buly, R., & Valencia, S. W. (2002). Below the bar: Profiles of students who fail state reading assessments. *Educational Evaluation and Policy Analysis, 24*(3), 219–239.

Burns, B. (2001). *Guided reading: A how-to for all grades*. Arlington Heights, IL: SkyLight.

Caldwell, J. S., & Leslie, L. (2005). *Intervention strategies to follow informal reading inventory assessment: So what do I do now?* Boston: Pearson Education.

Caldwell, K., & Gaine, T. (2000). *"The Phantom Tollbooth" and how the independent reading of good books improves students' reading performances*. Bloomington, IN: Reading and Clearinghouse on Communication Skills. (ERIC Document Reproduction Service No. ED449462)

Calkins, L. M. (1991). *Living between the lines*. Portsmouth, NH: Heinemann.

Calkins, L. M. (1994). *The art of teaching writing*. Portsmouth, NH: Heinemann.

Callella, T., Samoiloff, S., & Tom, D. (2001). *Making your word wall more interactive*. Huntington Beach, CA: Creative Teaching Press.

Camp, R. (1996). Response: The politics of methodology. In E. M. White, W. D. Lutz, & S. Kamusikiri (Eds.), *Assessment of writing: Politics, policies, practices* (pp. 97–99). New York: Modern Language Association of America.

Carey, S. (1985). Are children fundamentally different thinkers and learners from adults? In S. F. Chipman, J. W. Segal, & R. Glaser (Eds.), *Thinking and learning skills* (Vol. 2, pp. 485–517). Hillsdale, NJ: Erlbaum.

Carlisle, J. F. (2000). Awareness of the structure and meaning of morphologically complex words: Impact on reading. *Reading and Writing, 12*, 169–190.

Carlo, M. S., August, D., McLaughlin, B., Snow, C. E., Dressler, C., Lippma, D. N., et al. (2004). Closing the gap: Addressing the vocabulary needs of English-language learners in bilingual and mainstream classrooms. *Reading Research Quarterly, 39*, 188–215.

Carnine, D. W., Silbert, J., & Kame'enui, E. J. (1996). *Direct instruction reading* (3rd ed.). Upper Saddle River, NJ: Pearson Education.

Carnine, D. W., Silbert, J., Kame'enui, E. J., & Tarver, S. (2004). *Direct instruction reading* (4th ed.). Upper Saddle River, NJ: Pearson Education.

Carr, E. M. (1985). The vocabulary overview guide: A metacognitive strategy to improve vocabulary comprehension and retention. *Journal of Reading, 28*, 684–689.

Carr, E. M., & Wixson, K. K. (1986). Guidelines for evaluating vocabulary instruction. *Journal of Reading, 29*, 588–595.

Carroll, J. A., & Wilson, E. E. (1993). *Acts of teaching: How to teach writing*. Englewood, CO: Teacher Ideas Press.

Carroll, L. (1996) Jabberwocky. From *Through the looking-glass and what Alice found there*. Retrieved from *www.jabberwocky.com/carroll/jabber/jabberwocky.html* (Original work published 1872)

Carson, L., Kirby, J. R., & Hutchinson, N. L. (2000). Phonological processing, family support, academic self-concept as predictors of early reading. *Canadian Journal of Education, 25*, 310–327.

Carson-Dellosa, Inc. (1994). *Introducing word families through literature*. Greensboro, NC: Author.

Cassell, J., & Ryokai, K. (2001). Making space for voice: Technologies to support children's fantasy storytelling. *Personal Technologies, 5*(3), 203–224.

Catts, H. (1995). Early language impairments and developmental dyslexia. *Dyslexia: An International Journal of Research and Practice, 1*, 51–53.

Chall, J. S. (1967). *Learning to read: The great debate*. New York: McGraw-Hill.

Chall, J. S. (1991). American reading instruction: Science, art, and ideology. In W. Ellis (Ed.), *All language and the creation of literacy* (pp. 20–26). Baltimore: Orton Dyslexia Society.

Chall, J. S., Bissex, G., Conard, S., & Harris-Sharples, S. (1996). *Qualitative assessment of text difficulty: A practical guide for teachers and authors.* Cambridge, MA: Brookline Books.

Chall, J. S., Jacobs, V., & Baldwin, L. (1990). *The reading crises: Why poor children fall behind.* Cambridge, MA: Harvard University Press.

Chall, J. S., & Popp, H. M. (1996). *Teaching and assessing phonics: Why, what, when, how.* Cambridge, MA: Education Publishing Service.

Chard, D. J., & Dickson, S. V. (1999). Phonological awareness: Instructional and assessment guidelines. *Intervention in School and Clinic, 34,* 261–270.

Chard, D. J., & Osborn, J. (1998). *Suggestions for examining phonics and decoding instruction in supplementary reading programs.* Austin: Texas Education Agency.

Chard, D. J., Vaughn, S., & Tyler, B. (2002). A synthesis of research on effective interventions for building reading fluency with elementary students with learning disabilities. *Journal of Learning Disabilities, 35,* 386–407.

Cheney, A. (1984). *Teaching reading skills through the newspaper.* Newark, DE: International Reading Association.

Cheyney, W. J., & Cohen, E. J. (1999). *Focus on phonics: Assessment and instruction.* Bothell, WA: Wright Group.

Chiappone, L. L. (2003). A comparative study of English language learners reading storybooks in traditional print and digital formats. *Dissertation Abstracts International, 65*(1), 121.

Chomsky, N. (1965). *Aspects of the theory of syntax.* Cambridge, MA: MIT Press.

Chun, D., & Plass, J. (1996). Effects of multimedia annotations on vocabulary acquisition. *Modern Language Journal, 80,* 183–198.

Clark, K. F. (2004). What can I say besides "sound it out"?: Coaching word recognition in beginning reading. *The Reading Teacher, 57*(5), 440–449.

Clark, R. E. (1992). Dangers in the evaluation of instructional media. *Academic Medicine, 67*(12), 819–820.

Clay, M. M. (1966). *Emergent reading behavior.* Unpublished doctoral dissertation, University of Auckland, Auckland, New Zealand.

Clay, M. M. (1985). *The early detection of reading difficulties* (3rd ed.). Portsmouth, NH: Heinemann.

Clay, M. M. (1987). Implementing reading recovery: Systematic adaptations to an educational innovation. *New Zealand Journal of Educational Studies, 22,* 35–36.

Clay, M. M. (2001). *Change over time in children's literacy development.* Portsmouth, NH: Heinemann.

Clay, M. M., & Imlach, R. (1971). Juncture, pitch, and stress as reading behavior variables. *Journal of Verbal Learning and Verbal Behavior, 10,* 133–139.

Clinton, H. R. (1996). *It takes a village.* New York: Simon & Schuster.

Clymer, T. (1963). The utility of phonic generalizations in the primary grades. *The Reading Teacher, 16,* 252–258.

Cohen, E. J. K. (1996). *The effects of a holistic graphophonic intervention on the decoding performance of children with reading disabilities.* Unpublished doctoral dissertation, Florida International University.

Coleridge, S. T. (1907). *Biographia literaria.* London: Oxford University Press. (Original work published 1817)

Collier, V. P., & Thomas, W. P. (1989). How quickly can immigrants become proficient in school English? *Journal of Educational Issues of Language Minority Students, 5,* 26–38.

Colman, P. (1999). Nonfiction is literature too. *New Advocate, 12,* 215–223.

Comeau, L., Cormier, P., Grandmaison, È., & Lacroix, D. (1999). A longitudinal study of phonological processing skills in children learning to read in a second language. *Journal of Educational Psychology, 91*(1), 29–43.

Cook, L., & Friend, M. (1995). Co-teaching: Guidelines for effective practice. *Focus on Exceptional Children, 28,* 1–12.

Cooper, H. (1989). *Homework.* White Plains, NY: Longman.

Cooper, J. D. (2006). *Literacy: Helping children construct meaning.* Boston: Houghton Mifflin.

Cooter, R. B., Mills-House, E., Marrin, P., Mathews, B. A., Campbell, S., & Baker, T. (1999). Family and community involvement: The bedrock of reading success. *The Reading Teacher, 52,* 891–896.

Cotton, K. (2001). *Teaching composition: Research on effective practices.* Portland, OR: Northwest Regional Educational Laboratory.

Council for Exceptional Children. (1999). *ERIC/OSEP mini-library: Adapting curricular materials* (3 vols.). Reston, VA: Author.

Cramer, E., Schumm, J. S., Moreyra, A., & Young, J. (2005). *America Reads: Lessons learned from administrators, teachers, and students in a large urban school district.* Manuscript submitted for publication.

Cramer, R. L. (2004). *The language arts: A balanced approach to teaching reading, writing listening, talking, and thinking.* Boston: Allyn & Bacon.

Crocker, L. (2000). Review of the Woodcock–Muñoz Language Survey. *Mental Measurements Yearbook.* Retrieved from *web5s.silverplatter.com/webspirs/stark.wscustomer=cl4878&databases=yb*

Cromwell, S. (1997). Whole language and phonics: Can they work together. *Education World. Retrieved from www.education-world.com/a_curr/curr029.shtml*

Cuban, L. (2001). *Oversold and underused: Computers in the classroom.* Cambridge, MA: Harvard University Press.

Cummins, J. (1981). *Bilingualism and minority language children.* Toronto: Institute for Studies in Education.

Cummins, J. (1991). Interdependence of first- and second-language proficiency in bilingual children. In E. Bialystok (Ed.), *Language processes in bilingual children* (pp. 70–89). Cambridge, UK: Cambridge University Press.

Cummins, J. (2003). Reading and the bilingual student: Fact and friction. In G. G. Garcia (Ed.), *English learners: Reaching the highest level of English literacy* (pp. 2–33). Newark, DE: International Reading Association.

Cunningham, P. M. (1990). The Names Test: A quick assessment of decoding ability. *The Reading Teacher, 44,* 124–129.

Cunningham, P. M. (2005). *Phonics they use* (4th ed.). Boston: Pearson/Allyn & Bacon.

Cunningham, P. M., & Allington, R. L. (2002). *Classrooms that work: They can all read and write* (3rd ed.). New York: Longman.

Cunningham, P. M., & Hall, D. (1994a). *Making Big Words: Multi-level hands-on spelling and phonics activities.* New York: Good Apple.

Cunningham, P. M., & Hall, D. (1994b). *Making Words: Hands-on developmentally appropriate spelling and phonics activities.* New York: Good Apple.

Cunningham, P. M., Moore, S. A., Cunningham, J. W., & Moore, D. W. (2000). *Reading and writing in elementary classrooms: Strategies and observations* (4th ed.). New York: Longman.

Cunningham, A. E., & Stanovich, K. E. (1997). Early reading acquisition and its relation to reading experience and ability 10 years later. *Developmental Psychology, 33,* 934–945.

Cunningham, A. E., & Stanovich, K. E. (1998). What reading does for the mind. *American Educator, 22,* 8–15.

Dahlstrom, L. M. (2000). *Writing down the days: 365 creative journaling ideas for young people.* Minneapolis, MN: Free Spirit.

Dale, E., & Chall, J. (1948). A formula for predicting readability. *Educational Research Bulletin, 27,* 11–20.

Dale, E., & O'Rourke, J. (1971). *Techniques of teaching vocabulary.* Palo Alto, CA: Field.

Davidson, J., Coles, D., Noyes, P., & Terrell, C. (1991). Using computer-delivered natural speech to assist in the teaching of reading. *British Journal of Educational Technology, 22,* 110–118.

Davis, G. A., & Rimm, S. B. (2004). *Education of the gifted and talented* (5th ed.). Boston: Pearson Education.

Dechant, E. V. (1993). *Whole-language reading: A comprehensive teaching guide.* Lancaster, PA: Technomic.

Deem, D., Feely, L., Fullmer, C., Lienemann, D., & Moore, K. (2002). *Ready-to-go management kit for teaching genre: Dozens of engaging response activities to use with any book that help kids explore 10 genres independently.* New York: Scholastic.

Delgado-Gaitan, C. (1990, January). *Involving parents in the schools: A process of empowerment.* Paper presented at the University of California Symposium on Race, Ethnicity, and Schooling, Davis.

Dickson, S. V., & Bursuck, W. D. (1999). Implementing a model for preventing reading failure: A report from the field. *Learning Disabilities Research and Practice, 14,* 191–222.

Dickson, S. V., Simmons, D. C., & Kame'enui, E. J. (1995). *Text organization: Curricular and instructional implications for diverse learners.* Eugene: National Center to Improve the Tools of Educators, University of Oregon.

Dodge, B. (1997). *Some thoughts about WebQuests.* Retrieved from *http://edweb.sdsu.edu/courses/edtec596/about_webquests.html*

Dolch, E. W. (1942). *The basic sight word test.* Champaign, IL: Garrard.

Dole, J. A. (2003). *Comprehension instruction.* Paper presented at the National Higher Education Collaboration Seminar, Albuquerque, NM.

Dole, J. A., Duffy, G. G., Roehler, L. R., & Pearson, P. D. (1991). Moving from the old to the new: Research on reading comprehension instruction. *Review of Educational Research, 61*(2), 239–264.

Dougherty Stahl, K. A. (2004). Proof, practice, and promise: Comprehension strategy instruction in the primary grades. *The Reading Teacher, 57*(7), 598–609.

Dowhower, S. (1987). Effects of repeated reading on second-grade transitional readers' fluency and comprehension. *Reading Research Quarterly, 22(4), 389–406.*

Drucker, M. J. (2003). What reading teachers should know about ESL learners. *The Reading Teacher, 57*, 22–29.

Duffy, G. (1997). Powerful models or powerful teachers?: An argument for teacher-as-entrepreneur. In S. Stahl & D. Hayes (Eds.), *Instructional models in reading* (pp. 351–365). Mahwah, NJ: Erlbaum.

Duke, N. K. (2000). 3.6 minutes per day: The scarcity of informational texts in first grade. *Reading Research Quarterly, 35*, 202–224.

Duke, N. K., & Bennett-Armistead, V. S. (2003). *Reading and writing informational text in the primary grades: Research-based practices.* New York: Scholastic.

Duke, N. K., & Purcell-Gates, V. (2003). Genres at home and at school: Bridging the known to the new. *The Reading Teacher, 57*, 30–37.

Dunlap, G., dePerczel, M., Clarke, S., Wilson, D., Wright, S., White, R., et al. (1994). Choice making to promote adaptive behavior for students with emotional and behavioral challenges. *Journal of Applied Behavior Analysis, 27*, 505–518.

Duren, E. B. (2000). Critical multiculturalism and racism in children's literature. *Multicultural Education, 7*(3), 16–19.

Durkin, D. (1978–1979). What classroom observation reveals about reading comprehension instruction. *Reading Research Quarterly, 14*, 481–533.

Durkin, D. (1980). *Teaching young children to read* (3rd ed.). Boston: Allyn & Bacon.

Durkin, D. (1981). Reading comprehension instruction in five basal reading series. *Reading Research Quarterly, 16*, 515–544.

Durkin, D. (1984). Is there a match between what elementary teachers do and what basal reading manuals recommend? *The Reading Teacher, 37*, 734–744.

Dyson, A. H., & Freedman, S. W. (1991). Writing. In J. Flood, J. M. Jensen, D. Lapp, & J. R. Squire (Eds.), *Handbook of research on teaching the English language arts* (pp. 754–774). New York: Macmillan.

Echevarria, J., Vogt, M., & Short, D. (2000). *Making content comprehensible for English language learners: The SIOP model.* Boston: Allyn & Bacon.

Edelsky, C., Altwerger, B., & Flores, B. M. (1991). *Whole language: What's the difference* Portsmouth, NH: Heinemann.

Edwards, P. A. (2003). Introduction. In P. A. Mason & J. S. Schumm (Eds.), *Promising practices for urban reading instruction* (pp. 308–318). Newark, DE: International Reading Association.

Edwards, P. A. (2004). *Children's literacy development: Making it happen through school, family, and community involvement.* Boston: Allyn & Bacon.

Ehri, L. C. (1995). Phases of development in learning to read words by sight. *Journal of Research in Reading, 18*, 116–125.

Ehri, L. C. (1998). Grapheme–phoneme knowledge is essential for learning to read words in English. In J. Metsala & L. Ehri (Eds.), *Word recognition in beginning literacy* (pp. 3–40). Mahwah, NJ: Erlbaum.

Ehri, L. C., & McCormick, S. (1998). Phases of word learning: Implications for instruction with delayed and disabled readers. *Reading and Writing Quarterly, 14*, 135–163.

Eissenberg, T. E., & Rudner, L. M. (1988). Explaining test results to parents. *Practical Assessment, Research and Evaluation, 1*, 1–2.

Elbaum, B. E., Vaughn, S., Hughes, M. T., & Moody, S. W. (2000). How effective are one-to-one tutoring programs in reading for elementary students at risk for reading failure?: A meta-analysis of the intervention research. *Journal of Educational Psychology*, *92*, 605–619.

Elkind, D. (1981). *The hurried child.* Cambridge, MA: Perseus.

Elkind, D. (2001). *The hurried child* (3rd ed.). Cambridge, MA: Perseus.

Emig, J. (1971). *The composing processes of twelfth graders.* Urbana, IL: National Council of Teachers of English.

Englemann, S., & Bruner, E. (1969). *Distar reading program.* Chicago: Science Research Associates.

Englert, C. S., & Raphael, T. E. (1988). Constructive well-formed prose: Process, structure, and metacognitive knowledge. *Exceptional Children*, *3*, 98–113.

Englert, C. S., Raphael, T. E., & Anderson, L. M. (1989). *Cognitive strategy instruction in writing process.* East Lansing: Institute for Reseach on Teaching, Michigan State University.

Epstein, J. L. (1995). School/family/community partnerships: Caring for the children we share. *Phi Delta Kappan*, *76*, 705–707.

Erickson, G. C., Foster, K. C., Foster, D. F., Torgesen, J. K., & Packer, S. (1992). *DaisyQuest.* Austin, TX: PRO-ED.

Erickson, G. C., Foster, K. C., Foster, D. F., Torgesen, J. K., & Packer, S. (1993). *Daisy's castle.* Austin, TX: PRO-ED.

Fang, Z. (1996). Illustrations, text, and the child reader: What are pictures in children's storybooks for? *Reading Horizons*, *37*, 130–142.

Farnan, N., & Dahl, K. (2003). Children's writing: Research and practice. In J. Flood, D. Lapp, J. R. Squire, & J. M. Jensen (Eds.), *Handbook of research on the English language arts* (2nd ed., pp. 993–1007). Mahwah, NJ: Erlbaum.

Farstrup, A. E., & Samuels, S. J. (Eds.). (2002). *What research has to say about reading instruction* (3rd ed.). Newark, DE: International Reading Association.

Fashola, O. S. (2002). *Building effective after-school programs.* Thousand Oaks, CA: Corwin Press.

Fearn, L., & Farnan, N. (1998). *Writing effectively: Helping children master the conventions of writing.* Boston: Allyn & Bacon.

Fernald, G. M. (1943). *Remedial techniques in basic school subjects.* New York: McGraw-Hill.

Finney, S. (2003). *Independent reading activities that keep kids learning . . . while you teach small groups (grades 3–6).* New York: Scholastic.

Fisk, C., & Hurst, B. (2003). Paraphrasing for comprehension. *The Reading Teacher*, *57*, 182–185.

Fitzgerald, J., & Graves, M. F. (2004). *Scaffolding reading experiences for English-language learners.* Norwood, MA: Christopher-Gordon.

Flesch, R. (1955). *Why Johnny can't read.* New York: Harper & Row.

Fletcher, J. M. (Chair). (2004). *Important outcomes for children at risk for reading difficulties: Empirical, practical, and ethical issues in diagnosis and early intervention.* Symposium conducted at the University of Miami, Coral Gables, FL.

Fletcher, J. M., & Lyon, G. R. (1998). Reading: A research-based approach. In W. M. Evers (Ed.), *What's gone wrong in America's classrooms* (pp. 50–65). Stanford, CA: Hoover Institution Press.

Fletcher, R., & Portalupi, J. (2001). *Writing workshop: The essential guide.* Portsmouth, NH: Heinemann.

Flett, A., & Conderman, G. (2002). 20 ways to promote phonemic awareness. *Intervention in School and Clinic*, *37*, 242–245.

Flower, L., & Hayes, J. (1980). The dynamics of composing: Making plans and juggling constraints. In L. Gregg & E. Steinberg (Eds.), *Cognitive processes in writing* (pp. 31–50). Hillsdale, NJ: Erlbaum.

Flower, L., & Hayes, J. (1981). A cognitive process theory of writing. *College Composition and Communication*, *32*, 365–387.

Forgan, H. (1977). *The reading corner.* Santa Monica, CA: Goodyear.

Forgan, J. W., & Gonzalez-DeHass, A. (2004). How to infuse social skills training into literacy instruction. *Teaching Exceptional Children*, *36*, 24–30.

Foshay, R. (2000). *Instructional models: Four ways to integrate PLATO into the curriculum* (Technical Paper No. 6). Edina, MN: TRO Learning.

Foster, K. C., Erickson, G. C., Foster, D. F., Brinkman, D., & Torgesen, J. K. (1994). Computer administered instruction in phonological awareness: Evaluation of the DaisyQuest program. *Journal of Research and Development in Education*, *27*, 126–137.

Fountas, I. C., & Pinnell, G. S. (1996). *Guided reading: Good first teaching for all children.* Portsmouth, NH: Heinemann.

Fountas, I. C., & Pinnell, G. S. (1999). *Matching books to readers: Using leveled books in guided reading, K–3* Portsmouth, NH: Heinemann.

Fradd, S. H., & Klingner, J. K. (1995). *Classroom inclusion strategies for students learning English.* Austin, TX: PRO-ED.

Freeman, D. E., & Freeman, Y. S. (2000). *Teaching reading in multicultural classrooms.* Portsmouth, NH: Heinemann.

Freeman, Y. S., & Freeman, D. E. (1992). *Whole language for second language learners.* Portsmouth, NH: Heinemann.

Friend, M., & Bursuck, W. D. (2002). *Including students with special needs: A practical guide for classroom teachers.* Boston: Allyn & Bacon.

Friend, M., & Cook, L. (2002). *Interactions: Collaboration skills for school professionals* (4th ed.). Boston: Allyn & Bacon.

Fry, E. B. (1989). Reading formulas—maligned but valid. *Journal of Reading, 32,* 292–297.

Fry, E. B. (1998). An open letter to United States President Clinton. *The Reading Teacher, 51,* 366–370.

Fry, E. B. (1999). *Spelling book: Words most needed plus phonics by Dr. Fry.* Westminster, CA: Teacher Created Materials.

Fry, E. B., Kress, J. E., & Fountoukidis, D. L. (2000). *The reading teacher's book of lists* (4th ed.). Paramus, NJ: Prentice Hall.

Fuchs, D., Fuchs, L. S., Mathes, P. G., & Lipsey, M. W. (2000). Reading differences between low-achieving students with and without learning disabilities. In R. Gersten, E. P. Schiller, & S. Vaughn (Eds.), *Contemporary special education research: Syntheses of the knowledge base on critical instructional issues* (pp. 81–104). Mahwah, NJ: Erlbaum.

Fuchs, L. S., & Deno, S. L. (1991). Curriculum-based measurement: Current applications and future directions. *Exceptional Children, 57,* 466–501.

Fuchs, L. S., Fuchs, D., Hamlett, C. L., Walz, L., & Germann, G. (1993). Formative evaluation of academic progress: How much growth should we expect? *School Psychology Review, 22,* 27–48.

Fuchs, L. S., Fuchs, F., Hosp, M. K., & Jenkins, R. (2001). Oral reading fluency as an indicator of reading competence: A theoretical, empirical, and historical analysis. *Scientific Studies of Reading, 5*(3), 239–256.

Fulk, B. M., & King, K. (2001). Classwide peer tutoring at work. *Teaching Exceptional Children, 34*(2), 49–53.

Galda, L., & Cullinan, B. E. (2002). *Literature and the child* (5th ed.). Belmont, CA: Wadsworth.

Gambrell, L. B. (1985). Dialogue journals: Reading–writing interaction. *The Reading Teacher, 38,* 512–515.

Gambrell, L. B., Palmer, B. M., & Mazzoni, S. A. (1996). Assessing motivation to read. *The Reading Teacher, 49,* 518–533.

Gangi, J. M. (2004). *Encountering children's literature: An arts approach.* Boston: Allyn & Bacon.

Ganske, K. (2000). *Word journeys: Assessment-guided phonics, spelling, and vocabulary instruction.* New York: Guilford Press.

Ganske, K., Monroe, J. K., & Strickland, D. S. (2003). Questions teachers ask about struggling readers and writers. *The Reading Teacher, 57,* 118–128.

Garan, E. (2001). Beyond the smoke and mirrors: A critique of the National Reading Panel report on phonics. *Phi Delta Kappan, 82*(7), 500–506.

Garcia, G. E. (2003). The reading comprehension development and instruction of English language learners. In A. P. Sweet & C. E. Snow (Eds.), *Rethinking reading comprehension* (pp. 30–50). New York: Guilford Press.

Gee, J. P. (2003). *What video games have to teach us about learning and literacy.* New York: Paulgrave Macmillan.

Gentry, J. R., & Gillet, J. W. (1993). *Teaching kids to spell.* Portsmouth, NH: Heinemann.

Gerke, P. (1996). *Multicultural plays for children: Vol. 1 (grades 1–3) and Vol. 2 (grades 4–6).* Lyme, NH: Smith & Kraus.

Gersten, R. M., & Baker, S. (1999). *Teaching expressive writing to students with learning disabilities: A meta-analysis.* Eugene: University of Oregon.

Gersten, R. M., & Baker, S. (2000). What we know about effective practices for English language learners. *Exceptional Children, 66,* 454–470.

Gersten, R. M., Fuchs, L. S., Williams, J. P., & Baker, S. (2001). Teaching reading comprehension strategies to students with learning disabilities: A review of the research. *Review of Educational Research*, *71*, 279–320.

Gersten, R. M., & Jimenez, R. T. (1998). *Promoting learning for culturally and linguistically diverse students*. Belmont, CA: Wadsworth.

Giambo, D. A. (1999). *The effects of a phonological awareness intervention on the oral English proficiency and English vocabulary of Spanish-speaking kindergarten children*. Unpublished doctoral dissertation, University of Miami.

Gillet, J. W., & Temple, C. (1982). *Understanding reading problems*. Boston: Allyn & Bacon.

Gipe, J. P. (1979–1980). Investigating techniques for teaching words meanings. *Reading Research Quarterly*, *14*, 624–645.

Glass, G. (1973). *Teaching decoding as separate from reading*. Garden City, NY: Adelphi University Press.

Goh, D. S. (2004). *Assessment accommodations for diverse learners*. Boston: Allyn & Bacon.

Goldenberg, C. N. (1987). Low-income Hispanic parents' contributions to their first-grade children's word-recognition skills. *Anthropology and Education Quarterly, 18, 149–179.*

Good, R. H., Kaminski, R. A., Smith, S., Laimon, D., & Dill, S. (2001). *Dynamic Indicators of Basic Early Literacy Skills* (5th ed.). Eugene: University of Oregon.

Goodman, K. S. (1967). Reading: A psycholinguistic guessing game. *Journal of the Reading Specialist*, *6*, 125–135.

Goodman, K. S. (1986). *What's whole about whole language*. Portsmouth, NH: Heinemann.

Gordon, J., Vaughn, S., & Schumm, J. S. (1993). Spelling interventions: A review of literature and implications for instruction for students with learning disabilities. *Learning Disabilities Research and Practice*, *8*, 175–181.

Grabe, M., & Grabe, C. (2004). *Integrating technology for meaningful learning* (4th ed.). New York: Houghton Mifflin.

Grant, C. A., & Gomez, M. L. (2001). Journeying toward multicultural and social reconstructionist teaching and teacher education. In C. A. Grant & M. L. Gomez (Eds.), *Making school multicultural: Campus and classroom* (pp. 3–16). Upper Saddle River, NJ: Merrill.

Graves, D. H. (1978). *Balance the basics: Let them write*. New York: Ford Foundation.

Graves, D. H. (1983). *Writing: Teachers and children at work*. Portsmouth, NH: Heinemann.

Graves, D. H. (1994). *A fresh look at writing*. Portsmouth, NH: Heinemann.

Graves, D. H. (2003). *Writing: Teachers and children at work* (20th anniversary ed.). Portsmouth, NH: Heinemann.

Graves, M. F. (1986). Vocabulary learning and instruction. In E. Rothkopf (Ed.), *Review of research in education* (pp. 49–89). Washington, DC: American Educational Research Association.

Graves, M. F., Brunetti, G. J., & Slater, W. H. (1982). The reading vocabularies of primary-grade children of varying geographic and social backgrounds. In J. A. Harris & L. A. Harris (Eds.), *New inquiries in reading research and instruction* (pp. 99–104). Rochester, NY: National Reading Conference.

Graves, M. F., Cooke, C. L., & Laberge, M. J. (1983). Effects of previewing difficult short stories on low ability junior high school students' comprehension, recall, and attitudes. *Reading Research Quarterly*, *18*, 262–276.

Graves, M. F., & Slater, W. H. (1987). *The development of reading vocabularies in rural disadvantaged students, inner-city disadvantaged students, and middle class suburban students*. Paper presented at the meeting of the American Educational Research Association, Washington, D.C.

Greenleaf, C. L., Jimenez, R. T., & Roller, C. M. (2002). Reclaiming secondary reading interventions: From limited to rich conceptions, from narrow to broad conversations. *Reading Research Quarterly*, *37*, 484–496.

Greenwood, C. R., & Delquadri, J. (1995). Classwide peer tutoring and the prevention of school failure. *Preventing School Failure*, *39*(4), 21–25.

Gregory, G. H., & Chapman, C. (2001). *Differentiated instructional strategies: One size doesn't fit all*. Thousand Oaks, CA: Corwin Press.

Griffith, P. L., & Olson, M. W. (1992). Phonemic awareness helps beginning readers break the code. *The Reading Teacher*, *45*, 516–523.

Gunning, T. G. (2000). *Building words: A resource manual for teaching word analysis and spelling*. Upper Saddle River, NJ: Pearson Education.

Gunning, T. G. (2001). *Building words: A resource manual*. Needham Heights, MA: Allyn & Bacon.

Gunning, T. G. (2002). *Assessing and correcting reading and writing difficulties* (2nd ed.). Boston: Allyn & Bacon.

Hack, C., Hepler, S., & Hickman, J. (2001). *Children's literature in the elementary school* (7th ed.). Boston: McGraw-Hill.

Haggard, M. R. (1980). The vocabulary self-collection strategy: An active approach to word learning. *Journal of Reading*, *26*, 203–207.

Hall, C. J. (2002). The automatic cognate assumption: Evidence for the parasitic model of vocabulary development. *IRAL*, *40*, 69–87.

Hall, R. (1984). *Sniglets: Any word that doesn't appear in the dictionary, but should*. New York: Collier Books.

Hall, T. (2003). *Differentiated instruction*. Wakefield, MA: National Center on Accessing the General Curriculum. (Also available at *www.cast.org*)

Hallahan, D., Lloyd, J., Kauffman, J., Weiss, M., & Martinez, E. (2005). *Learning disabilities: Foundations, characteristics, and effective teaching* (3rd ed.). Boston: Pearson Education.

Hancock, M. R. (2000). *A celebration of literature and response: Children, books, and teachers in K–8 classrooms*. Upper Saddle River, NJ: Prentice Hall.

Hannon, P. (1987). Educational home visiting and the teaching of reading. *Educational Research, 29, 182–191.*

Harmon, J. M. (1998). Constructing word meanings: Strategies and perceptions of four middle school learners. *Journal of Literacy Research*, *30*, 561–599.

Harp, B. (2000). *The handbook of literacy assessment and evaluation* (2nd ed.). Norwood, MA: Christopher-Gordon.

Harris, A. J., & Sipay, E. R. (1980). *How to increase reading ability* (7th ed.). New York: Longman.

Harris, A. J., & Sipay, E. R. (1990). *How to increase reading ability* (9th ed.). New York: Longman.

Harris, K., & Graham, S. (1996). *Making the writing process work: Strategies for composition and self-regulation* (2nd ed.). Cambridge, MA: Brookline Books.

Harris, T. L., & Hodges, R. E. (Eds.) (1995). *The literacy dictionary: The vocabulary of reading and writing*: Newark, DE: International Reading Association.

Harry, B. (1992). Making sense of disability: Low-income, Puerto Rican parents' theories of the problem. *Exceptional Children, 59, 1, 27–40.*

Hart, B., & Risley, T. R. (1995). *Meaningful differences in the everyday experiences of young American children*. Baltimore: Brookes.

Hasbrouck, J. E., & Tindal, G. (1992). Curriculum-based oral reading fluency norms for students in grades 2 through 5. *Teaching Exceptional Children*, *24*, 41–44.

Heath, S. B. (1983). *Ways with words: Language, life, and work in communities and classrooms*. New York: Cambridge University Press.

Heckelman, R. G. (1969). A neurological impress method of remedial reading instruction. *Academic Therapy Quarterly*, *4*, 177–282.

Henderson, A. (1987). *The evidence continues to grow*. Columbia, MD: National Committee for Citizens in Education.

Hennings, D. G. (2000). Contextually relevant word study: Adolescent vocabulary development across the curriculum. *Journal of Adolescent and Adult Literacy*, *44*(3), 268–279.

Herrell, A., & Jordan, M. (2004). *Fifty strategies for teaching English language learners* (2nd ed.). Upper Saddle River, NJ: Pearson Education.

Heuston, D. H. (1996). *Background on reading research behind the Waterford Early Reading Program*. Sandy, UT: Waterford Institute.

Heuston, D., Fletcher-Flinn, C. M., & Gravatt, B. (1995). The efficacy of computer assisted instruction (CAI): A meta-analysis. *Journal of Educational Computing Research*, *12*, 219–241.

Hickman, P., Pollard-Durodola, S., & Vaughn, S. (2004). Storybook reading: Improving vocabulary and comprehension for English-language learners. *The Reading Teacher*, *57*(8), 720–730.

Hiebert, E., & Taylor, B. (1994). *Getting reading right from the start: Effective literacy Interventions*. Boston: Allyn & Bacon.

Hiebert, E. H. (2003, May). *The role of text in developing fluency: A comparison of two interventions*. Paper presented at the annual meeting of the American Educational Research Association, Chicago.

Hiebert, E. H., Pearson, P. D., Taylor, B. M., Richardson, V., & Paris, S. G. (1998). *Every child a reader:*

Applying reading research in the classroom. Ann Arbor, MI: Center for the Improvement of Early Reading Achievement.

Hoffman, J. V., Sailors, M., Duffy, G., & Beretvas, S. N. (2004). The effective elementary classroom literacy environment: Examining the validity of the TEX-IN3 observation system. *Journal of Literacy Research*, *36*, 303–334.

Hohn, W. E., & Ehri, L. (1983). Do alphabet letters help prereaders acquire phonemic segmentation skill? *Journal of Educational Psychology*, *75*, 752–762.

Holdaway, D. (1979). *The foundations of literacy*. Portsmouth, NH: Heinemann.

Holland, K., Bloome, D., & Solsken, J. (Eds.). (1994). *Alternative perspectives in assessing children's language and literacy*. Norwood, NJ: Ablex.

Holmes, B. C., & Roser, N. L. (1987). Five ways to assess readers' prior knowledge. *The Reading Teacher*, *40*, 646–649.

Hourcade, J. J., & Richardson, C. L. (1987). Parents as reading teachers. *Academic Therapy*, *22*(4), 381–383.

Hoyt, L. (2003). *Navigating informational texts: Easy and explicit strategies, K–5* [Videotapes]. Portsmouth, NH: Heinemann.

Hubbard, R. S., & Shorey, V. (2003). Worlds beneath the words: Writing workshop with second language learners. *Language Arts*, *81*(1), 52–61.

Huck, C., & Kiefer, B. (2004). *Children's literature in the elementary school* (8th ed.). Boston: McGraw-Hill.

Hudelson, S. (1984). "Kan yu ret an rayt en ingles": Children become literate in English as a second language. *TESOL Quarterly*, *18*, 221–238.

Huey, E. B. (1968). *The psychology and pedagogy of reading*. Cambridge, MA: MIT Press. (Original work published 1908)

Hughes, M. T. (1995). *Parent involvement in literacy instruction: Perceptions and practices of Hispanic parents of children with learning disabilities*. Unpublished doctoral dissertation, University of Miami.

Hughes, M. T., Valle-Riestra, D. M., & Arguelles, M. E. (2002). Experiences of Latino families with their child's special education program. *Multicultural Perspectives*, *4*, 11–17.

Idol, L. (1987). Group story mapping: A comprehension strategy for both skilled and unskilled readers. *Journal of Learning Disabilities*, *20*, 196–205.

Idol, L., Nevin, A., & Paolucci-Whitcomb, P. (1996). *Models of curriculum-based assessment: A blueprint for learning*. Austin, TX: PRO-ED.

International Reading Association. (1999, May). High-stakes assessment in reading: A position statement of the International Reading Association. *The Reading Teacher*, *53*(3), 257–264.

International Reading Association. (2002). *Evidence-based reading instruction: Putting the National Reading Panel report into practice*. Newark, DE: Author.

International Reading Association, Professional Standards and Ethics Committee. (2003). *Standards for reading professionals—revised 2003*. Newark, DE: Author.

Irvin, J. (1990). *Reading in the middle grades*. Boston: Allyn & Bacon.

Irwin, J. W. (1991). *Teaching reading comprehension processes* (2nd ed.). Englewood Cliffs, NJ: Prentic-Hall.

Irwin, J. W., & Baker, I. (1989). *Promoting active reading comprehension strategies: A resource book for teachers*. Englewood Cliffs, NJ: Prentice-Hall.

Isaacson, S. (1999). Instructionally relevant writing assessment. *Reading and Writing Quarterly*, *15*(1), 29–49.

Ivey, G. (2002). Building comprehension when they're still learning to read the words. In C. C. Block & M. Pressley (Eds.), *Comprehension instruction: Research-based best practices* (pp. 247–258). New York: Guilford Press.

Jacobs, J. E., & Paris, S. G. (1987). Children's metacognition about reading: Issues in definition, measurement, and instruction. *Educational Psychologist*, *22*, 313–332.

Jenkins, J. R., Fuchs, L. S., van den Broek, P., Espin, C., & Deno, S. L. (2003). Sources of individual differences in reading comprehension and reading fluency. *Journal of Educational Psychology*, *95*, 719–729.

Jimerson, S. R. (2001). Meta-analysis of grade retention research: Implications for practice in the 21st century. *School Psychology Review*, *30*, 420–437.

Jitendra, A. K., Edwards, L. L., Sacks, G., & Jacobson, L. A. (2004). What research says about vocabulary instruction for students with learning disabilities. *Exceptional Children, 70,* 299–322.

Johns, J., & Berglund, R. (2002). *Fluency: Questions, answers, evidence-based strategies.* Dubuque, IA: Kendall/Hunt.

Johns, J., & Galen, N. (1977). Reading instruction in the middle 50's: What tomorrow's teachers remember today. *Reading Horizons, 17,* 251–254.

Johns, J., Lenski, S. D., & Elish-Piper, L. (1999). *Reading and learning strategies for middle and high school students.* Dubuque, IA: Kendall/Hunt.

Johnson, D. (1981). A basic vocabulary for teaching beginning reading. *Elementary School Journal, 72,* 29–34.

Johnson, D. (2001). *Vocabulary in the elementary and middle school.* Boston: Allyn & Bacon.

Johnson, D., & Pearson, P. D. (1984). *Teaching reading vocabulary* (2nd ed.). New York: Holt, Rinehart & Winston.

Johnston, P. (1984). *Implications of basic research for the assessment of reading comprehension* (Technical Report No. 206). Urbana–Champaign: Center for the Study of Reading, University of Illinois.

Johnston, P. H. (1981). Assessment in reading. In P. D. Pearson, R. Barr, M. Kamil, & P. Mosenthal (Eds.), *Handbook of reading research* (Vol. 1, pp. 147–182). New York: Longman.

Johnston, P. H., & Allington, R. (1991). Remediation. In R. Barr, M. Kamil, P. Mosenthal, & P. D. Pearson (Eds.), *Handbook of reading research* (Vol. 2, pp. 984–1012). New York: Longman.

Jones, S. (2001). Teacher-friendly curriculum based assessment in spelling. *Teaching Exceptional Children, 34,* 32–38.

Jordan, A. M. (1974). *Children's classics.* Boston: Horn Books.

Jordan, A., & Wright, P. (2004, June 15). *The melody of writing: Tone, rhythm, and music in literature.* Paper presented at the 2004 Zelda Glazer Writing Institute, Miami, FL.

Juel, C. (1996). What makes literacy tutoring effective? *Reading Research Quarterly, 31,* 268–289.

Juel, C., Griffith, P., & Gough, P. (1986). The acquisition of literacy: A longitudinal study of children in first and second grades. *Journal of Educational Psychology, 78,* 243–255.

Kame'enui, E. J. (1995). Overcoming reading difficulties. *Reading and Writing Quarterly, 11,* 3–17.

Kame'enui, E. J., Dixon, R. C., & Carnine, D. (1987). Issues in the design of vocabulary instruction. In M. G. McKeown & M. E. Curtis (Eds.), *The nature of vocabulary acquisition* (pp. 129–146). Hillsdale, NJ: Erlbaum.

Kame'enui, E. J., & Simmons, D. C. (2000). *Planning and evaluation tool for effective schoolwide reading programs.* Eugene: Institute for the Development of Educational Achievement, University of Oregon.

Kame'enui, E. J., & Simmons, D. C. (2003). *Consumer's guide to evaluating a core reading program grades K–3: A critical elements analysis.* Retrieved from *www.idea.uoregon.edu*

Kame'enui, E. J., Simmons, D. C., & Cornachione, C. (2000). *A practical guide to reading assessments.* Newark, DE: International Reading Association.

Kear, D. J., Coffman, G. A., McKenna, M. C., & Ambrosio, A. L. (2000). Writing Attitude Survey. *The Reading Teacher, 54*(1), 16–23.

Kern, D., Andre, W., Schilke, R., Barton, J., & McGuire, M. C. (2003). Less is more: Preparing students for state writing assessments. *The Reading Teacher, 56,* 816–826.

Kibby, M. W. (1995). *Practical steps for informing literacy instruction: A diagnostic decision-making model.* Newark, DE: International Reading Association.

Kiefer, B. (1995). The literature-based movement: Yesterday, today, and tomorrow. *Emergency Librarian, 21,* 8–13.

Kletzien, S. B., & Dreher, M. J. (2004). *Informational text in K–3 classrooms: Helping children read and write.* Newark, DE: International Reading Association.

Klingner, J. K. (2003). Introduction to Reading Right 5. In P. A. Mason & J. S. Schumm (Eds.), *Promising practices for urban reading instruction* (pp. 222–228). Newark, DE: International Reading Association.

Klingner, J. K., Harry, B., & Felton, R. K. (2003). Understanding factors that contribute to disproportionality. *Journal of Special Education Leadership, 16,* 23–33.

Klingner, J. K., & Vaughn, S. (1999). Promoting reading comprehension, content learning and English acquisition through collaborative Strategic Reading. *The Reading Teacher, 52,* 738–747.

Klingner, J. K., Vaughn, S., Dimino, J., Schumm, J. S., & Bryant, D. (2002). *From clunk to click: Collaborative strategic reading.* Longmont, CO: Sopris West.

Klingner, J. K., Vaughn, S., & Schumm, J. D. (1998). Collaborative strategic reading in heterogeneous classrooms. *Elementary School Journal*, *99*, 3–21.

Knight, S. (1994). Dictionary use while reading: The effects on comprehension and vocabulary acquisition for students of different verbal abilities. *Modern Language Journal*, *78*, 285–299.

Kohn, A. (2000). *The case against standardized testing: Raising the scores, ruining the schools.* Portsmouth, NH: Heinemann.

Kohn, A., & Henkin, R. (2002). Poor teaching for poor kids. *Language Arts*, *79*, 251–255.

Kottmeyer, W. (1959). *Teacher's guide for remedial reading.* St. Louis, MO: McGraw Hill.

Krashen, S. (1982). *Principles and practices in second language acquisition.* Oxford: Pergamon.

Krashen, S. (2001). More smoke and mirrors: A critique of the National Reading Panel on fluency. *Phi Delta Kappan*, *83*, 118–121.

Krashen, S. (2003). False claims about phonemic awareness, phonics, skills vs. whole language, and recreational reading. *Nochildleft.com*, *1*(5). Retrieved from *www.nochildleft.com/2003/may03reading.html*

Kress, J. (1993). *The ESL teacher's book of lists.* Upper Saddle River, NJ: Prentice Hall.

Kristo, J., & Bamford, R. (2004). *Nonfiction in focus: A comprehensive framework for helping students become independent readers and writers of nonfiction, K–6.* New York: Scholastic.

Kroll, B. (1990). *Second language writing: Research insights for the classroom.* New York: Cambridge University Press.

Kuhn, M., & Stahl, S. (2000). *Fluency: A review of developmental and remedial practices.* Ann Arbor, MI: Center for the Improvement of Early Reading Achievement.

Kulik, J. A. (1994). Meta-analytic studies of findings on computer-based instruction. In E. Baker & H. O'Neils (Eds.), *Technology assessment in education and training* (pp. 9–33). Hillsdale, NJ: Erlbaum.

Kulik, C. C., & Kulik, J. A. (1991). Effectiveness of computer-based instruction: An updated analysis. *Computers in Human Behavior*, *7*, 75–94.

Kyle, D. W., McIntyre, E., Miller, K. B., & Moore, G. H. (2002). *Reaching out: A K–8 resource for connecting families and schools.* Thousand Oaks, CA: Corwin Press.

LaBerge, D., & Samuels, S. J. (1974). Toward a theory of automatic information processing in reading. *Cognitive Psychology*, *6*, 293–323.

Lane, H. B., & Pullen, P. C. (2004). *Phonological awareness assessment and instruction: A sound beginning.* Boston: Allyn & Bacon.

Lane, H. B., Pullen, P. C., Eisele, M. R., & Jordan, L. (2002). Preventing reading failure: Phonological awareness assessment and instruction. *Preventing School Failure*, *46*(3), 101–110.

Langer, J. A., Bartolomé, L., Vásquez, O., & Lucas T. (1990). Meaning construction in school literacy tasks: A study of bilingual students. *American Educational Research Journal*, *27*, 427–471.

Lapp, D., & Flood, J. (1997). Making the case (again) for integrated code instruction (point–counterpoint). *The Reading Teacher*, *50*, 696–698.

LaPray, M. H., & Ross, R. R. (1969). The graded word list: Quick gauge of reading ability. *Journal of Reading*, *12*, 305–307.

Larrick, N. (1965, September 11). The all-white world of children's literature. *Saturday Review*, pp. 63–65.

Leffa, V. J. (1992). Making foreign language texts comprehensible for beginners: An experiment with an electronic glossary. *System*, *20*, 63–73.

Leu, D. J., & Kinzer, C. K. (2003). *Effective literacy instruction, K–8: Implementing best practice* (5th ed.). Upper Saddle River, NJ: Merrill/Prentice Hall.

Leu, D. J., Leu, D. D., & Coiro, J. (2004). *Teaching with the Internet K–12: New literacies for new times* (4th ed.). Norwood, MA: Christopher-Gordon.

Levy, S., & Vaughn, S. (2002). An observational study of teachers' reading instruction of students with emotional or behavioral disorders. *Behavioral Disorders*, *27*, 215–235.

Liberman, I. Y., Shankweiler, D., & Liberman, A. M. (1989). The alphabetic principle and learning to read. In D. Shankweiler & I. Y. Lieberman (Eds.), *Phonology and reading disability: Solving the reading puzzle* (p. 1–33). Ann Arbor: University of Michigan Press.

Lindamood, P., & Lindamood, P. (2000). *The Lindamood phoneme sequencing program for reading, spelling, and speech.* Austin, TX: PRO-ED.

Little, A. (1990). The role of assessment re-examined in international context. In P. Broadfoot, R. Murphy, & H. Torrance (Eds.), *Changing educational assessment: International perspectives and trends* (pp. 9–23). New York: Routledge.

Lively, T., August, D., Snow, C. E., & Carlo, M. S. (2003). *Vocabulary improvement program for English language learners and their classmates.* Baltimore: Brookes.

Lloyd, S. (1993). *Jolly phonics.* Williston, VT: Jolly Learning.

Lopez-Reyna, N. (2002). Instructional strategies for English language learners with disabilities. In Illinois State Board of Education, *Serving English language learners with disabilities: A resource manual for Illinois educators.* Retrieved from *www.isbe.state.il.us/spec-ed/PDF/bilingual2002manual.pdf*

Lowery, R. M. (2003). Reading? The Star Fisher? Toward critical and sociological interpretations of immigrant literature. *Multicultural Education, 10*(3), 19–23.

Lubell, D. (1991). Spartan lotto-read. *Phi Delta Kappan, 73*, 257–258.

Lundberg, I., Olofsson, A., & Wall, S. (1980). Reading and spelling skills in the first school years predicted from phonemic awareness skills in kindergarten. *Scandinavian Journal of Psychology, 21*, 159–173.

MacIver, M. A., & Kemper, E. (2002). Research on direct instruction reading. *Journal of Education for Students Placed at Risk, 7*(2), 107–116.

Mangrum, C. T., & Forgan, H. W. (1979). *Developing competencies in teaching reading.* Columbus, OH: Merrill.

Manning, G., & Manning, L. (1984). What models of recreational reading make a difference. *Reading World, 23*, 275–380.

Manzo, A. V. (1969). The ReQuest procedure. *Journal of Reading, 13*, 123–126.

Market Data Retrieval. (2002). *Highlights from technology in education 2002.* Retrieved from *www.schooldata.com/publications3.htm*

Marriott, D., Kupperstein, J., Connelly, G., & Williams, C. (1997). *What are the other kids doing while you teach small groups?* Huntington Beach, CA: Creative Teaching Press.

Marston, D., Deno, S. L., Dongil, K., Diment, K., & Rogers, D. (1995). Comparison of reading intervention approaches for students with mild disabilities. *Exceptional Children, 62*, 20–37.

Marshall, J. (2002). *Are they really reading? Expanding SSR in the middle grades.* Portland, ME: Stenhouse.

Martinez, M. G., & McGee, L. M. (2000). Children's literature and reading instruction: Past, present, and future. *Reading Research Quarterly, 35*, 154–170.

Mason, M. H., Harris, K. R., & Graham, S. (2002). Every child has a story to tell: Self-regulated strategy development for story writing. *Education and Treatment of Children, 25*, 496–506.

Mason, P. A., & Schumm, J. S. (Eds.). (2003). *Promising practices for urban reading instruction.* Newark, DE: International Reading Association.

Masonheimer, P., Drum, P., & Ehri, L. (1984). Does environmental print identification lead children into word reading? *Journal of Reading Behavior, 6*, 257–272.

Mastropieri, M. A., & Scruggs, T. E. (1997). Best practices in promoting reading comprehension in students with learning disabilities: 1976–1996. *Remedial and Special Education, 18*, 197–213.

Mathes, P. (1995). Accommodating diversity through Peabody classwide peer tutoring. *Intervention in School and Clinic, 31*, 46–50.

Mathes, P., Clancy-Menchetti, J., & Torgesen, J. K. (2001). *K-PALS (Kindergarten Peer Assisted Literacy Strategies).* Longmont, CO: Sopris West.

Mathes, P., Fuchs, D., Fuchs, L. S., Henley, A. M., & Sanders, A. (1994). Increasing strategic reading practice with Peabody classwide peer tutoring. *Learning Disabilities Research and Practice, 8*(4), 233–243.

Mathes, P., Torgesen, J. K., Allen, S. H., & Alor, J. H. (2001). *First grade PALS (Peer Assisted Literacy Strategies).* Longmont, CO: Sopris West.

Mathews, M. M. (1966). *Teaching to read: Historically considered.* Chicago: University of Chicago Press.

May, F. (1998). *Reading as communication: To help children write and read.* Upper Saddle River, NJ: Merrill.

Mayer, R. E., Schustack, M. W., & Blanton, W. E. (1999). What do children learn from using computers in an informal, collaborative setting? *Educational Technology, 39*, 27–31.

McBride-Chang, C. (1999). The ABCs of the ABCs: The development of letter-name and letter-sound knowledge. *Merrill–Palmer Quarterly, 45*, 285–308.

McCabe, P. P. (2003). Enhancing self-efficacy for high-stakes reading tests. *The Reading Teacher, 57*, 12–21.

McCormick, S. (1994). A nonreader becomes a reader: A case study of literacy acquisition by a severely disabled reader. *Reading Research Quarterly*, *29*, 156–177.

McCormick, S. (1999). *Instructing students who have literacy problems* (4th ed.). Upper Saddle River, NJ: Prentice Hall.

McCormick, S. (2003). *Instructing students who have literacy problems.* Upper Saddle River, NJ: Prentice Hall.

McCormick, S., & Hill, D. S. (1984). An analysis of the effects of two procedures for increasing disabled readers' inferencing skills. *Journal of Educational Research*, *77*, 219–226.

McCracken, R. A., & McCracken, M. J. (1977). *Reading is only the tiger's tail.* San Rafael, CA: Leswing Press.

McElveen, S. A., & Dierking, C. C. (2001). Children's books as models to teach writing skills. *The Reading Teacher*, *54*, 362–364.

McGill-Franzen, A. (1994). Compensatory and special education: Is there accountability for learning and belief in children's potential? In E. H. Hiebert & B. M. Taylor (Eds.), *Getting reading right from the start: Effective literacy instruction* (pp. 3–35). Needham Heights, MA: Allyn & Bacon.

McKenna, M. C., & Kear, D. J. (1990). Measuring attitude toward reading: A new tool for teachers. *The Reading Teacher*, *43*, 626–639.

McKinney, J. D., Schumm, J. S., & Hocutt, A. (1999). *Preventing reading failure in at-risk kindergarten children.* (Field Initiated Research Project, CFDA No. 84–023C). Unpublished technical report.

McLaughlin, B. (1990). The development of bilingualism: Myth and reality. In A. Barona & E. Garcia (Eds.), *Children at risk: Poverty minority status and other issues in educational equity* (pp. 65–76). Washington, DC: National Association of School Psychologists.

McLaughlin, M., & DeVoogd, G. (2004). *Critical literacy: Enhancing students' comprehension of text.* New York: Scholastic.

McMillan, J. H. (2001). *Classroom assessment: Principles and practice for effective instruction* (2nd ed.). Boston: Allyn & Bacon.

McNair, J. C. (2003). "But *The Five Chinese Brothers* is one of my favorite books!": Conducting sociopolitical critiques of children's literature with pre-service teachers. *Journal of Children's Literature*, *29*(1), 46–54.

Meir, T. (2003). "Why can't she remember that?": The importance of storybook reading in multilingual, multicultural classrooms. *The Reading Teacher*, *57*(3), 242–252.

Mercer, C. D., & Mercer, A. R. (2005). *Teaching students with learning problems* (7th ed.). Upper Saddle River, NJ: Merrill/Prentice Hall

Miller, G. A., & Gildea, P. M. (1987). How children learn words. *Scientific American*, *257*, 94–99.

Mioduser, D., Tur-Kaspa, H., & Leitner, I. (2000). The learning value of computer-based instruction of early reading skills. *Journal of Computer Assisted Learning*, *16*, 54–63.

Mitchell, D. (2003). *Children's literature: An invitation to the world.* Boston: Allyn & Bacon.

Mitchell, M. J., & Fox, B. J. (2001). The effects of computer software for developing phonological awareness in low-progress readers. *Reading Research and Instruction*, *40*, 315–332.

Moats, L. C. (1999). *Teaching reading IS rocket science.* Washington, DC: American Federation of Teachers.

Moats, L. C. (2000). *Speech to print; Language essentials for teachers.* Baltimore: Brookes.

Moats, L. C. (2003). *Language essentials for teachers of reading and spelling.* Longmont, CO: Sopris West.

Monroe, M. (1932). *Children who cannot read.* Chicago: University of Chicago Press.

Montague, M., Maddux, C., & Dereshiwsky, M. (1990). Story grammar and learning disabled students' comprehension and production of narrative prose. *Journal of Learning Disabilities*, *23*, 190–197.

Montgomery, W. (2001). Creating culturally responsive, inclusive classrooms. *Teaching Exceptional Children*, pp. 4–9.

Moore, D., & Moore, S. (1992). Possible sentences: An update. In E. Dishner, T. Bean, J. Readence, & D. Moore (Eds.), *Reading in content areas: Improving classroom reading instruction* (3rd ed.). Dubuque, IA: Kendall/Hunt.

Morris, D., Bloodgood, J. W., Lomax, R. G., & Perney, J. (2003). Developmental steps in learning to read: A longitudinal study in kindergarten and first grade. *Reading Research Quarterly*, *38*, 302–328.

Morris, D., & Nelson, L. (1992). Supported oral reading with low-achieving second graders. *Reading Research and Instruction*, *32*, 49–63.

Morrow, L. M. (1997). *The radical middle: Balancing literacy instruction*. Paper presented at the annual meeting of the International Reading Association, Atlanta, GA.

Morrow, L. M. (2001). *Literacy development in the early years: Helping children read and write* (4th ed.). Boston: Allyn & Bacon.

Morrow, L. M., O'Connor, E. M., & Smith, J. K. (1990). Effects of a story reading program on the literacy development of at-risk kindergarten children. *Journal of Reading Behavior*, *22*, 255–275.

Morrow, L. M., & Paratore, J. (1993). Family literacy: Perspective and practices. *The Reading Teacher*, *47*, 194–200.

Mosenthal, P. (1984). Reading comprehension research from a classroom prospective. In J. Flood (Ed.), *Promoting reading comprehension* (pp. 16–29). Newark, DE: International Reading Association.

Moss, B. (2003). *Exploring the literature of fact: Children's nonfiction trade books in the elementary classroom*. New York: Guilford Press.

Moss, B. (2004). Teaching expository text structures through information trade book retellings. *The Reading Teacher*, *57*(8), 710–718.

Murphy, R. F., Penuel, W. R., Means, B., Korbak, C., Whaley, A., & Allen, J. E. (2002). *A review of recent evidence on the effectiveness of discrete educational software*. Washington, DC: U.S. Department of Education, Planning and Evaluation Service.

Murphy, S. (1998). *Fragile evidence: A critique of reading assessment*. Mahwah, NJ: Erlbaum.

Murphy, S. (1999). Assessing portfolios. In C. R. Cooper, & L. Odell (Eds.), *Evaluating writing: The role of teachers' knowledge about text* (pp. 114–135). Urbana, IL: National Council of Teachers of English.

Murray, B., Stahl, S., & Ivey, M. G. (1996). Develoing phoneme awareness through alphabet books. *Reading and Writing*, *8*, 307–322.

Myles, J. (2002). Second language writing and research: The writing process and error analysis in student texts. *TESL-EJ*, *6*, 1–20.

Nagel, G. K. (2001). *Effective grouping for literacy instruction*. Boston: Allyn & Bacon.

Nagy, W. E. (1998). *Teaching vocabulary to improve reading comprehension*. Urbana, IL: National Council of Teachers of English.

Nagy, W. E., & Anderson, R. C. (1984). How many words are there in printed school English? *Reading Research Quarterly*, *19*, 304–330.

Nagy, W. E., Garcia, G. E., Durgunoglu, A., & Hancin-Bhatt, B. (1993). Spanish–English bilingual use of cognates in English reading. *Journal of Reading Behavior*, *25*, 241–259.

Nagy, W. E., & Herman, P. (1987). Breadth and depth of vocabulary knowledge: Implications for acquisition and instruction. In M. McKeown & M. Curtis (Eds.), *The nature of vocabulary acquisition* (pp. 19–35). Hillsdale, NJ: Erlbaum.

National Center for Education Statistics. (1998). *NAEP 1998 writing report card for the nation and the states*. Retrieved from *http://nces.ed.gov/nationsreportcard/writing*

National Center for Education Statistics. (2000). *The condition of education*. Washington, DC: U.S. Department of Education.

National Reading Panel. (2000a). *Teaching children to read: An evidence-based assessment of the scientific research literature on reading and its implications for reading instruction*. Rockville, MD: National Institute of Child Health and Human Development.

National Reading Panel. (2000b). *Teaching children to read: An evidence-based assessment of the scientific research literature on reading and its implications for reading instruction: Reports of the subgroups*. Rockville, MD: National Institute of Child Health and Human Development.

Niemiec, R. P., & Walberg, H. J. (1985). Computers and achievement in the elementary schools. *Journal of Educational Computing Research*, *1*, 435–440.

Newman, S. B., Caperelli, B. J., & Kee, C. (1998). Literacy learning: A family matter. *The Reading Teacher*, *52*, 244–253.

Nicholson, T. (1998). The flashcard strikes back. *The Reading Teacher*, *52*, 188–192.

Nieto, S. (2000). *Affirming diversity*. Boston: Allyn & Bacon.

Nilsen, A. P., & Nilsen, D. F. (2002). Lessons in the teaching of vocabulary from September 11 and Harry Potter. *Journal of Adolescent and Adult Literacy*, *46*, 254–260.

Norton, D. E., & Norton, S. E. (2003). *Through the eyes of a child* (6th ed.). Upper Saddle River, NJ: Merrill/Prentice Hall.

Oczkus, L. D. (2003). *Reciprocal teaching at work: Strategies for improving comprehension.* Newark, DE: International Reading Association.

Odell, L. (1999). Assessing thinking: Glimpsing a mind at work. In C. R. Cooper & L. Odell (Eds.), *Evaluating writing: The role of teachers' knowledge about text* (pp. 7–22). Urbana, IL: National Council of Teachers of English.

Office of Educational Research and Improvement, U.S. Department of Education. (1998). *Talent and diversity: The emerging world of limited English proficient students in gifted education* (ORAD No. 98–1100). Retrieved from *www.ed.gov/pubs/TalentandDiversity/index.html*

Ogle, D. M. (1986). K-W-L: A teaching model that develops active reading of expository text. *The Reading Teacher, 39*(6), 564–570.

Olness, R. (2005). *Using literature to enhance writing instruction.* Newark, DE: International Reading Association.

Ortiz, A. (2001). *English language learners with special needs: Effective instructional strategies* (CAL Digest, EDO-FL-01-08). Retrieved from *www.cal.org/resources/digest/0108ortiz.html*

Orton, J. L. (1966). The Orton–Gillingham approach. In J. Money (Ed.), *The disabled reader* (pp. 119–146). Baltimore: Johns Hopkins University Press.

Otterbourg, S. D. (1998). *Using technology to strengthen employee and family involvement in education* (Research Report No. 1223-98 RR, The Educator's Reference Desk [ERIC]). Retrieved from *www.ed.gov/pubs/TechStrength/ex_summary.html*

Ouyang, R. (1993). *A meta-analysis: Effectiveness of computer-assisted instruction at the level of elementary education (K–6).* Unpublished doctoral dissertation, University of Indiana, Bloomington.

Ovando, C. J., Combs, M. C., & Collier, V. P. (Eds.). (2006). *Bilingual and ESL classrooms: Teaching in multicultural contexts* (4th ed.). Boston: McGraw-Hill.

Palincsar, A. (1984). The quest for meaning from expository text: A teacher guided journey. In G. Duffy, L. Roehler, & J. Mason (Eds.), *Comprehension instruction: Perspectives and suggestions* (pp. 251–264). New York: Longman.

Pang, V. O., Colvin, C., Tran, M., & Barba, R. H. (1992). Beyond chopsticks and dragons: Selecting Asian-American literature for children. *The Reading Teacher, 46,* 216–224.

Pappas, C. C. (1991). Young children's strategies in learning the "book language" of information books. *Discourse Processes, 14,* 203–225.

Pappas, C. C. (1993). Is narrative "primary"?: Some insights from kindergarteners' pretend readings of stories and information books. *Journal of Reading Behavior, 25*(1), 97–129.

Pappas, C. C., & Pettegrew, B. S. (1998). The role of genre in the psycholinguistic guessing game of reading. *Language Arts, 75*(1), 36–44.

Paris, S. G., Wasik, B. A., & Turner, J. C. (1991). The development of strategic readers. In R. Barr, M. L. Kamil, P. Mosenthal, & P. D. Pearson (Eds.), *Handbook of reading research* (Vol. 2, pp. 609–640). New York: Longman.

Paris, S. G., Wixson, K. K., & Palinscar, A. (1986). Instructional approaches to reading comprehension. In E. Z. Rothkopf (Ed.), *Review of research on education* (Vol. 13, pp. 91–128). Washington, DC: American Educational Research Association.

Patterson, W., Jacobs, H. J., O'Quin, K., Ceprano, M. A., & Blue, E. (2003). Investigating the effectiveness of an integrated learning system on early emergent readers. *Reading Research Quarterly, 38,* 172–207.

Pauk, W. (1962). *How to study in college.* Boston: Houghton Mifflin.

Pavalak, S. (1985). *Classroom activities for correcting specific reading problems.* New York: Parker.

Pavonetti, L. M., Brimmer, K. M., & Cipielewski, J. F. (2002). Accelerated Reader: What are the lasting effects on the reading habits of middle school students exposed to Accelerated Reader in elementary grades? *Journal of Adolescent and Adult Literacy, 46,* 300–312.

Peak, J. P., & Dewalt, M. W. (1994). Reading achievement effects of computerized reading management and enrichment. *ERS Spectrum, 12,* 31–55.

Pearson, P. D. (2001a). Life in the radical middle: A personal apology for a balanced view of reading. In R. Flippo (Ed.), *Reading researchers in search of common ground* (pp. 78–83). Newark, DE: International Reading Association.

Pearson, P. D. (2001b). *Reading in the twentieth century* (CIERA No. 01-08). Ann Arbor: Center for the Improvement of Early Reading Achievement, University of Michigan.

Pearson, P. D., & Duke, N. K. (2002). Comprehension instruction in the primary grades. In C. C. Block

& M. Pressley (Eds.), *Comprehension instruction: Research-based best practices* (pp. 247–258). New York: Guilford Press.

Pearson, P. D., & Fielding, L. (1991). Comprehension instruction. In R. Barr, M. L. Kamil, P. B. Mosenthal, & P. D. Pearson (Eds.), *Handbook of reading research* (Vol. 2, pp. 815–860). New York: Longman.

Pearson, P. D., & Johnson, D. D. (1978). *Teaching reading comprehension.* New York: Holt, Rinehart & Winston.

Pearson, P. D., & Harvey, S. (2004). *Nonfiction reading and writing workshops.* Des Moines, IA: National Geographic School Publishing.

Pearson, P. D., Roehler, L. R., Dole, J. A., & Duffy, G. G. (1992). Developing expertise in reading comprehension. In S. J. Samuel & A. E. Farstrup (Eds.), *What research has to say about reading instruction* (pp. 145–199). Newark, DE: International Reading Association.

Peregoy, S. F., & Boyle, O. F. (2001). *Reading, writing, and learning in ESL: A resource book for K–12 teachers* (3rd ed.). New York: Longman.

Peterson, S., & Phelps, P.H. (1991). Visual–auditory links: A structural analysis approach to increasing word power. *The Reading Teacher, 44,* 524–525.

Piaget, J., & Inhelder, B. (1969). *The psychology of the child.* New York: Basic Books.

Pierangelo, R., & Crane, R. (2000). *The special education yellow pages.* Upper Saddle River, NJ: Prentice Hall.

Pinnell, G. S., & Scharer, P. L. (2001). *Teaching for comprehension in reading, grades K–2: Strategies for helping children read with ease, confidence, and understanding.* New York: Scholastic.

Plass, J. L., Chun, D. M., Mayer, R. E., & Leutner, D. (1998). Supporting visual and verbal learning preferences in a second language multimedia learning environment. *Journal of Educational Psychology, 90,* 25–36.

Pratt, A. C., & Brady, S. (1988). Relation of phonological awareness to reading disability in children and adults. *Journal of Educational Psychology, 80,* 319–323.

Pressley, M. (2000). What should comprehension instruction be the instruction of? In M. L. Kamil, P. B. Mosenthal, P. D. Pearson, & R. Barr (Eds.), *Handbook of reading research* (Vol. 3, pp. 545–561). Mahwah, NJ: Erlbaum.

Pressley, M. (2002a). Comprehension strategy instruction: A turn-of-the-century status report. In C. C. Block & M. Pressley (Eds.), *Comprehension instruction: Research-based best practices* (pp. 11–27). New York: Guilford Press.

Pressley, M. (2002b). Metacognition and self-regulated comprehension. In A. E. Farstrup & S. J. Samuels (Eds.), *What research has to say about reading instruction* (3rd ed., pp. 291–309). Newark, DE: International Reading Association.

Pressley, M. (2003). A few things educators should know about instructional experiments. *The Reading Teacher, 57,* 64–71.

Pressley, M. (2006). *Reading instruction that works: The case for balanced teaching* (2nd ed.). New York: Guilford Press.

Pressley, M., Levin, J. R., & Delaney, H. D. (1982). The mnemonic keyword method. *Review of Educational Research, 52,* 6–91.

Pressley, M., Rankin, J., & Yokoi, L. (1996). A survey of instructional practices of primary teachers nominated as effective in promoting literacy. *Elementary School Journal, 96,* 363–384.

Preston, R. (1997). Literacies for life. *Adult Learning, 8,* 275–276.

Provenzo, E. F., Brett, A., & McCloskey, G. N. (2005). *Computers, curriculum, and cultural change: An introduction for teachers* (2nd ed.). Mahwah, NJ: Erlbaum.

Quiroaa, T., Lemos-Britton, Z., Mostafapour, E., Abbot, R. D., & Berninger, V. W. (2002). Phonological awareness and beginning reading in Spanish-speaking ESL first graders: Research into practice. *Journal of School Psychology, 40,* 85–111.

Radencich, M., Beers, P. G., & Schumm, J. S. (1993). *Handbook for the K–12 reading resource specialist.* Boston: Allyn & Bacon.

Raphael, T. E. (1982). Question-answering strategies for children. *The Reading Teacher, 36,* 186–191.

Raphael, T. E. (1986). Teaching question–answer relationships, revisited. *The Reading Teacher, 39,* 516–622.

Rashotte, C. A., & Torgesen, J. K. (1988). Repeated reading and reading fluency in learning disabled children. *Reading Research Quarterly, 20*(2), 180–188.

Rasinski, T. (2000). Speed does matter in reading. *The Reading Teacher, 54*(2), 146–151.

Rasinski, T. (2003). *The fluent reader: Oral reading strategies for building word recognition, fluency, and comprehension.* New York: Scholastic.

Ray, K. W. (1999). *Wondrous words: Writers and writing in the elementary classroom.* Urbana, IL: National Council of Teachers of English.

Readence, J. E., Bean, T. W., & Baldwin, R. S. (2000). *Content area literacy: An integrated approach* (8th ed.). Dubuque, IA: Kendall/Hunt.

Readence, J. R., Moore, D. W., & Rickelman, R. J. (2000). *Prereading activities for content area reading and learning* (3rd ed.). Newark, DE: International Reading Association.

Reardon-Anderson, J., Capps, R., & Fix, M. (2002). The health and well-being of children in immigrant families (Series B, No. B-52, November, 2002). Retrieved from *www.urban.org/UploadedPDF/310584_B52.pdf*

Reitsma, P. (1988). Reading practice for beginners: Effects of guided reading, reading-while-listening, and independent reading with computer-based speech feedback. *Reading Research Quarterly, 23*, 219–235.

Reutzel, R., & Cooter, R. B. (1999). *Balanced reading strategies and practices: Assessing and assisting readers with special needs.* Upper Saddle River, NJ: Prentice Hall.

Reutzel, D. R., & Fawson, P. C. (2002). *Your classroom library: New ways to give it more teaching power: Great teacher-tested and research-based strategies for organizing and using your library.* New York: Scholastic.

Rhodes, L. K. (Ed.). (1993). *Literary assessment: A handbook of instruments.* Portsmouth, NH: Heinemann.

Rhodes, L. K., & Shanklin, N. L. (1993). *Windows into literacy: Assessing learners, K–8.* Portsmouth, NH: Heinemann.

Riddle Buly, M., & Valencia, S. W. (2002). Below the bar: Profiles of students who fail state reading assessments. *Educational Evaluation and Policy Analysis, 24*, 219–239.

Ringenberg, K. (1991). Neurological impress method (NIM): A whole language procedure. *Notes on Literacy, 17*, 59–60.

Risko, V. J., & Bromley, K. (Eds.). (2001). *Collaboration for diverse learners: Viewpoints and practices.* Newark, DE: International Reading Association.

Rivera, O., Koorland, M., & Fueyo, V. (2002). Pupil-made pictorial prompts and fading for teaching sight words to a student with learning disabilities. *Education and Treatment of Children, 25*(2), 197–202.

Robertson, C., & Salter, W. (1995). *The phonological awareness kit.* East Moline, IL: Linguisystems.

Robyler, M. D. (2003). *Integrating educational technology into teaching* (3rd ed.). Upper Saddle River, NJ: Merrill/Prentice Hall.

Rodriguez, T. A. (2001). From the known to the unknown: Using cognates to teach English to Spanish-speaking literates. *The Reading Teacher, 54*, 744–746.

Roschelle, J. (1991). *Students' construction of physics knowledge: Learning about velocity and acceleration in a computer microworld.* Unpublished doctoral dissertation, University of California–Berkeley.

Rosenblatt, L. M. (1938). *Literature as exploration.* New York: Appleton-Century.

Rosenblatt, L. M. (1978). *The reader, the text, the poem: The transactional theory of the literary work.* Carbondale: Southern Illinois University Press.

Rosenshine, B., & Meister, C. (1994). Reciprocal teaching: A review of the research. *Review of Educational Research, 64*, 478–530.

Rothlein, L., & Meinbach, A. M. (1996). *Legacies: Using children's literature in the classroom.* New York: HarperCollins.

Ruddell, R. B. (1999). *Teaching children to read and write: Becoming an influential teacher* (2nd ed.). Boston: Allyn & Bacon.

Ruddell, R. B., & Ruddell, M. R. (1995). *Teaching children to read and write: Becoming an influential teacher.* Boston: Allyn & Bacon.

Rumelhart, D. E. (1976). *Toward an interactive model of reading* (Technical Report No. 56). San Diego: Center for Human Information Processing, University of California–San Diego.

Ryan, A. W. (1991). Meta-analysis of achievement effects of microcomputer applications in elementary schools. *Educational Administration Quarterly, 27*, 161–184.

Saenz, L. (2002). Examining the reading difficulty of secondary students with learning disabilities. *Remedial and Special Education, 23*, 31–42.

Sagally, K. (1997). *ArabTeX Version 3 overview: Short introduction.* Retrieved from *ftp://ftp.informatik.uni-stuttgart.de/pub/arabtex/arabtex.htm*

Samuels, J. (1979). The method of repeated readings. *The Reading Teacher, 50*, 376–382.

Savage, J. F. (2004). *Sound it out! Phonics in a comprehensive reading program* (2nd ed.). Boston: McGraw-Hill.

Scarborough, H. S., & Brady, S. A. (2002). Toward a common terminology for talking about speech and reading: A glossary of "Phon" words and related terms. *Journal of Literacy Research, 34*, 299–336.

Schmidt, P. R. (1999). Focus on research: Know thyself and understand others. *Language Arts, 76*, 332–340.

Schmitt, M. C. (1990). A questionnaire to measure children's awareness of strategic reading processes. *The Reading Teacher, 43*(7), 454–461.

Scholastic, Inc. (1999). *Read 180.* New York: Author.

Schumacher, J. B., Deshler, D. D., Alley, G. R., Warner, M. M., & Denton, P. H. (1984). Multipass: A learning strategy for improving reading comprehension. *Learning Disabilities Quarterly, 5*, 295–304.

Schumm, J. S. (2000). *School power.* Minneapolis, MN: Free Spirit.

Schumm, J. S. (2004). *How to help your child with homework* (3rd ed.). Minneapolis, MN: Free Spirit.

Schumm, J. S., Hughes, M. T., & Arguelles, M. E. (2001). Co-teaching: It takes more than ESP. In V. Risko & K. Bromley (Eds.), *Collaboration for diverse learners: Viewpoints and practices.* Newark, DE: International Reading Association.

Schumm, J. S., Leavell, A. G., Gordon, J., & Murfin, P. (1993). Literacy episodes: What we have learned from undergraduate tutors and at-risk elementary students. *Florida Reading Quarterly, 29*, 11–19.

Schumm, J. S., & Lopate, K. R. (1989). An 8-step instructional plan for teaching notetaking skills to middle school students. *Florida Reading Quarterly, 26*, 17–20.

Schumm, J. S., & Mangrum, C. T. (1991). FLIP: A framework for content area reading. *Journal of Reading, 35*, 120–125.

Schumm, J. S., & Radencich, M. C. (1984). Reader's/writer's workshop: An antidote for term paper terror. *Journal of Reading, 28*, 13–19.

Schumm, J. S., & Schumm, G. E., Jr. (1999). *The reading tutor's handbook: A commonsense guide to helping students read and write.* Minneapolis, MN: Free Spirit.

Schumm, J. S., & Vaughn, S. (1991). Making adaptations for mainstreamed students: Regular classroom teachers' perspectives. *Remedial and Special Education, 12*, 18–27.

Schumm, J. S., Vaughn, S., & Harris, J. (1997). Pyramid power for collaborative planning. *Teaching Exceptional Children, 29*(6), 62–66.

Schumm, J. S., Vaughn, S., & Leavell, A. G. (1994). Planning Pyramid: A framework for planning for diverse student needs during content area instruction. *The Reading Teacher, 47*, 2–10.

Schumm, J. S., Vaughn, S., & Moody, S. W. (2000). Grouping for reading instruction: Does one size fit all? *Journal of Learning Disabilities, 33, 477–488.*

Schumm, J. S., Vaughn, S., & Saumell, L. (1992). What teachers do when the textbook is tough: Students speak out. *Journal of Reading Behavior, 24*, 481–503.

Schwartz, R. M., & Raphael, T. E. (1985). Concept of definitions: A key to improving students' vocabulary. *The Reading Teacher, 39*, 198–205.

Scott, B. J., & Vitale, M. R. (2003). Teaching the writing process to students with LD. *Intervention in School and Clinic, 38*, 220–224.

Scott, J., & Nagy, W. (1997). Understanding the definitions of unfamiliar verbs. *Reading Research Quarterly, 32*, 184–200.

Scott-Simmons, D., Barker, J., & Cherry, N. (2003). Integrating research and story writing. *The Reading Teacher, 56*(8), 742–745.

Segalowitz, N., & Hébert, M. (1994). Phonological recoding in the first and second language reading of skilled bilinguals. In A. H. Cumming (Ed.), *Bilingual performance in reading and writing* (pp. 503–538). Ann Arbor: University of Michigan.

Serafini, F. (2000–2001). Three paradigms of assessment: Measurement, procedure, and inquiry. *The Reading Teacher, 54, 384–393.*

Shals, D. (1996). Essay reliability: Form and meaning. In E. M. White, W. D. Lutz, & S. Kamusikiri

(Eds.), *Assessment of writing: Politics, policies, practices* (pp. 76–96). New York: Modern Language Association of America.

Shanahan, T. (1988). The reading–writing relationship: Seven instructional principles. *The Reading Teacher, 41*, 636–647.

Shanahan, T. (Chair). (2003a, December). *National Literacy Panel on Language Minority Children and Youth: Findings from the Panel's research synthesis.* Symposium conducted at the 53rd annual meeting of the National Reading Conference, Scottsdale, AZ.

Shanahan, T. (2003b). Research-based reading instruction: Myths about the National Reading Panel report. *The Reading Teacher, 56*, 646–654.

Shanker, J. L., & Ekwall, E. E. (1999). *Ekwall–Shanker Reading Inventory* (4th ed.). Needham Heights, MA: Allyn & Bacon.

Shanker, J. L., & Ekwall, E. (2003). *Locating and correcting reading difficulties* (8th ed.). Upper Saddle River, NJ: Merill/Prentice Hall.

Shavelson, R. J., & Towne, L. (Eds.). (2002). *Scientific research in education.* Washington, DC: National Research Council, National Academy Press.

Shaywitz, S. (2003). *Overcoming dyslexia: A new and complete science-based program for reading problems at any level.* New York: Knopf.

Shefelbine, J. (1990). Student factors related to variability in learning word meanings from context. *Journal of Reading Behavior, 22*, 71–97.

Shepard, M. J., & Uhry, J. K. (1997). Teaching phonological recoding to young children with phonological processing deficits: The effect on sight-vocabulary acquisition. *Learning Disability Quarterly, 20*(2), 104–125.

Slaughter, J. P. (1993). *Beyond storybooks: Young children and the shared book experience.* Newark, DE: International Reading Association.

Smith, C., Tracey, E., & Weber, L. (1998). Motivating independent reading: The route to a lifetime of education. *Master's Action Research Project, 40–143.*

Smith, S. B., Simmons, D. C., & Kame'enui, E. J. (1995, February). *Synthesis of research on phonological awareness: Principles and implications for reading acquisition* (Technical Report No. 21). Eugene: National Center to Improve the Tools of Education, University of Oregon.

Snow, C. E. (1990). Rationales for native language instruction in the education of language minority children: Evidence from research. In A. Padilla, H. Fairchild, & C. Valadez (Eds.), *Bilingual education: Issues and strategies* (pp. 60–74). Newbury Park, CA: Sage.

Snow, C. E. (2002). *Reading for understanding: Toward an R&D program in reading comprehension.* Santa Monica, CA: Rand.

Snow, C. E., Burns, M. S., & Griffin, P. (Eds.). (1998). *Preventing reading difficulties in young children.* Washington, DC: National Academy Press.

Soodak, L. C. (2000). Performance assessment: Exploring issues of equity and fairness. *Reading and Writing Quarterly, 16*(3), 175–179.

Speck, B. (2000). Grading students' classroom writing: Issues and strategies. *ASHE-ERIC Higher Education Reports, 27*(3), 1–98.

Speece, D. L. (2004, November). *Response to instruction using curriculum-based measurement.* Paper presented at the National Higher Education Collaborative Seminar, Albuquerque, NM.

Spiegel, D. L., Fitzgerald, J., & Cunningham, J. (1993). Parental perceptions of preschoolers' literacy development: Implications for home–school partnerships. *Young Children, 48*(5), 74–79.

Stage, S. A., Sheppard, J., Davidson, M. M., & Browning, M. M. (2001). Prediction of first-graders' growth in oral reading fluency using kindergarten letter fluency, *Journal of School Psychology, 39*, 225–237.

Stahl, S. A., Duffy-Hester, A. M., & Stahl, K. A. D. (1998). Everything you wanted to know about phonics (but were afraid to ask). *Reading Research Quarterly, 33*, 338–355.

Stahl, S. A., Hare, V. C., Sinatra, R., & Gregory, J. F. (1991). Defining the role of prior knowledge and vocabulary in reading comprehension. *Journal of Reading Behavior, 18*, 309–319.

Stahl, S. A., & Jacobson, M. G. (1986). Vocabulary difficulty, prior knowledge, and text comprehension. *Journal of Reading Behavior, 18*, 309–323.

Stamboltzis, A., & Pumfrey, P. (2000). Reading across genres. *Support for Learning, 13*(2), 58–61.

Stanovich, K. E. (1980). Toward an interactive–compensatory model of individual differences in development of reading fluency. *Reading Research Quarterly, 16*(1), 32–71.

Stanovich, K. E. (1986). Matthew effects on reading: Some consequences of individual differences in the acquisition of literacy. *Reading Research Quarterly*, *21*, 360–407.

Stanovich, K. E. (1993–1994). Romance and reality. *The Reading Teacher*, *47*, 280–291.

Stanovich, K. E. (2000). *Progress in understanding reading: Scientific foundations and new frontiers.* New York: Guilford Press.

Stanovich, P. J., & Stanovich, K. E. (2003). *Using research and reason in education: How teachers can use scientifically based research to make curricular and instructional decisions.* Jessup, MD: National Institute for Literacy.

Staresina, L. (2003). Technology in education. *Education Week*. Retrieved from *www.edweek.org/rc/issues/technology-in-education*

Stauffer, R. G. (1969). *Teaching reading as a thinking process.* New York: Harper & Row.

Stauffer, R. G. (1970). *The language experience approach to the teaching of reading.* New York: Harper & Row.

Steffenson, M. S., Joag-dev, C., & Anderson, R. C. (1979). A cross-cultural perspective on reading comprehension. *Reading Research Quarterly*, *15*, 10–29.

Sternberg, R. J., & Powell, J. S. (1983). Comprehending verbal comprehension. *American Psychologist*, *38*, 878–893.

Stoodt-Hill, B. S., & Amspaugh-Corson, L. B. (2001). *Children's literature: Discovery for a lifetime.* Upper Saddle River, NJ: Prentice Hall.

Strichert, S. S., & Mangrum, C. T. (2001). *Teaching study skills and strategies to students with learning disabilities, attention deficit disorder, or special needs* (3rd ed.). Boston: Allyn & Bacon.

Strickland, D. S. (1998). *Teaching phonics today: A primer for educators.* Newark, DE: International Reading Association.

Strickland, D. S., Galda, L., & Cullinan, B. E. (2004). *Language arts: Learning and teaching.* Belmont, CA: Wadsworth.

Strickland, D. S., Ganske, K., & Monroe, J. K. (2002). *Supporting struggling readers and writers: Strategies for classroom interventions, 3–6.* Portland, ME: Stenhouse.

Strommen, E. F. (1993). "Does yours eat leaves?": Cooperative learning in an educational software task. *Journal of Computing Childhood Education, 4*, 45–56.

Sulzby, E. & Teale, W. H. (1991). Emergent literacy. In R. Barr, M. Kamil, P. Mosenthal, & P. D. Pearson (Eds.), *Handbook of reading research* (Vol. 2, pp. 727–757). New York: Longman.

Swanson, H. L. (2000). What instruction works for students with learning disabilities?: Summarizing the results from a meta-analysis of intervention studies. In R. Gersten, E. P Schiller, & S. Vaughn (Eds.), *Contemporary special education research: Syntheses of the knowledge base on critical instructional issues* (pp. 1–30). Mahwah, NJ: Erlbaum.

Sweet, A. P., & Snow, C. E. (Eds.). (2003). *Rethinking reading comprehension.* New York: Guilford Press.

Szedeli, B. (1993). From me to you: Publishing in the middle school. *English Journal*, *82*, 49–51.

Taba, H. (1967). *Teacher's handbook for elementary social studies.* Reading, MA: Addison-Wesley.

Tan, A., & Nicholson, T. (1997). Flashcards revisited: Training poor readers to read words faster improves their comprehension of text. *Journal of Educational Psychology*, *89*, 276–288.

Taylor, B., M., Anderson, R. C., Au, K. H., & Raphael, T. E. (2000). Discretion in the translation of research to policy: A case from beginning reading. *Educational Researcher*, *29*(6), 16–26.

Taylor, W. L. (1953). Cloze procedure: A new tool for measuring readability. *Journalism Quarterly*, *30*, 415–433.

Terban, M., & Brace, E. (2003). *Building your vocabulary.* New York: Scholastic.

Terban, M., & Devore, J. (1998). *Dictionary of idioms.* New York: Scholastic.

Thorndike, E. L. (1917). Reading as reasoning: A study of mistakes in paragraph reading. *Journal of Educational Psychology*, *8*, 323–332.

Tierney, R. J., & Pearson, P. D. (1984). Toward a composing model of reading. In. J. Jensen (Ed.), *Composing and comprehending* (pp. 33–46). Urbana, IL: National Council of Teachers of English.

Tierney, R. J., & Readence, J. E. (2004). *Reading strategies and practices: A compendium* (6th ed.). Boston: Allyn & Bacon.

Tierney, R. J., Readence, J. E., & Dishner, E. K. (1990). *Reading strategies and practices: A compendium* (3rd ed.). Boston: Allyn & Bacon.

Tomlinson, C. A. (2003). *Fulfilling the promise of the differentiated classroom: Strategies and tools for responsive teaching.* Alexandria, VA: Association for Supervision and Curriculum Development.

Tompkins, G. E. (2002). *Language arts: Content and teaching strategies* (5th ed.). Upper Saddle River, NJ: Prentice Hall.

Tompkins, G. E., & McGee, L. M. (1993). *Teaching reading with literature: Case studies to action plans.* New York: Macmillan.

Tonjes, M. J., & Zintz, M. V. (1987). *Teaching reading, thinking, and study skills in content classrooms.* Dubuque, IA: William C. Brown.

Topping, P., & Paul, T. (1999). Computer-assisted assessment of practice at reading: A large scale survey using accelerated reader data. *Reading and Writing Quarterly, 15*, 213–231.

Torgesen, J. K., & Barker, T. A. (1995). Computers as aids in the prevention and remediation of reading disabilities. *Learning Disability Quarterly, 18*, 76–87.

Torgesen, J. K., & Bryant, B. (1994). *Phonological awareness training for reading.* Austin, TX: PRO-ED.

Torgesen, J. K., & Mathes, P. G. (1998). *What every teacher should know about phonological awareness.* Tallahassee: Florida Department of Education, Division of Public Schools and Community Education, Bureau of Instructional Support and Community Services.

Torgesen, J. K., Wagner, R. K., & Rashotte, C. A. (1994). Longitudinal studies of phonological processes and reading. *Journal of Learning Disabilities, 27*, 276–286.

Torgesen, J. K., & Wagner, R. K. (1998). Alternative diagnostic approaches for specific developmental reading disabilities. *Learning Disabilities Research and Practice, 13*, 220–232.

Torgesen, J. K., Wagner, R. K., & Rashotte, C. A. (1997). Prevention and remediation of severe reading disabilities: Keeping the end in mind. *Scientific Studies of Reading, 1*, 217–234.

Townsend, J. S., Fu, D., & Lamme, L. L. (1997). Writing assessment: Multiple perspectives, multiple purposes. *Preventing School Failure, 41*, 71–76.

Trelease, J. (2001). *The read-aloud handbook* (5th ed.). New York: Penguin.

Treiman, R., Tincoff, R., Rodriguez, K., Mouzaki, A., & Francis, D. (1998). The foundations of literacy: Learning the sounds of letters. *Child Development, 69*, 524–540.

Trimbur, J. (1996). Response: Why do we test writing? In E. M. White, W. D. Lutz, & S. Kamusikiri (Eds.), *Assessment of writing: Politics, policies, practices* (pp. 45–48). New York: Modern Language Association of America.

Tunnell, M. O., & Jacobs, J. S. (2000). *Children's literature, briefly* (2nd ed.). Upper Saddle River, NJ: Merrill.

Turner, J. D., & Kim, Y. (2003). Afterword. In P. A. Mason & J. S. Schumm (Eds.), *Promising practices for urban reading instruction* (pp. 523–530). Newark, DE: International Reading Association.

Tyler, A., & Nagy, W. (1989). The acquisition of English derivational morphology. *Journal of Verbal Learning and Verbal Behavior, 14*, 638–647.

Tyner, B. (2004). *Small-group reading instruction: A differentiated teaching model for beginning and struggling readers.* Newark, DE: International Reading Association.

Unger, J., & Fleischman, S. (2004). Research matters: Is process writing the "write stuff"? *Educational Leadership, 62*, 90–91.

Vail, P. L. (1991). *Common ground: Whole language and phonics working together.* Rosemont, NJ: Modern Learning Press.

Valdez Pierce, L. (2003). Assessment. In C. J. Ovando, V. P. Collier, & M. C. Combs (Eds.), *Bilingual and ESL classrooms: Teaching in multicultural contexts* (3rd ed., pp. 322–357). Boston: McGraw-Hill.

Valencia, S. W. (2000). How will literacy be assessed in the next millennium? *Reading Research Quarterly, 35*, 244–250.

Valencia, S. W., & Pearson, P. D., & Peters, C. W. (1989). Theory and practice in statewide reading assessment: Closing the gap. *Educational Leadership, 46*, 57–63.

Valencia, S. W., & Riddle Buly, M. (2004). Behind test scores: What struggling readers *really* need. *The Reading Teacher, 57*, 520–531.

VanTassel-Baska, J. (1994). *Comprehensive curriculum for gifted learners* (2nd ed.). Needham Heights, MA: Allyn & Bacon.

Vasquez, V., Muise, M. R., Adamson, S. C., Heffernan, L., Chiola-Nakai, D., & Shear, J. (2003). *Setting the context: A critical take on using books in the classroom.* Newark, DE: International Reading Association.

Vaughn, S., Bos, C. S., & Schumm, J. S. (1997). *Teaching mainstreamed, diverse, and at-risk students in the general education classroom.* Boston: Allyn & Bacon.

Vaughn, S., Bos, C. S., & Schumm, J. S. (2003). *Teaching exceptional, diverse, and at-risk students in the general education classroom* (3rd ed.). Boston: Allyn & Bacon.

Vaughn, S., Hughes, M. T., Schumm, J. S., & Klingner, J. K. (1998). A collaborative effort to enhance reading and writing instruction in inclusive classrooms. *Learning Disabilities Quarterly, 21,* 211–226.

Vaughn, S., & Linan-Thompson, S. (2004). *Research-based methods of reading instruction: Grades K–3.* Alexandria, VA: Association for Supervision and Curriculum Development.

Vaughn, S., Linan-Thompson, S., & Elbaum, B. (2004). *Preventing reading difficulties: A three-tiered intervention model.* Retrieved from *www.texasreading.org/3tier/*

Vaughn, S., Moody, S., & Schumm, J. S. (1998). Broken promises: Reading instruction in the resource room. *Exceptional Children, 64,* 211–226.

Vaughn, S., & Schumm, J. S. (1995). Responsible inclusion for students with learning disabilities. *Journal of Learning Disabilities, 28*(5), 264–270, 290.

Vellutino, F. R. (2003). Individual differences as sources of variability in reading comprehension in elementary school children. In A. P. Sweet & C. E. Snow (Eds.), *Rethinking reading comprehension* (pp. 51–81). New York: Guilford Press.

Vygotsky, L. (1978). *Mind in society.* Cambridge, MA: Harvard University Press.

Walberg, H. J., & Tsai, S. (1983). Matthew effects in education. *American Educational Research Journal, 20,* 359–373.

Wald, S. (2000). *Spanish for dummies.* Foster City, CA: IDG Books Worldwide..

Walpole, S., & McKenna, M. C. (2004). *The literacy coach's handbook: A guide to research-based practice.* New York: Guilford Press.

Wasik, B. A. (1998). Using volunteers as reading tutors: Guidelines for successful practices. *The Reading Teacher, 51,* 562–573.

Warger, C. (2001). *Five homework strategies for teaching students with disabilities.* Arlington, VA: The ERIC Clearinghouse on Disabilities and Gifted Education, ERIC/OSEP Digest #E608.

Weller, D. L., Carpenter, S., & Holmes, C. T. (1998). Achievement gaines of low-achieving students using computer-assisted vs. regular instruction. *Psychological Reports, 83,* 834.

Wells, G. (2004). *An introduction to the role of language in the theoretical approaches of Vygotsky, Bakhtin, Halliday, and Hasan.* Lecture presented at the University of Miami Speakers Series on Literacy, Language and Culture, Coral Gables, FL.

Wenglinsky, H. (1998). *Does it compute?: The relationship between educational technology and student achievement in mathematics.* Princeton, NJ: Educational Testing Service.

White, E. M. (1996). Power and agenda setting in writing assessment. In E. M. White, W. D. Lutz, & S. Kamusikiri (Eds.), *Assessment of writing: Politics, policies, practices* (pp. 9–24). New York: Modern Language Association.

White, T., Graves, M., & Slater, W. (1990). Growth of reading vocabulary in diverse elementary schools: Decoding and word meaning. *Journal of Educational Psychology, 82,* 281–289.

Winograd, P., Paris, S., & Bridge, C. (1991). Improving the assessment of literacy. *The Reading Teacher, 45*(2), 108–116.

Wolcott, W. (1998). *An overview of writing assessment: Theory, research, and practice.* Urbana, IL: National Council of Teachers of English.

Wolfersberger, M. (2003). *L1 to L2 writing process and strategy transfer. A look at lower proficiency writers.* Retrieved from *www.writing.berkeley.edu/TESL-EJ/ej26/a6.html*

Wolfersberger, M. E., Reutzel, D. R., Sudweeks, R., & Fawson, P. C. (2004). Developing and validating the Classroom Literacy Environment Profile (CLEP): A tool for examining the "print richness" of early childhood and elementary classrooms. *Journal of Literacy Research, 36,* 211–272.

Wong Fillmore, L. (1991). When learning a second language means losing the first. *Early Childhood Research Quarterly, 6,* 324–346.

Wong Fillmore, L., & Valadez, C. (1986). Teaching bilingual learners. In M. C. Wittrock (Ed.), *Handbook of research on teaching* (3rd ed., pp. 648–685). New York: Macmillan.

Wood, K. D., Lapp, D., & Flood, J. (1992). *Guiding readers through text: A review of study guides.* Newark, DE: International Reading Association.

Woodward, A., & Elliott, D. L. (1992). Teacher professionalism school reform and textbooks. *Educational Horizons*, *70*(4), 176–180.

Wylie, R. E., & Durrell, D. D. (1970). Teaching vowels through phonograms. *Elementary English*, *47*, 787–791.

Yates, J. R., & Ortiz, A. (1998). Issues of culture and diversity affecting educators with diversity: A change in demography is reshaping America. In R. J. Anderson, C. E. Keller, & J. M. Karp (Eds.), *Enhancing diversity: Educators with disabilities in the education enterprise* (pp. 21–37). Washington, DC: Gallaudet University Press.

Yoon, J. (2002). Three decades of sustained silent reading: A meta-analytic review of the effects of SSR on attitude toward reading. *Reading Improvement*, *39*(4), 186–195.

Yopp, H. K. (1988). The validity and reliability of phonemic awareness tests. *Reading Research Quarterly*, *23*, 159–177.

Yopp, H. K. (1992). Developing phonemic awareness in young children. *The Reading Teacher*, *45*, 696–703.

Yopp, R. H., & Yopp, H. K. (2000). Sharing informational text with young children. *The Reading Teacher*, *53*, 410–423.

Young, J., Bolla, J., Schumm, J. S., Moreyra, A., & Exley, R. (2001). The South Florida America Reads Coalition: A synergistic effort. In L. M. Morrow & D. G. Woo (Eds.), *Tutoring programs for struggling readers: The America Reads challenge* (pp. 57–85). New York: Guilford Press.

Young, T. A. (Ed.). (2004). *Happily ever after: Sharing folk literature with elementary and middle school students.* Newark, DE: International Reading Association.

Zutell, J., & Rasinski, T. V. (1991). Training teachers to attend to their student's oral reading fluency. *Theory into Practice*, *30*(3), 211–216.

Index

Page numbers followed by *f* indicate figure; *t* indicate table